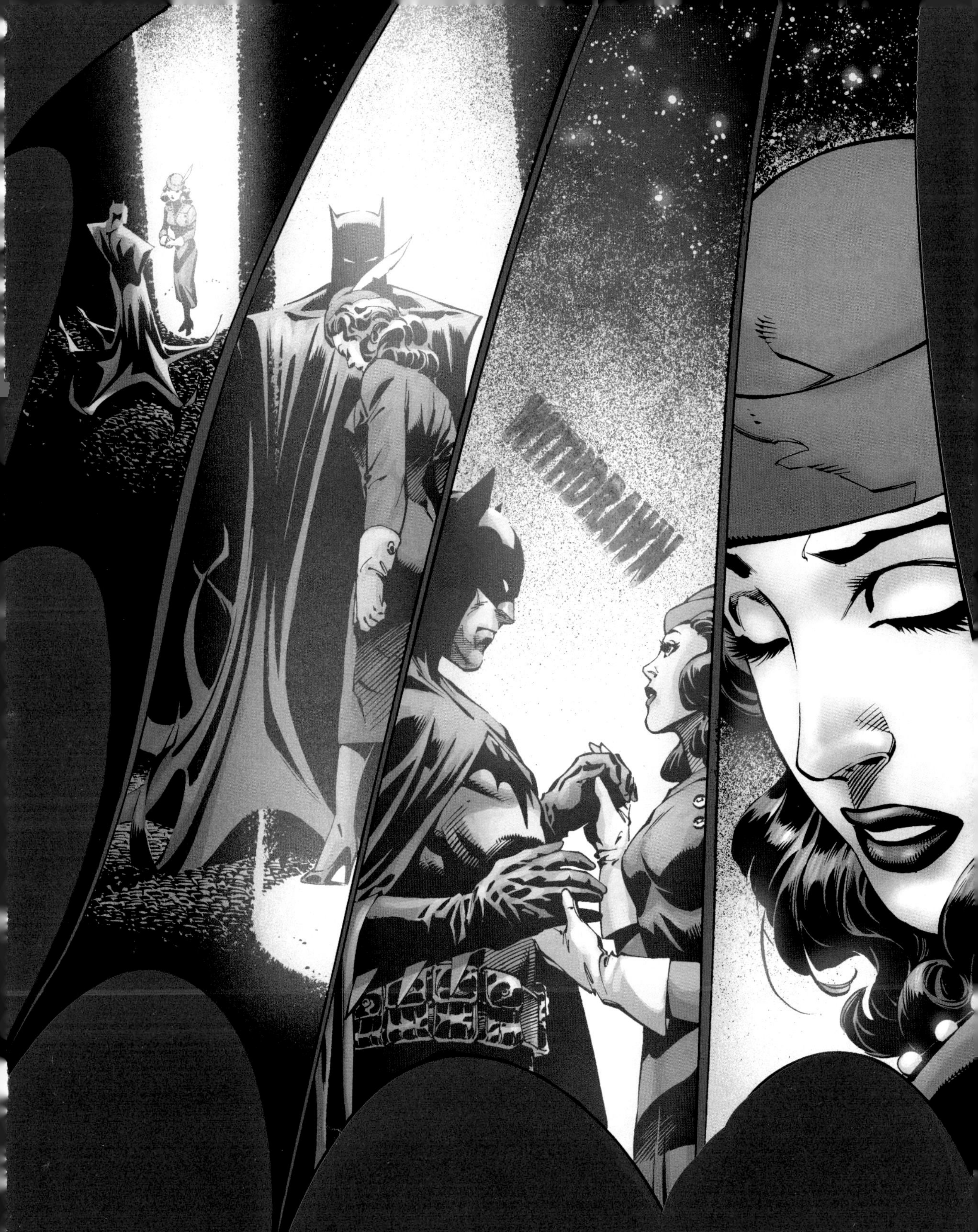

THE DC UNIVERSE by NEIL GAIMAN

THE DELUXE EDITION

NEIL GAIMAN
ALAN GRANT
MARK VERHEIDEN
Writers

ARTHUR ADAMS
MICHAEL ALLRED
JIM APARO
TERRY AUSTIN
SIMON BISLEY
PAT BRODERICK
MARK BUCKINGHAM
EDDIE CAMPBELL
DICK GIORDANO
MIKE HOFFMAN
SAM KIETH
TEDDY KRISTIANSEN
JASON LITTLE
BERNIE MIREAULT
KEVIN NOWLAN
ERIC SHANOWER
JOHN TOTLEBEN
MATT WAGNER
SCOTT WILLIAMS
Artists

LAURA ALLRED
MATT HOLLINGSWORTH
NANSI HOOLAHAN
TEDDY KRISTIANSEN
JOE MATT
TOM MCCRAW
KEVIN NOWLAN
ALEX SINCLAIR
Colorists

JOHN COSTANZA
ALBERT DE GUZMAN
JARED K. FLETCHER
TODD KLEIN
ROB LEIGH
AUGUSTIN MAS
BERNIE MIREAULT
NATE PIEKOS
Letterers

BRIAN BOLLAND
Dust Jacket Art

ANDY KUBERT
with ALEX SINCLAIR
FRANK MILLER with
MATT HOLLINGSWORTH
Case Art

MIKE CARLIN and
EDUARDO BARRETO
BRIAN BOLLAND
FRANK MILLER with
MATT HOLLINGSWORTH
ANDY KUBERT with
ALEX SINCLAIR
Original Series Covers

BATMAN created by Bob Kane
with Bill Finger
SUPERMAN created by Jerry
Siegel and Joe Shuster.
SUPERGIRL based on the
characters created by Jerry
Siegel and Joe Shuster
By special arrangement with
the Jerry Siegel family.
WONDER WOMAN created
by William Moulton Marston
KAMANDI created by
Jack Kirby
HAWKMAN created
by Gardner Fox
DEADMAN created
by Arnold Drake
METAMORPHO created
by Bob Haney and
Ramona Fradon

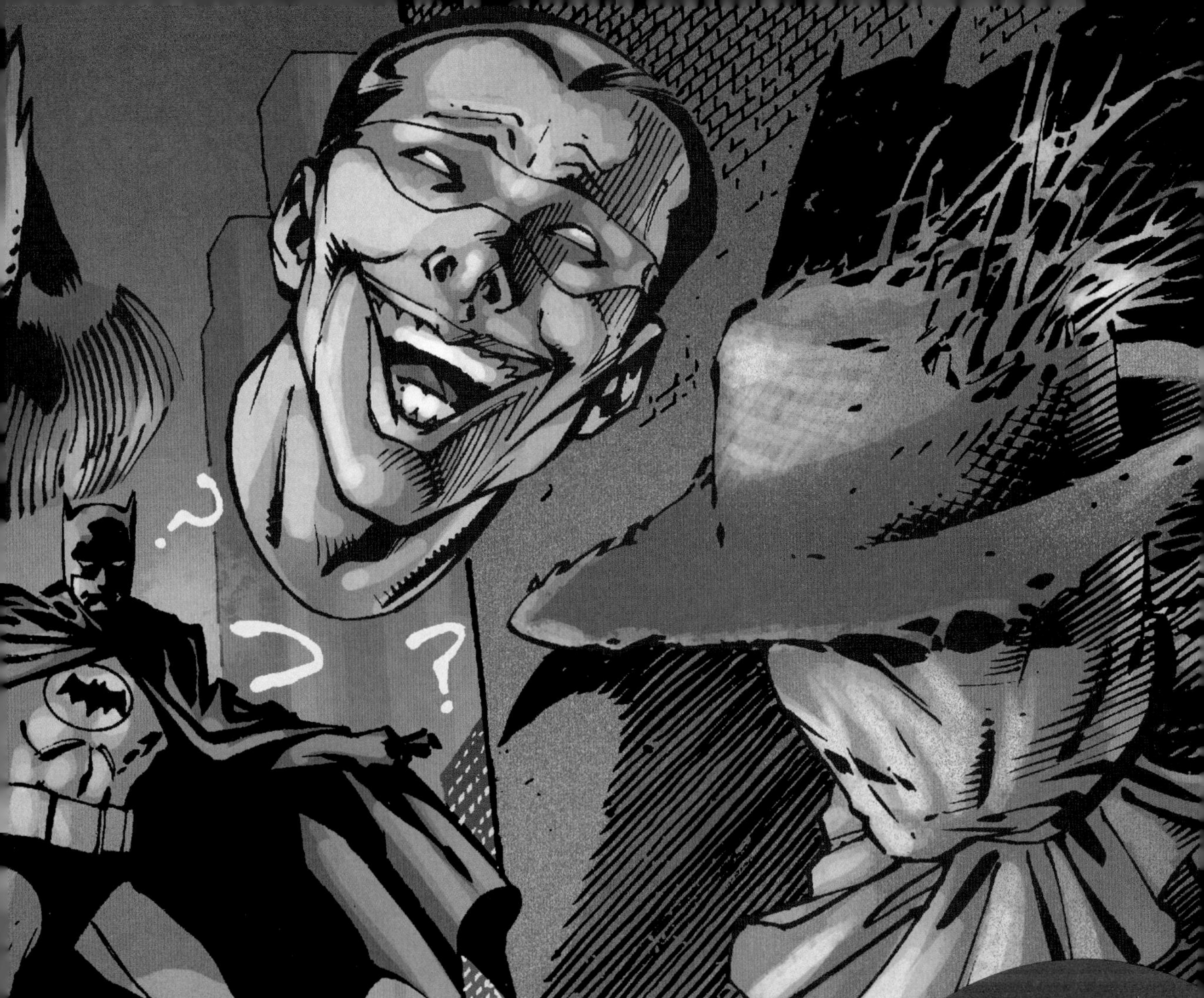

THE DC UNIVERSE by NEIL GAIMAN

THE DELUXE EDITION

MARK CHIARELLO	
MICHAEL MARTS	
SCOTT PETERSON	
BOB SCHRECK	
MARK WAID	Editors – Original Series
TOM PALMER JR.	Associate Editor – Original Series
FRANK BERRIOS	
JANELLE SIEGEL	
DARREN VINCENZO	Assistant Editors – Original Series
JEB WOODARD	Group Editor – Collected Editions
SCOTT NYBAKKEN	Editor – Collected Edition
STEVE COOK	Design Director – Books
CHRIS GRIGGS	Publication Design
BOB HARRAS	Senior VP – Editor-in-Chief, DC Comics
DIANE NELSON	President
DAN DIDIO and JIM LEE	Co-Publishers
GEOFF JOHNS	Chief Creative Officer
AMIT DESAI	Senior VP – Marketing & Global Franchise Management
NAIRI GARDINER	Senior VP – Finance
SAM ADES	VP – Digital Marketing
BOBBIE CHASE	VP – Talent Development
MARK CHIARELLO	Senior VP – Art, Design & Collected Editions
JOHN CUNNINGHAM	VP – Content Strategy
ANNE DEPIES	VP – Strategy Planning & Reporting
DON FALLETTI	VP – Manufacturing Operations
LAWRENCE GANEM	VP – Editorial Administration & Talent Relations
ALISON GILL	Senior VP – Manufacturing & Operations
HANK KANALZ	Senior VP – Editorial Strategy & Administration
JAY KOGAN	VP – Legal Affairs
DEREK MADDALENA	Senior VP – Sales & Business Development
JACK MAHAN	VP – Business Affairs
DAN MIRON	VP – Sales Planning & Trade Development
NICK NAPOLITANO	VP – Manufacturing Administration
CAROL ROEDER	VP – Marketing
EDDIE SCANNELL	VP – Mass Account & Digital Sales
COURTNEY SIMMONS	Senior VP – Publicity & Communications
JIM (SKI) SOKOLOWSKI	VP – Comic Book Specialty & Newsstand Sales
SANDY YI	Senior VP – Global Franchise Management

THE DC UNIVERSE BY NEIL GAIMAN: THE DELUXE EDITION

DC Comics
2900 West Alameda Ave.
Burbank, CA 91505
Printed by Transcontinental Interglobe, Beauceville, QC, Canada. 9/9/16.
First Printing.
ISBN: 978-1-4012-6488-8

Library of Congress Cataloging-in-Publication Data is available.

PEFC Certified
Printed on paper from sustainably managed forests and controlled sources
PEFC/01-31-106 www.pefc.org

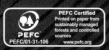

TABLE OF CONTENTS

All stories written by Neil Gaiman, unless otherwise noted

*This story was untitled in its original release.

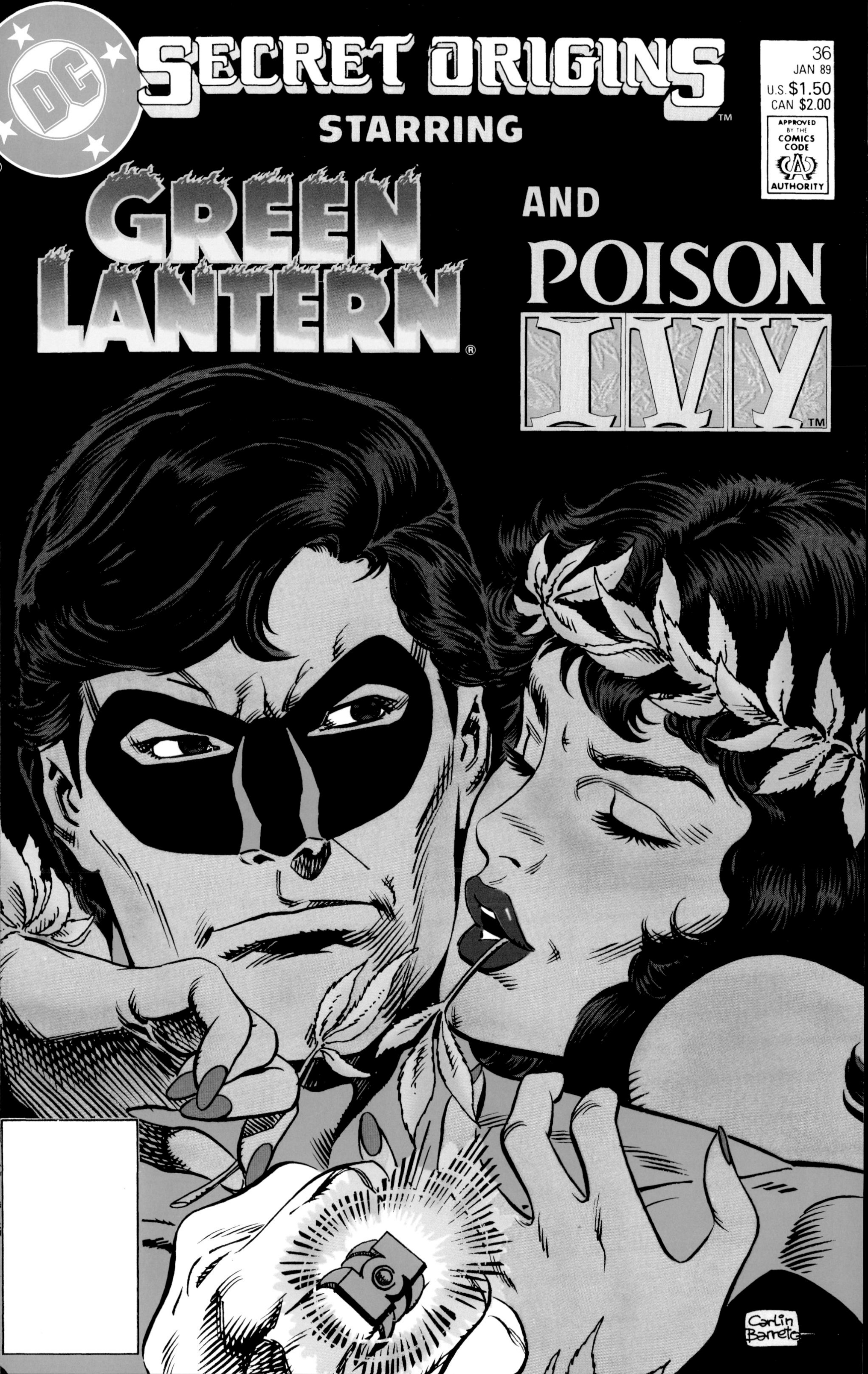
DC
SECRET ORIGINS™
STARRING
GREEN LANTERN®
AND
POISON IVY™
36
JAN 89
U.S. $1.50
CAN $2.00
APPROVED BY THE COMICS CODE AUTHORITY
Carlin
Barreto

PAVANE

I CAN SEE HER ON THE MONITOR, STROKING A LILY-OF-THE-VALLEY, STARING OUT AT THE HILL. SHE'S ALWAYS ON THE SCREEN: AT NIGHT IT SWITCHES TO INFRA-RED.

YOU CAN TURN DOWN THE SOUND, BUT YOU CAN'T TURN OFF THE PICTURE.

RETURN TO THE FILES. IT'S BEEN THREE DAYS NOW, AND THE MORE MATERIAL COMES IN, THE MORE CONFUSING IT GETS.

I'VE GOT TO TALK TO HER. TAKE THE FBI FILE, THE CIA FILE, GOTHAM POLICE FILE, PRISON SERVICES FILE, PRESS CUTTINGS FILE...

UH, GUARD? PRISONER ISLEY

YESSIR THIS WAY, SIR

DOWN ECHOING, DISINFECTED CORRIDORS, PAST A GROUP OF PRISONERS RETURNING FROM THE FARM.

THEY STARE AT ME HUNGRILY, WHISPER AND JOKE TO EACH OTHER COARSELY IN LOW VOICES.

I STARE STRAIGHT AHEAD, SWALLOW, PRETEND NOT TO NOTICE

DO THEY UPSET YOU?

WHAT? OH. N-NOOO, I CAN UNDERSTAND THAT THEY DON'T GET TO SEE MANY *MEN* IN *HERE*. IT DOESN'T BOTHER *ME* I'M A *PROFESSIONAL.*

THAT'S GOOD.

WHY?

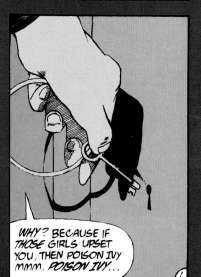

WHY? BECAUSE IF *THOSE* GIRLS UPSET YOU, THEN POISON IVY *mmm, POISON IVY...*

①

WRITTEN BY NEIL GAIMAN
ILLUSTRATED BY MARK BUCKINGHAM

LETTERED BY AGUSTIN MAS
SEPARATED BY NANSI HOOLAHAN

EDITED BY MARK WAID
POISON IVY CREATED BY BOB KANIGHER

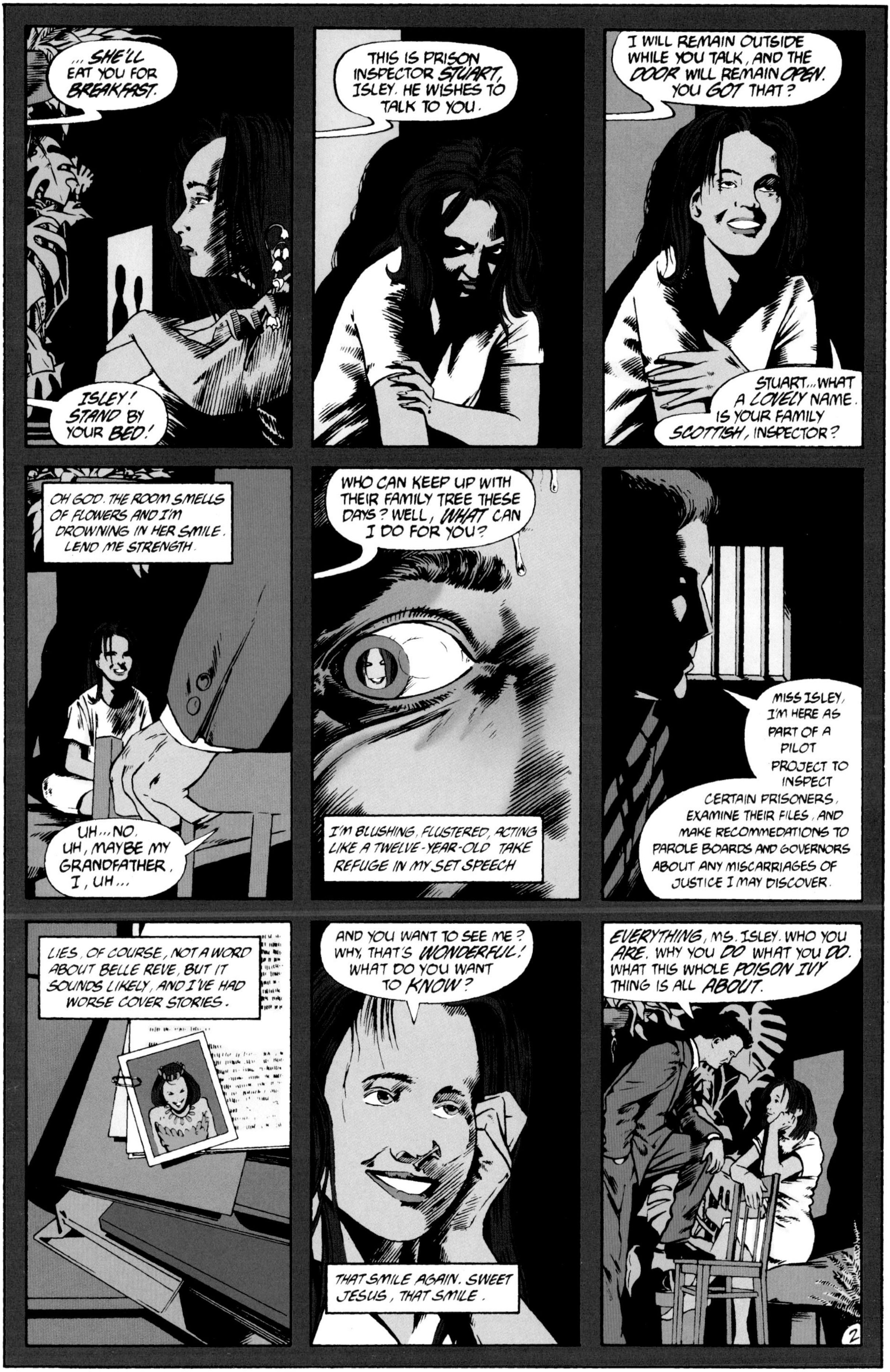
...SHE'LL EAT YOU FOR BREAKFAST.
ISLEY! STAND BY YOUR BED!
THIS IS PRISON INSPECTOR STUART, ISLEY. HE WISHES TO TALK TO YOU.
I WILL REMAIN OUTSIDE WHILE YOU TALK, AND THE DOOR WILL REMAIN OPEN. YOU GOT THAT?
STUART...WHAT A LOVELY NAME. IS YOUR FAMILY SCOTTISH, INSPECTOR?
OH GOD. THE ROOM SMELLS OF FLOWERS AND I'M DROWNING IN HER SMILE. LEND ME STRENGTH.
UH...NO. UH, MAYBE MY GRANDFATHER, I, UH...
WHO CAN KEEP UP WITH THEIR FAMILY TREE THESE DAYS? WELL, WHAT CAN I DO FOR YOU?
I'M BLUSHING, FLUSTERED, ACTING LIKE A TWELVE-YEAR-OLD. TAKE REFUGE IN MY SET SPEECH.
MISS ISLEY, I'M HERE AS PART OF A PILOT PROJECT TO INSPECT CERTAIN PRISONERS, EXAMINE THEIR FILES, AND MAKE RECOMMEDATIONS TO PAROLE BOARDS AND GOVERNORS ABOUT ANY MISCARRIAGES OF JUSTICE I MAY DISCOVER.
LIES, OF COURSE, NOT A WORD ABOUT BELLE REVE, BUT IT SOUNDS LIKELY, AND I'VE HAD WORSE COVER STORIES.
AND YOU WANT TO SEE ME? WHY, THAT'S WONDERFUL! WHAT DO YOU WANT TO KNOW?
THAT SMILE AGAIN. SWEET JESUS, THAT SMILE.
EVERYTHING, MS. ISLEY. WHO YOU ARE. WHY YOU DO WHAT YOU DO. WHAT THIS WHOLE POISON IVY THING IS ALL ABOUT.
2

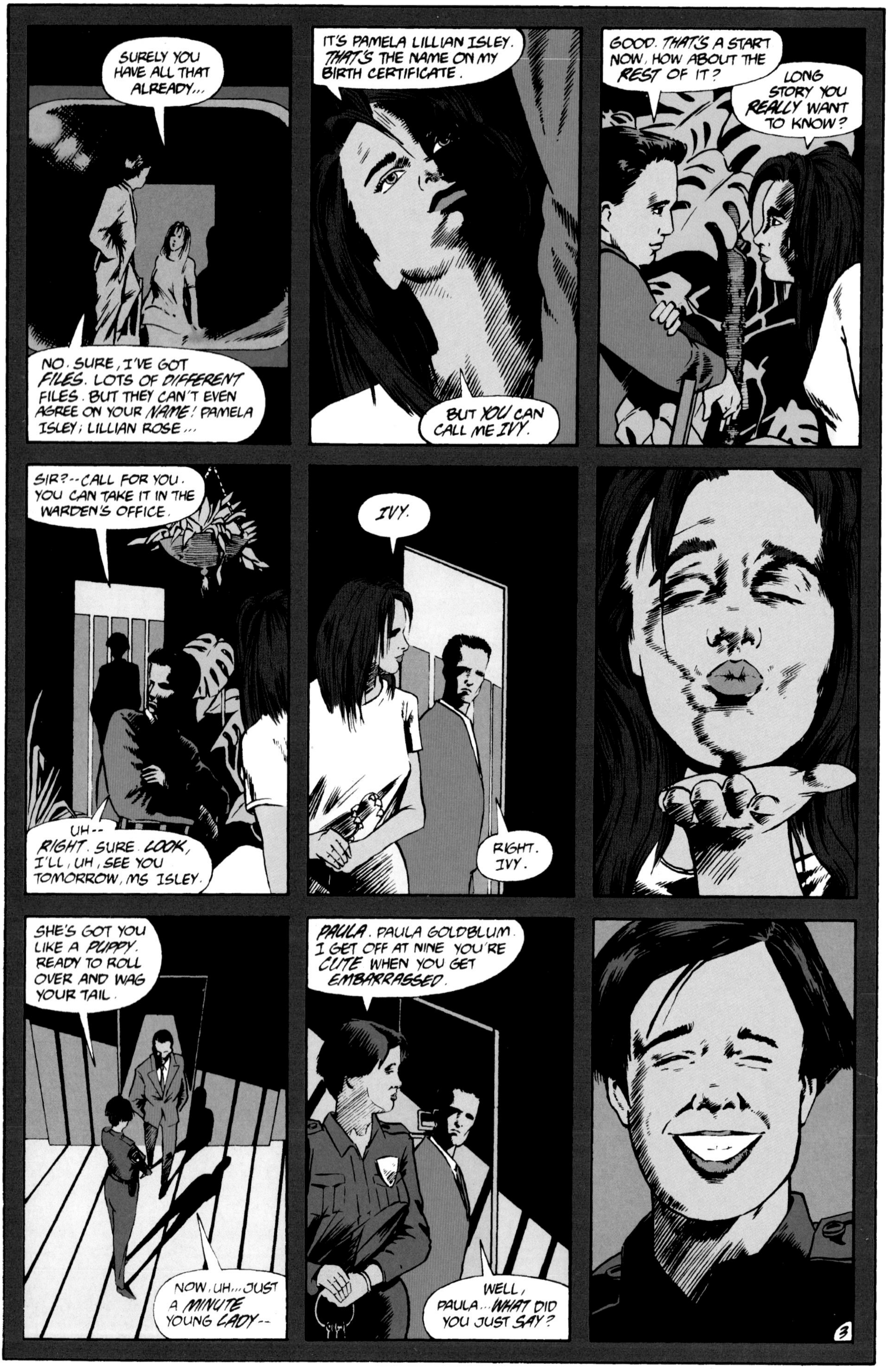
SURELY YOU HAVE ALL THAT ALREADY...
NO. SURE, I'VE GOT FILES. LOTS OF DIFFERENT FILES. BUT THEY CAN'T EVEN AGREE ON YOUR NAME! PAMELA ISLEY; LILLIAN ROSE...
IT'S PAMELA LILLIAN ISLEY. THAT'S THE NAME ON MY BIRTH CERTIFICATE.
BUT YOU CAN CALL ME IVY.
GOOD. THAT'S A START. NOW, HOW ABOUT THE REST OF IT?
LONG STORY. YOU REALLY WANT TO KNOW?
SIR?--CALL FOR YOU. YOU CAN TAKE IT IN THE WARDEN'S OFFICE.
UH--
RIGHT. SURE. LOOK, I'LL, UH, SEE YOU TOMORROW, MS ISLEY.
IVY.
RIGHT. IVY.
SHE'S GOT YOU LIKE A PUPPY. READY TO ROLL OVER AND WAG YOUR TAIL.
NOW, UH... JUST A MINUTE, YOUNG LADY--
PAULA. PAULA GOLDBLUM. I GET OFF AT NINE. YOU'RE CUTE WHEN YOU GET EMBARRASSED.
WELL, PAULA... WHAT DID YOU JUST SAY?
3

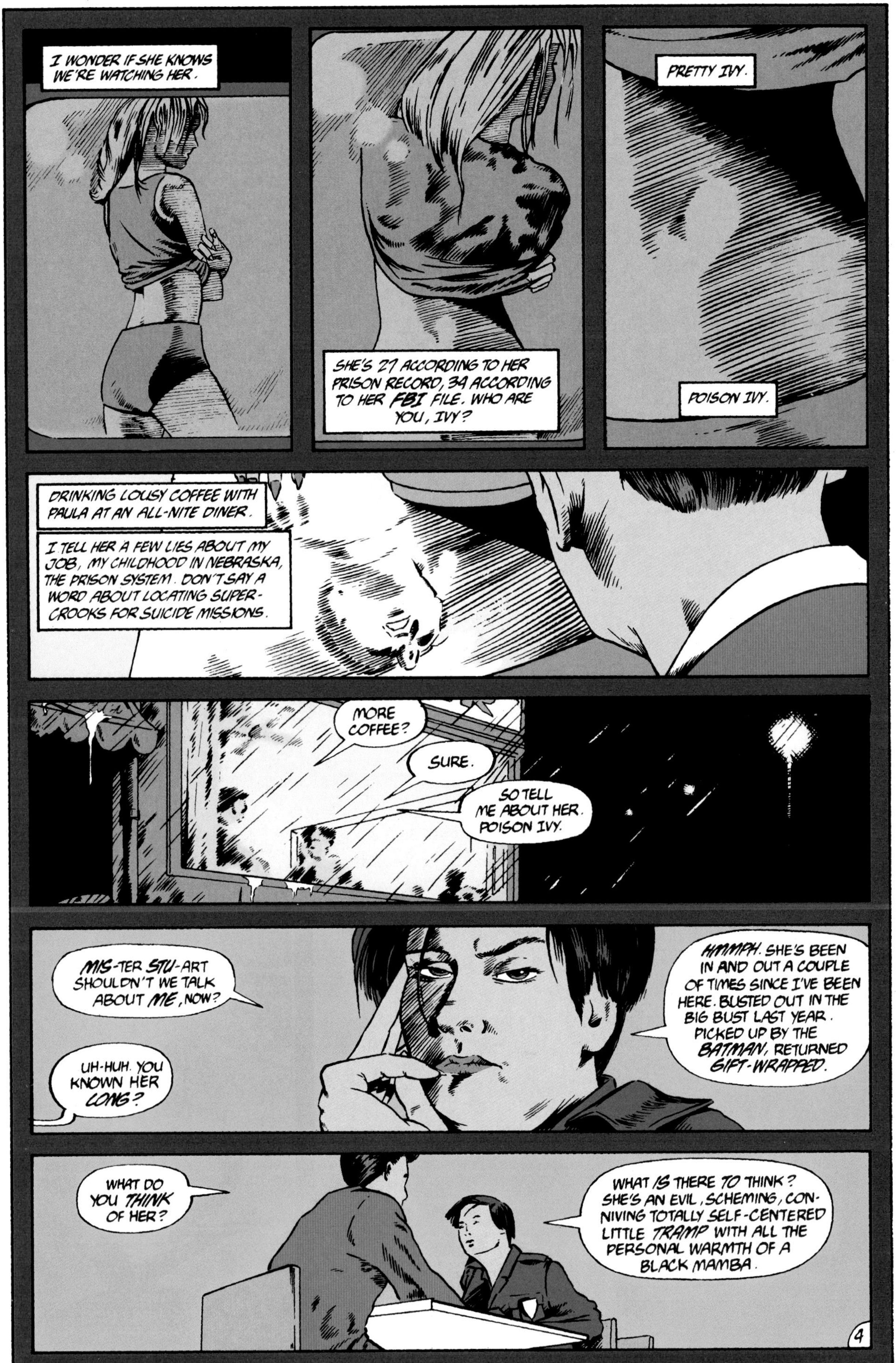

I WONDER IF SHE KNOWS WE'RE WATCHING HER.
SHE'S 27 ACCORDING TO HER PRISON RECORD, 34 ACCORDING TO HER FBI FILE. WHO ARE YOU, IVY?
PRETTY IVY.
POISON IVY.
DRINKING LOUSY COFFEE WITH PAULA AT AN ALL-NITE DINER.
I TELL HER A FEW LIES ABOUT MY JOB, MY CHILDHOOD IN NEBRASKA, THE PRISON SYSTEM. DON'T SAY A WORD ABOUT LOCATING SUPER-CROOKS FOR SUICIDE MISSIONS.
MORE COFFEE?
SURE.
SO TELL ME ABOUT HER. POISON IVY.
MIS-TER STU-ART SHOULDN'T WE TALK ABOUT ME, NOW?
UH-HUH. YOU KNOWN HER LONG?
HMMPH. SHE'S BEEN IN AND OUT A COUPLE OF TIMES SINCE I'VE BEEN HERE. BUSTED OUT IN THE BIG BUST LAST YEAR. PICKED UP BY THE BATMAN, RETURNED GIFT-WRAPPED.
WHAT DO YOU THINK OF HER?
WHAT IS THERE TO THINK? SHE'S AN EVIL, SCHEMING, CON-NIVING TOTALLY SELF-CENTERED LITTLE TRAMP WITH ALL THE PERSONAL WARMTH OF A BLACK MAMBA.
4

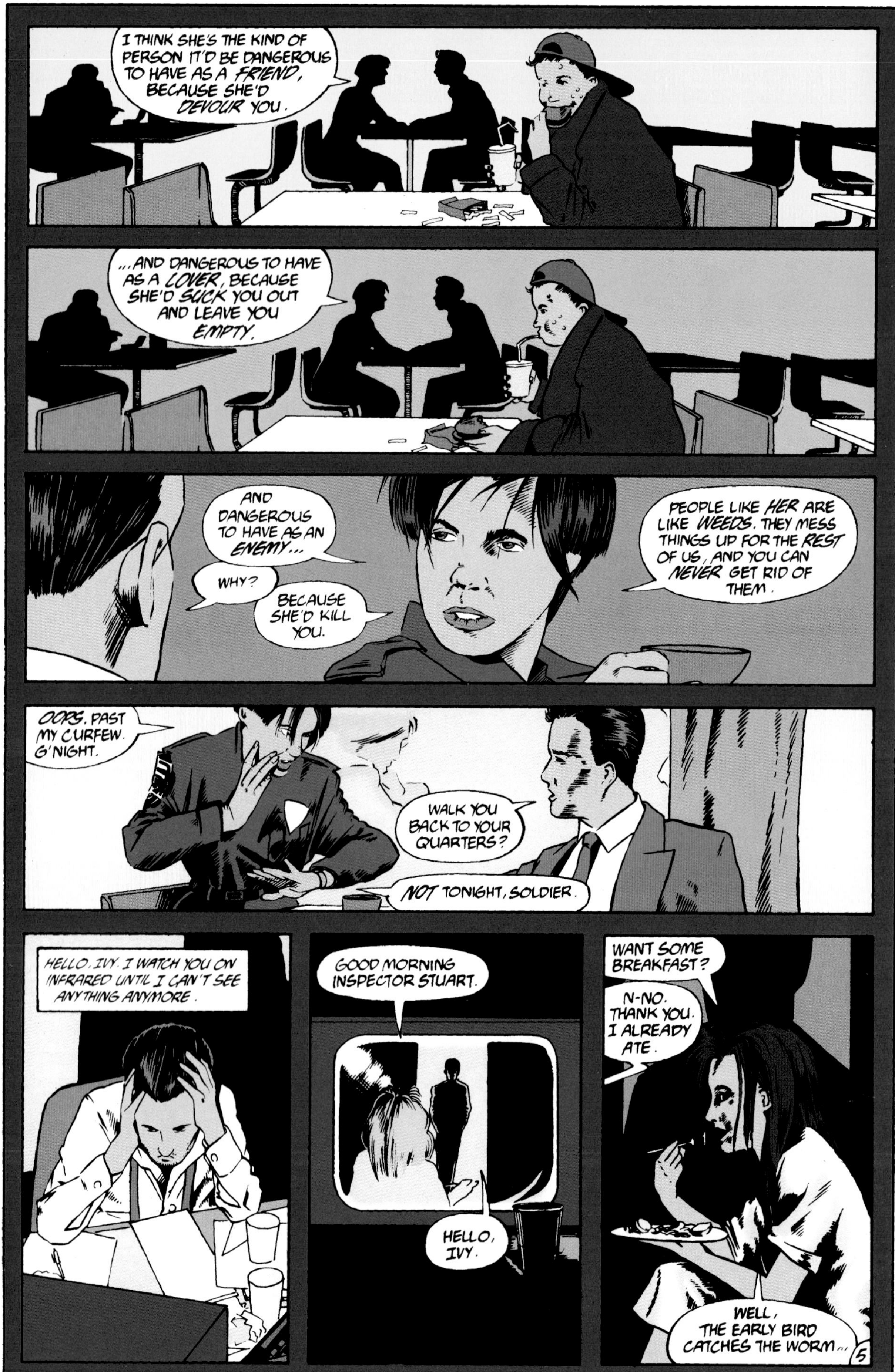
I THINK SHE'S THE KIND OF PERSON IT'D BE DANGEROUS TO HAVE AS A FRIEND, BECAUSE SHE'D DEVOUR YOU.
...AND DANGEROUS TO HAVE AS A LOVER, BECAUSE SHE'D SUCK YOU OUT AND LEAVE YOU EMPTY.
AND DANGEROUS TO HAVE AS AN ENEMY...
WHY?
BECAUSE SHE'D KILL YOU.
PEOPLE LIKE HER ARE LIKE WEEDS. THEY MESS THINGS UP FOR THE REST OF US, AND YOU CAN NEVER GET RID OF THEM.
OOPS. PAST MY CURFEW. G'NIGHT.
WALK YOU BACK TO YOUR QUARTERS?
NOT TONIGHT, SOLDIER.
HELLO, IVY. I WATCH YOU ON INFRARED UNTIL I CAN'T SEE ANYTHING ANYMORE.
GOOD MORNING INSPECTOR STUART.
HELLO, IVY.
WANT SOME BREAKFAST?
N-NO. THANK YOU. I ALREADY ATE.
WELL, THE EARLY BIRD CATCHES THE WORM...
5

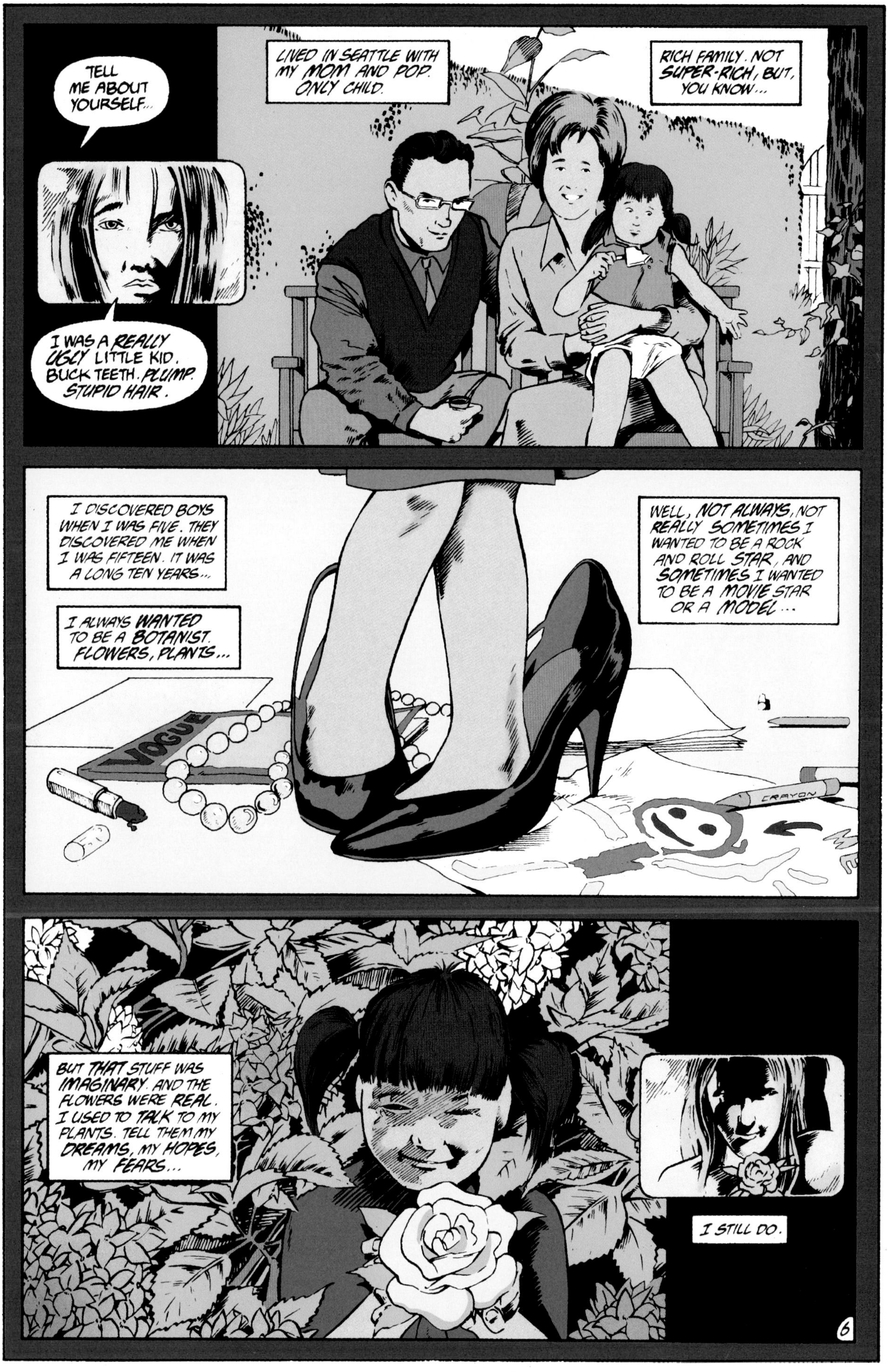
TELL ME ABOUT YOURSELF...
I WAS A REALLY UGLY LITTLE KID. BUCK TEETH. PLUMP. STUPID HAIR.
LIVED IN SEATTLE WITH MY MOM AND POP. ONLY CHILD.
RICH FAMILY. NOT SUPER-RICH, BUT, YOU KNOW...
I DISCOVERED BOYS WHEN I WAS FIVE. THEY DISCOVERED ME WHEN I WAS FIFTEEN. IT WAS A LONG TEN YEARS...
I ALWAYS WANTED TO BE A BOTANIST. FLOWERS, PLANTS...
WELL, NOT ALWAYS, NOT REALLY. SOMETIMES I WANTED TO BE A ROCK AND ROLL STAR, AND SOMETIMES I WANTED TO BE A MOVIE STAR OR A MODEL...
VOGUE
CRAYON
BUT THAT STUFF WAS IMAGINARY. AND THE FLOWERS WERE REAL. I USED TO TALK TO MY PLANTS. TELL THEM MY DREAMS, MY HOPES, MY FEARS...
I STILL DO.
6

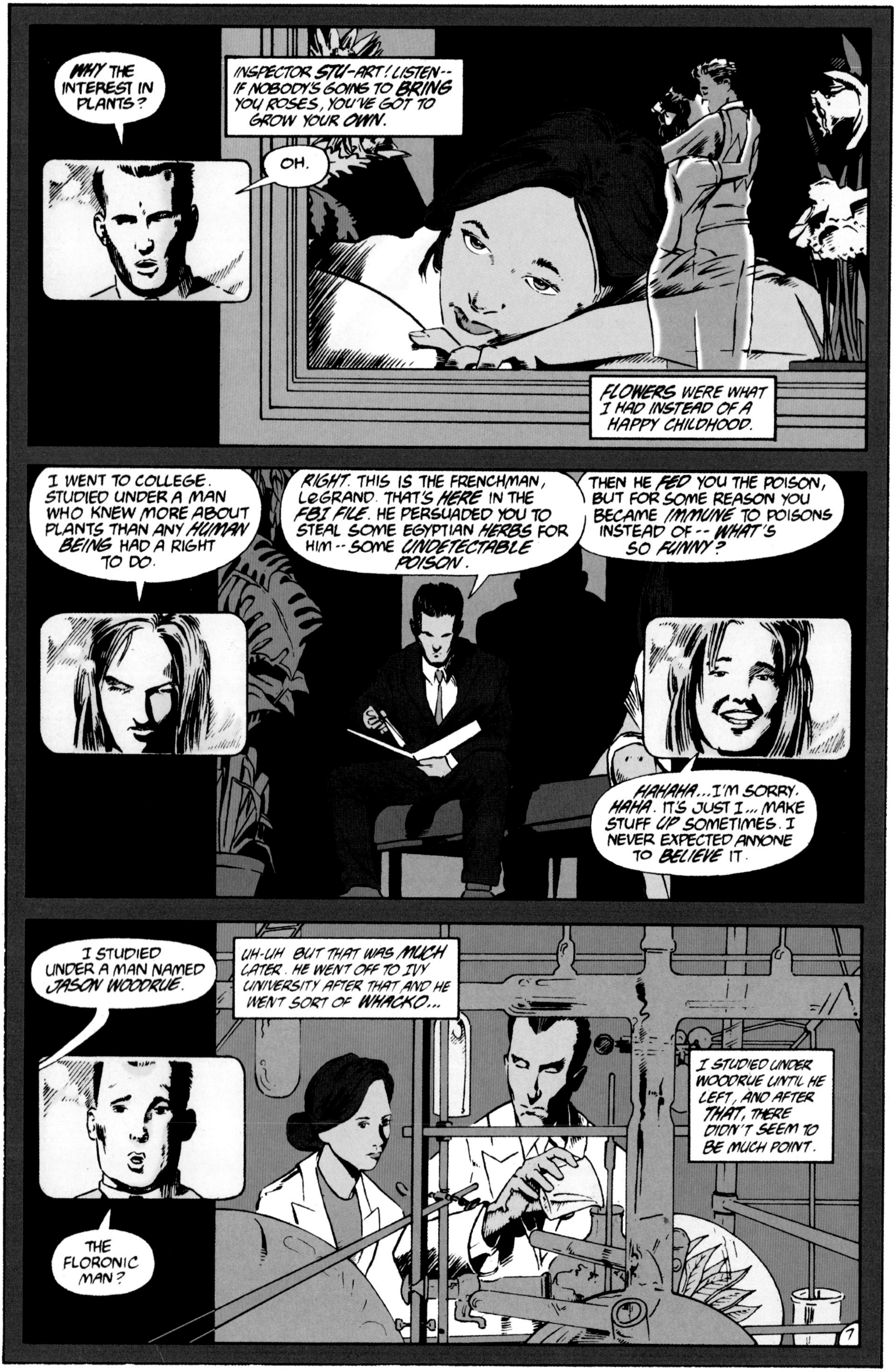
WHY THE INTEREST IN PLANTS?
INSPECTOR STU-ART! LISTEN-- IF NOBODY'S GOING TO BRING YOU ROSES, YOU'VE GOT TO GROW YOUR OWN.
OH.
FLOWERS WERE WHAT I HAD INSTEAD OF A HAPPY CHILDHOOD.
I WENT TO COLLEGE. STUDIED UNDER A MAN WHO KNEW MORE ABOUT PLANTS THAN ANY HUMAN BEING HAD A RIGHT TO DO.
RIGHT. THIS IS THE FRENCHMAN, LeGRAND. THAT'S HERE IN THE FBI FILE. HE PERSUADED YOU TO STEAL SOME EGYPTIAN HERBS FOR HIM -- SOME UNDETECTABLE POISON.
THEN HE FED YOU THE POISON, BUT FOR SOME REASON YOU BECAME IMMUNE TO POISONS INSTEAD OF -- WHAT'S SO FUNNY?
HAHAHA... I'M SORRY. HAHA. IT'S JUST I... MAKE STUFF UP SOMETIMES. I NEVER EXPECTED ANYONE TO BELIEVE IT.
I STUDIED UNDER A MAN NAMED JASON WOODRUE.
THE FLORONIC MAN?
UH-UH BUT THAT WAS MUCH LATER. HE WENT OFF TO IVY UNIVERSITY AFTER THAT AND HE WENT SORT OF WHACKO...
I STUDIED UNDER WOODRUE UNTIL HE LEFT, AND AFTER THAT, THERE DIDN'T SEEM TO BE MUCH POINT.
7

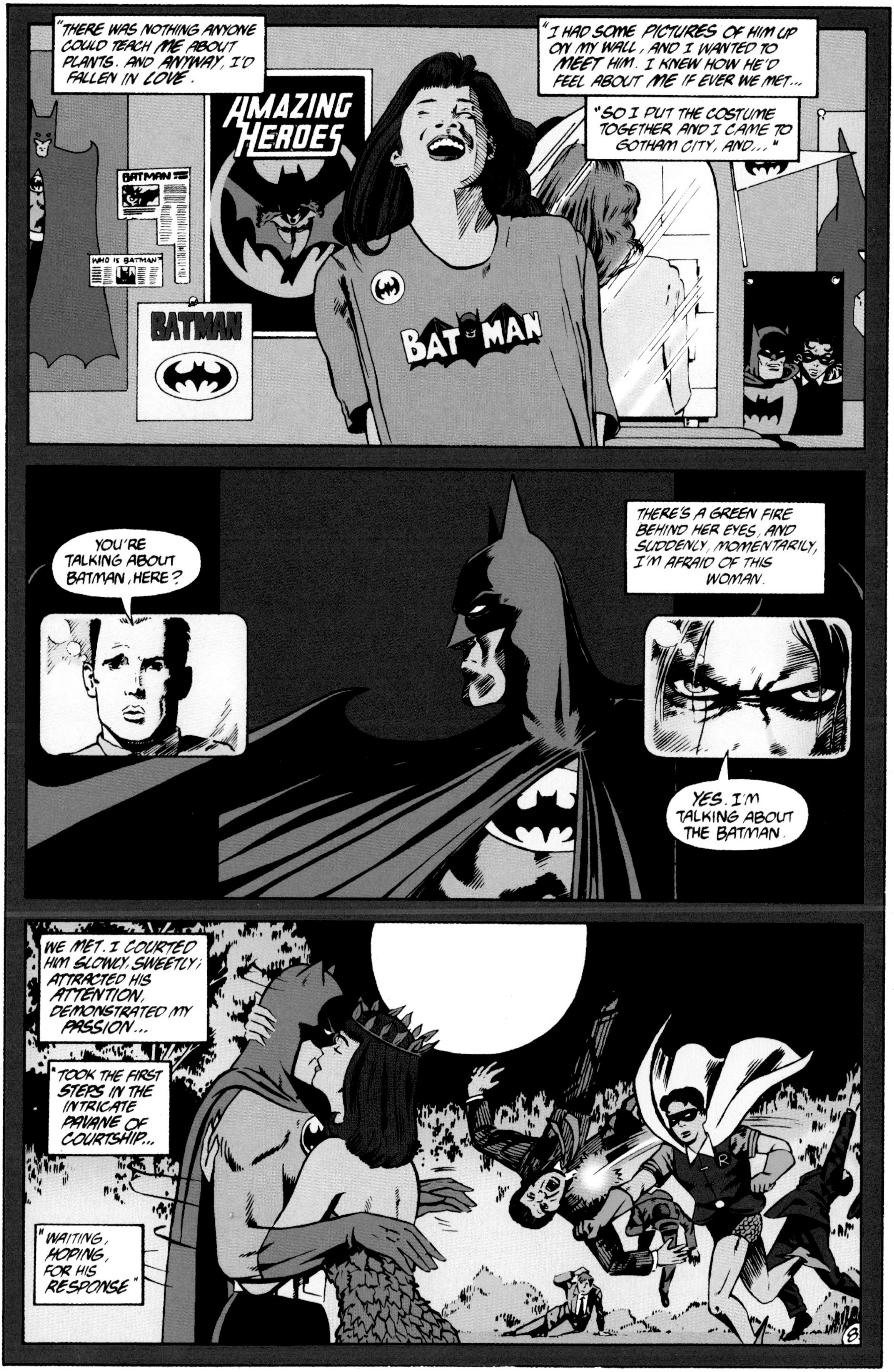
"THERE WAS NOTHING ANYONE COULD TEACH ME ABOUT PLANTS. AND ANYWAY, I'D FALLEN IN LOVE.
"I HAD SOME PICTURES OF HIM UP ON MY WALL, AND I WANTED TO MEET HIM. I KNEW HOW HE'D FEEL ABOUT ME IF EVER WE MET...
"SO I PUT THE COSTUME TOGETHER AND I CAME TO GOTHAM CITY, AND..."
AMAZING HEROES
BATMAN
WHO IS BATMAN?
BATMAN
BATMAN
YOU'RE TALKING ABOUT BATMAN, HERE?
THERE'S A GREEN FIRE BEHIND HER EYES, AND SUDDENLY, MOMENTARILY, I'M AFRAID OF THIS WOMAN.
YES. I'M TALKING ABOUT THE BATMAN.
WE MET. I COURTED HIM SLOWLY, SWEETLY; ATTRACTED HIS ATTENTION, DEMONSTRATED MY PASSION...
"TOOK THE FIRST STEPS IN THE INTRICATE PAVANE OF COURTSHIP...
"WAITING, HOPING, FOR HIS RESPONSE"

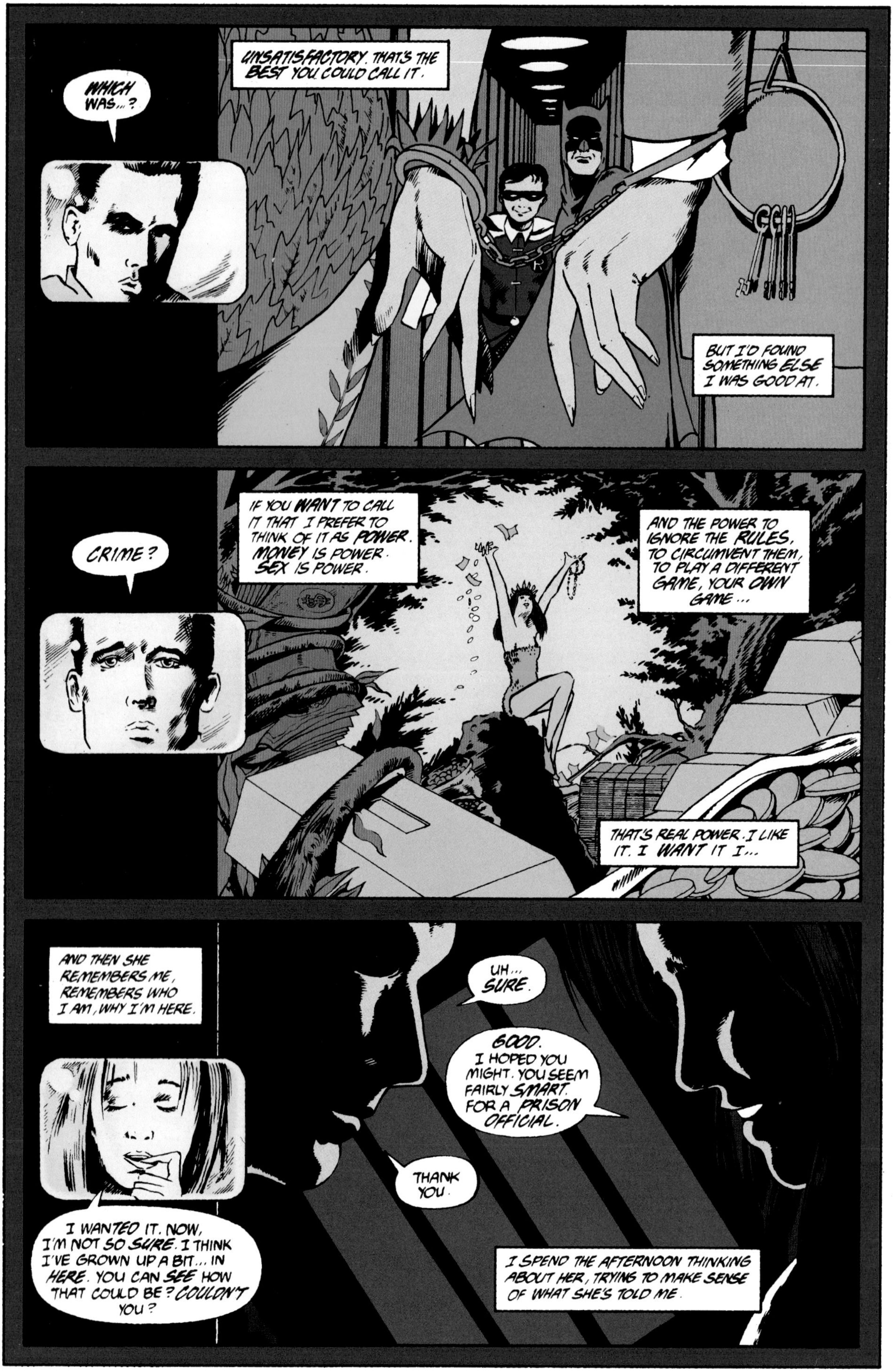
WHICH WAS...?
UNSATISFACTORY. THAT'S THE BEST YOU COULD CALL IT.
BUT I'D FOUND SOMETHING ELSE I WAS GOOD AT.
CRIME?
IF YOU WANT TO CALL IT THAT. I PREFER TO THINK OF IT AS POWER. MONEY IS POWER. SEX IS POWER.
AND THE POWER TO IGNORE THE RULES, TO CIRCUMVENT THEM, TO PLAY A DIFFERENT GAME, YOUR OWN GAME...
THAT'S REAL POWER. I LIKE IT. I WANT IT. I...
AND THEN SHE REMEMBERS ME, REMEMBERS WHO I AM, WHY I'M HERE.
I WANTED IT. NOW, I'M NOT SO SURE. I THINK I'VE GROWN UP A BIT... IN HERE. YOU CAN SEE HOW THAT COULD BE? COULDN'T YOU?
UH... SURE.
GOOD. I HOPED YOU MIGHT. YOU SEEM FAIRLY SMART. FOR A PRISON OFFICIAL.
THANK YOU.
I SPEND THE AFTERNOON THINKING ABOUT HER, TRYING TO MAKE SENSE OF WHAT SHE'S TOLD ME.

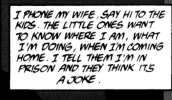
CALL FROM HEAD OFFICE SAYING THEY NEED RESULTS FAST: TASK FORCE X IS ALWAYS HUNGRY IT'S A LOUSY WAY TO MAKE A LIVING.

I PHONE MY WIFE, SAY HI TO THE KIDS. THE LITTLE ONES WANT TO KNOW WHERE I AM, WHAT I'M DOING, WHEN I'M COMING HOME. I TELL THEM I'M IN PRISON AND THEY THINK IT'S A JOKE.

IN THE AFTERNOON SHE READS A BOOK: FEMINIST TRASH. WATERS THE PLANTS STARES OUT OF THE WINDOW.

MORE COFFEE WITH PAULA.

WE GO BACK TO MY HOTEL ROOM TOGETHER.

DO NOT DISTURB

DURING THE NIGHT I DREAM AND CALL OUT A NAME, AND WAKE UP I'M SAYING "IVY, IVY," AND PAULA'S AWAKE NEXT TO ME SHE DOESN'T SAY ANYTHING, BUT I CAN TELL SHE'S AWAKE FROM HER BREATHING.

THEY TEACH US STUFF LIKE THAT IN THE AGENCY.

I PRETEND TO GO BACK TO SLEEP, AND SOON I REALLY DO.

PAULA'S GONE WHEN I WAKE UP: IT'S LIKE SHE WAS NEVER THERE AT ALL.

POISON IVY'S GOT ME ALL CONFUSED: I KEEP THINKING ABOUT HER. WHATEVER I'M DOING IS OVERLAID WITH FLASHES OF HER SMILE, HER HAIR, THE VERY SCENT OF HER...

MY THOUGHTS INTERTWINE AND TANGLE.

TANGLE LIKE...YEAH, LIKE IVY.

I GO DOWN TO THE WARDEN'S OFFICE. TELL HIM WHAT I'M GOING TO DO. HE PROTESTS. I PULL RANK, HE SHUTS UP CALLS THE GUARD CAPTAIN IN. BRIEFS HER, WE GO DOWN TOGETHER. I DON'T SEE PAULA ANYWHERE.

10

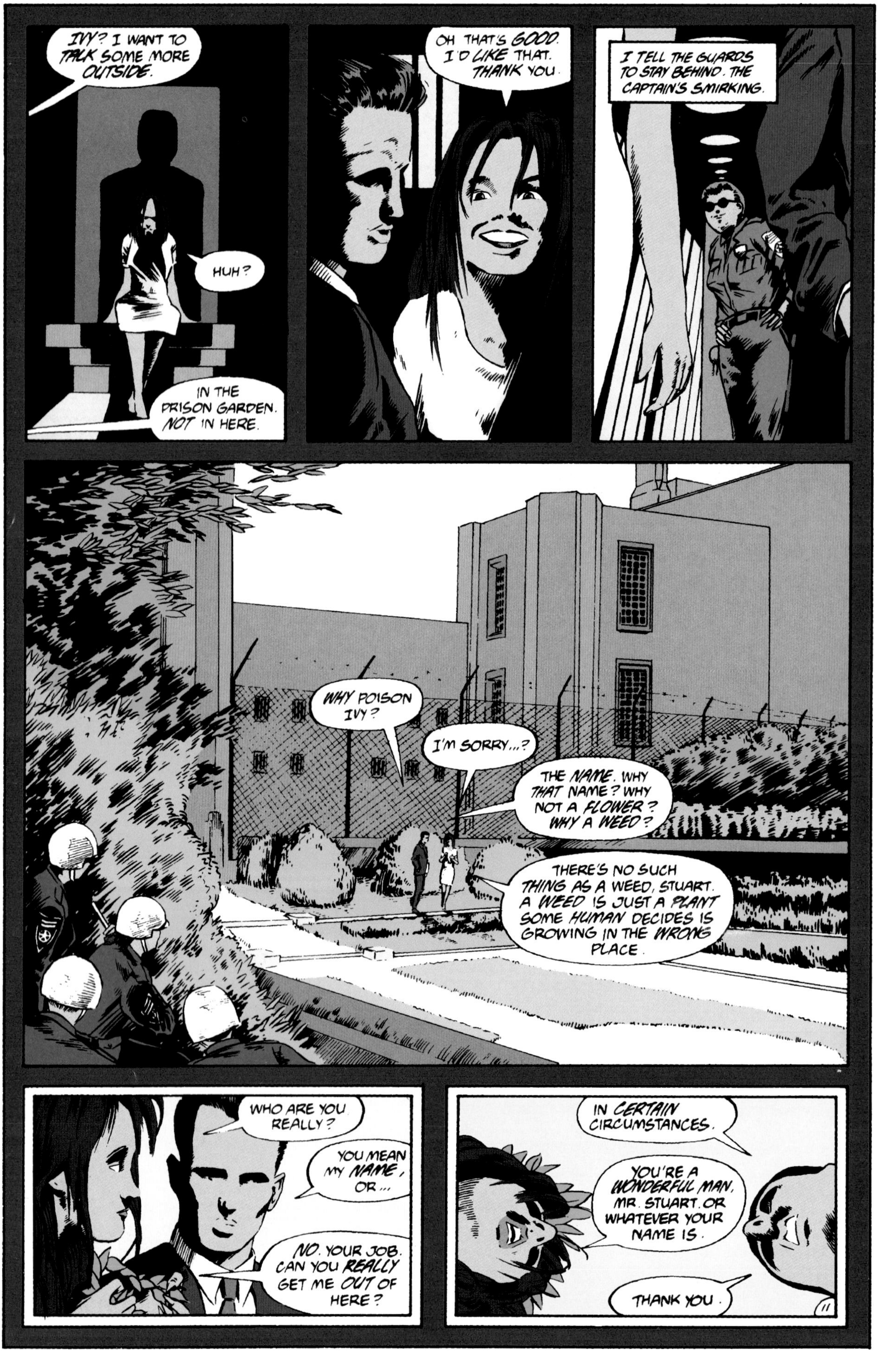
IVY? I WANT TO TALK SOME MORE OUTSIDE.
HUH?
IN THE PRISON GARDEN. NOT IN HERE.
OH THAT'S GOOD. I'D LIKE THAT. THANK YOU.
I TELL THE GUARDS TO STAY BEHIND. THE CAPTAIN'S SMIRKING.
WHY POISON IVY?
I'M SORRY...?
THE NAME. WHY THAT NAME? WHY NOT A FLOWER? WHY A WEED?
THERE'S NO SUCH THING AS A WEED, STUART. A WEED IS JUST A PLANT SOME HUMAN DECIDES IS GROWING IN THE WRONG PLACE.
WHO ARE YOU REALLY?
YOU MEAN MY NAME, OR...
NO. YOUR JOB. CAN YOU REALLY GET ME OUT OF HERE?
IN CERTAIN CIRCUMSTANCES.
YOU'RE A WONDERFUL MAN, MR. STUART. OR WHATEVER YOUR NAME IS.
THANK YOU.
11

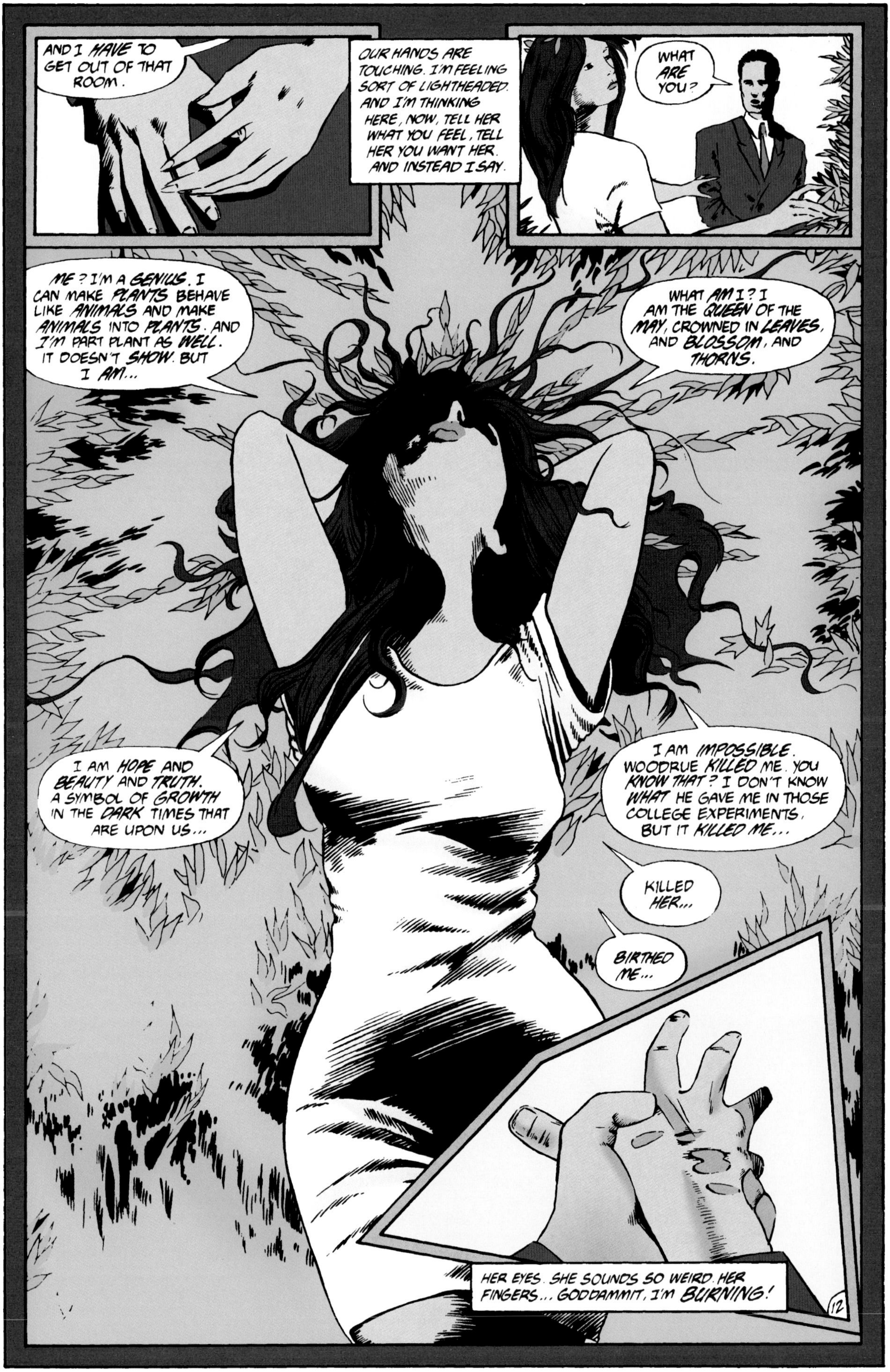
AND I HAVE TO GET OUT OF THAT ROOM.
OUR HANDS ARE TOUCHING. I'M FEELING SORT OF LIGHTHEADED. AND I'M THINKING HERE, NOW, TELL HER WHAT YOU FEEL, TELL HER YOU WANT HER. AND INSTEAD I SAY.
WHAT ARE YOU?
ME? I'M A GENIUS. I CAN MAKE PLANTS BEHAVE LIKE ANIMALS AND MAKE ANIMALS INTO PLANTS. AND I'M PART PLANT AS WELL. IT DOESN'T SHOW. BUT I AM...
WHAT AM I? I AM THE QUEEN OF THE MAY, CROWNED IN LEAVES, AND BLOSSOM, AND THORNS.
I AM HOPE AND BEAUTY AND TRUTH. A SYMBOL OF GROWTH IN THE DARK TIMES THAT ARE UPON US...
I AM IMPOSSIBLE. WOODRUE KILLED ME. YOU KNOW THAT? I DON'T KNOW WHAT HE GAVE ME IN THOSE COLLEGE EXPERIMENTS. BUT IT KILLED ME...
KILLED HER...
BIRTHED ME...
HER EYES. SHE SOUNDS SO WEIRD. HER FINGERS... GODDAMMIT, I'M BURNING!
12

WHAT *AM I?* I AM POISON IVY.

MY *HAND?* GODDAMMIT, WHAT HAVE YOU *DONE* TO MY HAND?

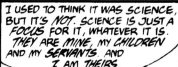

I USED TO THINK IT WAS SCIENCE, BUT IT'S *NOT.* SCIENCE IS JUST A *FOCUS* FOR IT, WHATEVER IT IS. THEY ARE *MINE,* MY *CHILDREN* AND MY *SERVANTS.* AND I AM THEIRS.

SO *THAT'S* WHY I HAVE TO GET *OUT.* DO YOU SEE? I CAN'T STAY *HERE* FOREVER. I WON'T LIVE *FOREVER...* WE *DON'T.* WE AREN'T ERL-KINGS. *THAT'S* WHY YOU HAVE TO LET ME OUT.

HELP! SOMEONE! GUARDS!

AT *NIGHT* THE EARTH MOTHER, NATURE, SHE *WHISPERS* TO ME.

SHE WHISPERS, *YOU ARE MY DAUGHTER. THE WORLD IS YOURS. WHATEVER YOU WANT IS YOURS, IVY...*

JUST REACH OUT AND TAKE IT.

NOW YOU *UNDERSTAND.* DON'T YOU. *THAT'S* WHY YOU HAVE TO LET ME *OUT* OF HERE...

WHAT *AM I?* DARLING, I'M POISON IVY.

GET *UP.* GET *BACK.* AWAY. NOW.

YOU WON'T *FORGET,* WILL YOU? YOU'LL GET ME OUT OF HERE...?

MY HAND IS SWOLLEN, THE MARKS OF HER FINGERS BURNED INTO THE FLESH. I FEEL SICK. I WATCH THEM AS THEY LEAD HER BACK TO HER CELL. MY FACE ITCHES WHERE SHE KISSED ME.

13

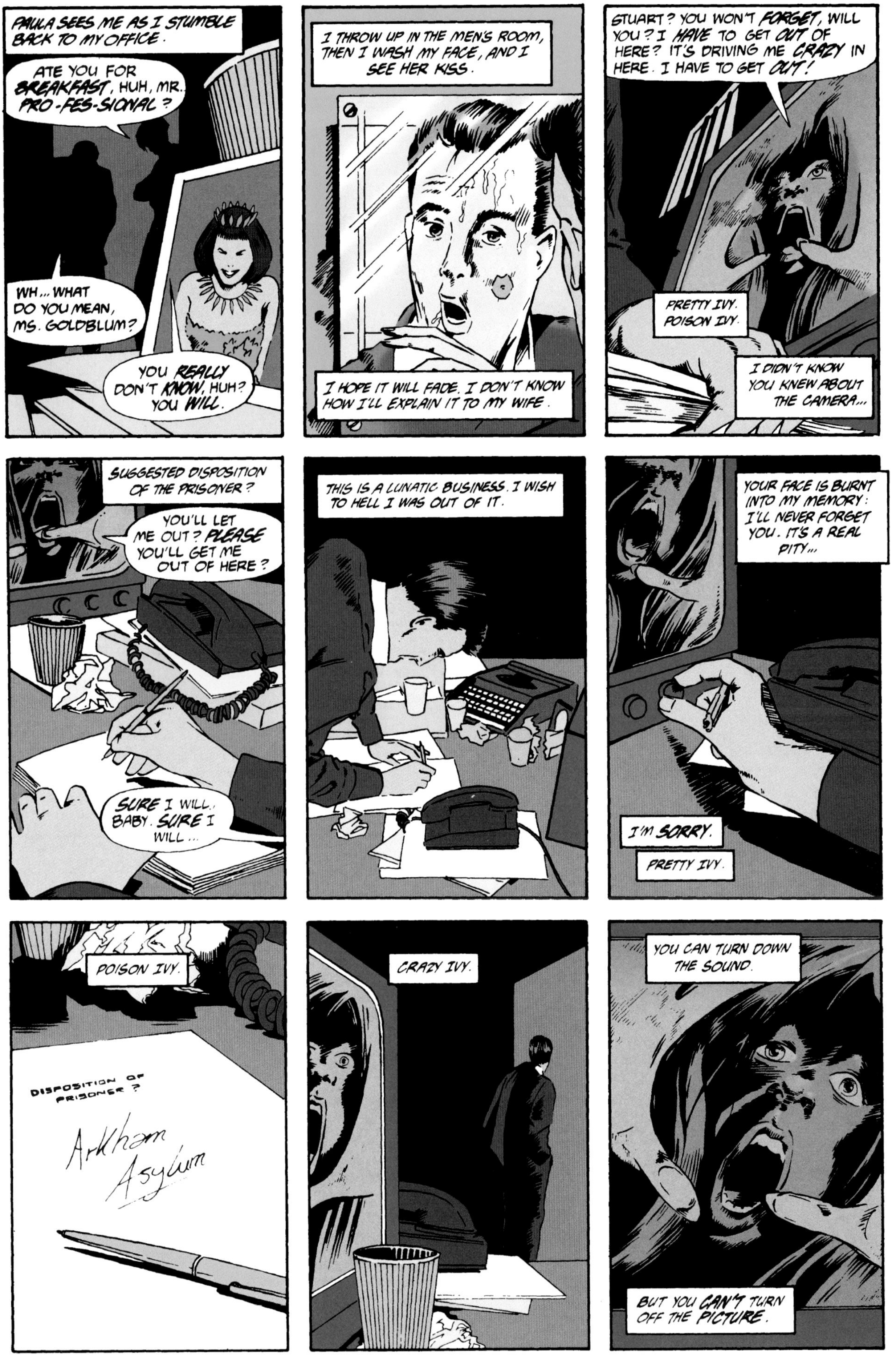
PAULA SEES ME AS I STUMBLE BACK TO MY OFFICE.
ATE YOU FOR BREAKFAST, HUH, MR. PRO-FES-SIONAL?
WH... WHAT DO YOU MEAN, MS. GOLDBLUM?
YOU REALLY DON'T KNOW, HUH? YOU WILL.
I THROW UP IN THE MEN'S ROOM, THEN I WASH MY FACE, AND I SEE HER KISS.
I HOPE IT WILL FADE. I DON'T KNOW HOW I'LL EXPLAIN IT TO MY WIFE.
STUART? YOU WON'T FORGET, WILL YOU? I HAVE TO GET OUT OF HERE? IT'S DRIVING ME CRAZY IN HERE. I HAVE TO GET OUT!
PRETTY IVY. POISON IVY.
I DIDN'T KNOW YOU KNEW ABOUT THE CAMERA...
SUGGESTED DISPOSITION OF THE PRISONER?
YOU'LL LET ME OUT? PLEASE YOU'LL GET ME OUT OF HERE?
SURE I WILL. BABY. SURE I WILL...
THIS IS A LUNATIC BUSINESS. I WISH TO HELL I WAS OUT OF IT.
YOUR FACE IS BURNT INTO MY MEMORY: I'LL NEVER FORGET YOU. IT'S A REAL PITY...
I'M SORRY.
PRETTY IVY.
POISON IVY.
DISPOSITION OF PRISONER?
Arkham Asylum
CRAZY IVY.
YOU CAN TURN DOWN THE SOUND.
BUT YOU CAN'T TURN OFF THE PICTURE.

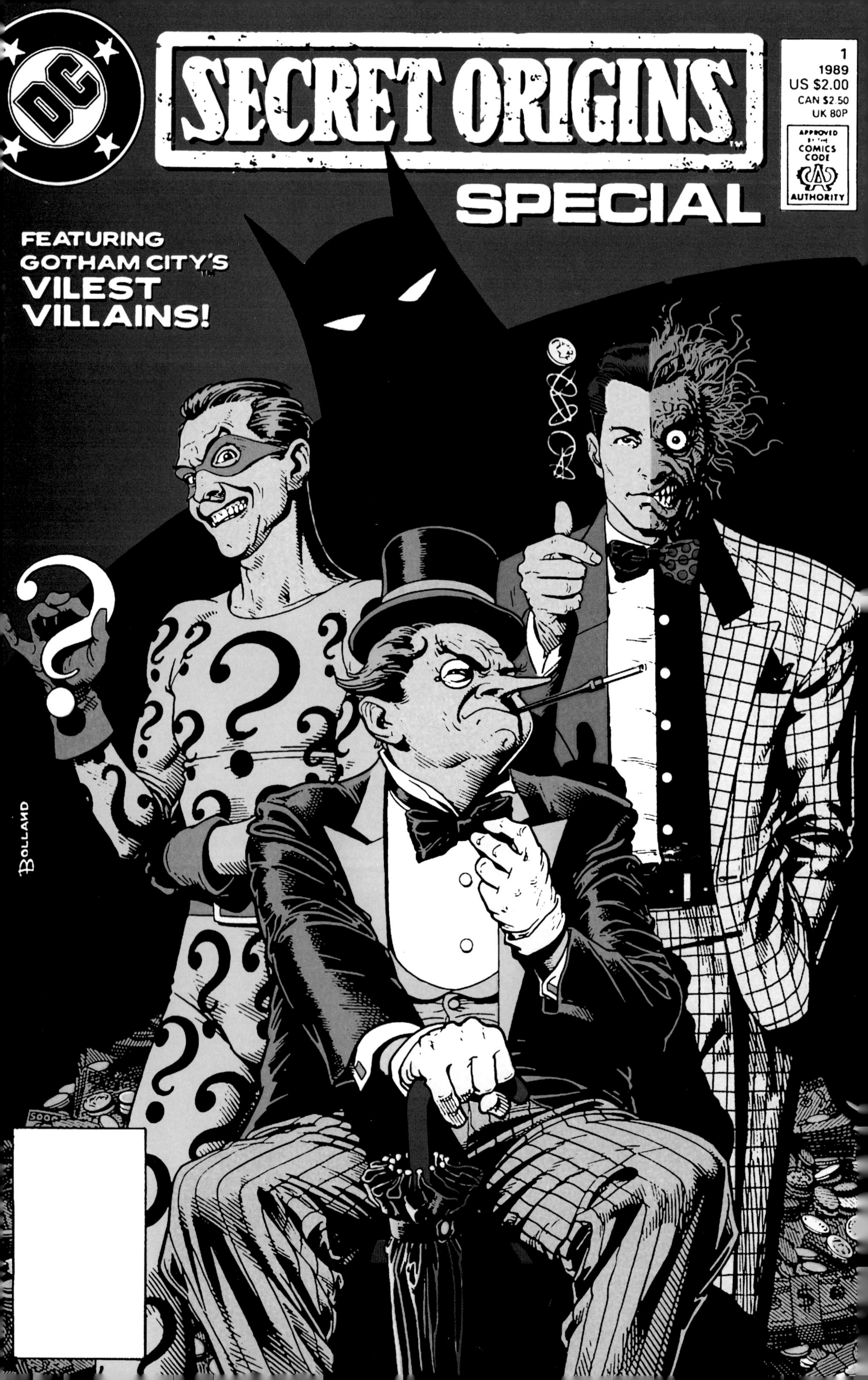
DC
SECRET ORIGINS
SPECIAL
1
1989
US $2.00
CAN $2.50
UK 80P
APPROVED BY THE COMICS CODE AUTHORITY
FEATURING GOTHAM CITY'S VILEST VILLAINS!
BOLLAND

EDITOR'S NOTE

This historic 64-page one-shot features three related tales set within a framing story authored by Neil Gaiman. Although two of these three chapters are scripted by other writers, they are included in this volume to preserve the integrity of the original narrative.

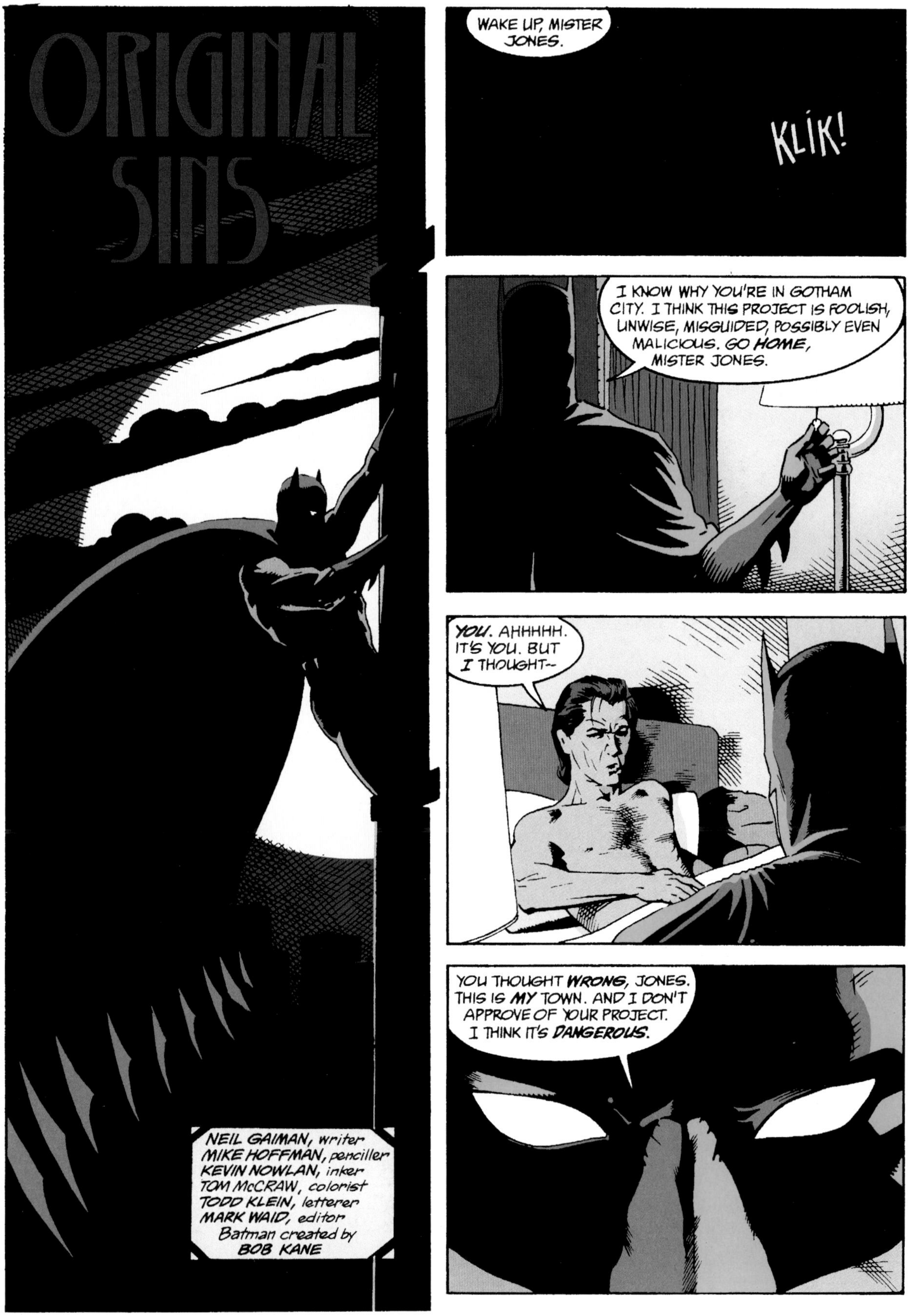
ORIGINAL SINS
NEIL GAIMAN, writer
MIKE HOFFMAN, penciller
KEVIN NOWLAN, inker
TOM McCRAW, colorist
TODD KLEIN, letterer
MARK WAID, editor
Batman created by
BOB KANE
WAKE UP, MISTER JONES.
KLIK!
I KNOW WHY YOU'RE IN GOTHAM CITY. I THINK THIS PROJECT IS FOOLISH, UNWISE, MISGUIDED, POSSIBLY EVEN MALICIOUS. GO HOME, MISTER JONES.
YOU. AHHHHH. IT'S YOU. BUT I THOUGHT--
YOU THOUGHT WRONG, JONES. THIS IS MY TOWN. AND I DON'T APPROVE OF YOUR PROJECT. I THINK IT'S DANGEROUS.

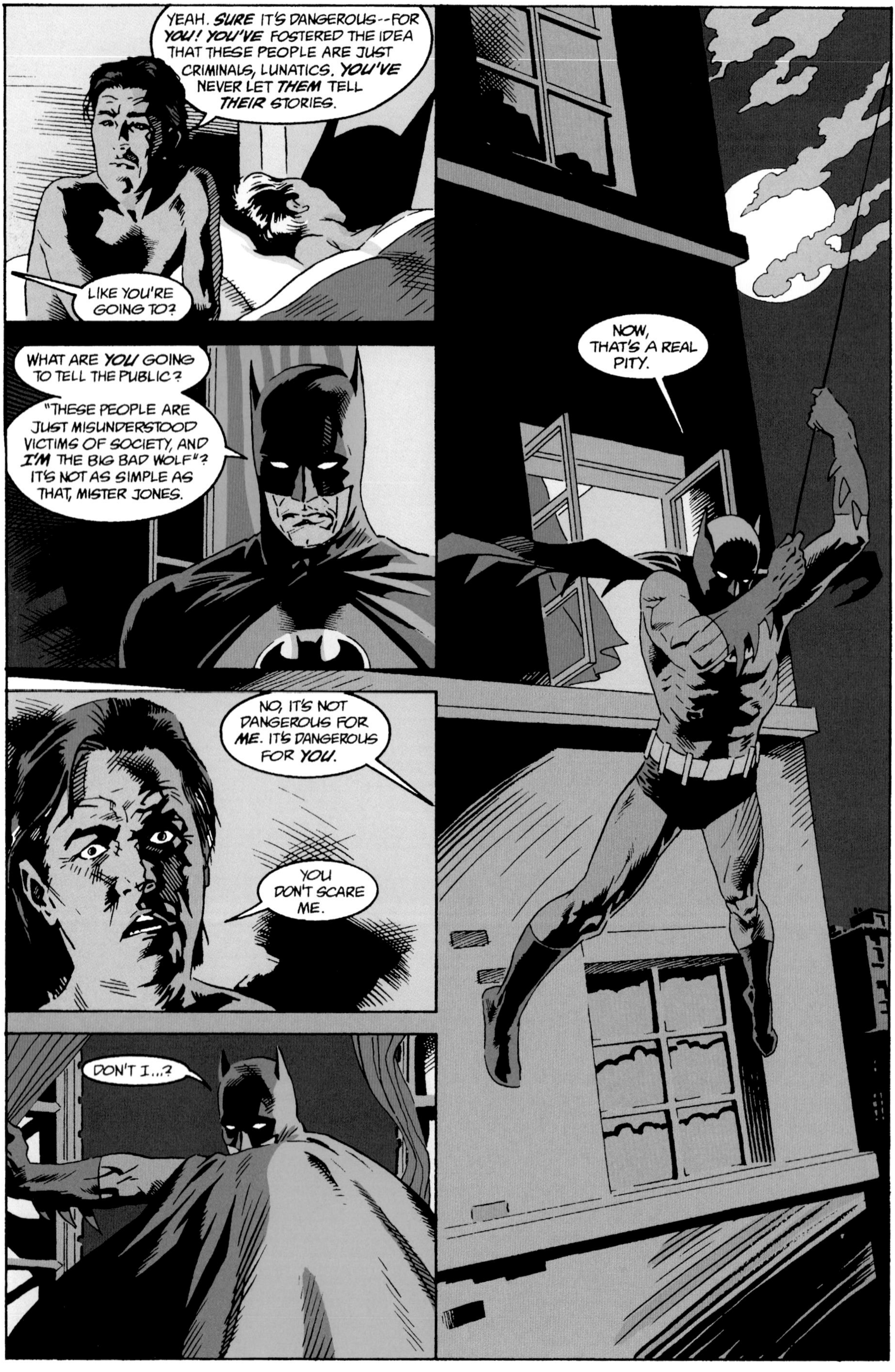
YEAH. SURE IT'S DANGEROUS--FOR YOU! YOU'VE FOSTERED THE IDEA THAT THESE PEOPLE ARE JUST CRIMINALS, LUNATICS. YOU'VE NEVER LET THEM TELL THEIR STORIES.
LIKE YOU'RE GOING TO?
WHAT ARE YOU GOING TO TELL THE PUBLIC?
"THESE PEOPLE ARE JUST MISUNDERSTOOD VICTIMS OF SOCIETY, AND I'M THE BIG BAD WOLF"? IT'S NOT AS SIMPLE AS THAT, MISTER JONES.
NO, IT'S NOT DANGEROUS FOR ME. IT'S DANGEROUS FOR YOU.
YOU DON'T SCARE ME.
DON'T I...?
NOW, THAT'S A REAL PITY.

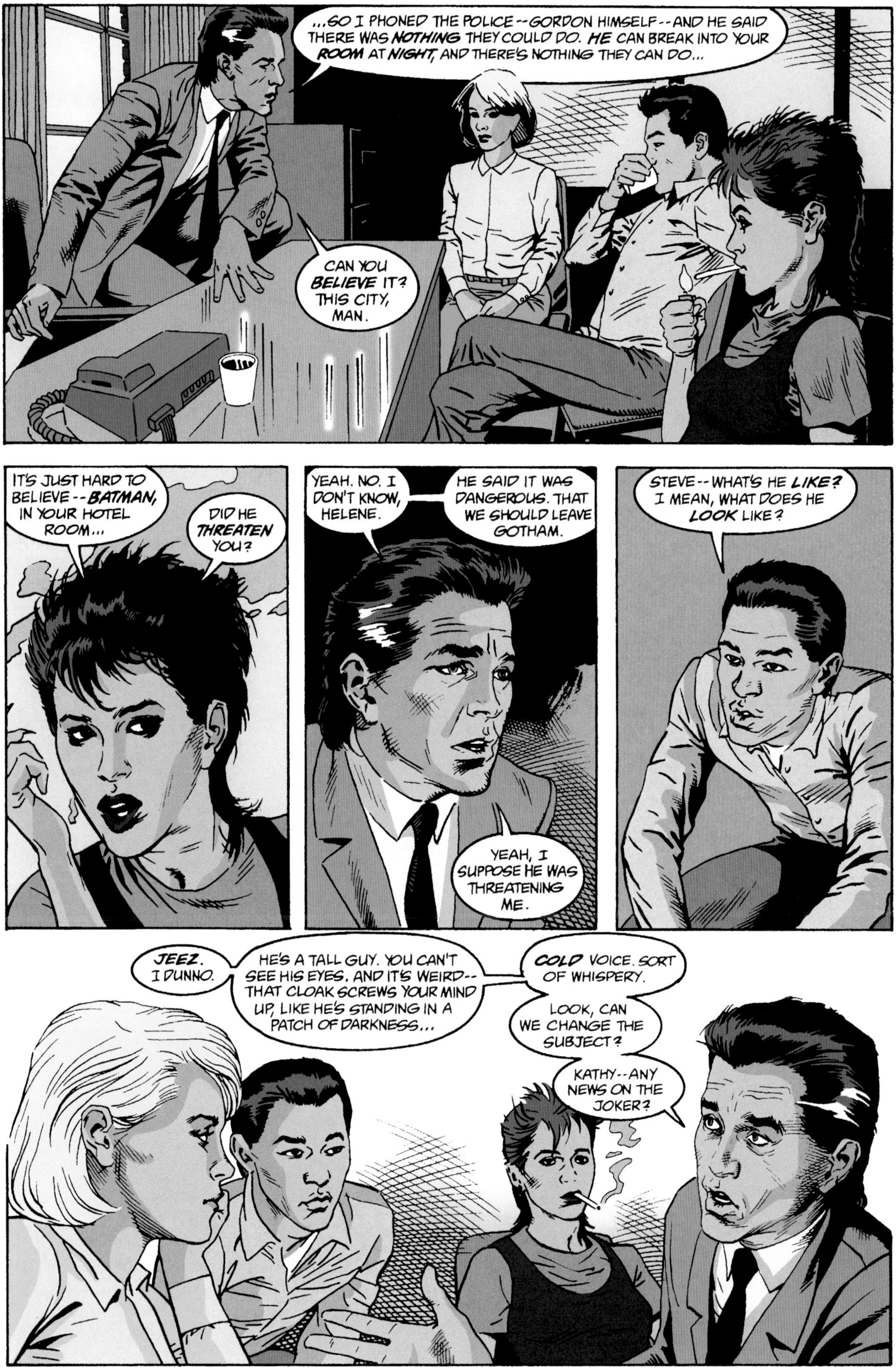
...SO I PHONED THE POLICE--GORDON HIMSELF--AND HE SAID THERE WAS NOTHING THEY COULD DO. HE CAN BREAK INTO YOUR ROOM AT NIGHT, AND THERE'S NOTHING THEY CAN DO...
CAN YOU BELIEVE IT? THIS CITY, MAN.
IT'S JUST HARD TO BELIEVE--BATMAN, IN YOUR HOTEL ROOM...
DID HE THREATEN YOU?
YEAH. NO. I DON'T KNOW, HELENE.
HE SAID IT WAS DANGEROUS. THAT WE SHOULD LEAVE GOTHAM.
YEAH, I SUPPOSE HE WAS THREATENING ME.
STEVE--WHAT'S HE LIKE? I MEAN, WHAT DOES HE LOOK LIKE?
JEEZ. I DUNNO.
HE'S A TALL GUY. YOU CAN'T SEE HIS EYES. AND IT'S WEIRD--THAT CLOAK SCREWS YOUR MIND UP, LIKE HE'S STANDING IN A PATCH OF DARKNESS...
COLD VOICE. SORT OF WHISPERY.
LOOK, CAN WE CHANGE THE SUBJECT?
KATHY--ANY NEWS ON THE JOKER?

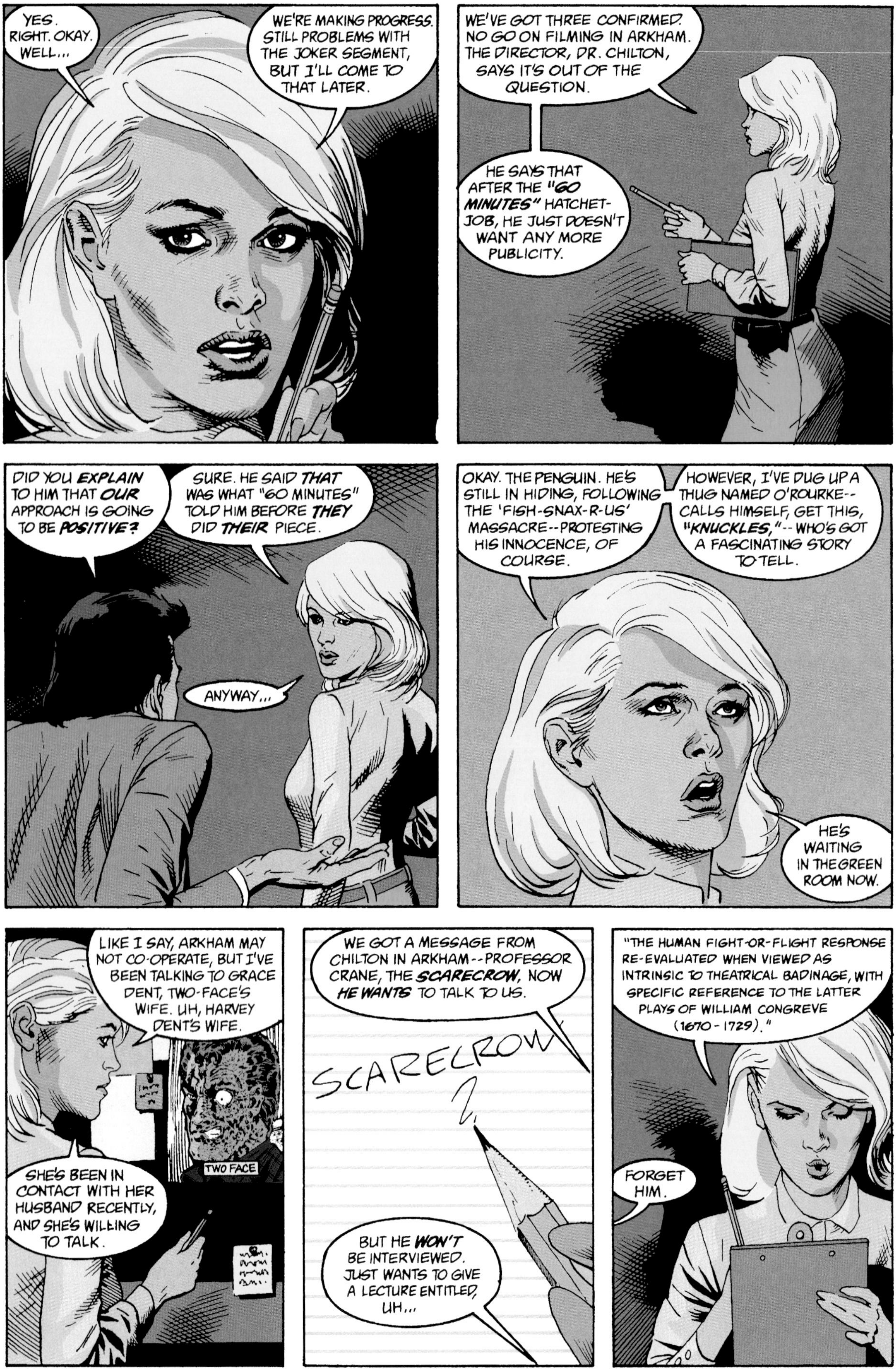

YES. RIGHT. OKAY. WELL...
WE'RE MAKING PROGRESS. STILL PROBLEMS WITH THE JOKER SEGMENT, BUT I'LL COME TO THAT LATER.
WE'VE GOT THREE CONFIRMED. NO GO ON FILMING IN ARKHAM. THE DIRECTOR, DR. CHILTON, SAYS IT'S OUT OF THE QUESTION.
HE SAYS THAT AFTER THE "60 MINUTES" HATCHET-JOB, HE JUST DOESN'T WANT ANY MORE PUBLICITY.
DID YOU EXPLAIN TO HIM THAT OUR APPROACH IS GOING TO BE POSITIVE?
SURE. HE SAID THAT WAS WHAT "60 MINUTES" TOLD HIM BEFORE THEY DID THEIR PIECE.
ANYWAY...
OKAY. THE PENGUIN. HE'S STILL IN HIDING, FOLLOWING THE 'FISH-SNAX-R-US' MASSACRE--PROTESTING HIS INNOCENCE, OF COURSE.
HOWEVER, I'VE DUG UP A THUG NAMED O'ROURKE--CALLS HIMSELF, GET THIS, "KNUCKLES,"--WHO'S GOT A FASCINATING STORY TO TELL.
HE'S WAITING IN THE GREEN ROOM NOW.
LIKE I SAY, ARKHAM MAY NOT CO-OPERATE, BUT I'VE BEEN TALKING TO GRACE DENT, TWO-FACE'S WIFE. UH, HARVEY DENT'S WIFE.
TWO FACE
SHE'S BEEN IN CONTACT WITH HER HUSBAND RECENTLY, AND SHE'S WILLING TO TALK.
WE GOT A MESSAGE FROM CHILTON IN ARKHAM--PROFESSOR CRANE, THE SCARECROW, NOW HE WANTS TO TALK TO US.
SCARECROW ?
BUT HE WON'T BE INTERVIEWED. JUST WANTS TO GIVE A LECTURE ENTITLED, UH...
"THE HUMAN FIGHT-OR-FLIGHT RESPONSE RE-EVALUATED WHEN VIEWED AS INTRINSIC TO THEATRICAL BADINAGE, WITH SPECIFIC REFERENCE TO THE LATTER PLAYS OF WILLIAM CONGREVE (1670 - 1729)."
FORGET HIM.

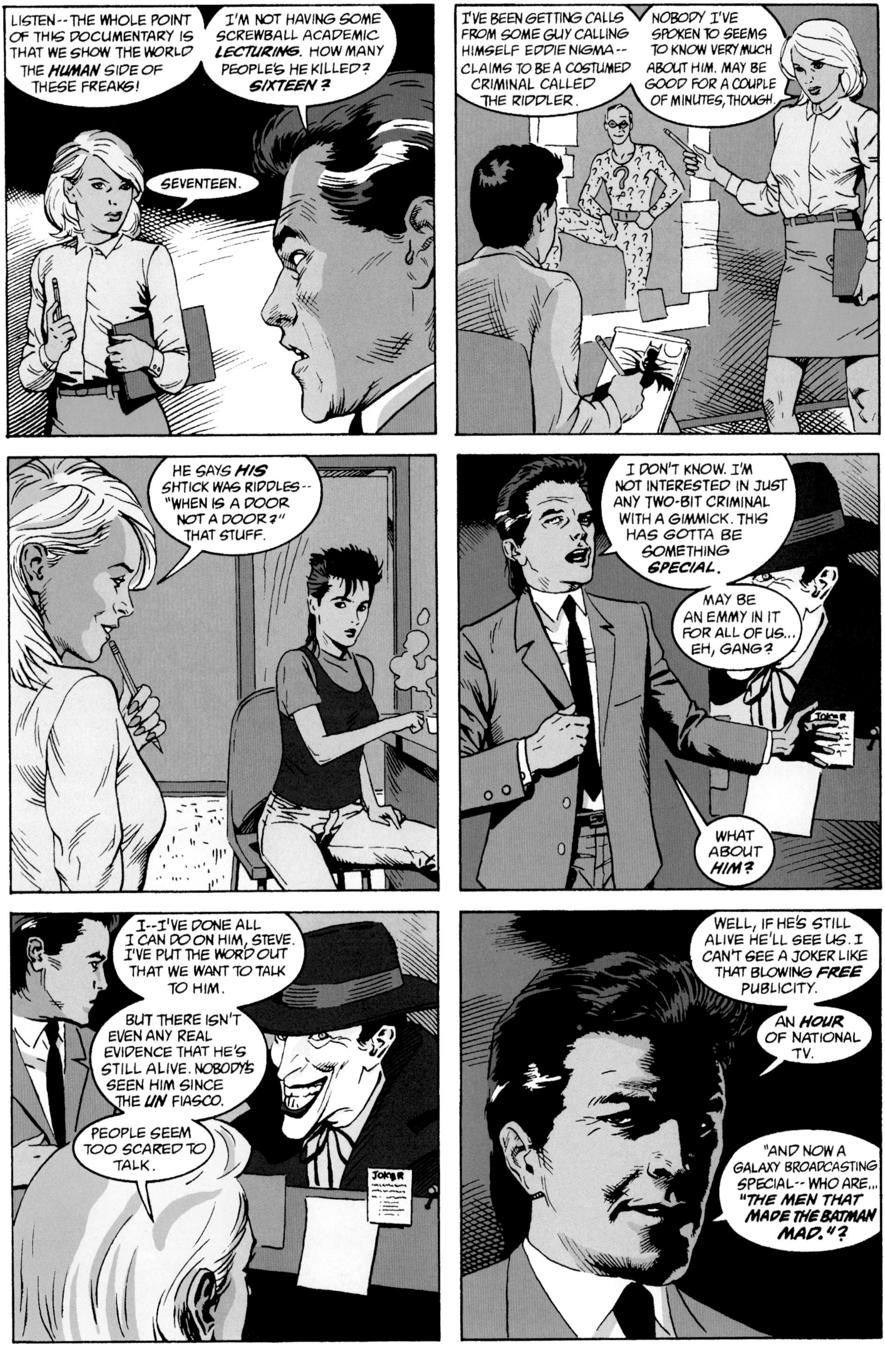
LISTEN--THE WHOLE POINT OF THIS DOCUMENTARY IS THAT WE SHOW THE WORLD THE HUMAN SIDE OF THESE FREAKS!
I'M NOT HAVING SOME SCREWBALL ACADEMIC LECTURING. HOW MANY PEOPLE'S HE KILLED? SIXTEEN?
SEVENTEEN.
I'VE BEEN GETTING CALLS FROM SOME GUY CALLING HIMSELF EDDIE NIGMA--CLAIMS TO BE A COSTUMED CRIMINAL CALLED THE RIDDLER.
NOBODY I'VE SPOKEN TO SEEMS TO KNOW VERY MUCH ABOUT HIM. MAY BE GOOD FOR A COUPLE OF MINUTES, THOUGH.
HE SAYS HIS SHTICK WAS RIDDLES--"WHEN IS A DOOR NOT A DOOR?" THAT STUFF.
I DON'T KNOW. I'M NOT INTERESTED IN JUST ANY TWO-BIT CRIMINAL WITH A GIMMICK. THIS HAS GOTTA BE SOMETHING SPECIAL.
MAY BE AN EMMY IN IT FOR ALL OF US... EH, GANG?
JOKER
WHAT ABOUT HIM?
I--I'VE DONE ALL I CAN DO ON HIM, STEVE. I'VE PUT THE WORD OUT THAT WE WANT TO TALK TO HIM.
BUT THERE ISN'T EVEN ANY REAL EVIDENCE THAT HE'S STILL ALIVE. NOBODY'S SEEN HIM SINCE THE UN FIASCO.
PEOPLE SEEM TOO SCARED TO TALK.
JOKER
WELL, IF HE'S STILL ALIVE HE'LL SEE US. I CAN'T SEE A JOKER LIKE THAT BLOWING FREE PUBLICITY.
AN HOUR OF NATIONAL TV.
"AND NOW A GALAXY BROADCASTING SPECIAL--WHO ARE... "THE MEN THAT MADE THE BATMAN MAD."?

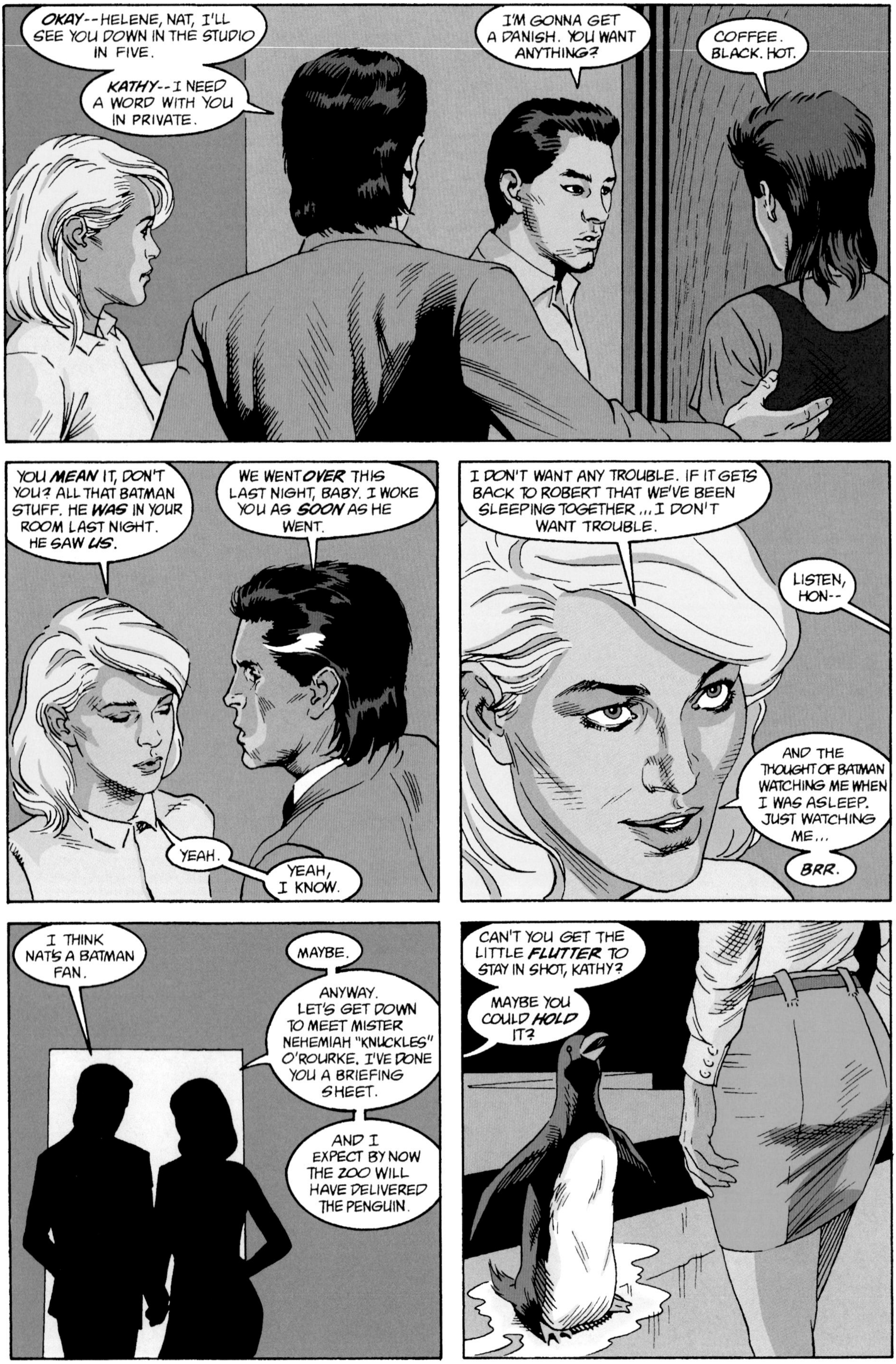
OKAY--HELENE, NAT, I'LL SEE YOU DOWN IN THE STUDIO IN FIVE.
KATHY--I NEED A WORD WITH YOU IN PRIVATE.
I'M GONNA GET A DANISH. YOU WANT ANYTHING?
COFFEE. BLACK. HOT.
YOU MEAN IT, DON'T YOU? ALL THAT BATMAN STUFF. HE WAS IN YOUR ROOM LAST NIGHT. HE SAW US.
WE WENT OVER THIS LAST NIGHT, BABY. I WOKE YOU AS SOON AS HE WENT.
YEAH.
YEAH, I KNOW.
I DON'T WANT ANY TROUBLE. IF IT GETS BACK TO ROBERT THAT WE'VE BEEN SLEEPING TOGETHER ... I DON'T WANT TROUBLE.
LISTEN, HON--
AND THE THOUGHT OF BATMAN WATCHING ME WHEN I WAS ASLEEP. JUST WATCHING ME...
BRR.
I THINK NAT'S A BATMAN FAN.
MAYBE.
ANYWAY. LET'S GET DOWN TO MEET MISTER NEHEMIAH "KNUCKLES" O'ROURKE. I'VE DONE YOU A BRIEFING SHEET.
AND I EXPECT BY NOW THE ZOO WILL HAVE DELIVERED THE PENGUIN.
CAN'T YOU GET THE LITTLE FLUTTER TO STAY IN SHOT, KATHY?
MAYBE YOU COULD HOLD IT?

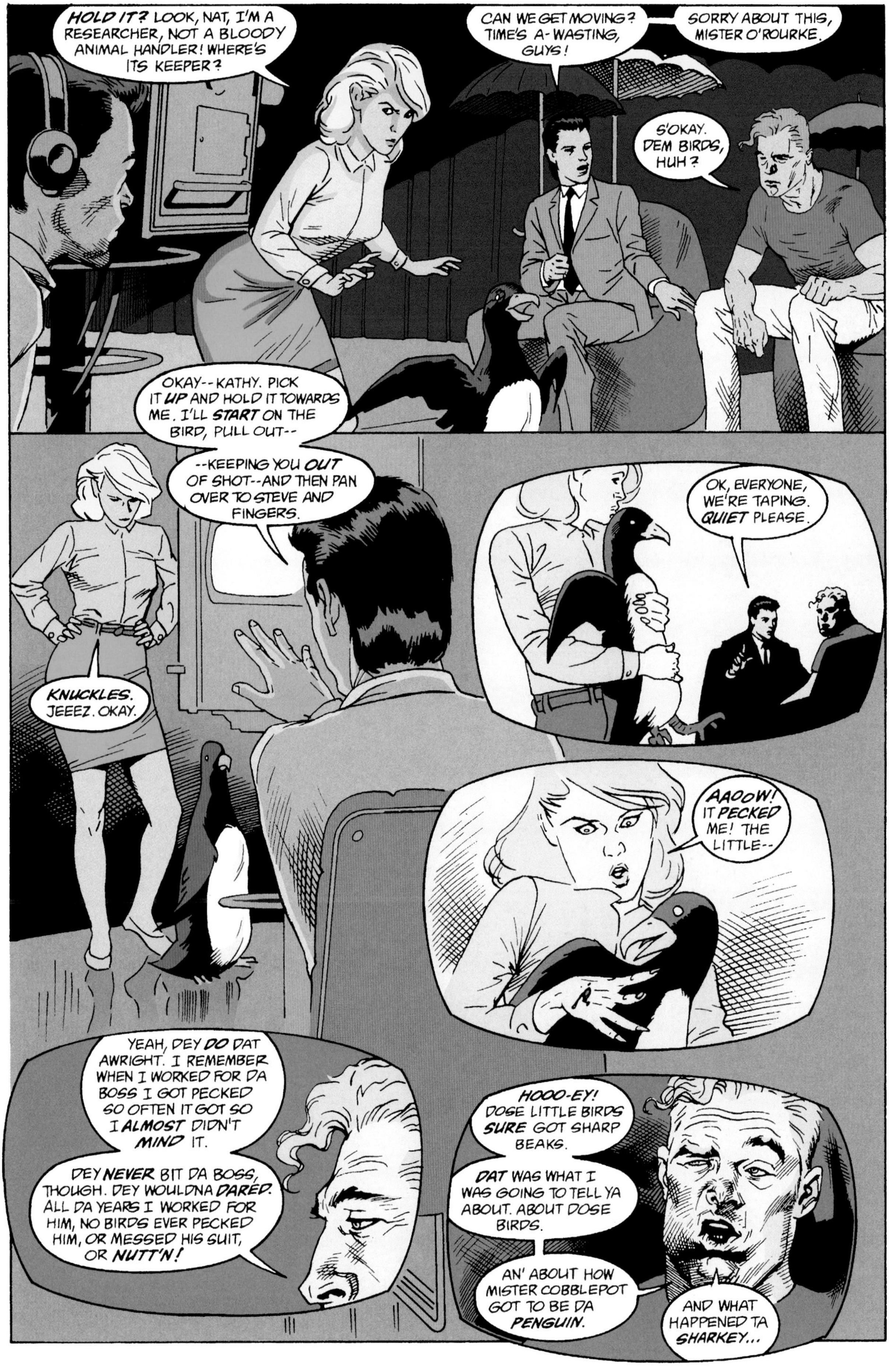
HOLD IT? LOOK, NAT, I'M A RESEARCHER, NOT A BLOODY ANIMAL HANDLER! WHERE'S ITS KEEPER?
CAN WE GET MOVING? TIME'S A-WASTING, GUYS!
SORRY ABOUT THIS, MISTER O'ROURKE.
S'OKAY. DEM BIRDS, HUH?
OKAY--KATHY. PICK IT UP AND HOLD IT TOWARDS ME. I'LL START ON THE BIRD, PULL OUT--
--KEEPING YOU OUT OF SHOT--AND THEN PAN OVER TO STEVE AND FINGERS.
KNUCKLES. JEEEZ. OKAY.
OK, EVERYONE, WE'RE TAPING. QUIET PLEASE.
AAOOW! IT PECKED ME! THE LITTLE--
YEAH, DEY DO DAT AWRIGHT. I REMEMBER WHEN I WORKED FOR DA BOSS I GOT PECKED SO OFTEN IT GOT SO I ALMOST DIDN'T MIND IT.
DEY NEVER BIT DA BOSS, THOUGH. DEY WOULDNA DARED. ALL DA YEARS I WORKED FOR HIM, NO BIRDS EVER PECKED HIM, OR MESSED HIS SUIT, OR NUTT'N!
HOOO-EY! DOSE LITTLE BIRDS SURE GOT SHARP BEAKS.
DAT WAS WHAT I WAS GOING TO TELL YA ABOUT. ABOUT DOSE BIRDS.
AN' ABOUT HOW MISTER COBBLEPOT GOT TO BE DA PENGUIN.
AND WHAT HAPPENED TA SHARKEY...

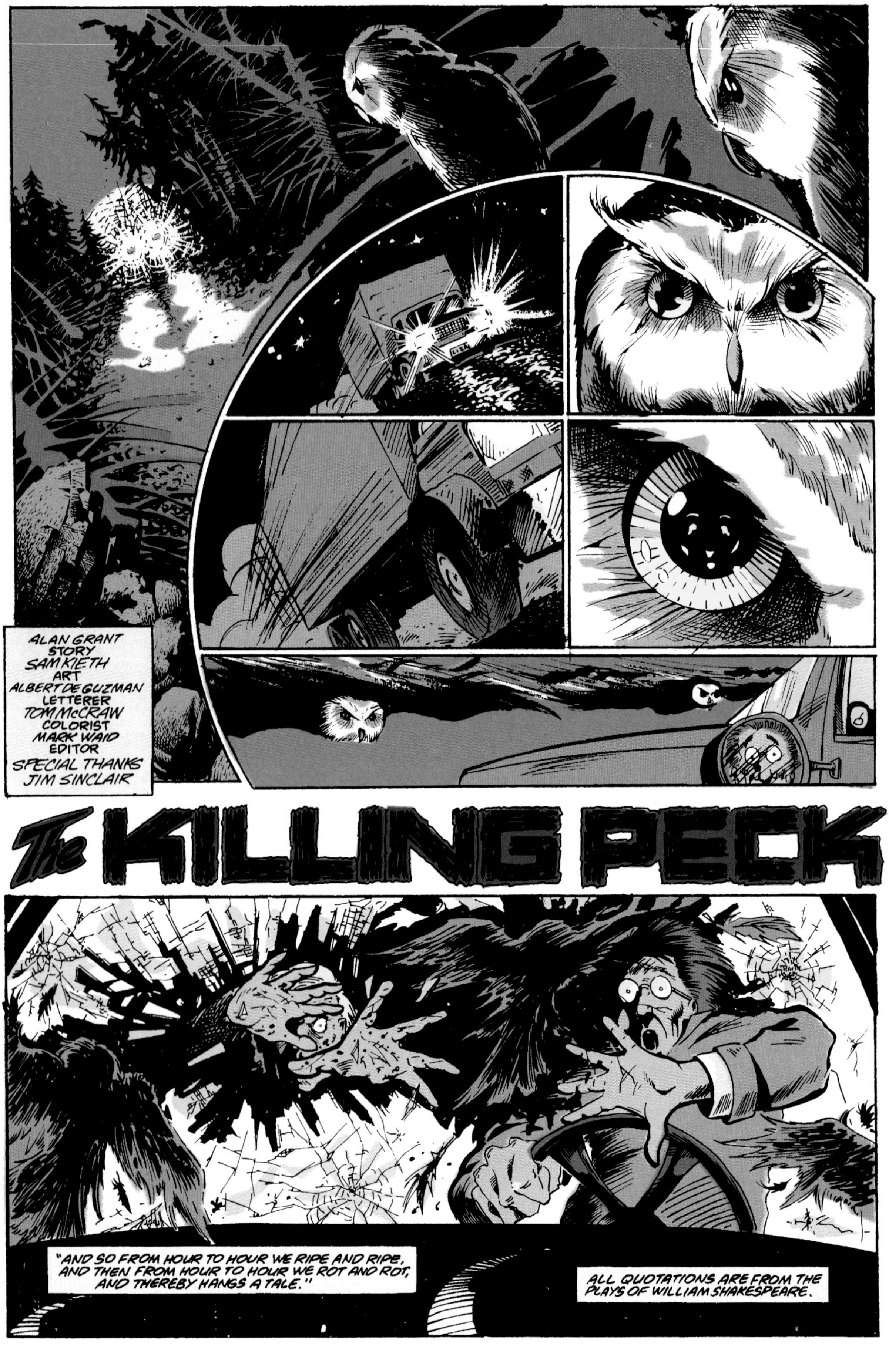
ALAN GRANT STORY
SAM KIETH ART
ALBERT DE GUZMAN LETTERER
TOM McCRAW COLORIST
MARK WAID EDITOR
SPECIAL THANKS JIM SINCLAIR
The KILLING PECK
"AND SO FROM HOUR TO HOUR WE RIPE AND RIPE, AND THEN FROM HOUR TO HOUR WE ROT AND ROT, AND THEREBY HANGS A TALE."
ALL QUOTATIONS ARE FROM THE PLAYS OF WILLIAM SHAKESPEARE.

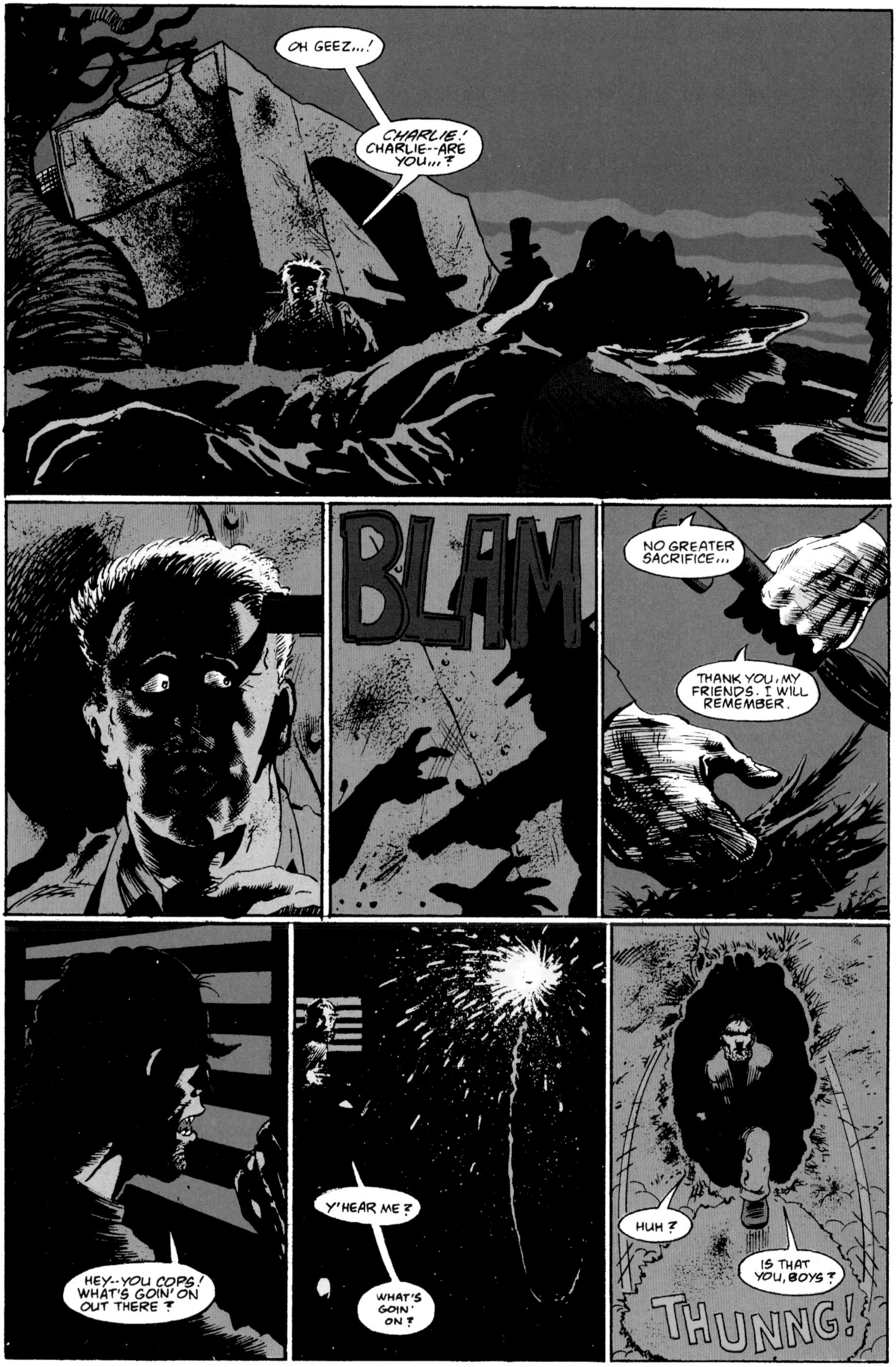
OH GEEZ...!
CHARLIE! CHARLIE--ARE YOU...?
BLAM
NO GREATER SACRIFICE...
THANK YOU, MY FRIENDS. I WILL REMEMBER.
HEY--YOU COPS! WHAT'S GOIN' ON OUT THERE?
Y'HEAR ME?
WHAT'S GOIN' ON?
HUH?
IS THAT YOU, BOYS?
THUNNG!

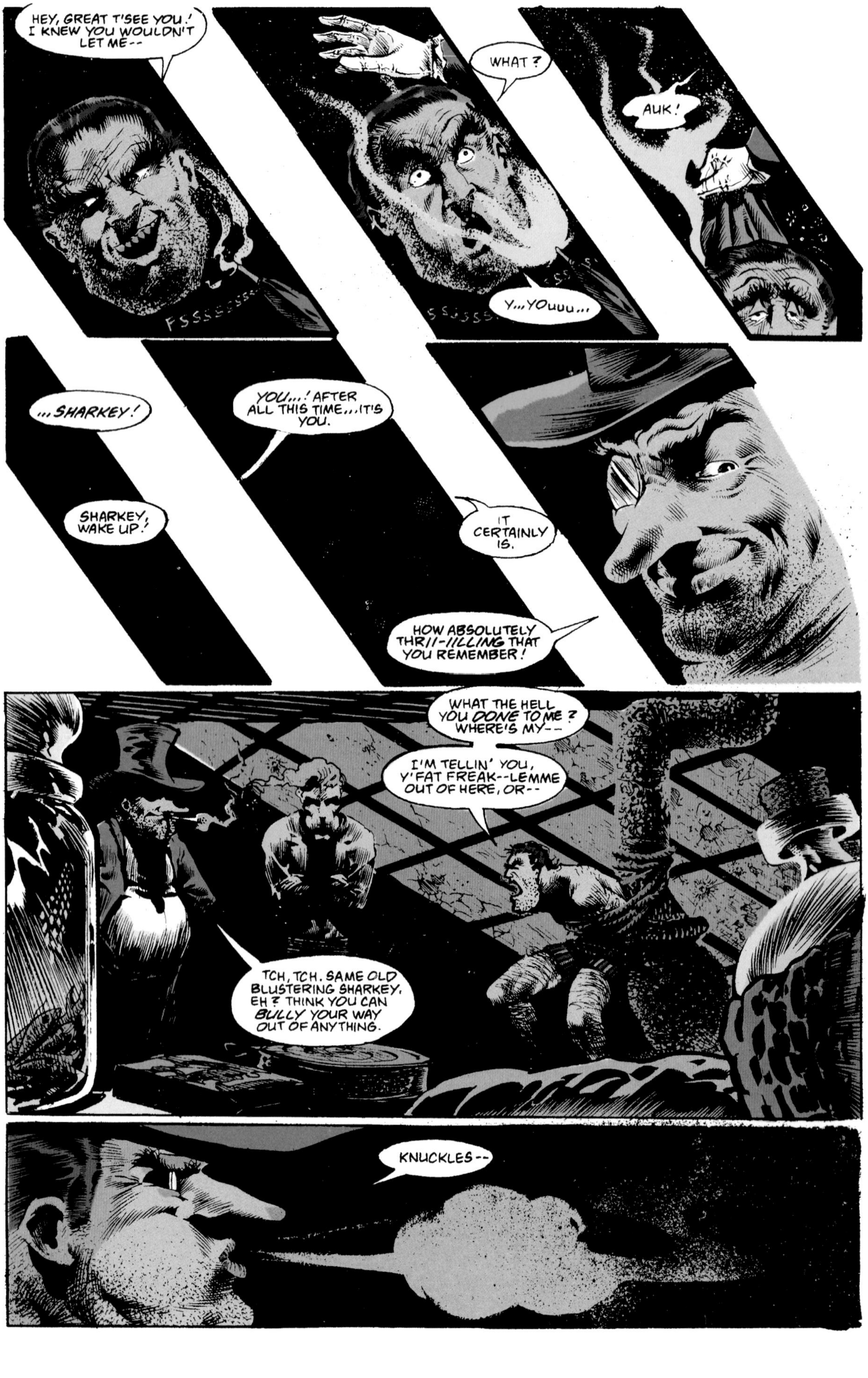
HEY, GREAT T'SEE YOU! I KNEW YOU WOULDN'T LET ME--
FSSSSSSSS
WHAT?
SSSSSS
Y...YOUuu...
AUK!
...SHARKEY!
SHARKEY, WAKE UP!
YOU...! AFTER ALL THIS TIME... IT'S YOU.
IT CERTAINLY IS.
HOW ABSOLUTELY THRI-ILLING THAT YOU REMEMBER!
WHAT THE HELL YOU DONE TO ME? WHERE'S MY--
I'M TELLIN' YOU, Y'FAT FREAK--LEMME OUT OF HERE, OR--
TCH, TCH. SAME OLD BLUSTERING SHARKEY, EH? THINK YOU CAN BULLY YOUR WAY OUT OF ANYTHING.
KNUCKLES--

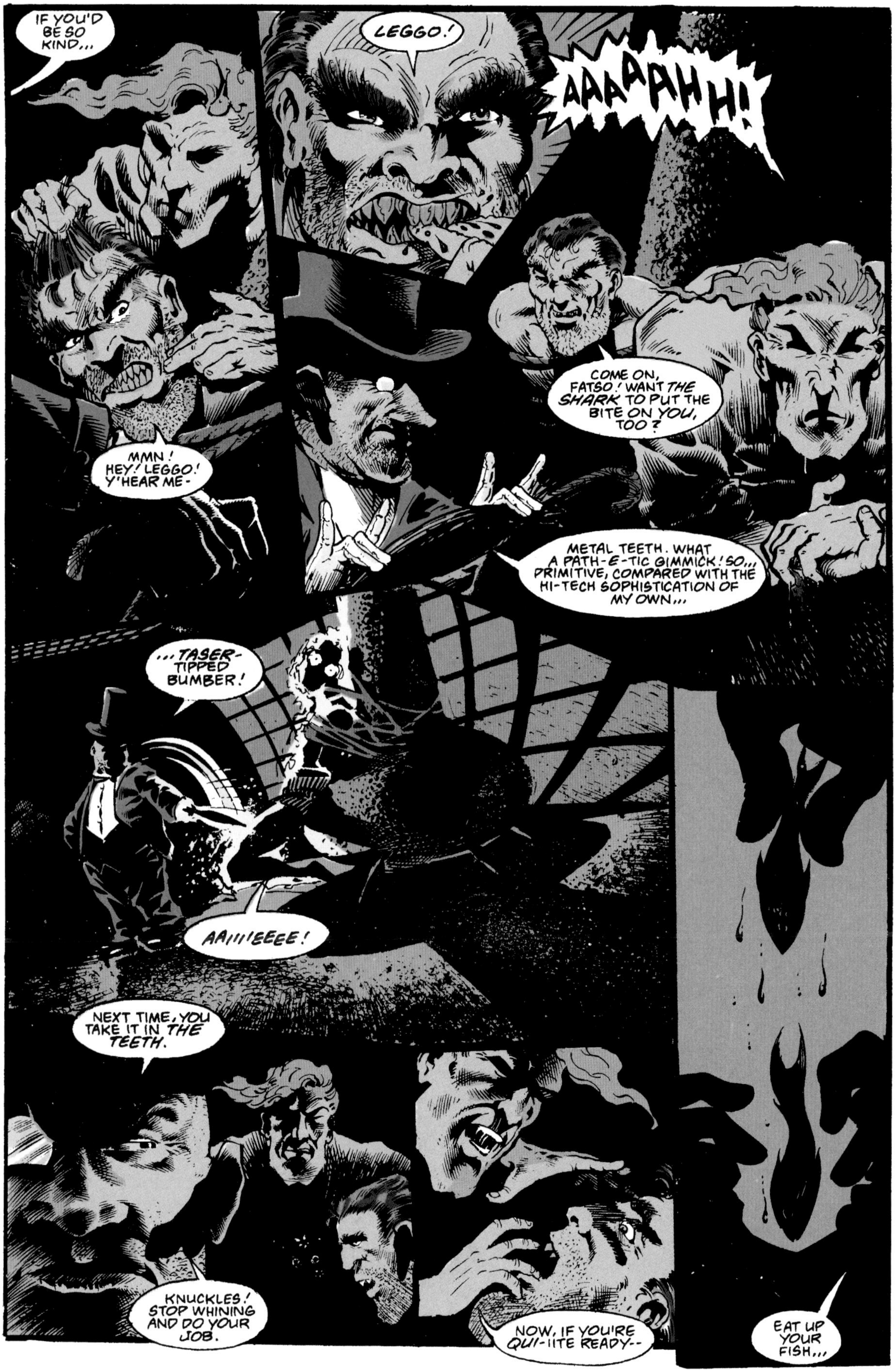

IF YOU'D BE SO KIND...
LEGGO!
AAAAAHH!
MMN! HEY! LEGGO! Y'HEAR ME-
COME ON, FATSO! WANT THE SHARK TO PUT THE BITE ON YOU, TOO?
METAL TEETH. WHAT A PATH-E-TIC GIMMICK! SO... PRIMITIVE, COMPARED WITH THE HI-TECH SOPHISTICATION OF MY OWN...
...TASER-TIPPED BUMBER!
AAIIIIEEEE!
NEXT TIME, YOU TAKE IT IN THE TEETH.
KNUCKLES! STOP WHINING AND DO YOUR JOB.
NOW, IF YOU'RE QUI-IITE READY--
EAT UP YOUR FISH...

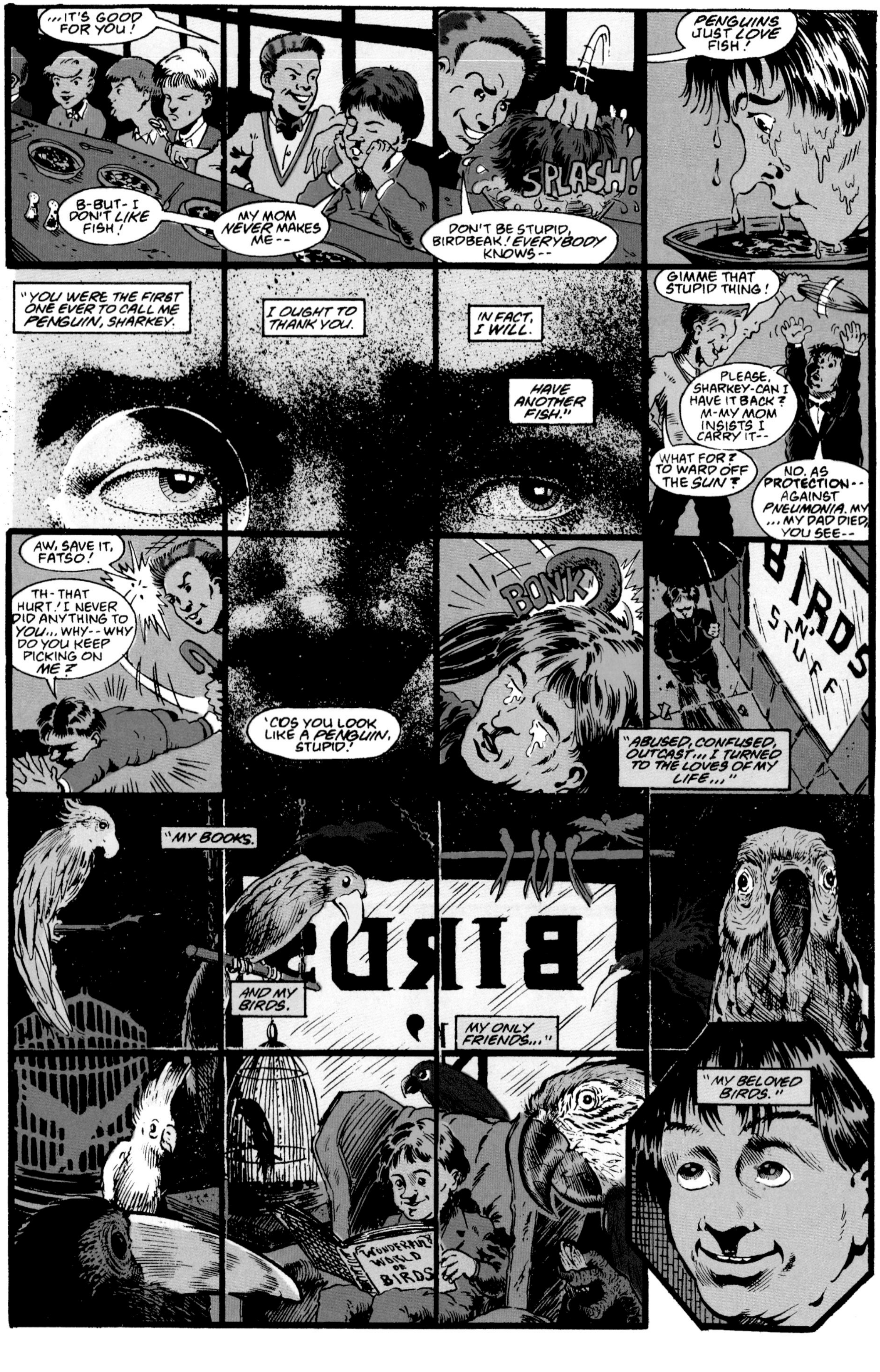
...IT'S GOOD FOR YOU!
B-BUT- I DON'T LIKE FISH!
MY MOM NEVER MAKES ME--
DON'T BE STUPID, BIRDBEAK! EVERYBODY KNOWS--
SPLASH!
PENGUINS JUST LOVE FISH!
"YOU WERE THE FIRST ONE EVER TO CALL ME PENGUIN, SHARKEY.
I OUGHT TO THANK YOU.
IN FACT, I WILL.
HAVE ANOTHER FISH."
GIMME THAT STUPID THING!
PLEASE, SHARKEY-CAN I HAVE IT BACK? M-MY MOM INSISTS I CARRY IT--
WHAT FOR? TO WARD OFF THE SUN?
NO, AS PROTECTION-- AGAINST PNEUMONIA. MY ... MY DAD DIED, YOU SEE--
AW, SAVE IT, FATSO!
TH-THAT HURT! I NEVER DID ANYTHING TO YOU... WHY--WHY DO YOU KEEP PICKING ON ME?
'COS YOU LOOK LIKE A PENGUIN, STUPID!
BONK
BIRDS N' STUFF
"ABUSED, CONFUSED, OUTCAST... I TURNED TO THE LOVES OF MY LIFE..."
"MY BOOKS.
BIRDS
AND MY BIRDS.
MY ONLY FRIENDS..."
WONDERFUL WORLD OF BIRDS
"MY BELOVED BIRDS."

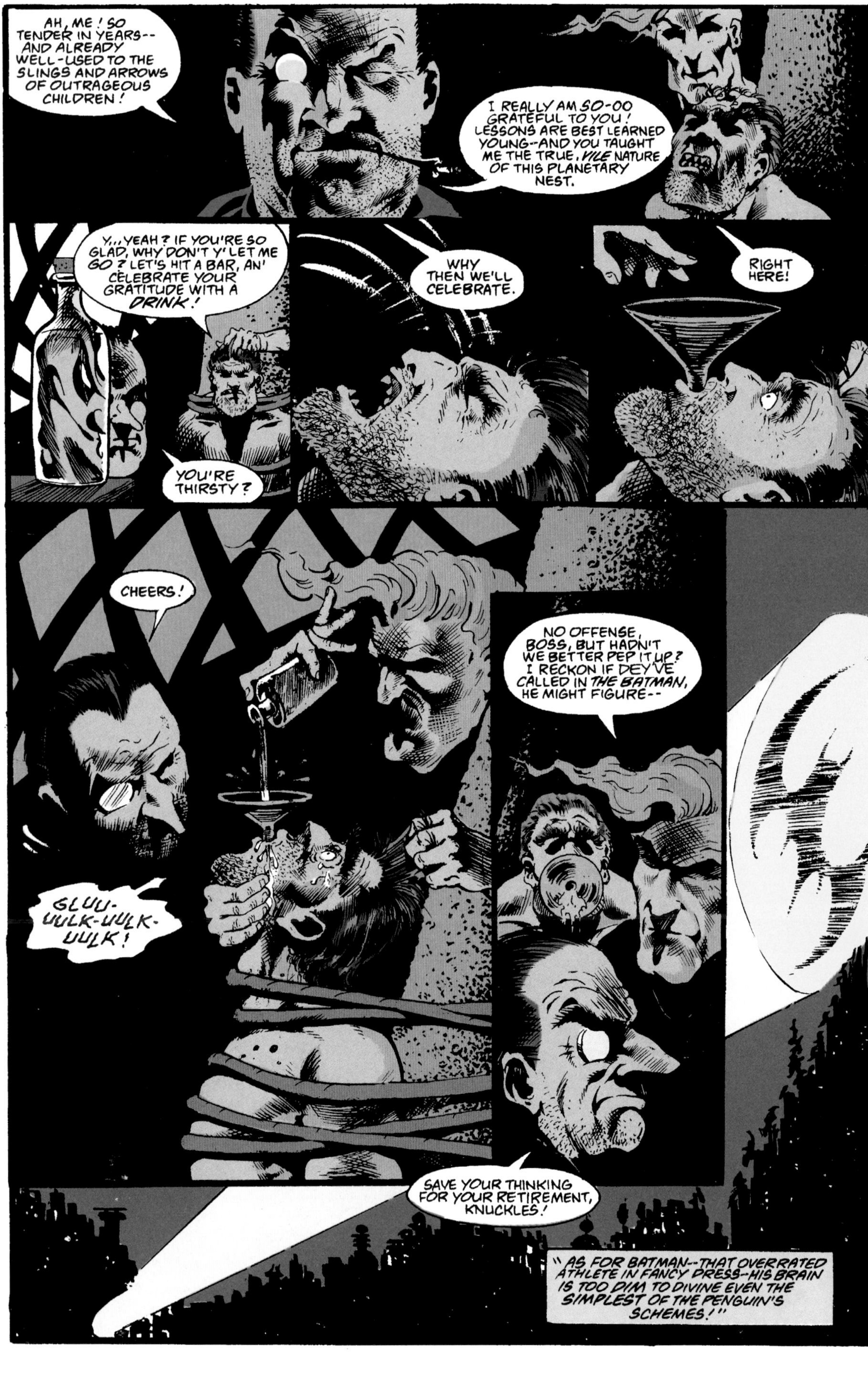
AH, ME! SO TENDER IN YEARS-- AND ALREADY WELL-USED TO THE SLINGS AND ARROWS OF OUTRAGEOUS CHILDREN!
I REALLY AM SO-OO GRATEFUL TO YOU! LESSONS ARE BEST LEARNED YOUNG--AND YOU TAUGHT ME THE TRUE, VILE NATURE OF THIS PLANETARY NEST.
Y...YEAH? IF YOU'RE SO GLAD, WHY DON'T Y' LET ME GO? LET'S HIT A BAR, AN' CELEBRATE YOUR GRATITUDE WITH A DRINK!
YOU'RE THIRSTY?
WHY THEN WE'LL CELEBRATE.
RIGHT HERE!
CHEERS!
GLUU-UULK-UULK-UULK!
NO OFFENSE, BOSS, BUT HADN'T WE BETTER PEP IT UP? I RECKON IF DEY'VE CALLED IN THE BATMAN, HE MIGHT FIGURE--
SAVE YOUR THINKING FOR YOUR RETIREMENT, KNUCKLES!
"AS FOR BATMAN--THAT OVERRATED ATHLETE IN FANCY DRESS--HIS BRAIN IS TOO DIM TO DIVINE EVEN THE SIMPLEST OF THE PENGUIN'S SCHEMES!"

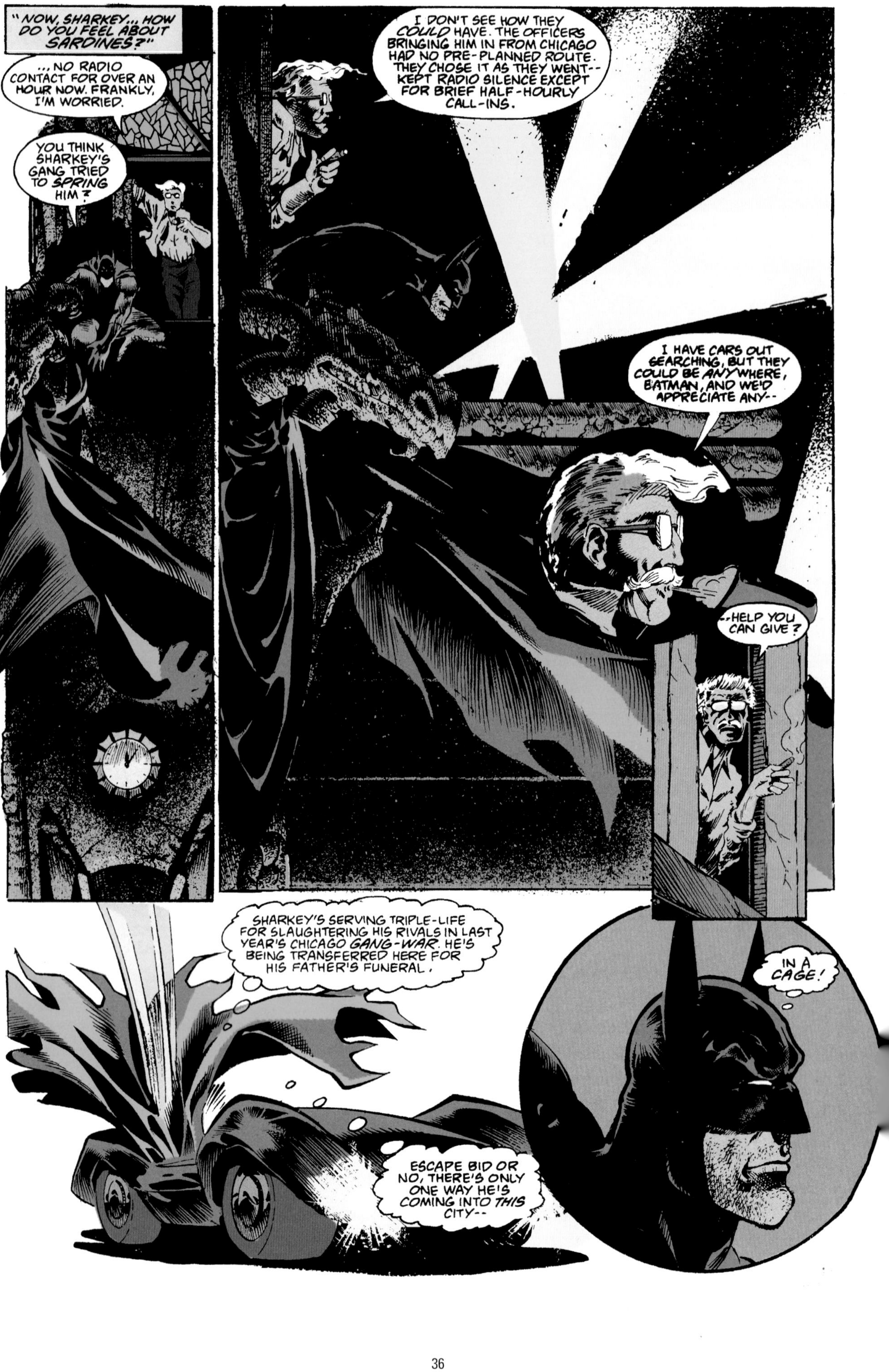
"NOW, SHARKEY... HOW DO YOU FEEL ABOUT SARDINES?"
...NO RADIO CONTACT FOR OVER AN HOUR NOW. FRANKLY, I'M WORRIED.
YOU THINK SHARKEY'S GANG TRIED TO SPRING HIM?
I DON'T SEE HOW THEY COULD HAVE. THE OFFICERS BRINGING HIM IN FROM CHICAGO HAD NO PRE-PLANNED ROUTE. THEY CHOSE IT AS THEY WENT-- KEPT RADIO SILENCE EXCEPT FOR BRIEF HALF-HOURLY CALL-INS.
I HAVE CARS OUT SEARCHING, BUT THEY COULD BE ANYWHERE, BATMAN, AND WE'D APPRECIATE ANY--
--HELP YOU CAN GIVE?
SHARKEY'S SERVING TRIPLE-LIFE FOR SLAUGHTERING HIS RIVALS IN LAST YEAR'S CHICAGO GANG-WAR. HE'S BEING TRANSFERRED HERE FOR HIS FATHER'S FUNERAL.
ESCAPE BID OR NO, THERE'S ONLY ONE WAY HE'S COMING INTO THIS CITY--
IN A CAGE!

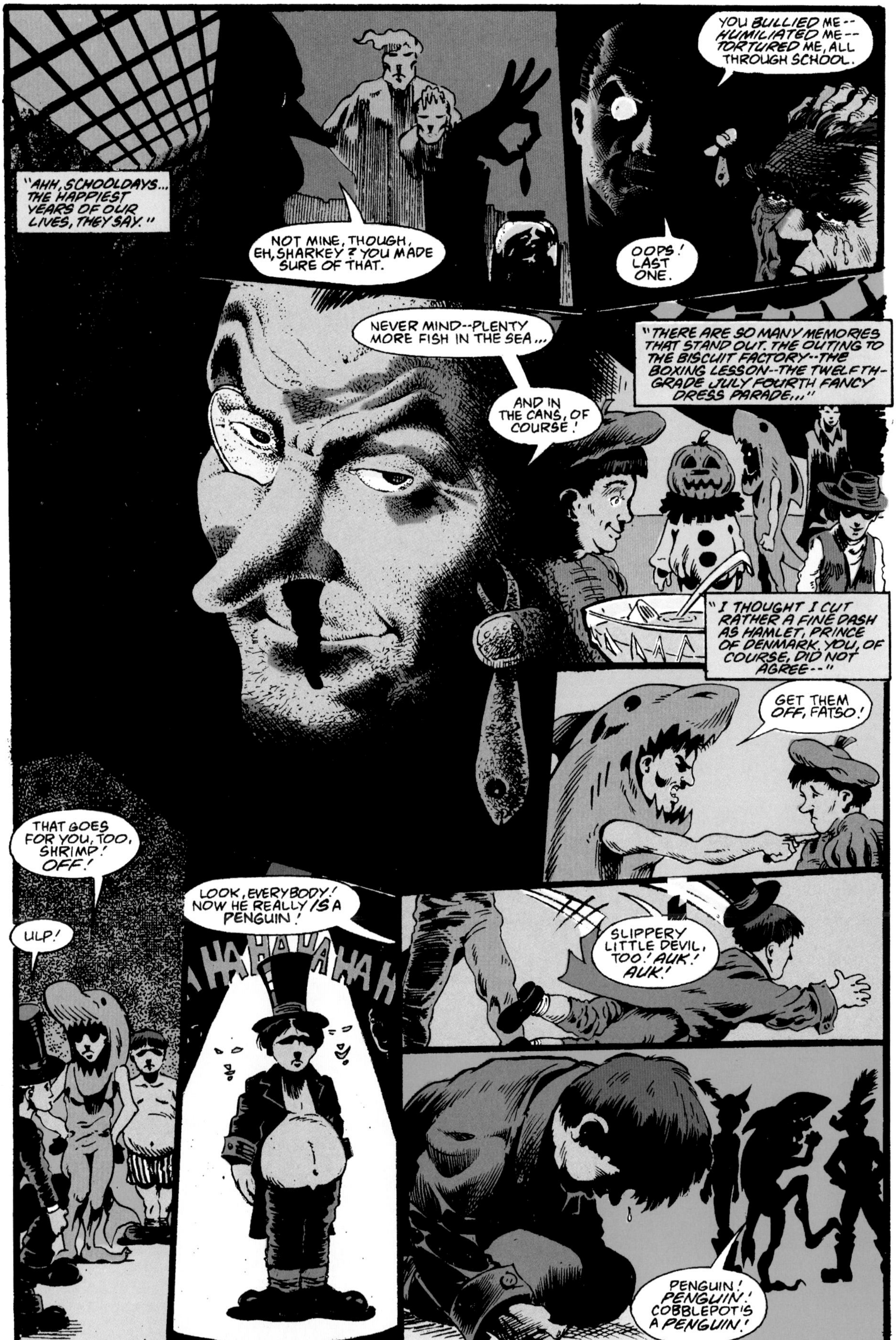
"AHH, SCHOOLDAYS... THE HAPPIEST YEARS OF OUR LIVES, THEY SAY."
NOT MINE, THOUGH, EH, SHARKEY? YOU MADE SURE OF THAT.
YOU BULLIED ME-- HUMILIATED ME-- TORTURED ME, ALL THROUGH SCHOOL.
OOPS! LAST ONE.
NEVER MIND--PLENTY MORE FISH IN THE SEA...
AND IN THE CANS, OF COURSE!
"THERE ARE SO MANY MEMORIES THAT STAND OUT. THE OUTING TO THE BISCUIT FACTORY--THE BOXING LESSON--THE TWELFTH-GRADE JULY FOURTH FANCY DRESS PARADE..."
"I THOUGHT I CUT RATHER A FINE DASH AS HAMLET, PRINCE OF DENMARK. YOU, OF COURSE, DID NOT AGREE--"
GET THEM OFF, FATSO!
THAT GOES FOR YOU, TOO, SHRIMP! OFF!
ULP!
LOOK, EVERYBODY! NOW HE REALLY IS A PENGUIN!
HA HA HA HA HA H
SLIPPERY LITTLE DEVIL, TOO! AUK! AUK!
PENGUIN! PENGUIN! COBBLEPOT'S A PENGUIN!

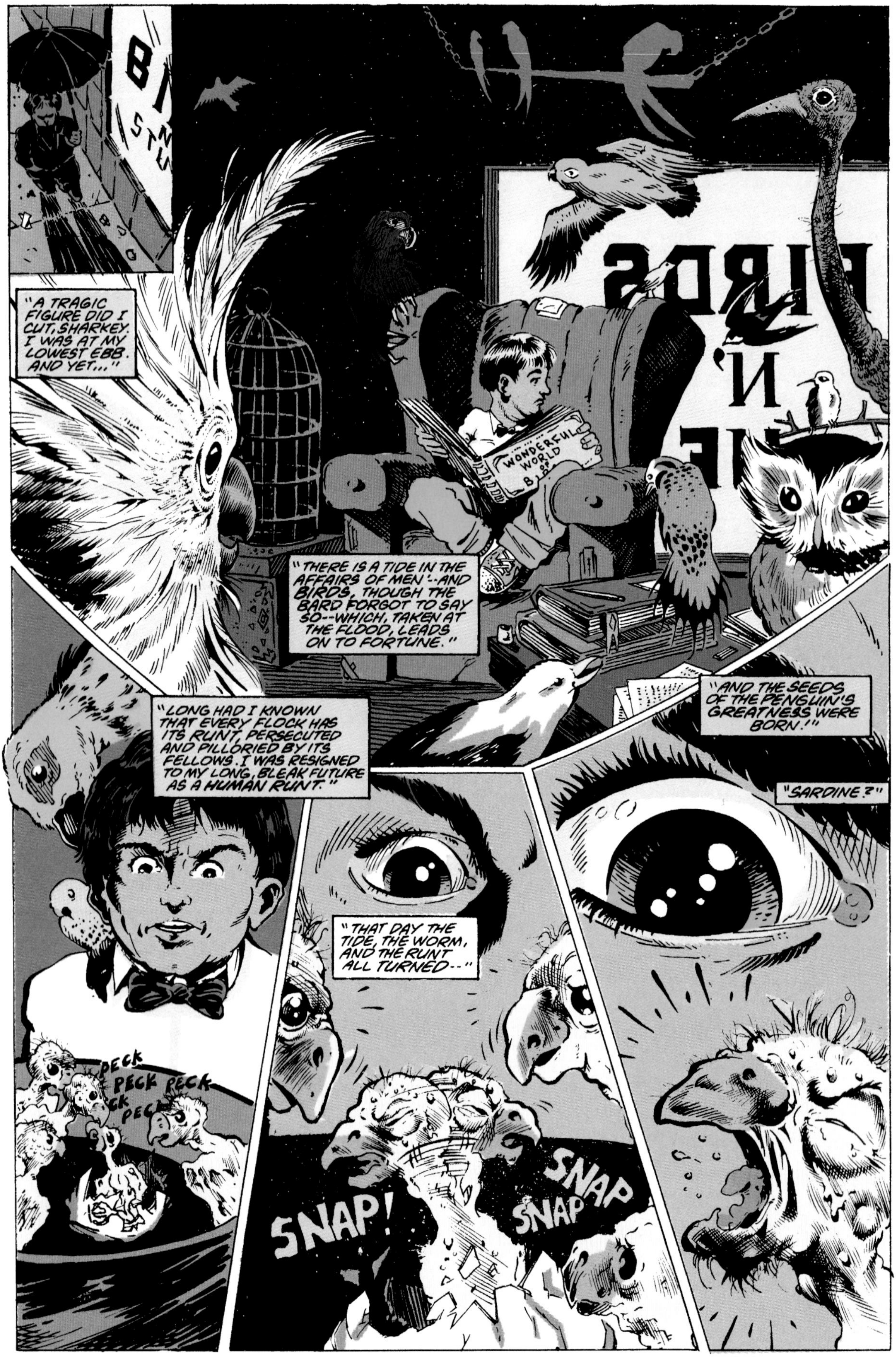
"A TRAGIC FIGURE DID I CUT, SHARKEY. I WAS AT MY LOWEST EBB. AND YET..."
WONDERFUL WORLD OF B
"THERE IS A TIDE IN THE AFFAIRS OF MEN--AND BIRDS, THOUGH THE BARD FORGOT TO SAY SO--WHICH, TAKEN AT THE FLOOD, LEADS ON TO FORTUNE."
"LONG HAD I KNOWN THAT EVERY FLOCK HAS ITS RUNT, PERSECUTED AND PILLORIED BY ITS FELLOWS. I WAS RESIGNED TO MY LONG, BLEAK FUTURE AS A HUMAN RUNT."
"AND THE SEEDS OF THE PENGUIN'S GREATNESS WERE BORN!"
"SARDINE?"
PECK PECK PECK
"THAT DAY THE TIDE, THE WORM, AND THE RUNT ALL TURNED--"
SNAP!
SNAP SNAP

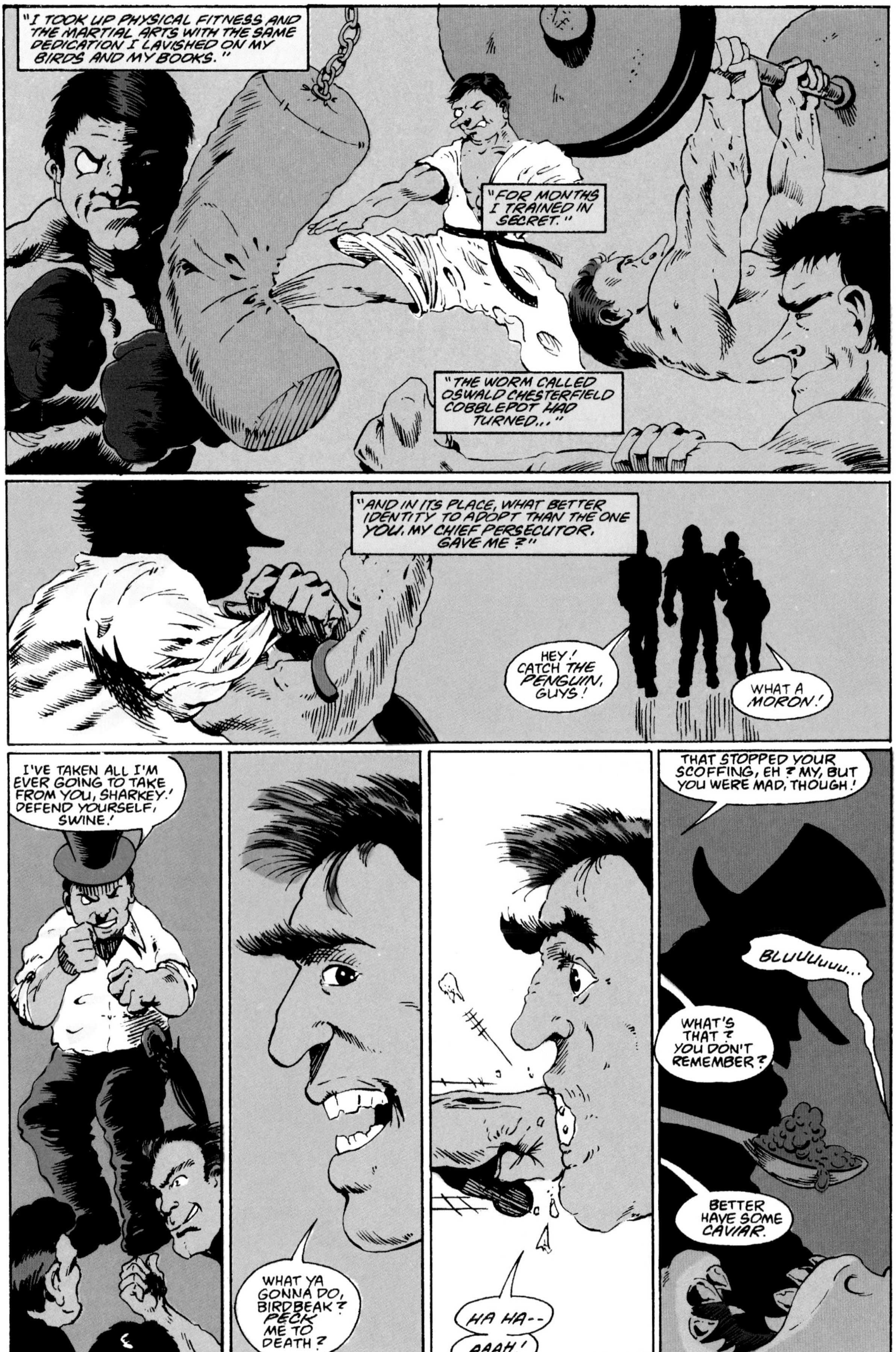
"I TOOK UP PHYSICAL FITNESS AND THE MARTIAL ARTS WITH THE SAME DEDICATION I LAVISHED ON MY BIRDS AND MY BOOKS."
"FOR MONTHS I TRAINED IN SECRET."
"THE WORM CALLED OSWALD CHESTERFIELD COBBLEPOT HAD TURNED..."
"AND IN ITS PLACE, WHAT BETTER IDENTITY TO ADOPT THAN THE ONE YOU, MY CHIEF PERSECUTOR, GAVE ME?"
HEY! CATCH THE PENGUIN, GUYS!
WHAT A MORON!
I'VE TAKEN ALL I'M EVER GOING TO TAKE FROM YOU, SHARKEY! DEFEND YOURSELF, SWINE!
WHAT YA GONNA DO, BIRDBEAK? PECK ME TO DEATH?
HA HA--
AAAH!
THAT STOPPED YOUR SCOFFING, EH? MY, BUT YOU WERE MAD, THOUGH!
BLUUUuuu...
WHAT'S THAT? YOU DON'T REMEMBER?
BETTER HAVE SOME CAVIAR.

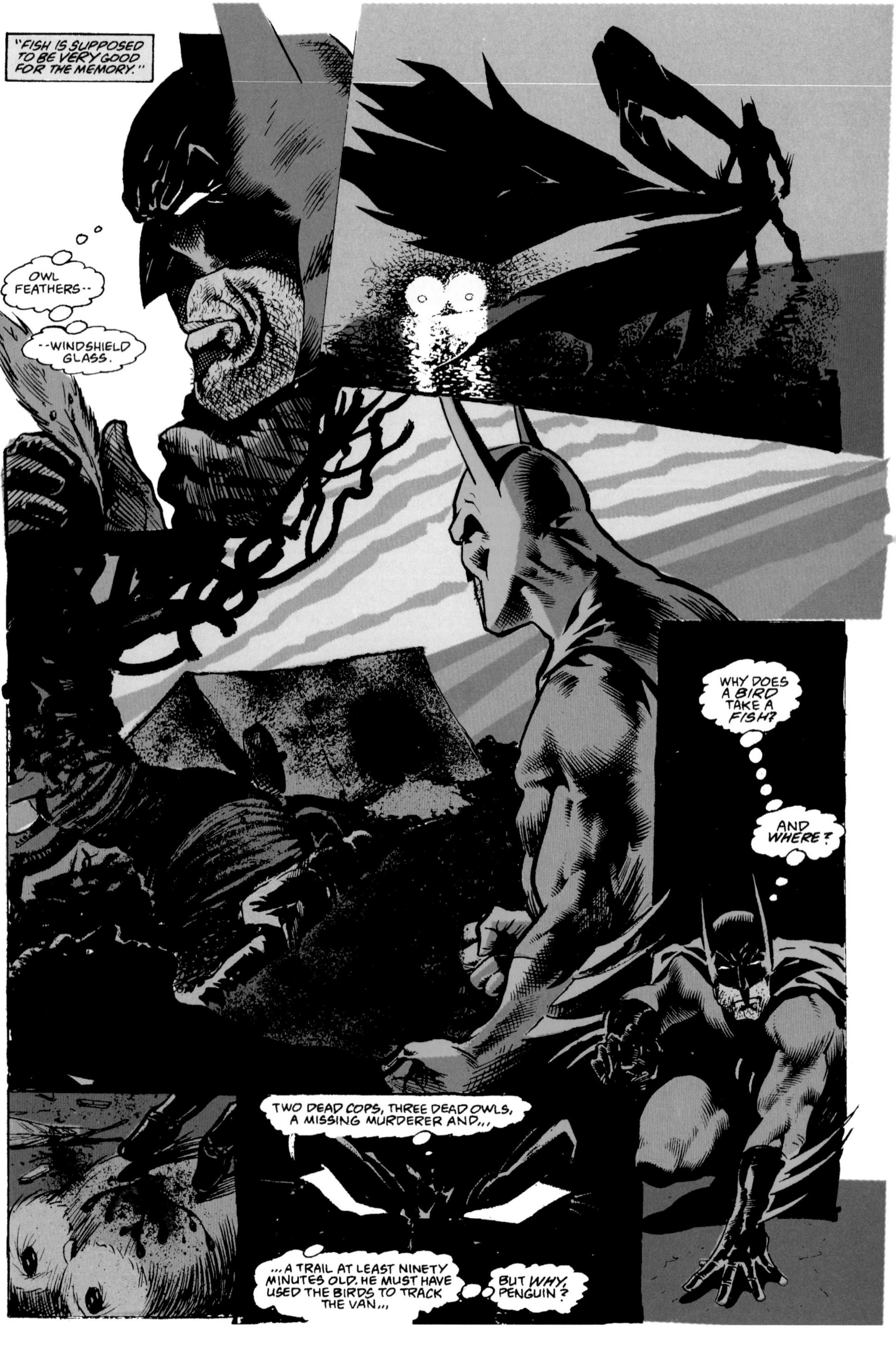
"FISH IS SUPPOSED TO BE VERY GOOD FOR THE MEMORY."
OWL FEATHERS--
--WINDSHIELD GLASS.
WHY DOES A BIRD TAKE A FISH?
AND WHERE?
TWO DEAD COPS, THREE DEAD OWLS, A MISSING MURDERER AND,,,
...A TRAIL AT LEAST NINETY MINUTES OLD. HE MUST HAVE USED THE BIRDS TO TRACK THE VAN...
BUT WHY, PENGUIN?

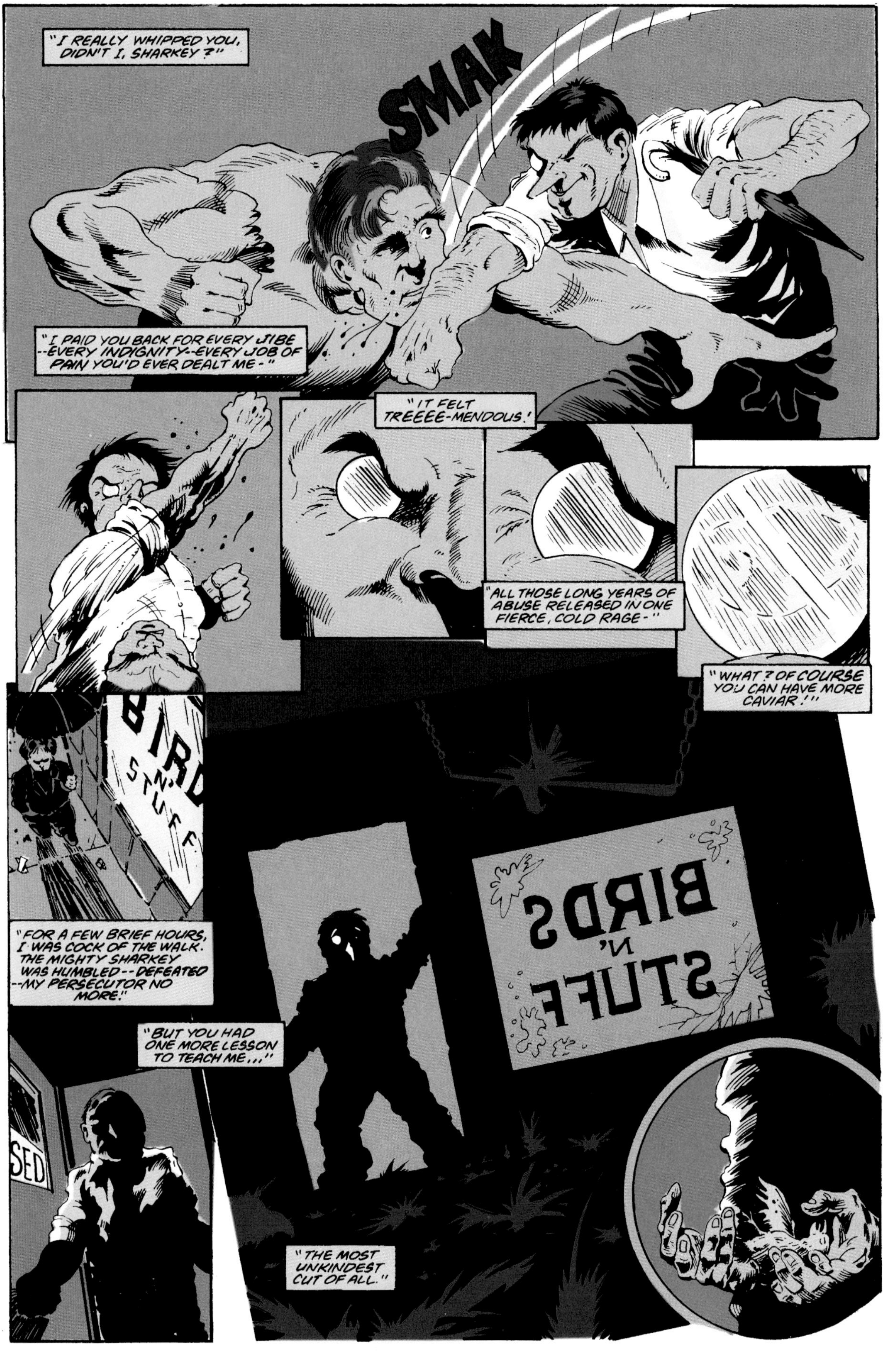
"I REALLY WHIPPED YOU, DIDN'T I, SHARKEY ?"
SMAK
"I PAID YOU BACK FOR EVERY JIBE --EVERY INDIGNITY--EVERY JOB OF PAIN YOU'D EVER DEALT ME -"
"IT FELT TREEEE-MENDOUS !
"ALL THOSE LONG YEARS OF ABUSE RELEASED IN ONE FIERCE, COLD RAGE -"
"WHAT ? OF COURSE YOU CAN HAVE MORE CAVIAR !"
BIRD N' STUFF
"FOR A FEW BRIEF HOURS, I WAS COCK OF THE WALK. THE MIGHTY SHARKEY WAS HUMBLED--DEFEATED --MY PERSECUTOR NO MORE."
BIRDS N' STUFF
"BUT YOU HAD ONE MORE LESSON TO TEACH ME..."
SED
"THE MOST UNKINDEST CUT OF ALL."

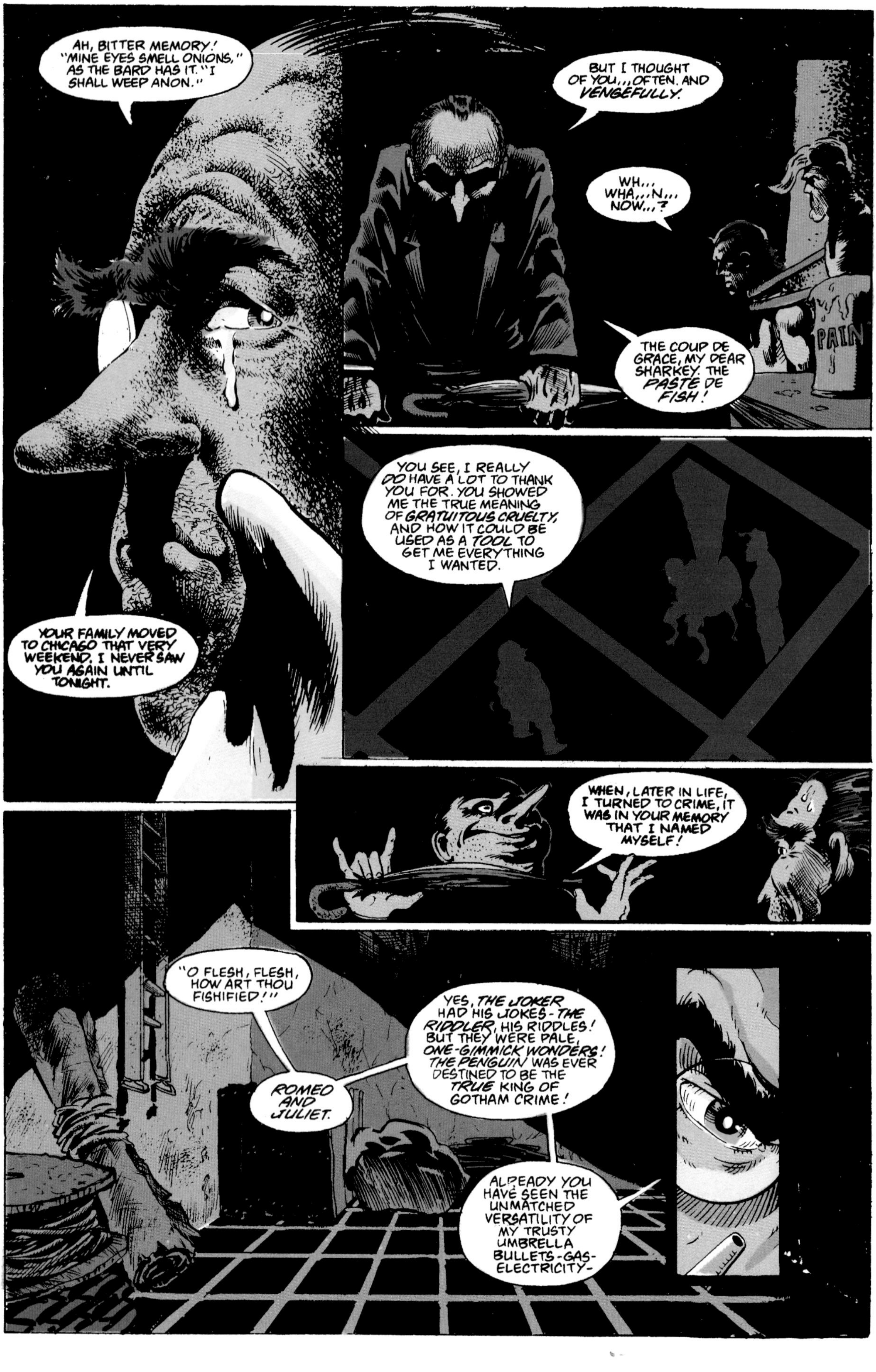

AH, BITTER MEMORY! "MINE EYES SMELL ONIONS," AS THE BARD HAS IT. "I SHALL WEEP ANON."
YOUR FAMILY MOVED TO CHICAGO THAT VERY WEEKEND. I NEVER SAW YOU AGAIN UNTIL TONIGHT.
BUT I THOUGHT OF YOU... OFTEN. AND VENGEFULLY.
WH... WHA... N... NOW...?
THE COUP DE GRACE, MY DEAR SHARKEY. THE PASTE DE FISH!
PAIN
YOU SEE, I REALLY DO HAVE A LOT TO THANK YOU FOR. YOU SHOWED ME THE TRUE MEANING OF GRATUITOUS CRUELTY, AND HOW IT COULD BE USED AS A TOOL TO GET ME EVERYTHING I WANTED.
WHEN, LATER IN LIFE, I TURNED TO CRIME, IT WAS IN YOUR MEMORY THAT I NAMED MYSELF!
"O FLESH, FLESH, HOW ART THOU FISHIFIED!"
ROMEO AND JULIET.
YES, THE JOKER HAD HIS JOKES - THE RIDDLER, HIS RIDDLES! BUT THEY WERE PALE, ONE-GIMMICK WONDERS! THE PENGUIN WAS EVER DESTINED TO BE THE TRUE KING OF GOTHAM CRIME!
ALREADY YOU HAVE SEEN THE UNMATCHED VERSATILITY OF MY TRUSTY UMBRELLA BULLETS - GAS - ELECTRICITY -

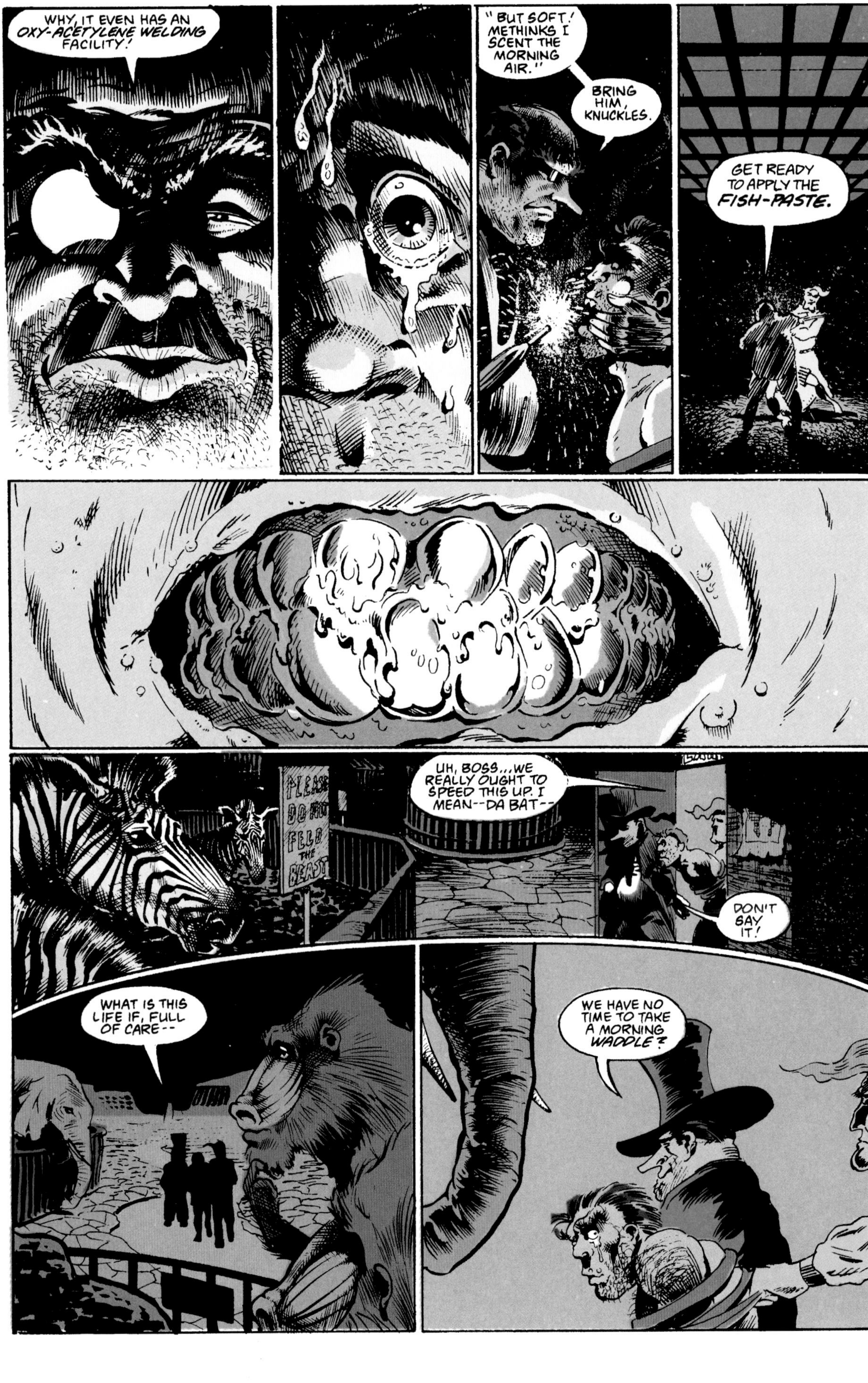
WHY, IT EVEN HAS AN OXY-ACETYLENE WELDING FACILITY!
"BUT SOFT! METHINKS I SCENT THE MORNING AIR."
BRING HIM, KNUCKLES.
GET READY TO APPLY THE FISH-PASTE.
UH, BOSS...WE REALLY OUGHT TO SPEED THIS UP. I MEAN--DA BAT--
DON'T SAY IT!
WHAT IS THIS LIFE IF, FULL OF CARE--
WE HAVE NO TIME TO TAKE A MORNING WADDLE?

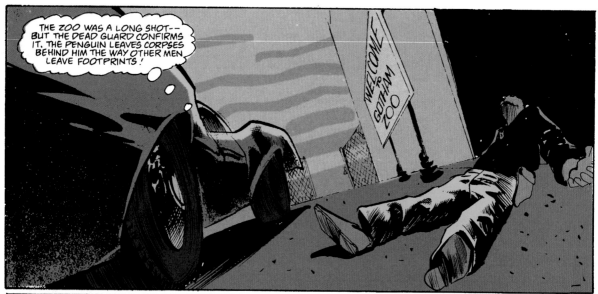

THE ZOO WAS A LONG SHOT-- BUT THE DEAD GUARD CONFIRMS IT. THE PENGUIN LEAVES CORPSES BEHIND HIM THE WAY OTHER MEN LEAVE FOOTPRINTS!

I'VE NEVER BEEN ABLE TO FIGURE IT. WHAT MAKES A MAN WHO COULD BE SUCCESSFUL IN ANY CAREER HE CHOSE TURN TO CRIME--TO *MURDER?*

AND HOW DOES A GANG-BOSS LIKE SHARKEY FIGURE IN HIS FOUL PLANS--?

TIGERS

THERE!

IT'S HIM!

I TOLD YOU, BOSS--

JUST SHUT UP AND KILL HIM, YOU FOOL!

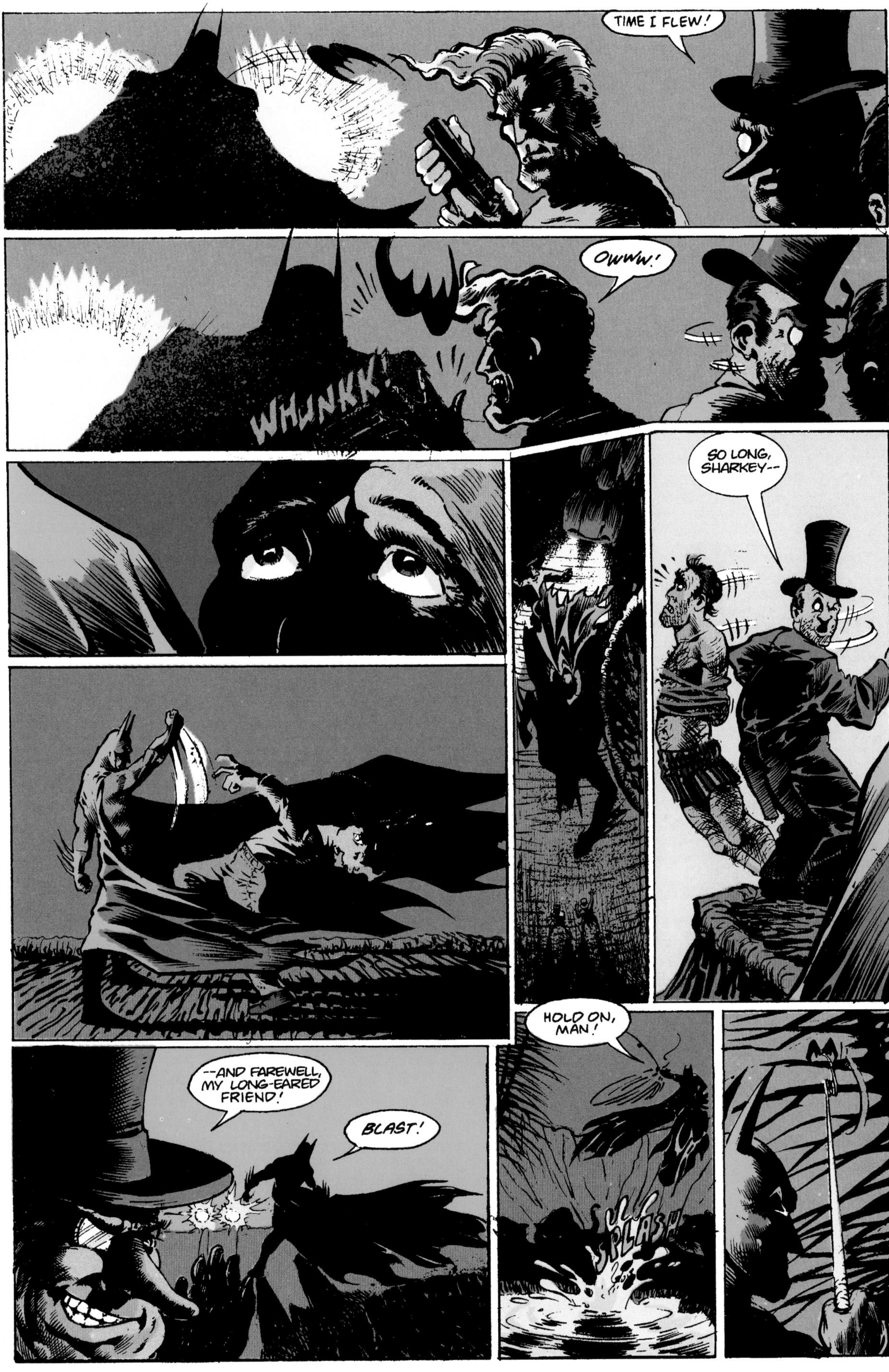
TIME I FLEW!
OWWW!
WHUNKK!
SO LONG, SHARKEY--
HOLD ON, MAN!
--AND FAREWELL, MY LONG-EARED FRIEND!
BLAST!
SPLASH!

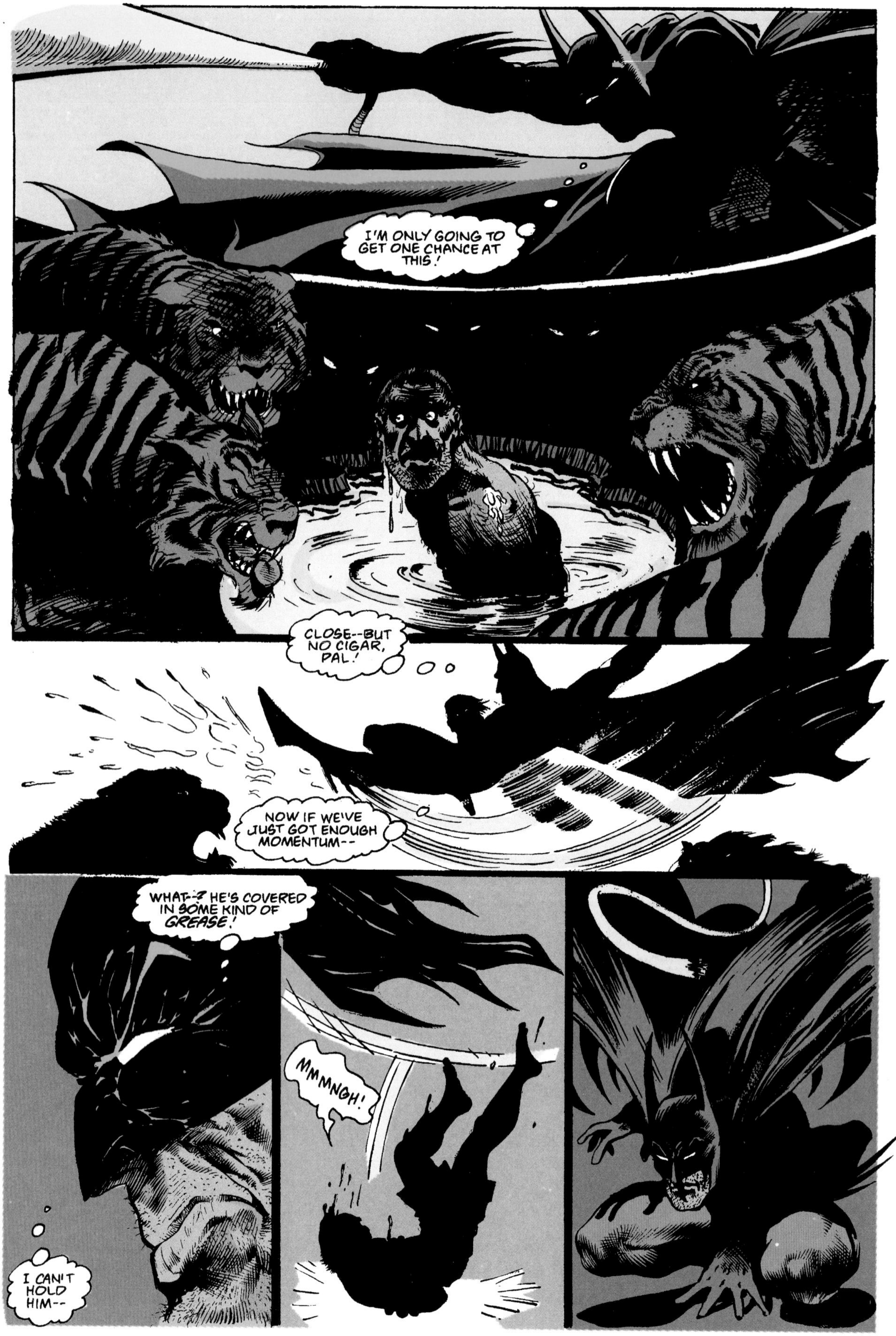
I'M ONLY GOING TO GET ONE CHANCE AT THIS!
CLOSE--BUT NO CIGAR, PAL!
NOW IF WE'VE JUST GOT ENOUGH MOMENTUM--
WHAT--? HE'S COVERED IN SOME KIND OF GREASE!
I CAN'T HOLD HIM--
MMMNGH!

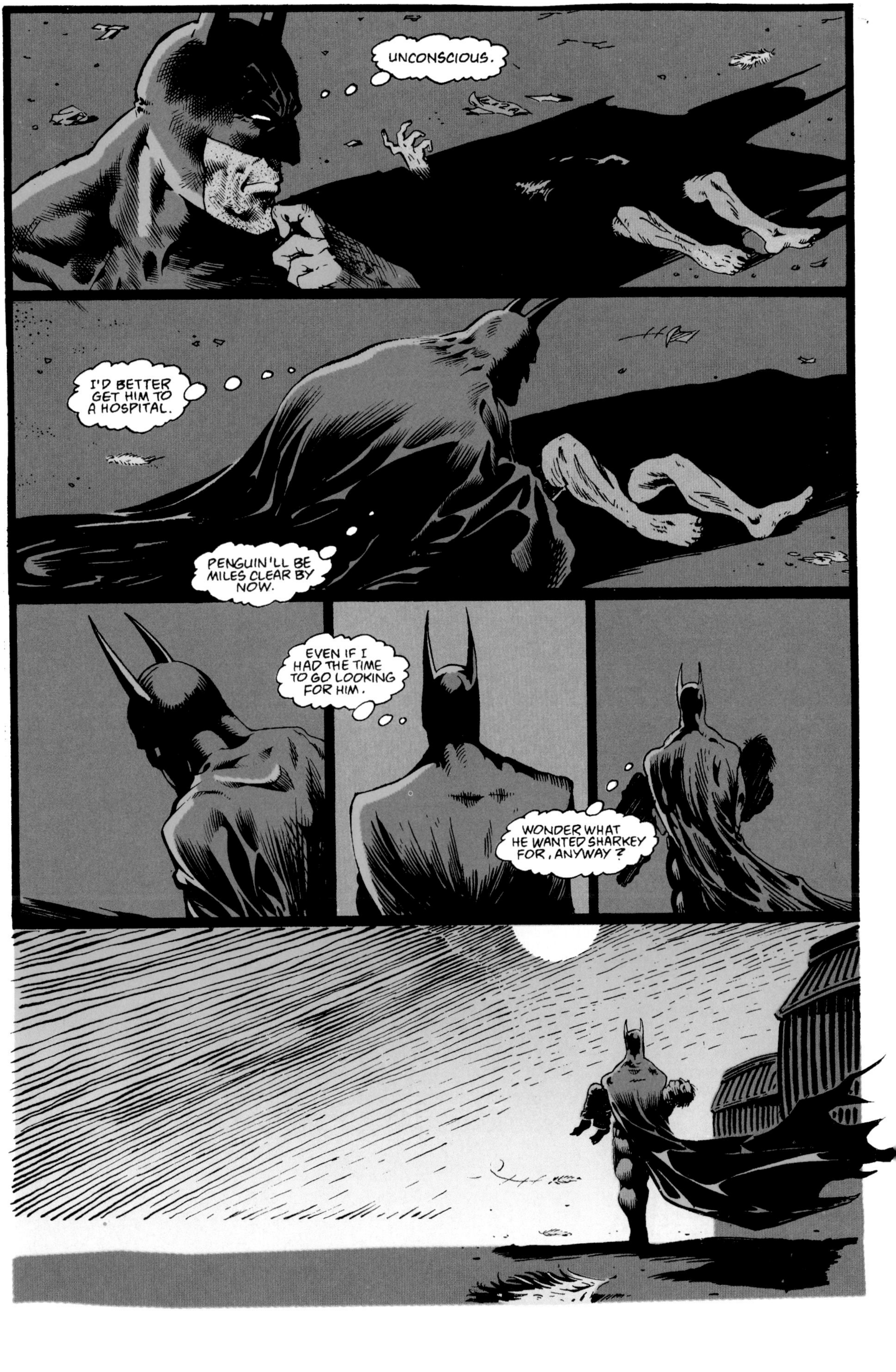
UNCONSCIOUS.
I'D BETTER GET HIM TO A HOSPITAL.
PENGUIN'LL BE MILES CLEAR BY NOW.
EVEN IF I HAD THE TIME TO GO LOOKING FOR HIM.
WONDER WHAT HE WANTED SHARKEY FOR, ANYWAY?

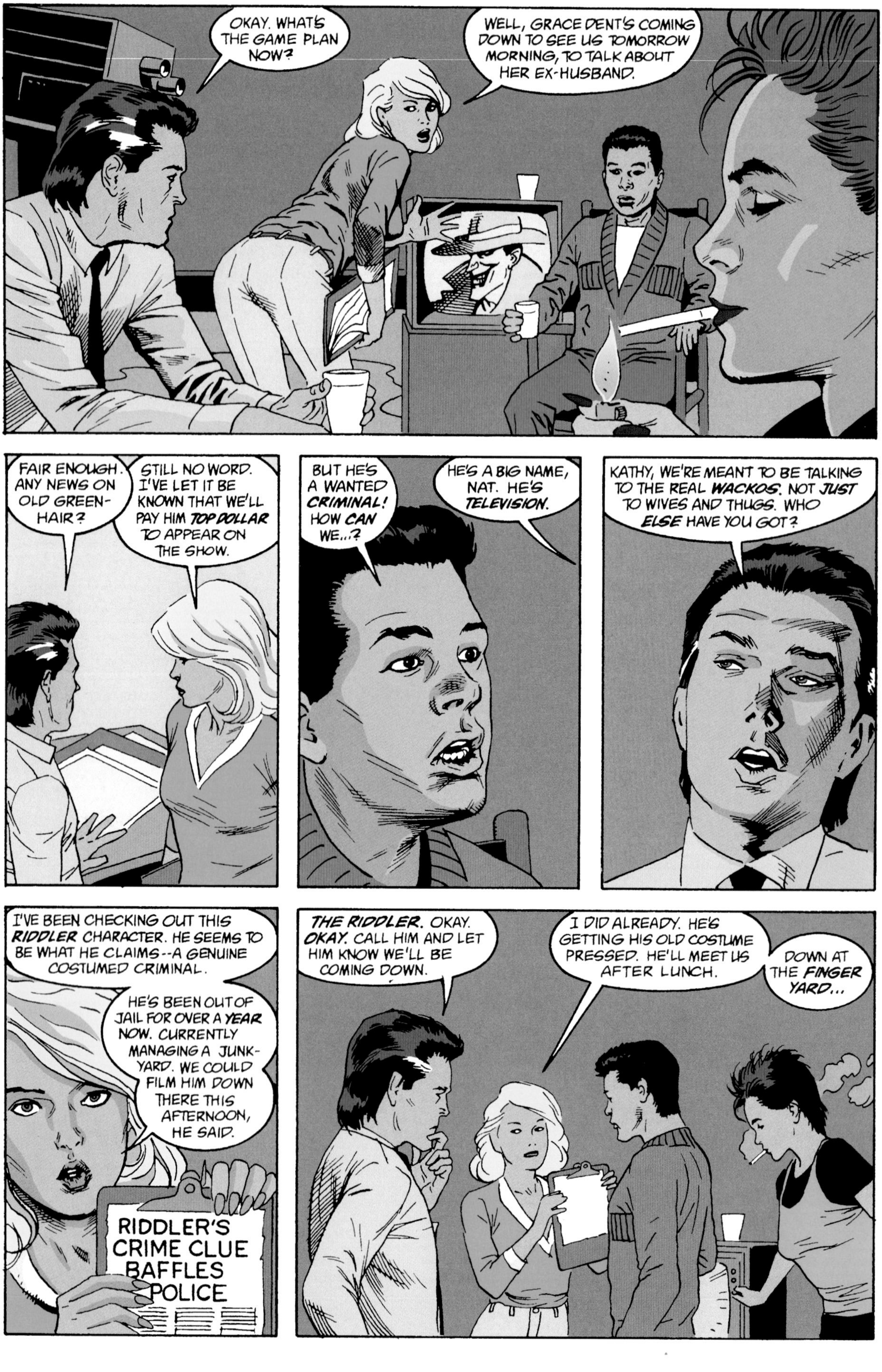
OKAY. WHAT'S THE GAME PLAN NOW?
WELL, GRACE DENT'S COMING DOWN TO SEE US TOMORROW MORNING, TO TALK ABOUT HER EX-HUSBAND.
FAIR ENOUGH. ANY NEWS ON OLD GREEN-HAIR?
STILL NO WORD. I'VE LET IT BE KNOWN THAT WE'LL PAY HIM TOP DOLLAR TO APPEAR ON THE SHOW.
BUT HE'S A WANTED CRIMINAL! HOW CAN WE...?
HE'S A BIG NAME, NAT. HE'S TELEVISION.
KATHY, WE'RE MEANT TO BE TALKING TO THE REAL WACKOS. NOT JUST TO WIVES AND THUGS. WHO ELSE HAVE YOU GOT?
I'VE BEEN CHECKING OUT THIS RIDDLER CHARACTER. HE SEEMS TO BE WHAT HE CLAIMS--A GENUINE COSTUMED CRIMINAL.
HE'S BEEN OUT OF JAIL FOR OVER A YEAR NOW. CURRENTLY MANAGING A JUNK-YARD. WE COULD FILM HIM DOWN THERE THIS AFTERNOON, HE SAID.
RIDDLER'S CRIME CLUE BAFFLES POLICE
THE RIDDLER. OKAY. OKAY. CALL HIM AND LET HIM KNOW WE'LL BE COMING DOWN.
I DID ALREADY. HE'S GETTING HIS OLD COSTUME PRESSED. HE'LL MEET US AFTER LUNCH.
DOWN AT THE FINGER YARD...

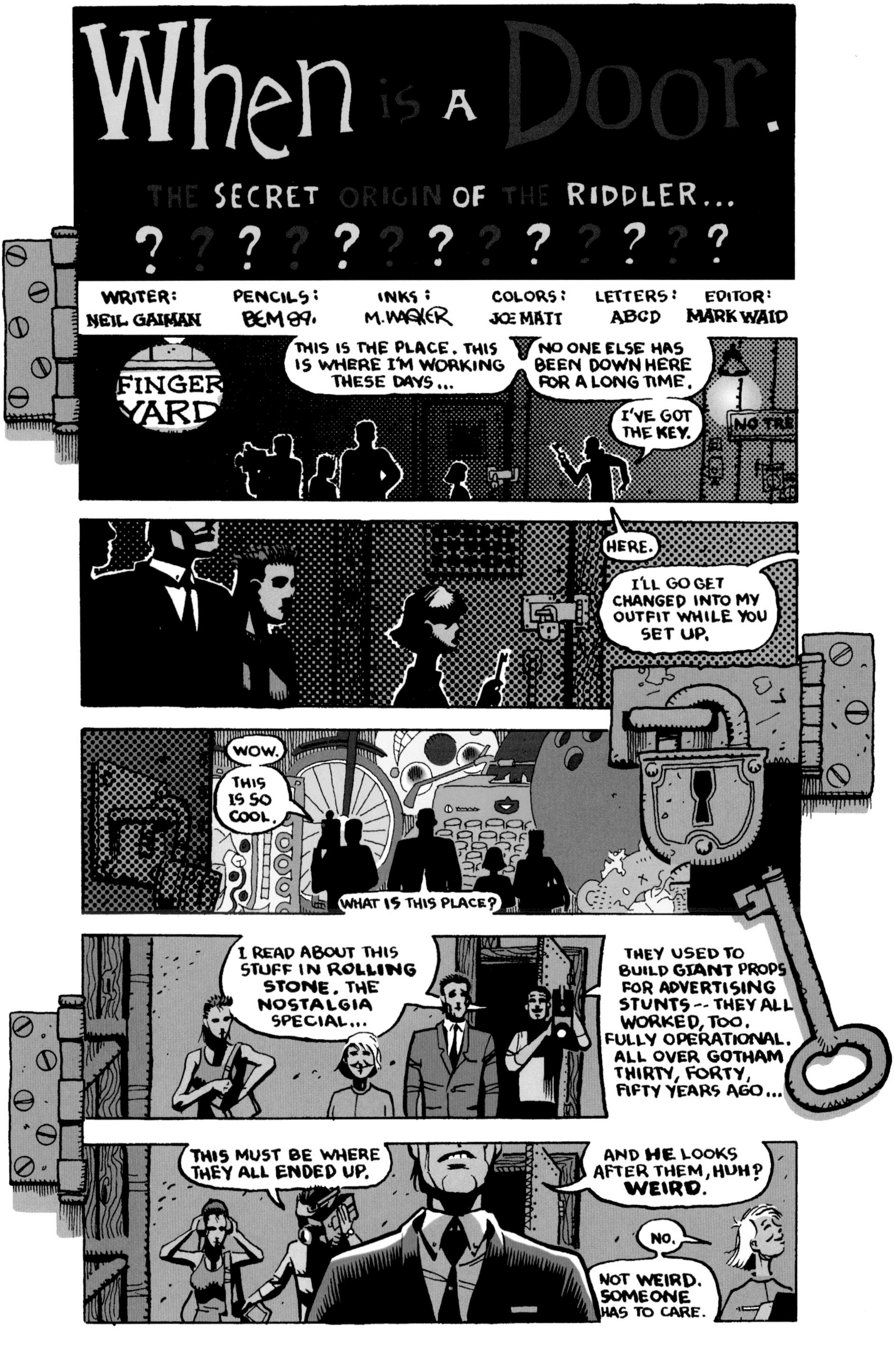

When is a Door.
THE SECRET ORIGIN OF THE RIDDLER...
WRITER: NEIL GAIMAN
PENCILS: BEM 89.
INKS: M. WAGNER
COLORS: JOE MATT
LETTERS: ABCD
EDITOR: MARK WAID
FINGER YARD
THIS IS THE PLACE. THIS IS WHERE I'M WORKING THESE DAYS...
NO ONE ELSE HAS BEEN DOWN HERE FOR A LONG TIME.
I'VE GOT THE KEY.
HERE.
I'LL GO GET CHANGED INTO MY OUTFIT WHILE YOU SET UP.
WOW.
THIS IS SO COOL.
WHAT IS THIS PLACE?
I READ ABOUT THIS STUFF IN ROLLING STONE. THE NOSTALGIA SPECIAL...
THEY USED TO BUILD GIANT PROPS FOR ADVERTISING STUNTS -- THEY ALL WORKED, TOO. FULLY OPERATIONAL. ALL OVER GOTHAM THIRTY, FORTY, FIFTY YEARS AGO...
THIS MUST BE WHERE THEY ALL ENDED UP.
AND HE LOOKS AFTER THEM, HUH? WEIRD.
NO.
NOT WEIRD. SOMEONE HAS TO CARE.

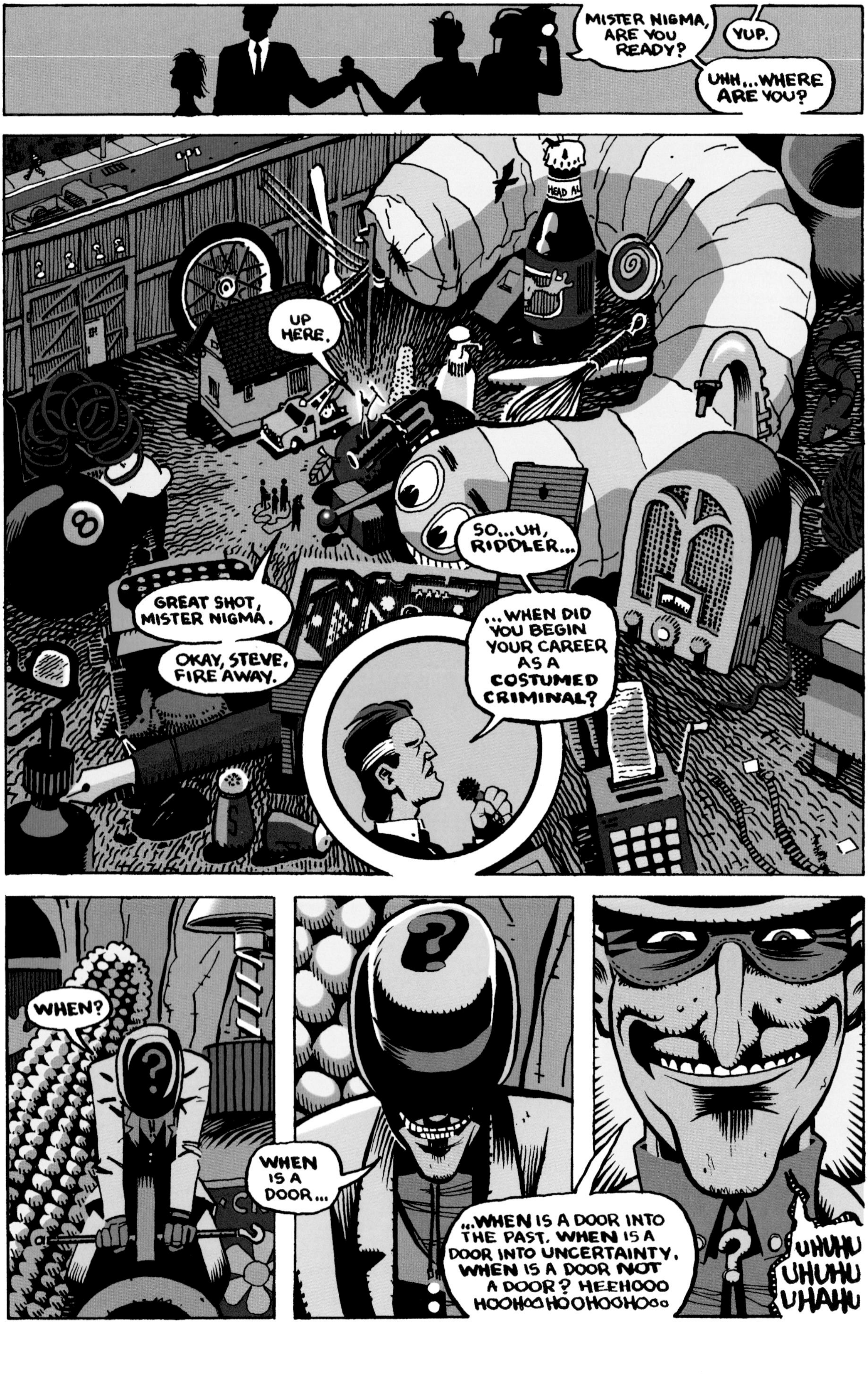
MISTER NIGMA, ARE YOU READY?
YUP.
UHH... WHERE ARE YOU?
UP HERE.
HEAD AL
GREAT SHOT, MISTER NIGMA.
OKAY, STEVE, FIRE AWAY.
SO... UH, RIDDLER...
...WHEN DID YOU BEGIN YOUR CAREER AS A COSTUMED CRIMINAL?
WHEN?
WHEN IS A DOOR...
...WHEN IS A DOOR INTO THE PAST, WHEN IS A DOOR INTO UNCERTAINTY, WHEN IS A DOOR NOT A DOOR? HEEHOOO HOOHOOHOOHOOHOOo
UHUHU UHUHU UHAHU

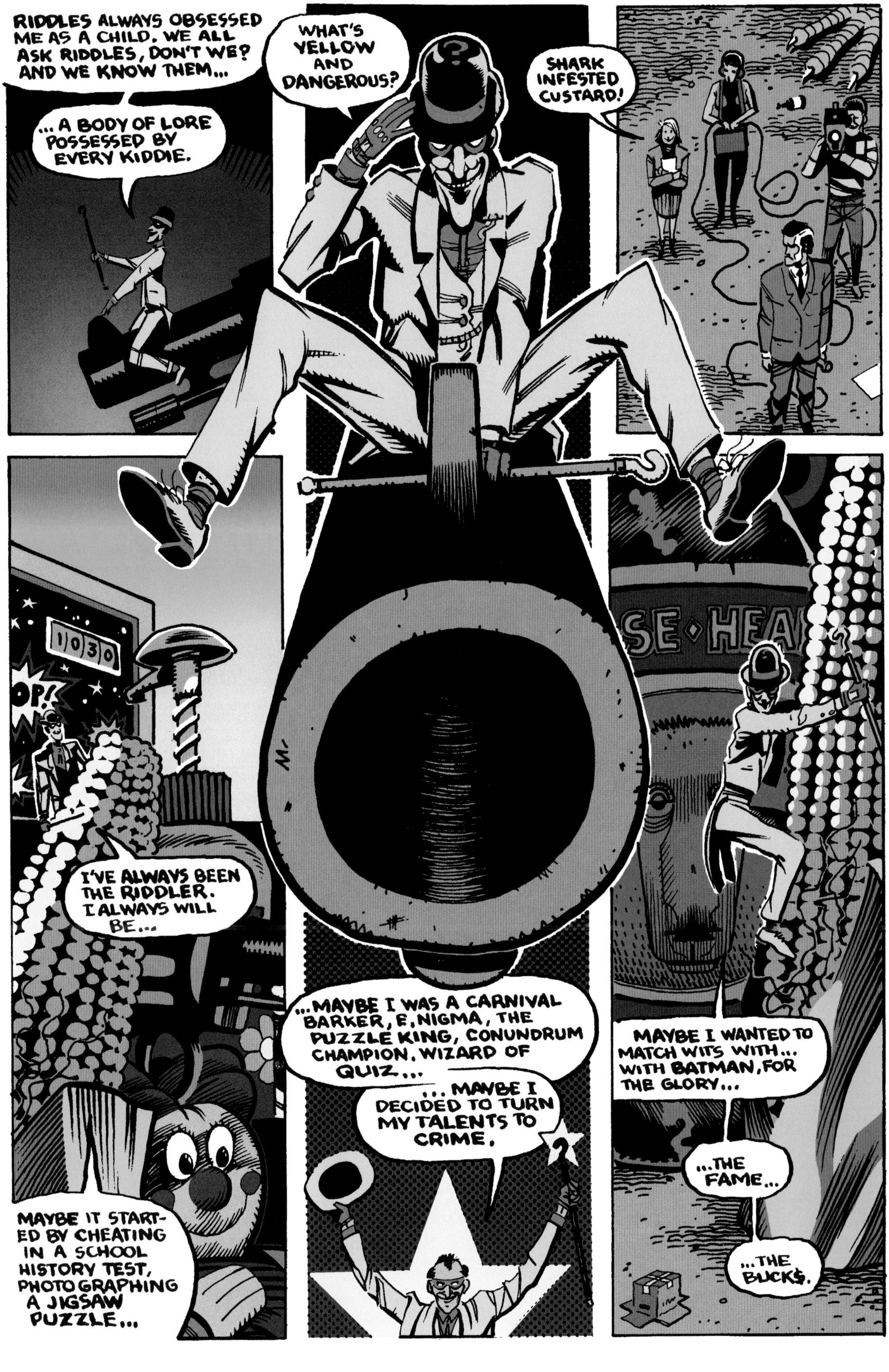
RIDDLES ALWAYS OBSESSED ME AS A CHILD. WE ALL ASK RIDDLES, DON'T WE? AND WE KNOW THEM...
...A BODY OF LORE POSSESSED BY EVERY KIDDIE.
WHAT'S YELLOW AND DANGEROUS?
SHARK INFESTED CUSTARD!
1030
OP!
SE◆HEA
I'VE ALWAYS BEEN THE RIDDLER. I ALWAYS WILL BE...
...MAYBE I WAS A CARNIVAL BARKER, E. NIGMA, THE PUZZLE KING, CONUNDRUM CHAMPION, WIZARD OF QUIZ...
...MAYBE I DECIDED TO TURN MY TALENTS TO CRIME.
MAYBE I WANTED TO MATCH WITS WITH... WITH BATMAN, FOR THE GLORY...
...THE FAME...
...THE BUCK$.
MAYBE IT STARTED BY CHEATING IN A SCHOOL HISTORY TEST, PHOTOGRAPHING A JIGSAW PUZZLE...

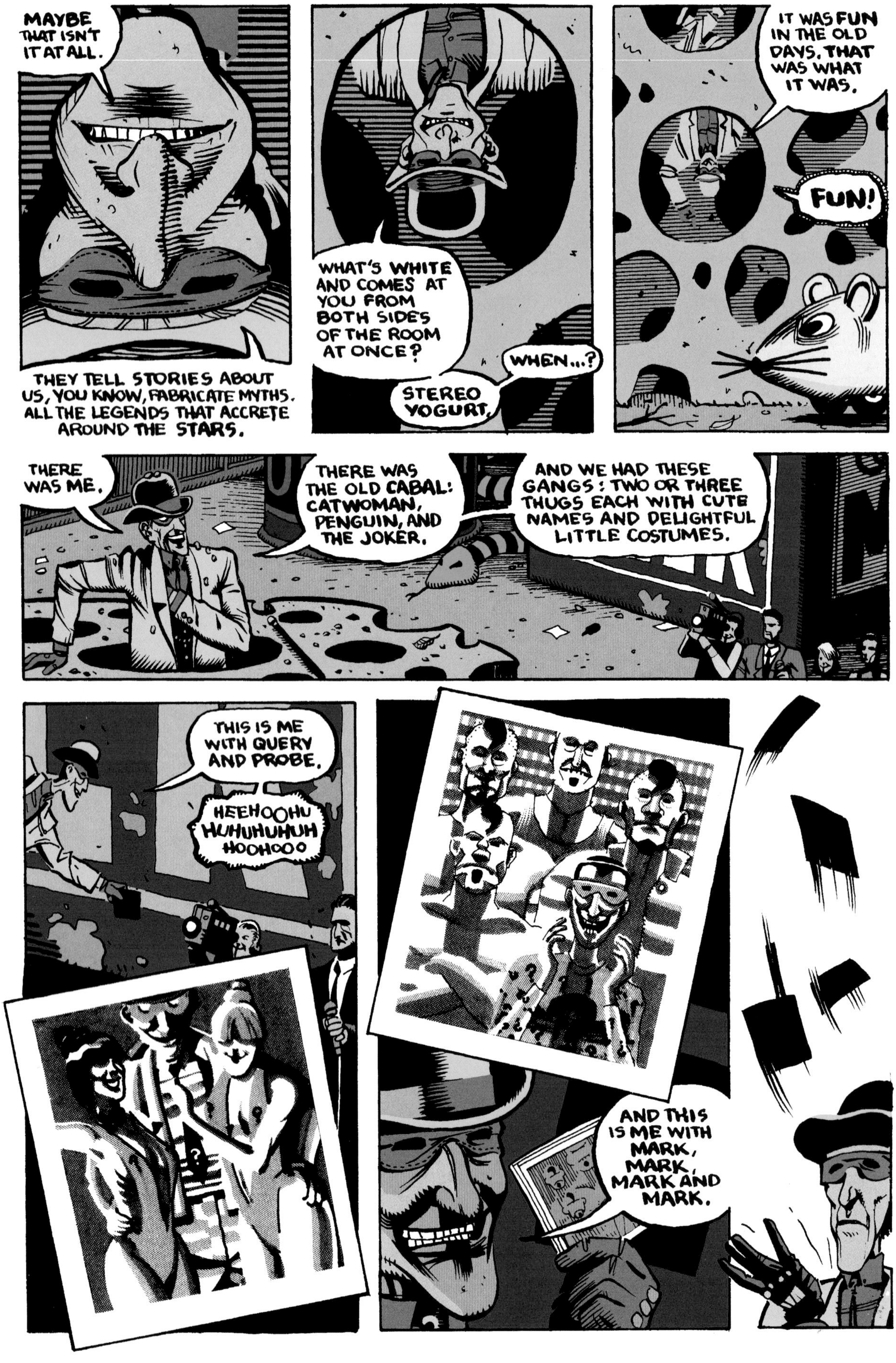
MAYBE THAT ISN'T IT AT ALL.
THEY TELL STORIES ABOUT US, YOU KNOW, FABRICATE MYTHS. ALL THE LEGENDS THAT ACCRETE AROUND THE STARS.
WHAT'S WHITE AND COMES AT YOU FROM BOTH SIDES OF THE ROOM AT ONCE?
WHEN...?
STEREO YOGURT.
IT WAS FUN IN THE OLD DAYS. THAT WAS WHAT IT WAS.
FUN!
THERE WAS ME.
THERE WAS THE OLD CABAL: CATWOMAN, PENGUIN, AND THE JOKER.
AND WE HAD THESE GANGS: TWO OR THREE THUGS EACH WITH CUTE NAMES AND DELIGHTFUL LITTLE COSTUMES.
THIS IS ME WITH QUERY AND PROBE.
HEEHOOHU HUHUHUHUH HOOHOOO
AND THIS IS ME WITH MARK, MARK, MARK AND MARK.

AND THERE WERE ALL THESE GUYS YOU NEVER SEE ANYMORE...

KING TUT.

EGG HEAD.

HOOHOO!

BOOK WORM.

MARSHA, QUEEN OF DIAMONDS.

WE HUNG OUT TOGETHER, DOWN AT THE 'WHAT A WAY TO GO-GO.'

IT WAS GREAT!

¿SIGH?

WHERE DID THEY ALL GO?

BATMAN AND ROBIN WERE PART OF THE FUN-- THEY WERE THE STRAIGHT MEN, BUT WE WERE THE STARS.

NO ONE EVER HURT ANYBODY. NOT REALLY.

NOBODY DIED.

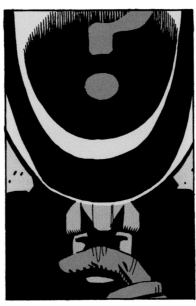

YOU LOOK AROUND THESE DAYS -- IT'S ALL DIFFERENT.

IT'S ALL CHANGED.

THE JOKER'S KILLING PEOPLE, FOR GOD'S SAKE!

DID I MISS SOMETHING?

WAS I AWAY WHEN THEY CHANGED THE RULES?

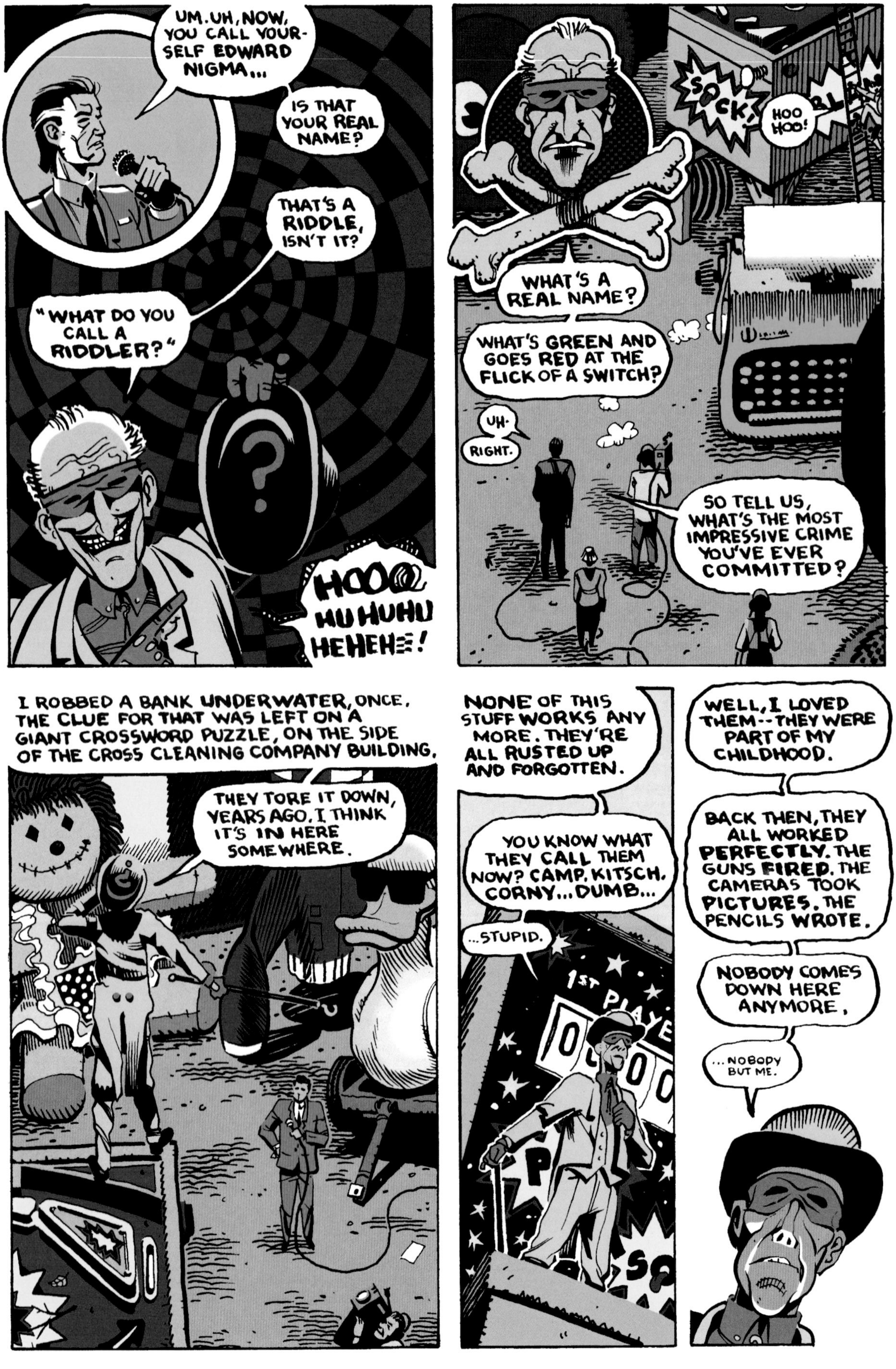
UM. UH, NOW, YOU CALL YOURSELF EDWARD NIGMA...
IS THAT YOUR REAL NAME?
THAT'S A RIDDLE, ISN'T IT?
"WHAT DO YOU CALL A RIDDLER?"
HOOO HU HUHU HEHEHE!
SOCK
HOO HOO!
WHAT'S A REAL NAME?
WHAT'S GREEN AND GOES RED AT THE FLICK OF A SWITCH?
UH.
RIGHT.
SO TELL US, WHAT'S THE MOST IMPRESSIVE CRIME YOU'VE EVER COMMITTED?
I ROBBED A BANK UNDERWATER, ONCE. THE CLUE FOR THAT WAS LEFT ON A GIANT CROSSWORD PUZZLE, ON THE SIDE OF THE CROSS CLEANING COMPANY BUILDING.
THEY TORE IT DOWN, YEARS AGO. I THINK IT'S IN HERE SOMEWHERE.
NONE OF THIS STUFF WORKS ANY MORE. THEY'RE ALL RUSTED UP AND FORGOTTEN.
YOU KNOW WHAT THEY CALL THEM NOW? CAMP, KITSCH, CORNY...DUMB...
...STUPID.
1ST PLAYE
WELL, I LOVED THEM-- THEY WERE PART OF MY CHILDHOOD.
BACK THEN, THEY ALL WORKED PERFECTLY. THE GUNS FIRED. THE CAMERAS TOOK PICTURES. THE PENCILS WROTE.
NOBODY COMES DOWN HERE ANYMORE,
...NOBODY BUT ME.

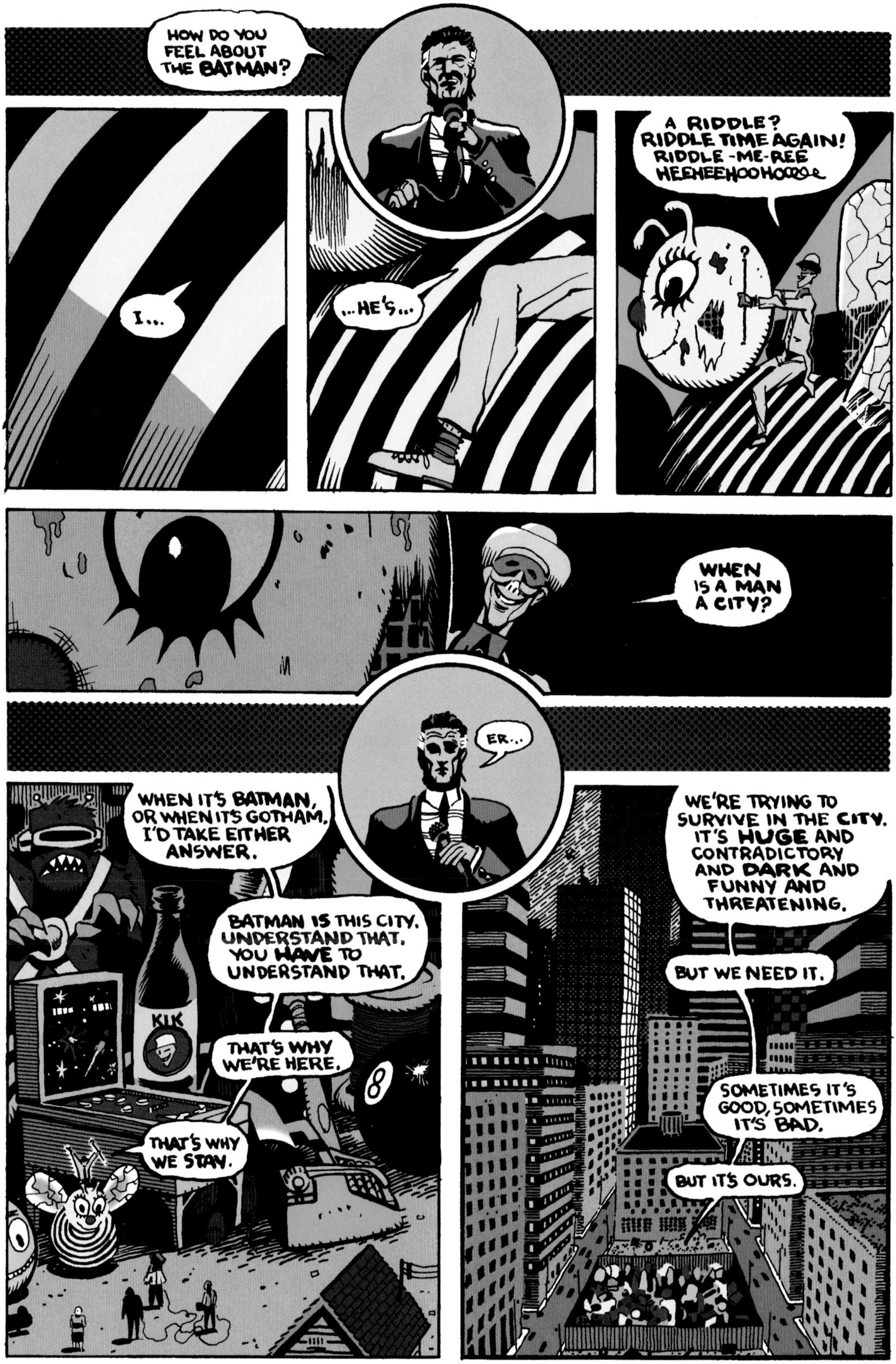
HOW DO YOU FEEL ABOUT THE BATMAN?
I...
...HE'S...
A RIDDLE? RIDDLE TIME AGAIN! RIDDLE-ME-REE HEEHEEHOOHOO
WHEN IS A MAN A CITY?
ER...
WHEN IT'S BATMAN, OR WHEN IT'S GOTHAM, I'D TAKE EITHER ANSWER.
BATMAN IS THIS CITY. UNDERSTAND THAT. YOU HAVE TO UNDERSTAND THAT.
THAT'S WHY WE'RE HERE.
THAT'S WHY WE STAY.
KIK
8
WE'RE TRYING TO SURVIVE IN THE CITY. IT'S HUGE AND CONTRADICTORY AND DARK AND FUNNY AND THREATENING.
BUT WE NEED IT.
SOMETIMES IT'S GOOD, SOMETIMES IT'S BAD.
BUT IT'S OURS.

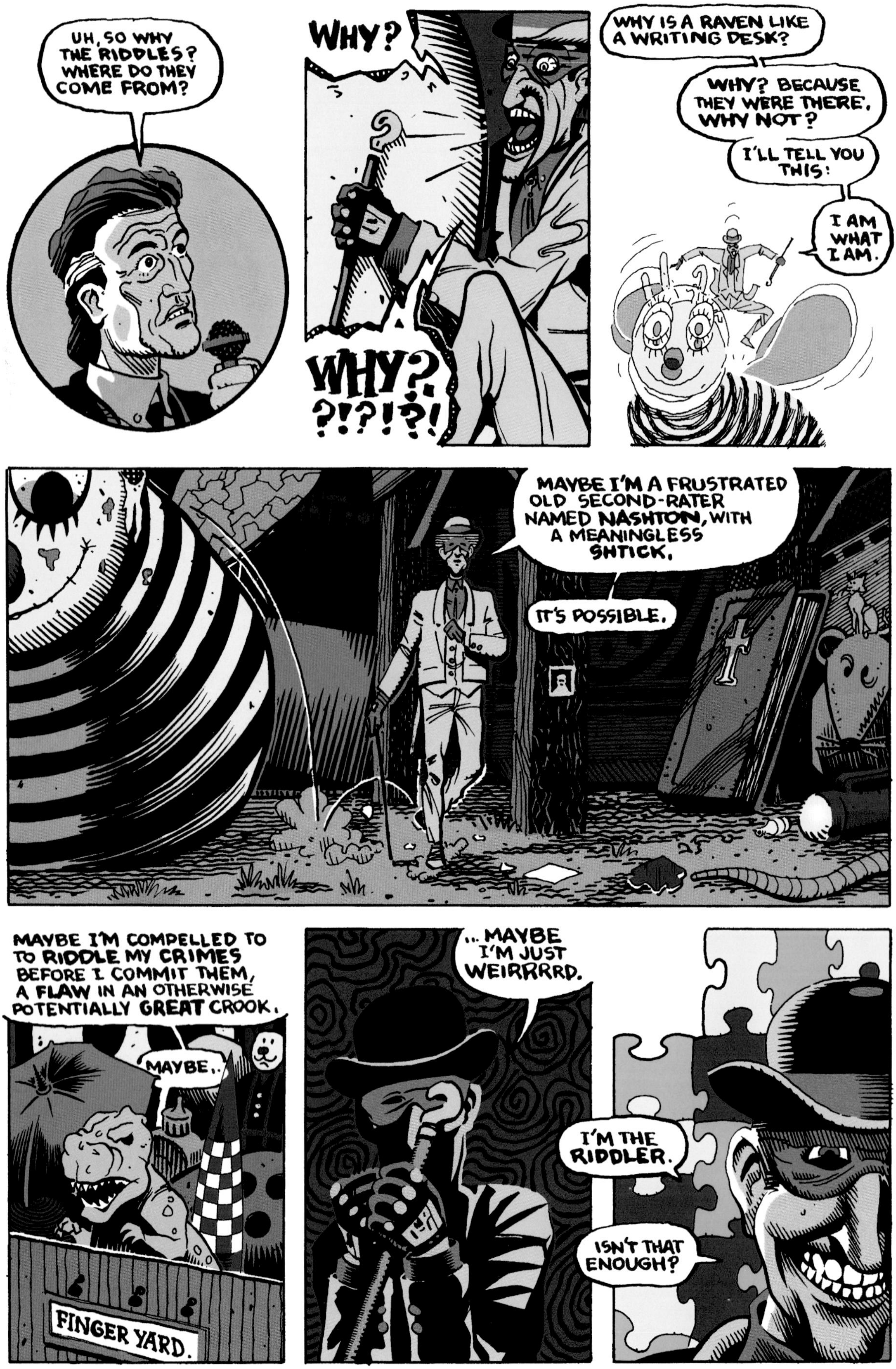
UH, SO WHY THE RIDDLES? WHERE DO THEY COME FROM?
WHY?
WHY?! ?!?!?!
WHY IS A RAVEN LIKE A WRITING DESK?
WHY? BECAUSE THEY WERE THERE. WHY NOT?
I'LL TELL YOU THIS:
I AM WHAT I AM.
MAYBE I'M A FRUSTRATED OLD SECOND-RATER NAMED NASHTON, WITH A MEANINGLESS SHTICK.
IT'S POSSIBLE.
MAYBE I'M COMPELLED TO TO RIDDLE MY CRIMES BEFORE I COMMIT THEM, A FLAW IN AN OTHERWISE POTENTIALLY GREAT CROOK.
MAYBE...
FINGER YARD.
...MAYBE I'M JUST WEIRRRRD.
I'M THE RIDDLER.
ISN'T THAT ENOUGH?

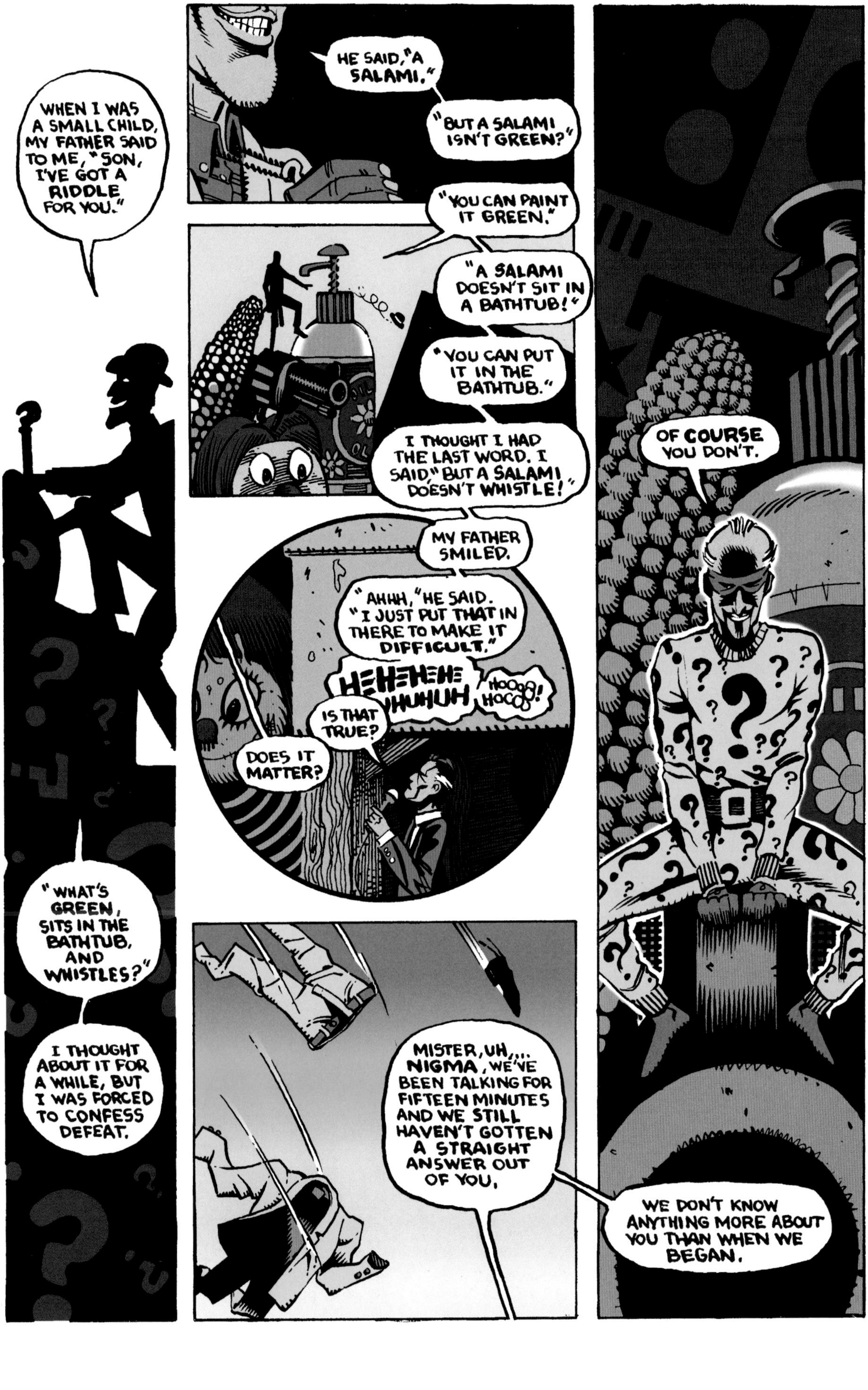

WHEN I WAS A SMALL CHILD, MY FATHER SAID TO ME, "SON, I'VE GOT A RIDDLE FOR YOU."
"WHAT'S GREEN, SITS IN THE BATHTUB, AND WHISTLES?"
I THOUGHT ABOUT IT FOR A WHILE, BUT I WAS FORCED TO CONFESS DEFEAT.
HE SAID, "A SALAMI."
"BUT A SALAMI ISN'T GREEN?"
"YOU CAN PAINT IT GREEN."
"A SALAMI DOESN'T SIT IN A BATHTUB!"
"YOU CAN PUT IT IN THE BATHTUB."
I THOUGHT I HAD THE LAST WORD. I SAID, "BUT A SALAMI DOESN'T WHISTLE!"
MY FATHER SMILED.
"AHHH," HE SAID. "I JUST PUT THAT IN THERE TO MAKE IT DIFFICULT."
HEHEHEHE HUHUHUH
HOOOO! HOOOO!
IS THAT TRUE?
DOES IT MATTER?
OF COURSE YOU DON'T.
MISTER, UH,... NIGMA, WE'VE BEEN TALKING FOR FIFTEEN MINUTES AND WE STILL HAVEN'T GOTTEN A STRAIGHT ANSWER OUT OF YOU,
WE DON'T KNOW ANYTHING MORE ABOUT YOU THAN WHEN WE BEGAN.

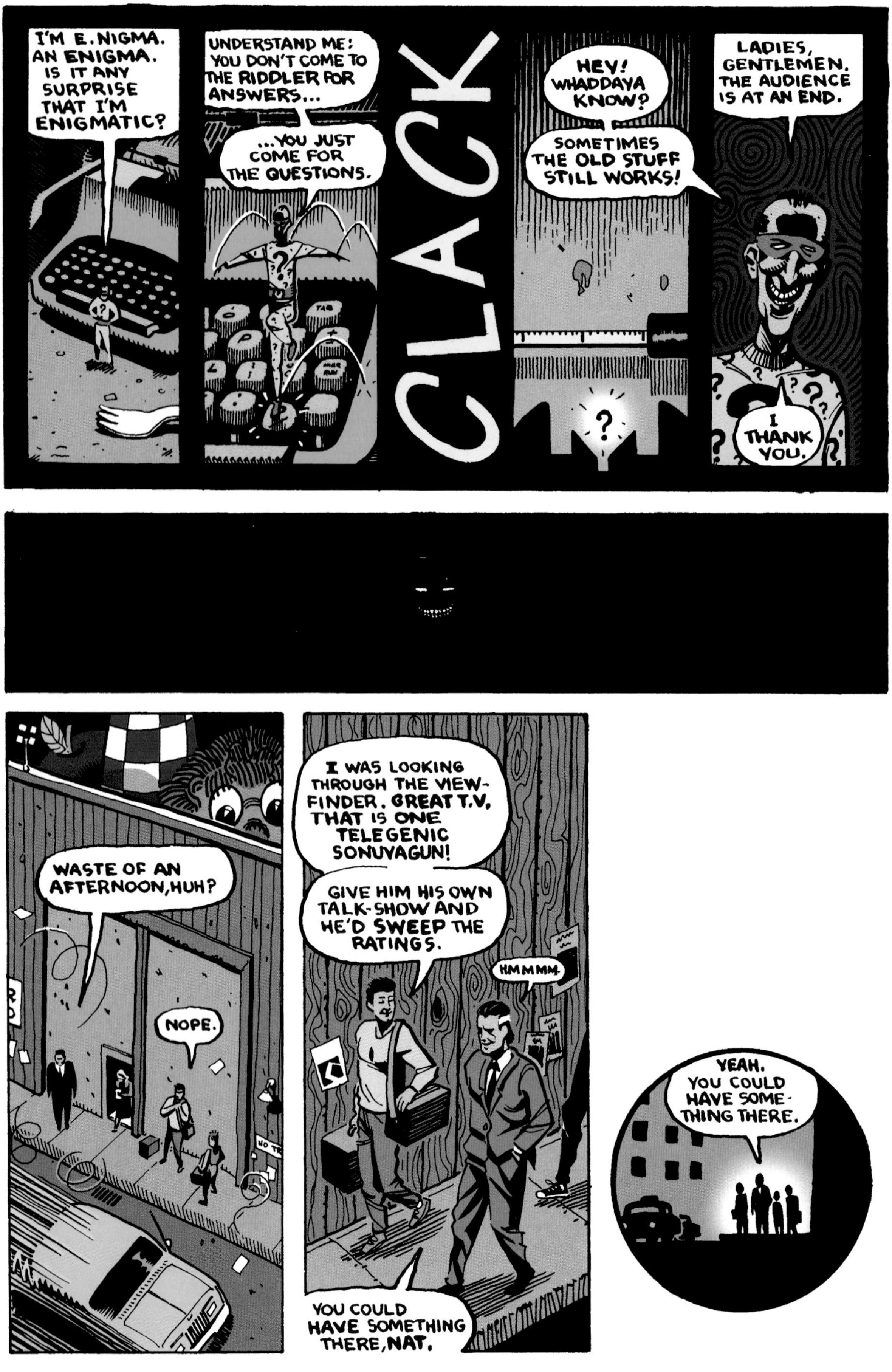
I'M E. NIGMA. AN ENIGMA. IS IT ANY SURPRISE THAT I'M ENIGMATIC?
UNDERSTAND ME: YOU DON'T COME TO THE RIDDLER FOR ANSWERS...
...YOU JUST COME FOR THE QUESTIONS.
CLACK
HEY! WHADDAYA KNOW?
SOMETIMES THE OLD STUFF STILL WORKS!
LADIES, GENTLEMEN. THE AUDIENCE IS AT AN END.
I THANK YOU.
WASTE OF AN AFTERNOON, HUH?
NOPE.
I WAS LOOKING THROUGH THE VIEW-FINDER. GREAT T.V. THAT IS ONE TELEGENIC SONUVAGUN!
GIVE HIM HIS OWN TALK-SHOW AND HE'D SWEEP THE RATINGS.
HMMMM.
YOU COULD HAVE SOMETHING THERE, NAT.
YEAH. YOU COULD HAVE SOME-THING THERE.

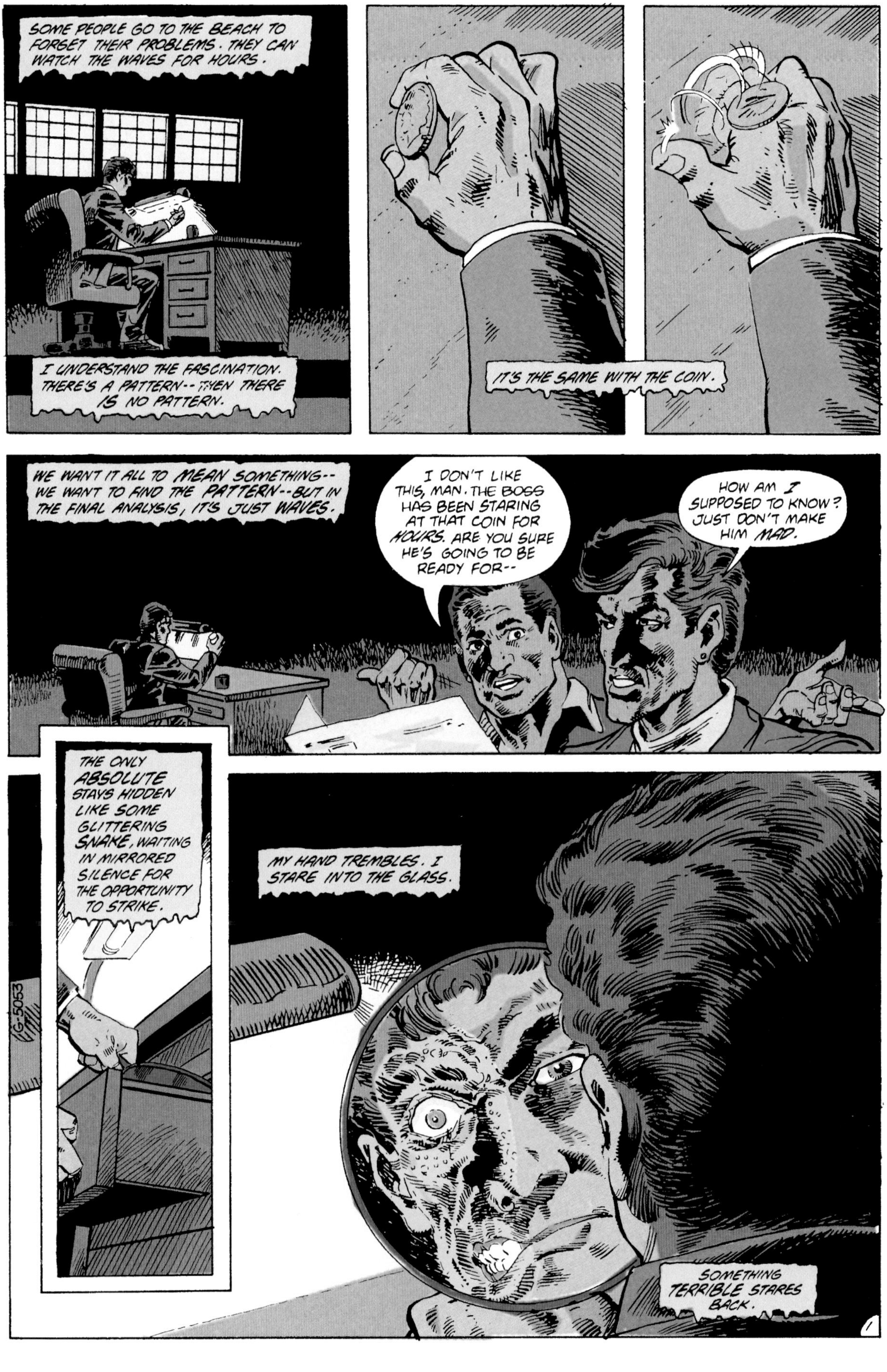
SOME PEOPLE GO TO THE BEACH TO FORGET THEIR PROBLEMS. THEY CAN WATCH THE WAVES FOR HOURS.
I UNDERSTAND THE FASCINATION. THERE'S A PATTERN--THEN THERE IS NO PATTERN.
IT'S THE SAME WITH THE COIN.
WE WANT IT ALL TO MEAN SOMETHING--WE WANT TO FIND THE PATTERN--BUT IN THE FINAL ANALYSIS, IT'S JUST WAVES.
I DON'T LIKE THIS, MAN. THE BOSS HAS BEEN STARING AT THAT COIN FOR HOURS. ARE YOU SURE HE'S GOING TO BE READY FOR--
HOW AM I SUPPOSED TO KNOW? JUST DON'T MAKE HIM MAD.
THE ONLY ABSOLUTE STAYS HIDDEN LIKE SOME GLITTERING SNAKE, WAITING IN MIRRORED SILENCE FOR THE OPPORTUNITY TO STRIKE.
MY HAND TREMBLES. I STARE INTO THE GLASS.
G-5053
SOMETHING TERRIBLE STARES BACK.
1

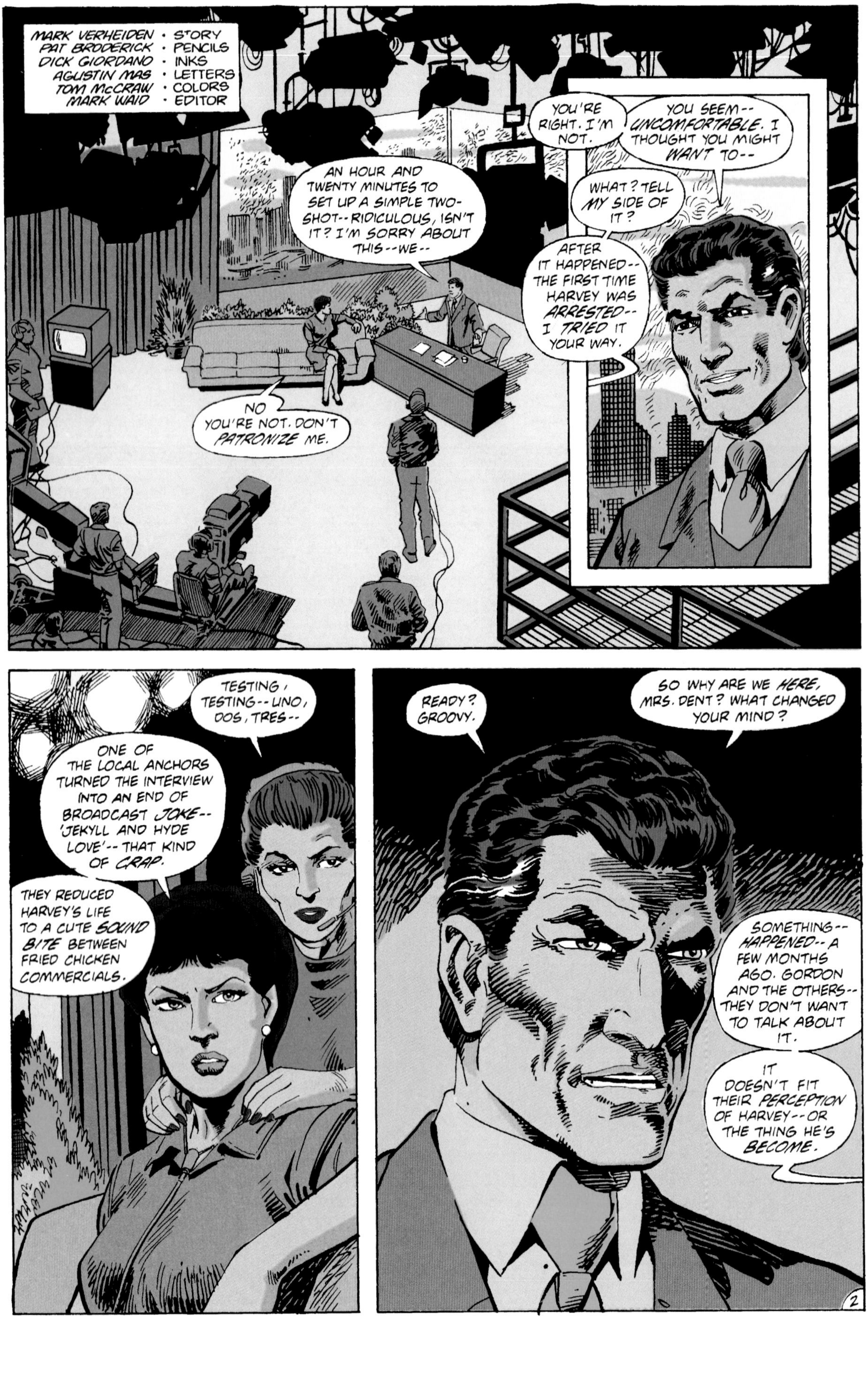
MARK VERHEIDEN • STORY
PAT BRODERICK • PENCILS
DICK GIORDANO • INKS
AGUSTIN MAS • LETTERS
TOM McCRAW • COLORS
MARK WAID • EDITOR
AN HOUR AND TWENTY MINUTES TO SET UP A SIMPLE TWO-SHOT--RIDICULOUS, ISN'T IT? I'M SORRY ABOUT THIS--WE--
NO YOU'RE NOT. DON'T PATRONIZE ME.
YOU SEEM--UNCOMFORTABLE. I THOUGHT YOU MIGHT WANT TO--
YOU'RE RIGHT. I'M NOT.
WHAT? TELL MY SIDE OF IT?
AFTER IT HAPPENED--THE FIRST TIME HARVEY WAS ARRESTED--I TRIED IT YOUR WAY.
TESTING, TESTING--UNO, DOS, TRES--
ONE OF THE LOCAL ANCHORS TURNED THE INTERVIEW INTO AN END OF BROADCAST JOKE--'JEKYLL AND HYDE LOVE'--THAT KIND OF CRAP.
THEY REDUCED HARVEY'S LIFE TO A CUTE SOUND BITE BETWEEN FRIED CHICKEN COMMERCIALS.
READY? GROOVY.
SO WHY ARE WE HERE, MRS. DENT? WHAT CHANGED YOUR MIND?
SOMETHING--HAPPENED--A FEW MONTHS AGO. GORDON AND THE OTHERS--THEY DON'T WANT TO TALK ABOUT IT.
IT DOESN'T FIT THEIR PERCEPTION OF HARVEY--OR THE THING HE'S BECOME.
2

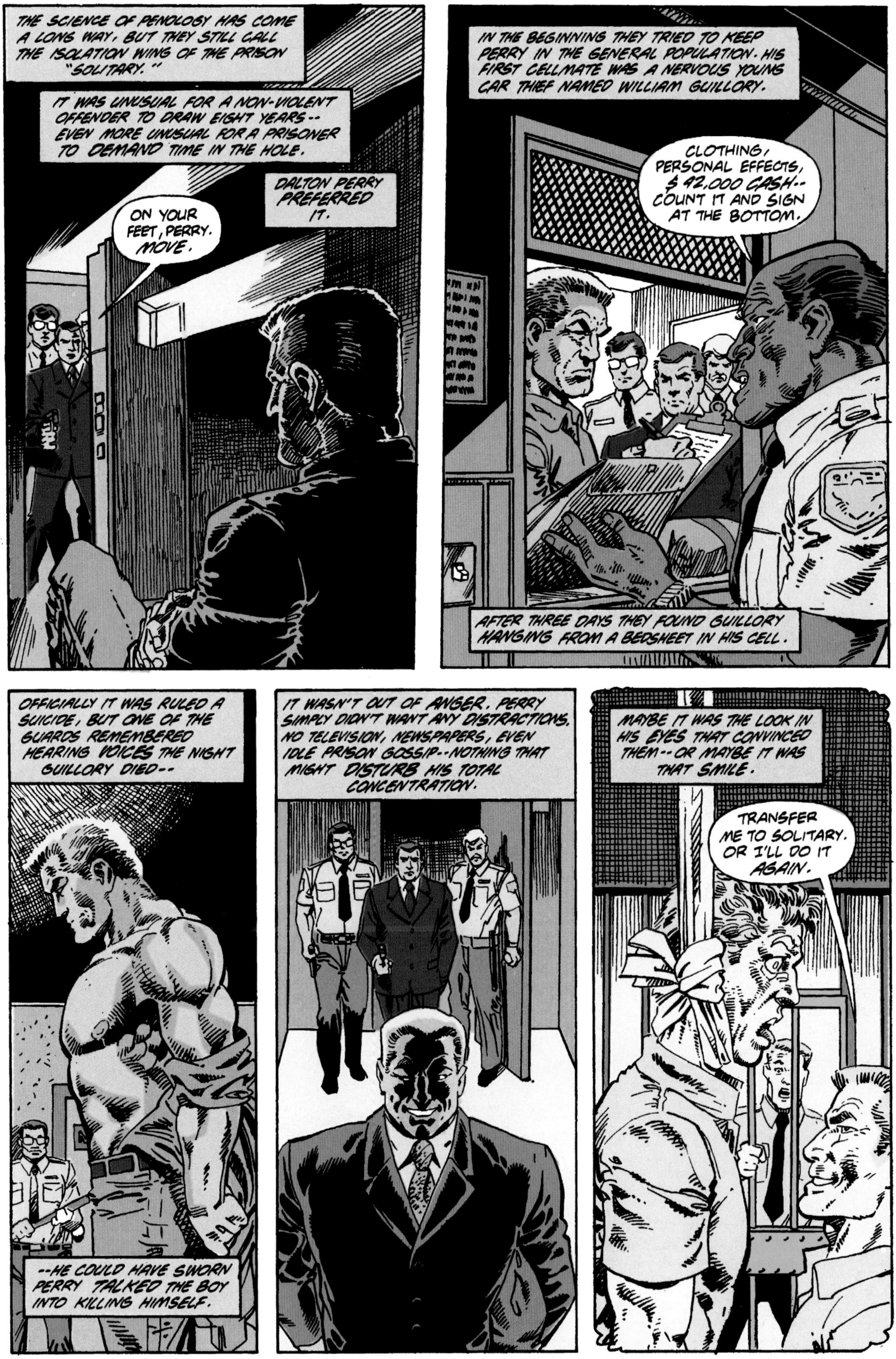
THE SCIENCE OF PENOLOGY HAS COME A LONG WAY, BUT THEY STILL CALL THE ISOLATION WING OF THE PRISON "SOLITARY."
IT WAS UNUSUAL FOR A NON-VIOLENT OFFENDER TO DRAW EIGHT YEARS-- EVEN MORE UNUSUAL FOR A PRISONER TO DEMAND TIME IN THE HOLE.
DALTON PERRY PREFERRED IT.
ON YOUR FEET, PERRY. MOVE.
IN THE BEGINNING THEY TRIED TO KEEP PERRY IN THE GENERAL POPULATION. HIS FIRST CELLMATE WAS A NERVOUS YOUNG CAR THIEF NAMED WILLIAM GUILLORY.
CLOTHING, PERSONAL EFFECTS, $42,000 CASH-- COUNT IT AND SIGN AT THE BOTTOM.
AFTER THREE DAYS THEY FOUND GUILLORY HANGING FROM A BEDSHEET IN HIS CELL.
OFFICIALLY IT WAS RULED A SUICIDE, BUT ONE OF THE GUARDS REMEMBERED HEARING VOICES THE NIGHT GUILLORY DIED--
--HE COULD HAVE SWORN PERRY TALKED THE BOY INTO KILLING HIMSELF.
IT WASN'T OUT OF ANGER. PERRY SIMPLY DIDN'T WANT ANY DISTRACTIONS. NO TELEVISION, NEWSPAPERS, EVEN IDLE PRISON GOSSIP--NOTHING THAT MIGHT DISTURB HIS TOTAL CONCENTRATION.
MAYBE IT WAS THE LOOK IN HIS EYES THAT CONVINCED THEM--OR MAYBE IT WAS THAT SMILE.
TRANSFER ME TO SOLITARY. OR I'LL DO IT AGAIN.

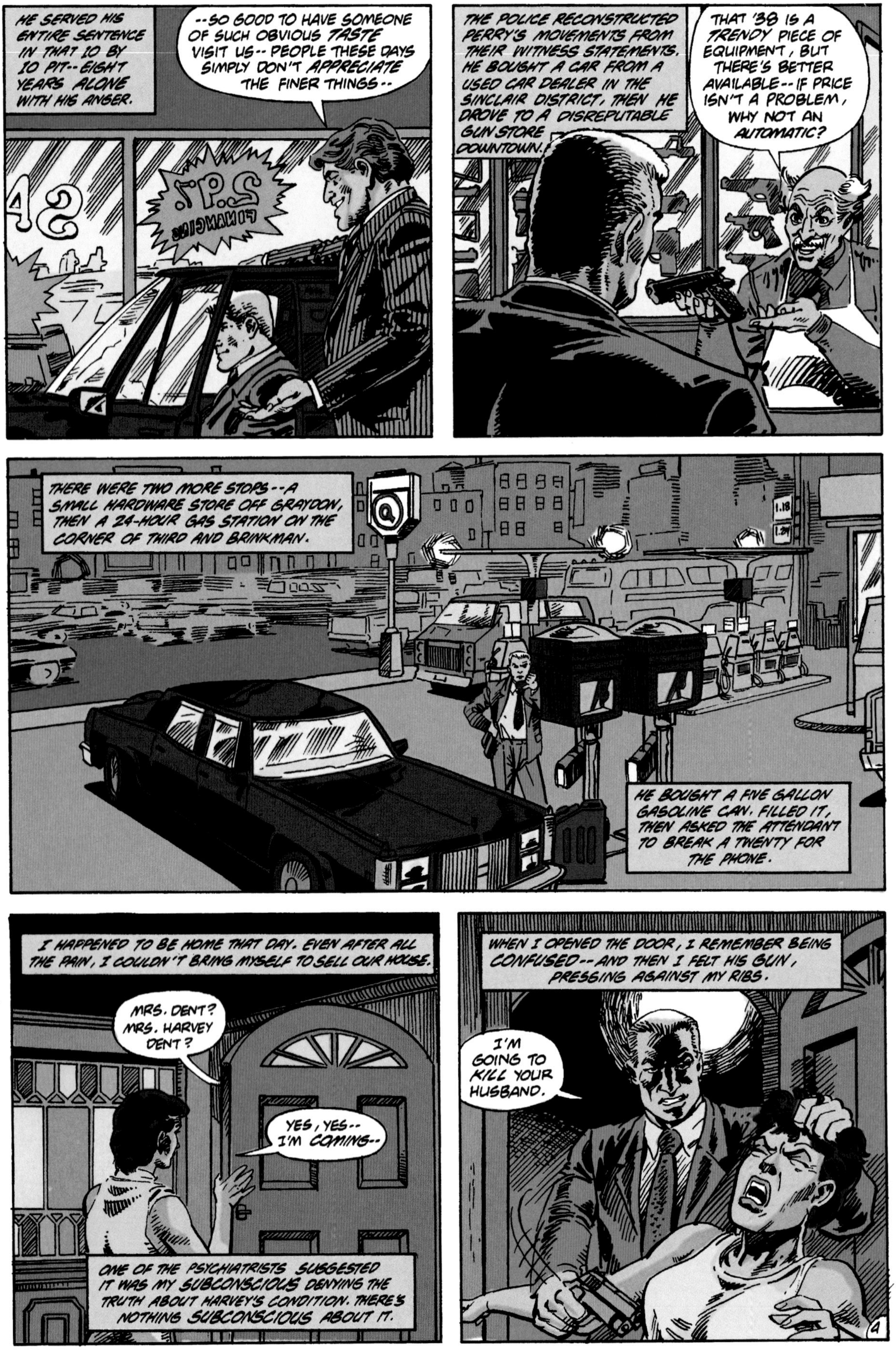
HE SERVED HIS ENTIRE SENTENCE IN THAT 10 BY 10 PIT--EIGHT YEARS ALONE WITH HIS ANGER.
--SO GOOD TO HAVE SOMEONE OF SUCH OBVIOUS TASTE VISIT US--PEOPLE THESE DAYS SIMPLY DON'T APPRECIATE THE FINER THINGS--
THE POLICE RECONSTRUCTED PERRY'S MOVEMENTS FROM THEIR WITNESS STATEMENTS. HE BOUGHT A CAR FROM A USED CAR DEALER IN THE SINCLAIR DISTRICT, THEN HE DROVE TO A DISREPUTABLE GUN STORE DOWNTOWN.
THAT '38 IS A TRENDY PIECE OF EQUIPMENT, BUT THERE'S BETTER AVAILABLE--IF PRICE ISN'T A PROBLEM, WHY NOT AN AUTOMATIC?
THERE WERE TWO MORE STOPS--A SMALL HARDWARE STORE OFF GRAYDON, THEN A 24-HOUR GAS STATION ON THE CORNER OF THIRD AND BRINKMAN.
HE BOUGHT A FIVE GALLON GASOLINE CAN, FILLED IT, THEN ASKED THE ATTENDANT TO BREAK A TWENTY FOR THE PHONE.
I HAPPENED TO BE HOME THAT DAY. EVEN AFTER ALL THE PAIN, I COULDN'T BRING MYSELF TO SELL OUR HOUSE.
MRS. DENT? MRS. HARVEY DENT?
YES, YES--I'M COMING--
ONE OF THE PSYCHIATRISTS SUGGESTED IT WAS MY SUBCONSCIOUS DENYING THE TRUTH ABOUT HARVEY'S CONDITION. THERE'S NOTHING SUBCONSCIOUS ABOUT IT.
WHEN I OPENED THE DOOR, I REMEMBER BEING CONFUSED--AND THEN I FELT HIS GUN, PRESSING AGAINST MY RIBS.
I'M GOING TO KILL YOUR HUSBAND.

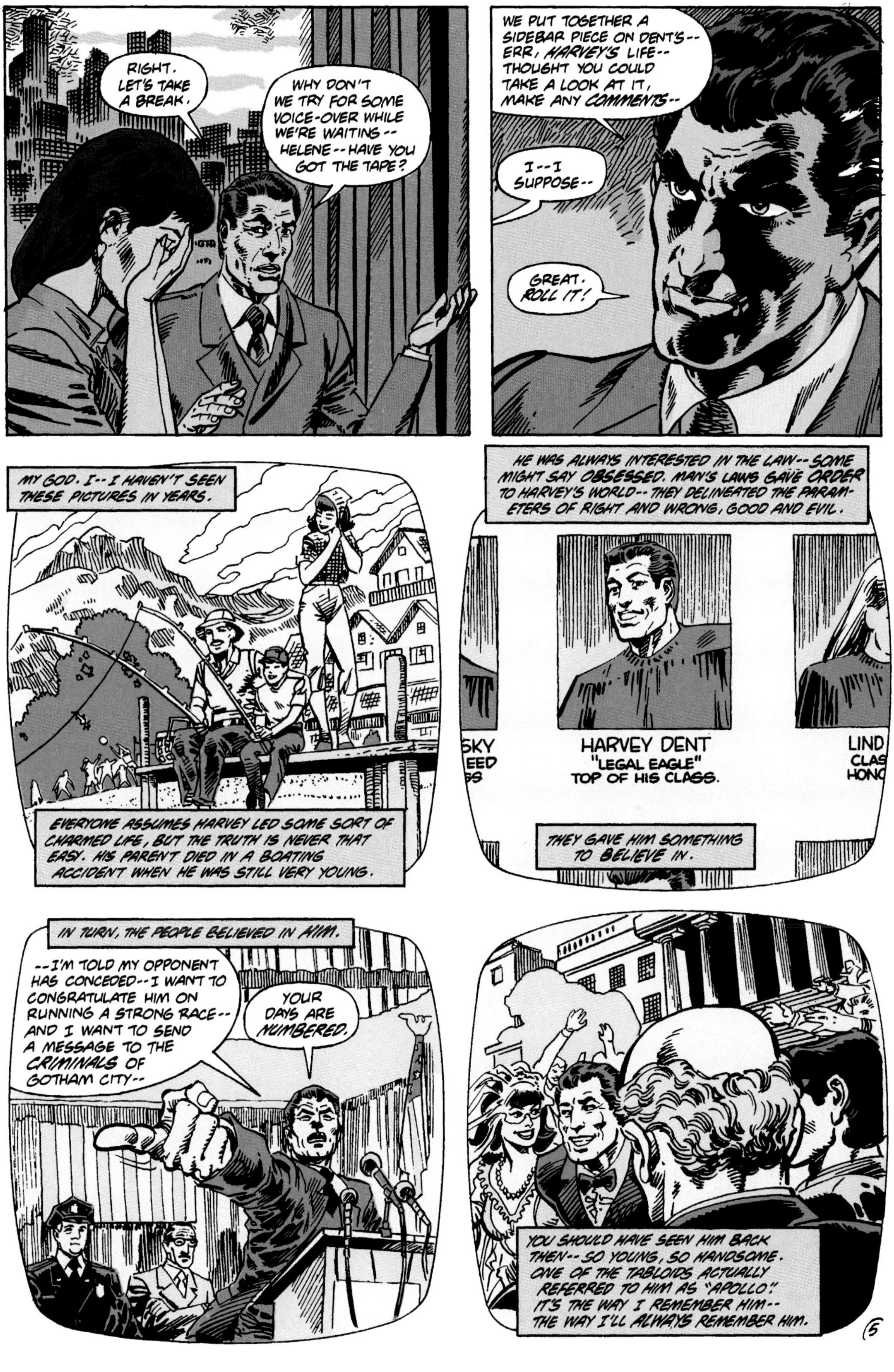
RIGHT. LET'S TAKE A BREAK.
WHY DON'T WE TRY FOR SOME VOICE-OVER WHILE WE'RE WAITING -- HELENE -- HAVE YOU GOT THE TAPE?
WE PUT TOGETHER A SIDEBAR PIECE ON DENT'S -- ERR, HARVEY'S LIFE -- THOUGHT YOU COULD TAKE A LOOK AT IT, MAKE ANY COMMENTS --
I -- I SUPPOSE --
GREAT. ROLL IT!
MY GOD. I -- I HAVEN'T SEEN THESE PICTURES IN YEARS.
EVERYONE ASSUMES HARVEY LED SOME SORT OF CHARMED LIFE, BUT THE TRUTH IS NEVER THAT EASY. HIS PARENT DIED IN A BOATING ACCIDENT WHEN HE WAS STILL VERY YOUNG.
HE WAS ALWAYS INTERESTED IN THE LAW -- SOME MIGHT SAY OBSESSED. MAN'S LAWS GAVE ORDER TO HARVEY'S WORLD -- THEY DELINEATED THE PARAMETERS OF RIGHT AND WRONG, GOOD AND EVIL.
HARVEY DENT
"LEGAL EAGLE"
TOP OF HIS CLASS.
THEY GAVE HIM SOMETHING TO BELIEVE IN.
IN TURN, THE PEOPLE BELIEVED IN HIM.
--I'M TOLD MY OPPONENT HAS CONCEDED -- I WANT TO CONGRATULATE HIM ON RUNNING A STRONG RACE -- AND I WANT TO SEND A MESSAGE TO THE CRIMINALS OF GOTHAM CITY --
YOUR DAYS ARE NUMBERED.
YOU SHOULD HAVE SEEN HIM BACK THEN -- SO YOUNG, SO HANDSOME. ONE OF THE TABLOIDS ACTUALLY REFERRED TO HIM AS "APOLLO." IT'S THE WAY I REMEMBER HIM -- THE WAY I'LL ALWAYS REMEMBER HIM.
5

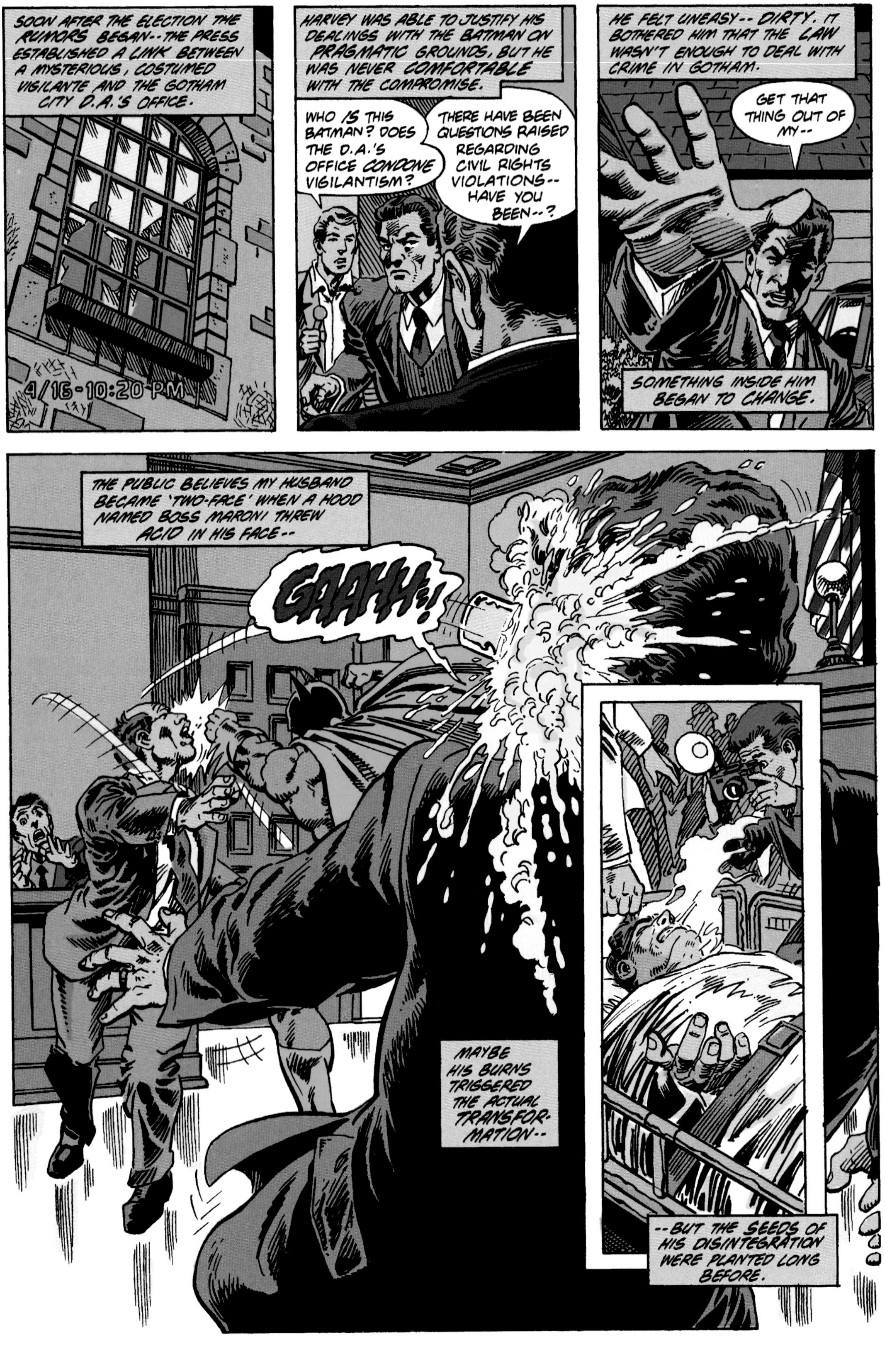
SOON AFTER THE ELECTION THE RUMORS BEGAN--THE PRESS ESTABLISHED A LINK BETWEEN A MYSTERIOUS, COSTUMED VIGILANTE AND THE GOTHAM CITY D.A.'S OFFICE.
4/16-10:20 PM
HARVEY WAS ABLE TO JUSTIFY HIS DEALINGS WITH THE BATMAN ON PRAGMATIC GROUNDS, BUT HE WAS NEVER COMFORTABLE WITH THE COMPROMISE.
WHO IS THIS BATMAN? DOES THE D.A.'S OFFICE CONDONE VIGILANTISM?
THERE HAVE BEEN QUESTIONS RAISED REGARDING CIVIL RIGHTS VIOLATIONS--HAVE YOU BEEN--?
HE FELT UNEASY--DIRTY. IT BOTHERED HIM THAT THE LAW WASN'T ENOUGH TO DEAL WITH CRIME IN GOTHAM.
GET THAT THING OUT OF MY--
SOMETHING INSIDE HIM BEGAN TO CHANGE.
THE PUBLIC BELIEVES MY HUSBAND BECAME 'TWO-FACE' WHEN A HOOD NAMED BOSS MARONI THREW ACID IN HIS FACE--
GAAHH!
MAYBE HIS BURNS TRIGGERED THE ACTUAL TRANSFORMATION--
--BUT THE SEEDS OF HIS DISINTEGRATION WERE PLANTED LONG BEFORE.

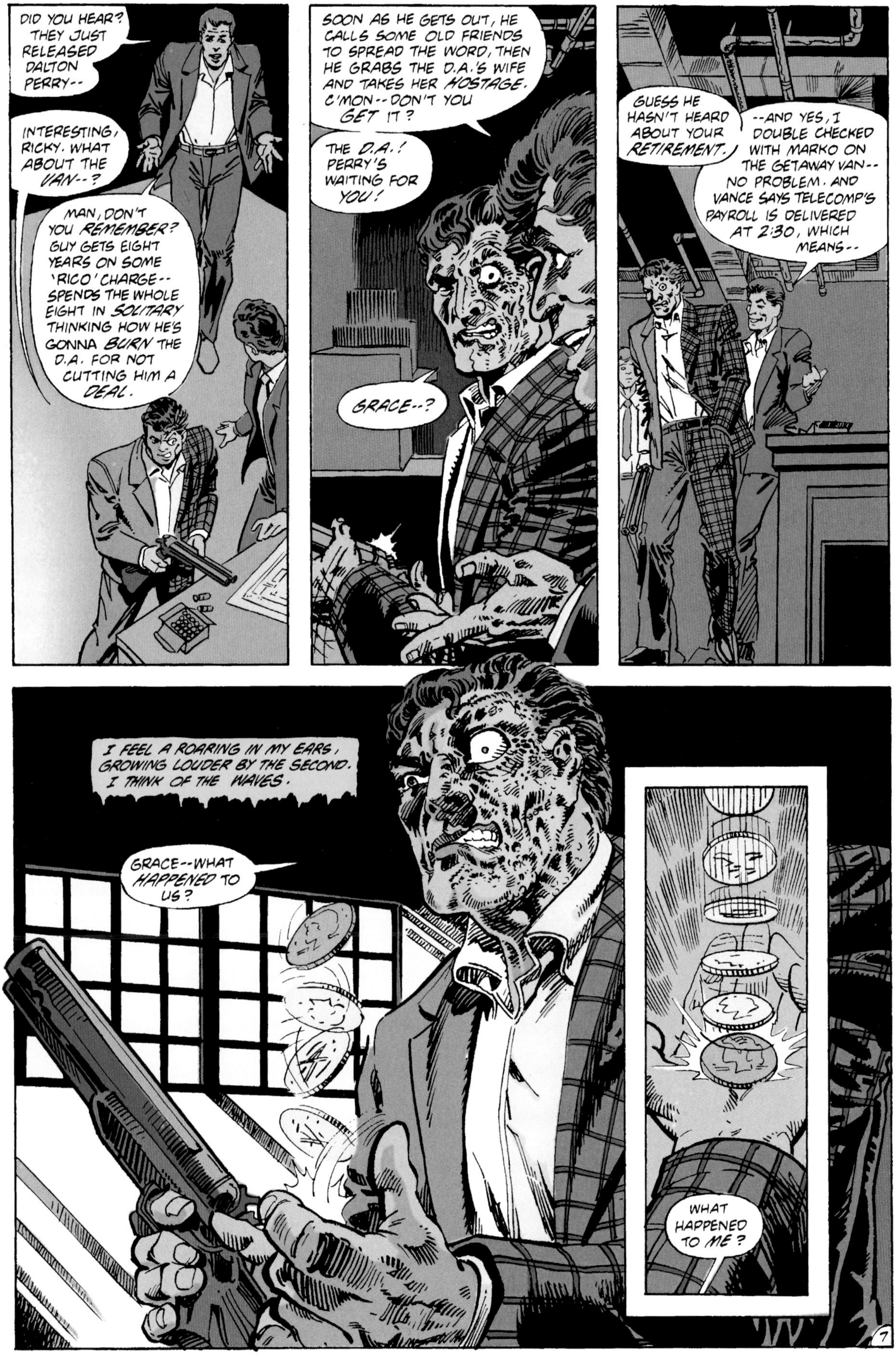
DID YOU HEAR? THEY JUST RELEASED DALTON PERRY--
INTERESTING, RICKY. WHAT ABOUT THE VAN--?
MAN, DON'T YOU REMEMBER? GUY GETS EIGHT YEARS ON SOME 'RICO' CHARGE--SPENDS THE WHOLE EIGHT IN SOLITARY THINKING HOW HE'S GONNA BURN THE D.A. FOR NOT CUTTING HIM A DEAL.
SOON AS HE GETS OUT, HE CALLS SOME OLD FRIENDS TO SPREAD THE WORD, THEN HE GRABS THE D.A.'S WIFE AND TAKES HER HOSTAGE. C'MON--DON'T YOU GET IT?
THE D.A.! PERRY'S WAITING FOR YOU!
GRACE--?
GUESS HE HASN'T HEARD ABOUT YOUR RETIREMENT.
--AND YES, I DOUBLE CHECKED WITH MARKO ON THE GETAWAY VAN--NO PROBLEM. AND VANCE SAYS TELECOMP'S PAYROLL IS DELIVERED AT 2:30, WHICH MEANS--
I FEEL A ROARING IN MY EARS, GROWING LOUDER BY THE SECOND. I THINK OF THE WAVES.
GRACE--WHAT HAPPENED TO US?
WHAT HAPPENED TO ME?
7

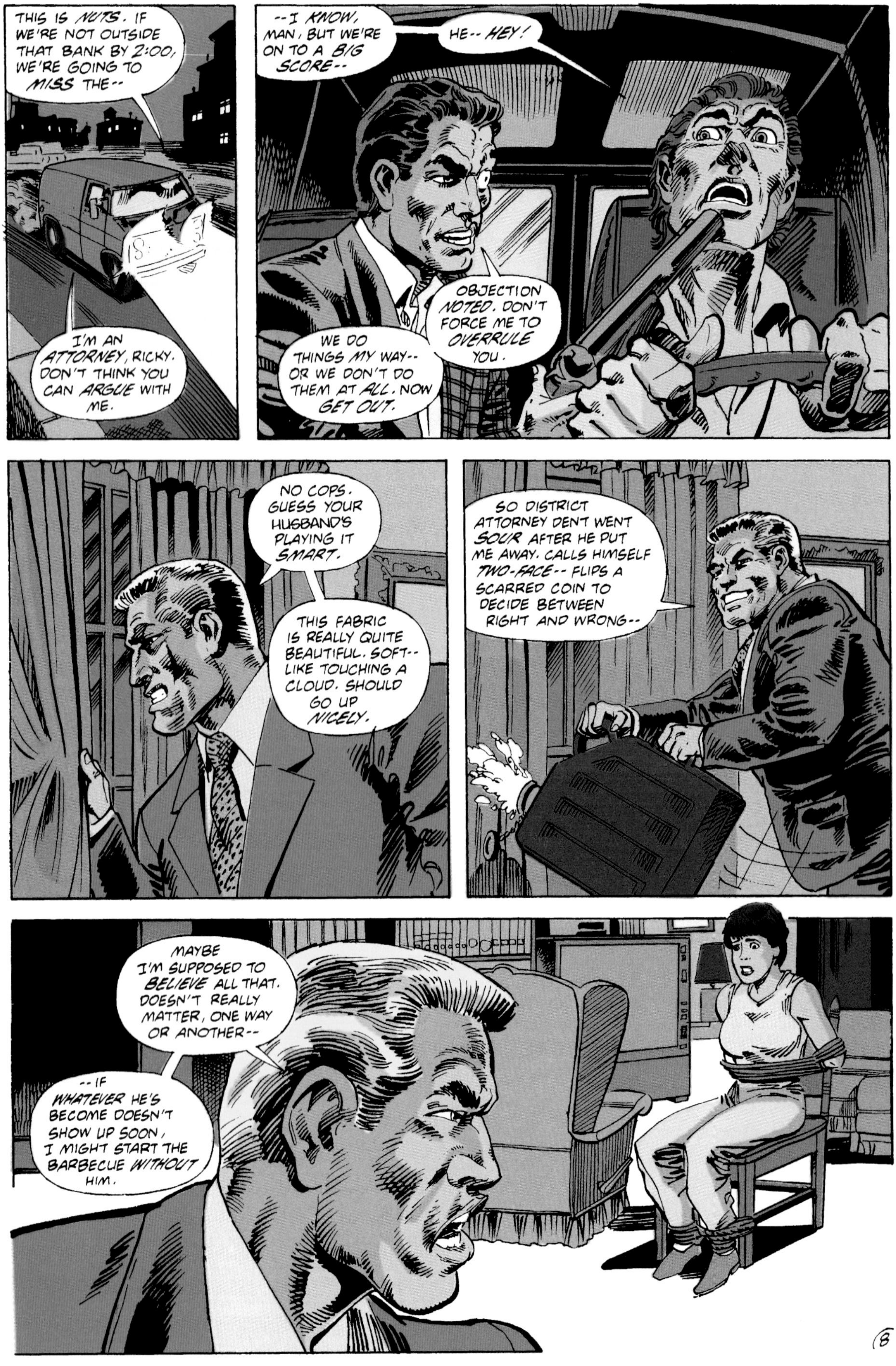
THIS IS NUTS. IF WE'RE NOT OUTSIDE THAT BANK BY 2:00, WE'RE GOING TO MISS THE--
I'M AN ATTORNEY, RICKY. DON'T THINK YOU CAN ARGUE WITH ME.
--I KNOW, MAN, BUT WE'RE ON TO A BIG SCORE--
HE-- HEY!
WE DO THINGS MY WAY-- OR WE DON'T DO THEM AT ALL. NOW GET OUT.
OBJECTION NOTED. DON'T FORCE ME TO OVERRULE YOU.
NO COPS. GUESS YOUR HUSBAND'S PLAYING IT SMART.
THIS FABRIC IS REALLY QUITE BEAUTIFUL. SOFT-- LIKE TOUCHING A CLOUD. SHOULD GO UP NICELY.
SO DISTRICT ATTORNEY DENT WENT SOUR AFTER HE PUT ME AWAY. CALLS HIMSELF TWO-FACE-- FLIPS A SCARRED COIN TO DECIDE BETWEEN RIGHT AND WRONG--
MAYBE I'M SUPPOSED TO BELIEVE ALL THAT. DOESN'T REALLY MATTER, ONE WAY OR ANOTHER--
--IF WHATEVER HE'S BECOME DOESN'T SHOW UP SOON, I MIGHT START THE BARBECUE WITHOUT HIM.
8

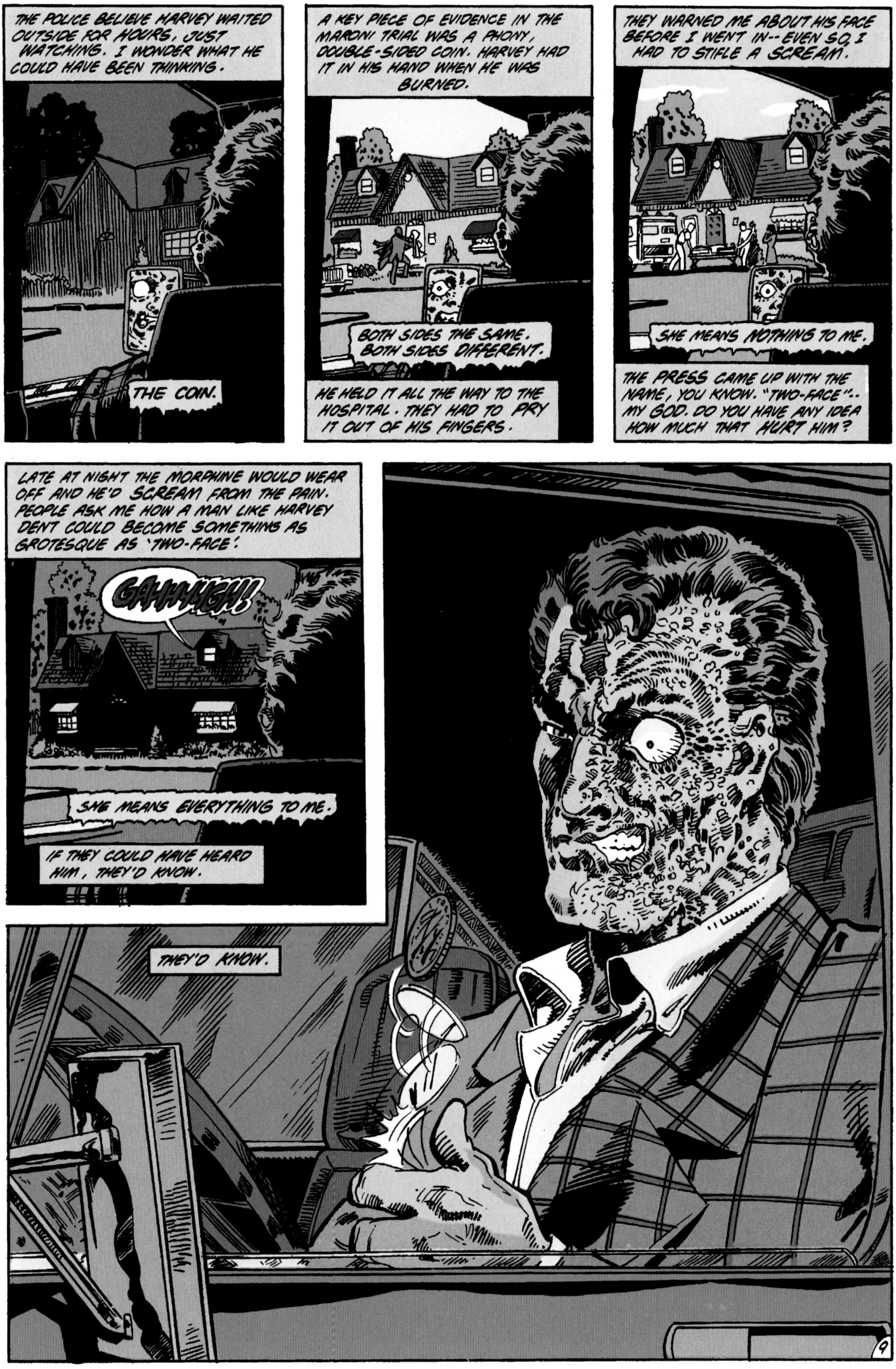
THE POLICE BELIEVE HARVEY WAITED OUTSIDE FOR HOURS, JUST WATCHING. I WONDER WHAT HE COULD HAVE BEEN THINKING.
THE COIN.
A KEY PIECE OF EVIDENCE IN THE MARONI TRIAL WAS A PHONY, DOUBLE-SIDED COIN. HARVEY HAD IT IN HIS HAND WHEN HE WAS BURNED.
BOTH SIDES THE SAME. BOTH SIDES DIFFERENT.
HE HELD IT ALL THE WAY TO THE HOSPITAL. THEY HAD TO PRY IT OUT OF HIS FINGERS.
THEY WARNED ME ABOUT HIS FACE BEFORE I WENT IN--EVEN SO, I HAD TO STIFLE A SCREAM.
SHE MEANS NOTHING TO ME.
THE PRESS CAME UP WITH THE NAME, YOU KNOW. "TWO-FACE"... MY GOD. DO YOU HAVE ANY IDEA HOW MUCH THAT HURT HIM?
LATE AT NIGHT THE MORPHINE WOULD WEAR OFF AND HE'D SCREAM FROM THE PAIN. PEOPLE ASK ME HOW A MAN LIKE HARVEY DENT COULD BECOME SOMETHING AS GROTESQUE AS 'TWO-FACE'.
GAHHHUGH!
SHE MEANS EVERYTHING TO ME.
IF THEY COULD HAVE HEARD HIM, THEY'D KNOW.
THEY'D KNOW.
9

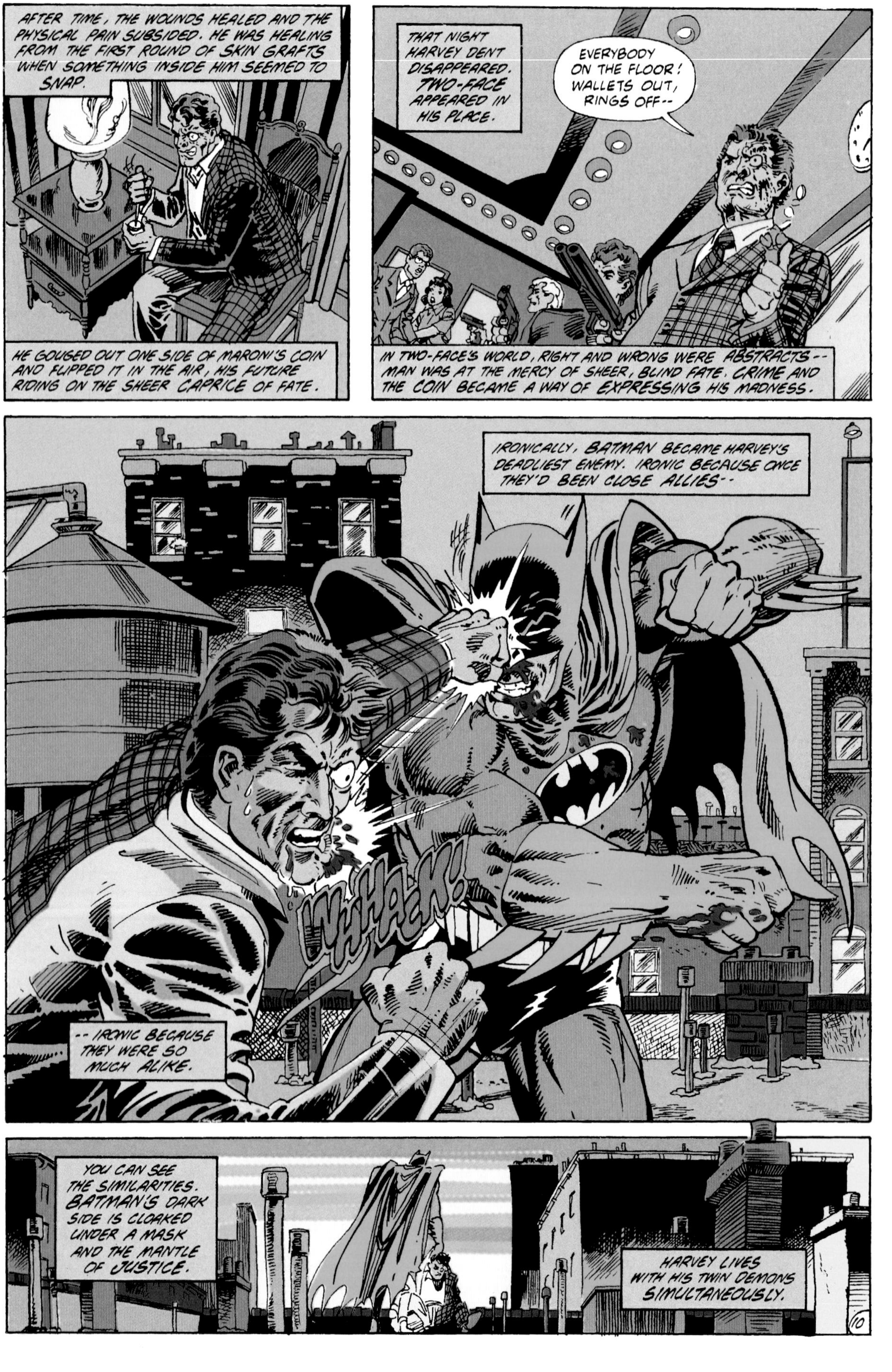
AFTER TIME, THE WOUNDS HEALED AND THE PHYSICAL PAIN SUBSIDED. HE WAS HEALING FROM THE FIRST ROUND OF SKIN GRAFTS WHEN SOMETHING INSIDE HIM SEEMED TO SNAP.
HE GOUGED OUT ONE SIDE OF MARONI'S COIN AND FLIPPED IT IN THE AIR, HIS FUTURE RIDING ON THE SHEER CAPRICE OF FATE.
THAT NIGHT HARVEY DENT DISAPPEARED. TWO-FACE APPEARED IN HIS PLACE.
EVERYBODY ON THE FLOOR! WALLETS OUT, RINGS OFF--
IN TWO-FACE'S WORLD, RIGHT AND WRONG WERE ABSTRACTS--MAN WAS AT THE MERCY OF SHEER, BLIND FATE. CRIME AND THE COIN BECAME A WAY OF EXPRESSING HIS MADNESS.
IRONICALLY, BATMAN BECAME HARVEY'S DEADLIEST ENEMY. IRONIC BECAUSE ONCE THEY'D BEEN CLOSE ALLIES--
WHHACK!
--IRONIC BECAUSE THEY WERE SO MUCH ALIKE.
YOU CAN SEE THE SIMILARITIES. BATMAN'S DARK SIDE IS CLOAKED UNDER A MASK AND THE MANTLE OF JUSTICE.
HARVEY LIVES WITH HIS TWIN DEMONS SIMULTANEOUSLY.
10

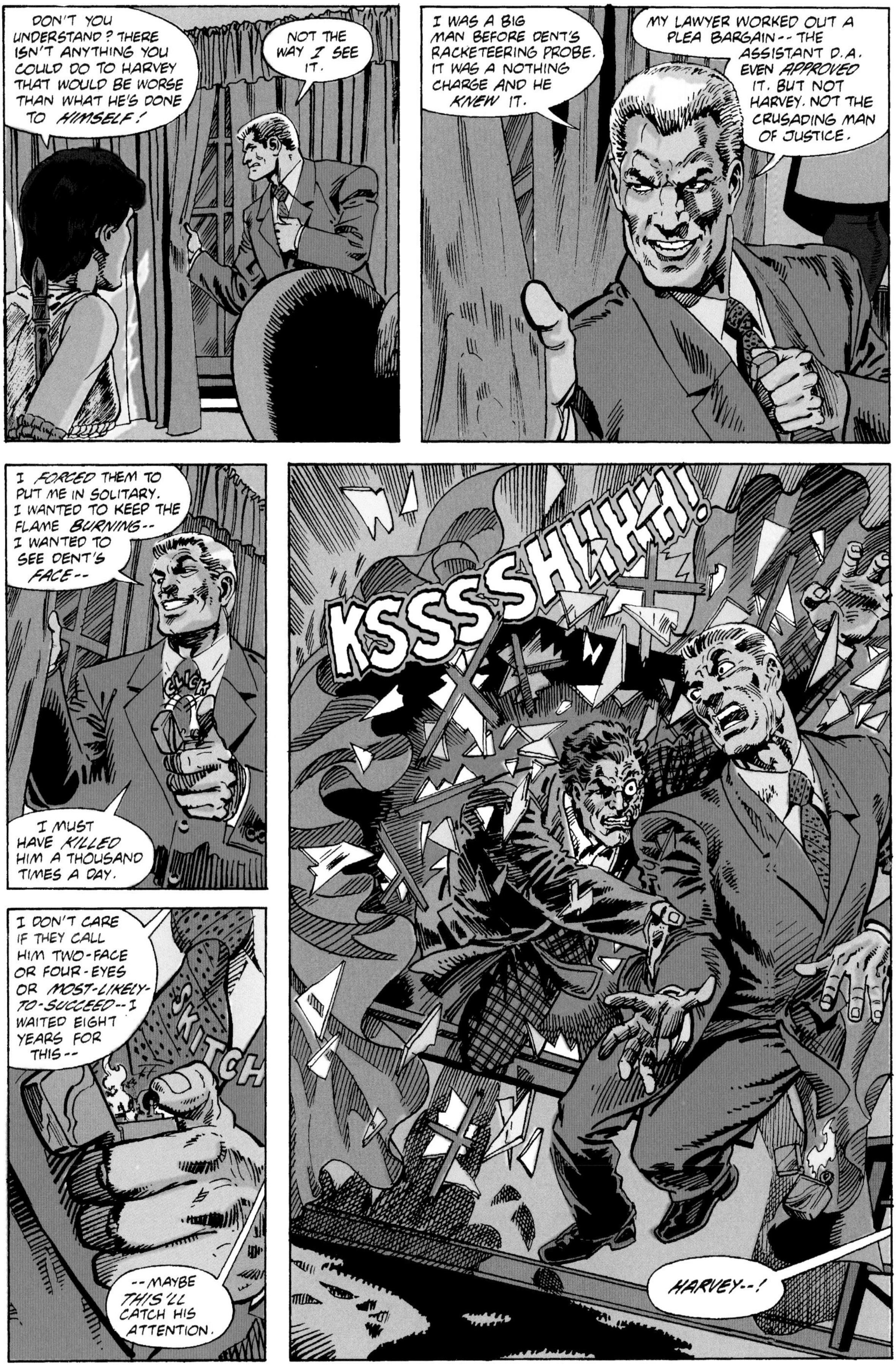
DON'T YOU UNDERSTAND? THERE ISN'T ANYTHING YOU COULD DO TO HARVEY THAT WOULD BE WORSE THAN WHAT HE'S DONE TO *HIMSELF!*
NOT THE WAY *I* SEE IT.
I WAS A BIG MAN BEFORE DENT'S RACKETEERING PROBE. IT WAS A NOTHING CHARGE AND HE *KNEW* IT.
MY LAWYER WORKED OUT A PLEA BARGAIN-- THE ASSISTANT D.A. EVEN *APPROVED* IT. BUT NOT HARVEY. NOT THE CRUSADING MAN OF JUSTICE.
I *FORCED* THEM TO PUT ME IN SOLITARY. I WANTED TO KEEP THE FLAME *BURNING*-- I WANTED TO SEE DENT'S *FACE*--
CLICK
I MUST HAVE *KILLED* HIM A THOUSAND TIMES A DAY.
I DON'T CARE IF THEY CALL HIM TWO-FACE OR FOUR-EYES OR *MOST-LIKELY-TO-SUCCEED*--I WAITED EIGHT YEARS FOR THIS--
SKITCH
--MAYBE *THIS'LL* CATCH HIS ATTENTION.
KSSSSHHKH!
HARVEY--!

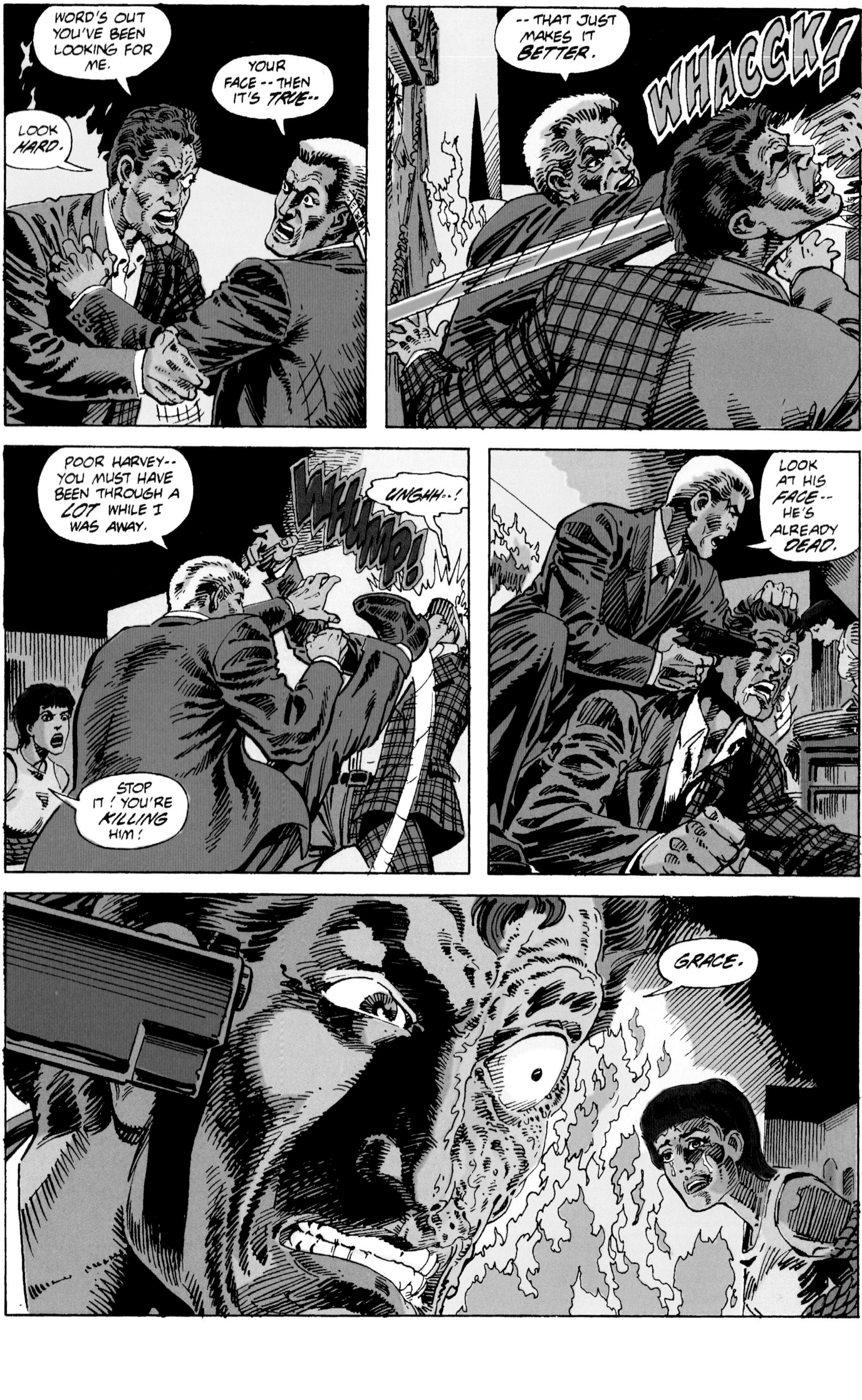
WORD'S OUT YOU'VE BEEN LOOKING FOR ME.
LOOK HARD.
YOUR FACE -- THEN IT'S TRUE --
-- THAT JUST MAKES IT BETTER.
WHACCK!
POOR HARVEY-- YOU MUST HAVE BEEN THROUGH A LOT WHILE I WAS AWAY.
WHUMP!
UNGHH--!
STOP IT! YOU'RE KILLING HIM!
LOOK AT HIS FACE-- HE'S ALREADY DEAD.
GRACE.

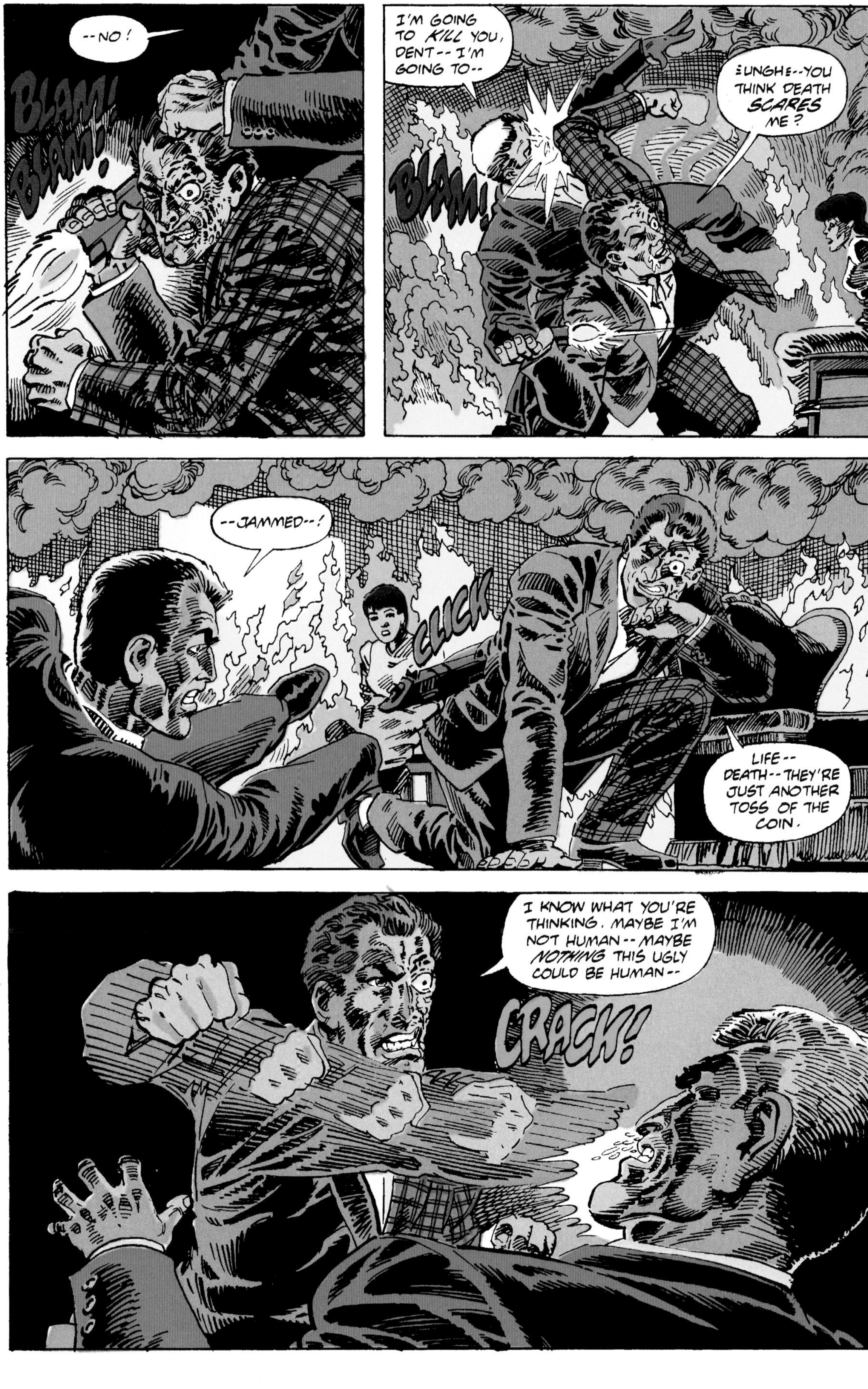
--NO!
BLAM! BLAM!
I'M GOING TO KILL YOU, DENT--I'M GOING TO--
BLAM!
UNGH--YOU THINK DEATH SCARES ME?
--JAMMED--!
CLICK
LIFE--DEATH--THEY'RE JUST ANOTHER TOSS OF THE COIN.
I KNOW WHAT YOU'RE THINKING. MAYBE I'M NOT HUMAN--MAYBE NOTHING THIS UGLY COULD BE HUMAN--
CRACK!

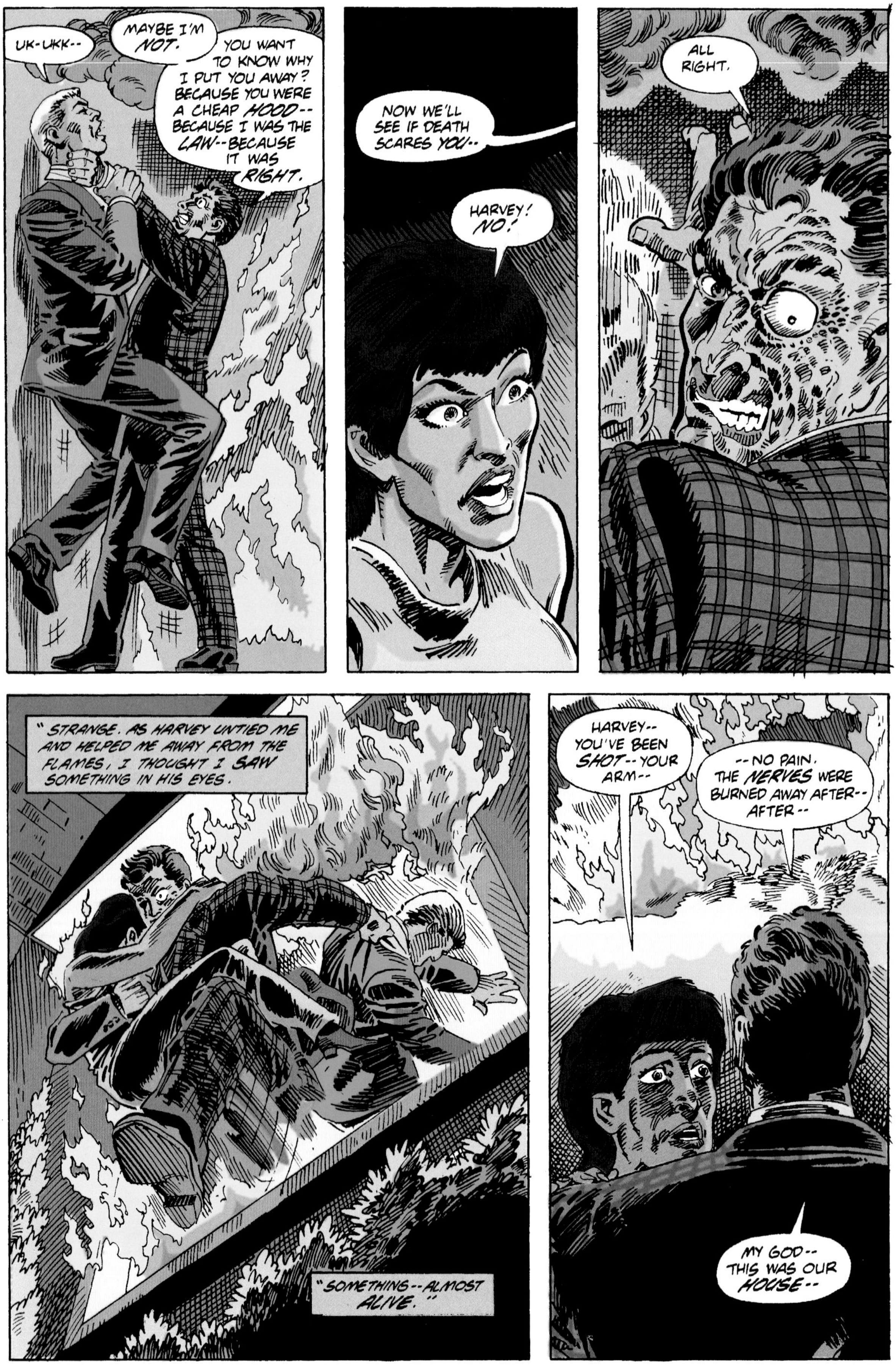
UK-UKK--
MAYBE I'M NOT.
YOU WANT TO KNOW WHY I PUT YOU AWAY? BECAUSE YOU WERE A CHEAP HOOD--BECAUSE I WAS THE LAW--BECAUSE IT WAS RIGHT.
NOW WE'LL SEE IF DEATH SCARES YOU--
HARVEY! NO!
ALL RIGHT.
"STRANGE. AS HARVEY UNTIED ME AND HELPED ME AWAY FROM THE FLAMES, I THOUGHT I SAW SOMETHING IN HIS EYES.
"SOMETHING--ALMOST ALIVE."
HARVEY--YOU'VE BEEN SHOT--YOUR ARM--
--NO PAIN. THE NERVES WERE BURNED AWAY AFTER--AFTER--
MY GOD--THIS WAS OUR HOUSE--

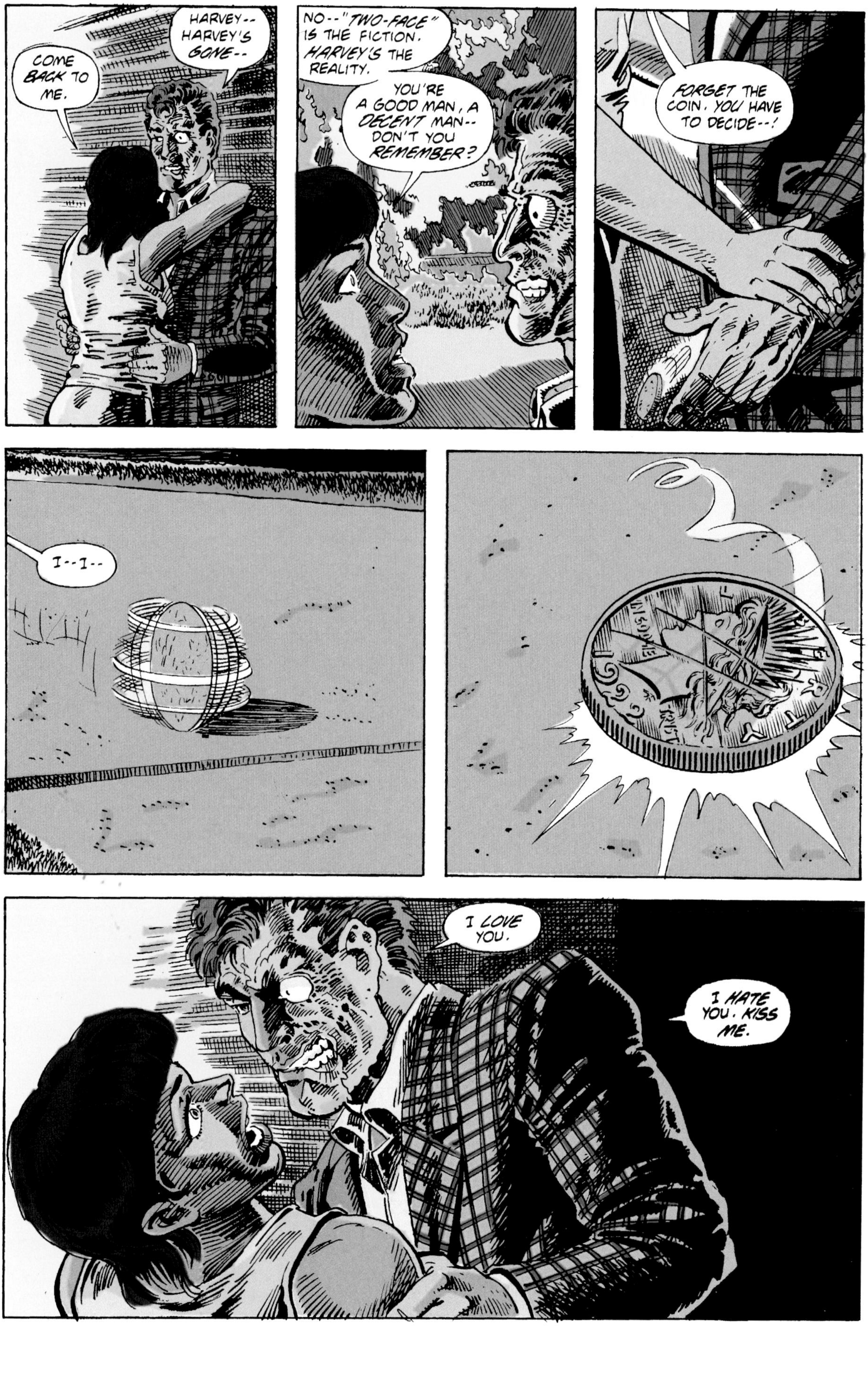
COME BACK TO ME.
HARVEY-- HARVEY'S GONE--
NO--"TWO-FACE" IS THE FICTION. HARVEY'S THE REALITY.
YOU'RE A GOOD MAN, A DECENT MAN-- DON'T YOU REMEMBER?
FORGET THE COIN. YOU HAVE TO DECIDE--!
I--I--
I LOVE YOU.
I HATE YOU. KISS ME.

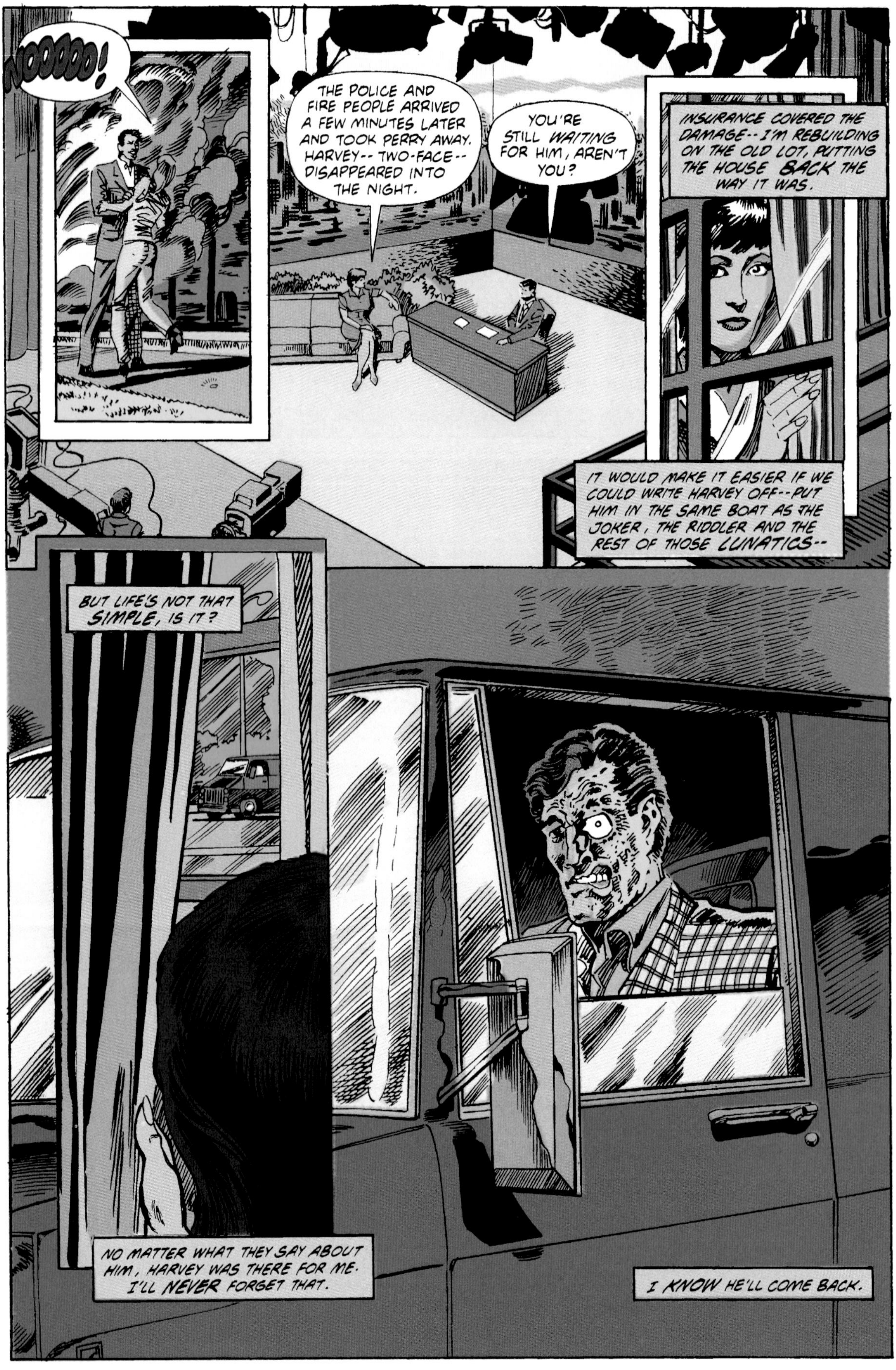
NOOOOO!
THE POLICE AND FIRE PEOPLE ARRIVED A FEW MINUTES LATER AND TOOK PERRY AWAY. HARVEY-- TWO-FACE-- DISAPPEARED INTO THE NIGHT.
YOU'RE STILL WAITING FOR HIM, AREN'T YOU?
INSURANCE COVERED THE DAMAGE-- I'M REBUILDING ON THE OLD LOT, PUTTING THE HOUSE BACK THE WAY IT WAS.
IT WOULD MAKE IT EASIER IF WE COULD WRITE HARVEY OFF--PUT HIM IN THE SAME BOAT AS THE JOKER, THE RIDDLER AND THE REST OF THOSE LUNATICS--
BUT LIFE'S NOT THAT SIMPLE, IS IT?
NO MATTER WHAT THEY SAY ABOUT HIM, HARVEY WAS THERE FOR ME. I'LL NEVER FORGET THAT.
I KNOW HE'LL COME BACK.

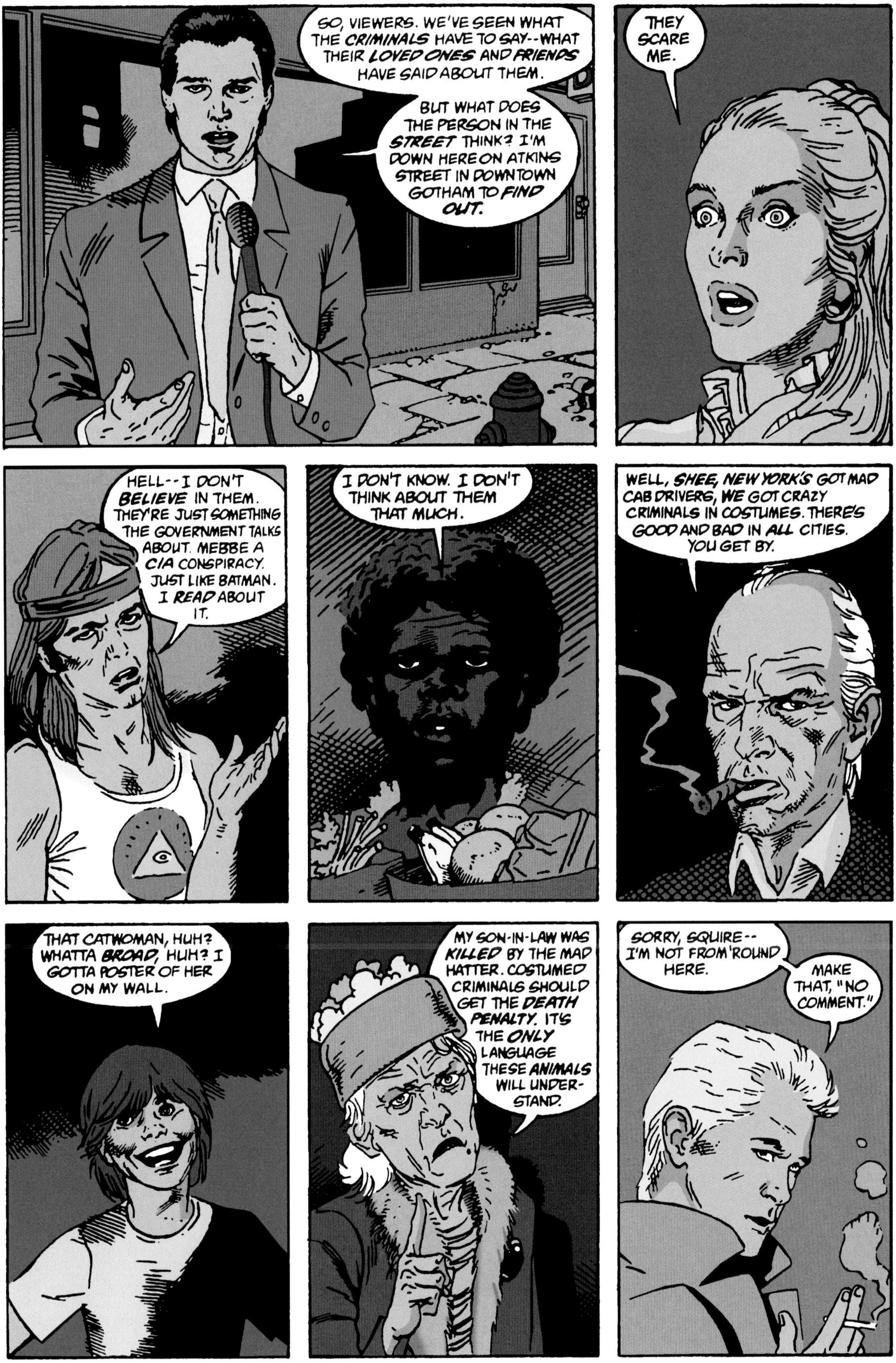
SO, VIEWERS. WE'VE SEEN WHAT THE CRIMINALS HAVE TO SAY--WHAT THEIR LOVED ONES AND FRIENDS HAVE SAID ABOUT THEM.
BUT WHAT DOES THE PERSON IN THE STREET THINK? I'M DOWN HERE ON ATKINS STREET IN DOWNTOWN GOTHAM TO FIND OUT.
THEY SCARE ME.
HELL--I DON'T BELIEVE IN THEM. THEY'RE JUST SOMETHING THE GOVERNMENT TALKS ABOUT. MEBBE A CIA CONSPIRACY. JUST LIKE BATMAN. I READ ABOUT IT.
I DON'T KNOW. I DON'T THINK ABOUT THEM THAT MUCH.
WELL, SHEE, NEW YORK'S GOT MAD CAB DRIVERS, WE GOT CRAZY CRIMINALS IN COSTUMES. THERE'S GOOD AND BAD IN ALL CITIES. YOU GET BY.
THAT CATWOMAN, HUH? WHATTA BROAD, HUH? I GOTTA POSTER OF HER ON MY WALL.
MY SON-IN-LAW WAS KILLED BY THE MAD HATTER. COSTUMED CRIMINALS SHOULD GET THE DEATH PENALTY. IT'S THE ONLY LANGUAGE THESE ANIMALS WILL UNDERSTAND.
SORRY, SQUIRE--I'M NOT FROM 'ROUND HERE.
MAKE THAT, "NO COMMENT."

WHEN I GROW UP I WANNA GET A COSTUME AND A GIMMICK AND BE THE ONE WHO *KILLS BATMAN.* THAT WOULD BE *SOOOO* COOL.

I HAD THAT PENGUIN IN MY CAB ONCE. BIG TIPPER. HE'S OKAY IN *MY* BOOK.

WE *HATE* THIS CITY. WE'RE MOVING TO FLORIDA WHEN *WE* RETIRE. YOU DON'T *GET* THOSE PEOPLE DOWN THERE.

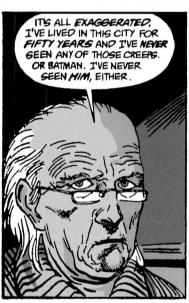

IT'S ALL *EXAGGERATED.* I'VE LIVED IN THIS CITY FOR *FIFTY YEARS* AND I'VE *NEVER* SEEN ANY OF THOSE CREEPS. OR BATMAN. I'VE NEVER SEEN *HIM,* EITHER.

MY MOMMY SAYS IF I'M BAD THE JOKER WILL COME AND GET ME.

WORRY ABOUT THEM? *LISTEN,* BUD, THE GARBAGE STRIKE'S IN ITS *FIFTH* WEEK, THE *ELEVATOR'S* ON THE FRITZ, AND MY *DAUGHTER'S* JUST JOINED A SKINHEAD ROCK BAND.

I GOT *BETTER* THINGS TO WORRY ABOUT.

MAN, THEY'RE CULTURAL *ICONS.* SPRINGSTEEN, THE JOKER, DONALD DUCK, AND *BOGART.* SAYS IT ALL, HUH?

SO, THERE WE HAVE IT.

HEROES OR VILLAINS, POP ICONS OR BOOGEYMEN--THE COSTUMED CRIMINALS OF GOTHAM CITY ARE HERE TO *STAY.*

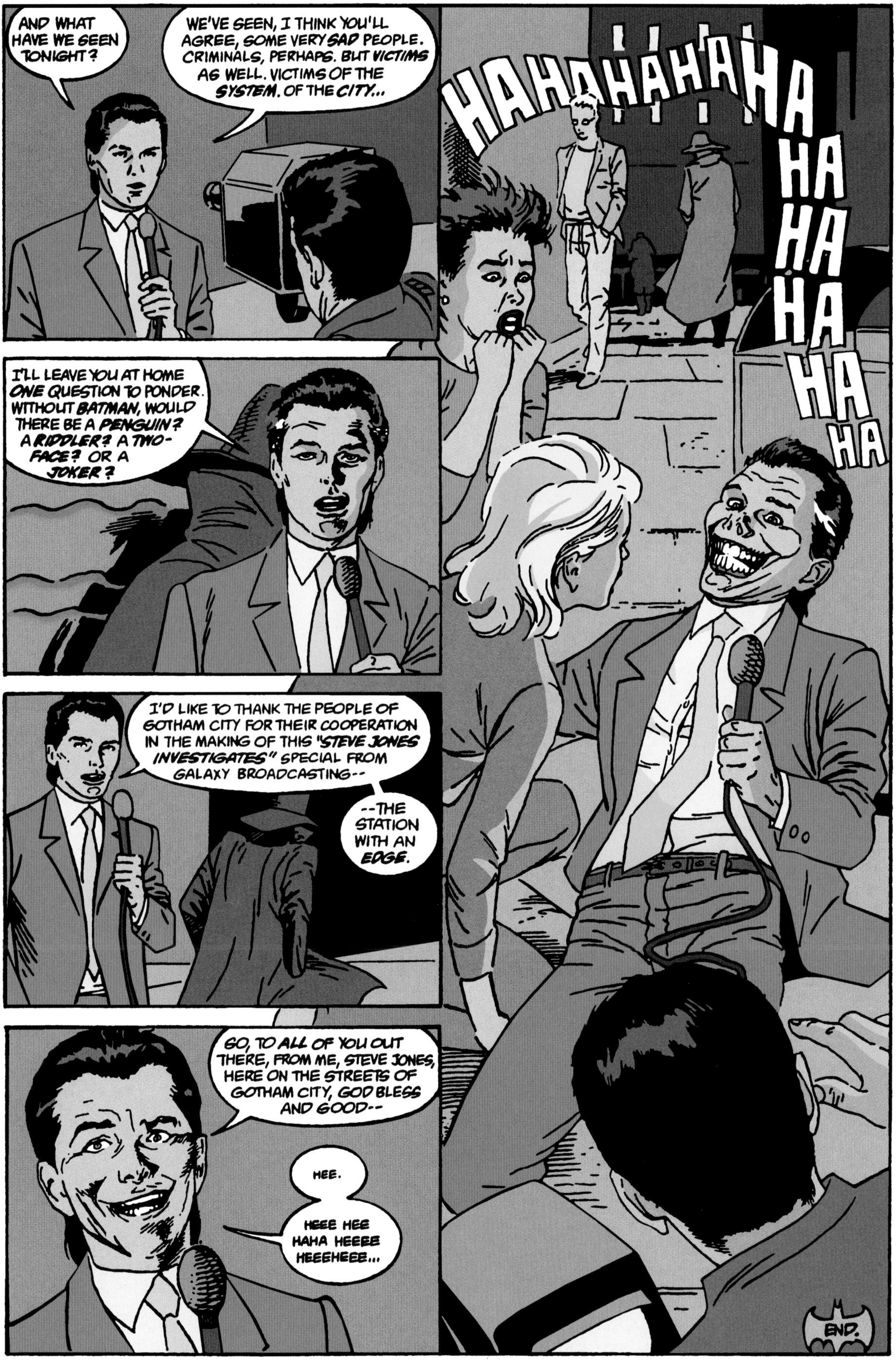
AND WHAT HAVE WE SEEN TONIGHT?
WE'VE SEEN, I THINK YOU'LL AGREE, SOME VERY SAD PEOPLE. CRIMINALS, PERHAPS. BUT VICTIMS AS WELL. VICTIMS OF THE SYSTEM. OF THE CITY...
I'LL LEAVE YOU AT HOME ONE QUESTION TO PONDER. WITHOUT BATMAN, WOULD THERE BE A PENGUIN? A RIDDLER? A TWO-FACE? OR A JOKER?
I'D LIKE TO THANK THE PEOPLE OF GOTHAM CITY FOR THEIR COOPERATION IN THE MAKING OF THIS "STEVE JONES INVESTIGATES" SPECIAL FROM GALAXY BROADCASTING--
--THE STATION WITH AN EDGE.
SO, TO ALL OF YOU OUT THERE, FROM ME, STEVE JONES, HERE ON THE STREETS OF GOTHAM CITY, GOD BLESS AND GOOD--
HEE.
HEEE HEE HAHA HEEEE HEEEHEEE...
HAHAHAHAHAHA HA HA HA HA HA HA HA HA HA HA
END.

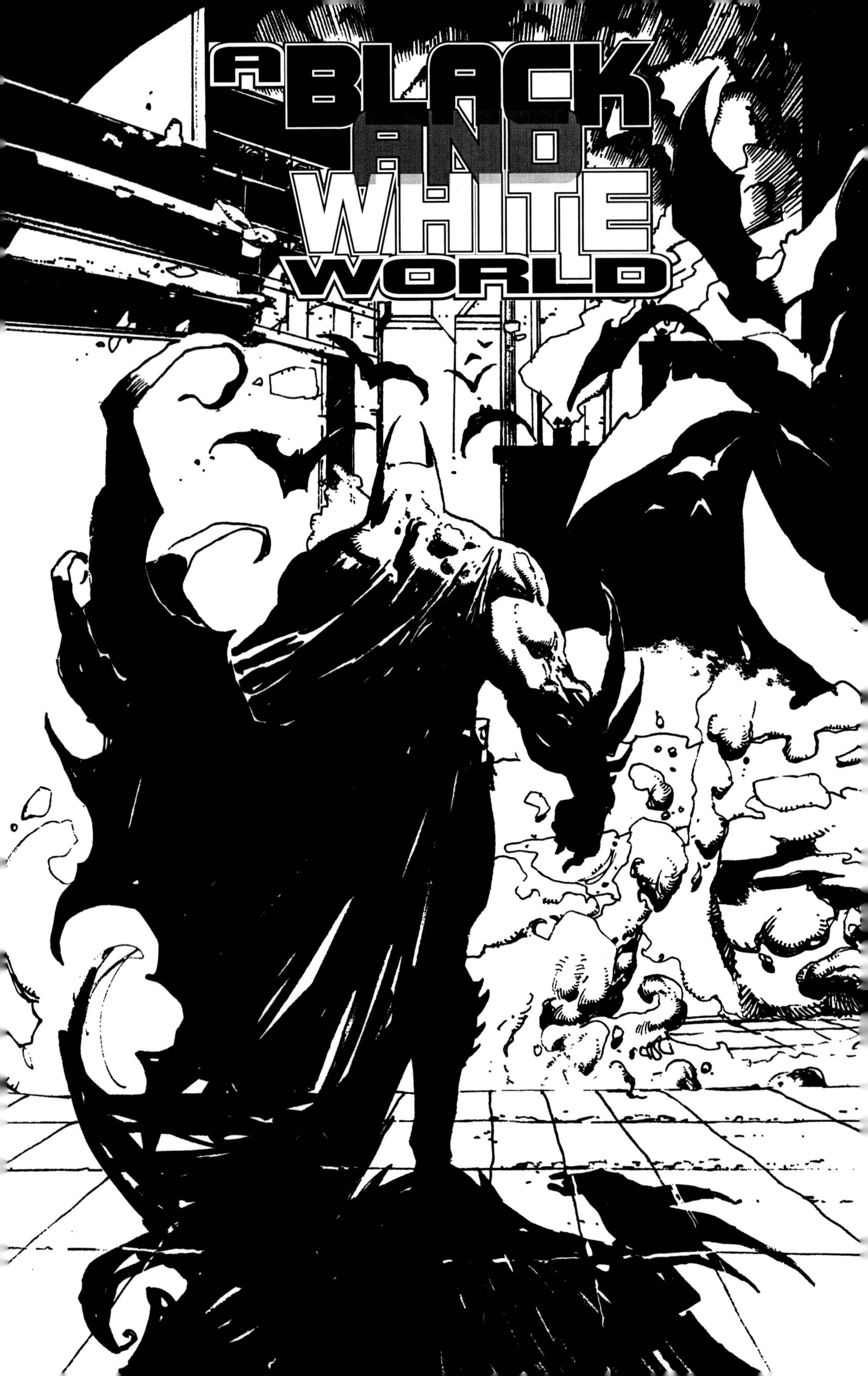
A BLACK AND WHITE WORLD

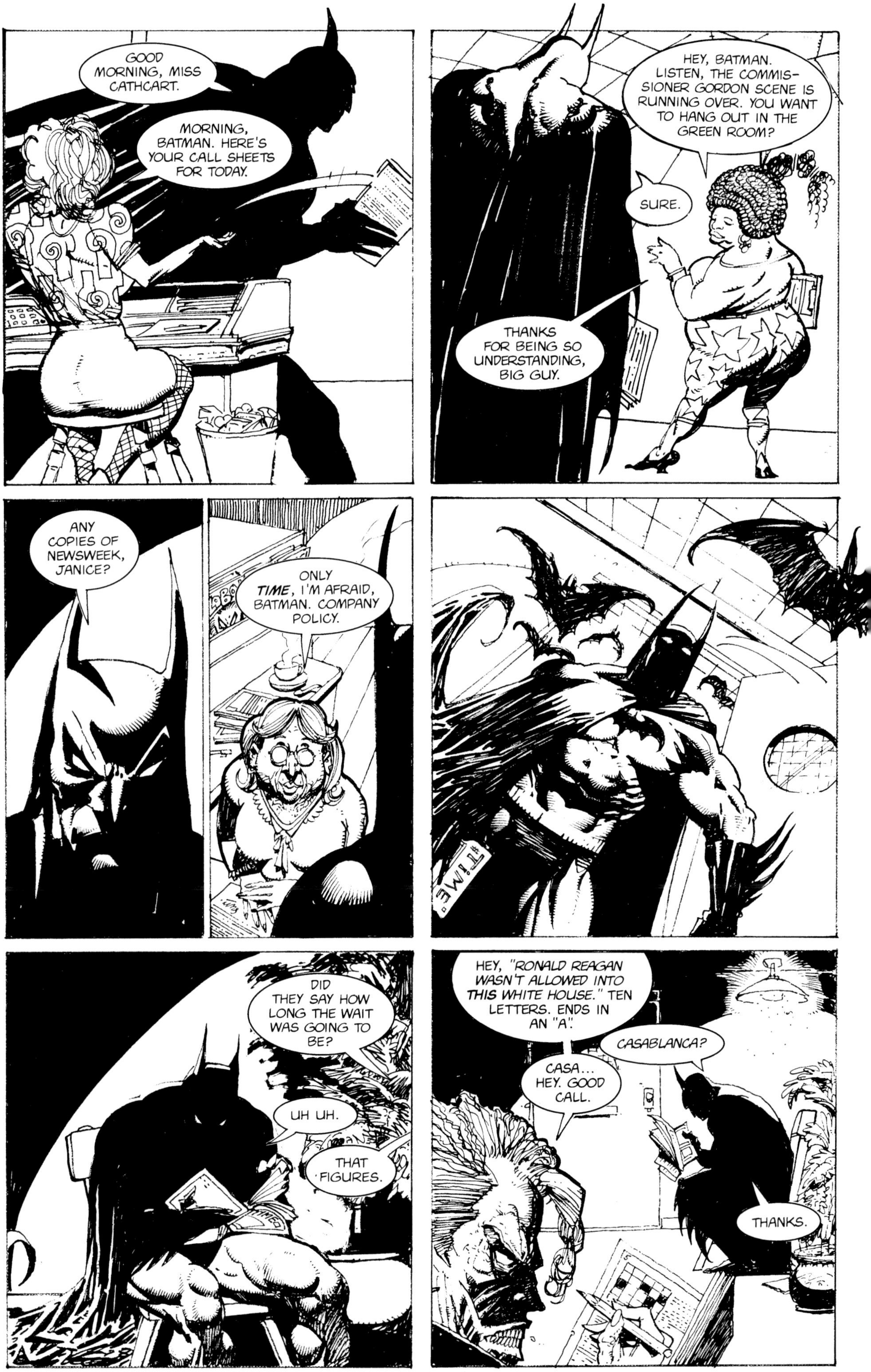
GOOD MORNING, MISS CATHCART.
MORNING, BATMAN. HERE'S YOUR CALL SHEETS FOR TODAY.
HEY, BATMAN. LISTEN, THE COMMISSIONER GORDON SCENE IS RUNNING OVER. YOU WANT TO HANG OUT IN THE GREEN ROOM?
SURE.
THANKS FOR BEING SO UNDERSTANDING, BIG GUY.
ANY COPIES OF NEWSWEEK, JANICE?
ONLY *TIME*, I'M AFRAID, BATMAN. COMPANY POLICY.
TIME
DID THEY SAY HOW LONG THE WAIT WAS GOING TO BE?
UH UH.
THAT FIGURES.
HEY, *"RONALD REAGAN WASN'T ALLOWED INTO* ***THIS*** *WHITE HOUSE."* TEN LETTERS. ENDS IN AN "A".
CASABLANCA?
CASA... HEY. GOOD CALL.
THANKS.

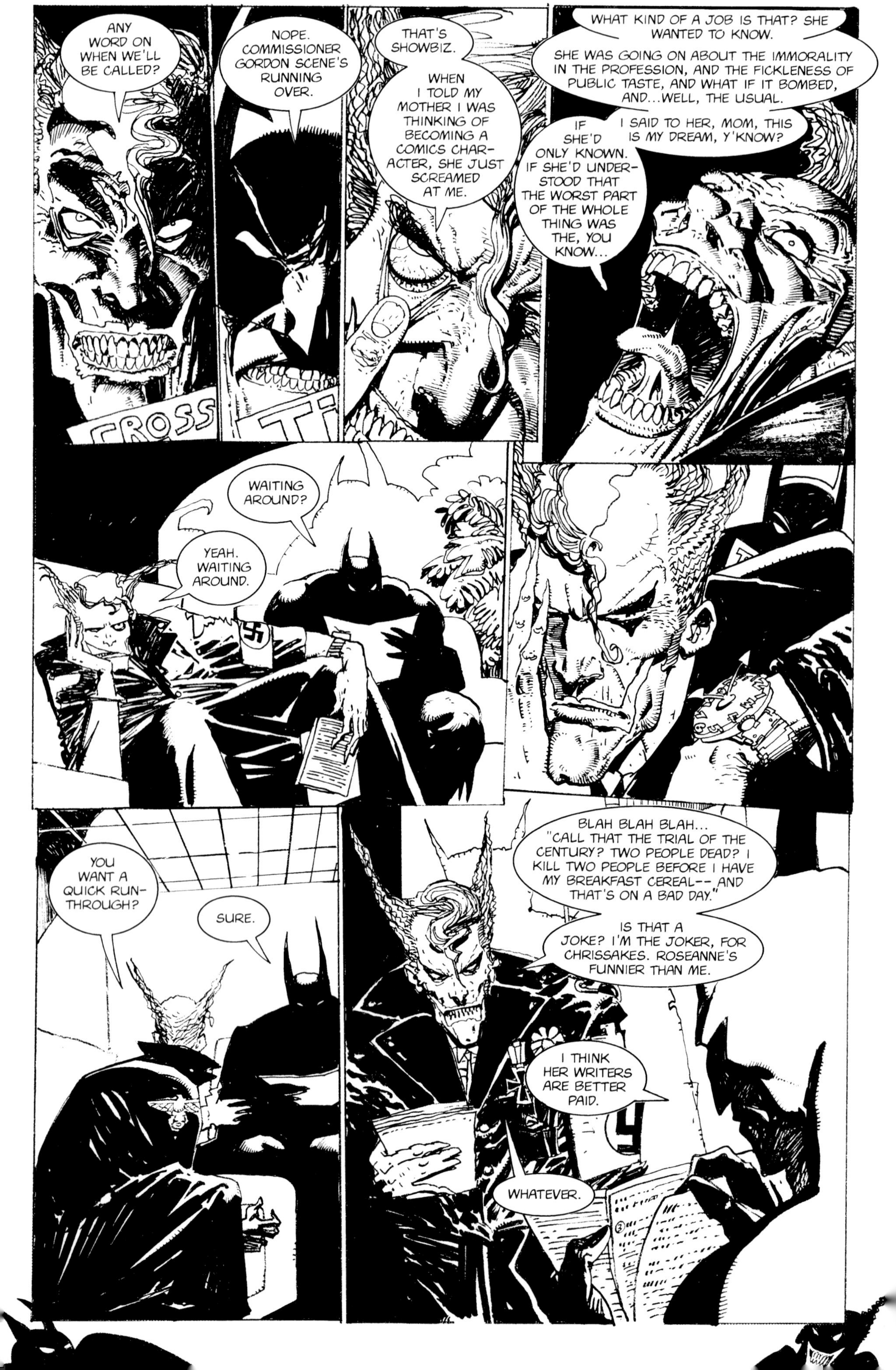
ANY WORD ON WHEN WE'LL BE CALLED?
NOPE. COMMISSIONER GORDON SCENE'S RUNNING OVER.
THAT'S SHOWBIZ.
WHEN I TOLD MY MOTHER I WAS THINKING OF BECOMING A COMICS CHARACTER, SHE JUST SCREAMED AT ME.
WHAT KIND OF A JOB IS THAT? SHE WANTED TO KNOW.
SHE WAS GOING ON ABOUT THE IMMORALITY IN THE PROFESSION, AND THE FICKLENESS OF PUBLIC TASTE, AND WHAT IF IT BOMBED, AND...WELL, THE USUAL.
I SAID TO HER, MOM, THIS IS MY DREAM, Y'KNOW?
IF SHE'D ONLY KNOWN. IF SHE'D UNDERSTOOD THAT THE WORST PART OF THE WHOLE THING WAS THE, YOU KNOW...
WAITING AROUND?
YEAH. WAITING AROUND.
YOU WANT A QUICK RUN-THROUGH?
SURE.
BLAH BLAH BLAH... "CALL THAT THE TRIAL OF THE CENTURY? TWO PEOPLE DEAD? I KILL TWO PEOPLE BEFORE I HAVE MY BREAKFAST CEREAL-- AND THAT'S ON A BAD DAY."
IS THAT A JOKE? I'M THE JOKER, FOR CHRISSAKES. ROSEANNE'S FUNNIER THAN ME.
I THINK HER WRITERS ARE BETTER PAID.
WHATEVER.

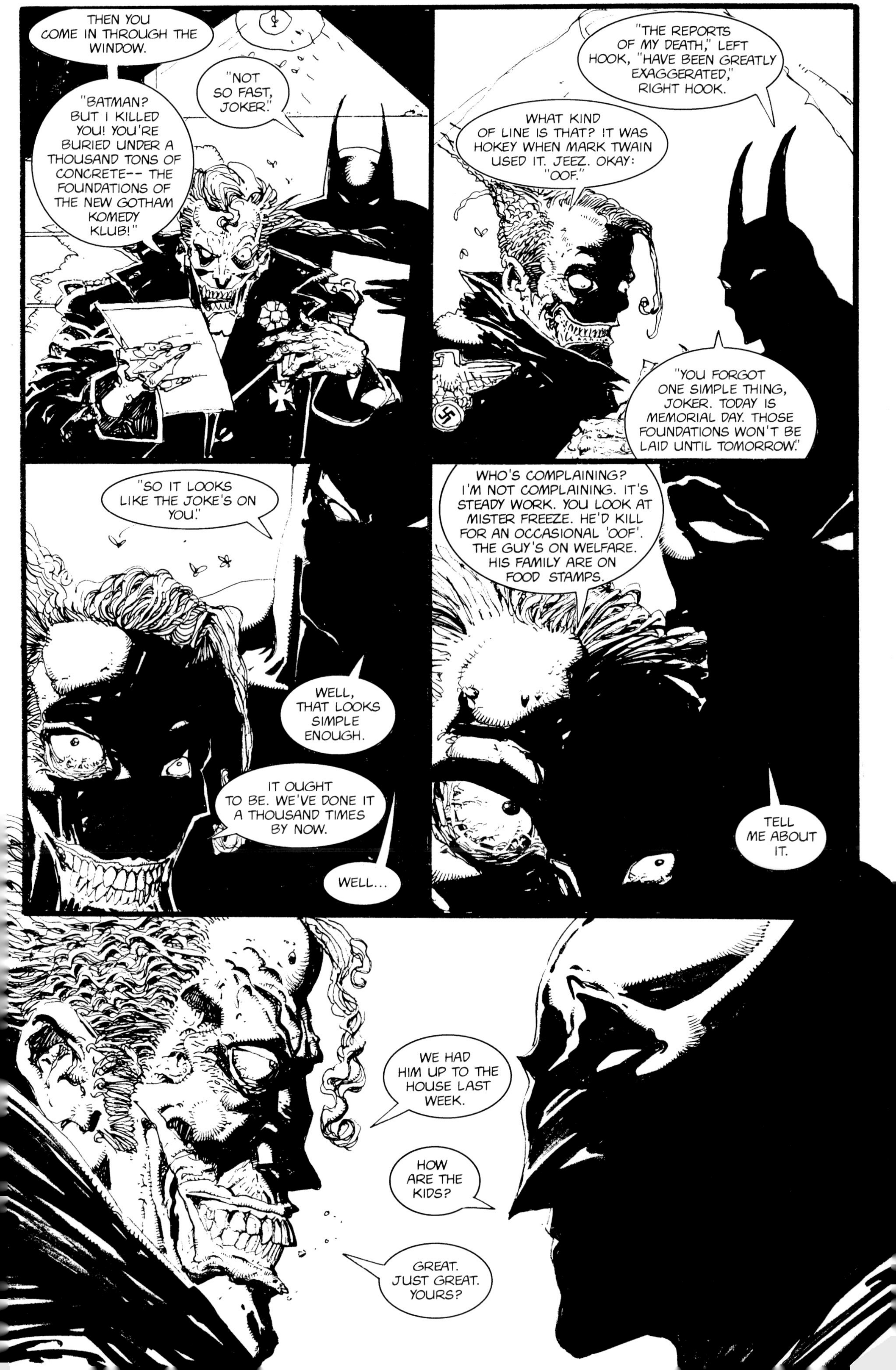
THEN YOU COME IN THROUGH THE WINDOW.
"BATMAN? BUT I KILLED YOU! YOU'RE BURIED UNDER A THOUSAND TONS OF CONCRETE-- THE FOUNDATIONS OF THE NEW GOTHAM KOMEDY KLUB!"
"NOT SO FAST, JOKER."
"THE REPORTS OF MY DEATH," LEFT HOOK, "HAVE BEEN GREATLY EXAGGERATED," RIGHT HOOK.
WHAT KIND OF LINE IS THAT? IT WAS HOKEY WHEN MARK TWAIN USED IT. JEEZ. OKAY: "OOF."
"YOU FORGOT ONE SIMPLE THING, JOKER. TODAY IS MEMORIAL DAY. THOSE FOUNDATIONS WON'T BE LAID UNTIL TOMORROW."
"SO IT LOOKS LIKE THE JOKE'S ON YOU."
WELL, THAT LOOKS SIMPLE ENOUGH.
IT OUGHT TO BE. WE'VE DONE IT A THOUSAND TIMES BY NOW.
WELL...
WHO'S COMPLAINING? I'M NOT COMPLAINING. IT'S STEADY WORK. YOU LOOK AT MISTER FREEZE. HE'D KILL FOR AN OCCASIONAL 'OOF'. THE GUY'S ON WELFARE. HIS FAMILY ARE ON FOOD STAMPS.
TELL ME ABOUT IT.
WE HAD HIM UP TO THE HOUSE LAST WEEK.
HOW ARE THE KIDS?
GREAT. JUST GREAT. YOURS?

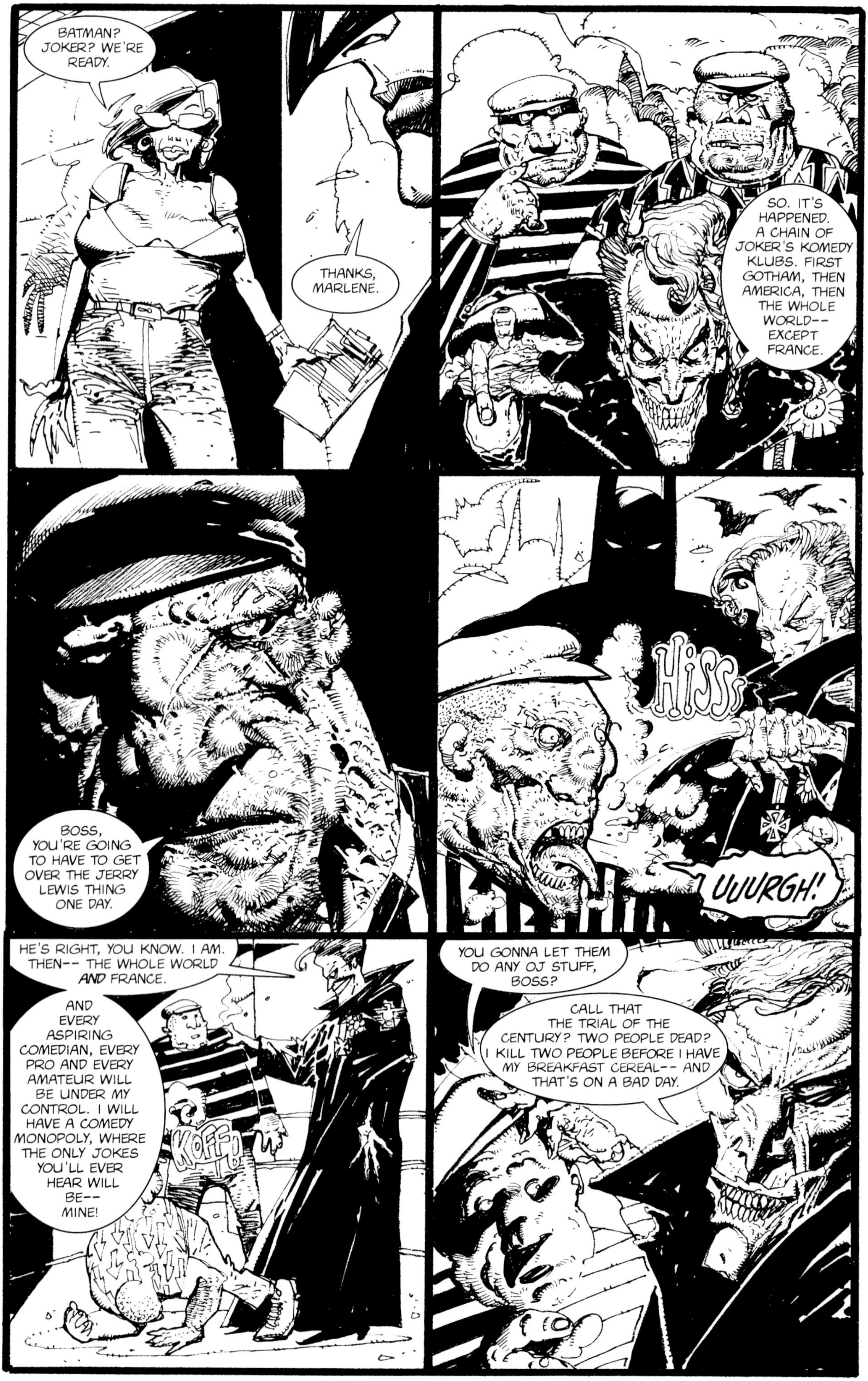
BATMAN? JOKER? WE'RE READY.
THANKS, MARLENE.
SO. IT'S HAPPENED. A CHAIN OF JOKER'S KOMEDY KLUBS. FIRST GOTHAM, THEN AMERICA, THEN THE WHOLE WORLD-- EXCEPT FRANCE.
BOSS, YOU'RE GOING TO HAVE TO GET OVER THE JERRY LEWIS THING ONE DAY.
HISSS
UUURGH!
HE'S RIGHT, YOU KNOW. I AM. THEN-- THE WHOLE WORLD AND FRANCE.
AND EVERY ASPIRING COMEDIAN, EVERY PRO AND EVERY AMATEUR WILL BE UNDER MY CONTROL. I WILL HAVE A COMEDY MONOPOLY, WHERE THE ONLY JOKES YOU'LL EVER HEAR WILL BE-- MINE!
KOFF!
YOU GONNA LET THEM DO ANY OJ STUFF, BOSS?
CALL THAT THE TRIAL OF THE CENTURY? TWO PEOPLE DEAD? I KILL TWO PEOPLE BEFORE I HAVE MY BREAKFAST CEREAL-- AND THAT'S ON A BAD DAY.

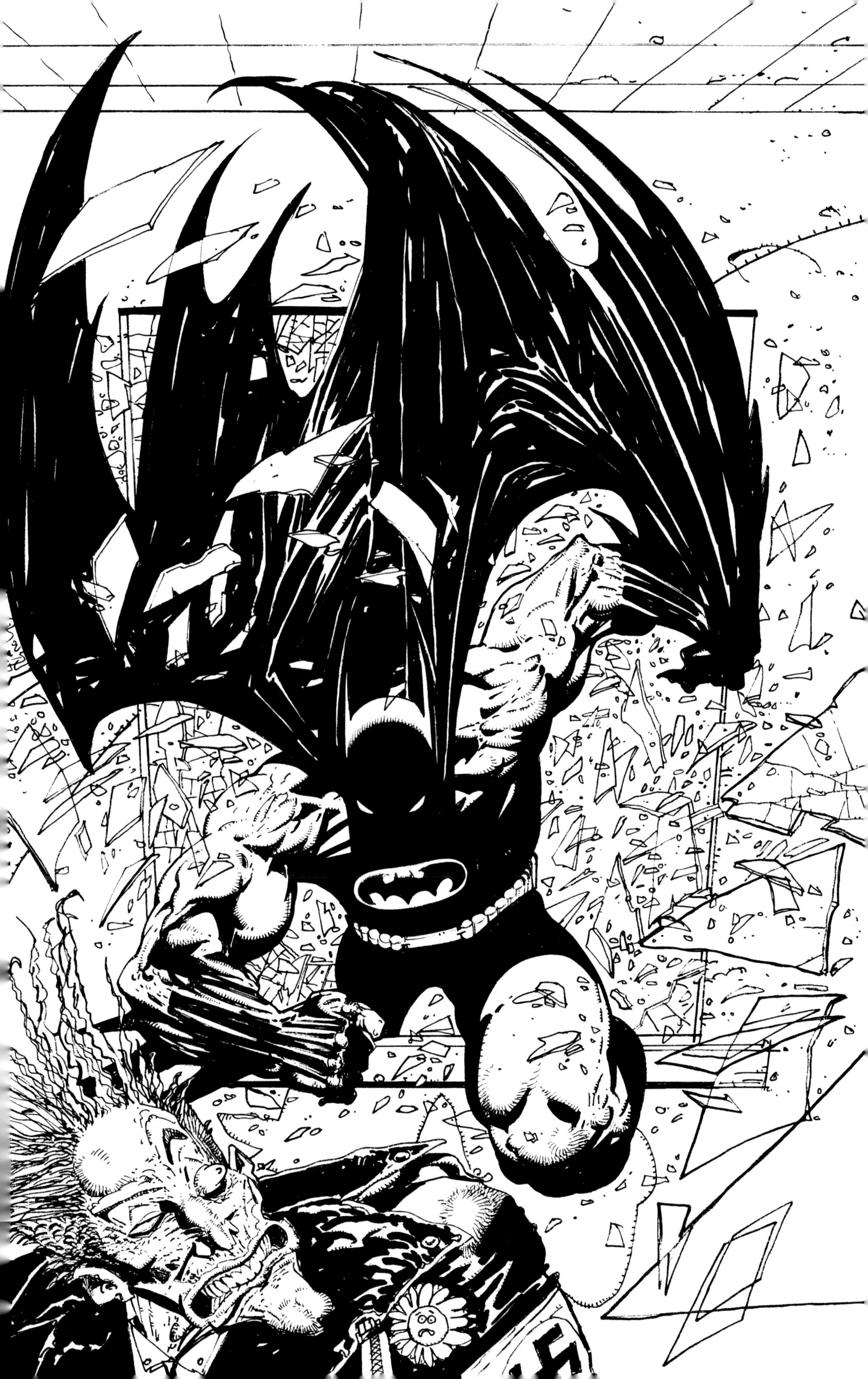

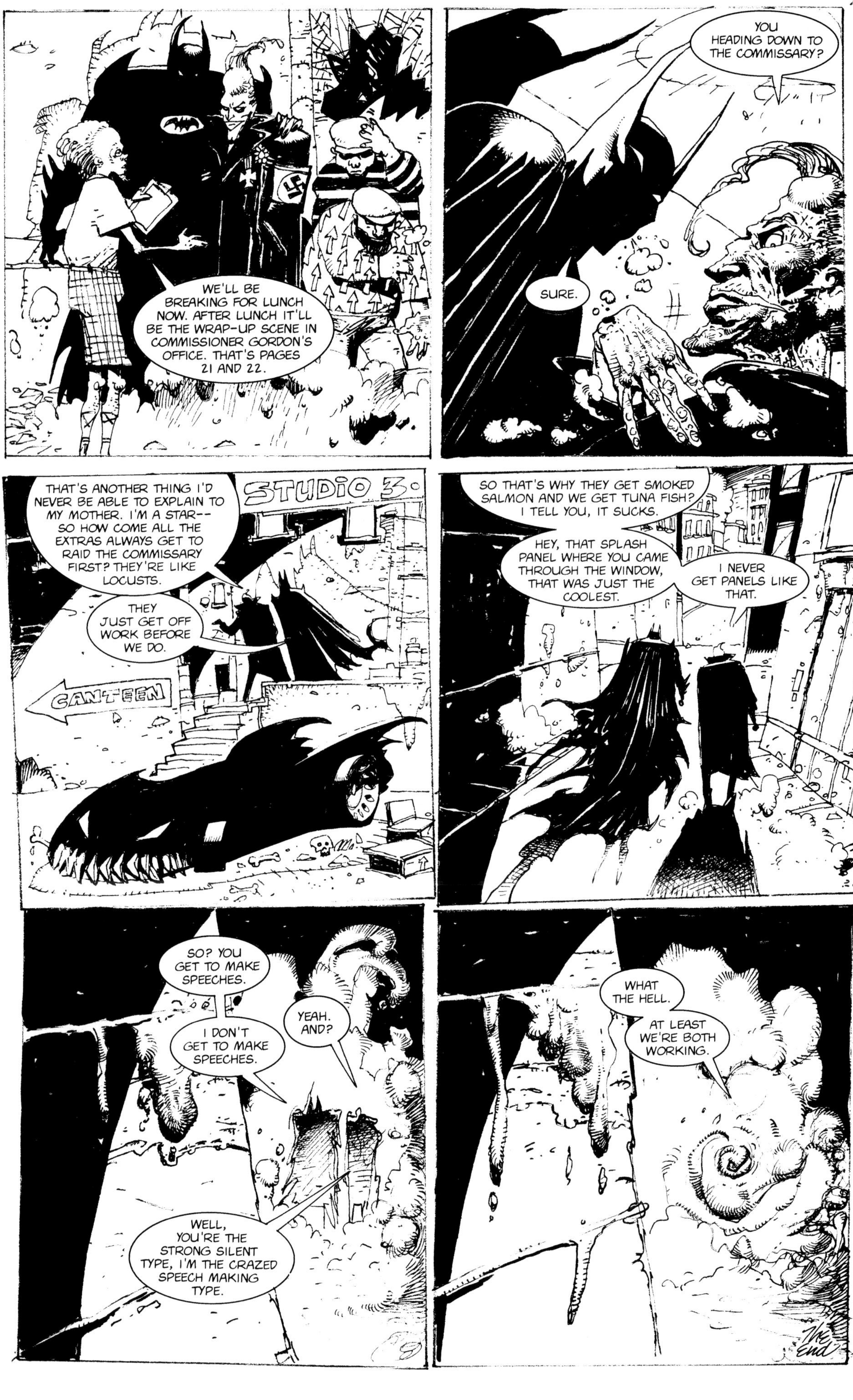
WE'LL BE BREAKING FOR LUNCH NOW. AFTER LUNCH IT'LL BE THE WRAP-UP SCENE IN COMMISSIONER GORDON'S OFFICE. THAT'S PAGES 21 AND 22.
YOU HEADING DOWN TO THE COMMISSARY?
SURE.
STUDIO 3
THAT'S ANOTHER THING I'D NEVER BE ABLE TO EXPLAIN TO MY MOTHER. I'M A STAR-- SO HOW COME ALL THE EXTRAS ALWAYS GET TO RAID THE COMMISSARY FIRST? THEY'RE LIKE LOCUSTS.
THEY JUST GET OFF WORK BEFORE WE DO.
CANTEEN
SO THAT'S WHY THEY GET SMOKED SALMON AND WE GET TUNA FISH? I TELL YOU, IT SUCKS.
HEY, THAT SPLASH PANEL WHERE YOU CAME THROUGH THE WINDOW, THAT WAS JUST THE COOLEST.
I NEVER GET PANELS LIKE THAT.
SO? YOU GET TO MAKE SPEECHES.
I DON'T GET TO MAKE SPEECHES.
YEAH. AND?
WELL, YOU'RE THE STRONG SILENT TYPE, I'M THE CRAZED SPEECH MAKING TYPE.
WHAT THE HELL.
AT LEAST WE'RE BOTH WORKING.
The End

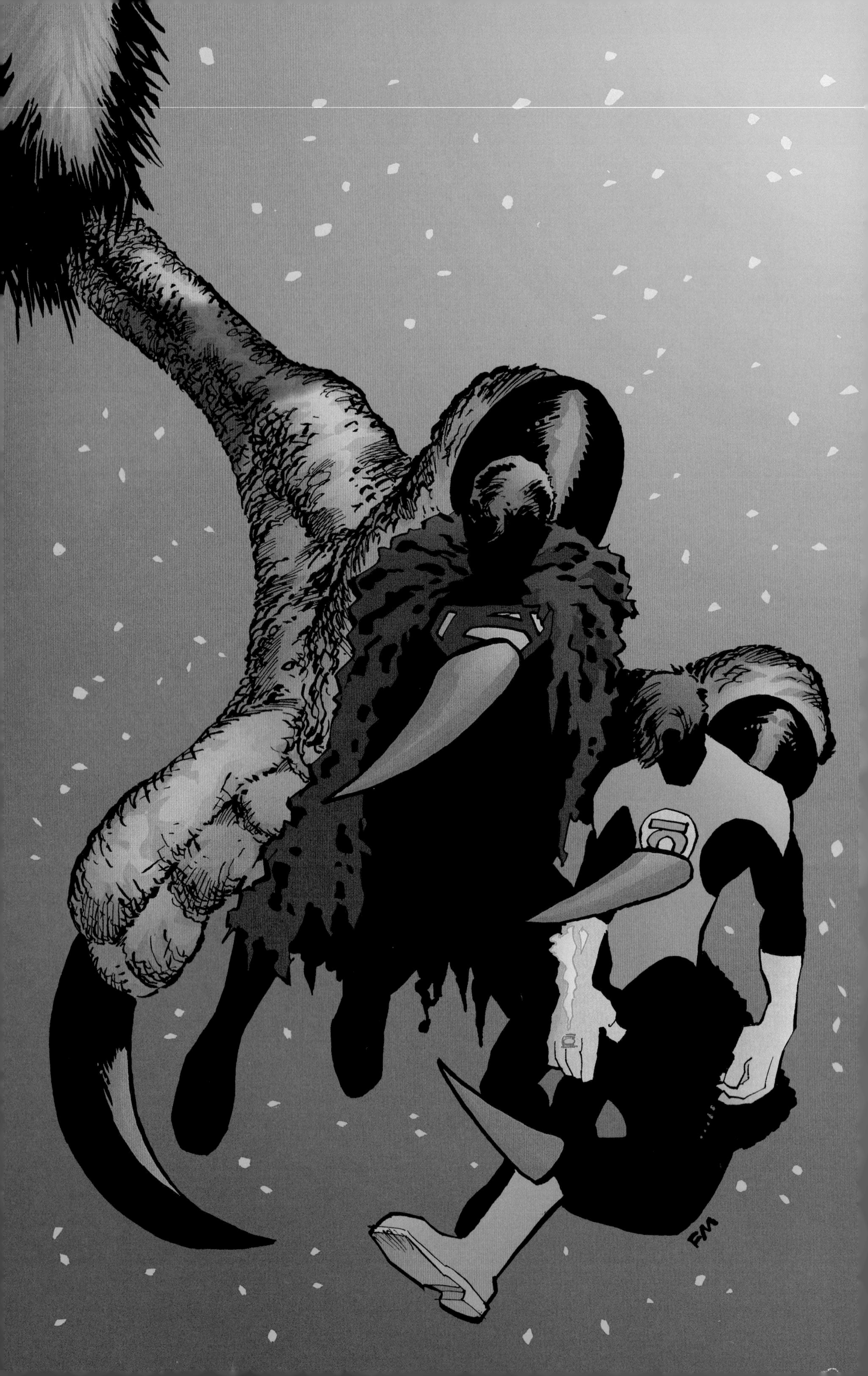
FM

PROLOGUE: 1949

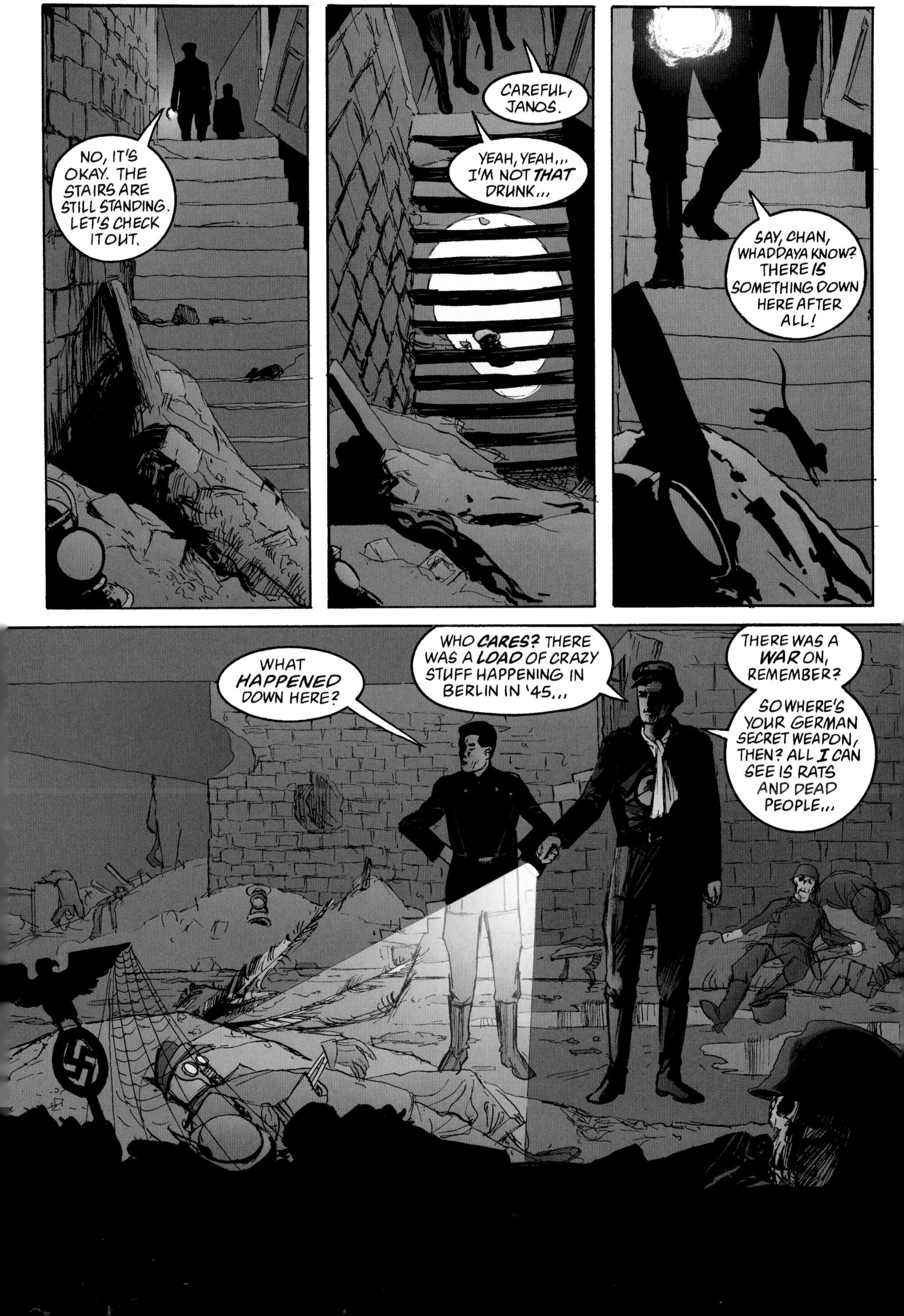

NO, IT'S OKAY. THE STAIRS ARE STILL STANDING. LET'S CHECK IT OUT.
CAREFUL, JANOS.
YEAH, YEAH... I'M NOT THAT DRUNK...
SAY, CHAN, WHADDAYA KNOW? THERE IS SOMETHING DOWN HERE AFTER ALL!
WHAT HAPPENED DOWN HERE?
WHO CARES? THERE WAS A LOAD OF CRAZY STUFF HAPPENING IN BERLIN IN '45...
THERE WAS A WAR ON, REMEMBER?
SO WHERE'S YOUR GERMAN SECRET WEAPON, THEN? ALL I CAN SEE IS RATS AND DEAD PEOPLE...

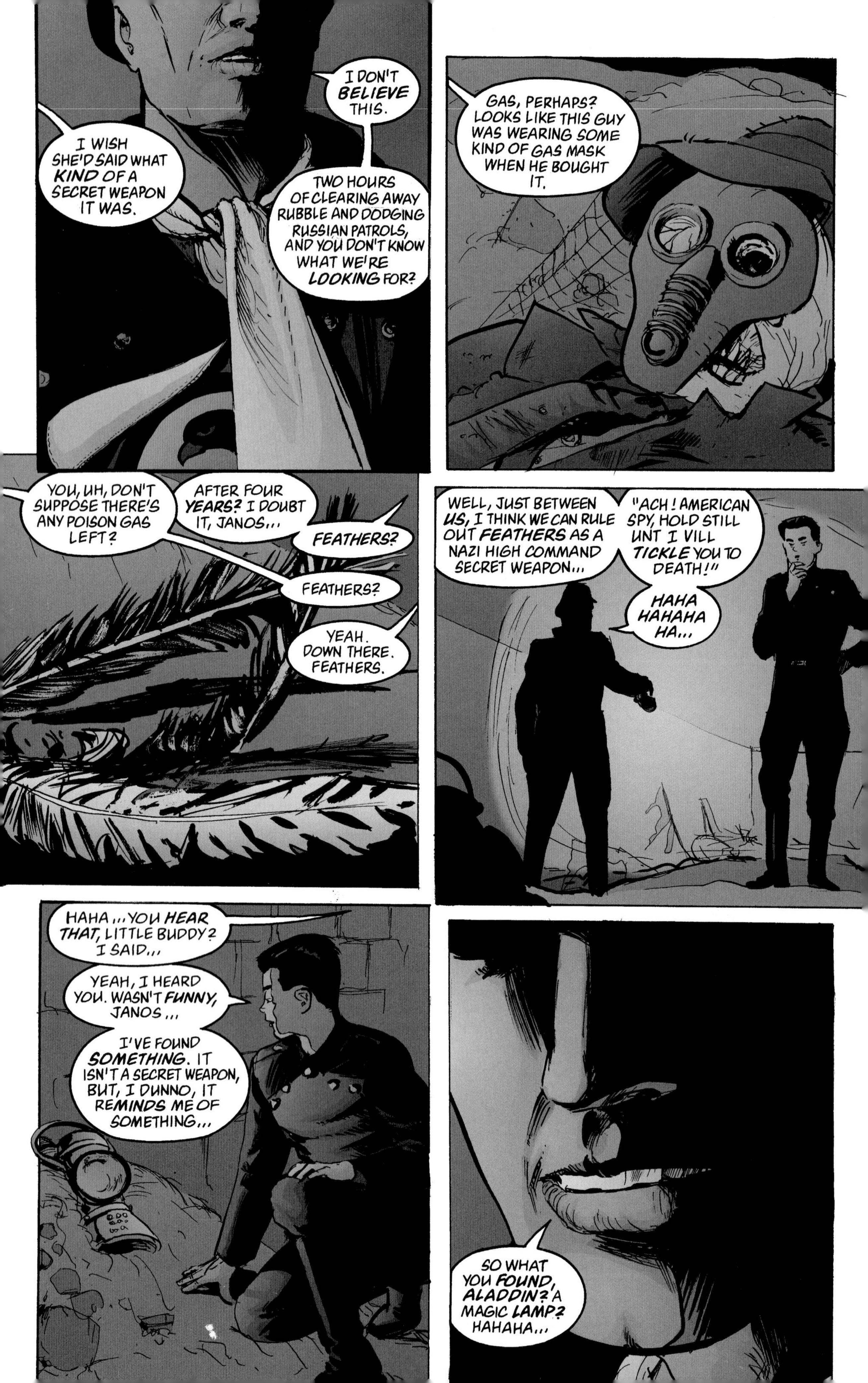
I WISH SHE'D SAID WHAT KIND OF A SECRET WEAPON IT WAS.
I DON'T BELIEVE THIS.
TWO HOURS OF CLEARING AWAY RUBBLE AND DODGING RUSSIAN PATROLS, AND YOU DON'T KNOW WHAT WE'RE LOOKING FOR?
GAS, PERHAPS? LOOKS LIKE THIS GUY WAS WEARING SOME KIND OF GAS MASK WHEN HE BOUGHT IT.
YOU, UH, DON'T SUPPOSE THERE'S ANY POISON GAS LEFT?
AFTER FOUR YEARS? I DOUBT IT, JANOS...
FEATHERS?
FEATHERS?
YEAH. DOWN THERE. FEATHERS.
WELL, JUST BETWEEN US, I THINK WE CAN RULE OUT FEATHERS AS A NAZI HIGH COMMAND SECRET WEAPON...
"ACH! AMERICAN SPY, HOLD STILL UNT I VILL TICKLE YOU TO DEATH!"
HAHA HAHAHA HA...
HAHA... YOU HEAR THAT, LITTLE BUDDY? I SAID...
YEAH, I HEARD YOU. WASN'T FUNNY, JANOS...
I'VE FOUND SOMETHING. IT ISN'T A SECRET WEAPON, BUT, I DUNNO, IT REMINDS ME OF SOMETHING...
SO WHAT YOU FOUND, ALADDIN? A MAGIC LAMP? HAHAHA...

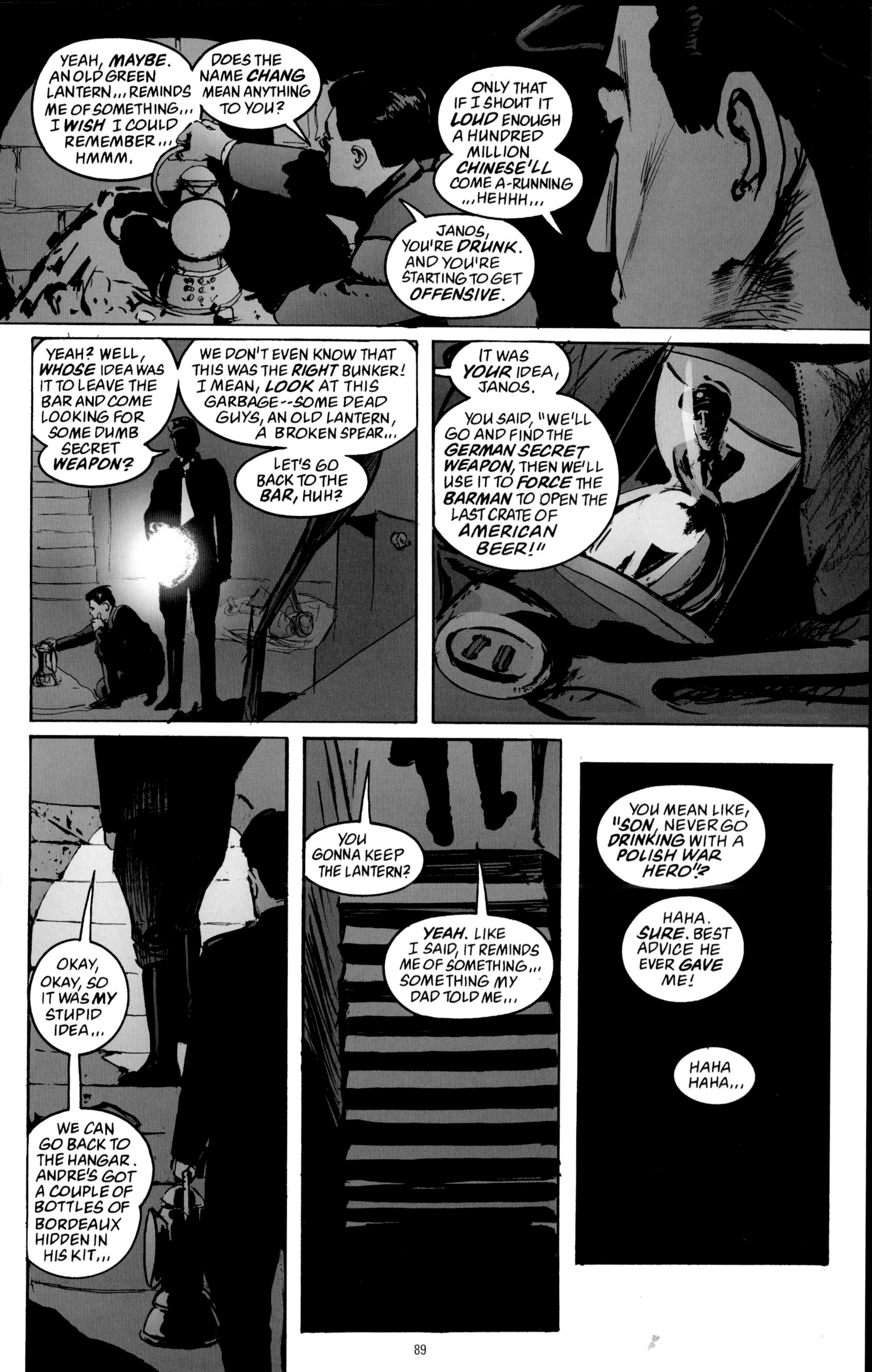
YEAH, MAYBE. AN OLD GREEN LANTERN... REMINDS ME OF SOMETHING... I WISH I COULD REMEMBER... HMMM.
DOES THE NAME CHANG MEAN ANYTHING TO YOU?
ONLY THAT IF I SHOUT IT LOUD ENOUGH A HUNDRED MILLION CHINESE'LL COME A-RUNNING ...HEHHH...
JANOS, YOU'RE DRUNK. AND YOU'RE STARTING TO GET OFFENSIVE.
YEAH? WELL, WHOSE IDEA WAS IT TO LEAVE THE BAR AND COME LOOKING FOR SOME DUMB SECRET WEAPON?
WE DON'T EVEN KNOW THAT THIS WAS THE RIGHT BUNKER! I MEAN, LOOK AT THIS GARBAGE--SOME DEAD GUYS, AN OLD LANTERN, A BROKEN SPEAR...
LET'S GO BACK TO THE BAR, HUH?
IT WAS YOUR IDEA, JANOS.
YOU SAID, "WE'LL GO AND FIND THE GERMAN SECRET WEAPON, THEN WE'LL USE IT TO FORCE THE BARMAN TO OPEN THE LAST CRATE OF AMERICAN BEER!"
OKAY, OKAY, SO IT WAS MY STUPID IDEA...
WE CAN GO BACK TO THE HANGAR. ANDRE'S GOT A COUPLE OF BOTTLES OF BORDEAUX HIDDEN IN HIS KIT...
YOU GONNA KEEP THE LANTERN?
YEAH. LIKE I SAID, IT REMINDS ME OF SOMETHING... SOMETHING MY DAD TOLD ME...
YOU MEAN LIKE, "SON, NEVER GO DRINKING WITH A POLISH WAR HERO"?
HAHA. SURE. BEST ADVICE HE EVER GAVE ME!
HAHA HAHA...

CHAPTER ONE: 1989

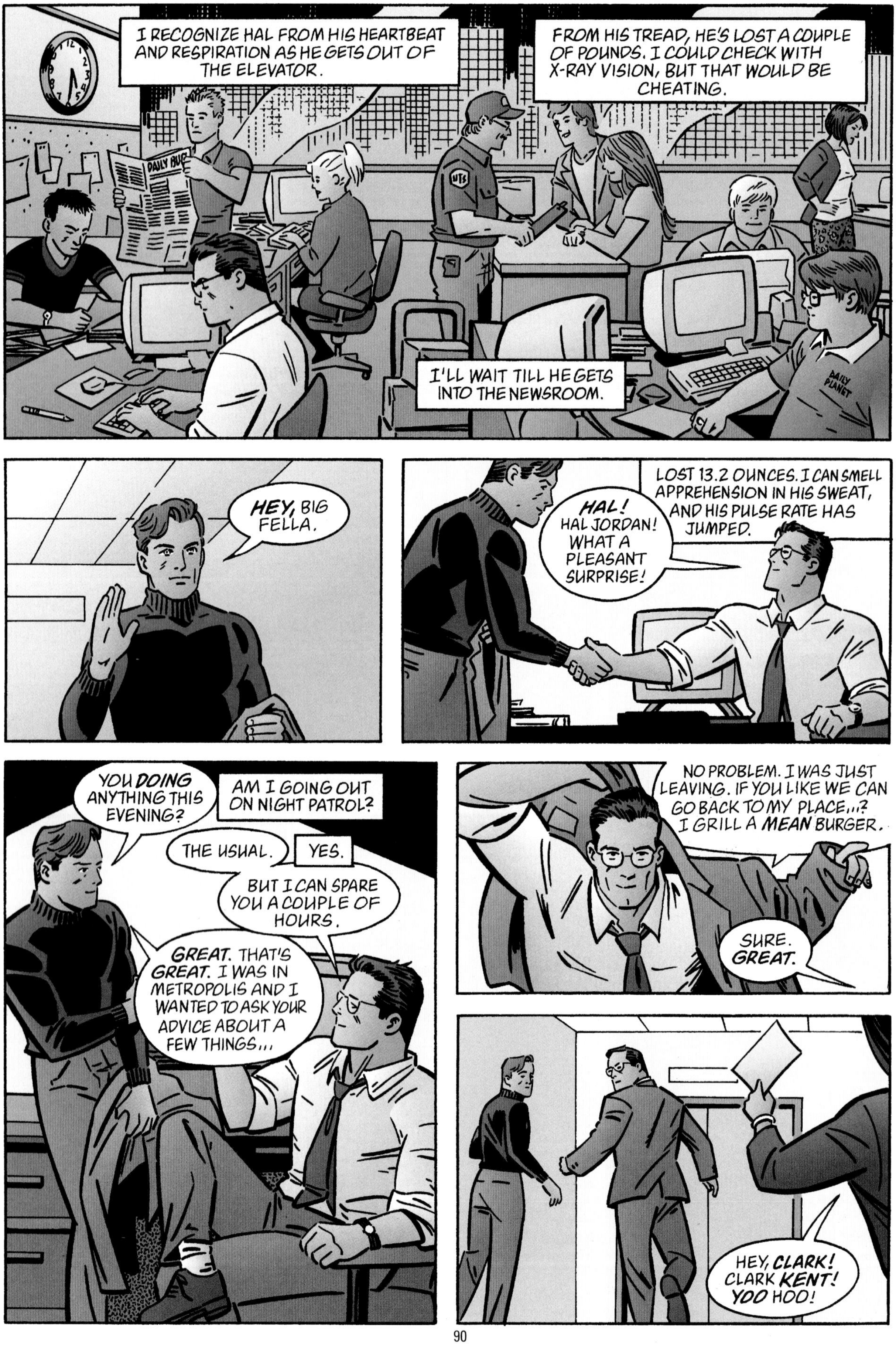

I RECOGNIZE HAL FROM HIS HEARTBEAT AND RESPIRATION AS HE GETS OUT OF THE ELEVATOR.
FROM HIS TREAD, HE'S LOST A COUPLE OF POUNDS. I COULD CHECK WITH X-RAY VISION, BUT THAT WOULD BE CHEATING.
DAILY BUGLE
DAILY PLANET
I'LL WAIT TILL HE GETS INTO THE NEWSROOM.
HEY, BIG FELLA.
LOST 13.2 OUNCES. I CAN SMELL APPREHENSION IN HIS SWEAT, AND HIS PULSE RATE HAS JUMPED.
HAL! HAL JORDAN! WHAT A PLEASANT SURPRISE!
YOU DOING ANYTHING THIS EVENING?
AM I GOING OUT ON NIGHT PATROL?
THE USUAL.
YES.
BUT I CAN SPARE YOU A COUPLE OF HOURS.
GREAT. THAT'S GREAT. I WAS IN METROPOLIS AND I WANTED TO ASK YOUR ADVICE ABOUT A FEW THINGS...
NO PROBLEM. I WAS JUST LEAVING. IF YOU LIKE WE CAN GO BACK TO MY PLACE...? I GRILL A MEAN BURGER.
SURE. GREAT.
HEY, CLARK! CLARK KENT! YOO HOO!

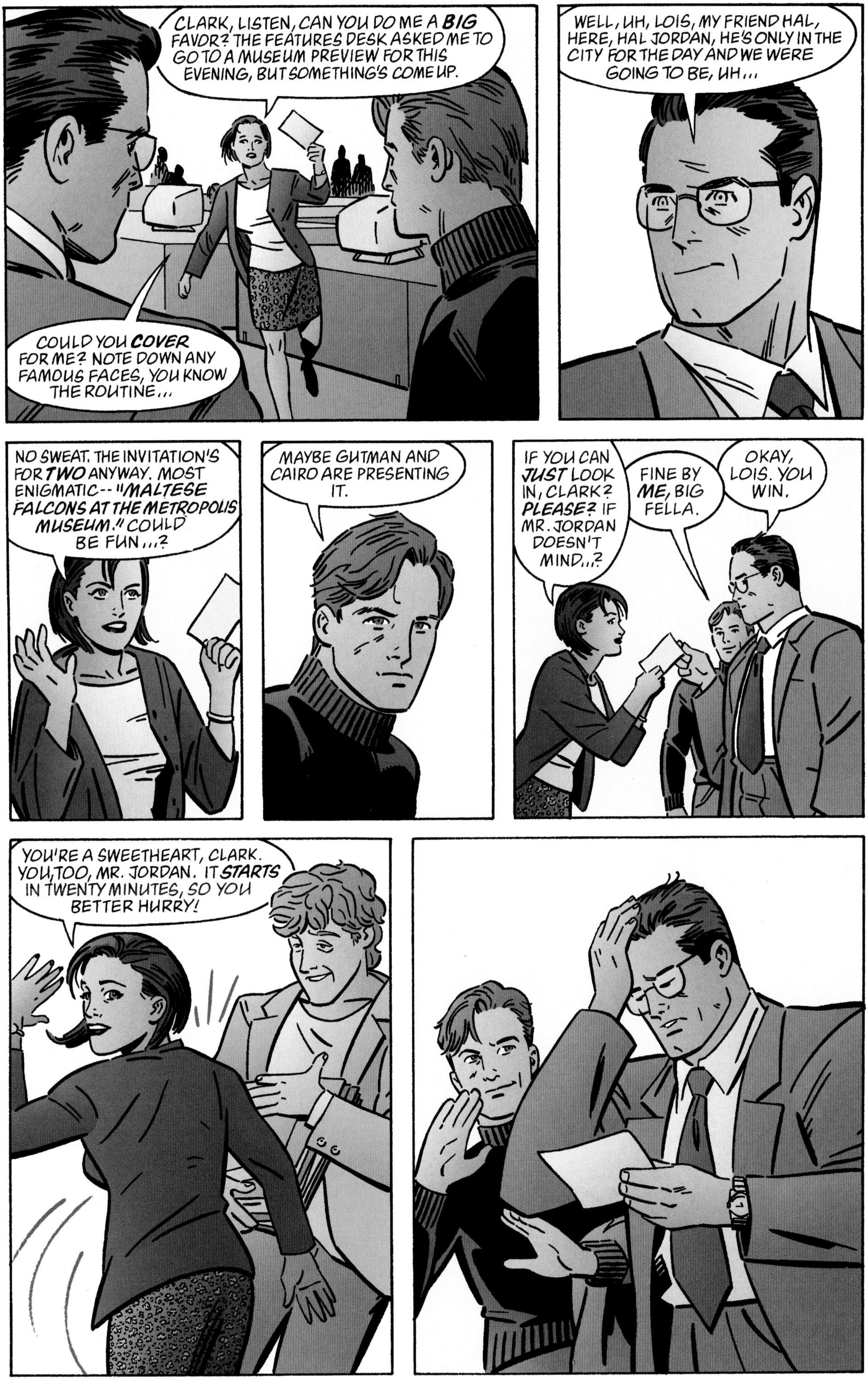
CLARK, LISTEN, CAN YOU DO ME A **BIG** FAVOR? THE FEATURES DESK ASKED ME TO GO TO A MUSEUM PREVIEW FOR THIS EVENING, BUT SOMETHING'S COME UP.
COULD YOU **COVER** FOR ME? NOTE DOWN ANY FAMOUS FACES, YOU KNOW THE ROUTINE...
WELL, UH, LOIS, MY FRIEND HAL, HERE, HAL JORDAN, HE'S ONLY IN THE CITY FOR THE DAY AND WE WERE GOING TO BE, UH...
NO SWEAT. THE INVITATION'S FOR **TWO** ANYWAY. MOST ENIGMATIC-- **"MALTESE FALCONS AT THE METROPOLIS MUSEUM."** COULD BE FUN...?
MAYBE GUTMAN AND CAIRO ARE PRESENTING IT.
IF YOU CAN **JUST** LOOK IN, CLARK? **PLEASE?** IF MR. JORDAN DOESN'T MIND...?
FINE BY **ME**, BIG FELLA.
OKAY, LOIS. YOU WIN.
YOU'RE A SWEETHEART, CLARK. YOU, TOO, MR. JORDAN. IT **STARTS** IN TWENTY MINUTES, SO YOU BETTER HURRY!

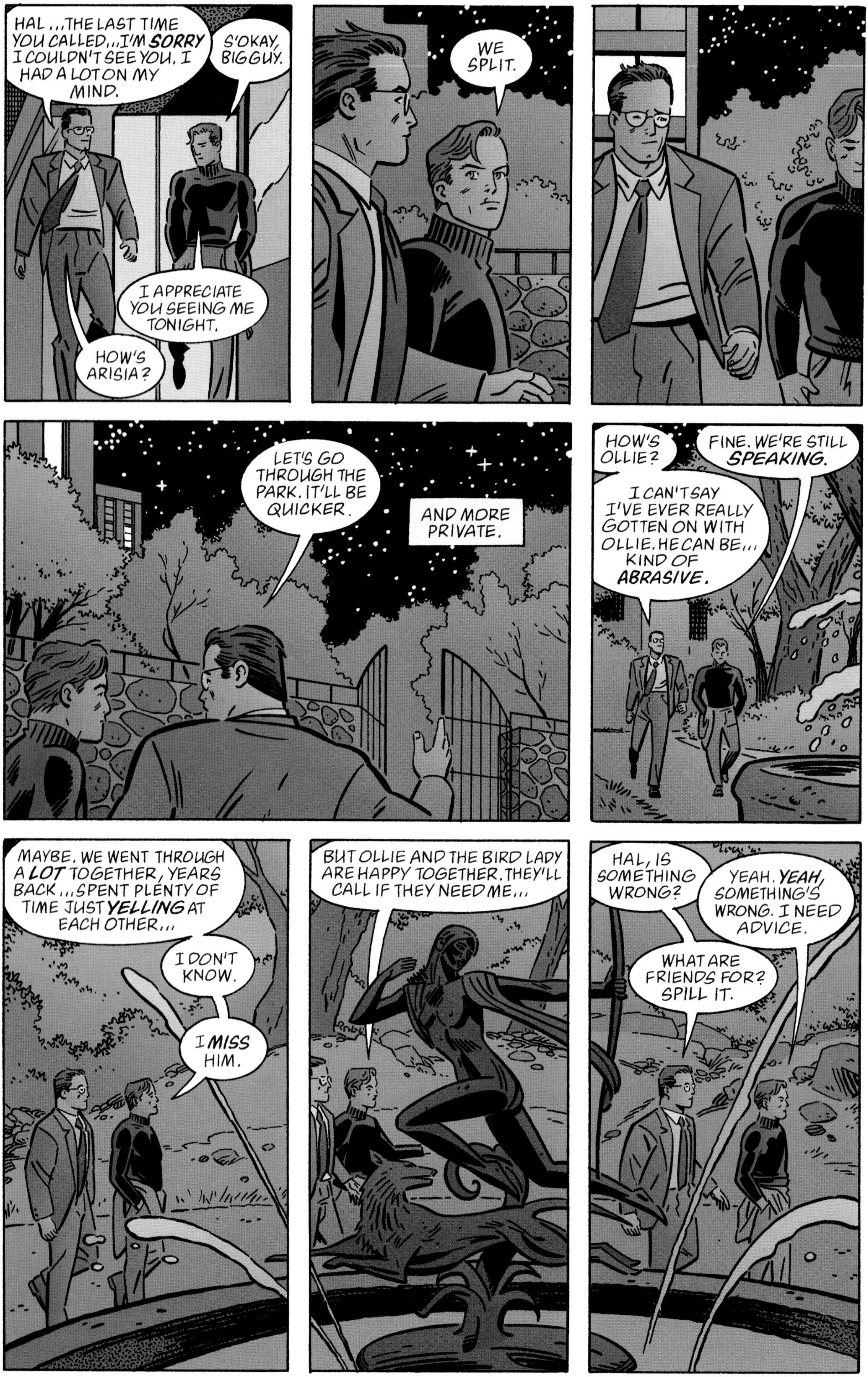
HAL ... THE LAST TIME YOU CALLED ... I'M SORRY I COULDN'T SEE YOU. I HAD A LOT ON MY MIND.
S'OKAY, BIG GUY.
I APPRECIATE YOU SEEING ME TONIGHT.
HOW'S ARISIA?
WE SPLIT.
LET'S GO THROUGH THE PARK. IT'LL BE QUICKER.
AND MORE PRIVATE.
HOW'S OLLIE?
FINE. WE'RE STILL SPEAKING.
I CAN'T SAY I'VE EVER REALLY GOTTEN ON WITH OLLIE. HE CAN BE ... KIND OF ABRASIVE.
MAYBE. WE WENT THROUGH A LOT TOGETHER, YEARS BACK ... SPENT PLENTY OF TIME JUST YELLING AT EACH OTHER ...
I DON'T KNOW.
I MISS HIM.
BUT OLLIE AND THE BIRD LADY ARE HAPPY TOGETHER. THEY'LL CALL IF THEY NEED ME ...
HAL, IS SOMETHING WRONG?
YEAH. YEAH, SOMETHING'S WRONG. I NEED ADVICE.
WHAT ARE FRIENDS FOR? SPILL IT.

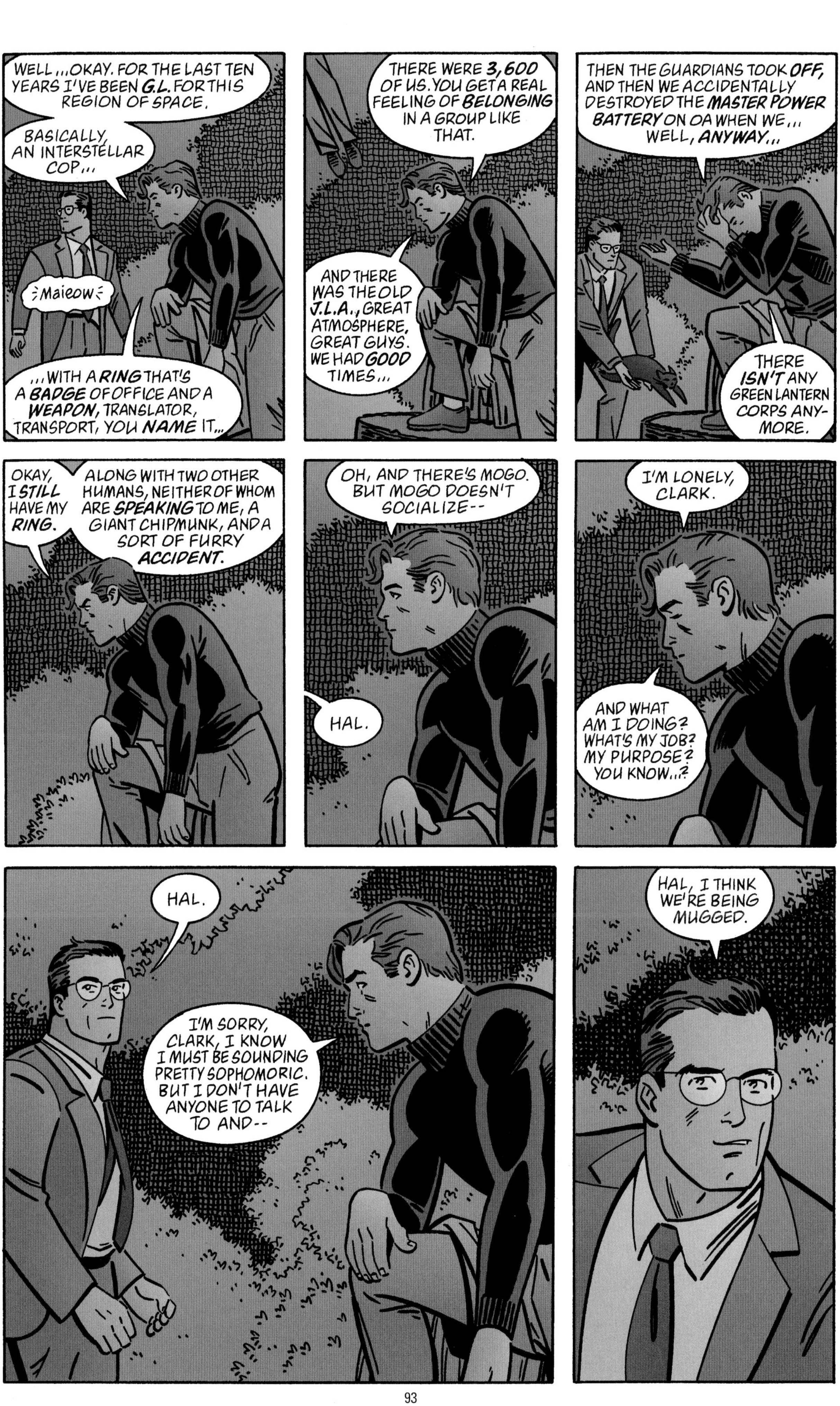
WELL ... OKAY. FOR THE LAST TEN YEARS I'VE BEEN G.L. FOR THIS REGION OF SPACE.
BASICALLY, AN INTERSTELLAR COP...
Maieow
...WITH A RING THAT'S A BADGE OF OFFICE AND A WEAPON, TRANSLATOR, TRANSPORT, YOU NAME IT...
THERE WERE 3,600 OF US. YOU GET A REAL FEELING OF BELONGING IN A GROUP LIKE THAT.
AND THERE WAS THE OLD J.L.A., GREAT ATMOSPHERE, GREAT GUYS. WE HAD GOOD TIMES...
THEN THE GUARDIANS TOOK OFF, AND THEN WE ACCIDENTALLY DESTROYED THE MASTER POWER BATTERY ON OA WHEN WE... WELL, ANYWAY...
THERE ISN'T ANY GREEN LANTERN CORPS ANY-MORE.
OKAY, I STILL HAVE MY RING.
ALONG WITH TWO OTHER HUMANS, NEITHER OF WHOM ARE SPEAKING TO ME, A GIANT CHIPMUNK, AND A SORT OF FURRY ACCIDENT.
OH, AND THERE'S MOGO. BUT MOGO DOESN'T SOCIALIZE--
HAL.
I'M LONELY, CLARK.
AND WHAT AM I DOING? WHAT'S MY JOB? MY PURPOSE? YOU KNOW...?
HAL.
I'M SORRY, CLARK, I KNOW I MUST BE SOUNDING PRETTY SOPHOMORIC. BUT I DON'T HAVE ANYONE TO TALK TO AND--
HAL, I THINK WE'RE BEING MUGGED.

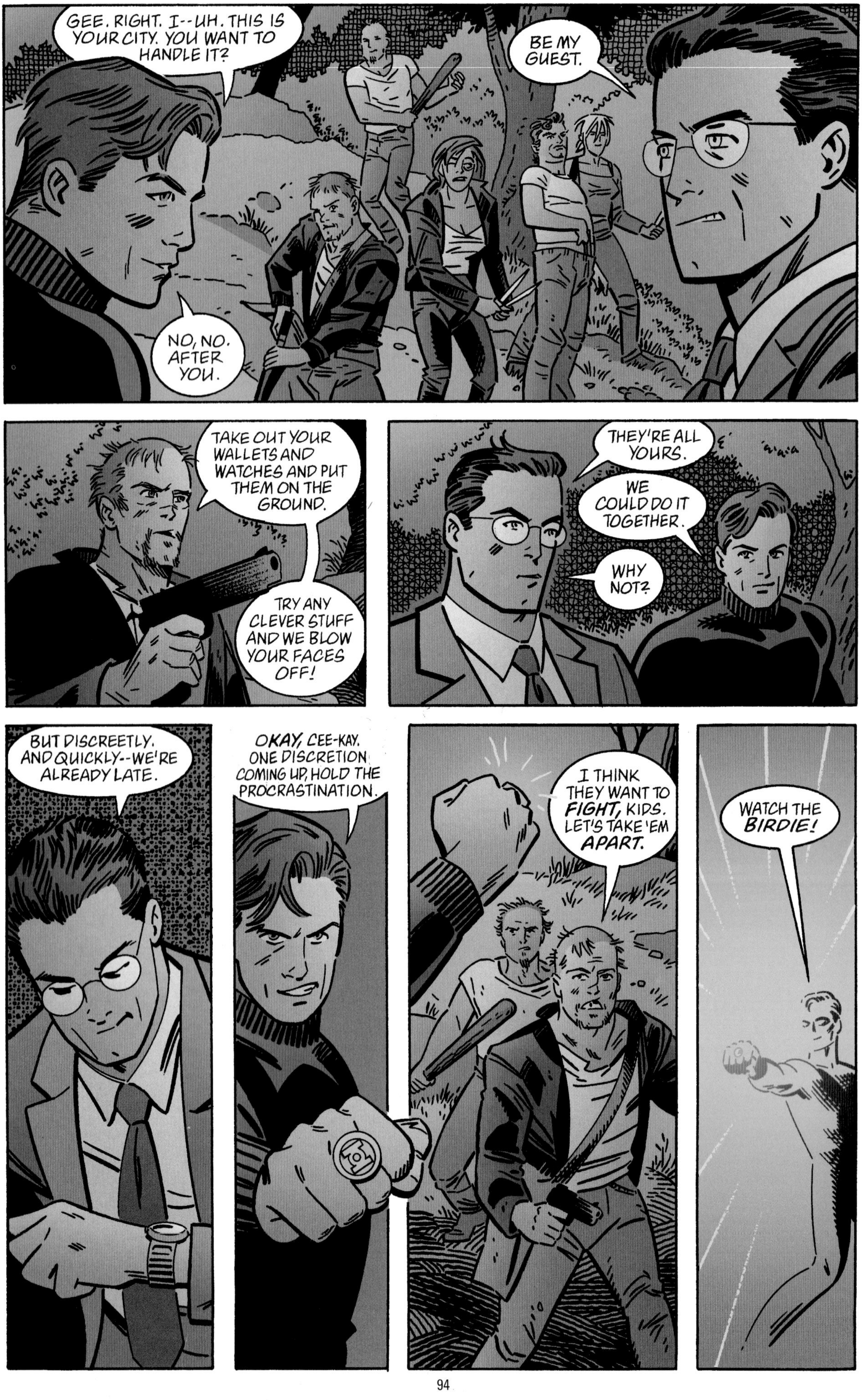
GEE. RIGHT. I--UH. THIS IS YOUR CITY. YOU WANT TO HANDLE IT?
BE MY GUEST.
NO, NO. AFTER YOU.
TAKE OUT YOUR WALLETS AND WATCHES AND PUT THEM ON THE GROUND.
TRY ANY CLEVER STUFF AND WE BLOW YOUR FACES OFF!
THEY'RE ALL YOURS.
WE COULD DO IT TOGETHER.
WHY NOT?
BUT DISCREETLY. AND QUICKLY--WE'RE ALREADY LATE.
OKAY, CEE-KAY. ONE DISCRETION COMING UP, HOLD THE PROCRASTINATION.
I THINK THEY WANT TO FIGHT, KIDS. LET'S TAKE 'EM APART.
WATCH THE BIRDIE!

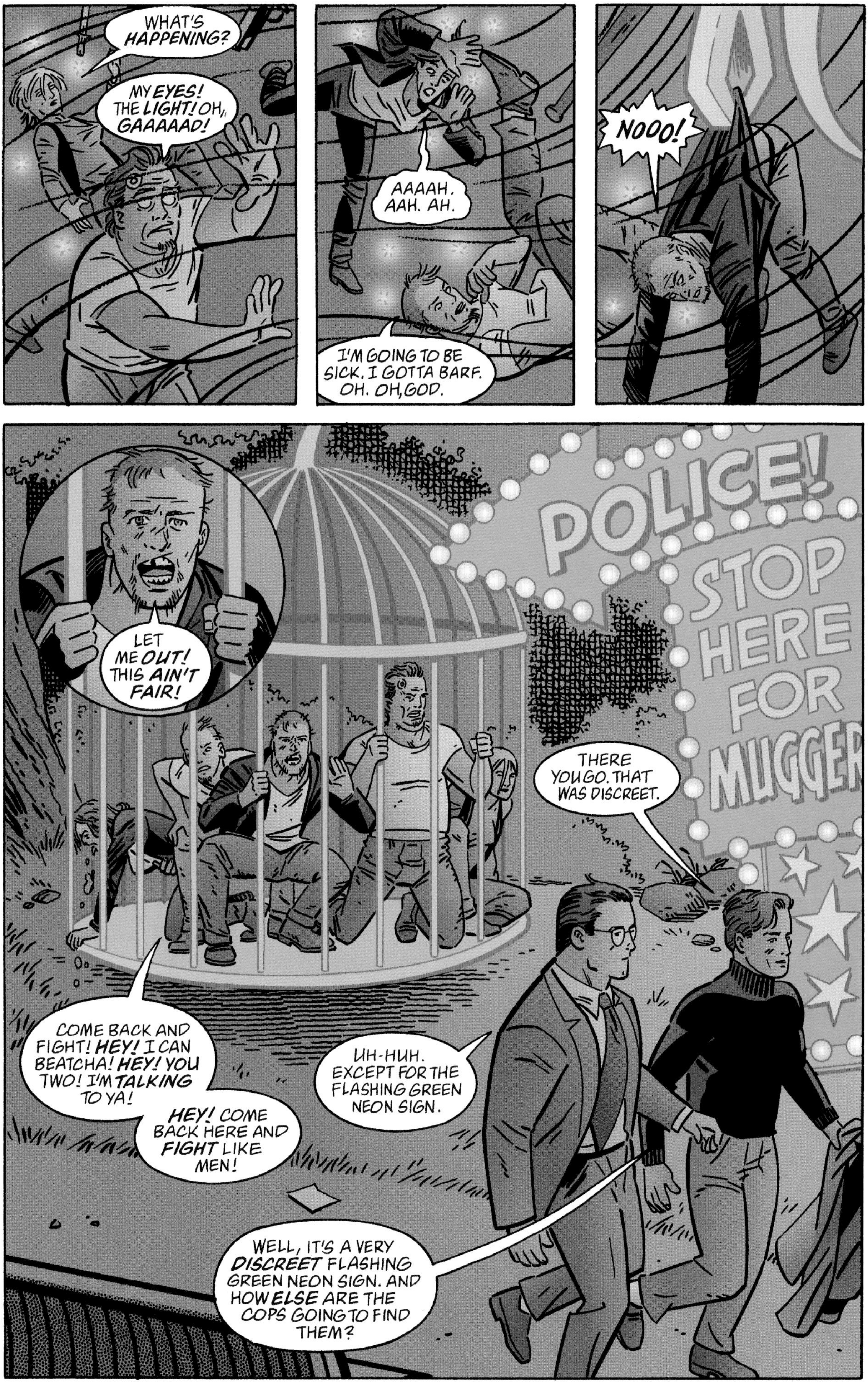
WHAT'S HAPPENING?
MY EYES! THE LIGHT! OH, GAAAAAD!
AAAAH. AAH. AH.
I'M GOING TO BE SICK. I GOTTA BARF. OH. OH, GOD.
NOOO!
POLICE! STOP HERE FOR MUGGER
LET ME OUT! THIS AIN'T FAIR!
THERE YOU GO. THAT WAS DISCREET.
UH-HUH. EXCEPT FOR THE FLASHING GREEN NEON SIGN.
COME BACK AND FIGHT! HEY! I CAN BEATCHA! HEY! YOU TWO! I'M TALKING TO YA!
HEY! COME BACK HERE AND FIGHT LIKE MEN!
WELL, IT'S A VERY DISCREET FLASHING GREEN NEON SIGN. AND HOW ELSE ARE THE COPS GOING TO FIND THEM?

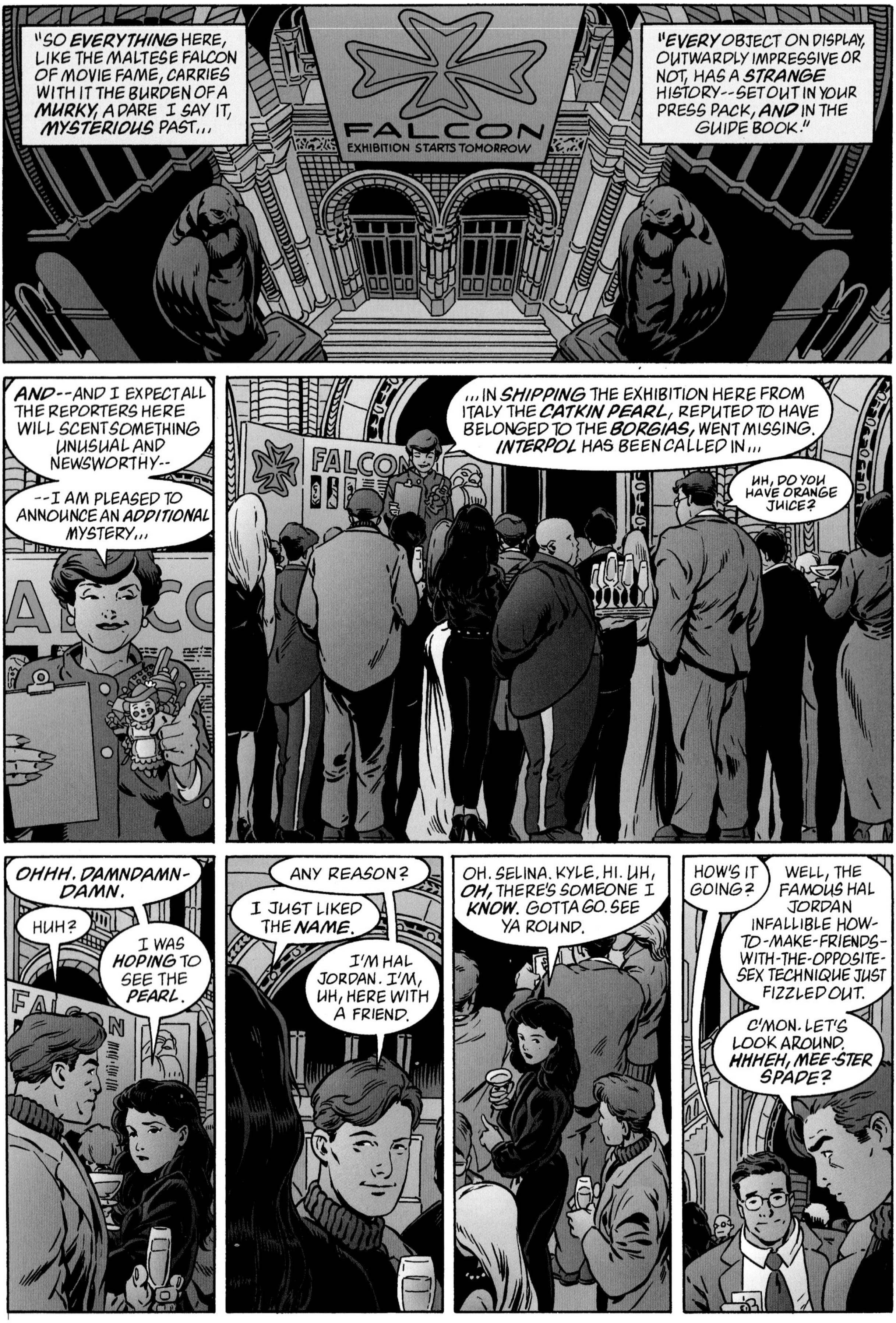
"SO EVERYTHING HERE, LIKE THE MALTESE FALCON OF MOVIE FAME, CARRIES WITH IT THE BURDEN OF A MURKY, A DARE I SAY IT, MYSTERIOUS PAST...
FALCON
EXHIBITION STARTS TOMORROW
"EVERY OBJECT ON DISPLAY, OUTWARDLY IMPRESSIVE OR NOT, HAS A STRANGE HISTORY--SET OUT IN YOUR PRESS PACK, AND IN THE GUIDE BOOK."
AND--AND I EXPECT ALL THE REPORTERS HERE WILL SCENT SOMETHING UNUSUAL AND NEWSWORTHY--
--I AM PLEASED TO ANNOUNCE AN ADDITIONAL MYSTERY...
...IN SHIPPING THE EXHIBITION HERE FROM ITALY THE CATKIN PEARL, REPUTED TO HAVE BELONGED TO THE BORGIAS, WENT MISSING. INTERPOL HAS BEEN CALLED IN...
UH, DO YOU HAVE ORANGE JUICE?
OHHH. DAMNDAMN-DAMN.
HUH?
I WAS HOPING TO SEE THE PEARL.
ANY REASON?
I JUST LIKED THE NAME.
I'M HAL JORDAN. I'M, UH, HERE WITH A FRIEND.
OH. SELINA. KYLE. HI. UH, OH, THERE'S SOMEONE I KNOW. GOTTA GO. SEE YA ROUND.
HOW'S IT GOING?
WELL, THE FAMOUS HAL JORDAN INFALLIBLE HOW-TO-MAKE-FRIENDS-WITH-THE-OPPOSITE-SEX TECHNIQUE JUST FIZZLED OUT.
C'MON. LET'S LOOK AROUND. HHHEH, MEE-STER SPADE?

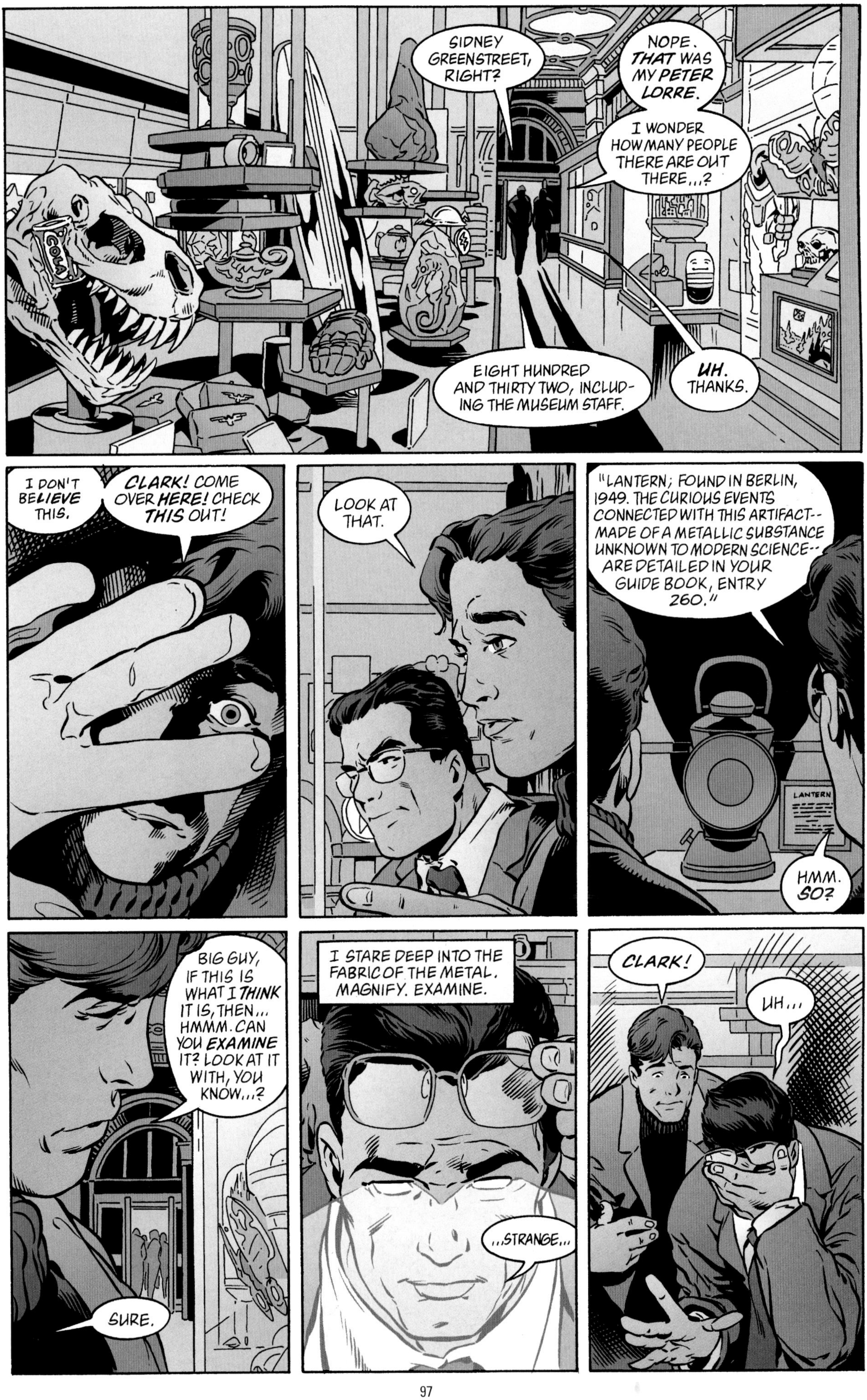
SIDNEY GREENSTREET, RIGHT?
NOPE. THAT WAS MY PETER LORRE.
I WONDER HOW MANY PEOPLE THERE ARE OUT THERE...?
EIGHT HUNDRED AND THIRTY TWO, INCLUDING THE MUSEUM STAFF.
UH. THANKS.
COLA
I DON'T BELIEVE THIS.
CLARK! COME OVER HERE! CHECK THIS OUT!
LOOK AT THAT.
"LANTERN; FOUND IN BERLIN, 1949. THE CURIOUS EVENTS CONNECTED WITH THIS ARTIFACT--MADE OF A METALLIC SUBSTANCE UNKNOWN TO MODERN SCIENCE--ARE DETAILED IN YOUR GUIDE BOOK, ENTRY 260."
LANTERN
HMM. SO?
BIG GUY, IF THIS IS WHAT I THINK IT IS, THEN... HMMM. CAN YOU EXAMINE IT? LOOK AT IT WITH, YOU KNOW...?
SURE.
I STARE DEEP INTO THE FABRIC OF THE METAL. MAGNIFY. EXAMINE.
...STRANGE...
CLARK!
UH...

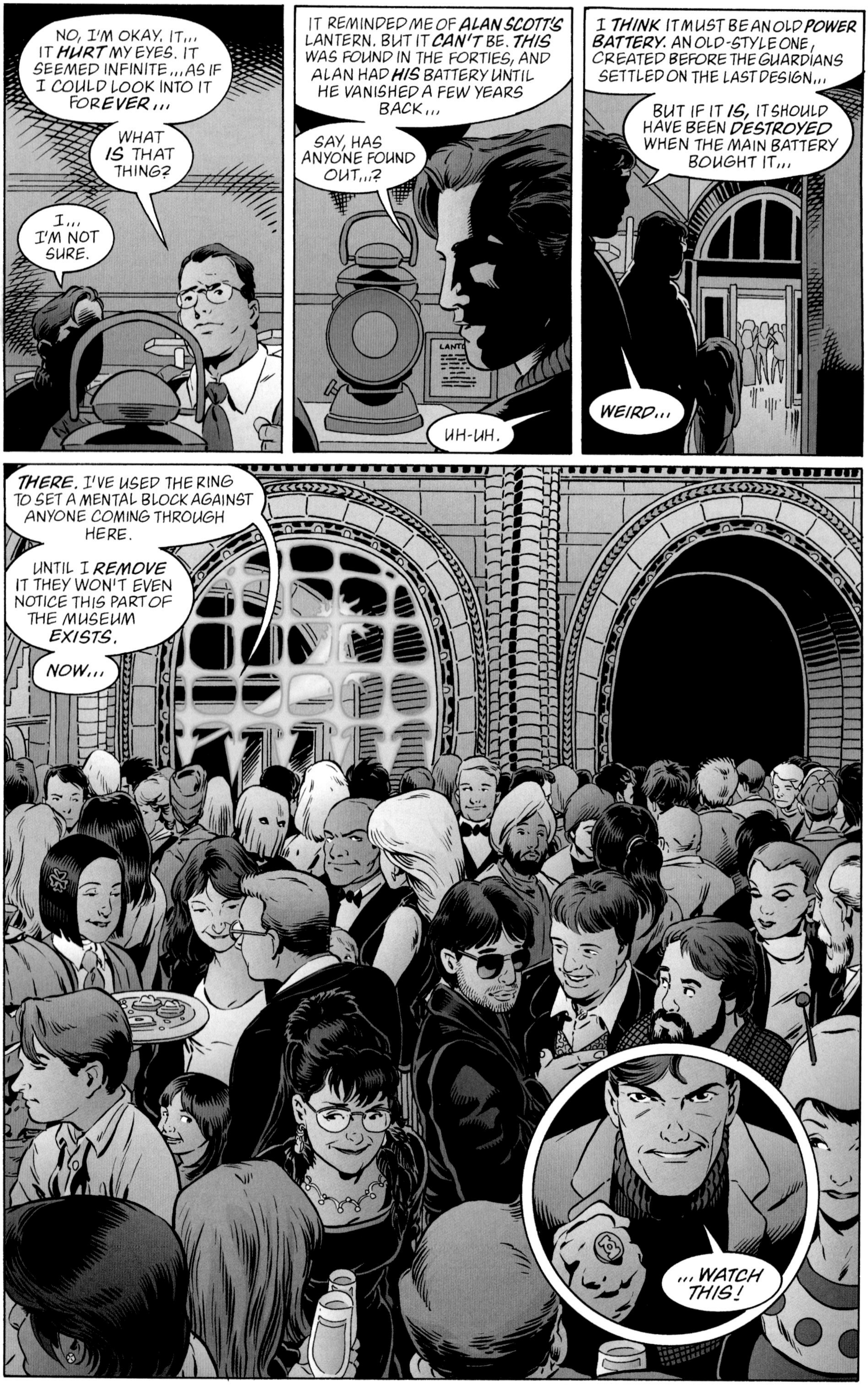
NO, I'M OKAY. IT... IT HURT MY EYES. IT SEEMED INFINITE... AS IF I COULD LOOK INTO IT FOREVER...
WHAT IS THAT THING?
I... I'M NOT SURE.
IT REMINDED ME OF ALAN SCOTT'S LANTERN. BUT IT CAN'T BE. THIS WAS FOUND IN THE FORTIES, AND ALAN HAD HIS BATTERY UNTIL HE VANISHED A FEW YEARS BACK...
SAY, HAS ANYONE FOUND OUT...?
UH-UH.
I THINK IT MUST BE AN OLD POWER BATTERY. AN OLD-STYLE ONE, CREATED BEFORE THE GUARDIANS SETTLED ON THE LAST DESIGN...
BUT IF IT IS, IT SHOULD HAVE BEEN DESTROYED WHEN THE MAIN BATTERY BOUGHT IT...
WEIRD...
THERE. I'VE USED THE RING TO SET A MENTAL BLOCK AGAINST ANYONE COMING THROUGH HERE.
UNTIL I REMOVE IT THEY WON'T EVEN NOTICE THIS PART OF THE MUSEUM EXISTS.
NOW...
...WATCH THIS!

I'M GONNA CHANGE. I COULDN'T *DO* THIS IF I WERE OFF-DUTY.

HAL...? WHAT ARE YOU *DOING?*

IF THIS *IS* THE POWER BATTERY I THINK THAT IT IS, THEN IT'S MY *DUTY* TO CHECK IT OUT.

THERE ARE 3,594 *EX*-GREEN LANTERNS OUT THERE, CLARK.

" I KNOW HOW *I'D* FEEL BETTER IF IT WAS ME THAT'D LOST *MY* RING. MY *POWER.* "

HAL--ARE YOU SURE THIS IS A GOOD IDEA?

YES. YES I AM.

...CLARK, HAVE YOU EVER SEEN ME TAKE MY *OATH?*

NO. NEVER.

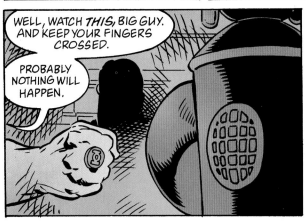

WELL, WATCH *THIS*, BIG GUY. AND KEEP YOUR FINGERS CROSSED.

PROBABLY NOTHING WILL HAPPEN.

OKAY...

IN *BRIGHTEST* DAY, IN *BLACKEST* NIGHT, NO EVIL SHALL ESCAPE MY *SIGHT*,...

LET THOSE WHO WORSHIP *EVIL'S* MIGHT *BEWARE* MY *POWER*,...

...GREEN *LANTERN'S* LIGHT!

WHOOMF!

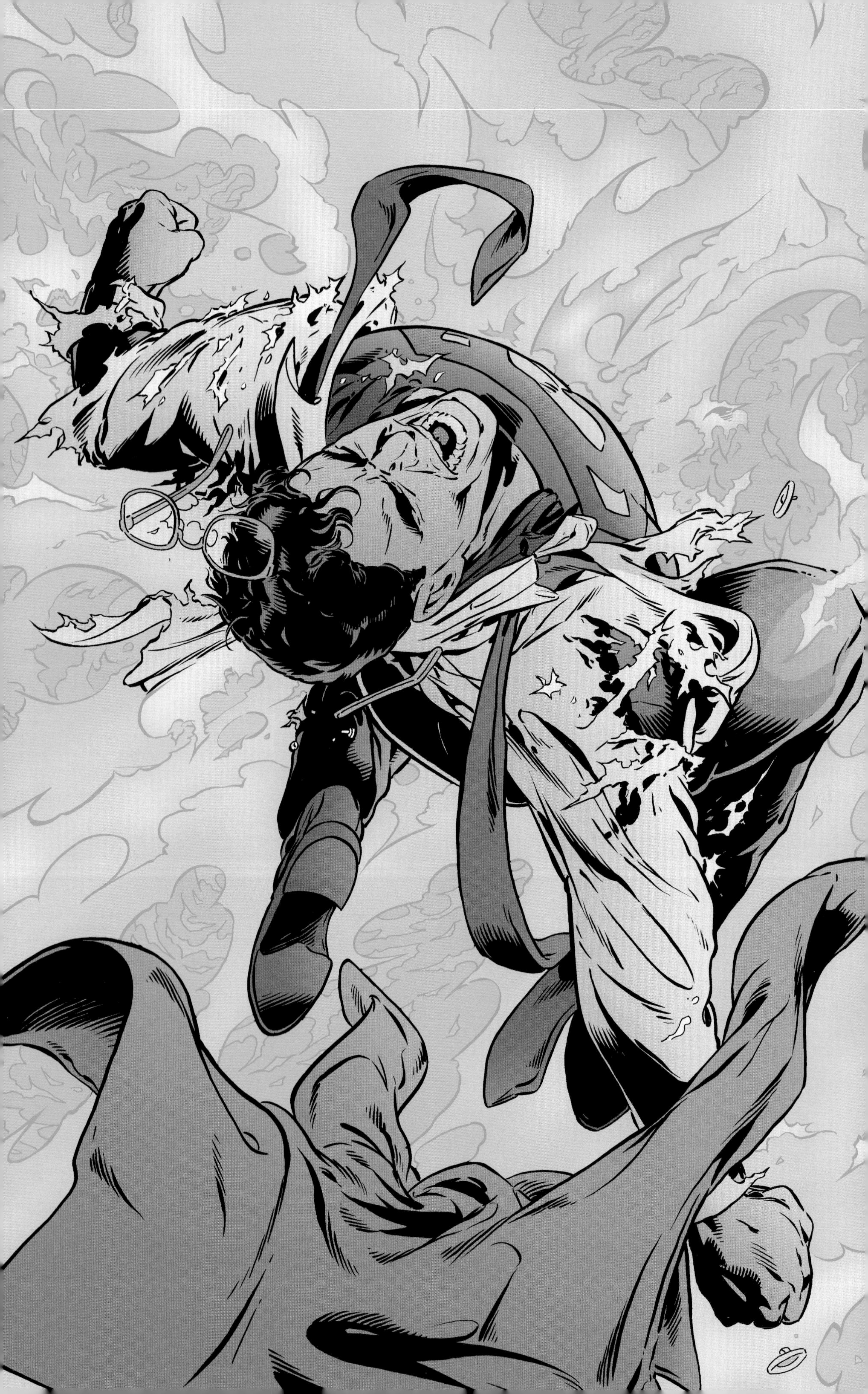

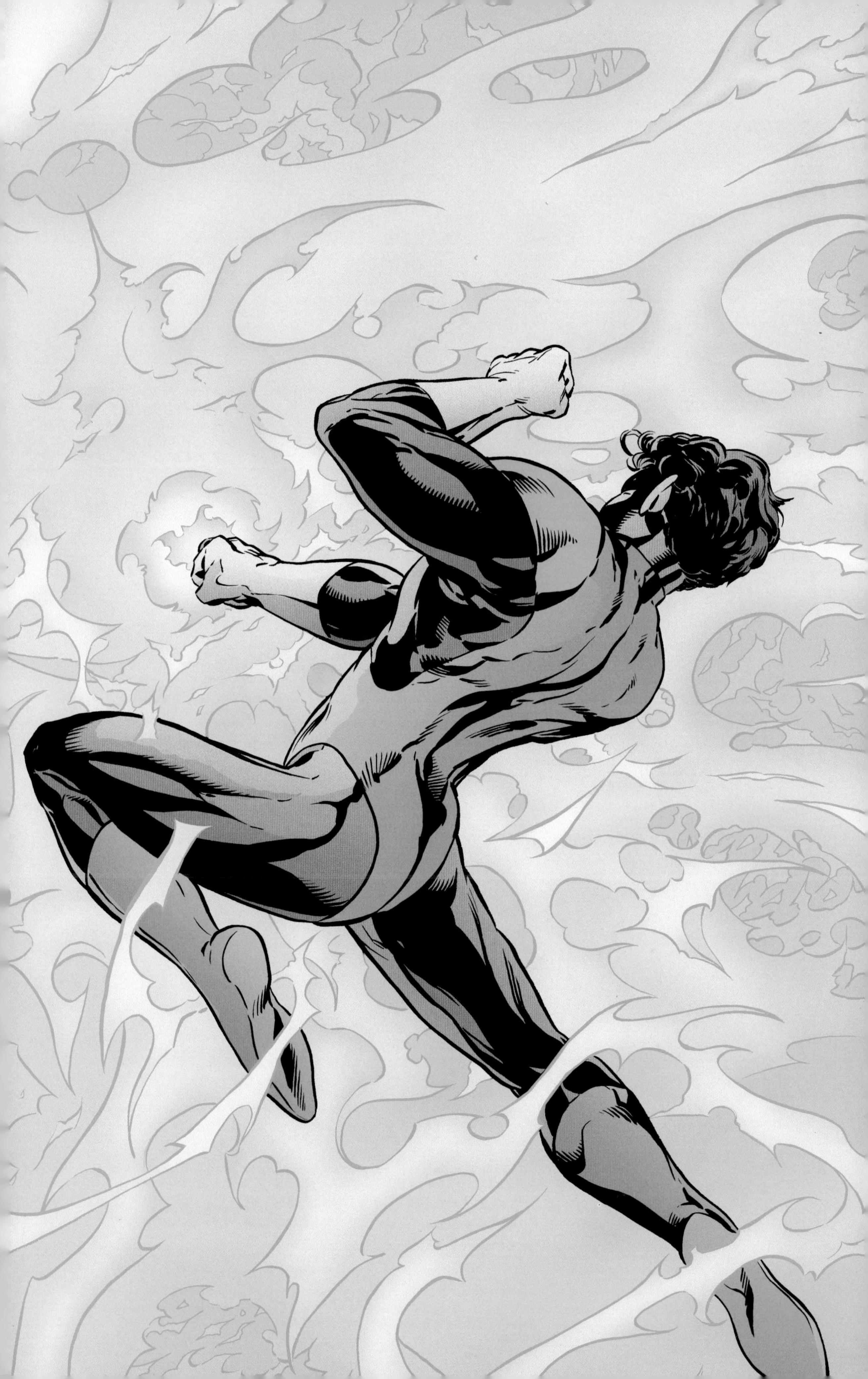

CHAPTER TWO

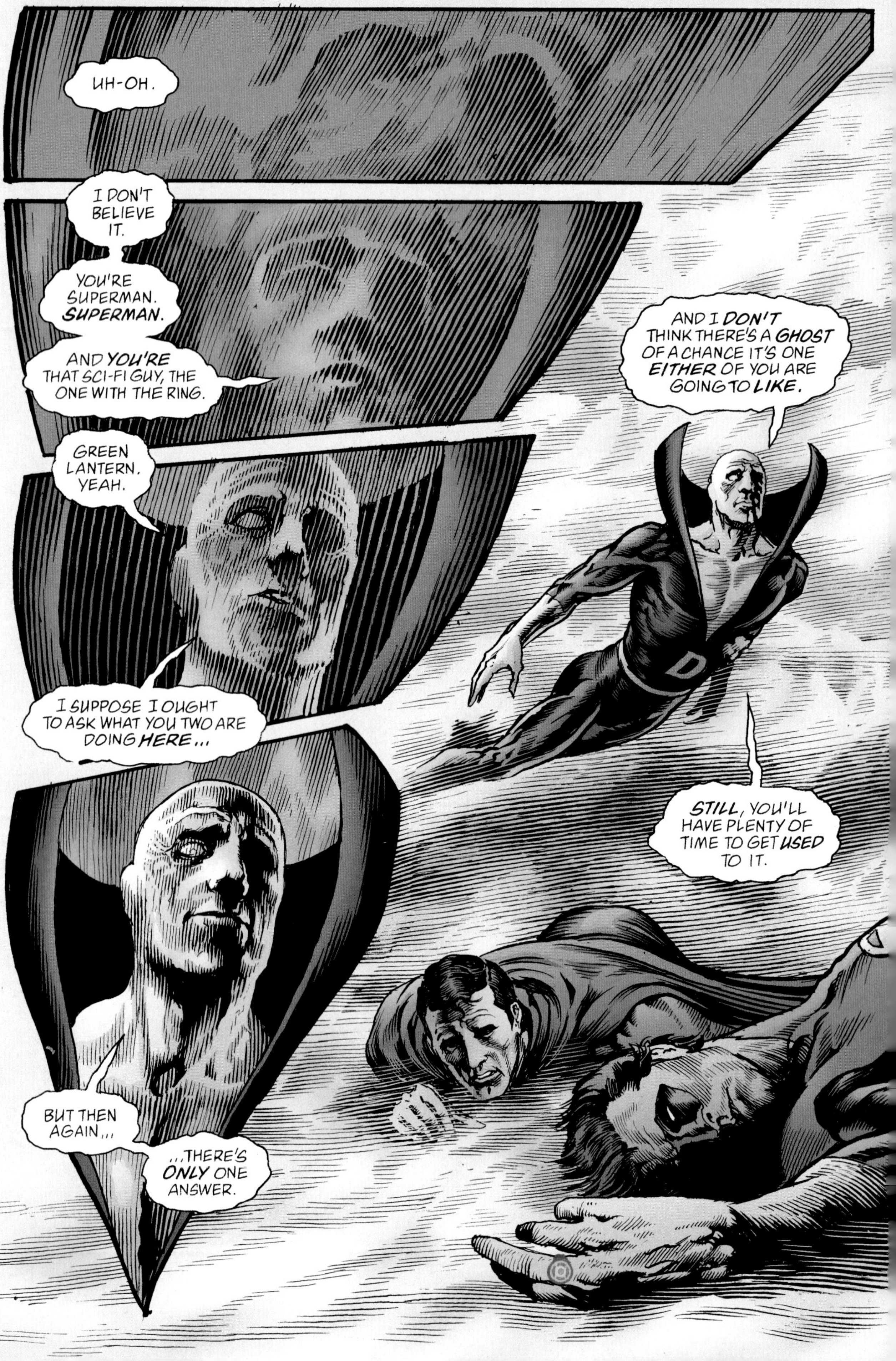
UH-OH.
I DON'T BELIEVE IT.
YOU'RE SUPERMAN. **SUPERMAN**.
AND **YOU'RE** THAT SCI-FI GUY, THE ONE WITH THE RING.
GREEN LANTERN. YEAH.
I SUPPOSE I OUGHT TO ASK WHAT YOU TWO ARE DOING **HERE**...
BUT THEN AGAIN...
...THERE'S **ONLY** ONE ANSWER.
AND I **DON'T** THINK THERE'S A **GHOST** OF A CHANCE IT'S ONE **EITHER** OF YOU ARE GOING TO **LIKE**.
STILL, YOU'LL HAVE PLENTY OF TIME TO GET **USED** TO IT.

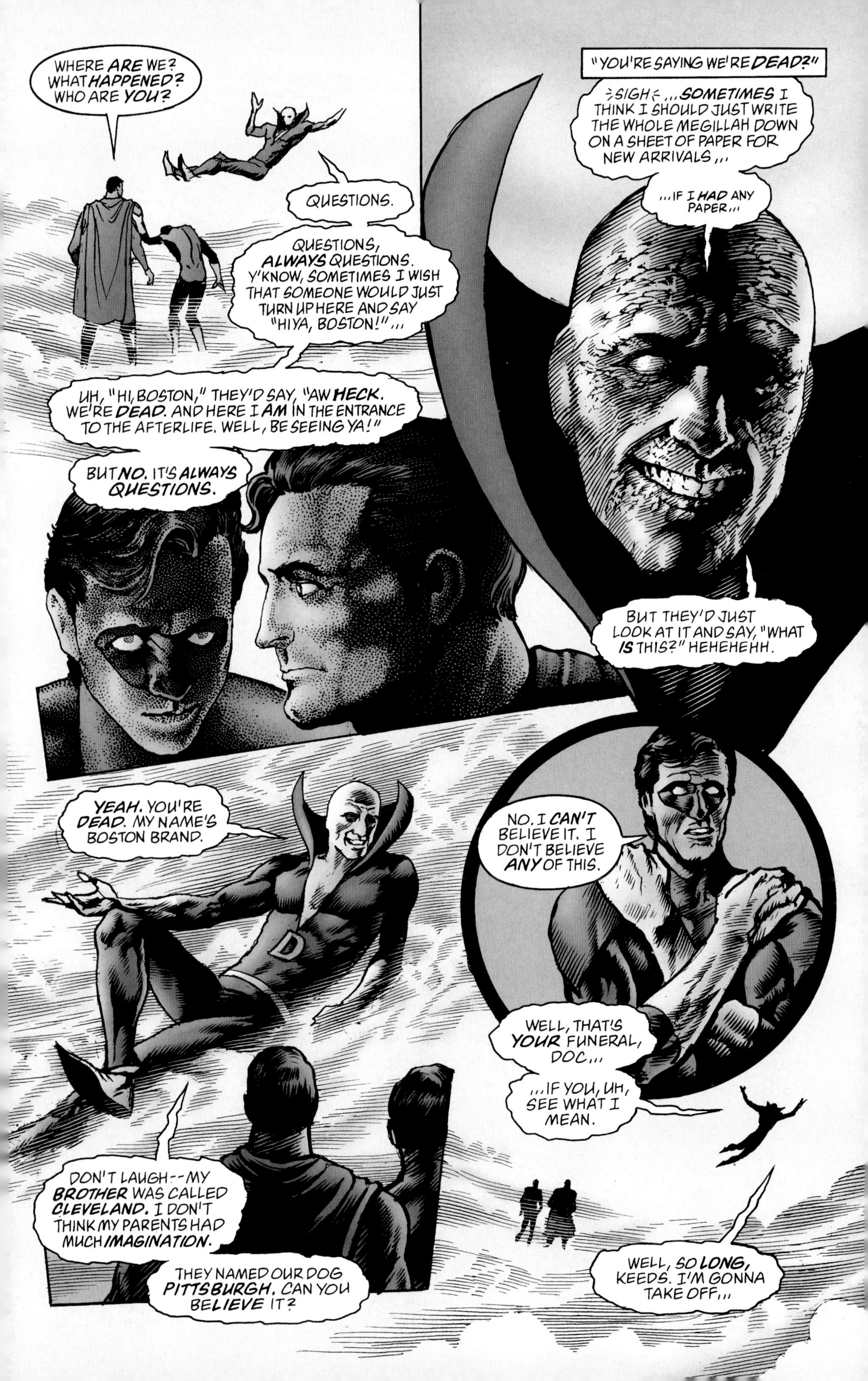
WHERE ARE WE? WHAT HAPPENED? WHO ARE YOU?
QUESTIONS.
QUESTIONS, ALWAYS QUESTIONS. Y'KNOW, SOMETIMES I WISH THAT SOMEONE WOULD JUST TURN UP HERE AND SAY "HIYA, BOSTON!"...
UH, "HI, BOSTON," THEY'D SAY, "AW HECK. WE'RE DEAD. AND HERE I AM IN THE ENTRANCE TO THE AFTERLIFE. WELL, BE SEEING YA!"
BUT NO. IT'S ALWAYS QUESTIONS.
"YOU'RE SAYING WE'RE DEAD?"
≥SIGH≤... SOMETIMES I THINK I SHOULD JUST WRITE THE WHOLE MEGILLAH DOWN ON A SHEET OF PAPER FOR NEW ARRIVALS...
...IF I HAD ANY PAPER...
BUT THEY'D JUST LOOK AT IT AND SAY, "WHAT IS THIS?" HEHEHEHH.
YEAH. YOU'RE DEAD. MY NAME'S BOSTON BRAND.
DON'T LAUGH--MY BROTHER WAS CALLED CLEVELAND. I DON'T THINK MY PARENTS HAD MUCH IMAGINATION.
THEY NAMED OUR DOG PITTSBURGH. CAN YOU BELIEVE IT?
NO. I CAN'T BELIEVE IT. I DON'T BELIEVE ANY OF THIS.
WELL, THAT'S YOUR FUNERAL, DOC...
...IF YOU, UH, SEE WHAT I MEAN.
WELL, SO LONG, KEEDS. I'M GONNA TAKE OFF...

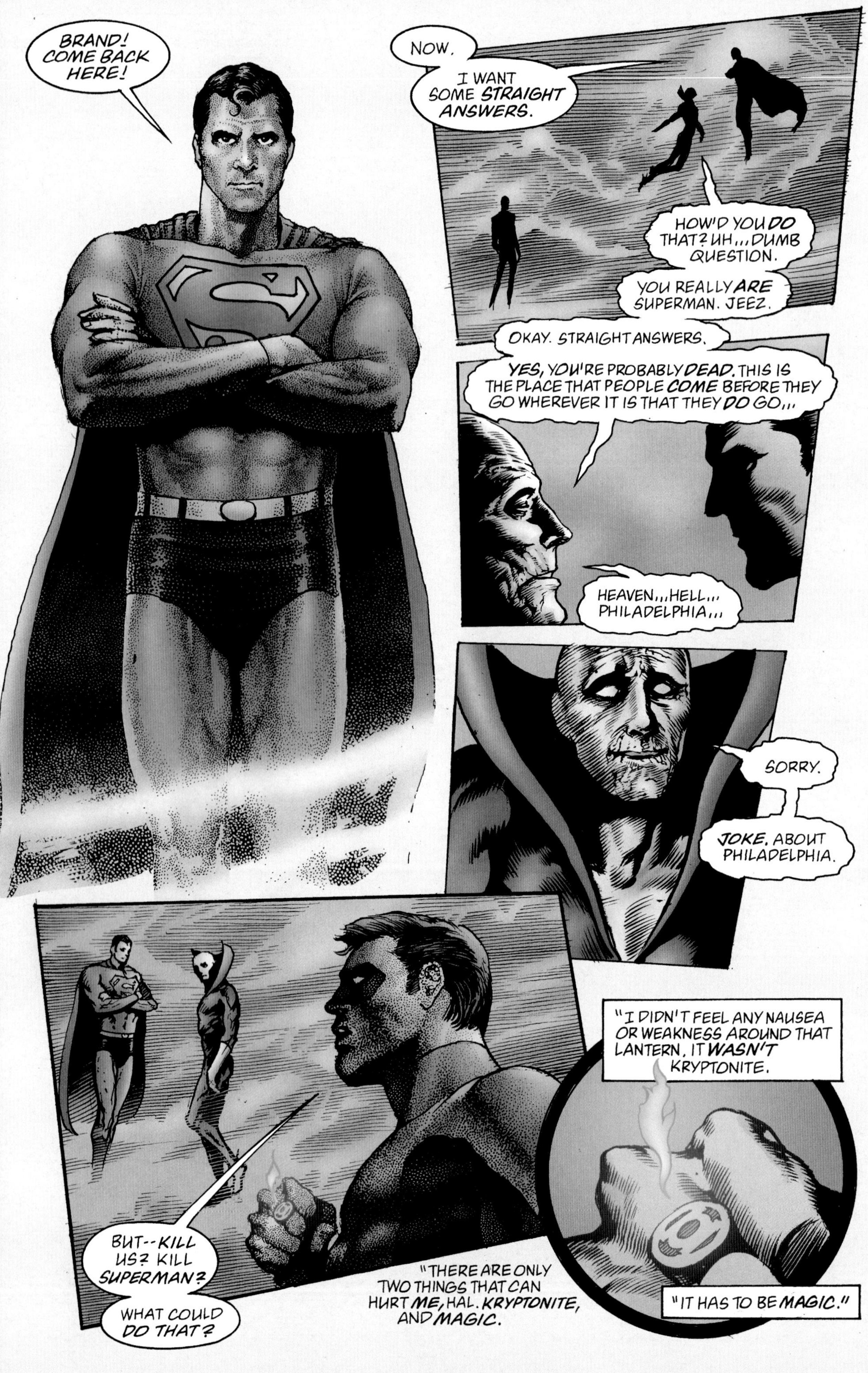

BRAND! COME BACK HERE!
NOW.
I WANT SOME STRAIGHT ANSWERS.
HOW'D YOU DO THAT? UH... DUMB QUESTION.
YOU REALLY ARE SUPERMAN. JEEZ.
OKAY. STRAIGHT ANSWERS.
YES, YOU'RE PROBABLY DEAD. THIS IS THE PLACE THAT PEOPLE COME BEFORE THEY GO WHEREVER IT IS THAT THEY DO GO...
HEAVEN... HELL... PHILADELPHIA...
SORRY.
JOKE. ABOUT PHILADELPHIA.
BUT--KILL US? KILL SUPERMAN?
WHAT COULD DO THAT?
"THERE ARE ONLY TWO THINGS THAT CAN HURT ME, HAL. KRYPTONITE, AND MAGIC.
"I DIDN'T FEEL ANY NAUSEA OR WEAKNESS AROUND THAT LANTERN. IT WASN'T KRYPTONITE.
"IT HAS TO BE MAGIC."

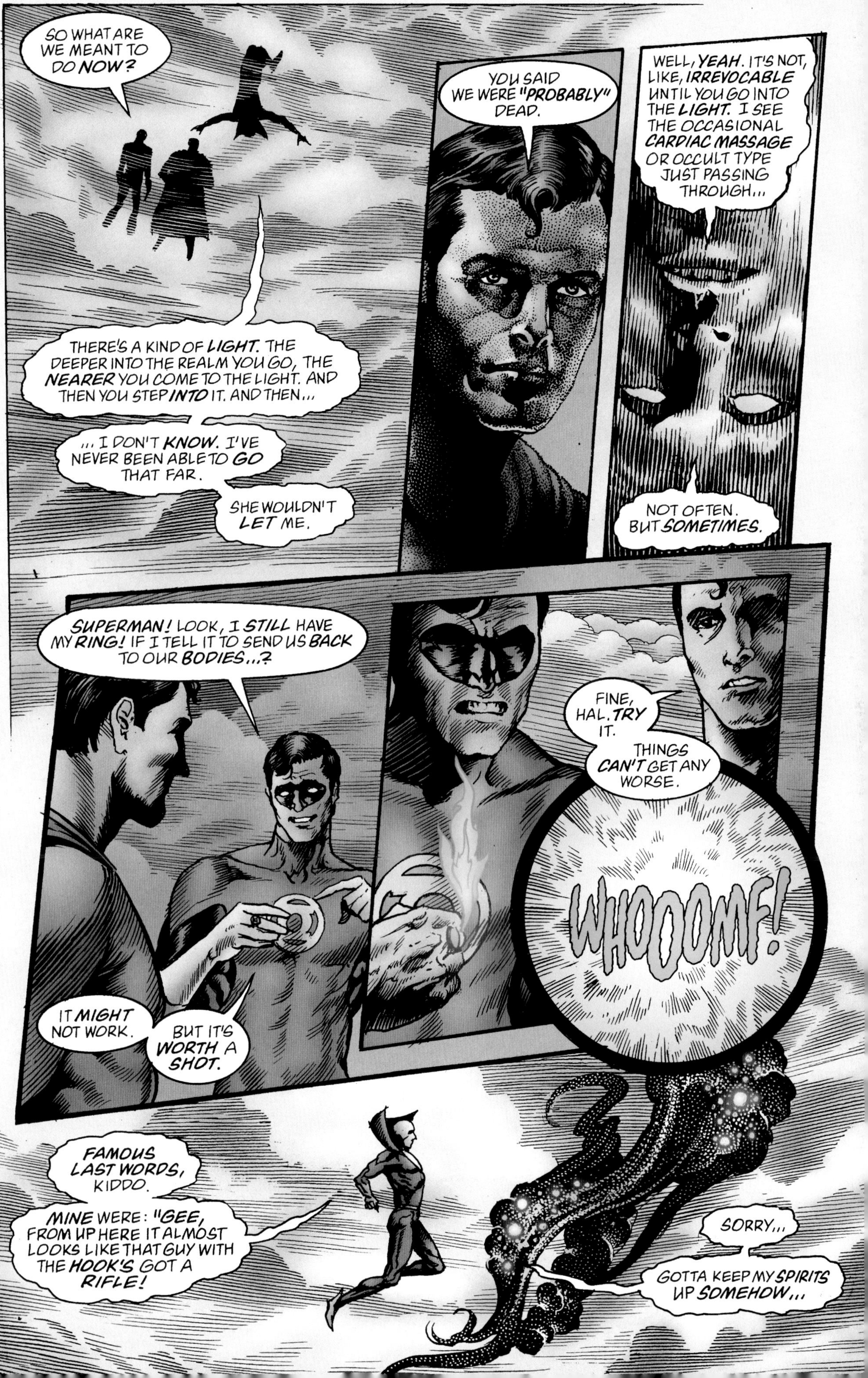

SO WHAT ARE WE MEANT TO DO NOW?
THERE'S A KIND OF LIGHT. THE DEEPER INTO THE REALM YOU GO, THE NEARER YOU COME TO THE LIGHT. AND THEN YOU STEP INTO IT. AND THEN...
...I DON'T KNOW. I'VE NEVER BEEN ABLE TO GO THAT FAR.
SHE WOULDN'T LET ME.
YOU SAID WE WERE "PROBABLY" DEAD.
WELL, YEAH. IT'S NOT, LIKE, IRREVOCABLE UNTIL YOU GO INTO THE LIGHT. I SEE THE OCCASIONAL CARDIAC MASSAGE OR OCCULT TYPE JUST PASSING THROUGH...
NOT OFTEN. BUT SOMETIMES.
SUPERMAN! LOOK, I STILL HAVE MY RING! IF I TELL IT TO SEND US BACK TO OUR BODIES...?
IT MIGHT NOT WORK.
BUT IT'S WORTH A SHOT.
FINE, HAL. TRY IT.
THINGS CAN'T GET ANY WORSE.
WHOOOMF!
FAMOUS LAST WORDS, KIDDO.
MINE WERE: "GEE, FROM UP HERE IT ALMOST LOOKS LIKE THAT GUY WITH THE HOOK'S GOT A RIFLE!
SORRY...
GOTTA KEEP MY SPIRITS UP SOMEHOW...

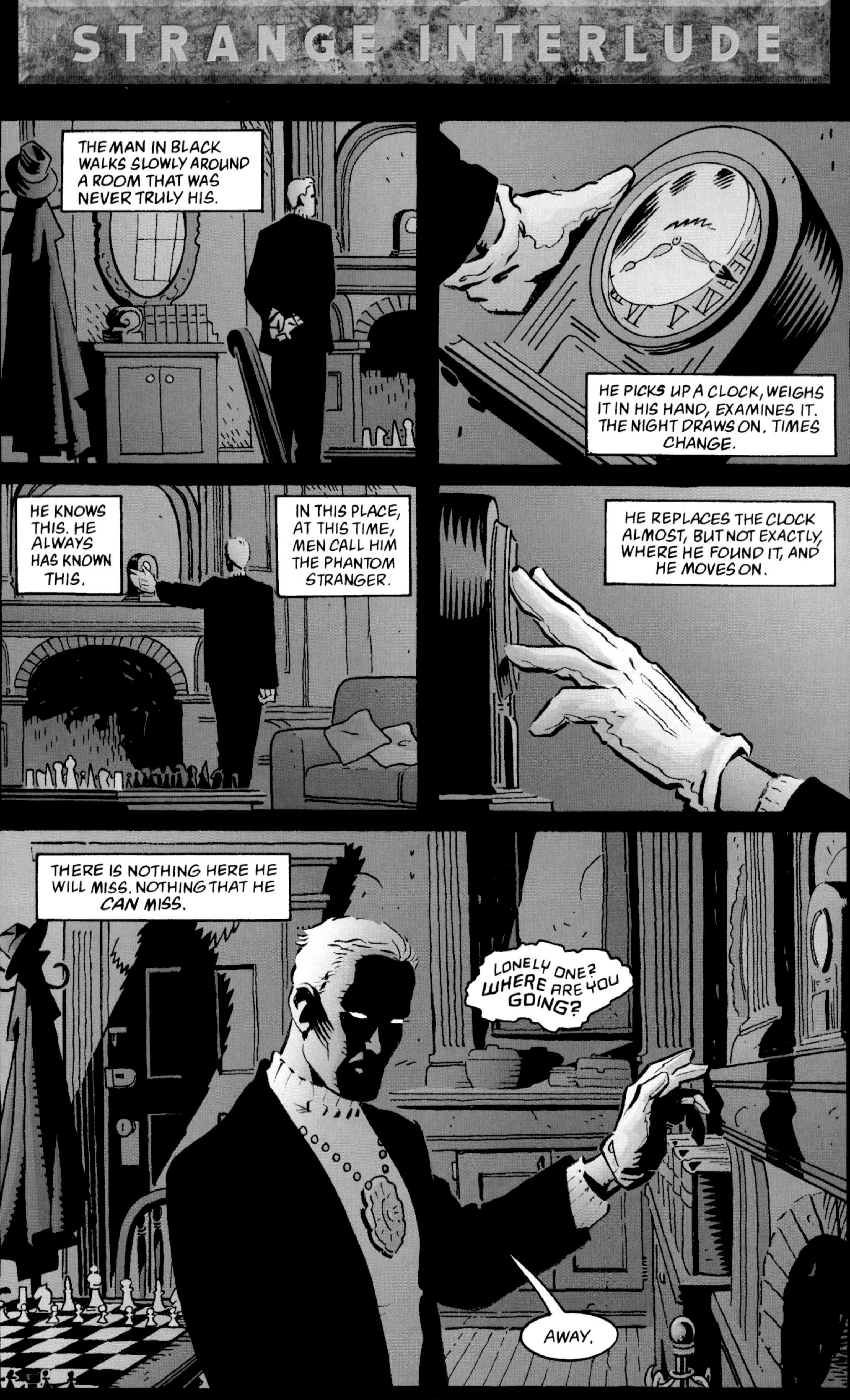
STRANGE INTERLUDE
THE MAN IN BLACK WALKS SLOWLY AROUND A ROOM THAT WAS NEVER TRULY HIS.
HE PICKS UP A CLOCK, WEIGHS IT IN HIS HAND, EXAMINES IT. THE NIGHT DRAWS ON. TIMES CHANGE.
HE KNOWS THIS. HE ALWAYS HAS KNOWN THIS.
IN THIS PLACE, AT THIS TIME, MEN CALL HIM THE PHANTOM STRANGER.
HE REPLACES THE CLOCK ALMOST, BUT NOT EXACTLY, WHERE HE FOUND IT, AND HE MOVES ON.
THERE IS NOTHING HERE HE WILL MISS. NOTHING THAT HE CAN MISS.
LONELY ONE? WHERE ARE YOU GOING?
AWAY.

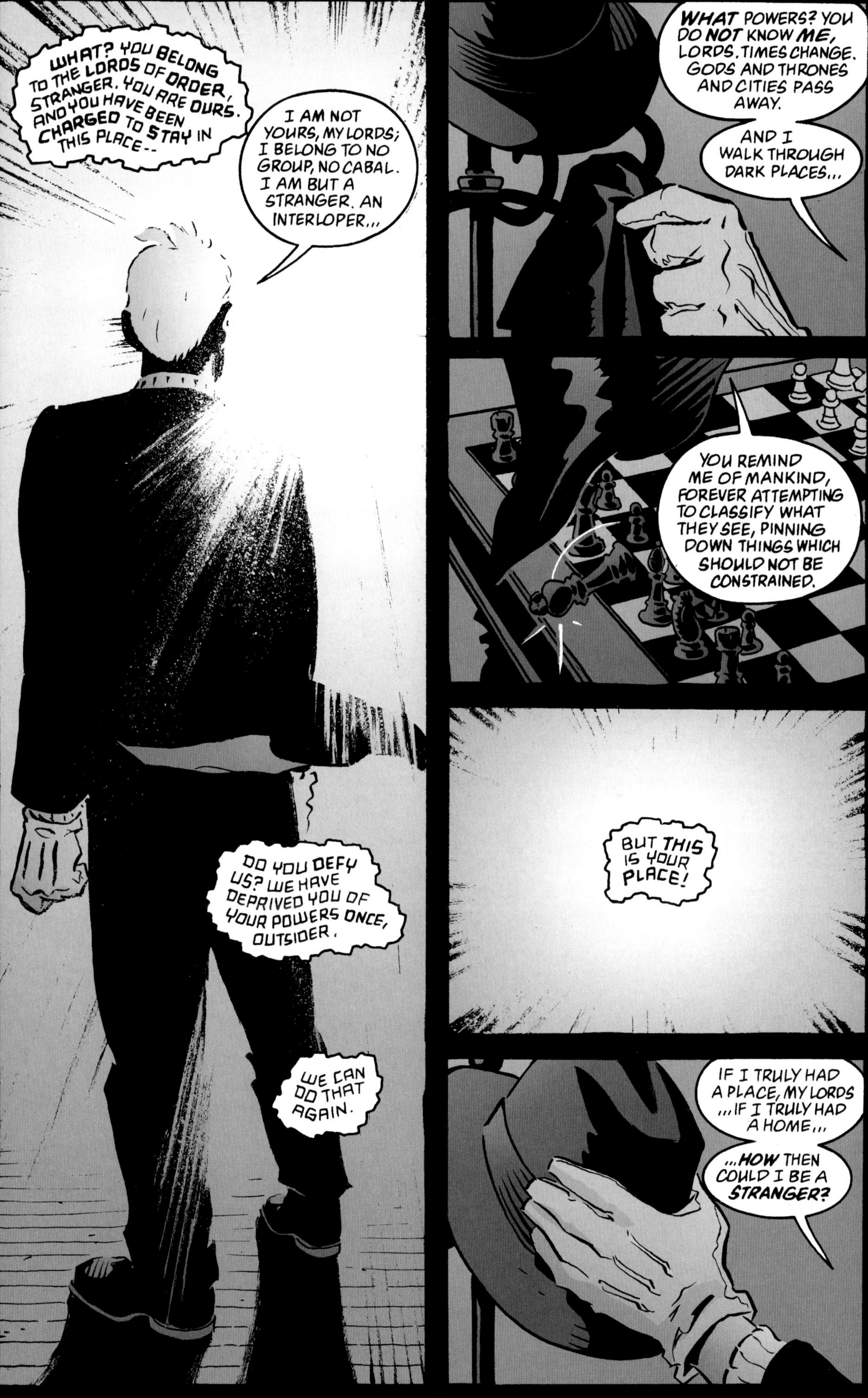

WHAT? YOU BELONG TO THE LORDS OF ORDER, STRANGER. YOU ARE OURS. AND YOU HAVE BEEN CHARGED TO STAY IN THIS PLACE--
I AM NOT YOURS, MY LORDS; I BELONG TO NO GROUP, NO CABAL. I AM BUT A STRANGER. AN INTERLOPER...
DO YOU DEFY US? WE HAVE DEPRIVED YOU OF YOUR POWERS ONCE, OUTSIDER.
WE CAN DO THAT AGAIN.
WHAT POWERS? YOU DO NOT KNOW ME, LORDS. TIMES CHANGE. GODS AND THRONES AND CITIES PASS AWAY.
AND I WALK THROUGH DARK PLACES...
YOU REMIND ME OF MANKIND, FOREVER ATTEMPTING TO CLASSIFY WHAT THEY SEE, PINNING DOWN THINGS WHICH SHOULD NOT BE CONSTRAINED.
BUT THIS IS YOUR PLACE!
IF I TRULY HAD A PLACE, MY LORDS ...IF I TRULY HAD A HOME...
...HOW THEN COULD I BE A STRANGER?

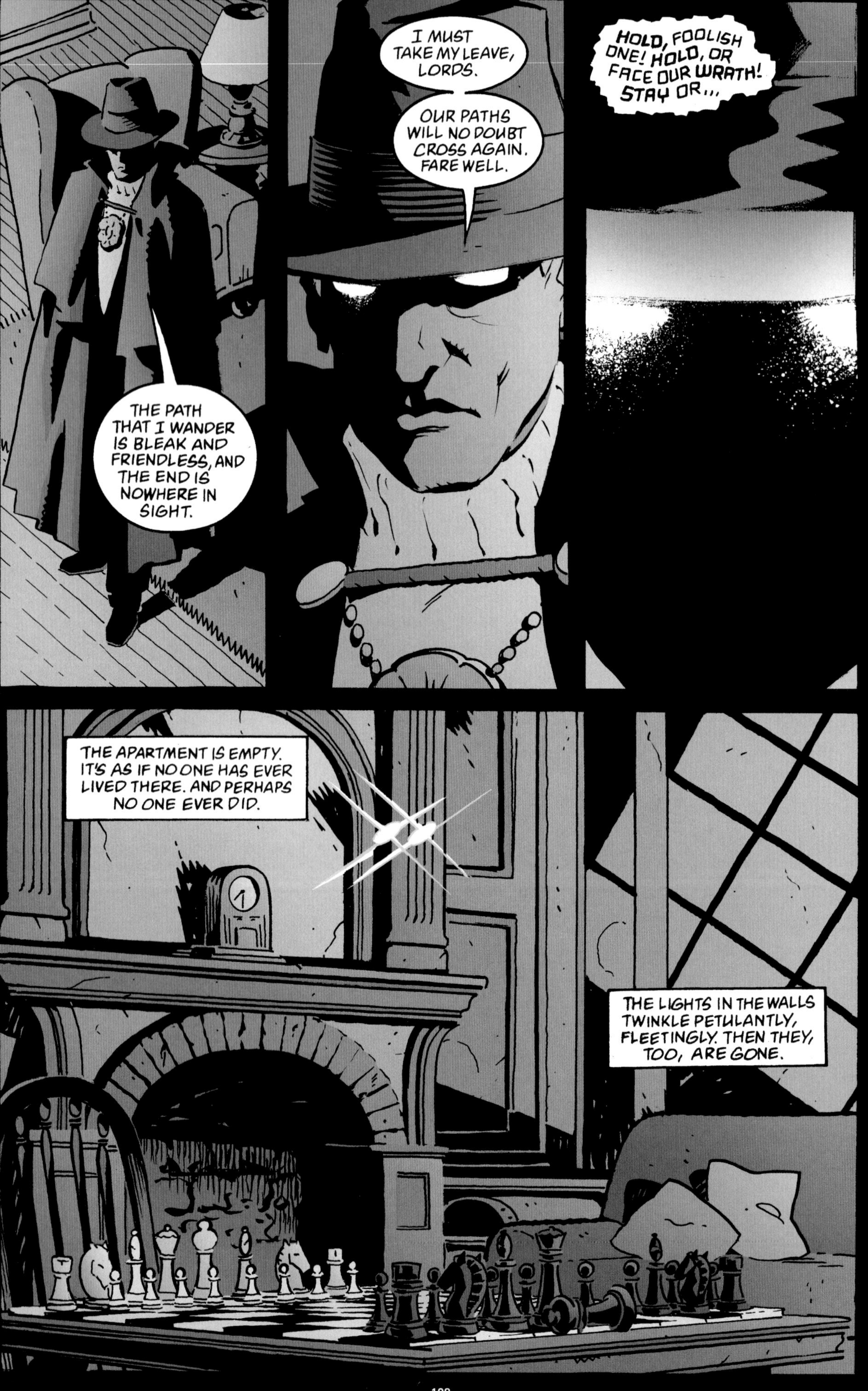
THE PATH THAT I WANDER IS BLEAK AND FRIENDLESS, AND THE END IS NOWHERE IN SIGHT.
I MUST TAKE MY LEAVE, LORDS.
OUR PATHS WILL NO DOUBT CROSS AGAIN. FARE WELL.
HOLD, FOOLISH ONE! HOLD, OR FACE OUR WRATH! STAY OR...
THE APARTMENT IS EMPTY. IT'S AS IF NO ONE HAS EVER LIVED THERE. AND PERHAPS NO ONE EVER DID.
THE LIGHTS IN THE WALLS TWINKLE PETULANTLY, FLEETINGLY. THEN THEY, TOO, ARE GONE.

CHAPTER THREE

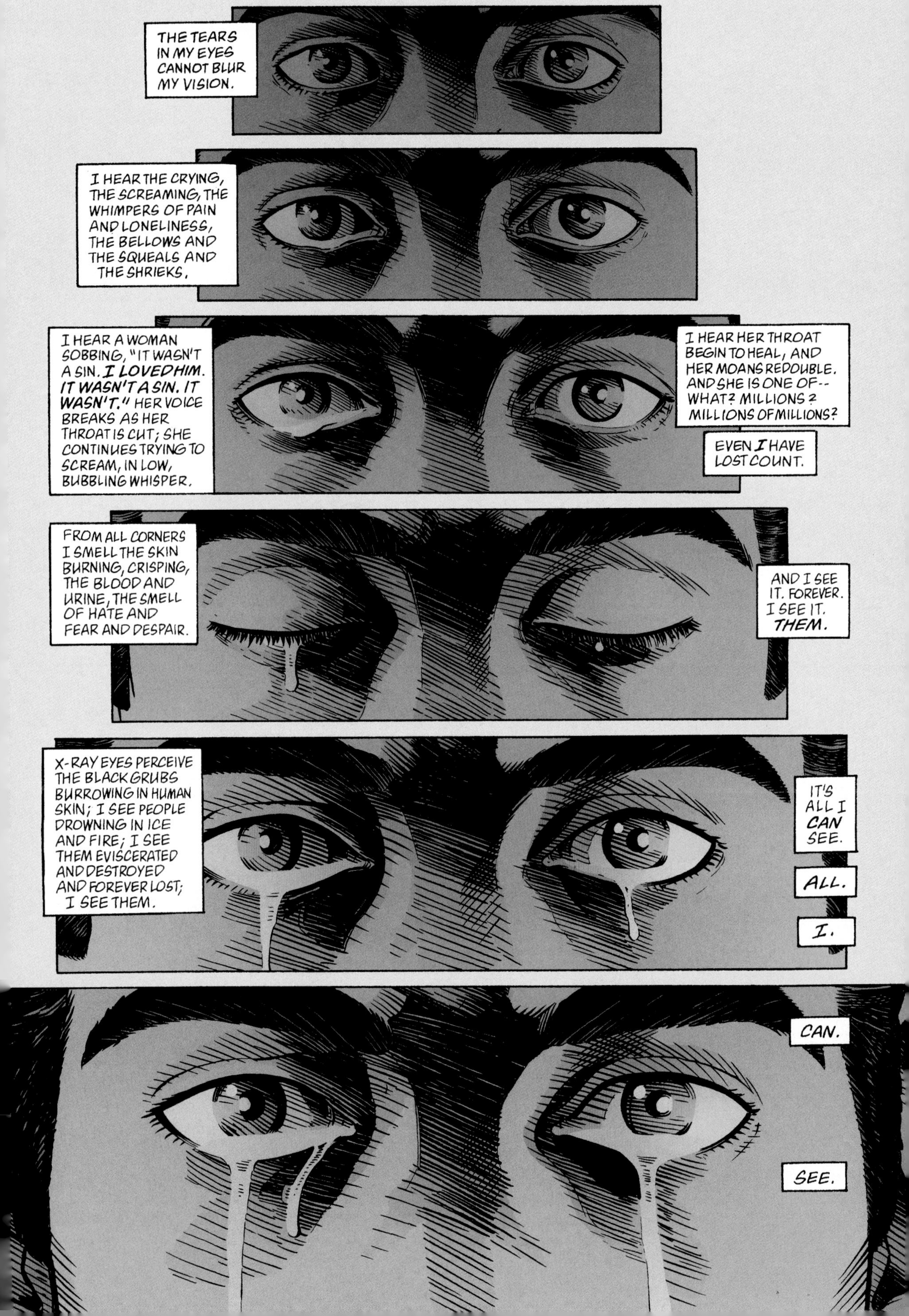
THE TEARS IN MY EYES CANNOT BLUR MY VISION.
I HEAR THE CRYING, THE SCREAMING, THE WHIMPERS OF PAIN AND LONELINESS, THE BELLOWS AND THE SQUEALS AND THE SHRIEKS.
I HEAR A WOMAN SOBBING, "IT WASN'T A SIN. I LOVED HIM. IT WASN'T A SIN. IT WASN'T." HER VOICE BREAKS AS HER THROAT IS CUT; SHE CONTINUES TRYING TO SCREAM, IN LOW, BUBBLING WHISPER.
I HEAR HER THROAT BEGIN TO HEAL, AND HER MOANS REDOUBLE. AND SHE IS ONE OF-- WHAT? MILLIONS? MILLIONS OF MILLIONS?
EVEN I HAVE LOST COUNT.
FROM ALL CORNERS I SMELL THE SKIN BURNING, CRISPING, THE BLOOD AND URINE, THE SMELL OF HATE AND FEAR AND DESPAIR.
AND I SEE IT. FOREVER. I SEE IT. THEM.
X-RAY EYES PERCEIVE THE BLACK GRUBS BURROWING IN HUMAN SKIN; I SEE PEOPLE DROWNING IN ICE AND FIRE; I SEE THEM EVISCERATED AND DESTROYED AND FOREVER LOST; I SEE THEM.
IT'S ALL I CAN SEE.
ALL.
I.
CAN.
SEE.

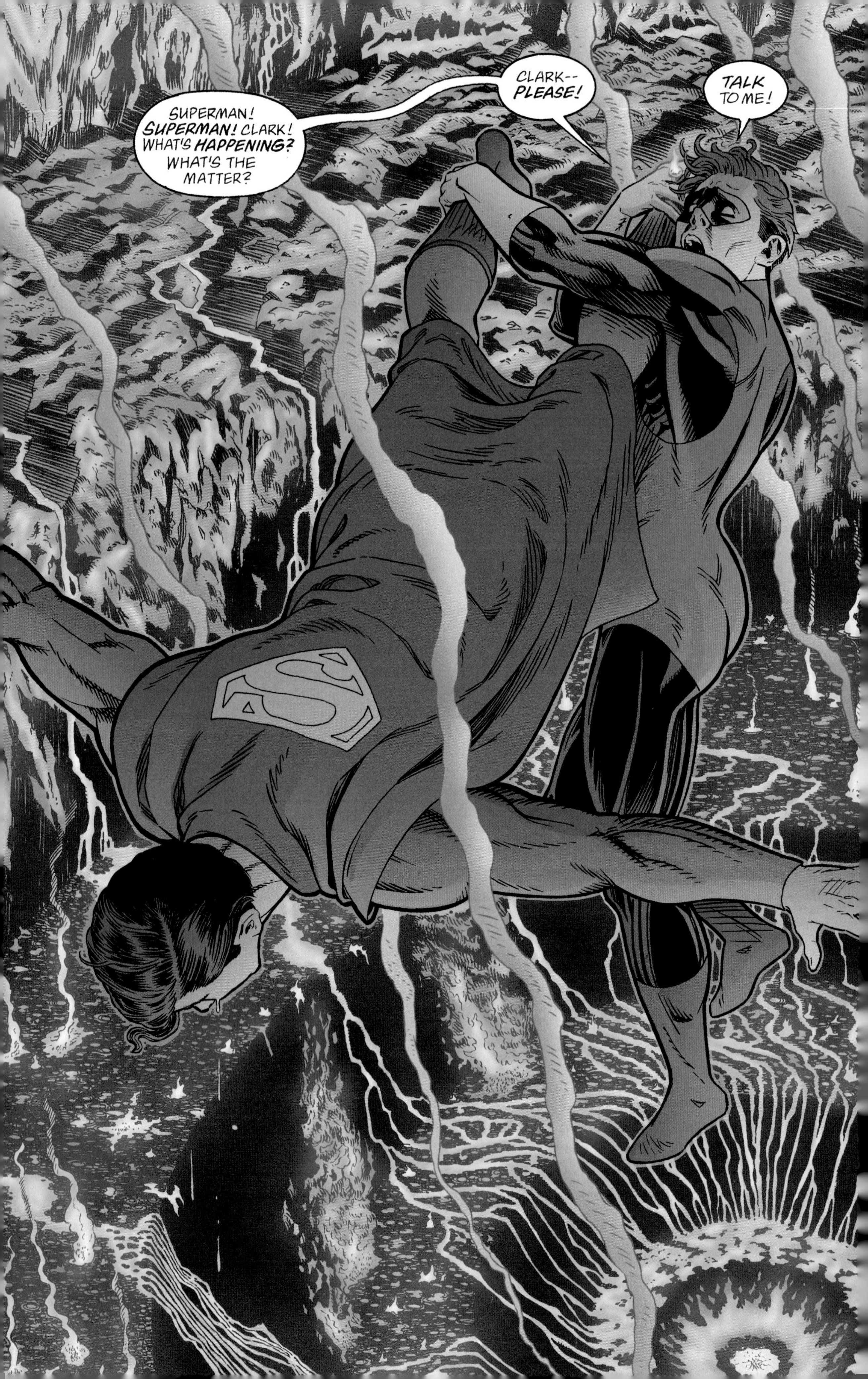
SUPERMAN! **SUPERMAN!** CLARK! WHAT'S **HAPPENING?** WHAT'S THE MATTER?
CLARK-- **PLEASE!**
TALK TO ME!

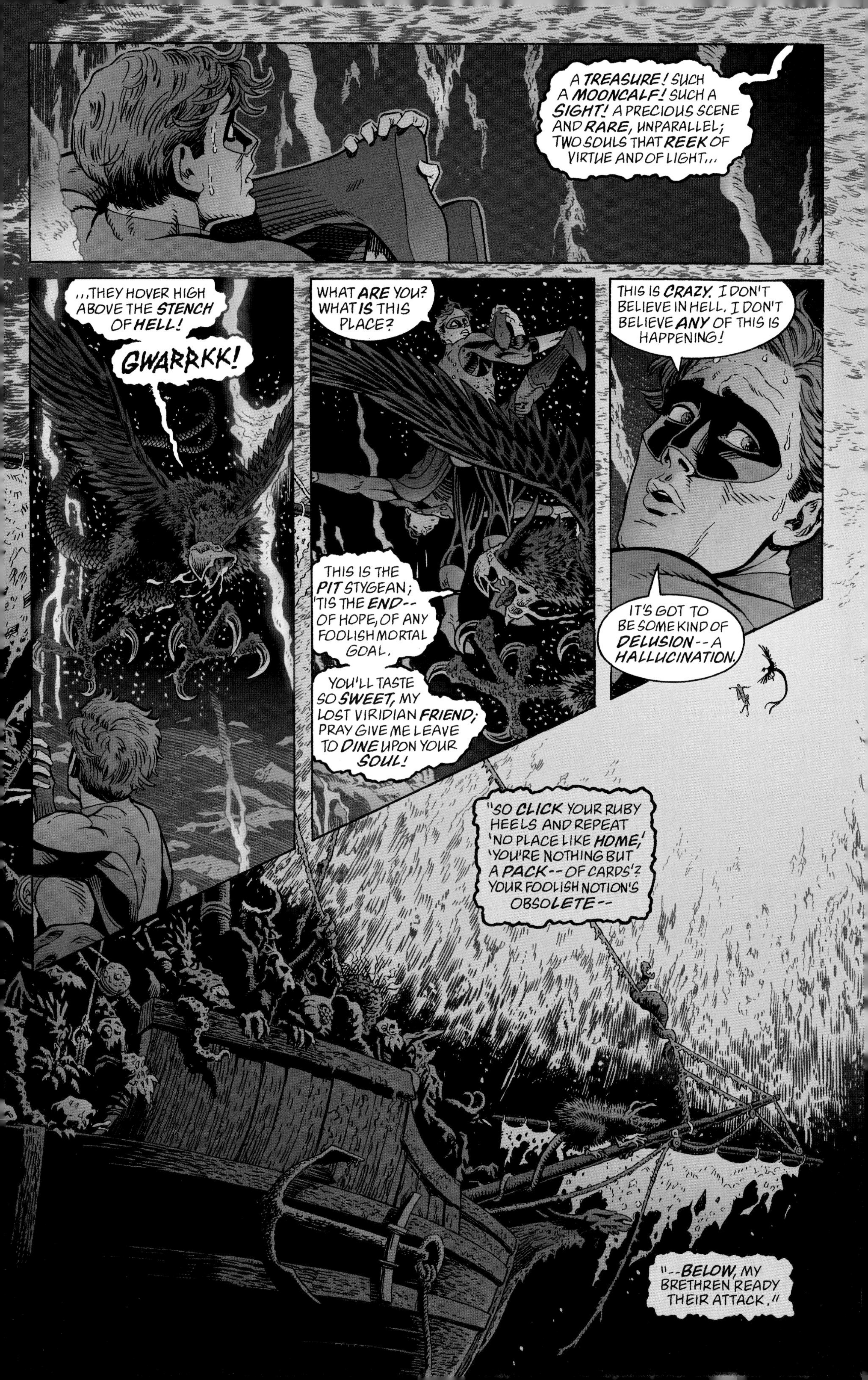
A TREASURE! SUCH A MOONCALF! SUCH A SIGHT! A PRECIOUS SCENE AND RARE, UNPARALLEL; TWO SOULS THAT REEK OF VIRTUE AND OF LIGHT...
...THEY HOVER HIGH ABOVE THE STENCH OF HELL!
GWARRKK!
WHAT ARE YOU? WHAT IS THIS PLACE?
THIS IS THE PIT STYGEAN; 'TIS THE END-- OF HOPE, OF ANY FOOLISH MORTAL GOAL.
YOU'LL TASTE SO SWEET, MY LOST VIRIDIAN FRIEND; PRAY GIVE ME LEAVE TO DINE UPON YOUR SOUL!
THIS IS CRAZY. I DON'T BELIEVE IN HELL. I DON'T BELIEVE ANY OF THIS IS HAPPENING!
IT'S GOT TO BE SOME KIND OF DELUSION--A HALLUCINATION.
"SO CLICK YOUR RUBY HEELS AND REPEAT 'NO PLACE LIKE HOME,' 'YOU'RE NOTHING BUT A PACK--OF CARDS'? YOUR FOOLISH NOTION'S OBSOLETE--
"--BELOW, MY BRETHREN READY THEIR ATTACK."

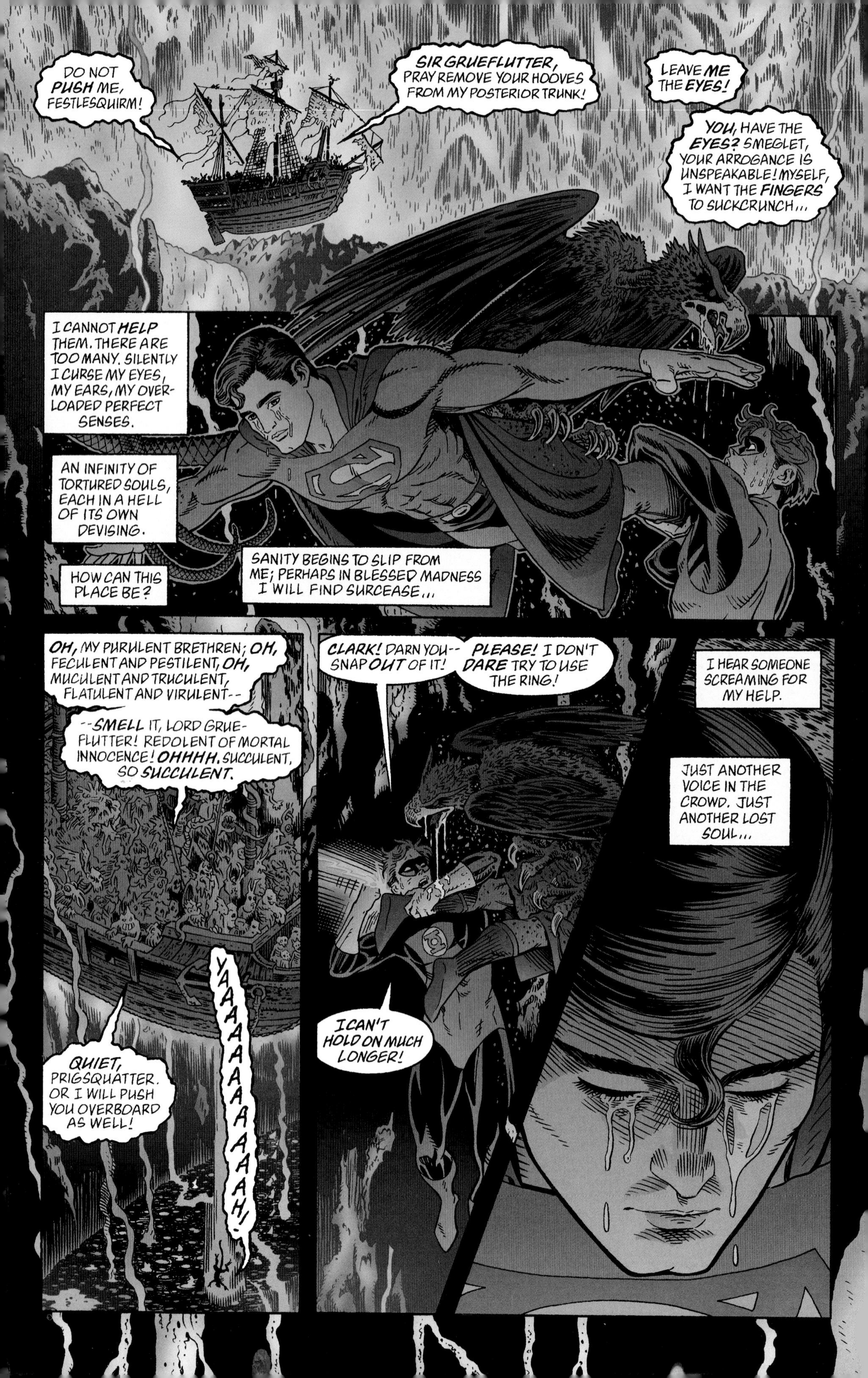

DO NOT PUSH ME, FESTLESQUIRM!
SIR GRUEFLUTTER, PRAY REMOVE YOUR HOOVES FROM MY POSTERIOR TRUNK!
LEAVE ME THE EYES!
YOU, HAVE THE EYES? SMEGLET, YOUR ARROGANCE IS UNSPEAKABLE! MYSELF, I WANT THE FINGERS TO SUCKCRUNCH...
I CANNOT HELP THEM. THERE ARE TOO MANY. SILENTLY I CURSE MY EYES, MY EARS, MY OVER-LOADED PERFECT SENSES.
AN INFINITY OF TORTURED SOULS, EACH IN A HELL OF ITS OWN DEVISING.
HOW CAN THIS PLACE BE?
SANITY BEGINS TO SLIP FROM ME; PERHAPS IN BLESSED MADNESS I WILL FIND SURCEASE...
OH, MY PURULENT BRETHREN; OH, FECULENT AND PESTILENT, OH, MUCULENT AND TRUCULENT, FLATULENT AND VIRULENT--
--SMELL IT, LORD GRUE-FLUTTER! REDOLENT OF MORTAL INNOCENCE! OHHHH. SUCCULENT, SO SUCCULENT.
YAAAAAAAAAAAAAH!
QUIET, PRIGSQUATTER. OR I WILL PUSH YOU OVERBOARD AS WELL!
CLARK! DARN YOU-- SNAP OUT OF IT!
PLEASE! I DON'T DARE TRY TO USE THE RING!
I CAN'T HOLD ON MUCH LONGER!
I HEAR SOMEONE SCREAMING FOR MY HELP.
JUST ANOTHER VOICE IN THE CROWD. JUST ANOTHER LOST SOUL...

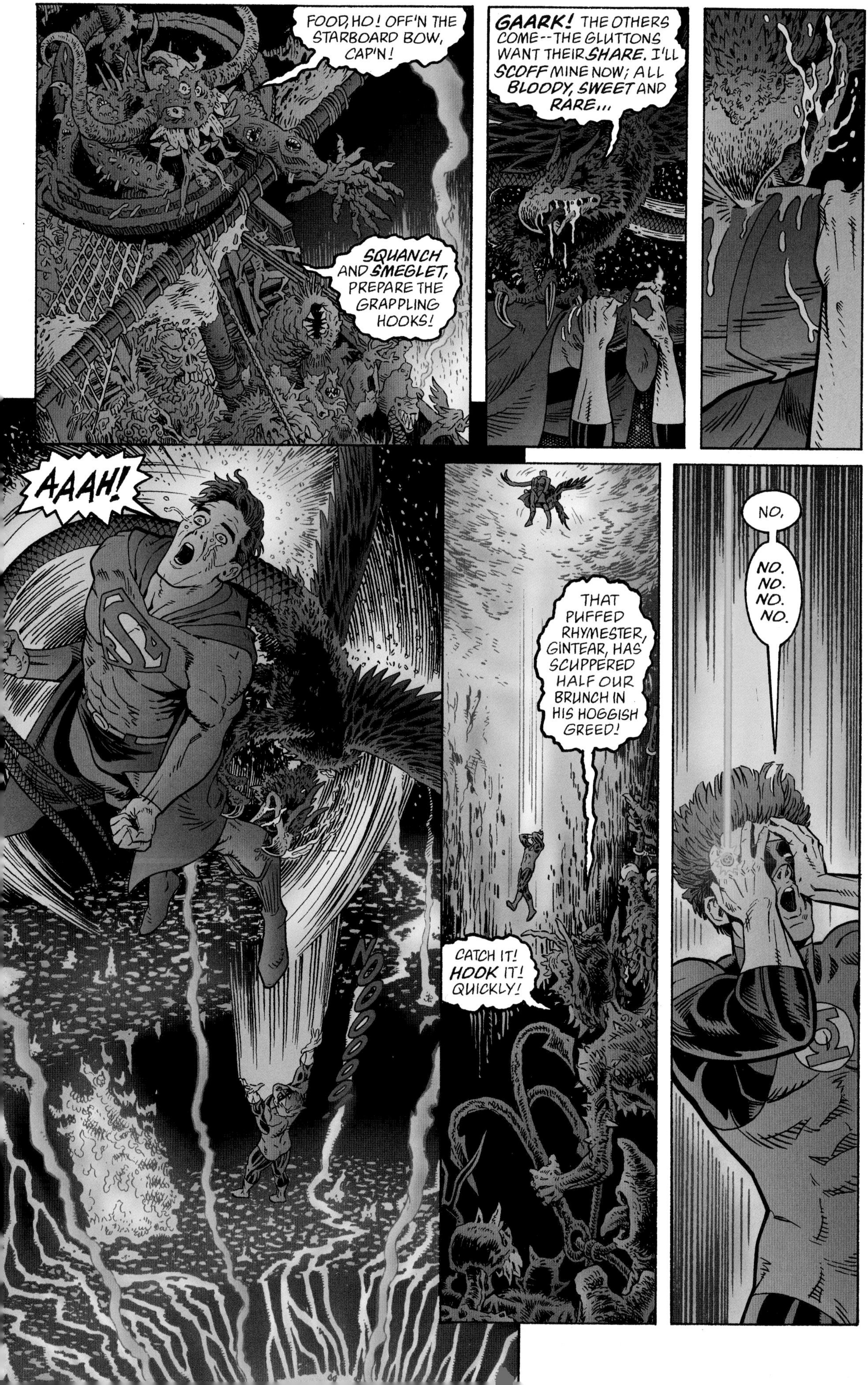
FOOD, HO! OFF'N THE STARBOARD BOW, CAP'N!
SQUANCH AND SMEGLET, PREPARE THE GRAPPLING HOOKS!
GAARK! THE OTHERS COME--THE GLUTTONS WANT THEIR SHARE. I'LL SCOFF MINE NOW; ALL BLOODY, SWEET AND RARE...
AAAH!
THAT PUFFED RHYMESTER, GINTEAR, HAS SCUPPERED HALF OUR BRUNCH IN HIS HOGGISH GREED!
CATCH IT! HOOK IT! QUICKLY!
NO,
NO. NO. NO. NO.

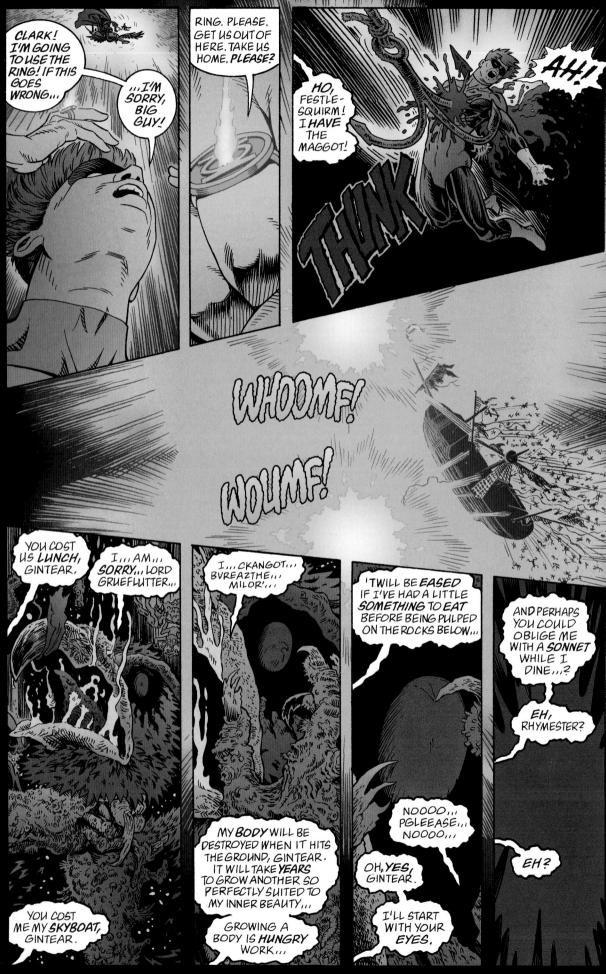

CLARK! I'M GOING TO USE THE RING! IF THIS GOES WRONG...

...I'M SORRY, BIG GUY!

RING. PLEASE. GET US OUT OF HERE. TAKE US HOME. PLEASE?

HO, FESTLE-SQUIRM! I HAVE THE MAGGOT!

THUNK

AH!

WHOOMF!

WOUMF!

YOU COST US LUNCH, GINTEAR.

I...AM... SORRY... LORD GRUEFLUTTER...

YOU COST ME MY SKYBOAT, GINTEAR.

I...CKANGOT... BVREAZTHE MILOR'...

MY BODY WILL BE DESTROYED WHEN IT HITS THE GROUND, GINTEAR. IT WILL TAKE YEARS TO GROW ANOTHER SO PERFECTLY SUITED TO MY INNER BEAUTY...

GROWING A BODY IS HUNGRY WORK...

'TWILL BE EASED IF I'VE HAD A LITTLE SOMETHING TO EAT BEFORE BEING PULPED ON THE ROCKS BELOW...

NOOOO... PGLEEASE... NOOOO...

OH, YES, GINTEAR.

I'LL START WITH YOUR EYES.

AND PERHAPS YOU COULD OBLIGE ME WITH A SONNET WHILE I DINE...?

EH, RHYMESTER?

EH?

STRANGE INTERLUDE

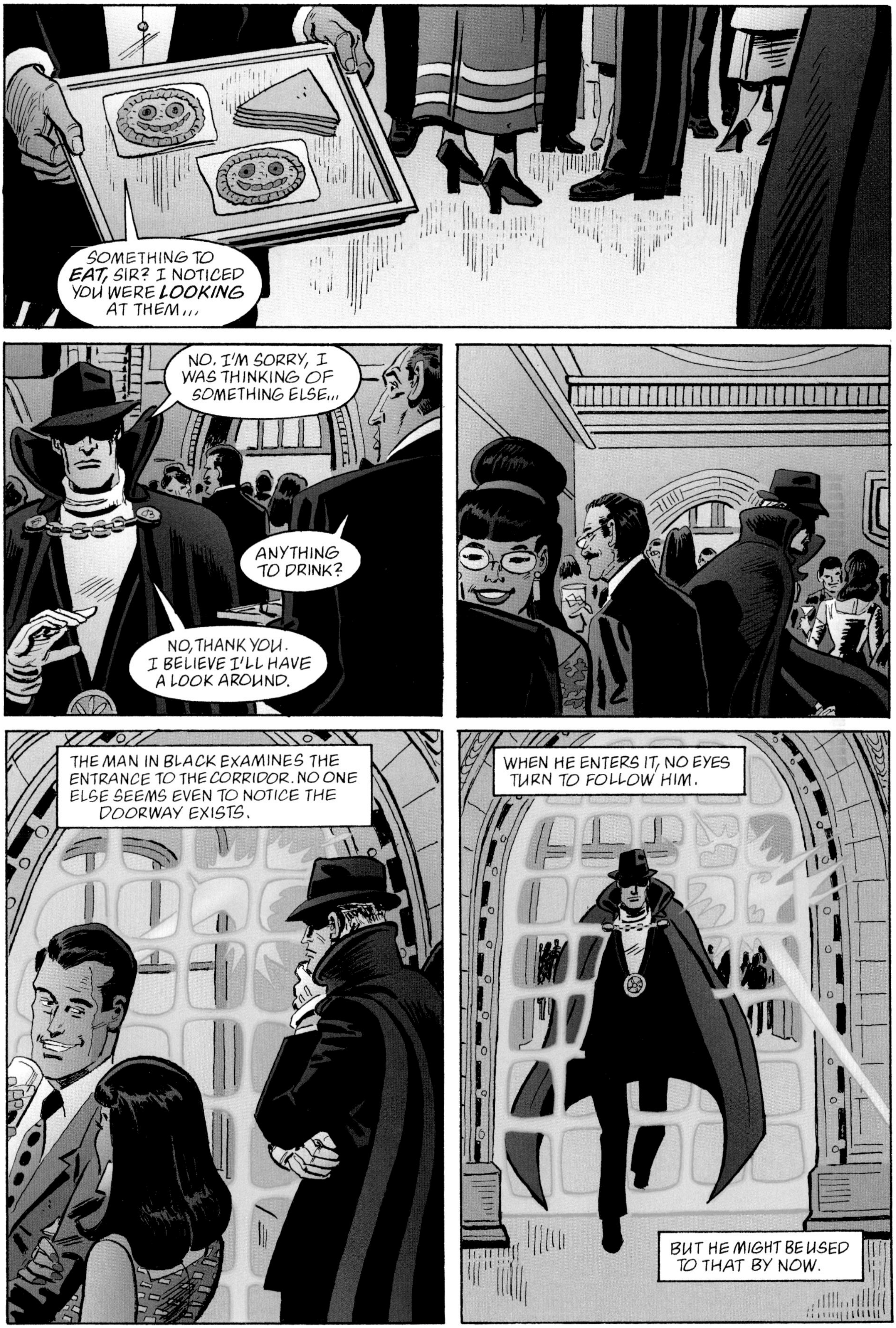

SOMETHING TO EAT, SIR? I NOTICED YOU WERE LOOKING AT THEM...
NO. I'M SORRY, I WAS THINKING OF SOMETHING ELSE...
ANYTHING TO DRINK?
NO, THANK YOU. I BELIEVE I'LL HAVE A LOOK AROUND.
THE MAN IN BLACK EXAMINES THE ENTRANCE TO THE CORRIDOR. NO ONE ELSE SEEMS EVEN TO NOTICE THE DOORWAY EXISTS.
WHEN HE ENTERS IT, NO EYES TURN TO FOLLOW HIM.
BUT HE MIGHT BE USED TO THAT BY NOW.

THEY ARE BADLY DAMAGED, THE OAN PAWN EVEN MORE THAN THE ALIEN. ONE REPAIRS THEM AS BEST ONE CAN.

IT IS THE LEAST ONE CAN DO.

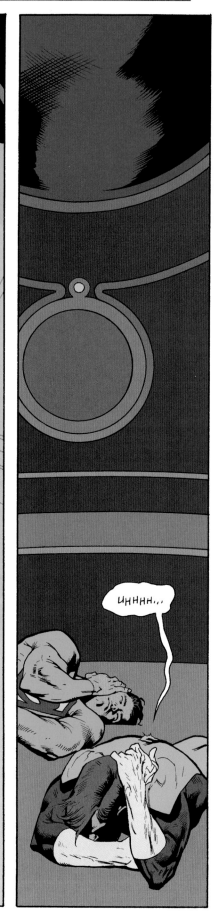

UHHHH...

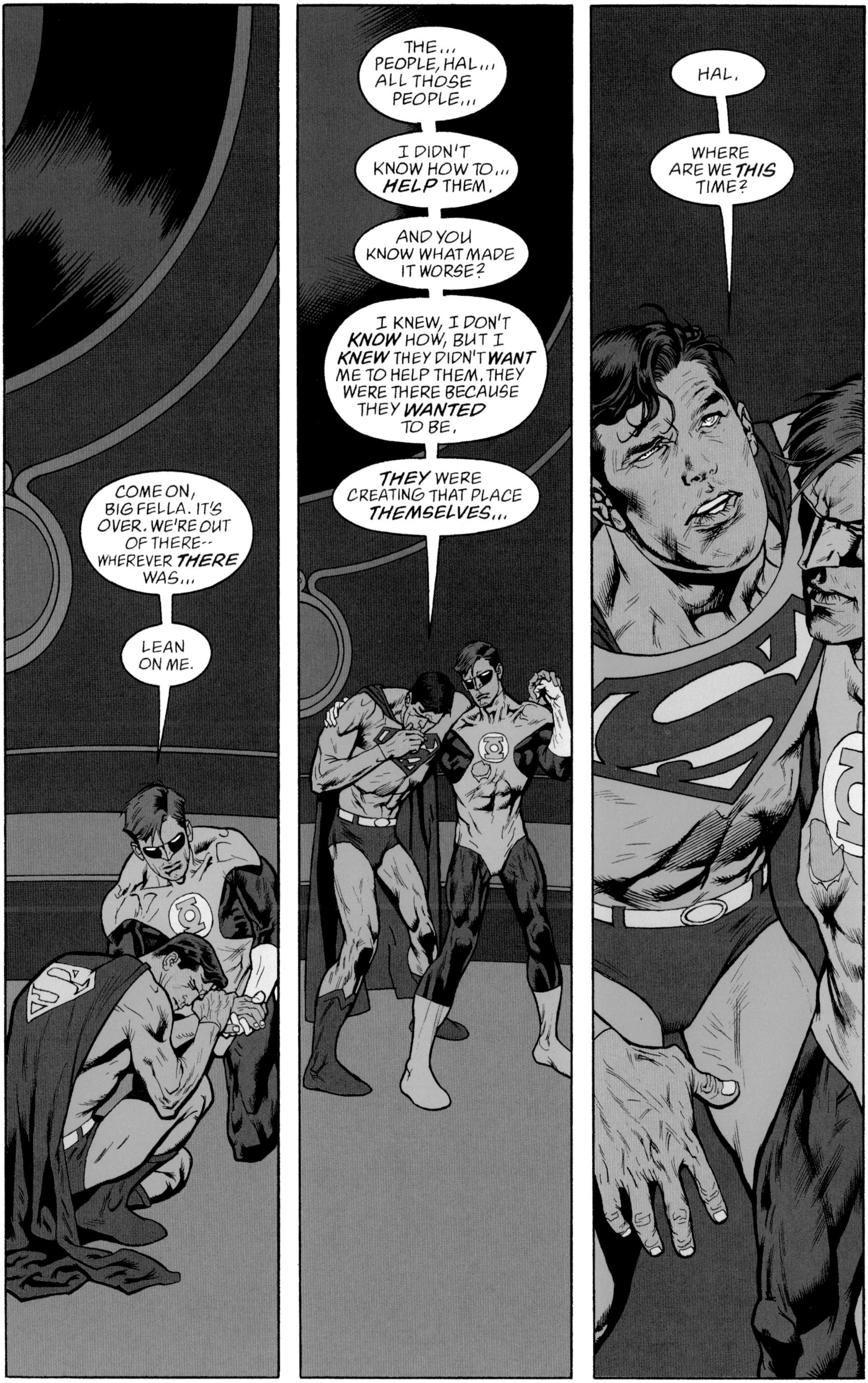
COME ON, BIG FELLA. IT'S OVER. WE'RE OUT OF THERE-- WHEREVER **THERE** WAS...
LEAN ON ME.
THE... PEOPLE, HAL... ALL THOSE PEOPLE...
I DIDN'T KNOW HOW TO... **HELP** THEM.
AND YOU KNOW WHAT MADE IT WORSE?
I KNEW, I DON'T **KNOW** HOW, BUT I **KNEW** THEY DIDN'T **WANT** ME TO HELP THEM. THEY WERE THERE BECAUSE THEY **WANTED** TO BE.
THEY WERE CREATING THAT PLACE **THEMSELVES**...
HAL.
WHERE ARE WE **THIS** TIME?

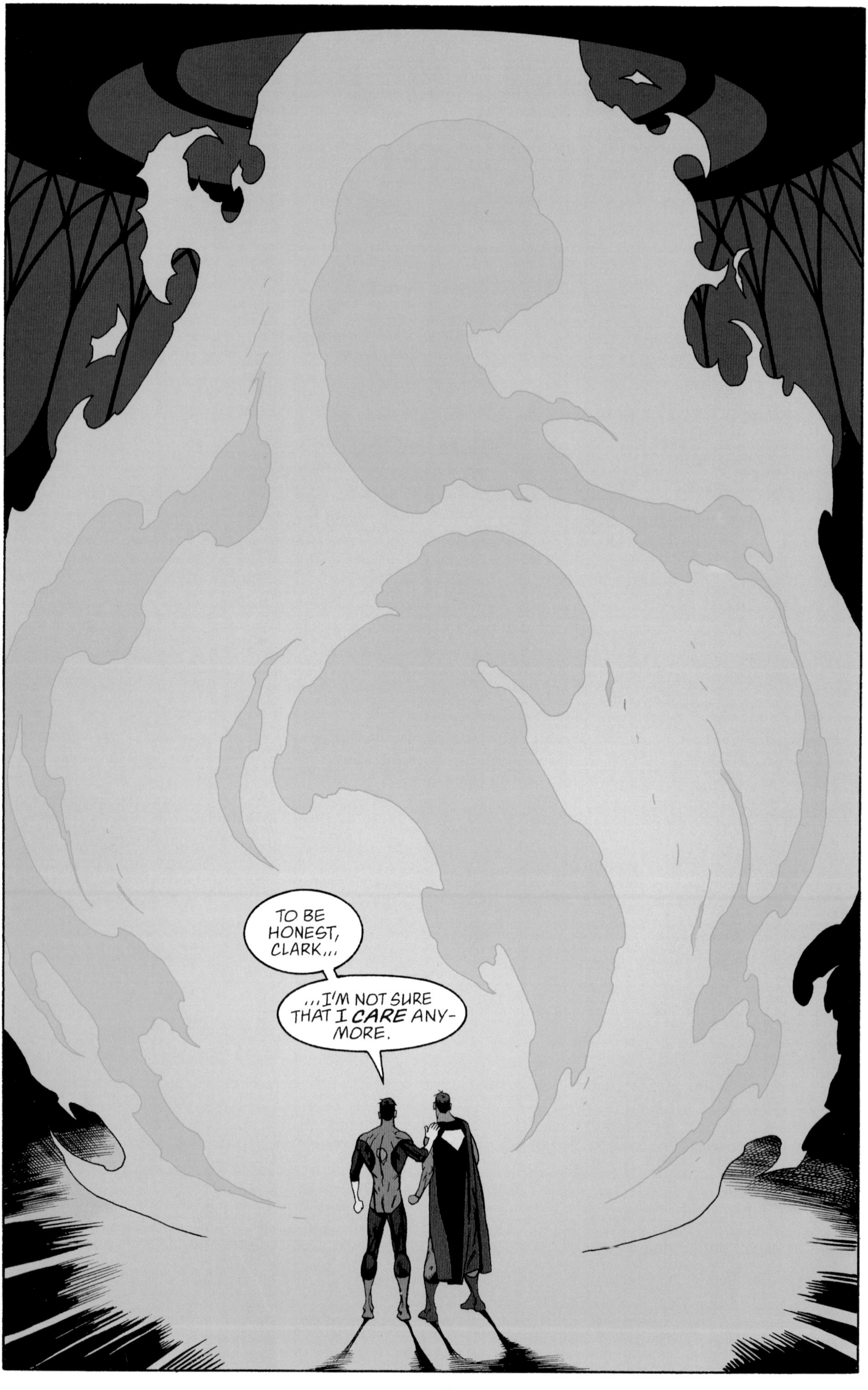
TO BE HONEST, CLARK...
...I'M NOT SURE THAT I CARE ANY-MORE.

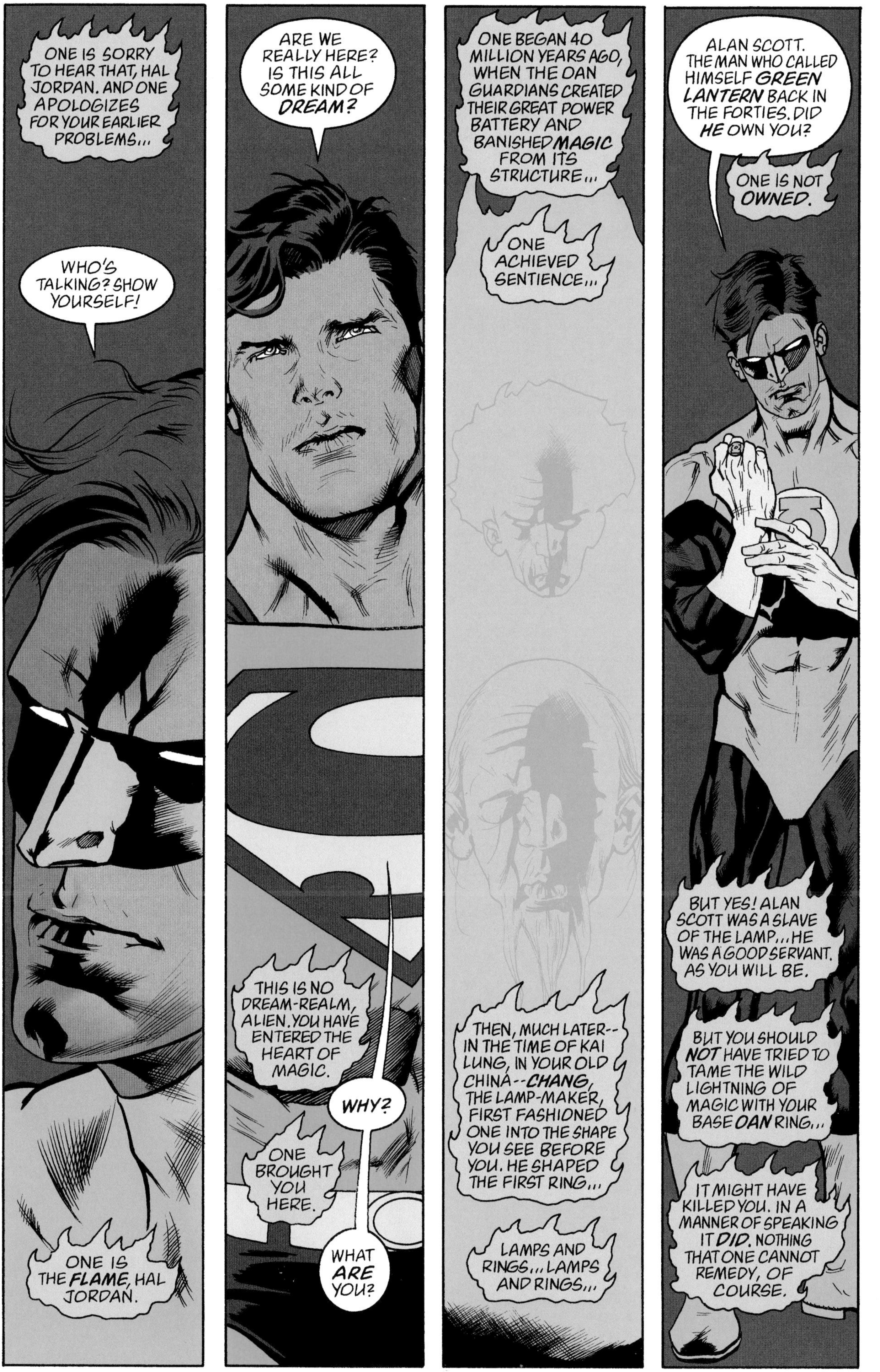
ONE IS SORRY TO HEAR THAT, HAL JORDAN. AND ONE APOLOGIZES FOR YOUR EARLIER PROBLEMS...
WHO'S TALKING? SHOW YOURSELF!
ONE IS THE FLAME, HAL JORDAN.
ARE WE REALLY HERE? IS THIS ALL SOME KIND OF DREAM?
THIS IS NO DREAM-REALM, ALIEN. YOU HAVE ENTERED THE HEART OF MAGIC.
WHY?
ONE BROUGHT YOU HERE.
WHAT ARE YOU?
ONE BEGAN 40 MILLION YEARS AGO, WHEN THE OAN GUARDIANS CREATED THEIR GREAT POWER BATTERY AND BANISHED MAGIC FROM ITS STRUCTURE...
ONE ACHIEVED SENTIENCE...
THEN, MUCH LATER-- IN THE TIME OF KAI LUNG, IN YOUR OLD CHINA--CHANG, THE LAMP-MAKER, FIRST FASHIONED ONE INTO THE SHAPE YOU SEE BEFORE YOU. HE SHAPED THE FIRST RING...
LAMPS AND RINGS... LAMPS AND RINGS...
ALAN SCOTT. THE MAN WHO CALLED HIMSELF GREEN LANTERN BACK IN THE FORTIES. DID HE OWN YOU?
ONE IS NOT OWNED.
BUT YES! ALAN SCOTT WAS A SLAVE OF THE LAMP... HE WAS A GOOD SERVANT. AS YOU WILL BE.
BUT YOU SHOULD NOT HAVE TRIED TO TAME THE WILD LIGHTNING OF MAGIC WITH YOUR BASE OAN RING...
IT MIGHT HAVE KILLED YOU. IN A MANNER OF SPEAKING IT DID. NOTHING THAT ONE CANNOT REMEDY, OF COURSE.

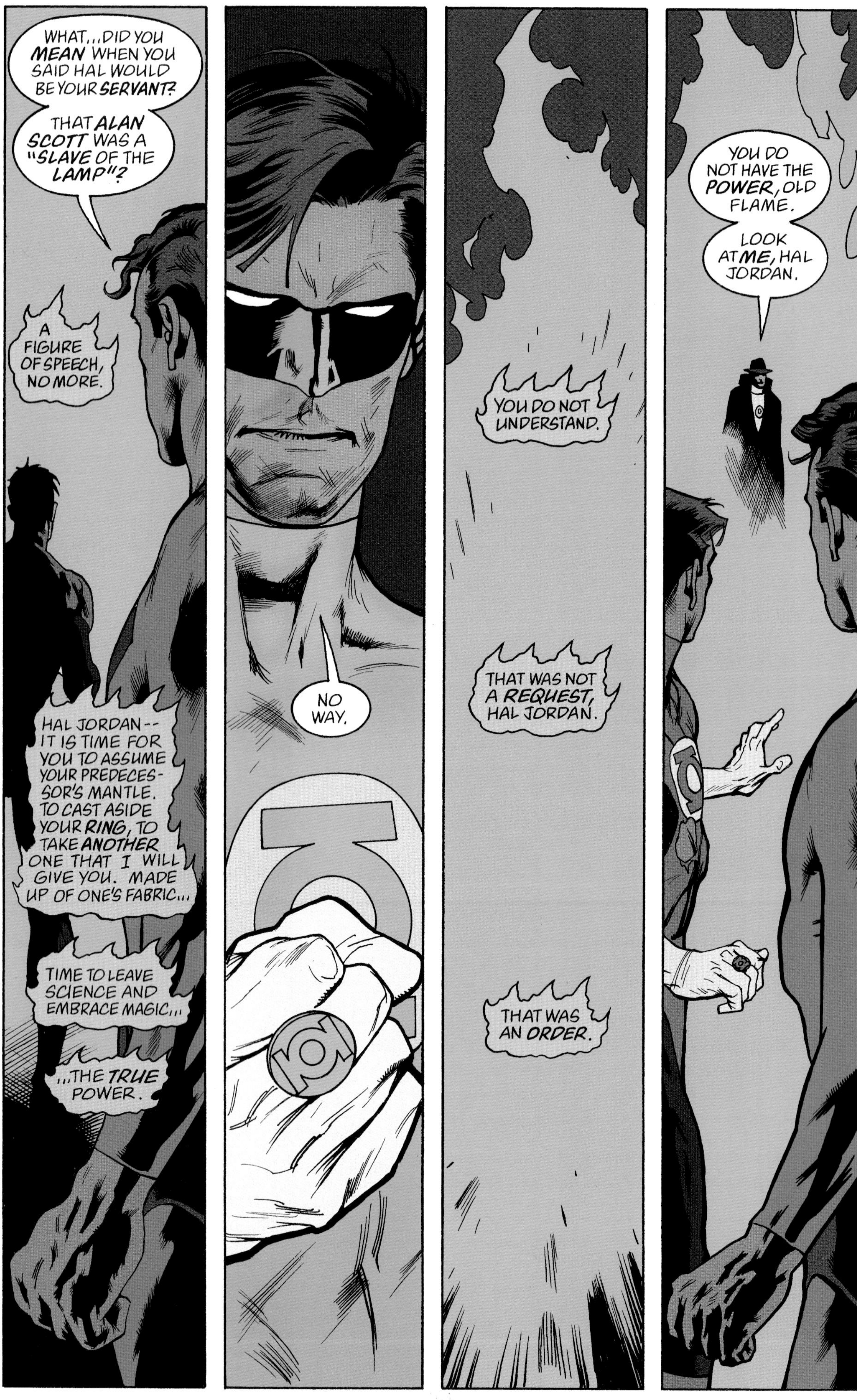
WHAT...DID YOU MEAN WHEN YOU SAID HAL WOULD BE YOUR SERVANT?
THAT ALAN SCOTT WAS A "SLAVE OF THE LAMP"?
A FIGURE OF SPEECH, NO MORE.
HAL JORDAN-- IT IS TIME FOR YOU TO ASSUME YOUR PREDECES-SOR'S MANTLE. TO CAST ASIDE YOUR RING, TO TAKE ANOTHER ONE THAT I WILL GIVE YOU. MADE UP OF ONE'S FABRIC...
TIME TO LEAVE SCIENCE AND EMBRACE MAGIC...
...THE TRUE POWER.
NO WAY.
YOU DO NOT UNDERSTAND.
THAT WAS NOT A REQUEST, HAL JORDAN.
THAT WAS AN ORDER.
YOU DO NOT HAVE THE POWER, OLD FLAME.
LOOK AT ME, HAL JORDAN.

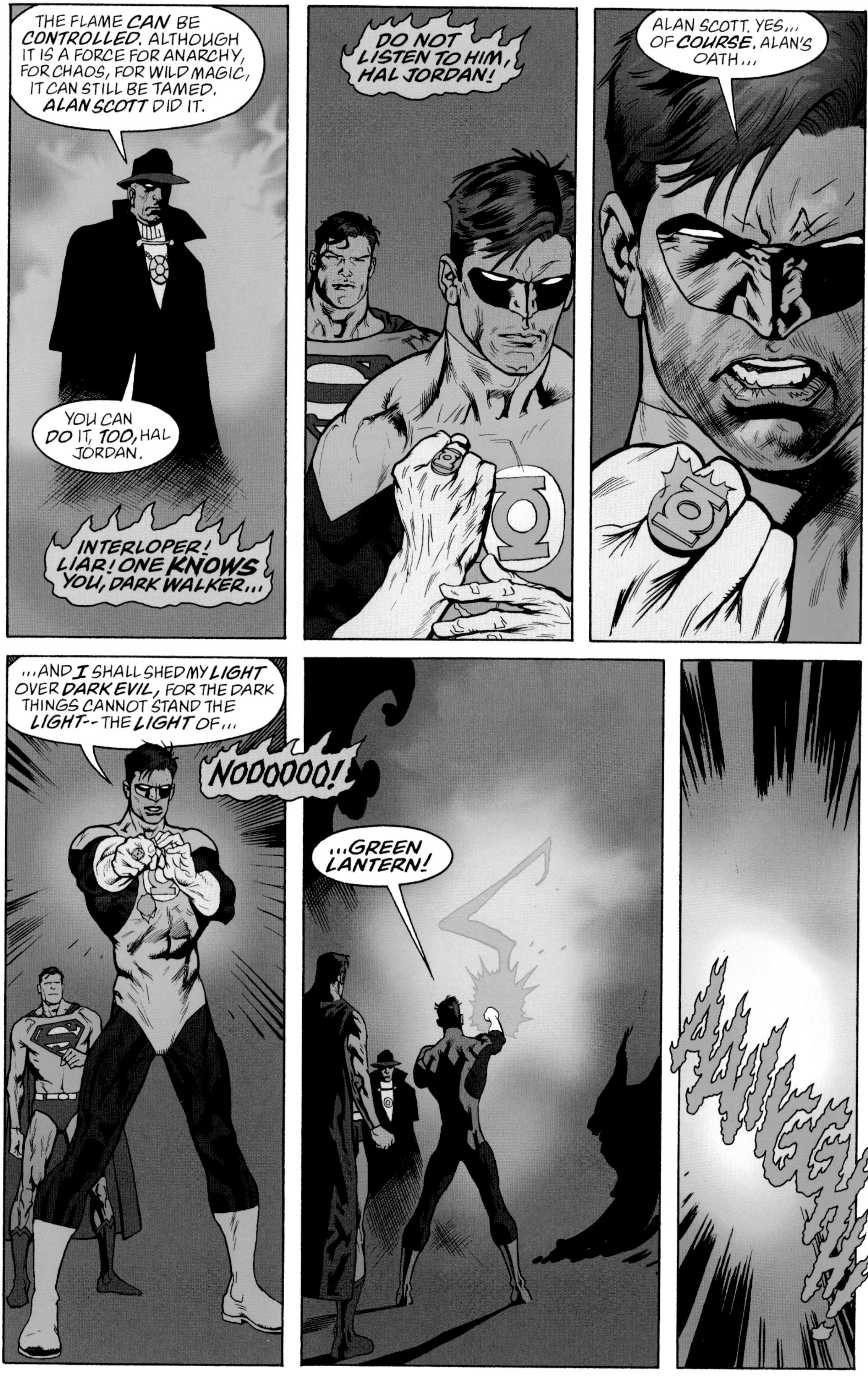
THE FLAME CAN BE CONTROLLED. ALTHOUGH IT IS A FORCE FOR ANARCHY, FOR CHAOS, FOR WILD MAGIC, IT CAN STILL BE TAMED. ALAN SCOTT DID IT.
YOU CAN DO IT, TOO, HAL JORDAN.
INTERLOPER! LIAR! ONE KNOWS YOU, DARK WALKER...
DO NOT LISTEN TO HIM, HAL JORDAN!
ALAN SCOTT. YES... OF COURSE. ALAN'S OATH...
...AND I SHALL SHED MY LIGHT OVER DARK EVIL, FOR THE DARK THINGS CANNOT STAND THE LIGHT-- THE LIGHT OF...
NOOOOOO!
...GREEN LANTERN!
AIIIGGH!

IT IS OVER.

I WILL TAKE THE LAMP. ONE DAY, PERHAPS, THE GREEN FLAME WILL BE FREED, AND THE WILD OLD DAYS OF HIGH MAGIC WILL RETURN....

ONE DAY,...

...BUT NOT YET.

WAIT!

HOW DO WE GET BACK TO OUR BODIES? WHAT'S HAPPENING?

WHO ARE YOU, STRANGER?

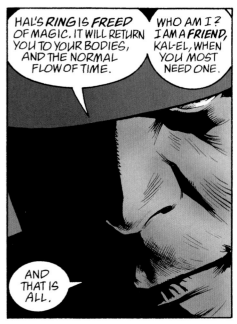

HAL'S RING IS FREED OF MAGIC. IT WILL RETURN YOU TO YOUR BODIES, AND THE NORMAL FLOW OF TIME.

WHO AM I? I AM A FRIEND, KAL-EL, WHEN YOU MOST NEED ONE.

AND THAT IS ALL.

HAL?

IT'LL BE FINE, SUPERMAN, I KNOW IT WILL.

OKAY, RING. GO FOR IT!

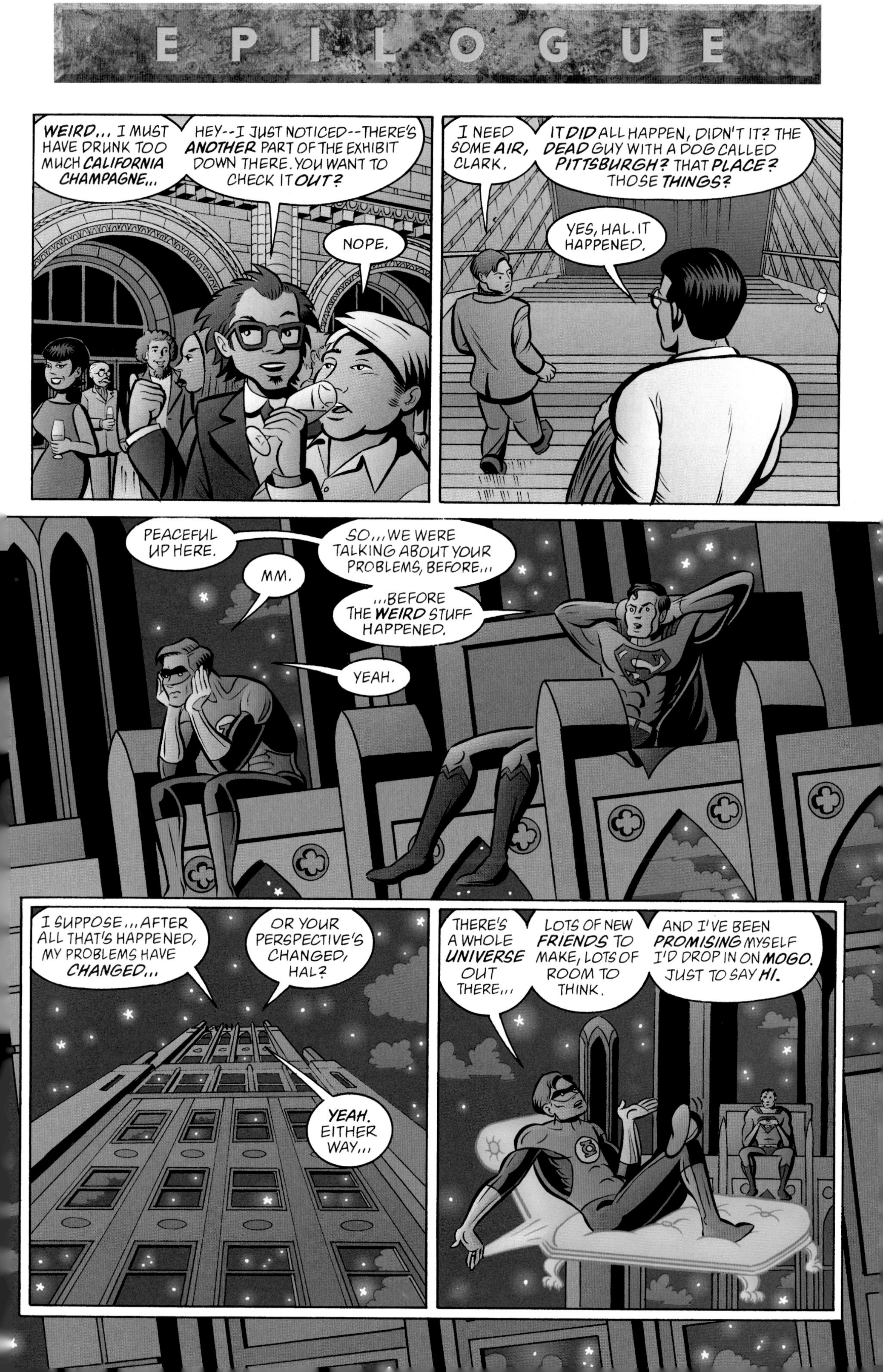
EPILOGUE
WEIRD... I MUST HAVE DRUNK TOO MUCH CALIFORNIA CHAMPAGNE...
HEY--I JUST NOTICED--THERE'S ANOTHER PART OF THE EXHIBIT DOWN THERE. YOU WANT TO CHECK IT OUT?
NOPE.
I NEED SOME AIR, CLARK.
IT DID ALL HAPPEN, DIDN'T IT? THE DEAD GUY WITH A DOG CALLED PITTSBURGH? THAT PLACE? THOSE THINGS?
YES, HAL. IT HAPPENED.
PEACEFUL UP HERE.
SO... WE WERE TALKING ABOUT YOUR PROBLEMS, BEFORE...
MM.
...BEFORE THE WEIRD STUFF HAPPENED.
YEAH.
I SUPPOSE... AFTER ALL THAT'S HAPPENED, MY PROBLEMS HAVE CHANGED...
OR YOUR PERSPECTIVE'S CHANGED, HAL?
YEAH. EITHER WAY...
THERE'S A WHOLE UNIVERSE OUT THERE...
LOTS OF NEW FRIENDS TO MAKE, LOTS OF ROOM TO THINK.
AND I'VE BEEN PROMISING MYSELF I'D DROP IN ON MOGO. JUST TO SAY HI.

HAL, IT'S BEEN *REAL* GOOD SEEING YOU.

YOU, *TOO*, BIG FELLA. *YOU, TOO.*

HAL, IF YOU *EVER* NEED SOMEONE TO TALK TO, WELL, YOU KNOW MY NUMBER.

YES. I APPRECIATE IT.

FILM FORUM
MICHAEL DOUGLAS
FATAL ATTRACTION
RETROSPECTIVE

ATAL ATTRACTION TROSPECTIVE

I WONDER WHAT CLARK EXPERIENCED IN THE *ABYSS...*?

I DON'T SUPPOSE I'LL EVER KNOW.

I'M NOT ENTIRELY SURE I *WANT* TO.

FILM FORUM
MICHAEL DOUGLAS
ACTION

AEL DOUGLAS
ACTION
ROSPECTIVE

TAKE CARE, BIG GUY! THE PLACE IS ALL YOURS!

IF YOU SEE WHAT I MEAN.

AFTERWORD

Stories set in alternate timelines and alternate universes have been a staple of comics for longer than most of us have been alive. All the what-ifs and if-onlys and Imaginary Stories, all the tales of things that could not actually have happened in the real world without bringing the comic to an abrupt end. The might-have-beens.

The comic you have just read is not one of them. The comics universe in which it is set is, pretty much, the DC Universe we are familiar with, albeit the DC Universe of 12 years ago.

The alternate universe it comes from is ours.

It was written pre-SANDMAN (the Hell of the tale is recognizably Alan Moore's from his SAGA OF THE SWAMP THING ANNUAL, "Down Among the Dead Men," not mine; and the idea of Superman in Hell was Alan's as well) at the request of editor Mark Waid, who had seen and liked what I had done on the as-yet-unpublished BLACK ORCHID, and who had wondered if I would be interested in bringing ACTION COMICS WEEKLY to a conclusion.

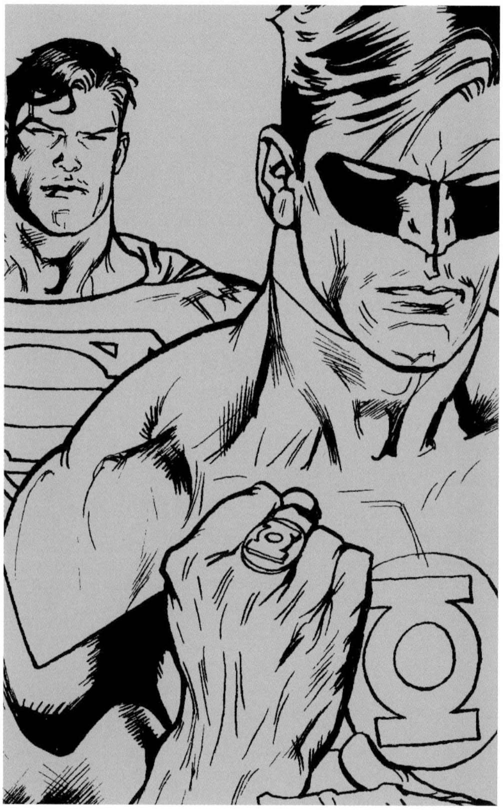

ACTION COMICS WEEKLY had been an experimental anthology comic. It asked the question, "Would readers want an anthology series of individual serialized stories featuring Green Lantern, Catwoman, Deadman, the Phantom Stranger, the Demon, the Blackhawks and, of course, Superman?"

The answer was, "No." They didn't want it. At DC it was felt that ACTION COMICS WEEKLY was much more trouble than it was worth. A new ACTION COMICS monthly title would pick up the numbering from where ACTION WEEKLY left off. But before it did, Mark Waid wanted to know, would I be interested in writing a story with all of the ACTION COMICS characters in it? Enthusiastically, I said yes, and I began to write.

It was like a puzzle assignment: fit all the ACTION COMICS DC characters into one story—and by the way, could I get the Phantom Stranger out of the New York apartment he was currently living in (or at least inhabiting) and out into the world?

Yup, I said. Not a problem. Nothing to it.

My enthusiasm was undiminished after being told that the Demon had to be taken out of the story—I simply created an anagrammatic demon creature to replace him, whose dialogue consisted of one sonnet.

I even prided myself on using plot threads from ACTION COMICS WEEKLY, like the one in which Green Lantern (who was then the Man Without Fear, Hal Jordan), undergoing an emotional crisis, telephones his oldest friends, and none of them want to speak to him—not even Superman, whom he phones at work at the *Daily Planet*.

It became a story of two old friends—one of whom was having problems, while the other wasn't—and the places I could take them. I wrote it in a week. I loved writing it. I loved getting to play with these characters, like a kid with new toys or a young playwright with a troupe of veteran actors he'd always loved. Dammit, it was fun.

I FedExed off the script. Mark Waid loved it. We started talking about artists. I suggested an unknown young talent named Mark Buckingham as an artist for one of the chapters. I was relieved. I went off to the Milford Writers' Conference, in a small seaside hotel at Milford-on-Sea, and soon found myself standing in a hallway talking on the pay phone to America on a crackly long-distance line. America, in this case, was Superman editor Mike Carlin. There was a problem.

There had been a continuity miscommunication discovered regarding DC's earlier reboot of Superman, in the week between my writing the story and its arriving on Mike Carlin's desk. The change-winds had blown, and the nature of reality had shifted.

It had been decided that too many people knew Superman's secret identity. It wasn't special anymore. So from now on, the only people who would know it would be Mr. and Mrs. Kent and Pete Ross, and maybe Mr. Mxyzptlk. Nobody else. Certainly not Green Lantern.

"Maybe they could meet stopping a bank robbery," suggested Mike, a little desperately. "I mean, I really like the story. It's just, it can't happen."

I said I didn't really think so, and we agreed to let it go. The story wasn't printed, I was paid off, and the matter was forgotten.

And that was, pretty much, the last time I played in the DC Universe sandpit. After that, I went and built my own, and when I used DC characters, they were, on the whole, the forgotten ones and the jokes, like Element Girl and Prez—the ones nobody seemed to care about except me.

But the story never quite died. I stole a joke from Boston Brand, and gave it back to him in THE BOOKS OF MAGIC. And when people would ask if I ever felt the urge to write Superman, or Green Lantern, I would reply, genuinely puzzled, "But I did."

Years passed. THE SANDMAN was written and one day it was finished. Karen Berger asked me if she could publish the tryout story I had written for her in the planned MIDNIGHT DAYS collection, if I still had a copy of the script. I did, and I sent it off to her. And then I had an idea for something else we could put into MIDNIGHT DAYS.

I phoned Mike Carlin.

"You remember that ACTION COMICS WEEKLY script I wrote all those years ago?" I asked him.

"Yes," he said.

"Is that continuity stuff still a problem?" I asked. "Or would it be okay to publish these days?"

He allowed as to how it would be absolutely fine by him, and he suggested it might be something Bob Schreck would like to play with. He was on his way out to New York to become a DC Comics editor. I thought that was a great idea and left a message on Bob's voicemail, asking if he'd be interested in it. He said it was the first message he listened to on his first day at work. He said it was a very good way to begin. He said he'd love to do it.

We found one immediate problem: I no longer had a copy of the script. Hadn't had one for years. Neither did DC Comics. But, I remembered, I had once photocopied a printout of the script for Brian Hibbs at San Francisco's Comix Experience, and while he no longer had it, he was able to track down a friend, James Barry, for whom he had copied it and get it back to me. (Thanks, Brian. Thanks, James.)

All the hard work after that was Bob Schreck's— and the various artists involved. To whom, my thanks.

Reading this over I felt—well, odd, really. But good odd. It was like reading a comic that had blown here from an alternate universe. The one in which I wrote this story and everything went just fine, and I went on to write a bunch of DC Universe stuff (while I was writing this I was figuring out ways to fix the mess that Hal Jordan and the Green Lantern Corps had become at the time) rather than just loving it from afar.

—Neil Gaiman
2000

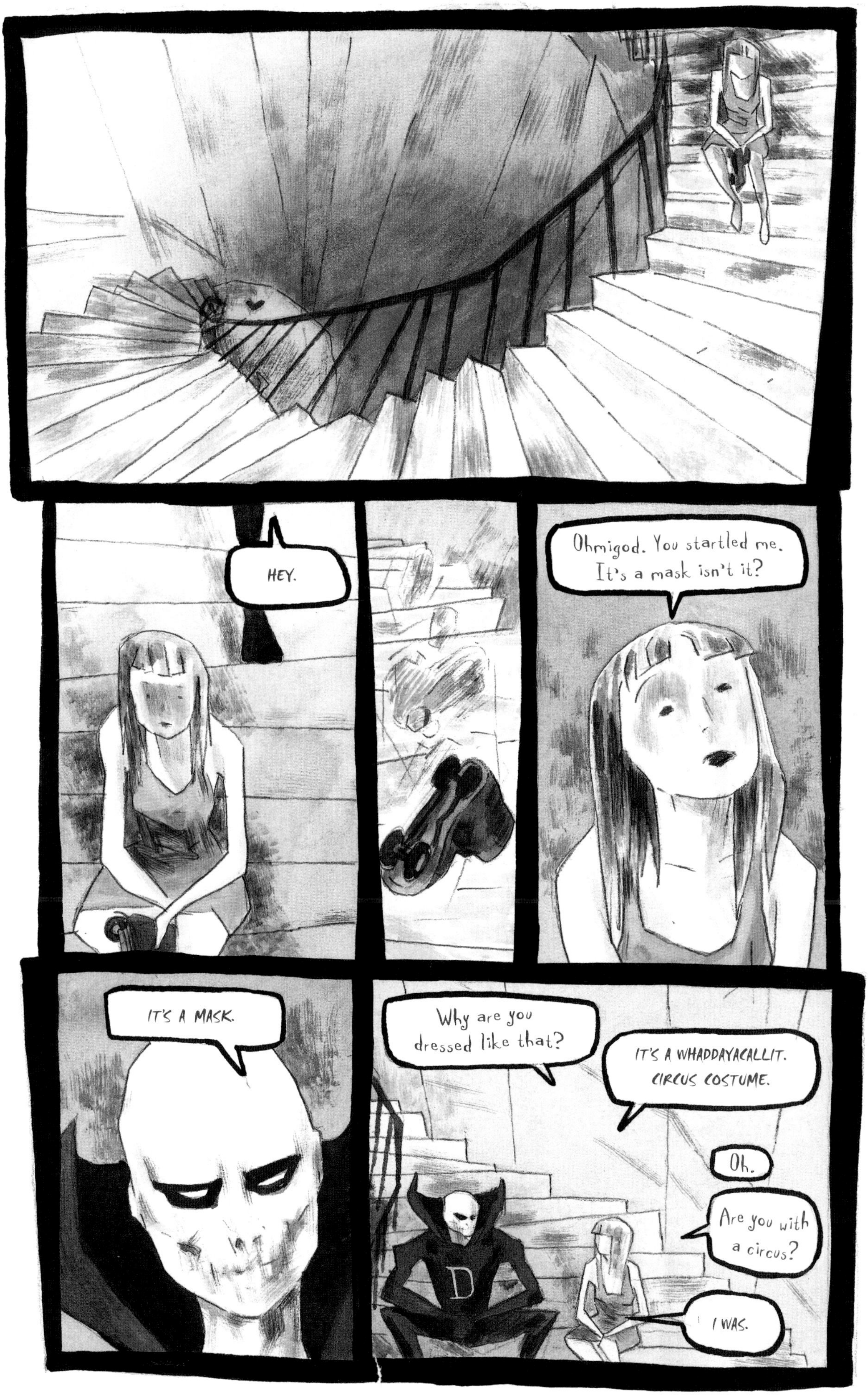
HEY.
Ohmigod. You startled me. It's a mask isn't it?
IT'S A MASK.
Why are you dressed like that?
IT'S A WHADDAYACALLIT. CIRCUS COSTUME.
Oh.
Are you with a circus?
I WAS.

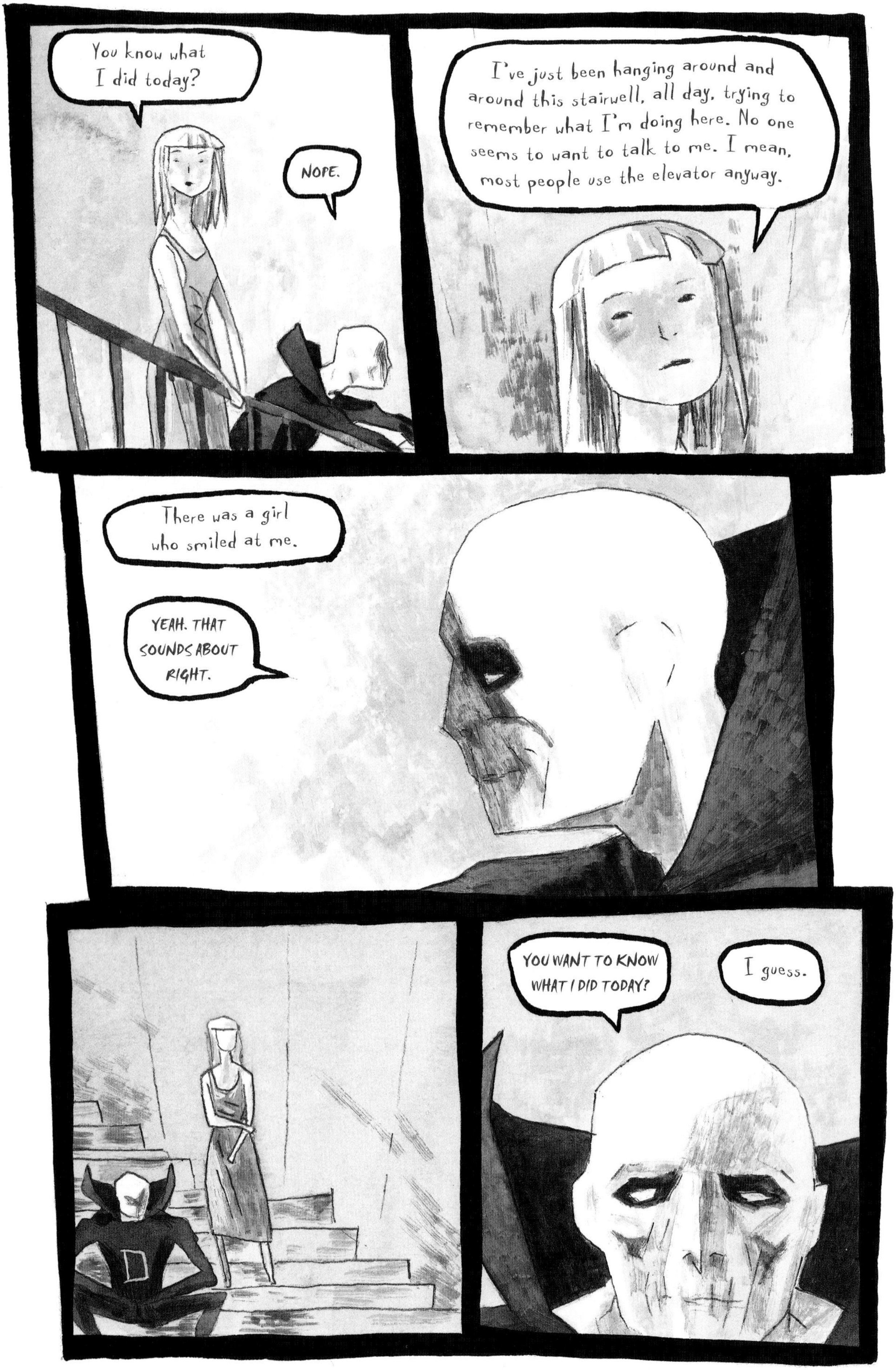
You know what I did today?
NOPE.
I've just been hanging around and around this stairwell, all day, trying to remember what I'm doing here. No one seems to want to talk to me. I mean, most people use the elevator anyway.
There was a girl who smiled at me.
YEAH. THAT SOUNDS ABOUT RIGHT.
YOU WANT TO KNOW WHAT I DID TODAY?
I guess.

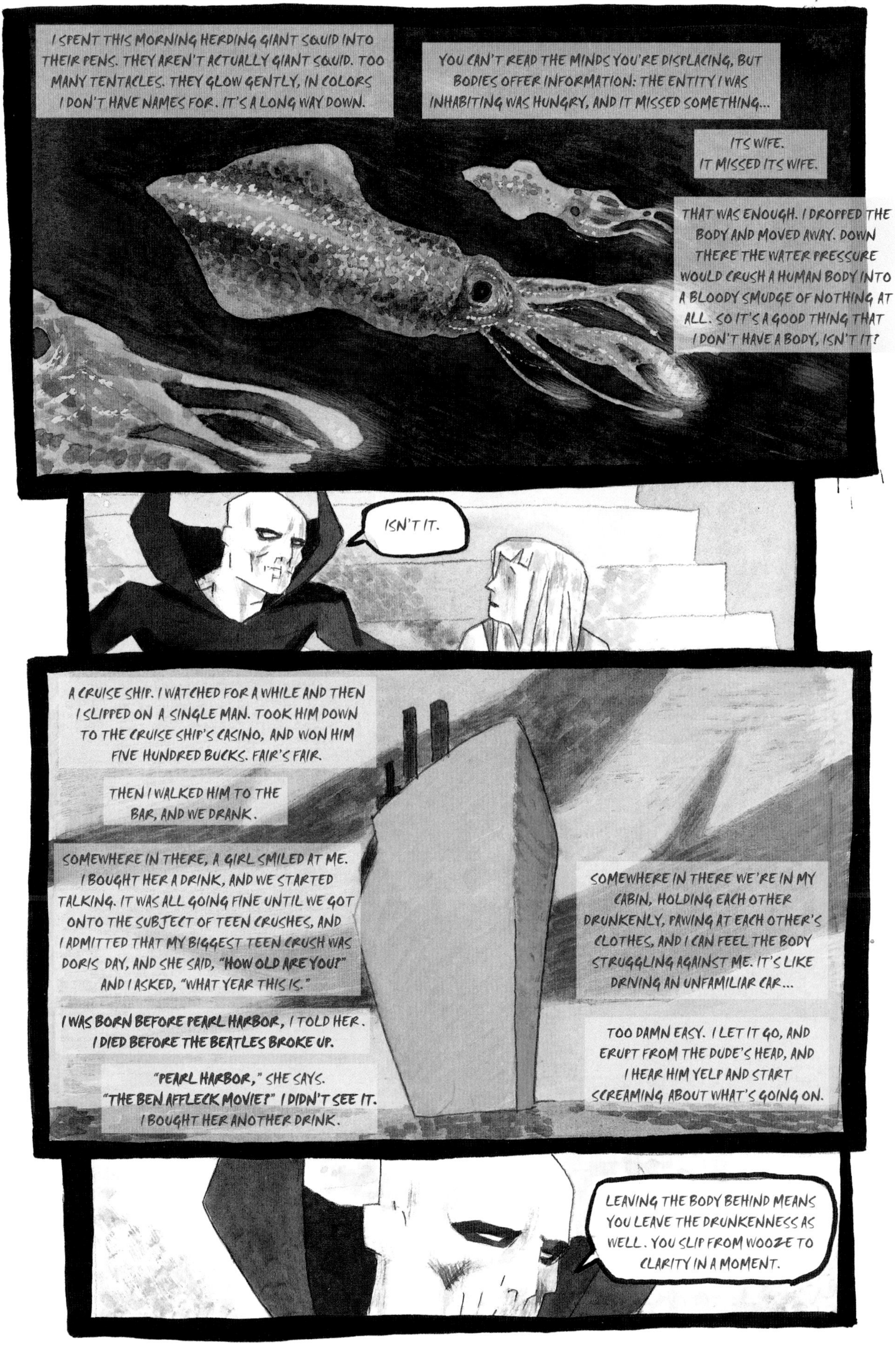
I SPENT THIS MORNING HERDING GIANT SQUID INTO THEIR PENS. THEY AREN'T ACTUALLY GIANT SQUID. TOO MANY TENTACLES. THEY GLOW GENTLY, IN COLORS I DON'T HAVE NAMES FOR. IT'S A LONG WAY DOWN.
YOU CAN'T READ THE MINDS YOU'RE DISPLACING, BUT BODIES OFFER INFORMATION: THE ENTITY I WAS INHABITING WAS HUNGRY, AND IT MISSED SOMETHING...
ITS WIFE. IT MISSED ITS WIFE.
THAT WAS ENOUGH. I DROPPED THE BODY AND MOVED AWAY. DOWN THERE THE WATER PRESSURE WOULD CRUSH A HUMAN BODY INTO A BLOODY SMUDGE OF NOTHING AT ALL. SO IT'S A GOOD THING THAT I DON'T HAVE A BODY, ISN'T IT?
ISN'T IT.
A CRUISE SHIP. I WATCHED FOR A WHILE AND THEN I SLIPPED ON A SINGLE MAN. TOOK HIM DOWN TO THE CRUISE SHIP'S CASINO, AND WON HIM FIVE HUNDRED BUCKS. FAIR'S FAIR.
THEN I WALKED HIM TO THE BAR, AND WE DRANK.
SOMEWHERE IN THERE, A GIRL SMILED AT ME. I BOUGHT HER A DRINK, AND WE STARTED TALKING. IT WAS ALL GOING FINE UNTIL WE GOT ONTO THE SUBJECT OF TEEN CRUSHES, AND I ADMITTED THAT MY BIGGEST TEEN CRUSH WAS DORIS DAY, AND SHE SAID, "HOW OLD ARE YOU?" AND I ASKED, "WHAT YEAR THIS IS."
I WAS BORN BEFORE PEARL HARBOR, I TOLD HER. I DIED BEFORE THE BEATLES BROKE UP.
"PEARL HARBOR," SHE SAYS. "THE BEN AFFLECK MOVIE?" I DIDN'T SEE IT. I BOUGHT HER ANOTHER DRINK.
SOMEWHERE IN THERE WE'RE IN MY CABIN, HOLDING EACH OTHER DRUNKENLY, PAWING AT EACH OTHER'S CLOTHES, AND I CAN FEEL THE BODY STRUGGLING AGAINST ME. IT'S LIKE DRIVING AN UNFAMILIAR CAR...
TOO DAMN EASY. I LET IT GO, AND ERUPT FROM THE DUDE'S HEAD, AND I HEAR HIM YELP AND START SCREAMING ABOUT WHAT'S GOING ON.
LEAVING THE BODY BEHIND MEANS YOU LEAVE THE DRUNKENNESS AS WELL. YOU SLIP FROM WOOZE TO CLARITY IN A MOMENT.

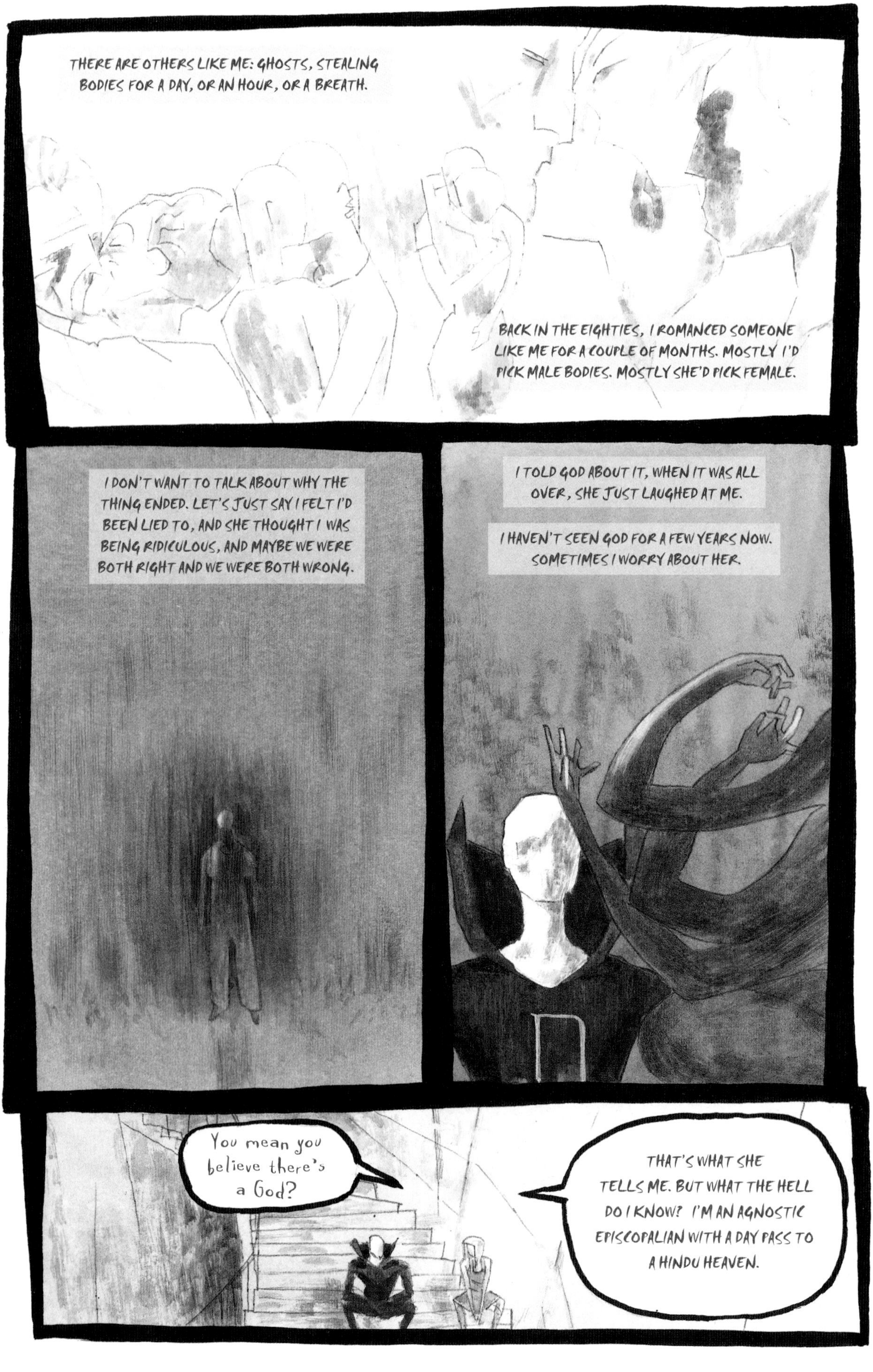
THERE ARE OTHERS LIKE ME: GHOSTS, STEALING BODIES FOR A DAY, OR AN HOUR, OR A BREATH.
BACK IN THE EIGHTIES, I ROMANCED SOMEONE LIKE ME FOR A COUPLE OF MONTHS. MOSTLY I'D PICK MALE BODIES. MOSTLY SHE'D PICK FEMALE.
I DON'T WANT TO TALK ABOUT WHY THE THING ENDED. LET'S JUST SAY I FELT I'D BEEN LIED TO, AND SHE THOUGHT I WAS BEING RIDICULOUS, AND MAYBE WE WERE BOTH RIGHT AND WE WERE BOTH WRONG.
I TOLD GOD ABOUT IT, WHEN IT WAS ALL OVER, SHE JUST LAUGHED AT ME.
I HAVEN'T SEEN GOD FOR A FEW YEARS NOW. SOMETIMES I WORRY ABOUT HER.
You mean you believe there's a God?
THAT'S WHAT SHE TELLS ME. BUT WHAT THE HELL DO I KNOW? I'M AN AGNOSTIC EPISCOPALIAN WITH A DAY PASS TO A HINDU HEAVEN.

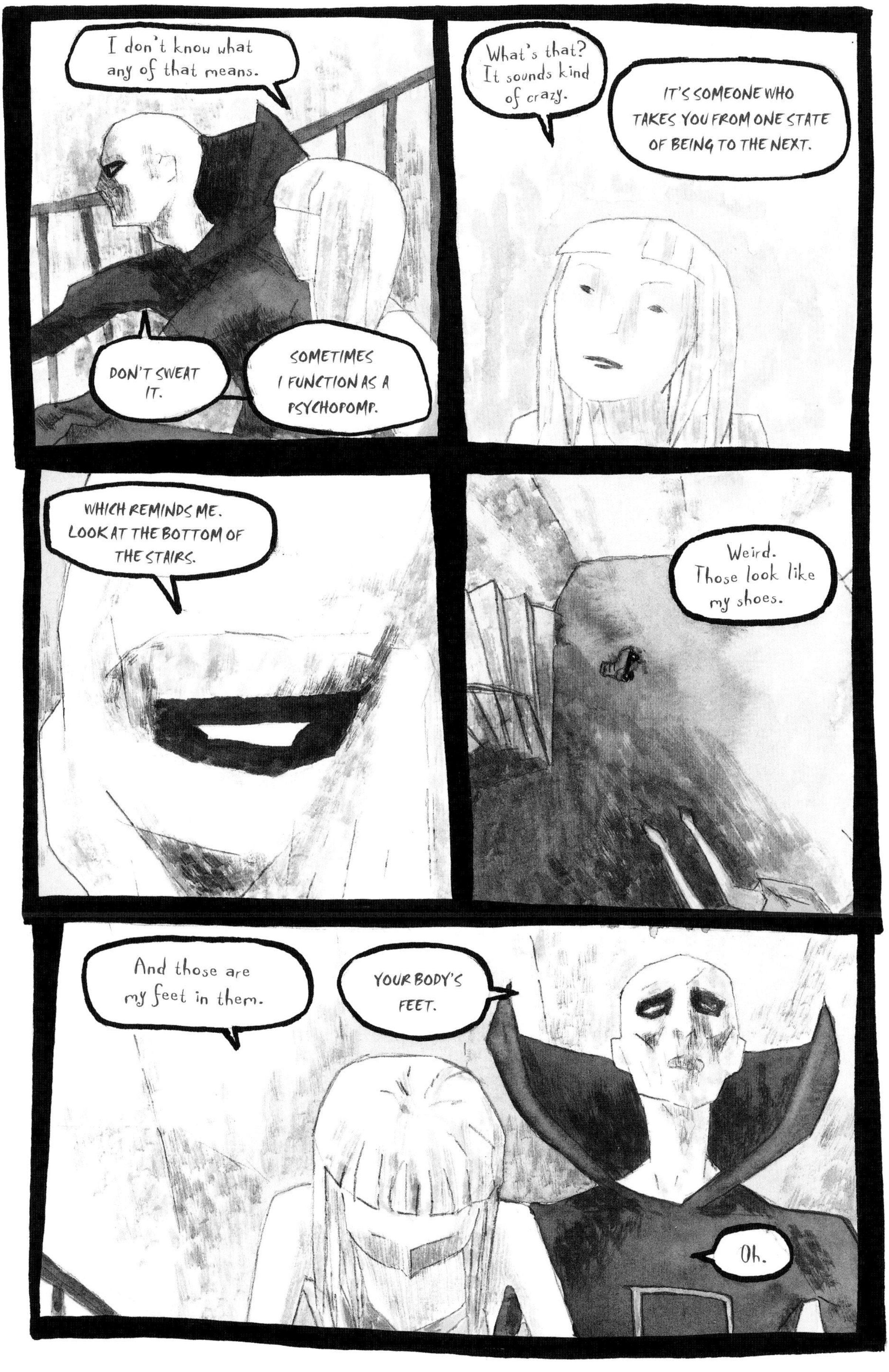
I don't know what any of that means.
DON'T SWEAT IT.
SOMETIMES I FUNCTION AS A PSYCHOPOMP.
What's that? It sounds kind of crazy.
IT'S SOMEONE WHO TAKES YOU FROM ONE STATE OF BEING TO THE NEXT.
WHICH REMINDS ME. LOOK AT THE BOTTOM OF THE STAIRS.
Weird. Those look like my shoes.
And those are my feet in them.
YOUR BODY'S FEET.
Oh.

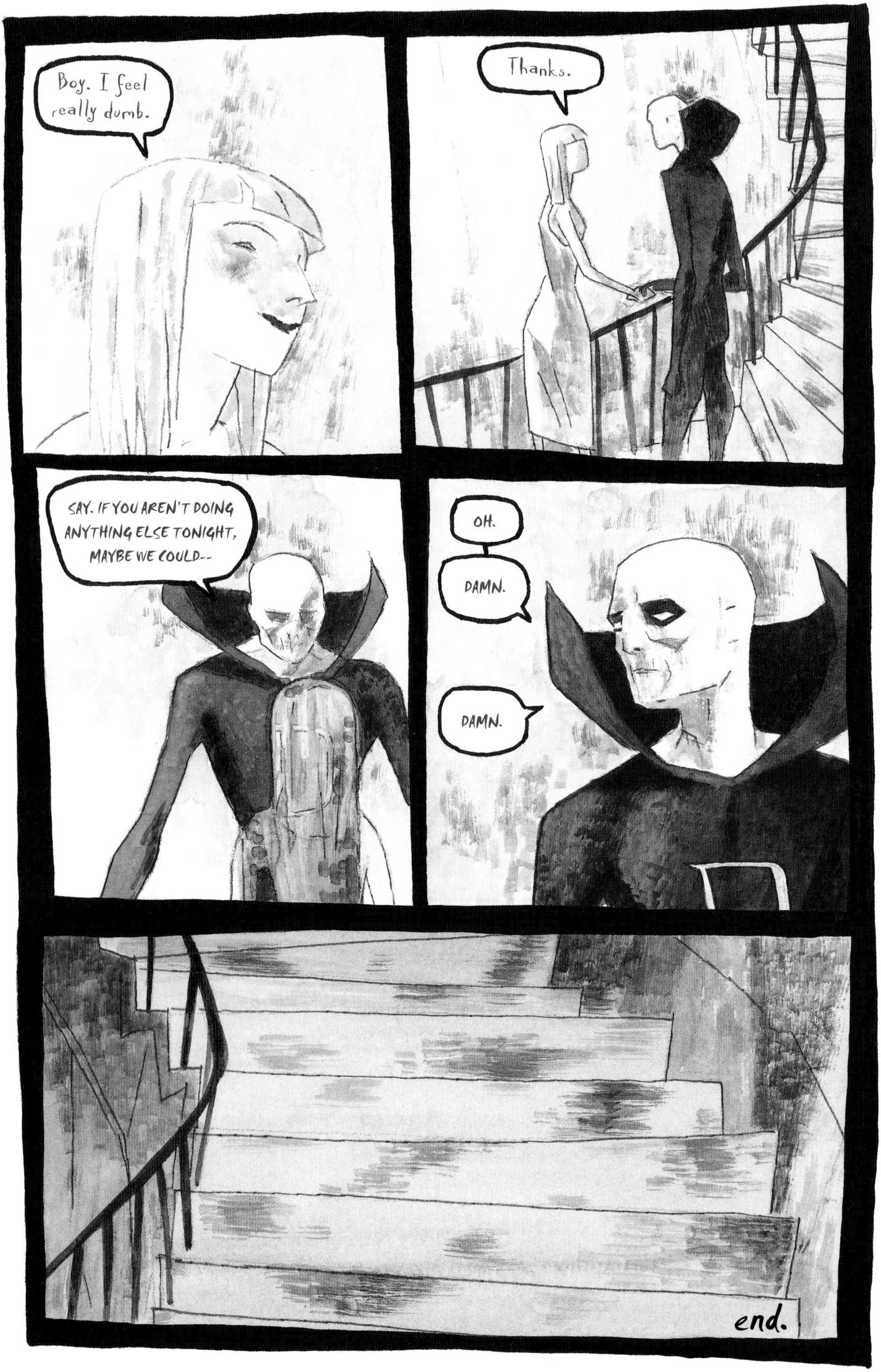

Boy. I feel really dumb.
Thanks.
SAY. IF YOU AREN'T DOING ANYTHING ELSE TONIGHT, MAYBE WE COULD--
OH.
DAMN.
DAMN.
end.

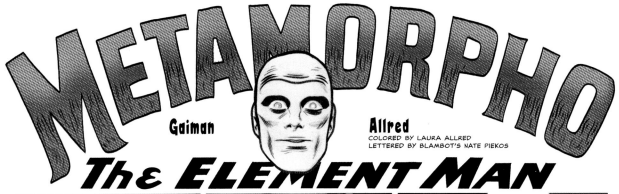

METAMORPHO

Gaiman · Allred

COLORED BY LAURA ALLRED
LETTERED BY BLAMBOT'S NATE PIEKOS

The ELEMENT MAN

MASON? REX MASON? WHERE IS THAT FREAK?

I NEED THE HOVERPLANE CREWED AND READY IN THE NEXT FIVE MINUTES.

AND I NEED REX MASON!

SHALL I FIND HIM FOR YOU, MASTER?

I COULD RELEASE THE DOGS...?

NO POINT. HE'D JUST BLAST THEM WITH CHLORINE, LIKE HE DID WITH THE LAST PACK.

WHERE IS HE? HE WAS MEANT TO BE ON CALL.

EXCUSE ME, MR. STAGG. I BELIEVE THE ELEMENT MAN'S PRESENCE WAS ALREADY REQUESTED THIS MORNING. MISS SAPPHIRE HAD HIM TAKE HER TO THE BEACH.

AW HECK! I KNEW SAPPH'S FONDNESS FOR GIANT CLAMS WOULD GET HER INTO TROUBLE.

SHE WAS HOPING FOR THE MOTHER OF ALL PEARL NECKLACES AND NOW SHE'S TRAPPED.

AND THOSE SHARKS DON'T LOOK FRIENDLY...

SORRY, SHARKIE--BITE ON AN IRON LEG AND YOU LOSE YOUR TEETH...

WHILE A QUICK BLAST OF FROZEN NITROGEN WILL TAKE CARE OF SAPPHIRE'S GIANT CLAM.

REX! YOU DARLING! YOU SAVED MY LIFE AGAIN.

AW. GEE, SAPPH. ANY ELEMENTAL FREAK WITH METAMORPHIC POWERS AND A CRUSH ON YOU WOULDA DONE THE SAME--

MASON, YOU MISBEGOTTEN MORON!

HEY, STAGGSIE, WHAT'S SHAKING?

JOWLS AND PAUNCH MOSTLY, MASON. THANK YOU FOR ASKING.

THE LEGENDARY STAR OF ATLANTIS DIAMOND HAS BEEN LOCATED, AND MY SPIES HAVE PAID DEARLY FOR THE LOCATION. THE MEMBERS OF THE FIRST EXPEDITION WERE ALL KILLED, APART FROM ONE MAN.

I NEED YOU--AND YOUR ELEMENTAL POWERS TO HELP BRING THE STAR BACK SAFELY.

IT'S OKAY, JAVA. I CAN TOWEL MYSELF OFF.

THE STAR OF ATLANTIS DIAMOND? HEY, POPPA? CAN I COME ALONG?

I'M AFRAID NOT, MY DARLING DAUGHTER. THIS JOURNEY IS MUCH TOO DANGEROUS FOR A GIRL.

OKAY, STAGGSY. I'LL BITE. WHERE IS THIS LOST TEMPLE? SOUTH AMERICA? AFRICA?

METAMORPHO CREATED BY BOB HANEY AND RAMONA FRADON

SIMON STAGG
BILLIONAIRE WITH A PLAN

JAVA
NEANDERTHAL MANSERVANT

SAPPHIRE STAGG
THE GAL WITH THE MOST

REX MASON
THE ELEMENT MAN, NATCH--EVERYBODY'S FAVORITE FREAK!

ELEMENT GIRL
CIA SECRET WEAPON

MYSTERY VILLAIN
TO BE REVEALED

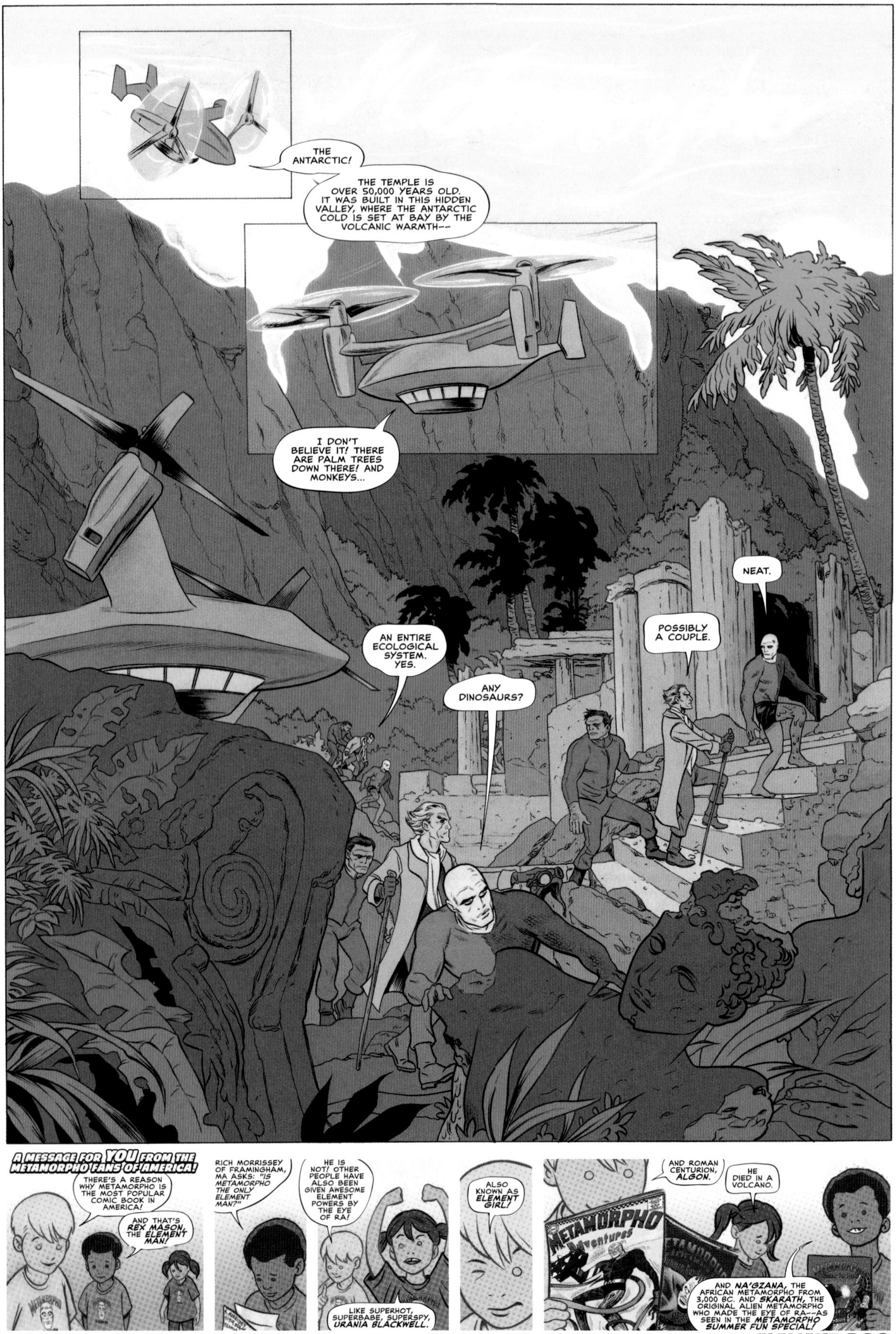
THE ANTARCTIC!
THE TEMPLE IS OVER 50,000 YEARS OLD. IT WAS BUILT IN THIS HIDDEN VALLEY, WHERE THE ANTARCTIC COLD IS SET AT BAY BY THE VOLCANIC WARMTH--
I DON'T BELIEVE IT! THERE ARE PALM TREES DOWN THERE! AND MONKEYS...
AN ENTIRE ECOLOGICAL SYSTEM. YES.
ANY DINOSAURS?
POSSIBLY A COUPLE.
NEAT.
A MESSAGE FOR YOU FROM THE METAMORPHO FANS OF AMERICA!
THERE'S A REASON WHY METAMORPHO IS THE MOST POPULAR COMIC BOOK IN AMERICA!
AND THAT'S REX MASON, THE ELEMENT MAN!
RICH MORRISSEY OF FRAMINGHAM, MA ASKS: "IS METAMORPHO THE ONLY ELEMENT MAN?"
HE IS NOT! OTHER PEOPLE HAVE ALSO BEEN GIVEN AWESOME ELEMENT POWERS BY THE EYE OF RA!
LIKE SUPERHOT, SUPERBABE, SUPERSPY, URANIA BLACKWELL.
ALSO KNOWN AS ELEMENT GIRL!
AND ROMAN CENTURION, ALGON.
HE DIED IN A VOLCANO.
AND NA'GZANA, THE AFRICAN METAMORPHO FROM 3,000 BC. AND SKARATH, THE ORIGINAL ALIEN METAMORPHO WHO MADE THE EYE OF RA--AS SEEN IN THE METAMORPHO SUMMER FUN SPECIAL!
METAMORPHO Adventures

KIDS! IF YOUR LETTER IS USED, YOU GET A YEAR'S FREE SUBSCRIPTION TO METAMORPHO'S CANINE PAL, ELEMENT DOG.

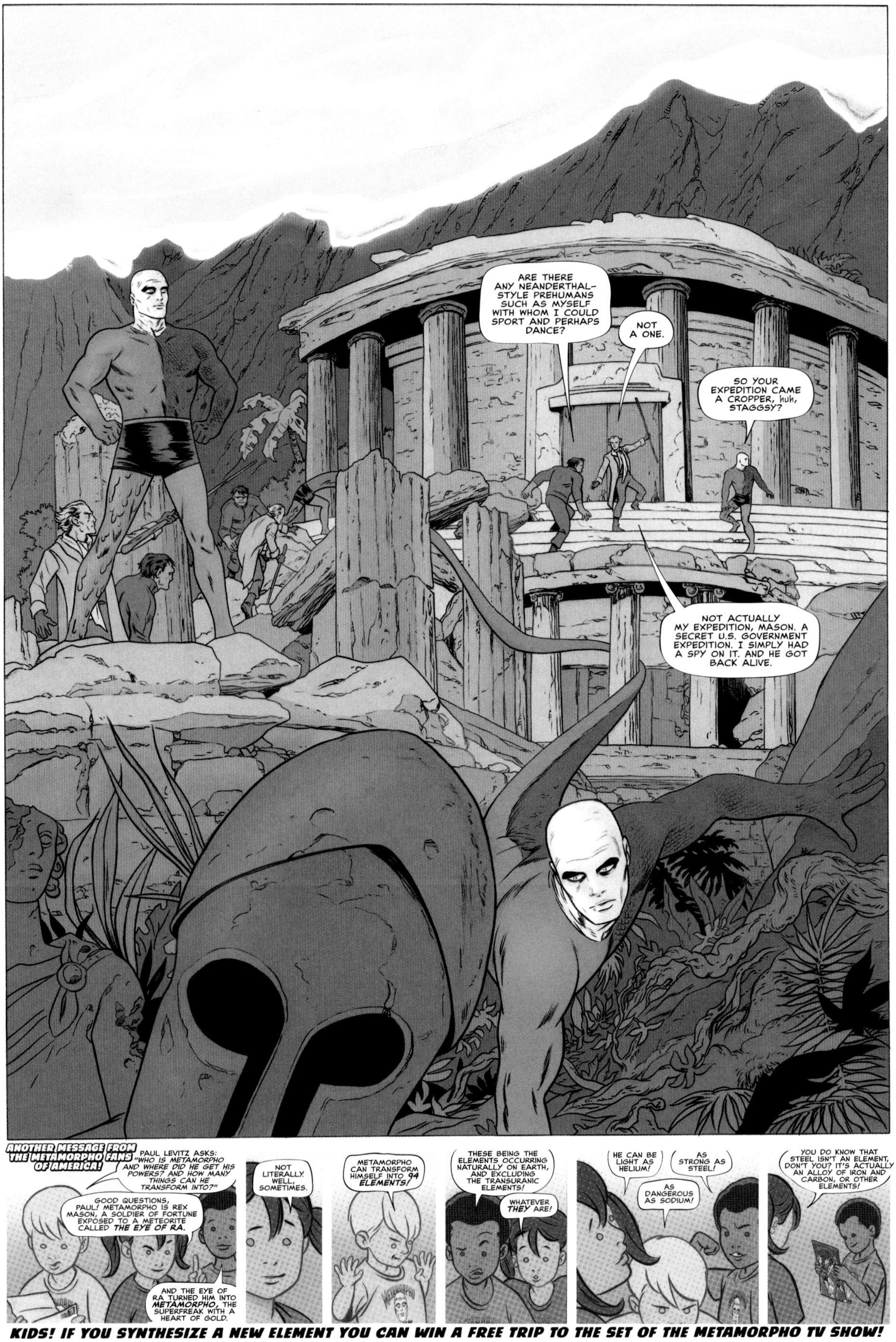
ARE THERE ANY NEANDERTHAL-STYLE PREHUMANS SUCH AS MYSELF WITH WHOM I COULD SPORT AND PERHAPS DANCE?
NOT A ONE.
SO YOUR EXPEDITION CAME A CROPPER, huh, STAGGSY?
NOT ACTUALLY MY EXPEDITION, MASON. A SECRET U.S. GOVERNMENT EXPEDITION. I SIMPLY HAD A SPY ON IT. AND HE GOT BACK ALIVE.
ANOTHER MESSAGE FROM THE METAMORPHO FANS OF AMERICA!
PAUL LEVITZ ASKS: "WHO IS METAMORPHO AND WHERE DID HE GET HIS POWERS? AND HOW MANY THINGS CAN HE TRANSFORM INTO?"
GOOD QUESTIONS, PAUL! METAMORPHO IS REX MASON, A SOLDIER OF FORTUNE EXPOSED TO A METEORITE CALLED THE EYE OF RA.
AND THE EYE OF RA TURNED HIM INTO METAMORPHO, THE SUPERFREAK WITH A HEART OF GOLD.
NOT LITERALLY. WELL, SOMETIMES.
METAMORPHO CAN TRANSFORM HIMSELF INTO 94 ELEMENTS!
THESE BEING THE ELEMENTS OCCURRING NATURALLY ON EARTH, AND EXCLUDING THE TRANSURANIC ELEMENTS!
WHATEVER THEY ARE!
HE CAN BE LIGHT AS HELIUM!
AS STRONG AS STEEL!
AS DANGEROUS AS SODIUM!
YOU DO KNOW THAT STEEL ISN'T AN ELEMENT, DON'T YOU? IT'S ACTUALLY AN ALLOY OF IRON AND CARBON, OR OTHER ELEMENTS!
KIDS! IF YOU SYNTHESIZE A NEW ELEMENT YOU CAN WIN A FREE TRIP TO THE SET OF THE METAMORPHO TV SHOW!

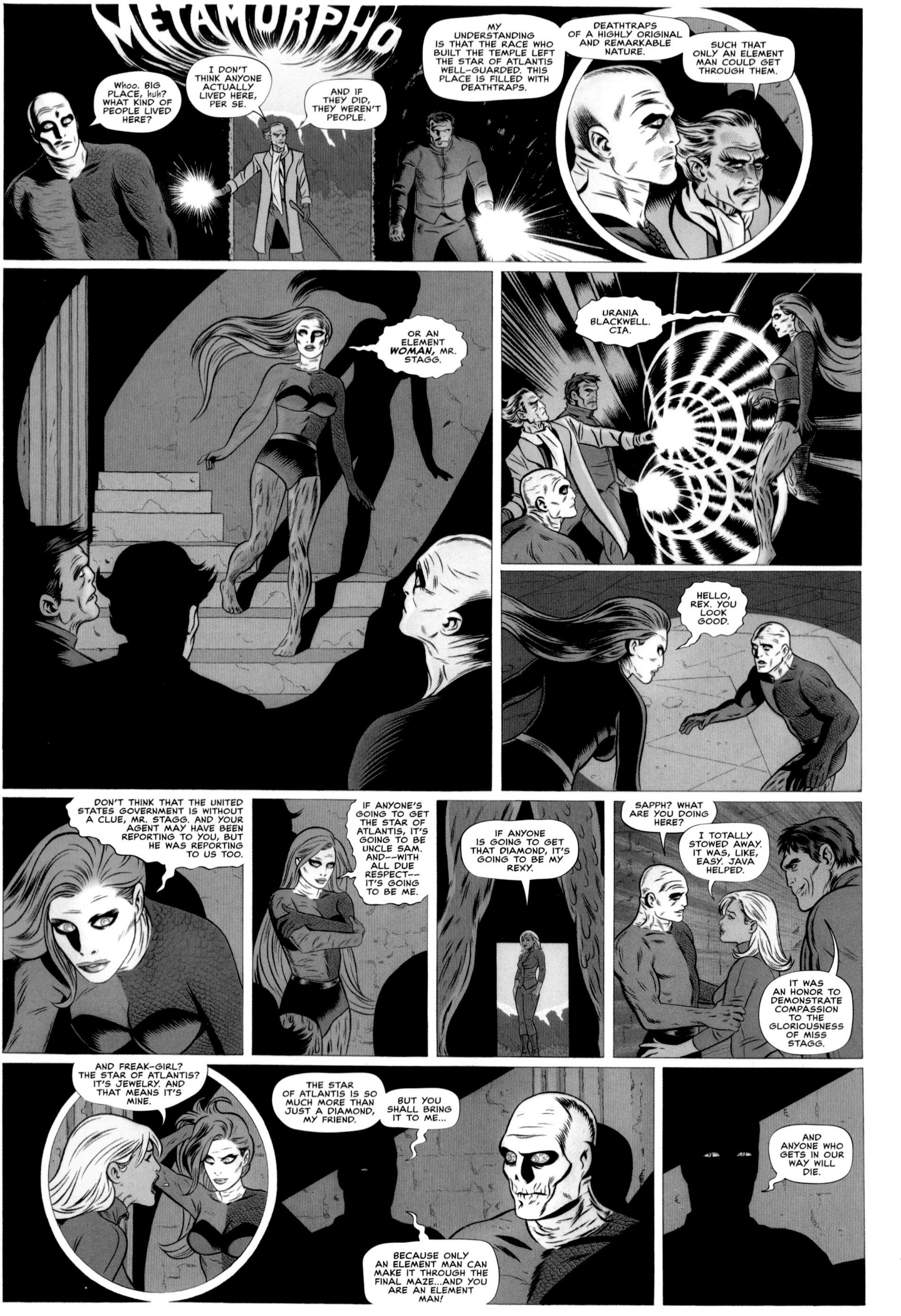
METAMORPHO
Whoo. BIG PLACE, huh? WHAT KIND OF PEOPLE LIVED HERE?
I DON'T THINK ANYONE ACTUALLY LIVED HERE, PER SE.
AND IF THEY DID, THEY WEREN'T PEOPLE.
MY UNDERSTANDING IS THAT THE RACE WHO BUILT THE TEMPLE LEFT THE STAR OF ATLANTIS WELL-GUARDED. THIS PLACE IS FILLED WITH DEATHTRAPS.
DEATHTRAPS OF A HIGHLY ORIGINAL AND REMARKABLE NATURE.
SUCH THAT ONLY AN ELEMENT MAN COULD GET THROUGH THEM.
OR AN ELEMENT WOMAN, MR. STAGG.
URANIA BLACKWELL. CIA.
HELLO, REX. YOU LOOK GOOD.
DON'T THINK THAT THE UNITED STATES GOVERNMENT IS WITHOUT A CLUE, MR. STAGG. AND YOUR AGENT MAY HAVE BEEN REPORTING TO YOU, BUT HE WAS REPORTING TO US TOO.
IF ANYONE'S GOING TO GET THE STAR OF ATLANTIS, IT'S GOING TO BE UNCLE SAM. AND--WITH ALL DUE RESPECT--IT'S GOING TO BE ME.
IF ANYONE IS GOING TO GET THAT DIAMOND, IT'S GOING TO BE MY REXY.
SAPPH? WHAT ARE YOU DOING HERE?
I TOTALLY STOWED AWAY. IT WAS, LIKE, EASY. JAVA HELPED.
IT WAS AN HONOR TO DEMONSTRATE COMPASSION TO THE GLORIOUSNESS OF MISS STAGG.
AND FREAK-GIRL? THE STAR OF ATLANTIS? IT'S JEWELRY. AND THAT MEANS IT'S MINE.
THE STAR OF ATLANTIS IS SO MUCH MORE THAN JUST A DIAMOND, MY FRIEND.
BUT YOU SHALL BRING IT TO ME...
BECAUSE ONLY AN ELEMENT MAN CAN MAKE IT THROUGH THE FINAL MAZE...AND YOU ARE AN ELEMENT MAN!
AND ANYONE WHO GETS IN OUR WAY WILL DIE.

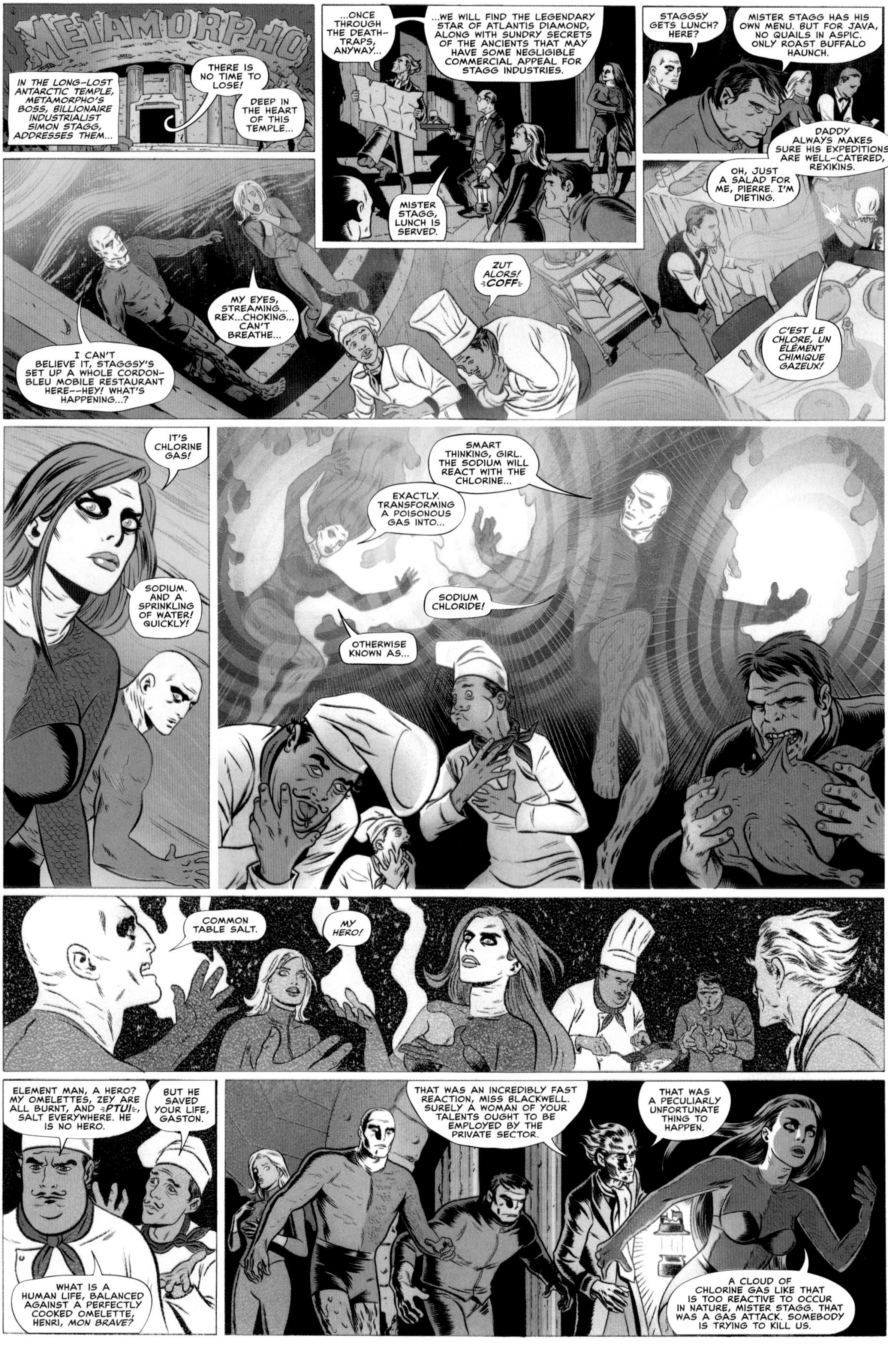
METAMORPHO
IN THE LONG-LOST ANTARCTIC TEMPLE, METAMORPHO'S BOSS, BILLIONAIRE INDUSTRIALIST SIMON STAGG, ADDRESSES THEM...
THERE IS NO TIME TO LOSE!
DEEP IN THE HEART OF THIS TEMPLE...
...ONCE THROUGH THE DEATH-TRAPS, ANYWAY...
...WE WILL FIND THE LEGENDARY STAR OF ATLANTIS DIAMOND, ALONG WITH SUNDRY SECRETS OF THE ANCIENTS THAT MAY HAVE SOME NEGLIGIBLE COMMERCIAL APPEAL FOR STAGG INDUSTRIES.
MISTER STAGG, LUNCH IS SERVED.
STAGGSY GETS LUNCH? HERE?
MISTER STAGG HAS HIS OWN MENU. BUT FOR JAVA, NO QUAILS IN ASPIC. ONLY ROAST BUFFALO HAUNCH.
DADDY ALWAYS MAKES SURE HIS EXPEDITIONS ARE WELL-CATERED, REXIKINS.
OH, JUST A SALAD FOR ME, PIERRE. I'M DIETING.
I CAN'T BELIEVE IT, STAGGSY'S SET UP A WHOLE CORDON-BLEU MOBILE RESTAURANT HERE--HEY! WHAT'S HAPPENING...?
MY EYES, STREAMING... REX...CHOKING... CAN'T BREATHE...
ZUT ALORS! COFF
C'EST LE CHLORE, UN ÉLÉMENT CHIMIQUE GAZEUX!
IT'S CHLORINE GAS!
SODIUM. AND A SPRINKLING OF WATER! QUICKLY!
SMART THINKING, GIRL. THE SODIUM WILL REACT WITH THE CHLORINE...
EXACTLY. TRANSFORMING A POISONOUS GAS INTO...
SODIUM CHLORIDE!
OTHERWISE KNOWN AS...
COMMON TABLE SALT.
MY HERO!
ELEMENT MAN, A HERO? MY OMELETTES, ZEY ARE ALL BURNT, AND PTU! SALT EVERYWHERE. HE IS NO HERO.
BUT HE SAVED YOUR LIFE, GASTON.
WHAT IS A HUMAN LIFE, BALANCED AGAINST A PERFECTLY COOKED OMELETTE, HENRI, MON BRAVE?
THAT WAS AN INCREDIBLY FAST REACTION, MISS BLACKWELL. SURELY A WOMAN OF YOUR TALENTS OUGHT TO BE EMPLOYED BY THE PRIVATE SECTOR.
THAT WAS A PECULIARLY UNFORTUNATE THING TO HAPPEN.
A CLOUD OF CHLORINE GAS LIKE THAT IS TOO REACTIVE TO OCCUR IN NATURE, MISTER STAGG. THAT WAS A GAS ATTACK. SOMEBODY IS TRYING TO KILL US.

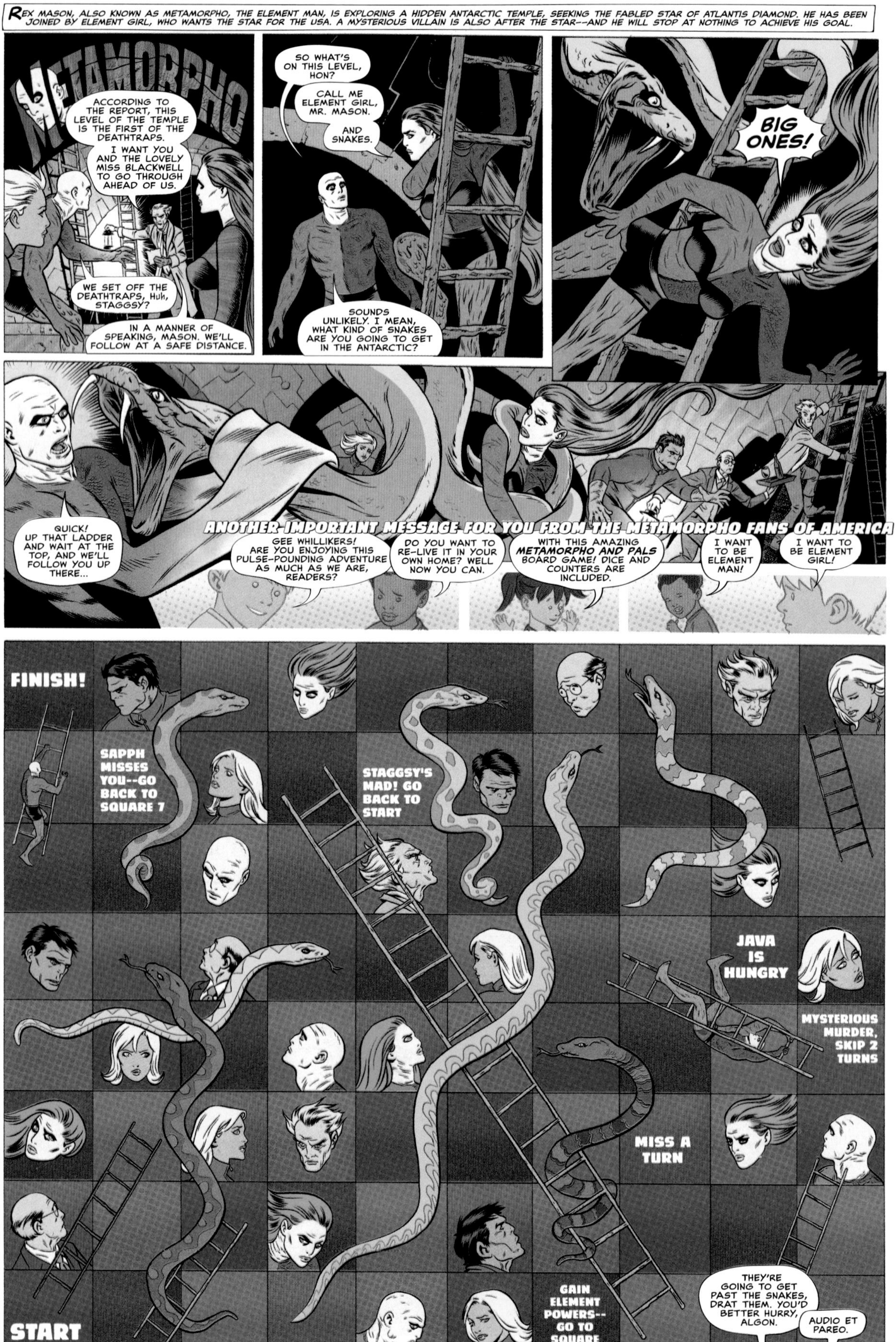
REX MASON, ALSO KNOWN AS METAMORPHO, THE ELEMENT MAN, IS EXPLORING A HIDDEN ANTARCTIC TEMPLE, SEEKING THE FABLED STAR OF ATLANTIS DIAMOND. HE HAS BEEN JOINED BY ELEMENT GIRL, WHO WANTS THE STAR FOR THE USA. A MYSTERIOUS VILLAIN IS ALSO AFTER THE STAR--AND HE WILL STOP AT NOTHING TO ACHIEVE HIS GOAL.
METAMORPHO
ACCORDING TO THE REPORT, THIS LEVEL OF THE TEMPLE IS THE FIRST OF THE DEATHTRAPS.
I WANT YOU AND THE LOVELY MISS BLACKWELL TO GO THROUGH AHEAD OF US.
WE SET OFF THE DEATHTRAPS, HUH, STAGGSY?
IN A MANNER OF SPEAKING, MASON. WE'LL FOLLOW AT A SAFE DISTANCE.
SO WHAT'S ON THIS LEVEL, HON?
CALL ME ELEMENT GIRL, MR. MASON.
AND SNAKES.
SOUNDS UNLIKELY. I MEAN, WHAT KIND OF SNAKES ARE YOU GOING TO GET IN THE ANTARCTIC?
BIG ONES!
QUICK! UP THAT LADDER AND WAIT AT THE TOP, AND WE'LL FOLLOW YOU UP THERE...
ANOTHER IMPORTANT MESSAGE FOR YOU FROM THE METAMORPHO FANS OF AMERICA
GEE WHILLIKERS! ARE YOU ENJOYING THIS PULSE-POUNDING ADVENTURE AS MUCH AS WE ARE, READERS?
DO YOU WANT TO RE-LIVE IT IN YOUR OWN HOME? WELL NOW YOU CAN.
WITH THIS AMAZING METAMORPHO AND PALS BOARD GAME! DICE AND COUNTERS ARE INCLUDED.
I WANT TO BE ELEMENT MAN!
I WANT TO BE ELEMENT GIRL!
FINISH!
SAPPH MISSES YOU--GO BACK TO SQUARE 7
STAGGSY'S MAD! GO BACK TO START
JAVA IS HUNGRY
MYSTERIOUS MURDER, SKIP 2 TURNS
MISS A TURN
GAIN ELEMENT POWERS--GO TO SQUARE 58
START
THEY'RE GOING TO GET PAST THE SNAKES, DRAT THEM. YOU'D BETTER HURRY, ALGON.
AUDIO ET PAREO.

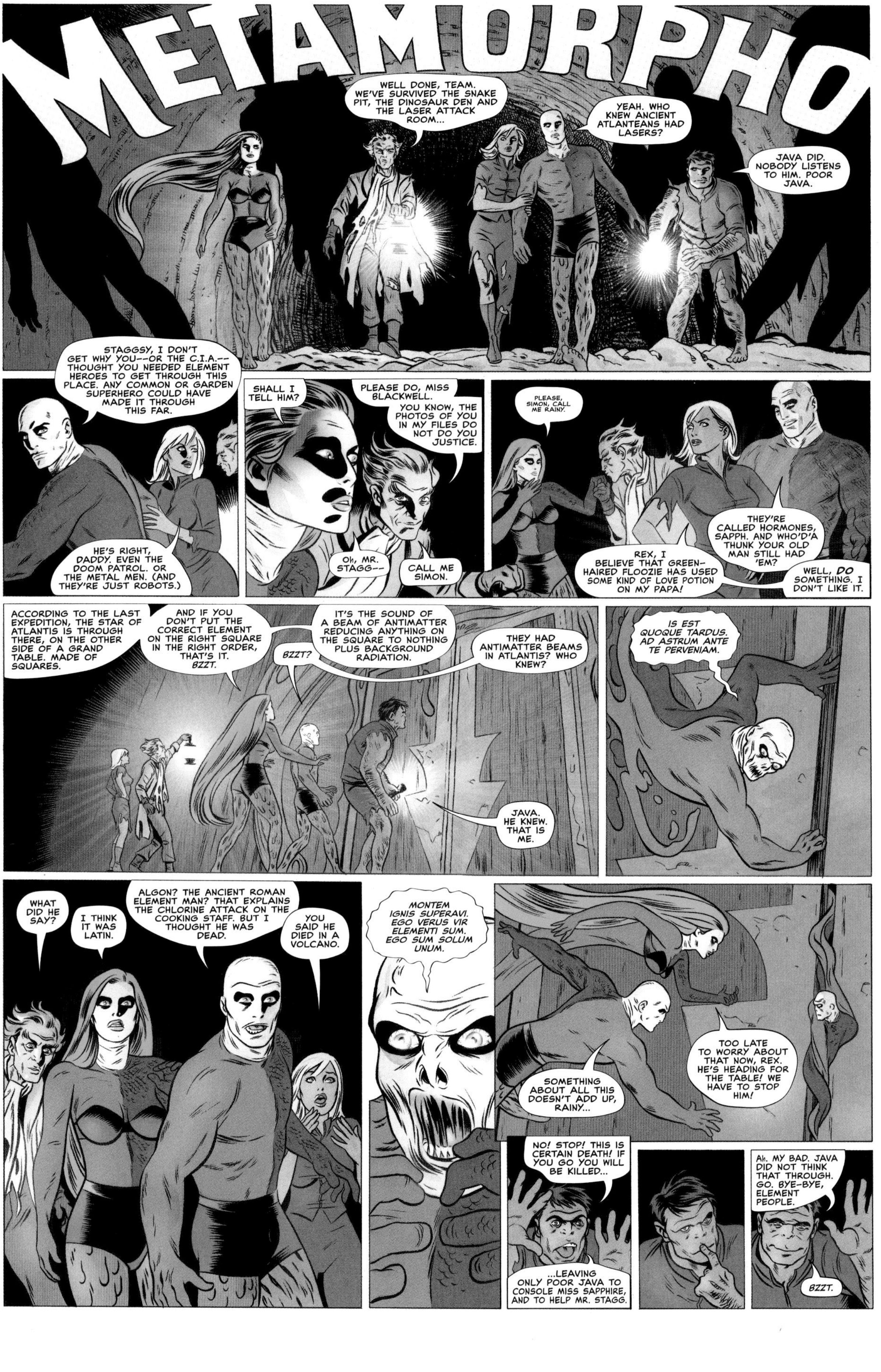
METAMORPHO
WELL DONE, TEAM. WE'VE SURVIVED THE SNAKE PIT, THE DINOSAUR DEN AND THE LASER ATTACK ROOM...
YEAH. WHO KNEW ANCIENT ATLANTEANS HAD LASERS?
JAVA DID. NOBODY LISTENS TO HIM. POOR JAVA.
STAGGSY, I DON'T GET WHY YOU--OR THE C.I.A.--THOUGHT YOU NEEDED ELEMENT HEROES TO GET THROUGH THIS PLACE. ANY COMMON OR GARDEN SUPERHERO COULD HAVE MADE IT THROUGH THIS FAR.
HE'S RIGHT, DADDY. EVEN THE DOOM PATROL. OR THE METAL MEN. (AND THEY'RE JUST ROBOTS.)
SHALL I TELL HIM?
PLEASE DO, MISS BLACKWELL.
YOU KNOW, THE PHOTOS OF YOU IN MY FILES DO NOT DO YOU JUSTICE.
Oh, MR. STAGG--
CALL ME SIMON.
PLEASE, SIMON, CALL ME RAINY.
THEY'RE CALLED HORMONES, SAPPH. AND WHO'D'A THUNK YOUR OLD MAN STILL HAD 'EM?
REX, I BELIEVE THAT GREEN-HAIRED FLOOZIE HAS USED SOME KIND OF LOVE POTION ON MY PAPA!
WELL, DO SOMETHING. I DON'T LIKE IT.
ACCORDING TO THE LAST EXPEDITION, THE STAR OF ATLANTIS IS THROUGH THERE, ON THE OTHER SIDE OF A GRAND TABLE. MADE OF SQUARES.
AND IF YOU DON'T PUT THE CORRECT ELEMENT ON THE RIGHT SQUARE IN THE RIGHT ORDER, THAT'S IT. BZZT.
BZZT?
IT'S THE SOUND OF A BEAM OF ANTIMATTER REDUCING ANYTHING ON THE SQUARE TO NOTHING PLUS BACKGROUND RADIATION.
THEY HAD ANTIMATTER BEAMS IN ATLANTIS? WHO KNEW?
JAVA. HE KNEW. THAT IS ME.
IS EST QUOQUE TARDUS. AD ASTRUM ANTE TE PERVENIAM.
WHAT DID HE SAY?
I THINK IT WAS LATIN.
ALGON? THE ANCIENT ROMAN ELEMENT MAN? THAT EXPLAINS THE CHLORINE ATTACK ON THE COOKING STAFF. BUT I THOUGHT HE WAS DEAD.
YOU SAID HE DIED IN A VOLCANO.
MONTEM IGNIS SUPERAVI. EGO VERUS VIR ELEMENTI SUM. EGO SUM SOLUM UNUM.
SOMETHING ABOUT ALL THIS DOESN'T ADD UP, RAINY...
TOO LATE TO WORRY ABOUT THAT NOW, REX. HE'S HEADING FOR THE TABLE! WE HAVE TO STOP HIM!
NO! STOP! THIS IS CERTAIN DEATH! IF YOU GO YOU WILL BE KILLED...
...LEAVING ONLY POOR JAVA TO CONSOLE MISS SAPPHIRE, AND TO HELP MR. STAGG.
Ah. MY BAD. JAVA DID NOT THINK THAT THROUGH. GO. BYE-BYE, ELEMENT PEOPLE.
BZZT.

REX MASON, THE EVER-LOVING ELEMENT MAN, AND URANIA BLACKWELL, THE GLAMOROUS ELEMENT GAL, ARE IN A MYSTERIOUS ANTARCTIC TEMPLE, IN A RACE AGAINST TIME WITH AN EVIL ROMAN ELEMENT MAN FOR THE LEGENDARY STAR OF ATLANTIS. YOU KNOW. THE USUAL.

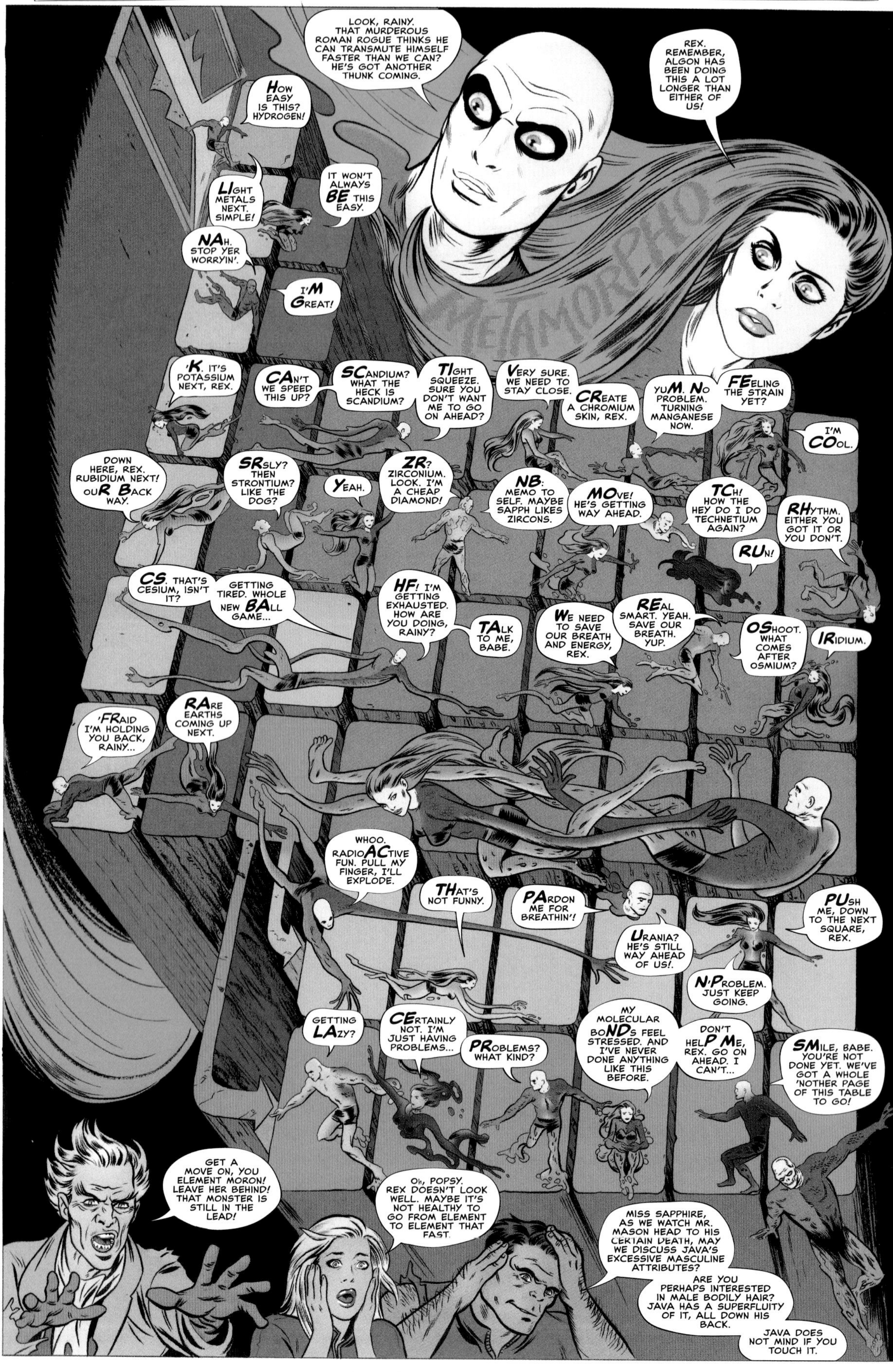
LOOK, RAINY. THAT MURDEROUS ROMAN ROGUE THINKS HE CAN TRANSMUTE HIMSELF FASTER THAN WE CAN? HE'S GOT ANOTHER THUNK COMING.
REX. REMEMBER, ALGON HAS BEEN DOING THIS A LOT LONGER THAN EITHER OF US!
HOW EASY IS THIS? HYDROGEN!
LIGHT METALS NEXT. SIMPLE!
IT WON'T ALWAYS BE THIS EASY.
NAH. STOP YER WORRYIN'.
I'M GREAT!
METAMORPHO
'K. IT'S POTASSIUM NEXT, REX.
CAN'T WE SPEED THIS UP?
SCANDIUM? WHAT THE HECK IS SCANDIUM?
TIGHT SQUEEZE. SURE YOU DON'T WANT ME TO GO ON AHEAD?
VERY SURE. WE NEED TO STAY CLOSE.
CREATE A CHROMIUM SKIN, REX.
YUM. NO PROBLEM. TURNING MANGANESE NOW.
FEELING THE STRAIN YET?
I'M COOL.
DOWN HERE, REX. RUBIDIUM NEXT! OUR BACK WAY.
SRSLY? THEN STRONTIUM? LIKE THE DOG?
YEAH.
ZR? ZIRCONIUM. LOOK. I'M A CHEAP DIAMOND!
NB: MEMO TO SELF. MAYBE SAPPH LIKES ZIRCONS.
MOVE! HE'S GETTING WAY AHEAD.
TCH! HOW THE HEY DO I DO TECHNETIUM AGAIN?
RHYTHM. EITHER YOU GOT IT OR YOU DON'T.
RUN!
CS. THAT'S CESIUM, ISN'T IT?
GETTING TIRED. WHOLE NEW BALL GAME...
HF! I'M GETTING EXHAUSTED. HOW ARE YOU DOING, RAINY?
TALK TO ME, BABE.
WE NEED TO SAVE OUR BREATH AND ENERGY, REX.
REAL SMART. YEAH. SAVE OUR BREATH. YUP.
OSHOOT. WHAT COMES AFTER OSMIUM?
IRIDIUM.
'FRAID I'M HOLDING YOU BACK, RAINY...
RARE EARTHS COMING UP NEXT.
WHOO. RADIOACTIVE FUN. PULL MY FINGER, I'LL EXPLODE.
THAT'S NOT FUNNY.
PARDON ME FOR BREATHIN'!
URANIA? HE'S STILL WAY AHEAD OF US!.
PUSH ME, DOWN TO THE NEXT SQUARE, REX.
N·PROBLEM. JUST KEEP GOING.
GETTING LAZY?
CERTAINLY NOT. I'M JUST HAVING PROBLEMS...
PROBLEMS? WHAT KIND?
MY MOLECULAR BONDS FEEL STRESSED. AND I'VE NEVER DONE ANYTHING LIKE THIS BEFORE.
DON'T HELP ME, REX. GO ON AHEAD. I CAN'T...
SMILE, BABE. YOU'RE NOT DONE YET. WE'VE GOT A WHOLE 'NOTHER PAGE OF THIS TABLE TO GO!
GET A MOVE ON, YOU ELEMENT MORON! LEAVE HER BEHIND! THAT MONSTER IS STILL IN THE LEAD!
OH, POPSY. REX DOESN'T LOOK WELL. MAYBE IT'S NOT HEALTHY TO GO FROM ELEMENT TO ELEMENT THAT FAST.
MISS SAPPHIRE, AS WE WATCH MR. MASON HEAD TO HIS CERTAIN DEATH, MAY WE DISCUSS JAVA'S EXCESSIVE MASCULINE ATTRIBUTES?
ARE YOU PERHAPS INTERESTED IN MALE BODILY HAIR? JAVA HAS A SUPERFLUITY OF IT, ALL DOWN HIS BACK.
JAVA DOES NOT MIND IF YOU TOUCH IT.

REX MASON, A.K.A METAMORPHO THE ELEMENT MAN, AND URANIA BLACKWELL, ELEMENT GIRL, ARE RACING ACROSS A GIANT TABLE OF ELEMENTS IN AN ANTARCTIC TEMPLE, IN A TRANSMUTATIONAL RACE AGAINST TIME WITH ALGON, THE ORIGINAL ELEMENT MAN.

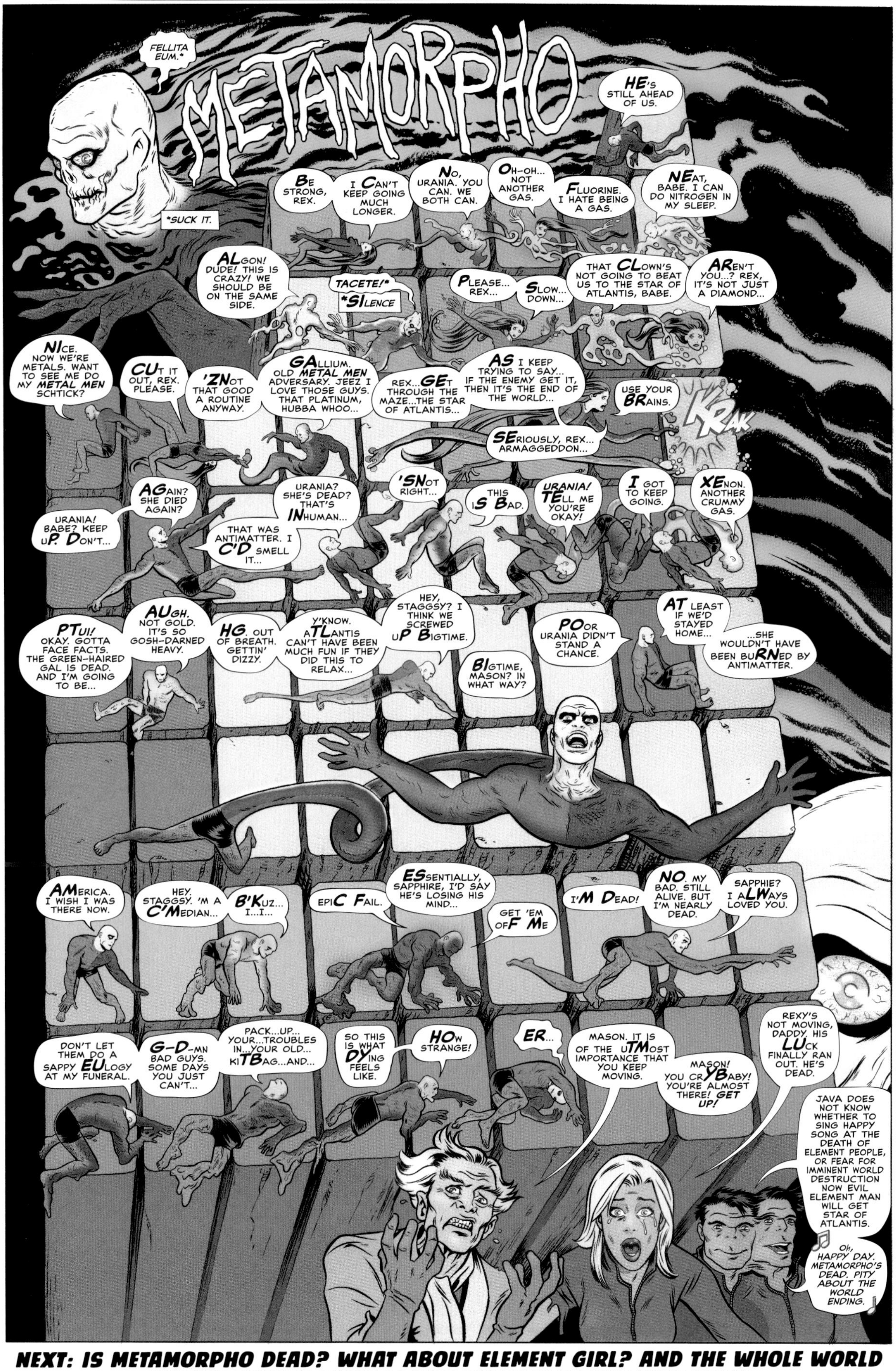
FELLITA EUM.*
METAMORPHO
*SUCK IT.
HE'S STILL AHEAD OF US.
BE STRONG, REX.
I CAN'T KEEP GOING MUCH LONGER.
NO, URANIA. YOU CAN. WE BOTH CAN.
OH-OH... NOT ANOTHER GAS.
FLUORINE. I HATE BEING A GAS.
NEAT, BABE. I CAN DO NITROGEN IN MY SLEEP.
ALGON! DUDE! THIS IS CRAZY! WE SHOULD BE ON THE SAME SIDE.
TACETE!*
*SILENCE
PLEASE... REX...
SLOW... DOWN...
THAT CLOWN'S NOT GOING TO BEAT US TO THE STAR OF ATLANTIS, BABE.
AREN'T YOU...? REX, IT'S NOT JUST A DIAMOND...
NICE. NOW WE'RE METALS. WANT TO SEE ME DO MY METAL MEN SCHTICK?
CUT IT OUT, REX. PLEASE.
'ZNOT THAT GOOD A ROUTINE ANYWAY.
GALLIUM. OLD METAL MEN ADVERSARY. JEEZ I LOVE THOSE GUYS. THAT PLATINUM, HUBBA WHOO...
REX...GET THROUGH THE MAZE...THE STAR OF ATLANTIS...
AS I KEEP TRYING TO SAY... IF THE ENEMY GET IT, THEN IT'S THE END OF THE WORLD...
USE YOUR BRAINS.
KRAK
SERIOUSLY, REX... ARMAGGEDDON...
URANIA! BABE? KEEP UP. DON'T...
AGAIN? SHE DIED AGAIN?
THAT WAS ANTIMATTER. I C'D SMELL IT...
URANIA? SHE'S DEAD? THAT'S INHUMAN...
'SNOT RIGHT...
THIS IS BAD.
URANIA! TELL ME YOU'RE OKAY!
I GOT TO KEEP GOING.
XENON. ANOTHER CRUMMY GAS.
PTUI! OKAY. GOTTA FACE FACTS. THE GREEN-HAIRED GAL IS DEAD. AND I'M GOING TO BE...
AUGH. NOT GOLD. IT'S SO GOSH-DARNED HEAVY.
HG. OUT OF BREATH. GETTIN' DIZZY.
Y'KNOW. ATLANTIS CAN'T HAVE BEEN MUCH FUN IF THEY DID THIS TO RELAX...
HEY, STAGGSY? I THINK WE SCREWED UP BIGTIME.
BIGTIME, MASON? IN WHAT WAY?
POOR URANIA DIDN'T STAND A CHANCE.
AT LEAST IF WE'D STAYED HOME...
...SHE WOULDN'T HAVE BEEN BURNED BY ANTIMATTER.
AMERICA. I WISH I WAS THERE NOW.
HEY. STAGGSY. 'M A C'MEDIAN...
B'KUZ... I...I...
EPIC FAIL.
ESSENTIALLY, SAPPHIRE, I'D SAY HE'S LOSING HIS MIND...
GET 'EM OFF ME
I'M DEAD!
NO. MY BAD. STILL ALIVE. BUT I'M NEARLY DEAD.
SAPPHIE? I ALWAYS LOVED YOU.
DON'T LET THEM DO A SAPPY EULOGY AT MY FUNERAL.
G-D-MN BAD GUYS. SOME DAYS YOU JUST CAN'T...
PACK...UP... YOUR...TROUBLES IN...YOUR OLD... KITBAG...AND...
SO THIS IS WHAT DYING FEELS LIKE.
HOW STRANGE!
ER...
MASON. IT IS OF THE UTMOST IMPORTANCE THAT YOU KEEP MOVING.
MASON! YOU CRYBABY! YOU'RE ALMOST THERE! GET UP!
REXY'S NOT MOVING, DADDY. HIS LUCK FINALLY RAN OUT. HE'S DEAD.
JAVA DOES NOT KNOW WHETHER TO SING HAPPY SONG AT THE DEATH OF ELEMENT PEOPLE, OR FEAR FOR IMMINENT WORLD DESTRUCTION NOW EVIL ELEMENT MAN WILL GET STAR OF ATLANTIS.
OH, HAPPY DAY. METAMORPHO'S DEAD. PITY ABOUT THE WORLD ENDING.

NEXT: IS METAMORPHO DEAD? WHAT ABOUT ELEMENT GIRL? AND THE WHOLE WORLD ENDING THING? WHAT ABOUT THAT? FIND OUT NEXT WEEK...

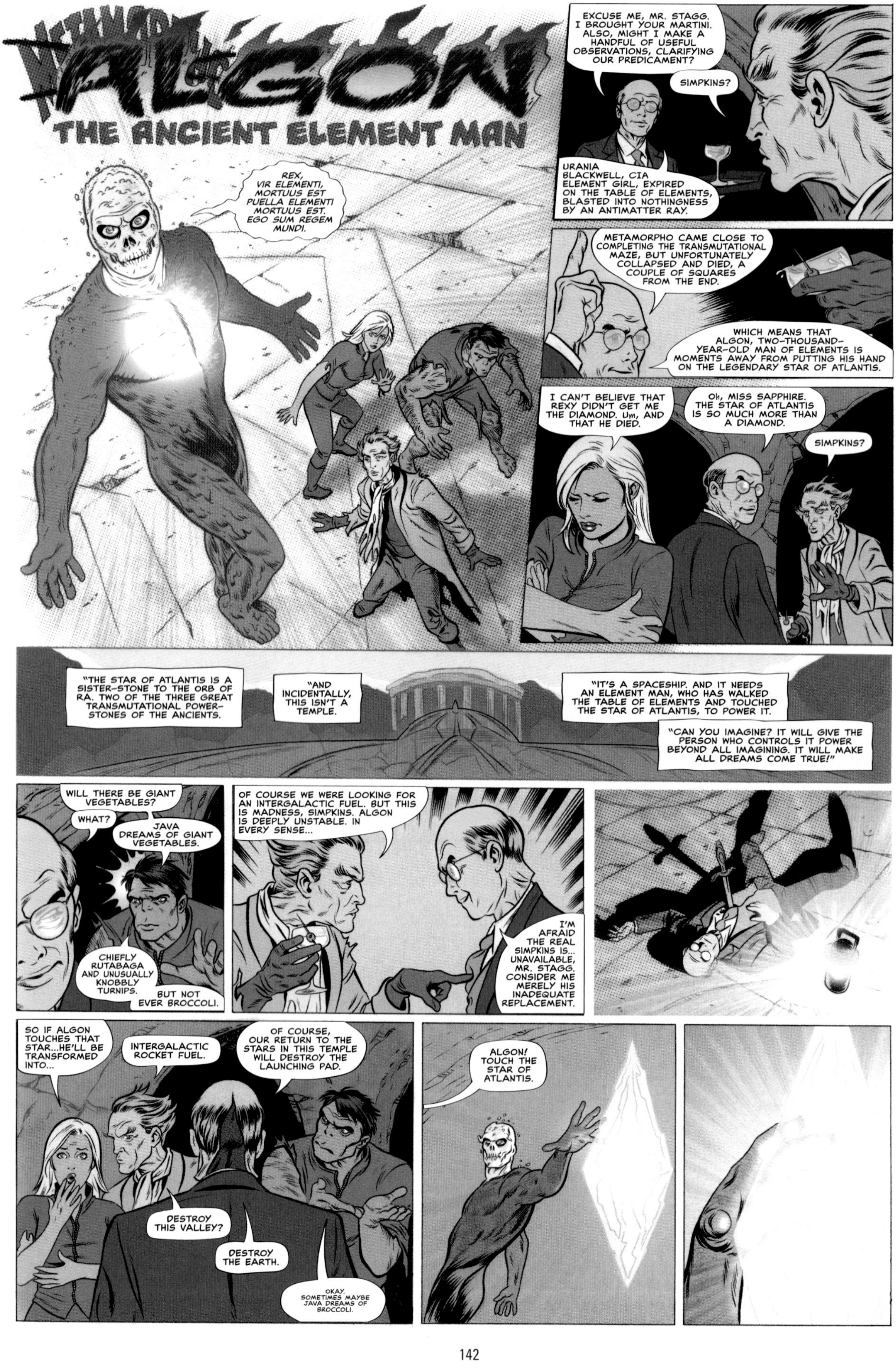

ALGON
THE ANCIENT ELEMENT MAN
REX, VIR ELEMENTI, MORTUUS EST PUELLA ELEMENTI MORTUUS EST. EGO SUM REGEM MUNDI.
EXCUSE ME, MR. STAGG. I BROUGHT YOUR MARTINI. ALSO, MIGHT I MAKE A HANDFUL OF USEFUL OBSERVATIONS, CLARIFYING OUR PREDICAMENT?
SIMPKINS?
URANIA BLACKWELL, CIA ELEMENT GIRL, EXPIRED ON THE TABLE OF ELEMENTS, BLASTED INTO NOTHINGNESS BY AN ANTIMATTER RAY.
METAMORPHO CAME CLOSE TO COMPLETING THE TRANSMUTATIONAL MAZE, BUT UNFORTUNATELY COLLAPSED AND DIED, A COUPLE OF SQUARES FROM THE END.
WHICH MEANS THAT ALGON, TWO-THOUSAND-YEAR-OLD MAN OF ELEMENTS IS MOMENTS AWAY FROM PUTTING HIS HAND ON THE LEGENDARY STAR OF ATLANTIS.
I CAN'T BELIEVE THAT REXY DIDN'T GET ME THE DIAMOND. Um, AND THAT HE DIED.
Oh, MISS SAPPHIRE. THE STAR OF ATLANTIS IS SO MUCH MORE THAN A DIAMOND.
SIMPKINS?
"THE STAR OF ATLANTIS IS A SISTER-STONE TO THE ORB OF RA. TWO OF THE THREE GREAT TRANSMUTATIONAL POWER-STONES OF THE ANCIENTS.
"AND INCIDENTALLY, THIS ISN'T A TEMPLE.
"IT'S A SPACESHIP. AND IT NEEDS AN ELEMENT MAN, WHO HAS WALKED THE TABLE OF ELEMENTS AND TOUCHED THE STAR OF ATLANTIS, TO POWER IT.
"CAN YOU IMAGINE? IT WILL GIVE THE PERSON WHO CONTROLS IT POWER BEYOND ALL IMAGINING. IT WILL MAKE ALL DREAMS COME TRUE!"
WILL THERE BE GIANT VEGETABLES?
WHAT?
JAVA DREAMS OF GIANT VEGETABLES.
CHIEFLY RUTABAGA AND UNUSUALLY KNOBBLY TURNIPS.
BUT NOT EVER BROCCOLI.
OF COURSE WE WERE LOOKING FOR AN INTERGALACTIC FUEL. BUT THIS IS MADNESS, SIMPKINS. ALGON IS DEEPLY UNSTABLE. IN EVERY SENSE...
I'M AFRAID THE REAL SIMPKINS IS... UNAVAILABLE, MR. STAGG. CONSIDER ME MERELY HIS INADEQUATE REPLACEMENT.
SO IF ALGON TOUCHES THAT STAR...HE'LL BE TRANSFORMED INTO...
INTERGALACTIC ROCKET FUEL.
OF COURSE, OUR RETURN TO THE STARS IN THIS TEMPLE WILL DESTROY THE LAUNCHING PAD.
DESTROY THIS VALLEY?
DESTROY THE EARTH.
OKAY. SOMETIMES MAYBE JAVA DREAMS OF BROCCOLI.
ALGON! TOUCH THE STAR OF ATLANTIS.

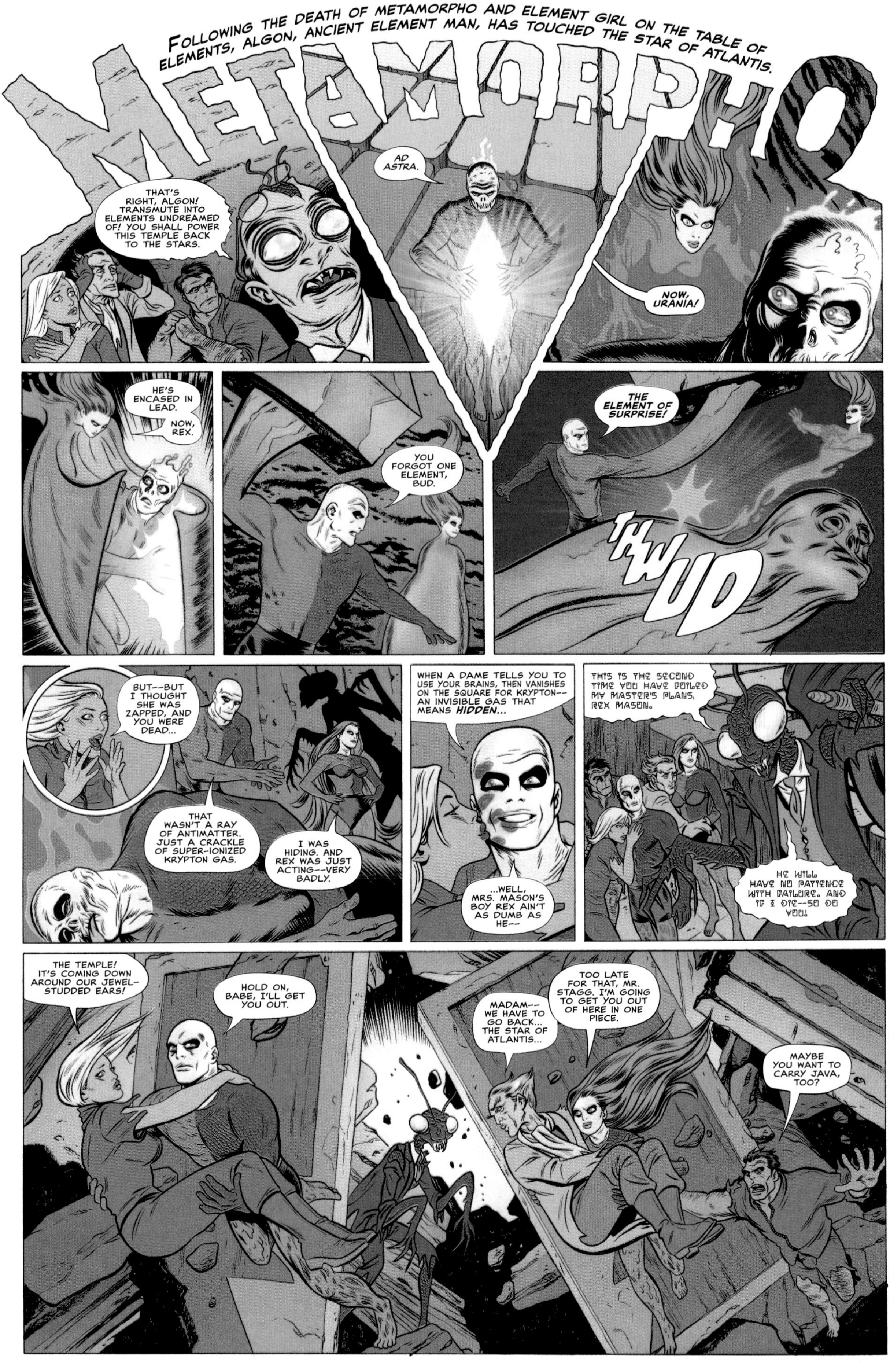
FOLLOWING THE DEATH OF METAMORPHO AND ELEMENT GIRL ON THE TABLE OF ELEMENTS, ALGON, ANCIENT ELEMENT MAN, HAS TOUCHED THE STAR OF ATLANTIS.
METAMORPHO
THAT'S RIGHT, ALGON! TRANSMUTE INTO ELEMENTS UNDREAMED OF! YOU SHALL POWER THIS TEMPLE BACK TO THE STARS.
AD ASTRA.
NOW, URANIA!
HE'S ENCASED IN LEAD.
NOW, REX.
YOU FORGOT ONE ELEMENT, BUD.
THE ELEMENT OF SURPRISE!
THWUD
BUT--BUT I THOUGHT SHE WAS ZAPPED, AND YOU WERE DEAD...
THAT WASN'T A RAY OF ANTIMATTER. JUST A CRACKLE OF SUPER-IONIZED KRYPTON GAS.
I WAS HIDING. AND REX WAS JUST ACTING--VERY BADLY.
WHEN A DAME TELLS YOU TO USE YOUR BRAINS, THEN VANISHES ON THE SQUARE FOR KRYPTON--AN INVISIBLE GAS THAT MEANS HIDDEN...
...WELL, MRS. MASON'S BOY REX AIN'T AS DUMB AS HE--
THIS IS THE SECOND TIME YOU HAVE FOILED MY MASTER'S PLANS, REX MASON.
HE WILL HAVE NO PATIENCE WITH FAILURE. AND IF I DIE--SO DO YOU!
THE TEMPLE! IT'S COMING DOWN AROUND OUR JEWEL-STUDDED EARS!
HOLD ON, BABE, I'LL GET YOU OUT.
MADAM--WE HAVE TO GO BACK... THE STAR OF ATLANTIS...
TOO LATE FOR THAT, MR. STAGG. I'M GOING TO GET YOU OUT OF HERE IN ONE PIECE.
MAYBE YOU WANT TO CARRY JAVA, TOO?

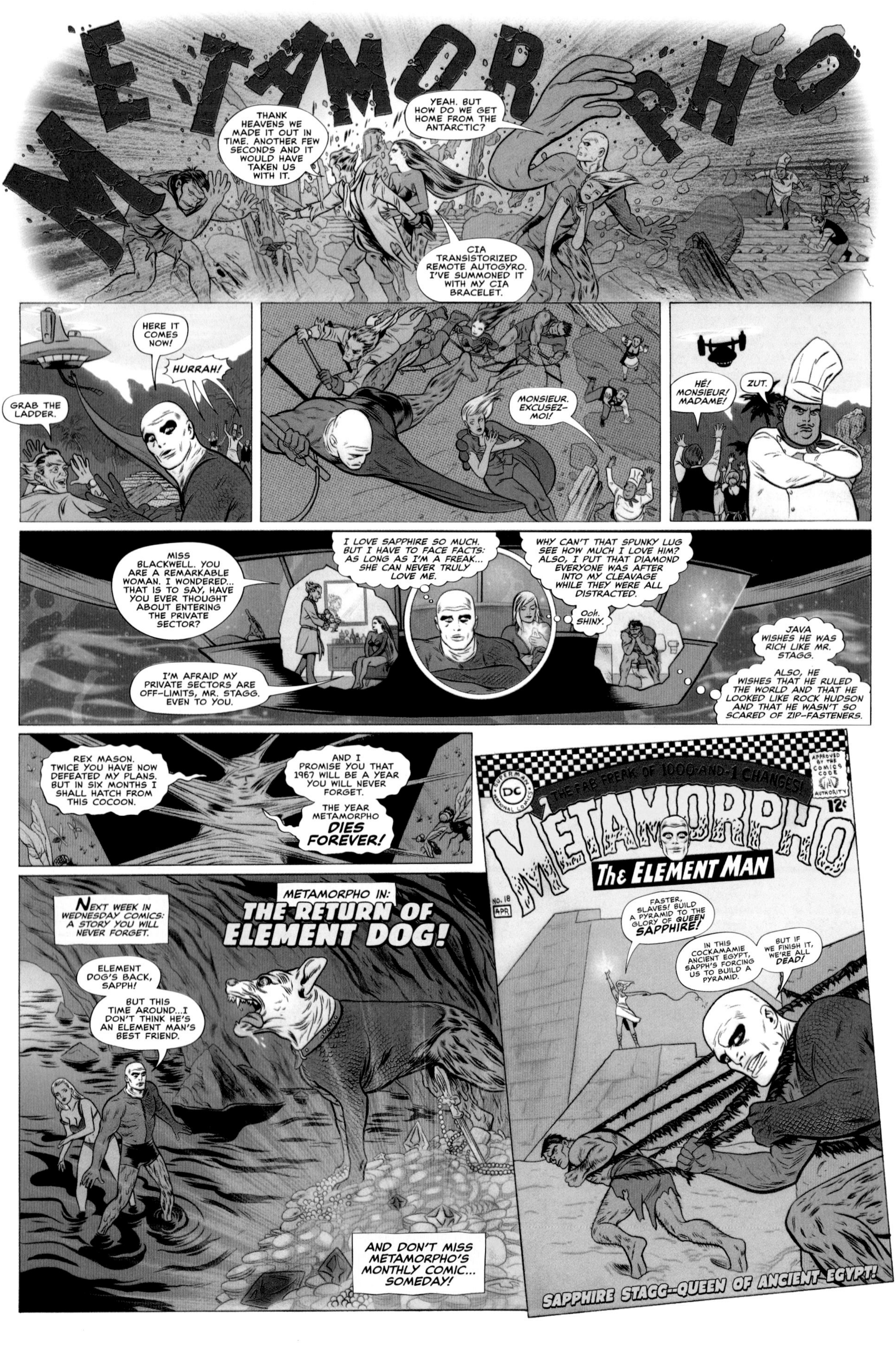
METAMORPHO
THANK HEAVENS WE MADE IT OUT IN TIME. ANOTHER FEW SECONDS AND IT WOULD HAVE TAKEN US WITH IT.
YEAH. BUT HOW DO WE GET HOME FROM THE ANTARCTIC?
CIA TRANSISTORIZED REMOTE AUTOGYRO. I'VE SUMMONED IT WITH MY CIA BRACELET.
HERE IT COMES NOW!
HURRAH!
GRAB THE LADDER.
MONSIEUR. EXCUSEZ-MOI!
HÉ! MONSIEUR! MADAME!
ZUT.
MISS BLACKWELL. YOU ARE A REMARKABLE WOMAN. I WONDERED... THAT IS TO SAY, HAVE YOU EVER THOUGHT ABOUT ENTERING THE PRIVATE SECTOR?
I LOVE SAPPHIRE SO MUCH. BUT I HAVE TO FACE FACTS: AS LONG AS I'M A FREAK... SHE CAN NEVER TRULY LOVE ME.
WHY CAN'T THAT SPUNKY LUG SEE HOW MUCH I LOVE HIM? ALSO, I PUT THAT DIAMOND EVERYONE WAS AFTER INTO MY CLEAVAGE WHILE THEY WERE ALL DISTRACTED.
Ooh. SHINY.
I'M AFRAID MY PRIVATE SECTORS ARE OFF-LIMITS, MR. STAGG. EVEN TO YOU.
JAVA WISHES HE WAS RICH LIKE MR. STAGG.
ALSO, HE WISHES THAT HE RULED THE WORLD AND THAT HE LOOKED LIKE ROCK HUDSON AND THAT HE WASN'T SO SCARED OF ZIP-FASTENERS.
REX MASON. TWICE YOU HAVE NOW DEFEATED MY PLANS. BUT IN SIX MONTHS I SHALL HATCH FROM THIS COCOON.
AND I PROMISE YOU THAT 1967 WILL BE A YEAR YOU WILL NEVER FORGET.
THE YEAR METAMORPHO DIES FOREVER!
NEXT WEEK IN WEDNESDAY COMICS: A STORY YOU WILL NEVER FORGET.
METAMORPHO IN: THE RETURN OF ELEMENT DOG!
ELEMENT DOG'S BACK, SAPPH!
BUT THIS TIME AROUND...I DON'T THINK HE'S AN ELEMENT MAN'S BEST FRIEND.
AND DON'T MISS METAMORPHO'S MONTHLY COMIC... SOMEDAY!
APPROVED BY THE COMICS CODE AUTHORITY
DC
THE FAB FREAK OF 1000-AND-1 CHANGES!
12¢
METAMORPHO
The ELEMENT MAN
NO. 18 APR
FASTER, SLAVES! BUILD A PYRAMID TO THE GLORY OF QUEEN SAPPHIRE!
IN THIS COCKAMAMIE ANCIENT EGYPT, SAPPH'S FORCING US TO BUILD A PYRAMID.
BUT IF WE FINISH IT, WE'RE ALL DEAD!
SAPPHIRE STAGG--QUEEN OF ANCIENT EGYPT!

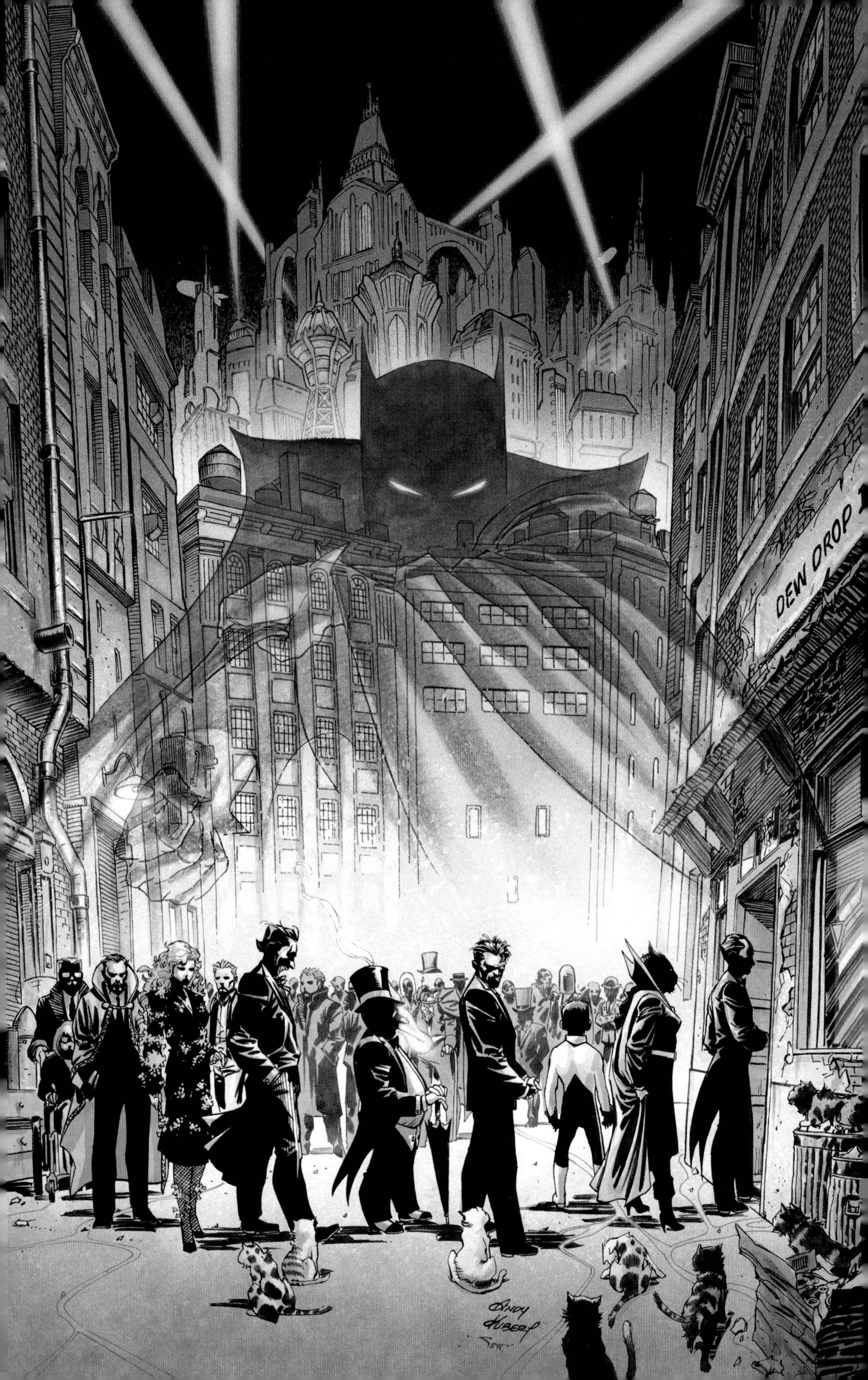
DEW DROP
ANDY KUBERT

BATMAN #686 variant cover art by Alex Ross

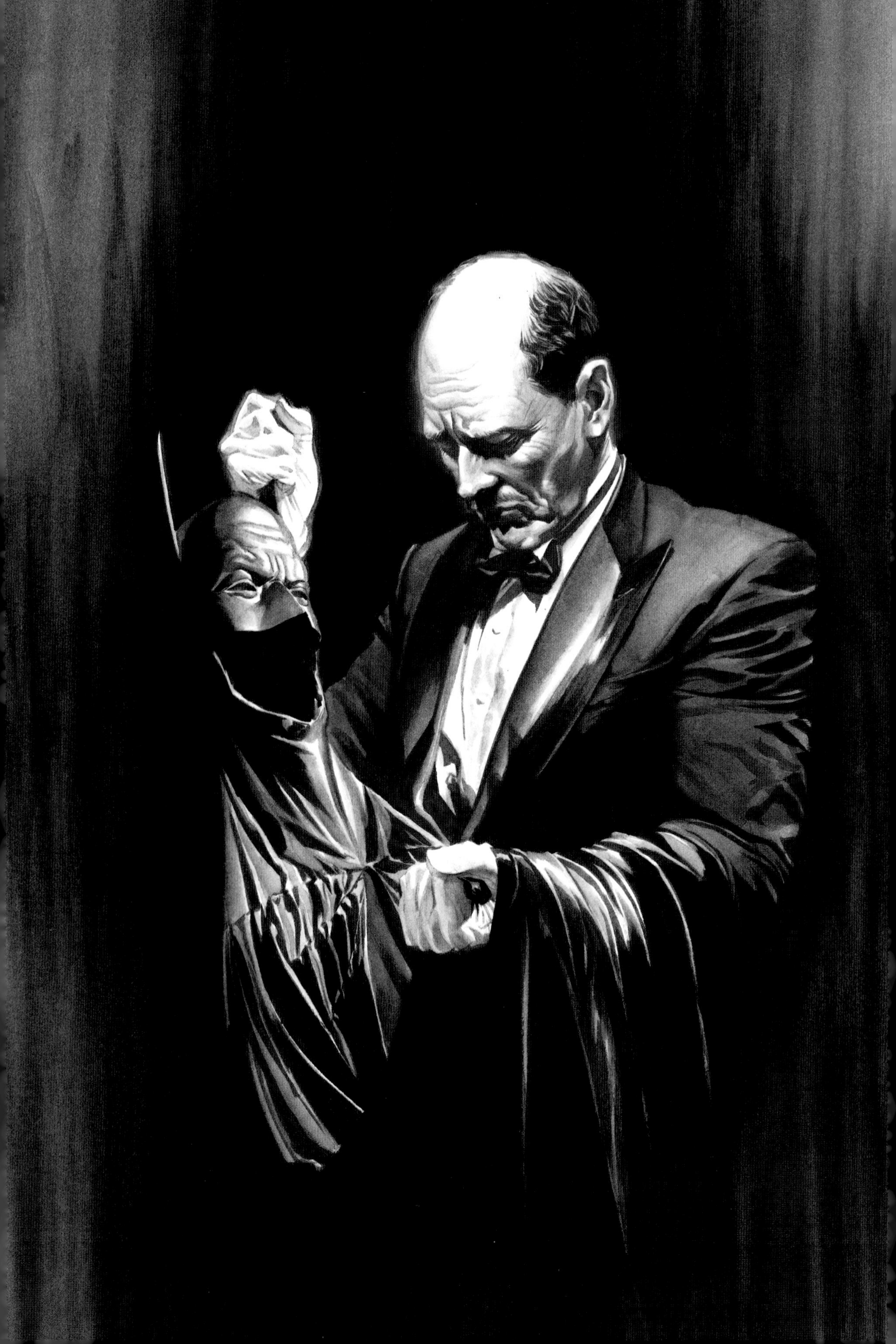

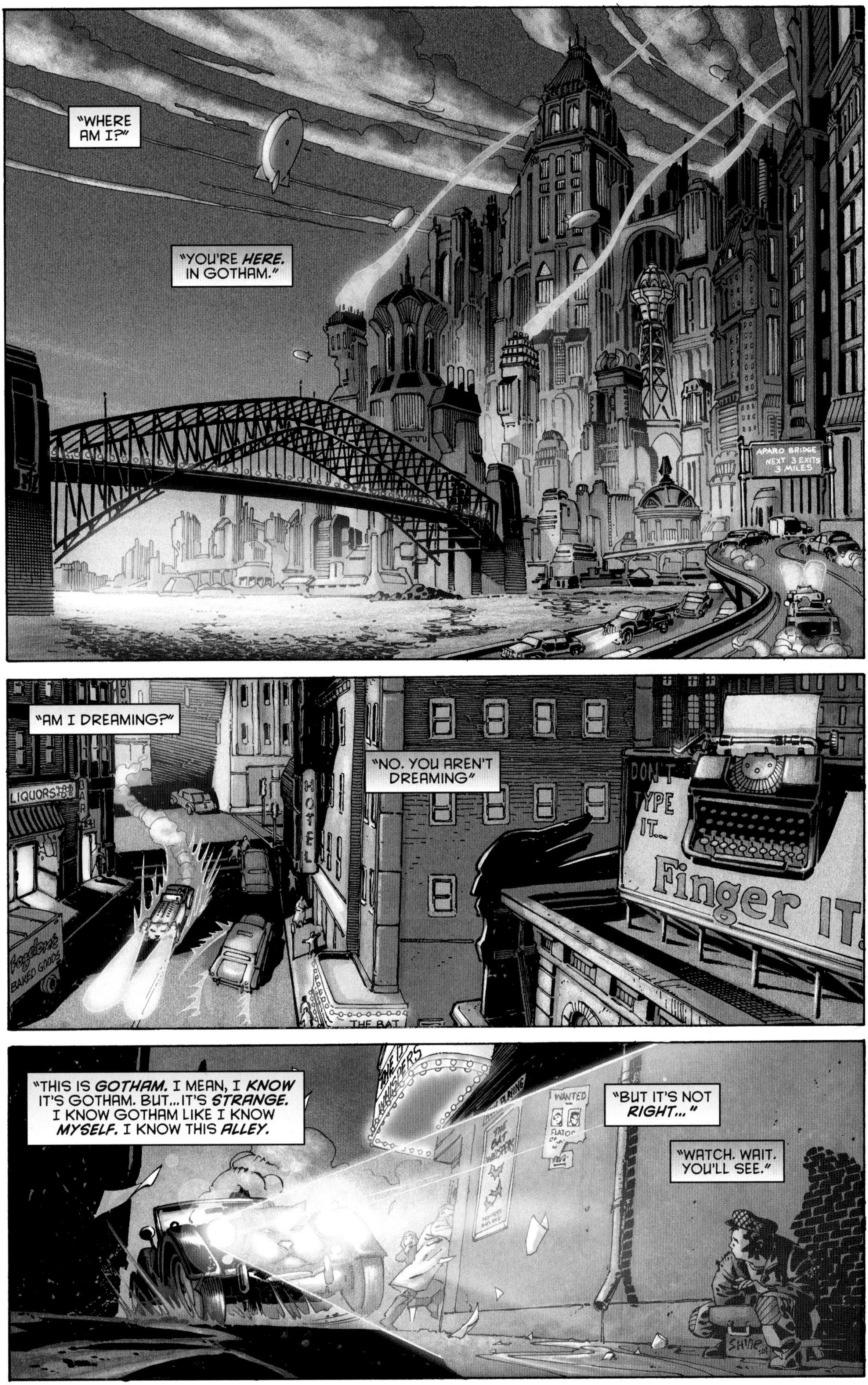
"WHERE AM I?"
"YOU'RE *HERE.* IN GOTHAM."
APARO BRIDGE NEXT 3 EXITS 3 MILES
"AM I DREAMING?"
LIQUORS
HOTEL
"NO. YOU AREN'T DREAMING"
DON'T TYPE IT...
Finger IT!
BAKED GOODS
THE BAT
"THIS IS *GOTHAM.* I MEAN, I *KNOW* IT'S GOTHAM. BUT...IT'S *STRANGE.* I KNOW GOTHAM LIKE I KNOW *MYSELF.* I KNOW THIS *ALLEY.*
WANTED
"BUT IT'S NOT *RIGHT...*"
"WATCH. WAIT. YOU'LL SEE."

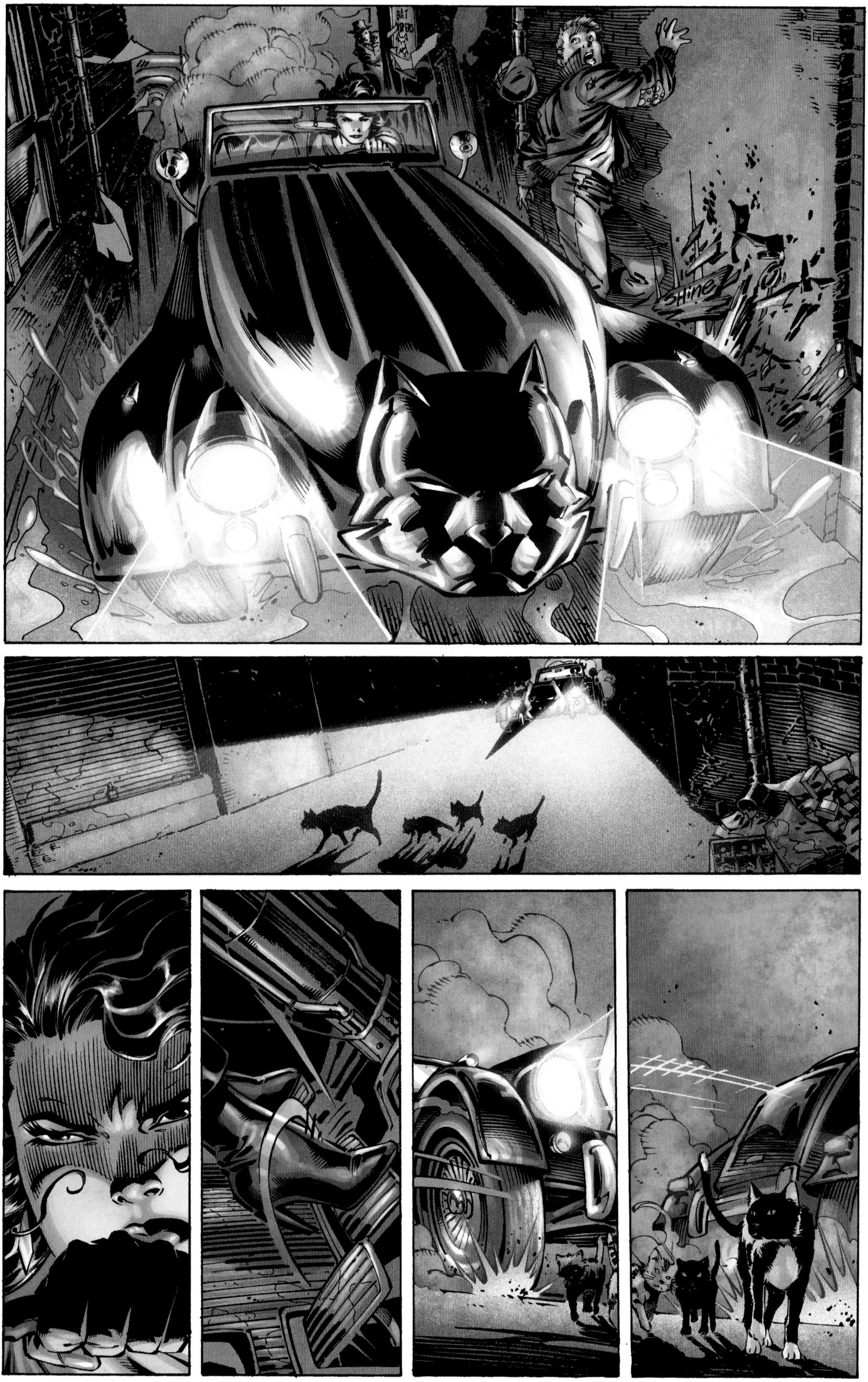
SHINE

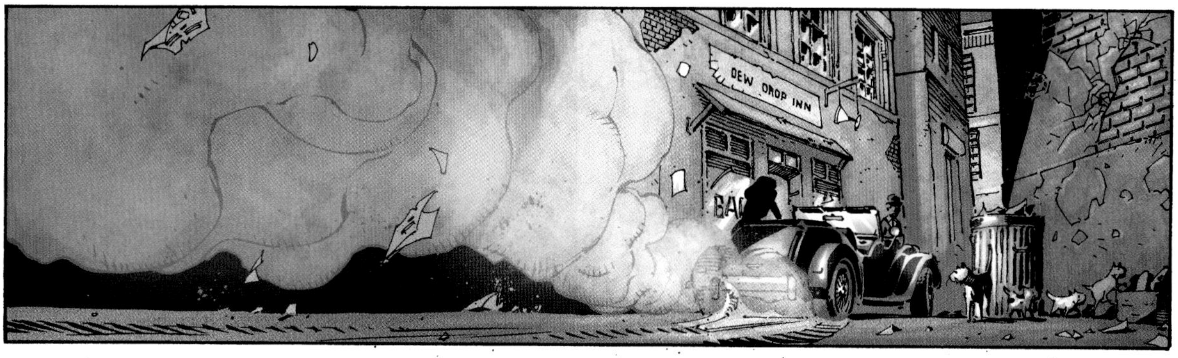
DEW DROP INN

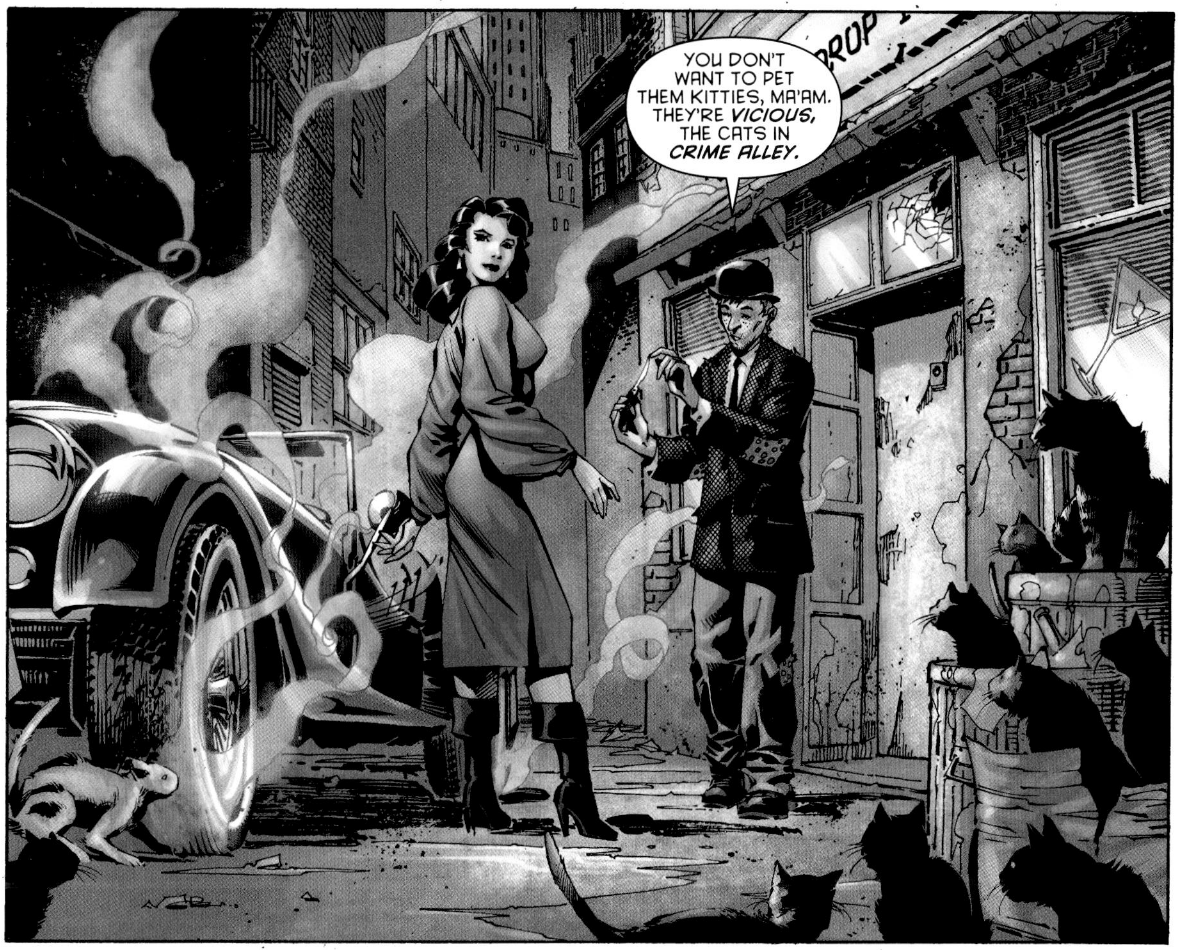
YOU DON'T WANT TO PET THEM KITTIES, MA'AM. THEY'RE VICIOUS, THE CATS IN CRIME ALLEY.

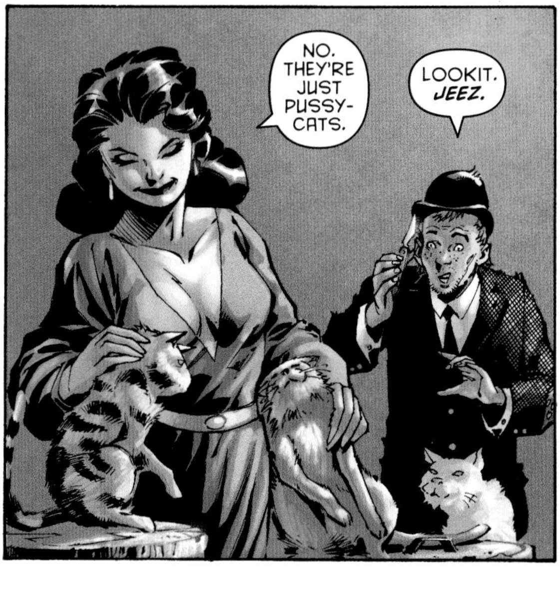
NO. THEY'RE JUST PUSSY-CATS.
LOOKIT. JEEZ.

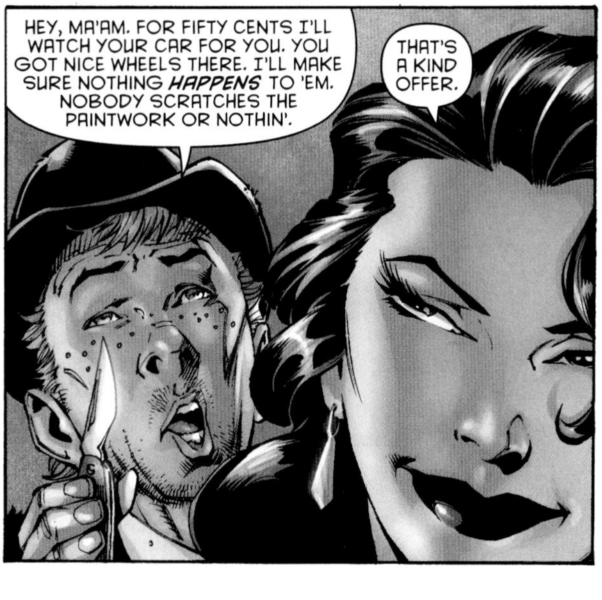
HEY, MA'AM. FOR FIFTY CENTS I'LL WATCH YOUR CAR FOR YOU. YOU GOT NICE WHEELS THERE. I'LL MAKE SURE NOTHING HAPPENS TO 'EM. NOBODY SCRATCHES THE PAINTWORK OR NOTHIN'.
THAT'S A KIND OFFER.

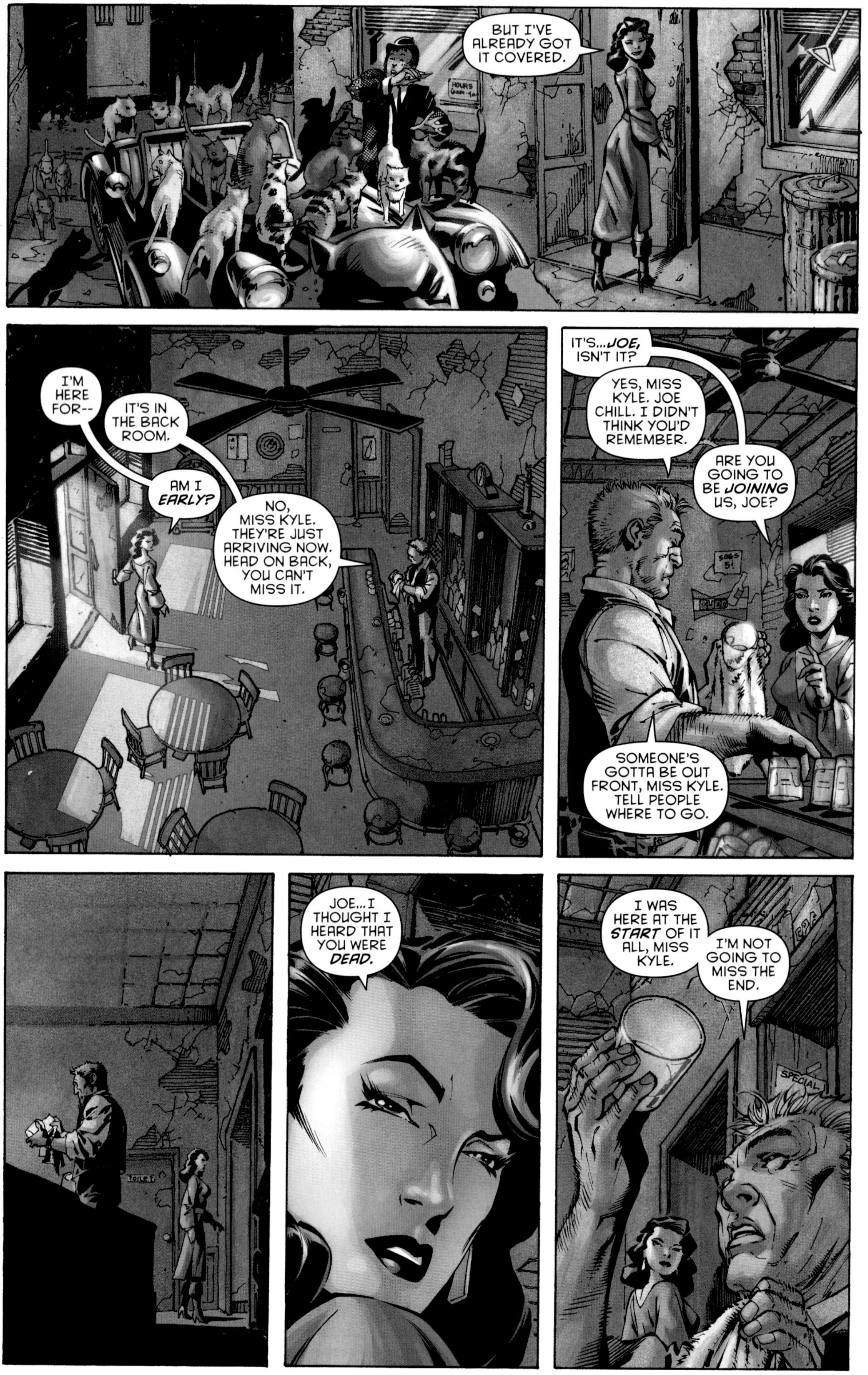
BUT I'VE ALREADY GOT IT COVERED.
HOURS 6am-1a
I'M HERE FOR--
IT'S IN THE BACK ROOM.
AM I EARLY?
NO, MISS KYLE. THEY'RE JUST ARRIVING NOW. HEAD ON BACK, YOU CAN'T MISS IT.
IT'S...JOE, ISN'T IT?
YES, MISS KYLE. JOE CHILL. I DIDN'T THINK YOU'D REMEMBER.
ARE YOU GOING TO BE JOINING US, JOE?
SOMEONE'S GOTTA BE OUT FRONT, MISS KYLE. TELL PEOPLE WHERE TO GO.
TOILET
JOE...I THOUGHT I HEARD THAT YOU WERE DEAD.
I WAS HERE AT THE START OF IT ALL, MISS KYLE.
I'M NOT GOING TO MISS THE END.
SPECIAL

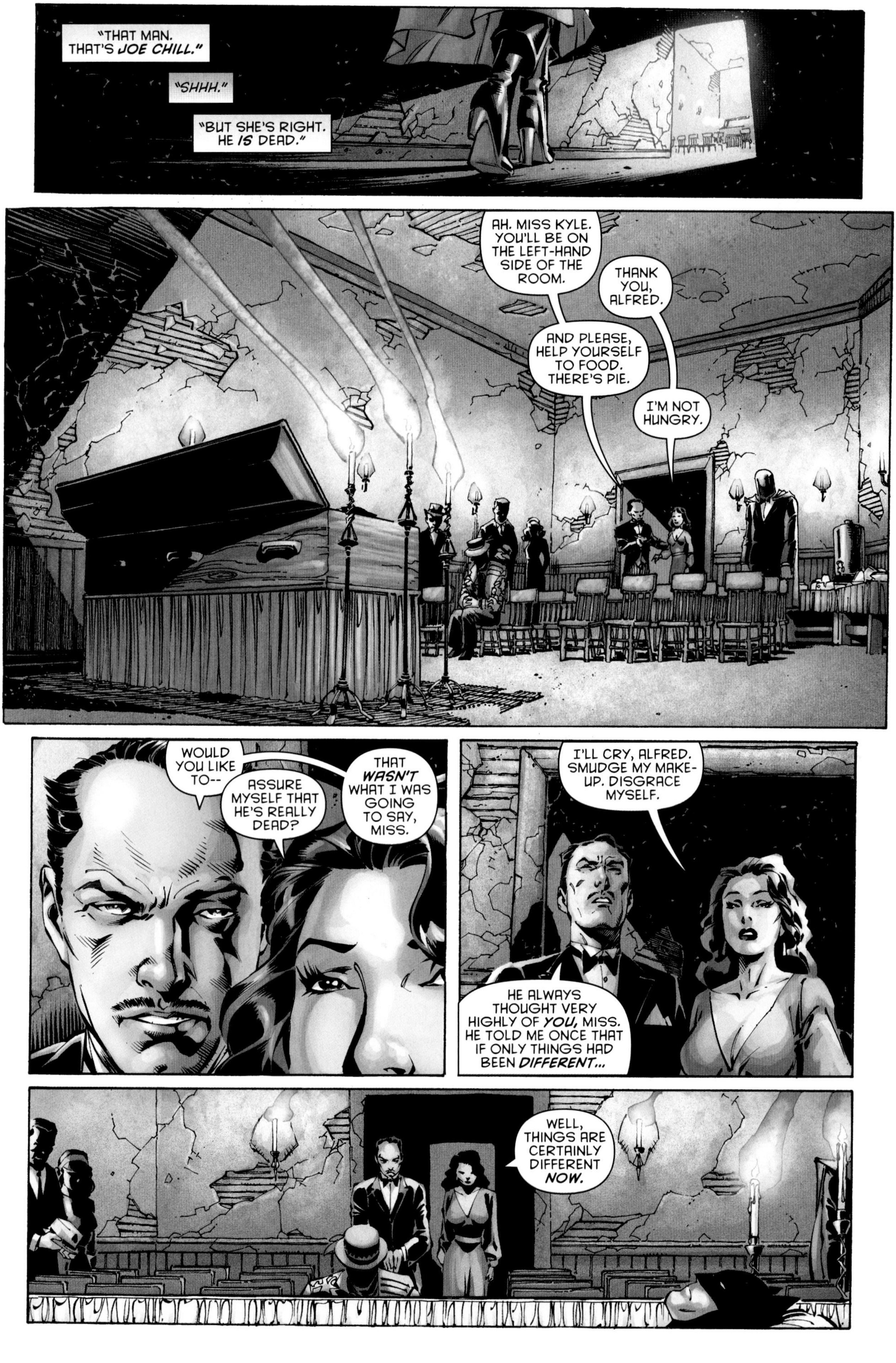
"THAT MAN. THAT'S JOE CHILL."
"SHHH."
"BUT SHE'S RIGHT. HE IS DEAD."
AH. MISS KYLE. YOU'LL BE ON THE LEFT-HAND SIDE OF THE ROOM.
THANK YOU, ALFRED.
AND PLEASE, HELP YOURSELF TO FOOD. THERE'S PIE.
I'M NOT HUNGRY.
WOULD YOU LIKE TO--
ASSURE MYSELF THAT HE'S REALLY DEAD?
THAT WASN'T WHAT I WAS GOING TO SAY, MISS.
I'LL CRY, ALFRED. SMUDGE MY MAKE-UP. DISGRACE MYSELF.
HE ALWAYS THOUGHT VERY HIGHLY OF YOU, MISS. HE TOLD ME ONCE THAT IF ONLY THINGS HAD BEEN DIFFERENT...
WELL, THINGS ARE CERTAINLY DIFFERENT NOW.

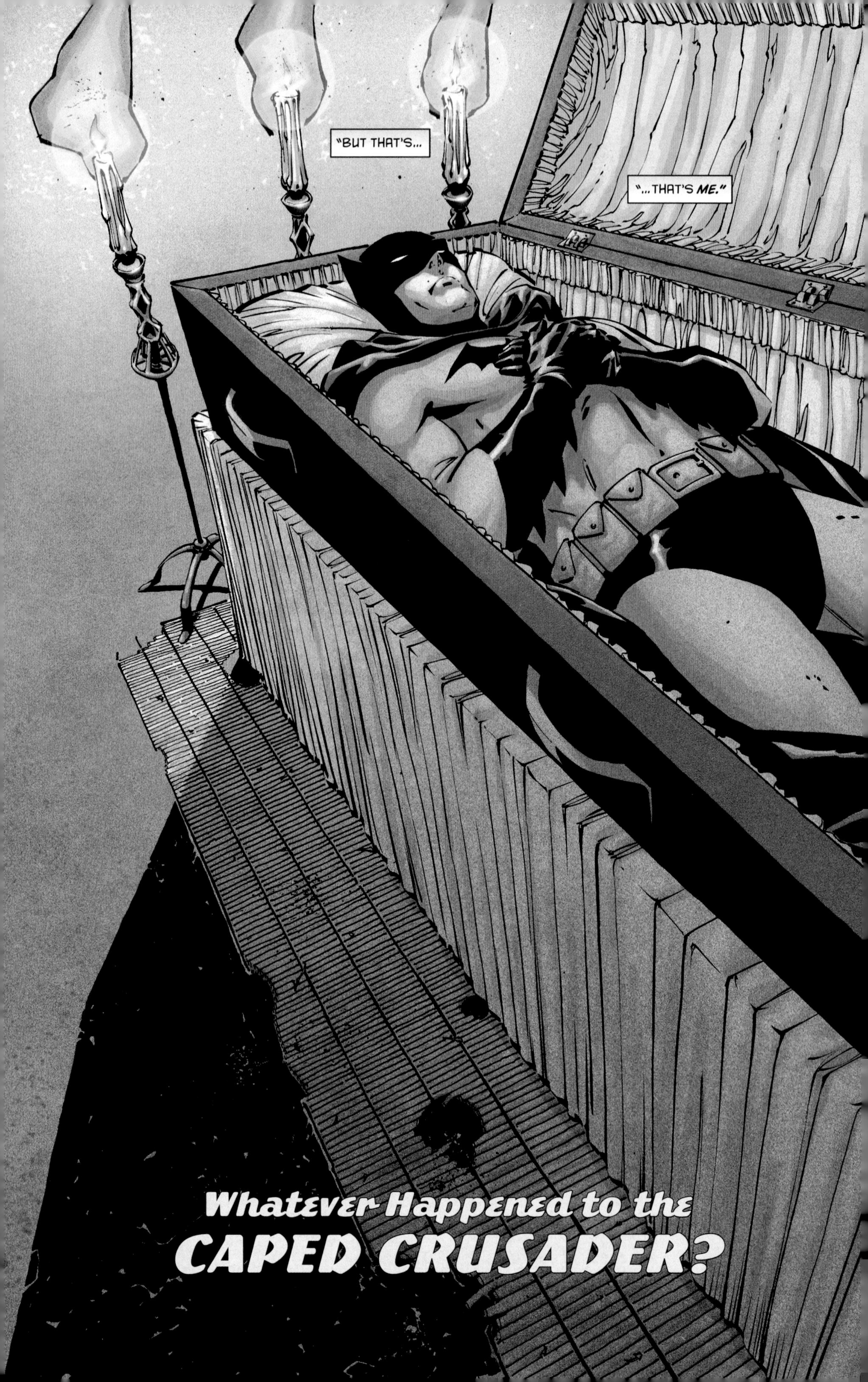
"BUT THAT'S...
"...THAT'S ME."
Whatever Happened to the
CAPED CRUSADER?

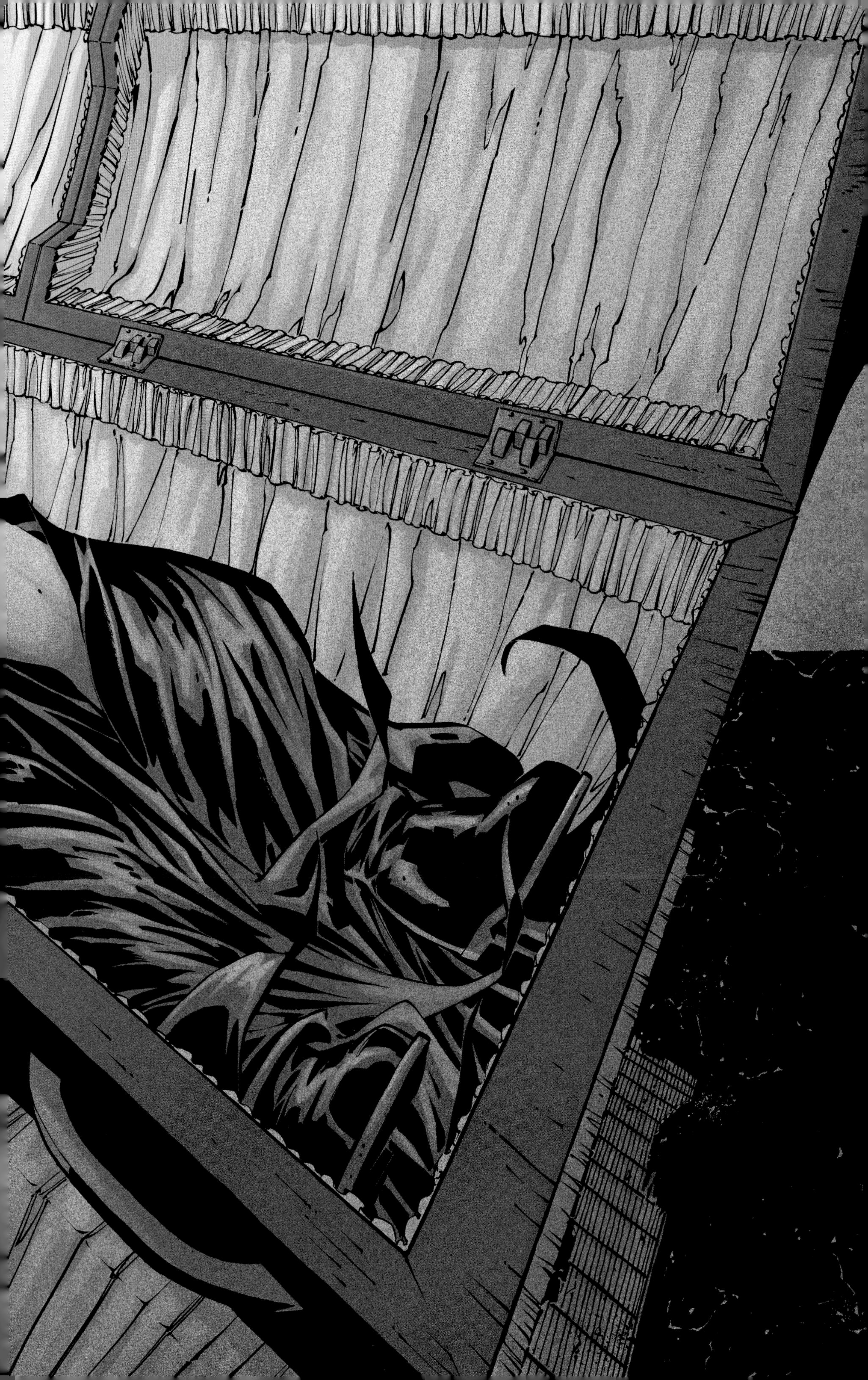

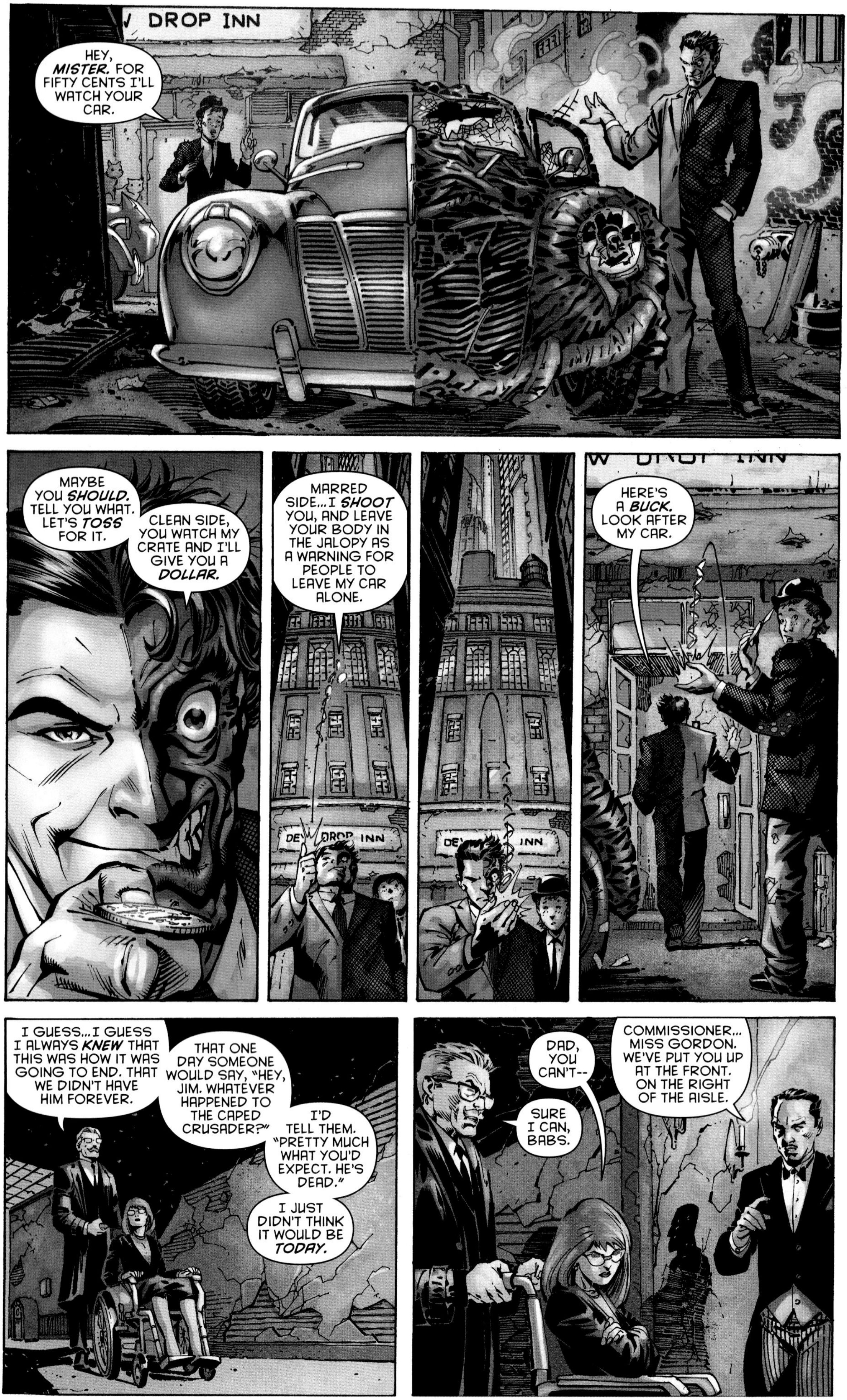
W DROP INN
HEY, MISTER. FOR FIFTY CENTS I'LL WATCH YOUR CAR.
MAYBE YOU SHOULD. TELL YOU WHAT. LET'S TOSS FOR IT.
CLEAN SIDE, YOU WATCH MY CRATE AND I'LL GIVE YOU A DOLLAR.
MARRED SIDE...I SHOOT YOU, AND LEAVE YOUR BODY IN THE JALOPY AS A WARNING FOR PEOPLE TO LEAVE MY CAR ALONE.
DROP INN
INN
HERE'S A BUCK. LOOK AFTER MY CAR.
I GUESS...I GUESS I ALWAYS KNEW THAT THIS WAS HOW IT WAS GOING TO END. THAT WE DIDN'T HAVE HIM FOREVER.
THAT ONE DAY SOMEONE WOULD SAY, "HEY, JIM. WHATEVER HAPPENED TO THE CAPED CRUSADER?"
I'D TELL THEM. "PRETTY MUCH WHAT YOU'D EXPECT. HE'S DEAD."
I JUST DIDN'T THINK IT WOULD BE TODAY.
DAD, YOU CAN'T--
SURE I CAN, BABS.
COMMISSIONER... MISS GORDON. WE'VE PUT YOU UP AT THE FRONT. ON THE RIGHT OF THE AISLE.

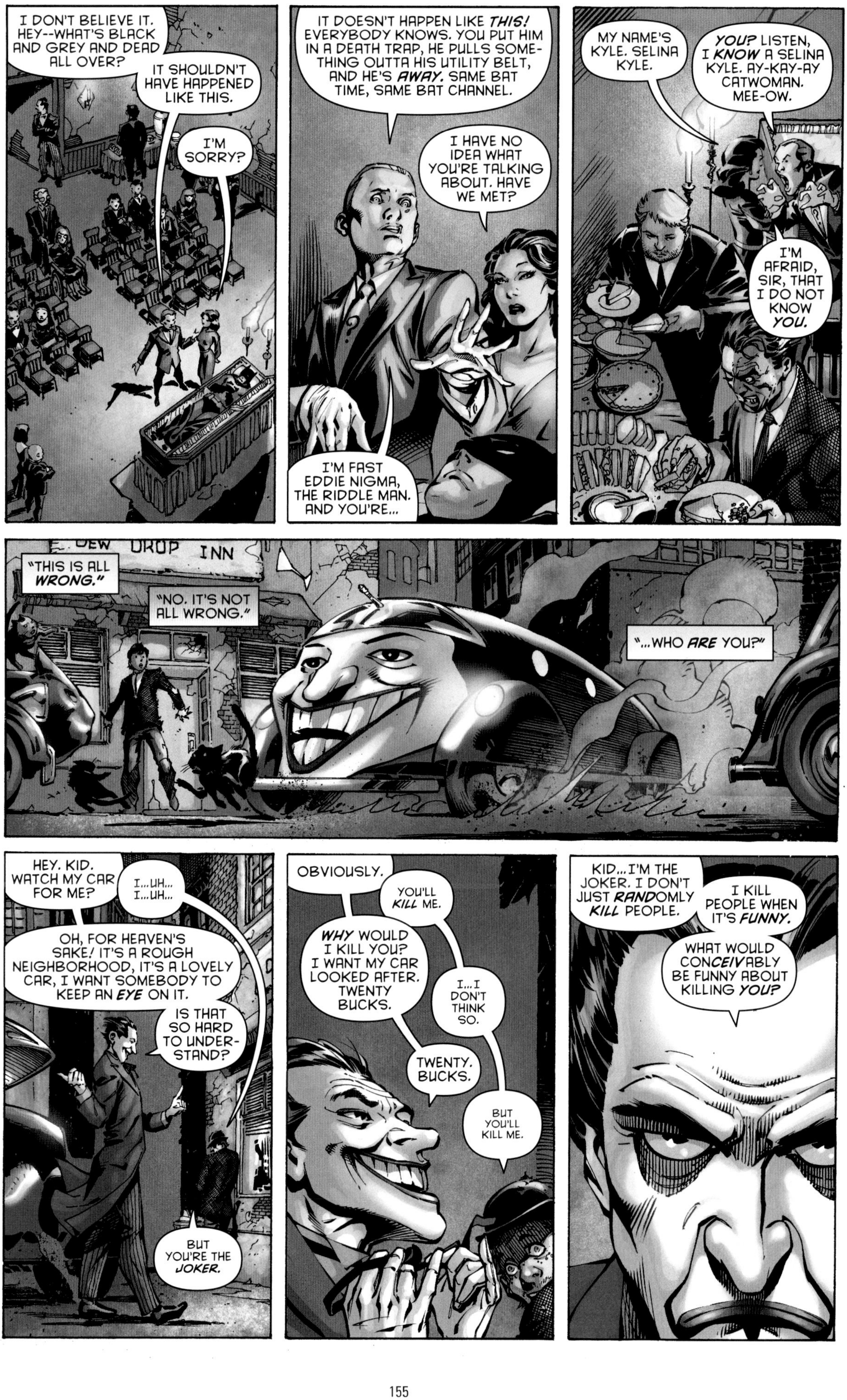
I DON'T BELIEVE IT. HEY--WHAT'S BLACK AND GREY AND DEAD ALL OVER?
IT SHOULDN'T HAVE HAPPENED LIKE THIS.
I'M SORRY?
IT DOESN'T HAPPEN LIKE THIS! EVERYBODY KNOWS. YOU PUT HIM IN A DEATH TRAP, HE PULLS SOMETHING OUTTA HIS UTILITY BELT, AND HE'S AWAY. SAME BAT TIME, SAME BAT CHANNEL.
I HAVE NO IDEA WHAT YOU'RE TALKING ABOUT. HAVE WE MET?
I'M FAST EDDIE NIGMA, THE RIDDLE MAN. AND YOU'RE...
MY NAME'S KYLE. SELINA KYLE.
YOU? LISTEN, I KNOW A SELINA KYLE. AY-KAY-AY CATWOMAN. MEE-OW.
I'M AFRAID, SIR, THAT I DO NOT KNOW YOU.
DEW DROP INN
"THIS IS ALL WRONG."
"NO. IT'S NOT ALL WRONG."
"...WHO ARE YOU?"
HEY. KID. WATCH MY CAR FOR ME?
I...UH... I...UH...
OH, FOR HEAVEN'S SAKE! IT'S A ROUGH NEIGHBORHOOD, IT'S A LOVELY CAR, I WANT SOMEBODY TO KEEP AN EYE ON IT.
IS THAT SO HARD TO UNDERSTAND?
BUT YOU'RE THE JOKER.
OBVIOUSLY.
YOU'LL KILL ME.
WHY WOULD I KILL YOU? I WANT MY CAR LOOKED AFTER. TWENTY BUCKS.
I...I DON'T THINK SO.
TWENTY. BUCKS.
BUT YOU'LL KILL ME.
KID...I'M THE JOKER. I DON'T JUST RANDOMLY KILL PEOPLE.
I KILL PEOPLE WHEN IT'S FUNNY.
WHAT WOULD CONCEIVABLY BE FUNNY ABOUT KILLING YOU?

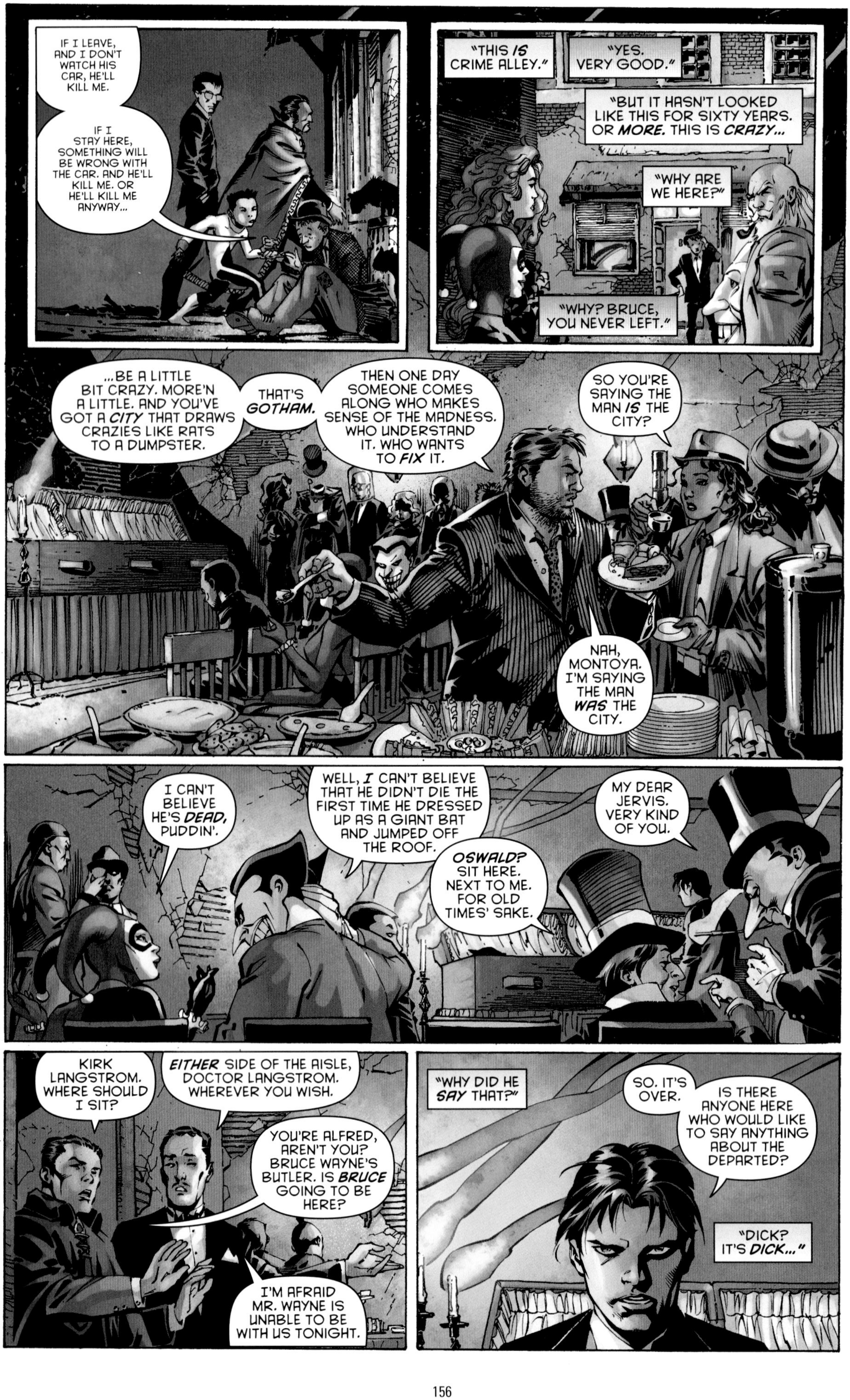
IF I LEAVE, AND I DON'T WATCH HIS CAR, HE'LL KILL ME.
IF I STAY HERE, SOMETHING WILL BE WRONG WITH THE CAR. AND HE'LL KILL ME. OR HE'LL KILL ME ANYWAY...
"THIS IS CRIME ALLEY."
"YES. VERY GOOD."
"BUT IT HASN'T LOOKED LIKE THIS FOR SIXTY YEARS. OR MORE. THIS IS CRAZY...
"WHY ARE WE HERE?"
"WHY? BRUCE, YOU NEVER LEFT."
...BE A LITTLE BIT CRAZY. MORE'N A LITTLE. AND YOU'VE GOT A CITY THAT DRAWS CRAZIES LIKE RATS TO A DUMPSTER.
THAT'S GOTHAM.
THEN ONE DAY SOMEONE COMES ALONG WHO MAKES SENSE OF THE MADNESS. WHO UNDERSTAND IT. WHO WANTS TO FIX IT.
SO YOU'RE SAYING THE MAN IS THE CITY?
NAH, MONTOYA. I'M SAYING THE MAN WAS THE CITY.
I CAN'T BELIEVE HE'S DEAD, PUDDIN'.
WELL, I CAN'T BELIEVE THAT HE DIDN'T DIE THE FIRST TIME HE DRESSED UP AS A GIANT BAT AND JUMPED OFF THE ROOF.
OSWALD? SIT HERE. NEXT TO ME. FOR OLD TIMES' SAKE.
MY DEAR JERVIS. VERY KIND OF YOU.
KIRK LANGSTROM. WHERE SHOULD I SIT?
EITHER SIDE OF THE AISLE, DOCTOR LANGSTROM. WHEREVER YOU WISH.
YOU'RE ALFRED, AREN'T YOU? BRUCE WAYNE'S BUTLER. IS BRUCE GOING TO BE HERE?
I'M AFRAID MR. WAYNE IS UNABLE TO BE WITH US TONIGHT.
"WHY DID HE SAY THAT?"
SO. IT'S OVER.
IS THERE ANYONE HERE WHO WOULD LIKE TO SAY ANYTHING ABOUT THE DEPARTED?
"DICK? IT'S DICK..."

I WOULD.

HELLO. MY NAME IS *SELINA KYLE.* I WAS *SADIE KELOWSKI* WHEN I WAS A KID, BUT THAT WAS TOO LONG AGO. I'VE KNOWN THE DEPARTED SINCE...WELL, IT WAS A COUPLE OF YEARS BEFORE PEARL HARBOR.

I GUESS THAT *DATES* ME.

I WANT TO TELL YOU WHAT KIND OF A *MAN* HE WAS.

AND *HOW* HE DIED. I SHOULD TELL YOU *THAT.*

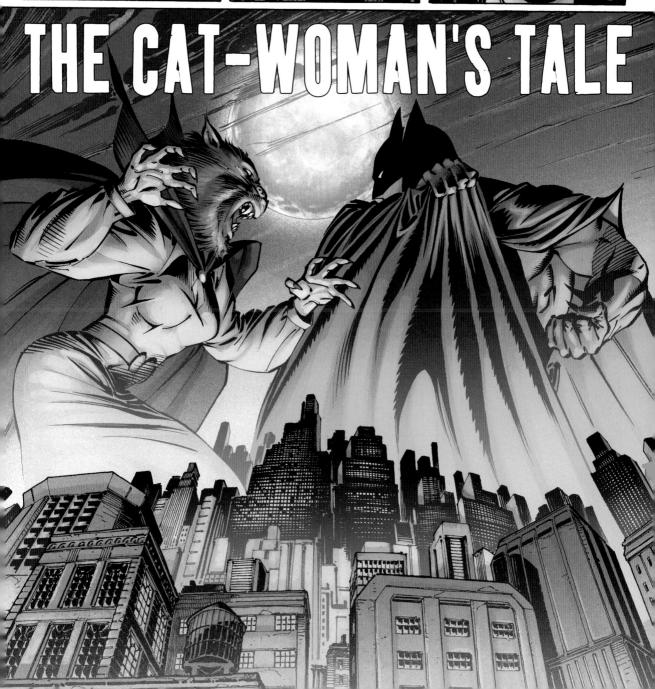

THE CAT-WOMAN'S TALE

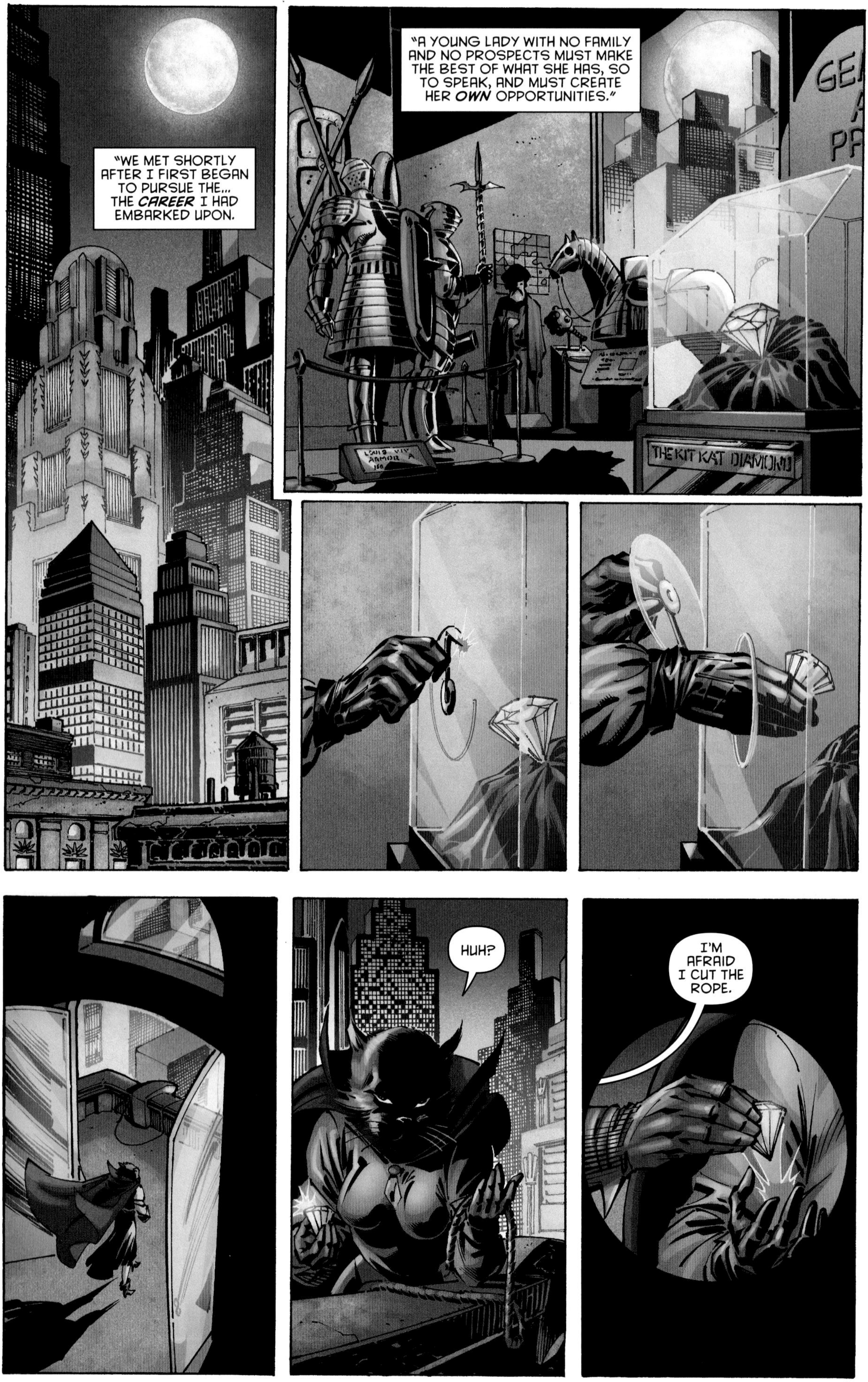
"WE MET SHORTLY AFTER I FIRST BEGAN TO PURSUE THE... THE CAREER I HAD EMBARKED UPON.
"A YOUNG LADY WITH NO FAMILY AND NO PROSPECTS MUST MAKE THE BEST OF WHAT SHE HAS, SO TO SPEAK, AND MUST CREATE HER OWN OPPORTUNITIES."
THE KIT KAT DIAMOND
HUH?
I'M AFRAID I CUT THE ROPE.

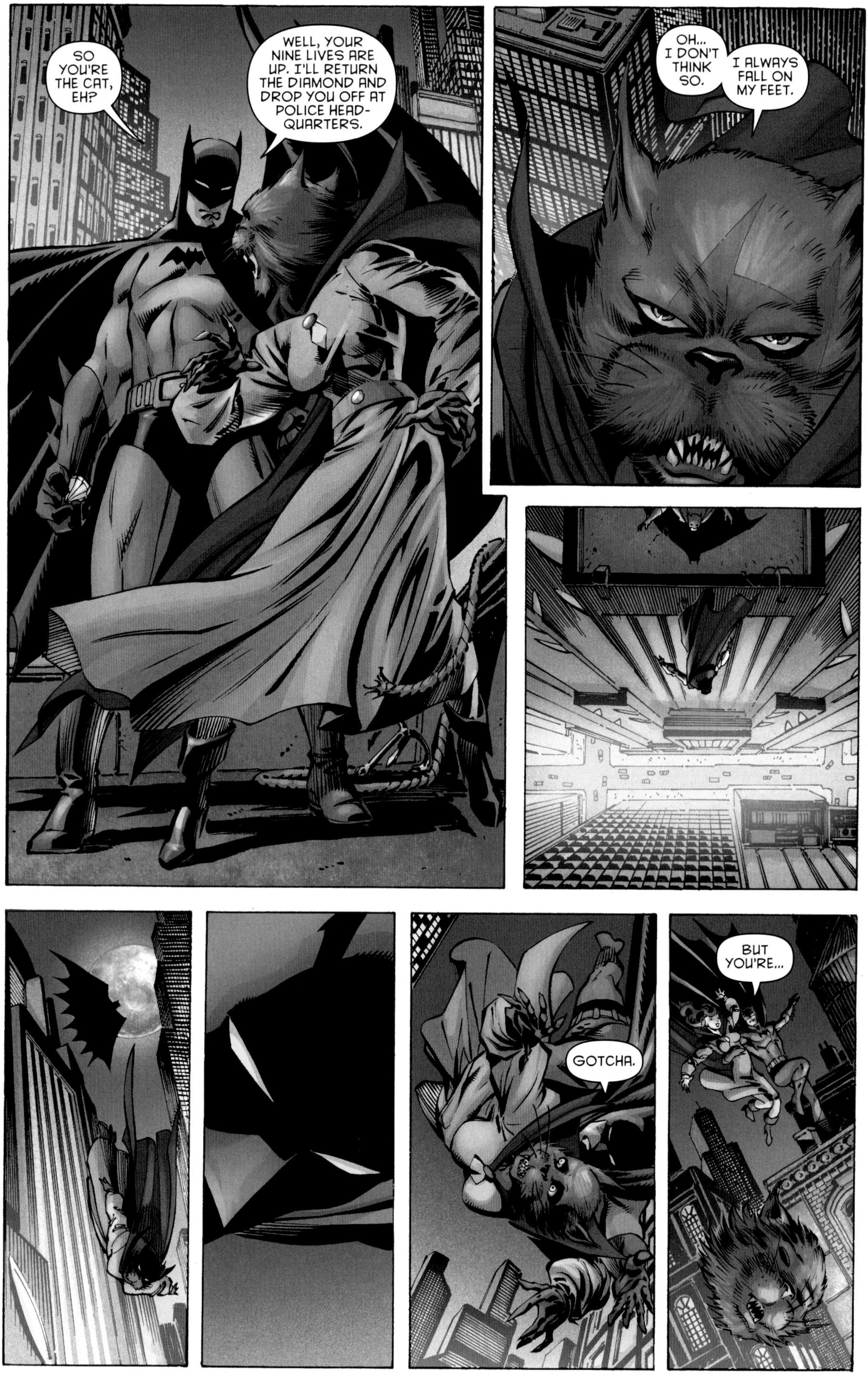
SO YOU'RE THE CAT, EH?
WELL, YOUR NINE LIVES ARE UP. I'LL RETURN THE DIAMOND AND DROP YOU OFF AT POLICE HEAD-QUARTERS.
OH... I DON'T THINK SO.
I ALWAYS FALL ON MY FEET.
GOTCHA.
BUT YOU'RE...

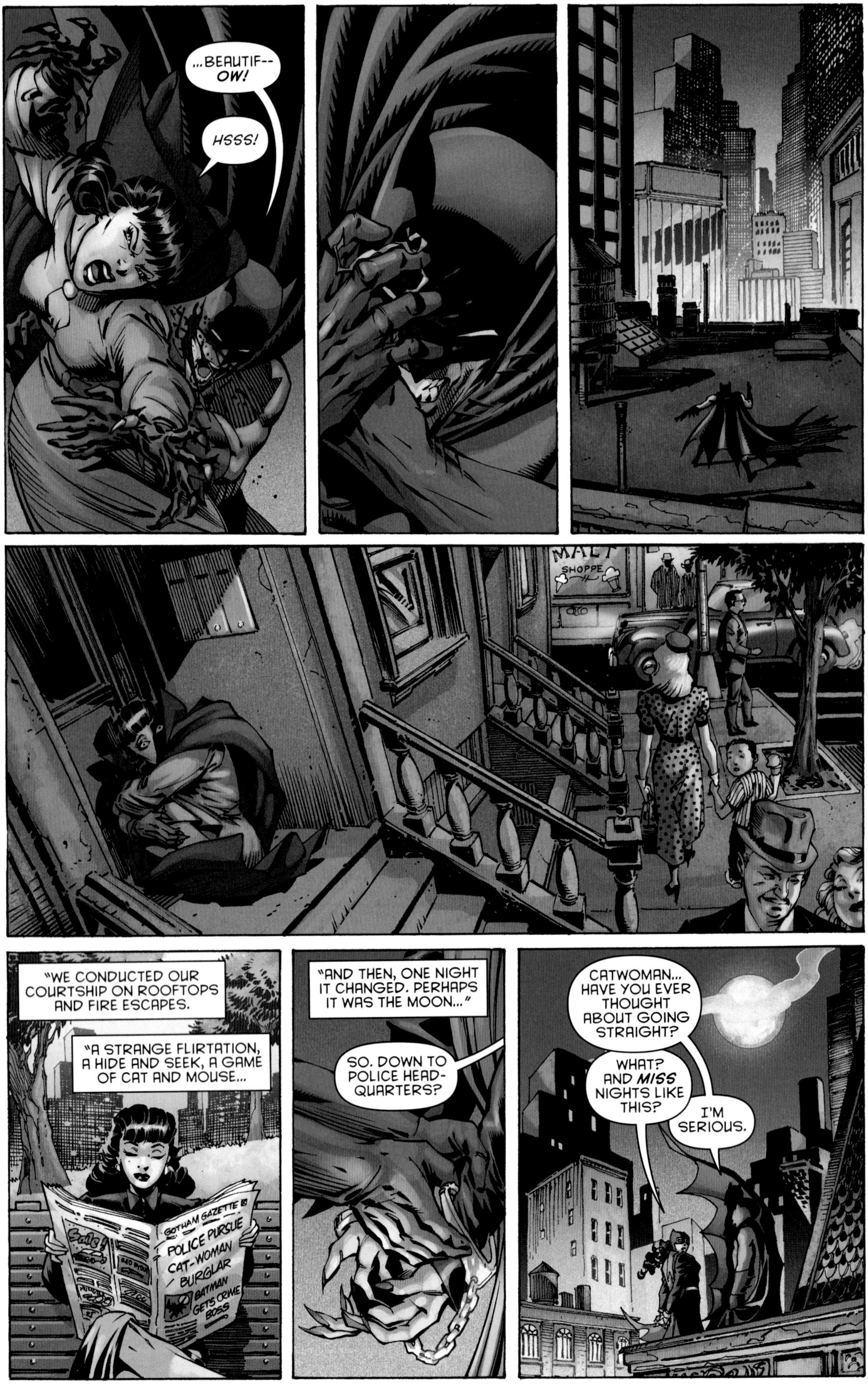
...BEAUTIF--
OW!
HSSS!
MALT
SHOPPE
"WE CONDUCTED OUR COURTSHIP ON ROOFTOPS AND FIRE ESCAPES.
"A STRANGE FLIRTATION, A HIDE AND SEEK, A GAME OF CAT AND MOUSE...
GOTHAM GAZETTE
POLICE PURSUE CAT-WOMAN BURGLAR
BATMAN GETS CRIME BOSS
"AND THEN, ONE NIGHT IT CHANGED. PERHAPS IT WAS THE MOON..."
SO. DOWN TO POLICE HEAD-QUARTERS?
CATWOMAN... HAVE YOU EVER THOUGHT ABOUT GOING STRAIGHT?
WHAT? AND *MISS* NIGHTS LIKE THIS?
I'M SERIOUS.

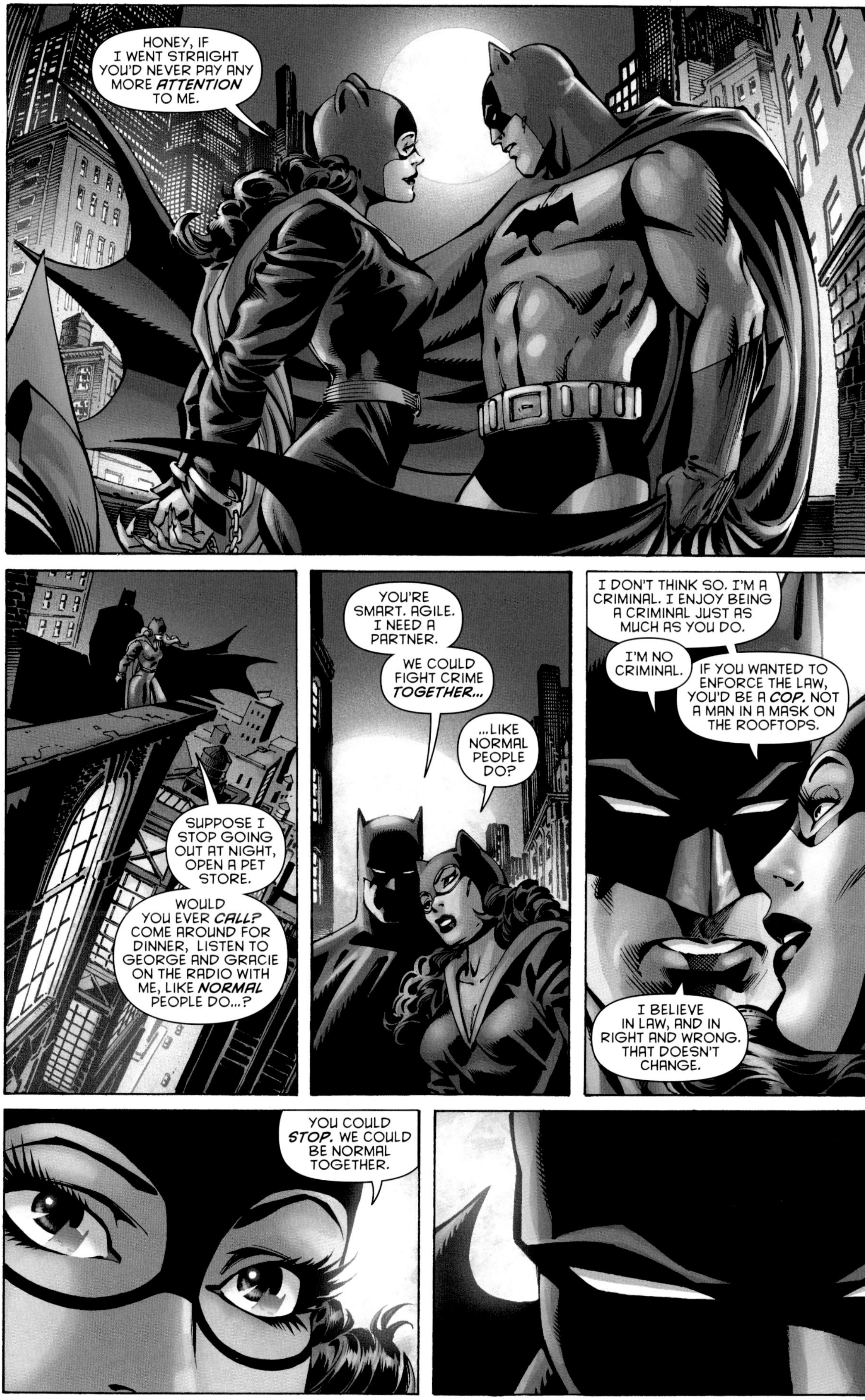
HONEY, IF I WENT STRAIGHT YOU'D NEVER PAY ANY MORE *ATTENTION* TO ME.
SUPPOSE I STOP GOING OUT AT NIGHT, OPEN A PET STORE.
WOULD YOU EVER *CALL?* COME AROUND FOR DINNER, LISTEN TO GEORGE AND GRACIE ON THE RADIO WITH ME, LIKE *NORMAL* PEOPLE DO...?
YOU'RE SMART. AGILE. I NEED A PARTNER.
WE COULD FIGHT CRIME *TOGETHER...*
...LIKE NORMAL PEOPLE DO?
I DON'T THINK SO. I'M A CRIMINAL. I ENJOY BEING A CRIMINAL JUST AS MUCH AS YOU DO.
I'M NO CRIMINAL.
IF YOU WANTED TO ENFORCE THE LAW, YOU'D BE A *COP.* NOT A MAN IN A MASK ON THE ROOFTOPS.
I BELIEVE IN LAW, AND IN RIGHT AND WRONG. THAT DOESN'T CHANGE.
YOU COULD *STOP.* WE COULD BE NORMAL TOGETHER.

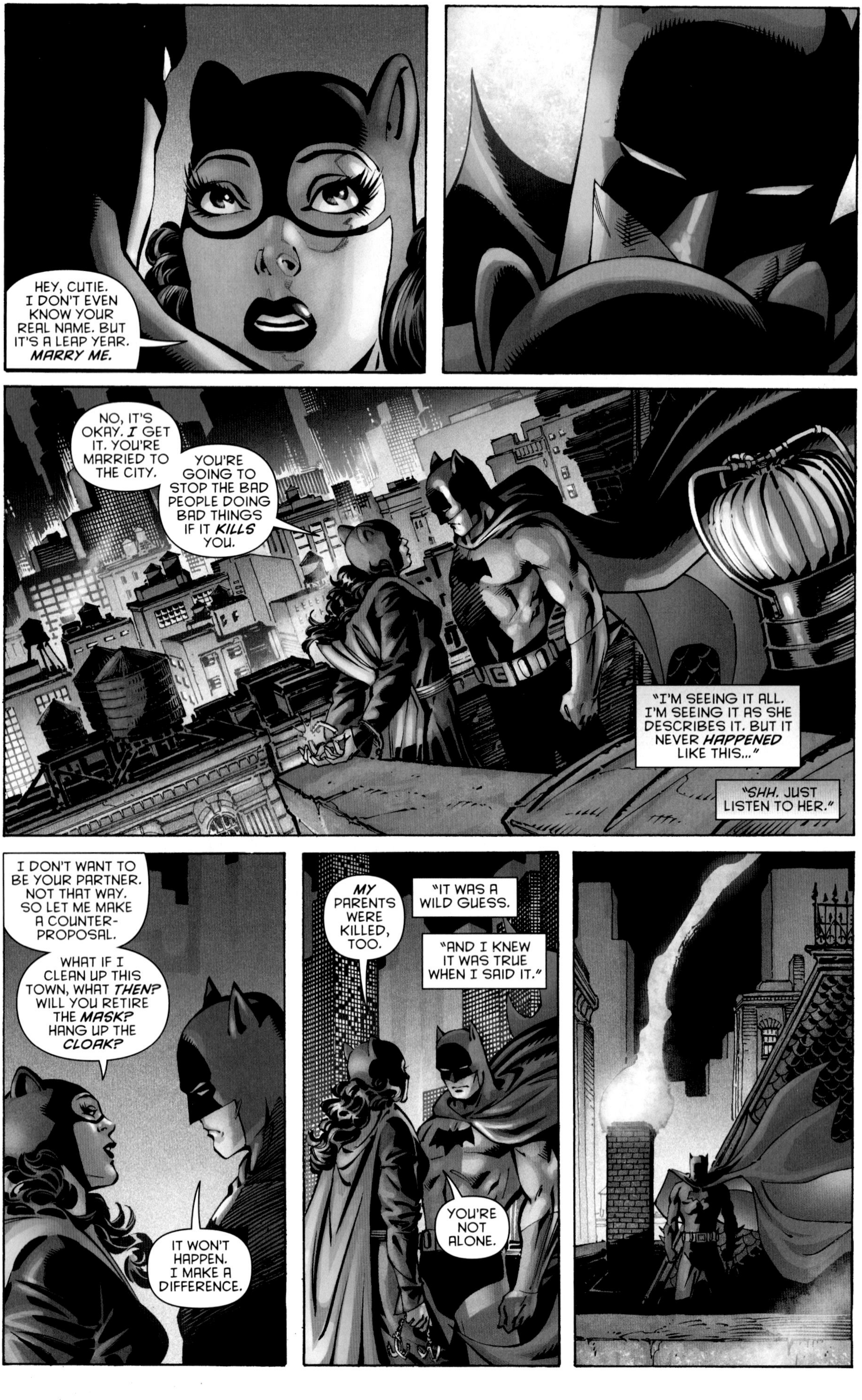
HEY, CUTIE. I DON'T EVEN KNOW YOUR REAL NAME. BUT IT'S A LEAP YEAR. MARRY ME.
NO, IT'S OKAY. I GET IT. YOU'RE MARRIED TO THE CITY.
YOU'RE GOING TO STOP THE BAD PEOPLE DOING BAD THINGS IF IT KILLS YOU.
"I'M SEEING IT ALL. I'M SEEING IT AS SHE DESCRIBES IT. BUT IT NEVER HAPPENED LIKE THIS..."
"SHH. JUST LISTEN TO HER."
I DON'T WANT TO BE YOUR PARTNER. NOT THAT WAY. SO LET ME MAKE A COUNTER-PROPOSAL.
WHAT IF I CLEAN UP THIS TOWN, WHAT THEN? WILL YOU RETIRE THE MASK? HANG UP THE CLOAK?
IT WON'T HAPPEN. I MAKE A DIFFERENCE.
MY PARENTS WERE KILLED, TOO.
"IT WAS A WILD GUESS.
"AND I KNEW IT WAS TRUE WHEN I SAID IT."
YOU'RE NOT ALONE.

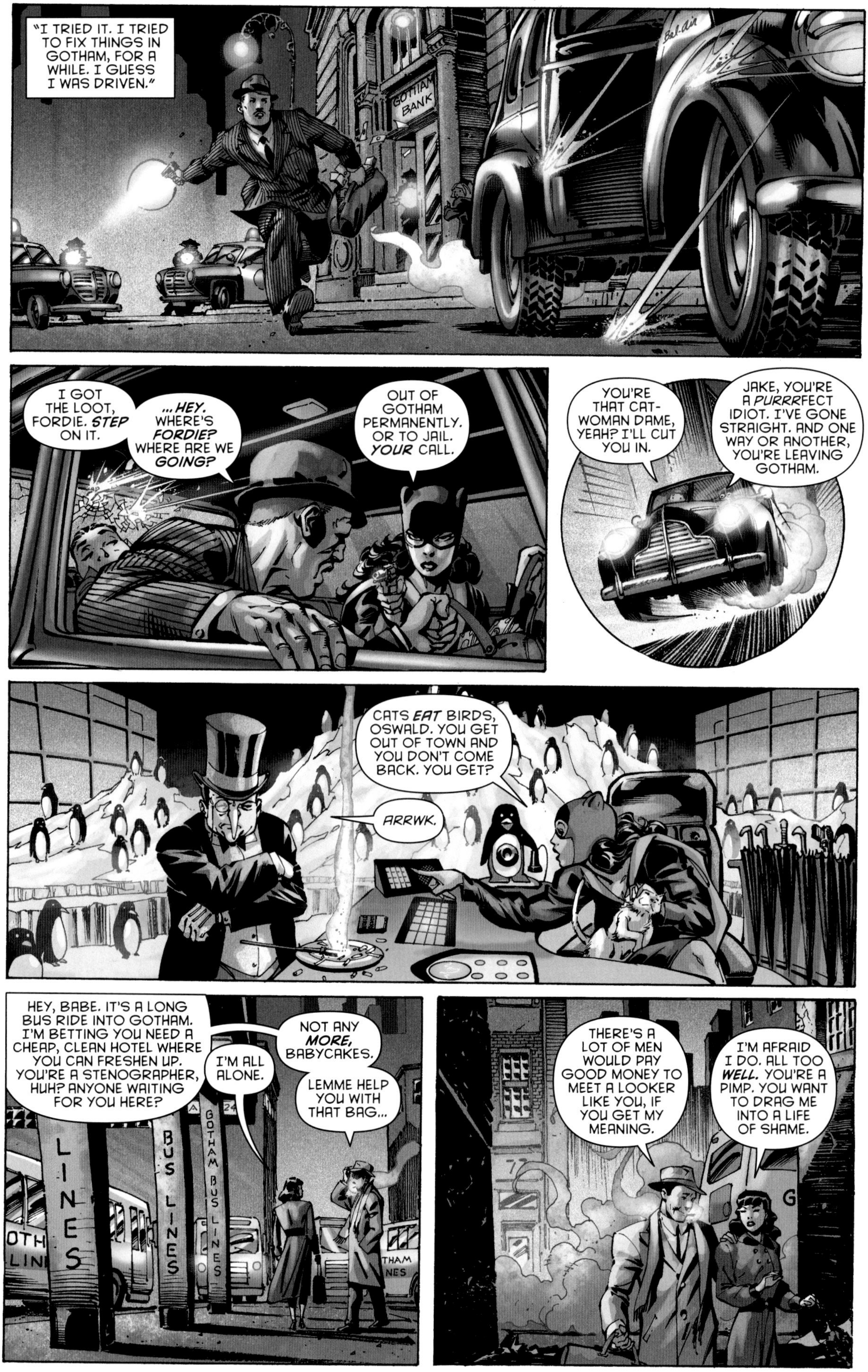
"I TRIED IT. I TRIED TO FIX THINGS IN GOTHAM, FOR A WHILE. I GUESS I WAS DRIVEN."
GOTHAM BANK
I GOT THE LOOT, FORDIE. STEP ON IT.
...HEY. WHERE'S FORDIE? WHERE ARE WE GOING?
OUT OF GOTHAM PERMANENTLY. OR TO JAIL. YOUR CALL.
YOU'RE THAT CAT-WOMAN DAME, YEAH? I'LL CUT YOU IN.
JAKE, YOU'RE A PURRRFECT IDIOT. I'VE GONE STRAIGHT. AND ONE WAY OR ANOTHER, YOU'RE LEAVING GOTHAM.
CATS EAT BIRDS, OSWALD. YOU GET OUT OF TOWN AND YOU DON'T COME BACK. YOU GET?
ARRWK.
HEY, BABE. IT'S A LONG BUS RIDE INTO GOTHAM. I'M BETTING YOU NEED A CHEAP, CLEAN HOTEL WHERE YOU CAN FRESHEN UP. YOU'RE A STENOGRAPHER, HUH? ANYONE WAITING FOR YOU HERE?
I'M ALL ALONE.
NOT ANY MORE, BABYCAKES.
LEMME HELP YOU WITH THAT BAG...
LINES
BUS LINES
GOTHAM BUS LINES
THERE'S A LOT OF MEN WOULD PAY GOOD MONEY TO MEET A LOOKER LIKE YOU, IF YOU GET MY MEANING.
I'M AFRAID I DO. ALL TOO WELL. YOU'RE A PIMP. YOU WANT TO DRAG ME INTO A LIFE OF SHAME.

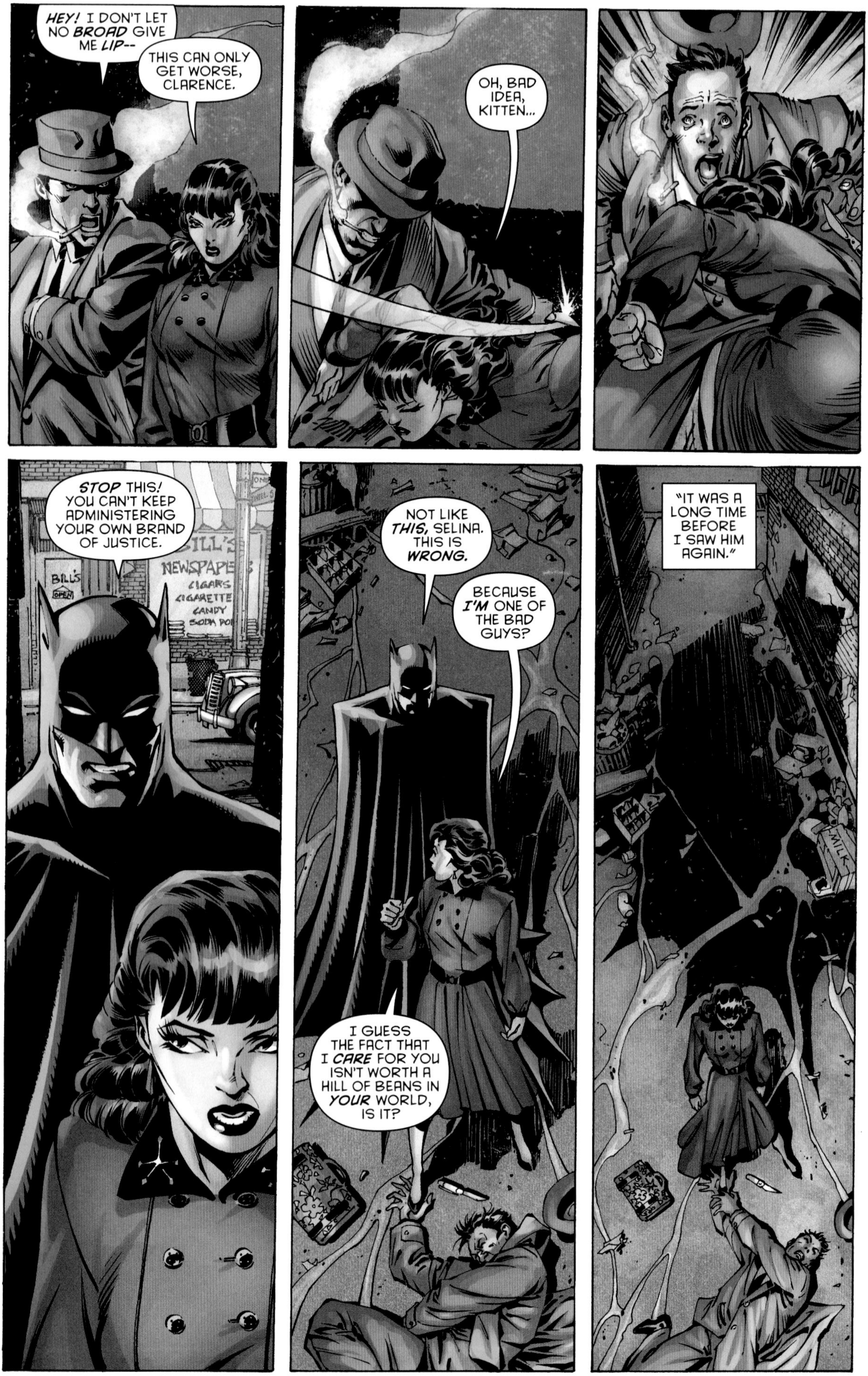
HEY! I DON'T LET NO BROAD GIVE ME LIP--
THIS CAN ONLY GET WORSE, CLARENCE.
OH, BAD IDEA, KITTEN...
STOP THIS! YOU CAN'T KEEP ADMINISTERING YOUR OWN BRAND OF JUSTICE.
BILL'S
NEWSPAPERS
CIGARS
CIGARETTES
CANDY
SODA POP
NOT LIKE THIS, SELINA. THIS IS WRONG.
BECAUSE I'M ONE OF THE BAD GUYS?
I GUESS THE FACT THAT I CARE FOR YOU ISN'T WORTH A HILL OF BEANS IN YOUR WORLD, IS IT?
"IT WAS A LONG TIME BEFORE I SAW HIM AGAIN."
MILK

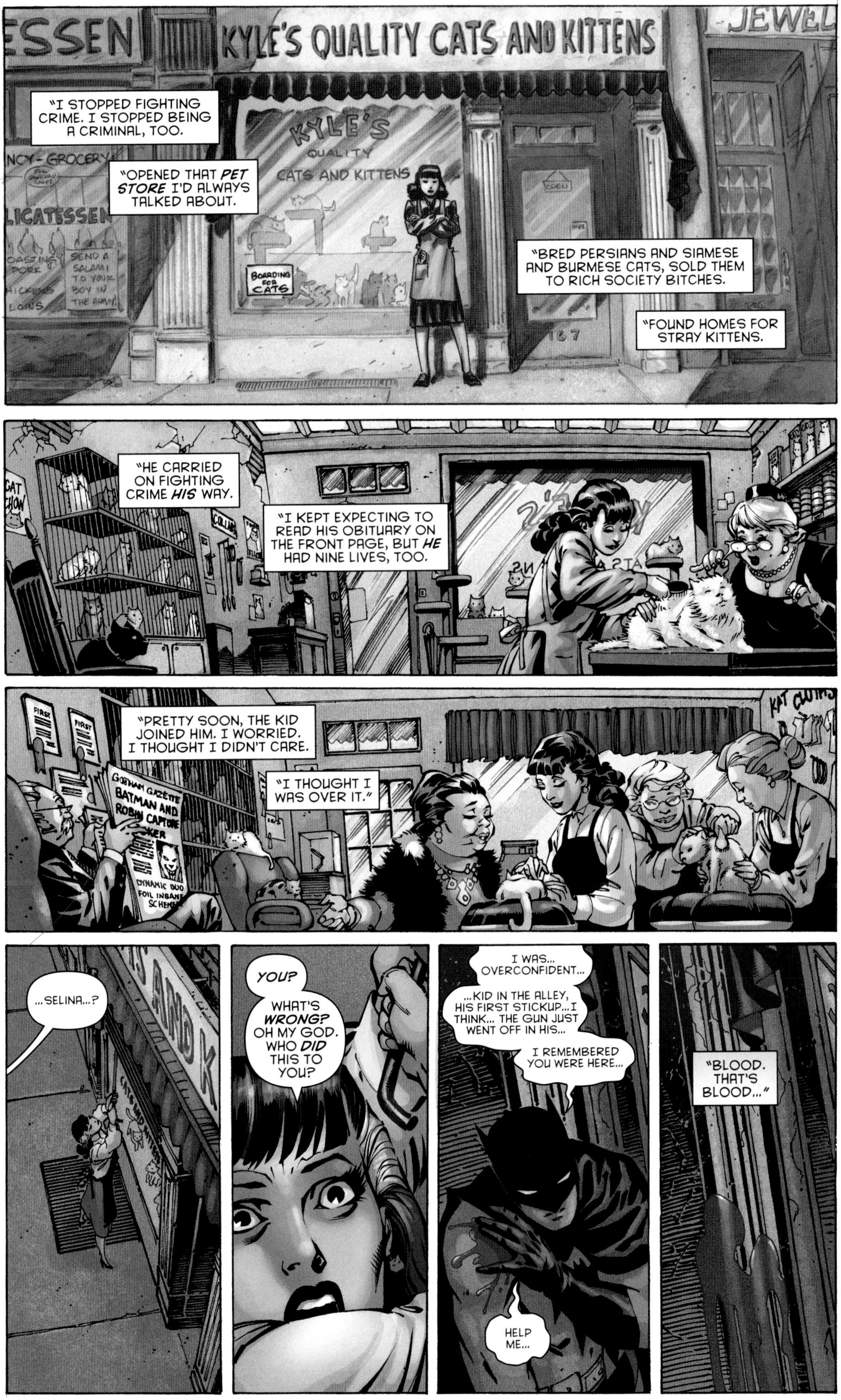
KYLE'S QUALITY CATS AND KITTENS
"I STOPPED FIGHTING CRIME. I STOPPED BEING A CRIMINAL, TOO.
"OPENED THAT PET STORE I'D ALWAYS TALKED ABOUT.
"BRED PERSIANS AND SIAMESE AND BURMESE CATS, SOLD THEM TO RICH SOCIETY BITCHES.
"FOUND HOMES FOR STRAY KITTENS.
"HE CARRIED ON FIGHTING CRIME HIS WAY.
"I KEPT EXPECTING TO READ HIS OBITUARY ON THE FRONT PAGE, BUT HE HAD NINE LIVES, TOO.
"PRETTY SOON, THE KID JOINED HIM. I WORRIED. I THOUGHT I DIDN'T CARE.
"I THOUGHT I WAS OVER IT."
GOTHAM GAZETTE
BATMAN AND ROBIN CAPTURE
DYNAMIC DUO FOIL INSANE SCHEME
...SELINA...?
YOU?
WHAT'S WRONG? OH MY GOD. WHO DID THIS TO YOU?
I WAS... OVERCONFIDENT...
...KID IN THE ALLEY, HIS FIRST STICKUP...I THINK... THE GUN JUST WENT OFF IN HIS...
I REMEMBERED YOU WERE HERE...
HELP ME...
"BLOOD. THAT'S BLOOD..."

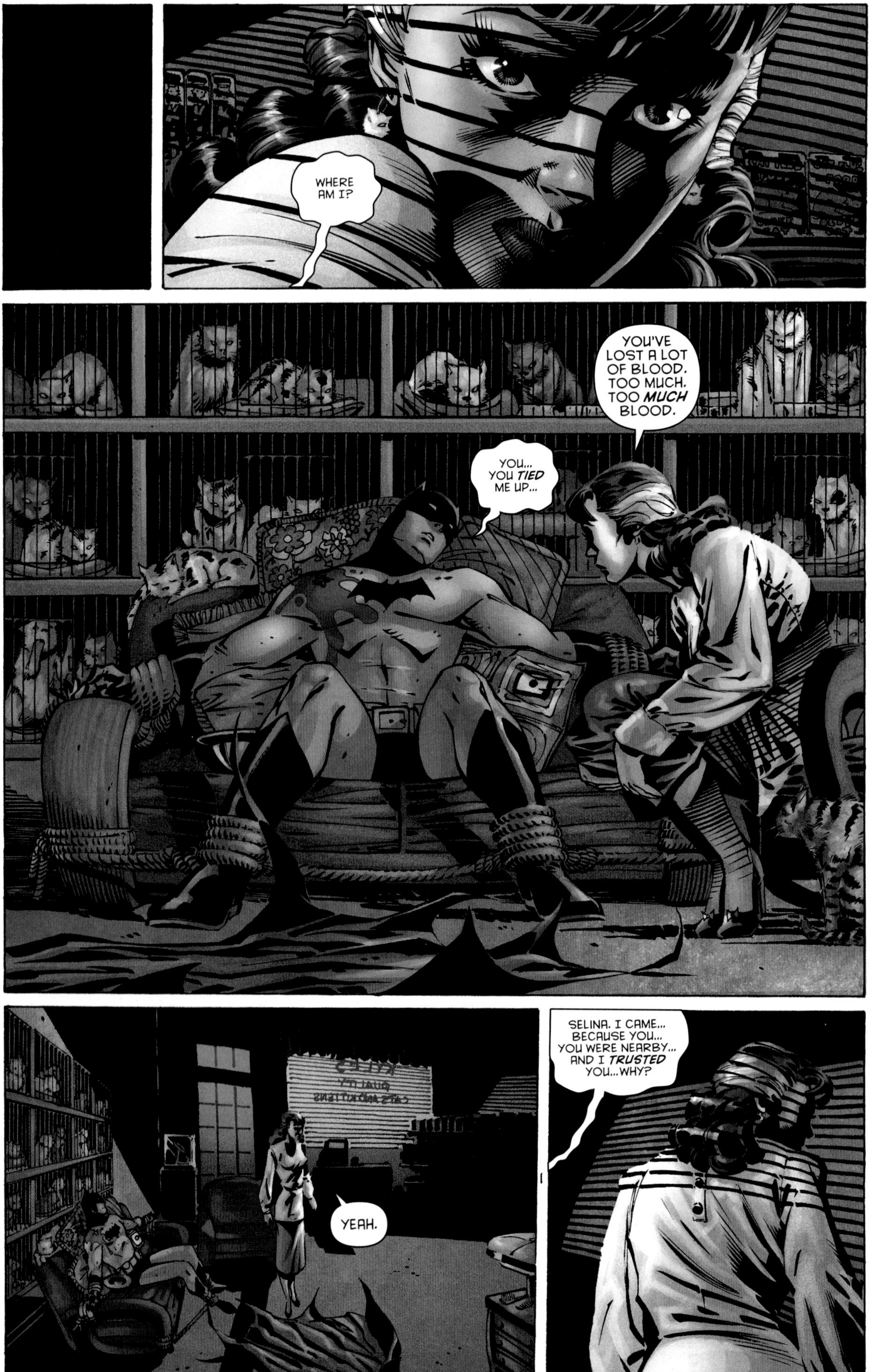
WHERE AM I?
YOU'VE LOST A LOT OF BLOOD. TOO MUCH. TOO *MUCH* BLOOD.
YOU... YOU *TIED* ME UP...
YEAH.
SELINA. I CAME... BECAUSE YOU... YOU WERE NEARBY... AND I *TRUSTED* YOU...WHY?

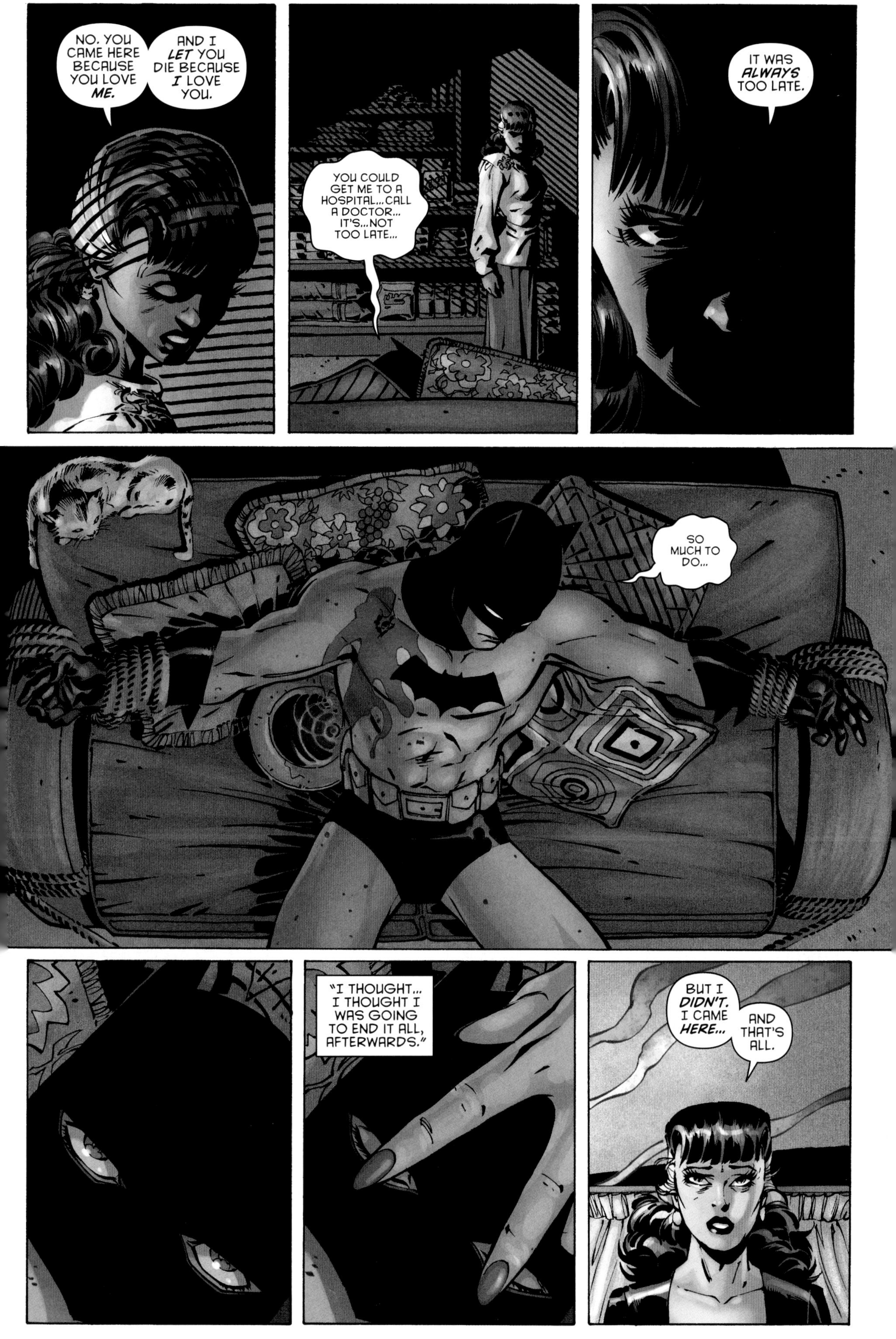
NO. YOU CAME HERE BECAUSE YOU LOVE *ME.*
AND I *LET* YOU DIE BECAUSE *I* LOVE YOU.
YOU COULD GET ME TO A HOSPITAL... CALL A DOCTOR... IT'S... NOT TOO LATE...
IT WAS *ALWAYS* TOO LATE.
SO MUCH TO DO...
"I THOUGHT... I THOUGHT I WAS GOING TO END IT ALL, AFTERWARDS."
BUT I *DIDN'T.* I CAME *HERE...*
AND THAT'S ALL.

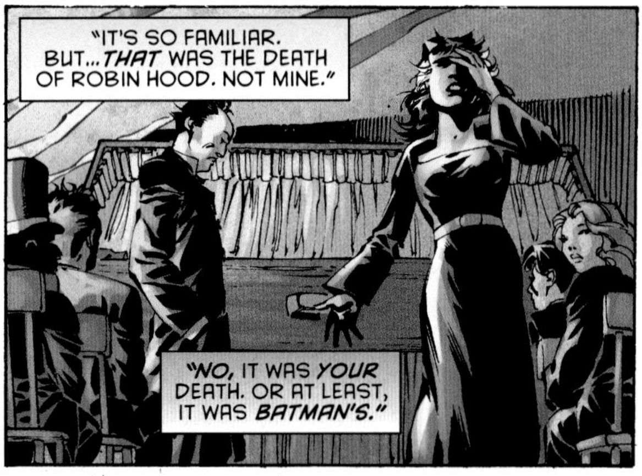
"IT'S SO FAMILIAR. BUT...THAT WAS THE DEATH OF ROBIN HOOD. NOT MINE."
"NO, IT WAS YOUR DEATH. OR AT LEAST, IT WAS BATMAN'S."

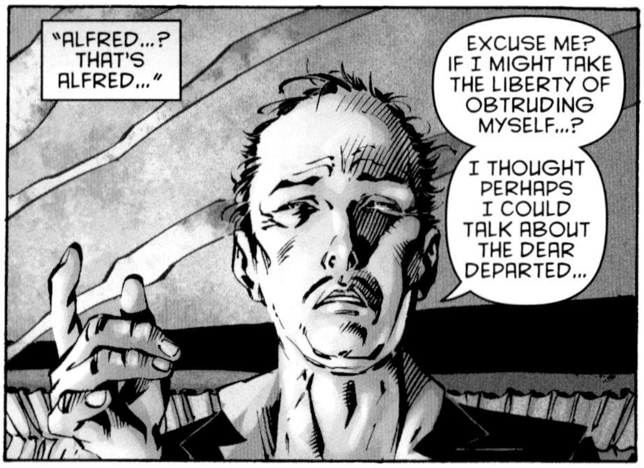
"ALFRED...? THAT'S ALFRED..."
EXCUSE ME? IF I MIGHT TAKE THE LIBERTY OF OBTRUDING MYSELF...?
I THOUGHT PERHAPS I COULD TALK ABOUT THE DEAR DEPARTED...

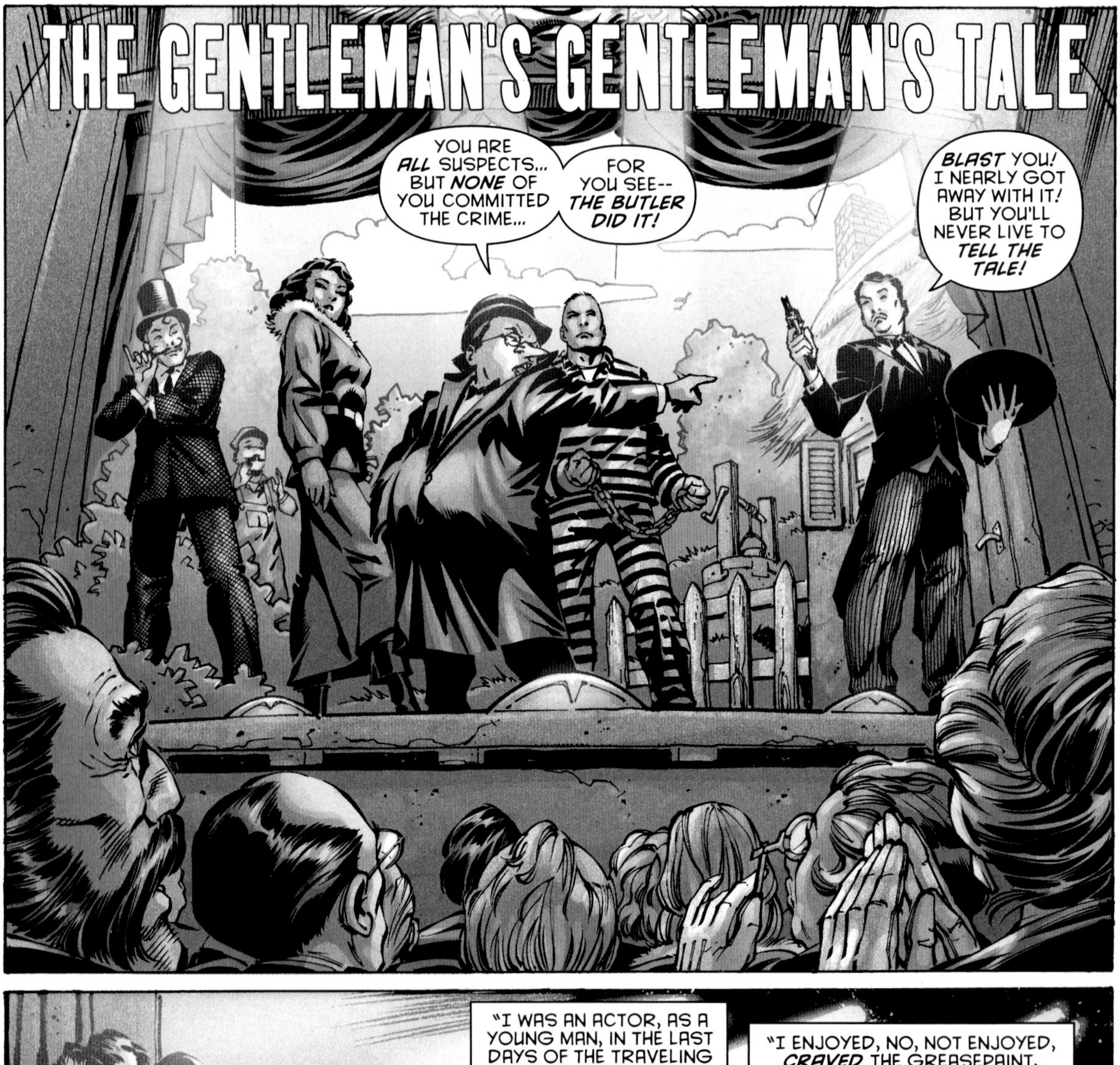
THE GENTLEMAN'S GENTLEMAN'S TALE
YOU ARE ALL SUSPECTS... BUT NONE OF YOU COMMITTED THE CRIME...
FOR YOU SEE-- THE BUTLER DID IT!
BLAST YOU! I NEARLY GOT AWAY WITH IT! BUT YOU'LL NEVER LIVE TO TELL THE TALE!

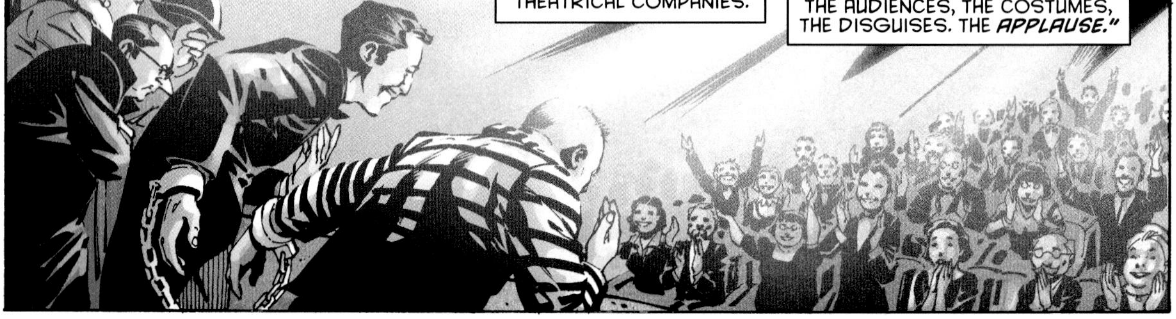
"I WAS AN ACTOR, AS A YOUNG MAN, IN THE LAST DAYS OF THE TRAVELING THEATRICAL COMPANIES.
"I ENJOYED, NO, NOT ENJOYED, CRAVED THE GREASEPAINT, THE AUDIENCES, THE COSTUMES, THE DISGUISES. THE APPLAUSE."

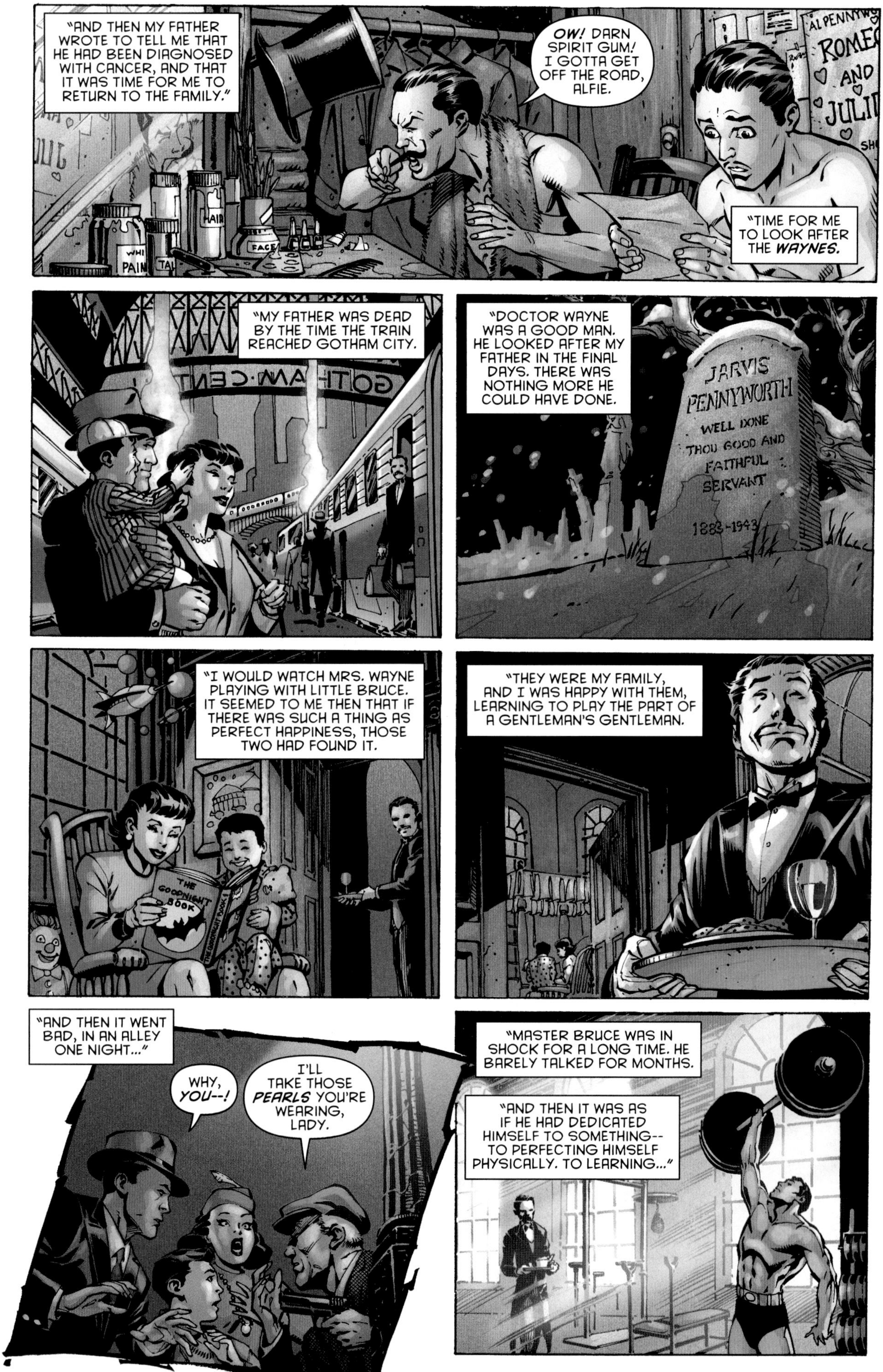
"AND THEN MY FATHER WROTE TO TELL ME THAT HE HAD BEEN DIAGNOSED WITH CANCER, AND THAT IT WAS TIME FOR ME TO RETURN TO THE FAMILY."
OW! DARN SPIRIT GUM! I GOTTA GET OFF THE ROAD, ALFIE.
"TIME FOR ME TO LOOK AFTER THE WAYNES.
"MY FATHER WAS DEAD BY THE TIME THE TRAIN REACHED GOTHAM CITY.
"DOCTOR WAYNE WAS A GOOD MAN. HE LOOKED AFTER MY FATHER IN THE FINAL DAYS. THERE WAS NOTHING MORE HE COULD HAVE DONE.
JARVIS PENNYWORTH
WELL DONE THOU GOOD AND FAITHFUL SERVANT
1883-1943
"I WOULD WATCH MRS. WAYNE PLAYING WITH LITTLE BRUCE. IT SEEMED TO ME THEN THAT IF THERE WAS SUCH A THING AS PERFECT HAPPINESS, THOSE TWO HAD FOUND IT.
THE GOODNIGHT BOOK
"THEY WERE MY FAMILY, AND I WAS HAPPY WITH THEM, LEARNING TO PLAY THE PART OF A GENTLEMAN'S GENTLEMAN.
"AND THEN IT WENT BAD, IN AN ALLEY ONE NIGHT..."
WHY, YOU--!
I'LL TAKE THOSE PEARLS YOU'RE WEARING, LADY.
"MASTER BRUCE WAS IN SHOCK FOR A LONG TIME. HE BARELY TALKED FOR MONTHS.
"AND THEN IT WAS AS IF HE HAD DEDICATED HIMSELF TO SOMETHING-- TO PERFECTING HIMSELF PHYSICALLY. TO LEARNING..."

"THE YEARS FLEW BY. I WAS THERE THE FIRST TIME HE RODE OUT AS A MASKED VIGILANTE.

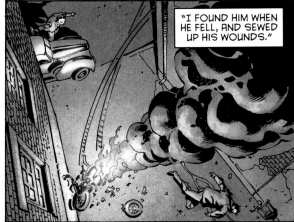

"I FOUND HIM WHEN HE FELL, AND SEWED UP HIS WOUNDS."

AND THEN HE BEGAN DRESSING AS A *BAT*...

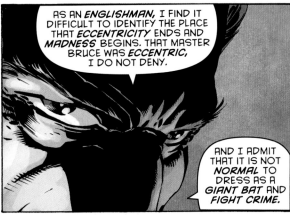

AS AN *ENGLISHMAN*, I FIND IT DIFFICULT TO IDENTIFY THE PLACE THAT *ECCENTRICITY* ENDS AND *MADNESS* BEGINS. THAT MASTER BRUCE WAS *ECCENTRIC*, I DO NOT DENY.

AND I ADMIT THAT IT IS NOT *NORMAL* TO DRESS AS A *GIANT BAT* AND *FIGHT CRIME.*

"BUT DOING IT MADE HIM *HAPPIER* THAN I HAD SEEN HIM IN A LONG, LONG TIME.

"THE BLACK MOODS THAT HAD STARTED WHEN HIS PARENTS WERE KILLED *RECEDED.*

"HE *SMILED*, SOMETIMES.

"AND THEN THE SMILE BEGAN TO FADE. HE *STILL* WENT OUT AT NIGHT. SOMETIMES HE FOUND CRIMINALS IN THE ACT OF COMMITTING CRIMES, AND STOPPED THEM.

"MOSTLY, HE DID *NOT.*

"HE WAS MOVING *AWAY* FROM ME, AWAY FROM THE WORLD, AND THE BLACK MOOD WAS TAKING OVER.

"DID I DO *RIGHT?* I BELIEVED SO AT THE TIME."

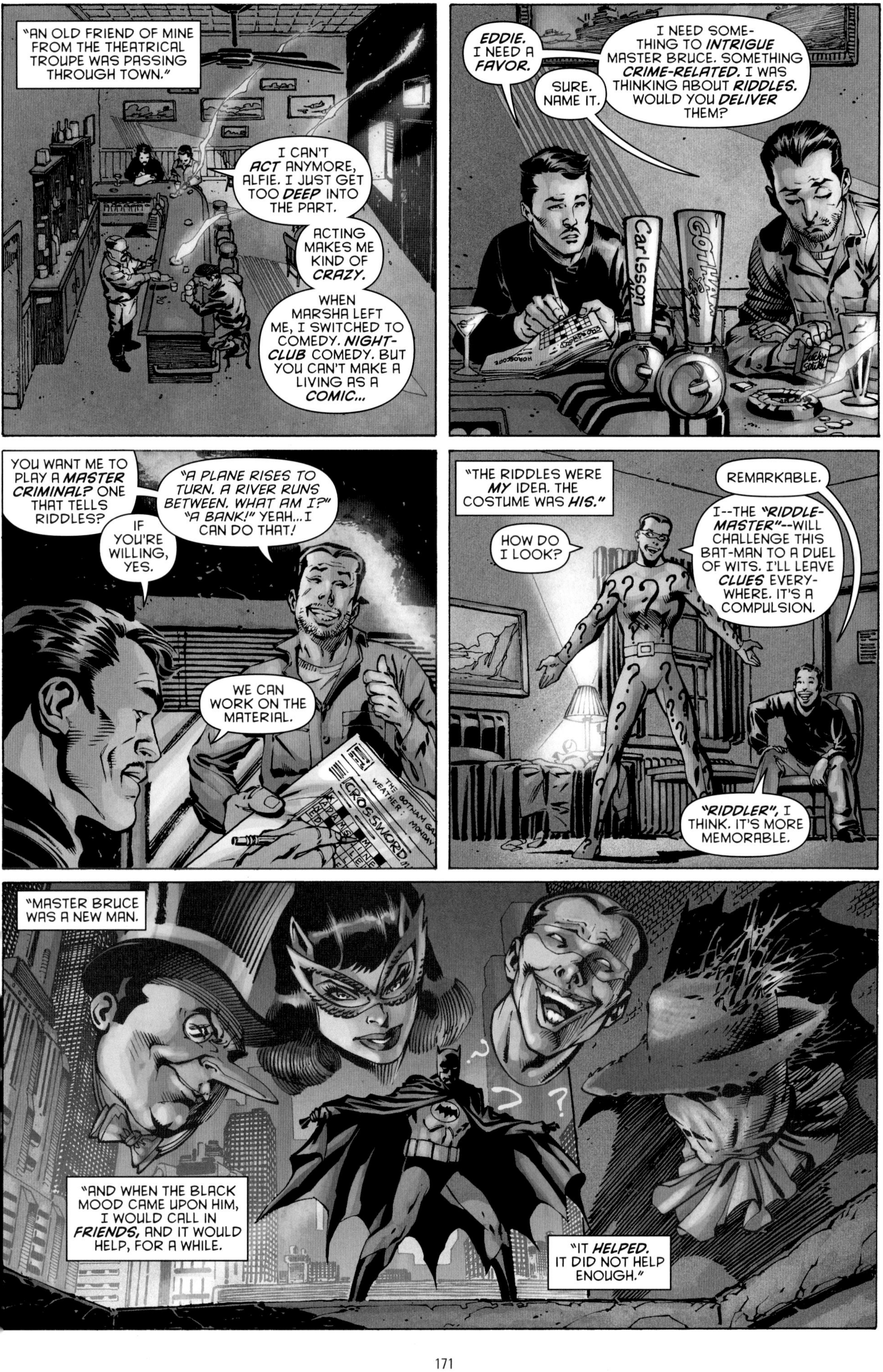
"AN OLD FRIEND OF MINE FROM THE THEATRICAL TROUPE WAS PASSING THROUGH TOWN."
I CAN'T *ACT* ANYMORE, ALFIE. I JUST GET TOO *DEEP* INTO THE PART.
ACTING MAKES ME KIND OF *CRAZY.*
WHEN MARSHA LEFT ME, I SWITCHED TO COMEDY. *NIGHT-CLUB* COMEDY. BUT YOU CAN'T MAKE A LIVING AS A *COMIC...*
EDDIE. I NEED A *FAVOR.*
SURE. NAME IT.
I NEED SOME-THING TO *INTRIGUE* MASTER BRUCE. SOMETHING *CRIME-RELATED.* I WAS THINKING ABOUT *RIDDLES.* WOULD YOU *DELIVER* THEM?
YOU WANT ME TO PLAY A *MASTER CRIMINAL?* ONE THAT TELLS RIDDLES?
IF YOU'RE WILLING, YES.
"A PLANE RISES TO TURN. A RIVER RUNS BETWEEN. WHAT AM I?" "A BANK!" YEAH...I CAN DO THAT!
WE CAN WORK ON THE MATERIAL.
CROSSWORD
"THE RIDDLES WERE *MY* IDEA. THE COSTUME WAS *HIS.*"
HOW DO I LOOK?
REMARKABLE.
I--THE *"RIDDLE-MASTER"*--WILL CHALLENGE THIS BAT-MAN TO A DUEL OF WITS. I'LL LEAVE *CLUES* EVERY-WHERE. IT'S A COMPULSION.
"RIDDLER", I THINK. IT'S MORE MEMORABLE.
"MASTER BRUCE WAS A NEW MAN.
"AND WHEN THE BLACK MOOD CAME UPON HIM, I WOULD CALL IN *FRIENDS,* AND IT WOULD HELP, FOR A WHILE.
"IT *HELPED.* IT DID NOT HELP ENOUGH."

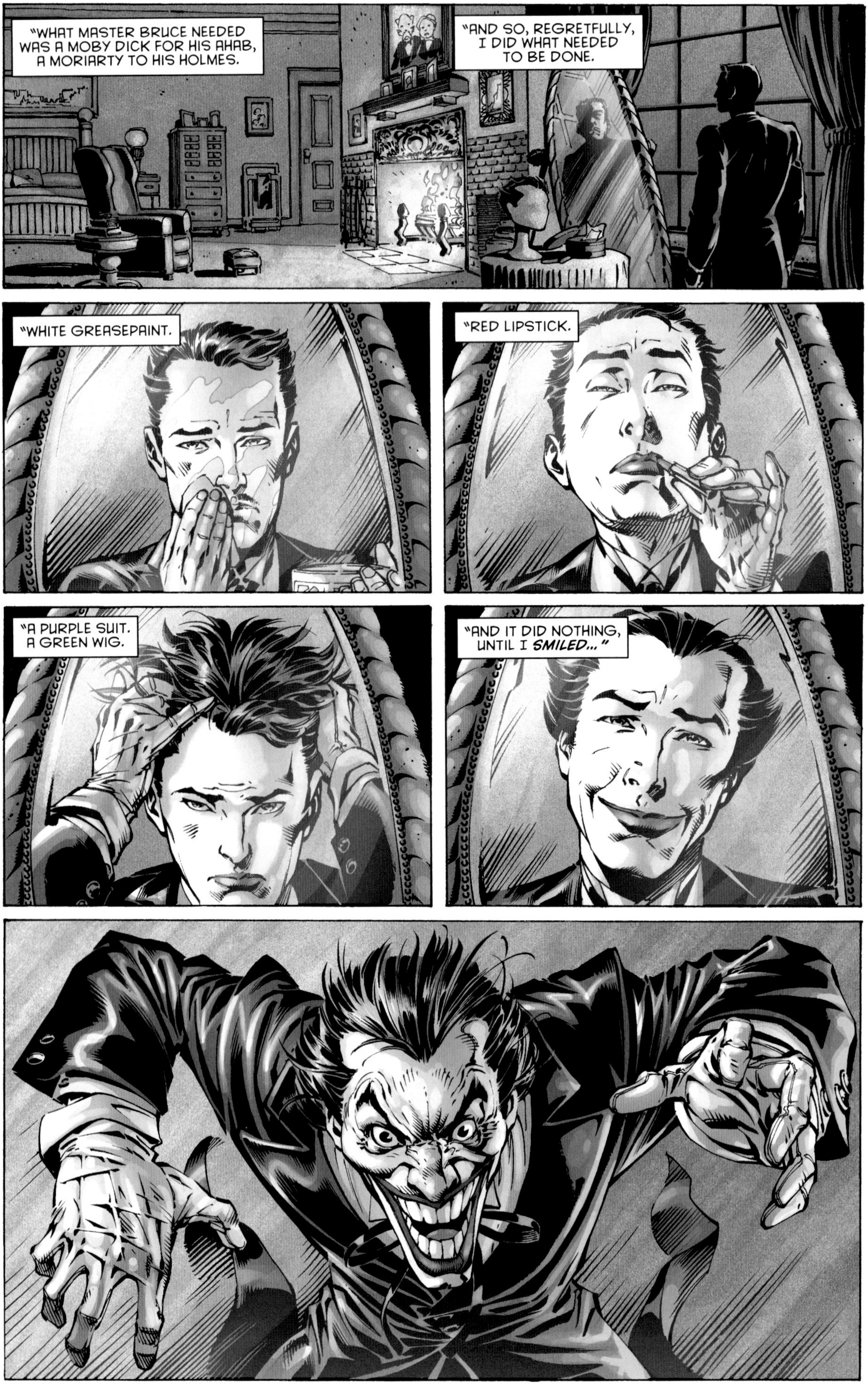
"WHAT MASTER BRUCE NEEDED WAS A MOBY DICK FOR HIS AHAB, A MORIARTY TO HIS HOLMES.
"AND SO, REGRETFULLY, I DID WHAT NEEDED TO BE DONE.
"WHITE GREASEPAINT.
"RED LIPSTICK.
"A PURPLE SUIT. A GREEN WIG.
"AND IT DID NOTHING, UNTIL I *SMILED...*"

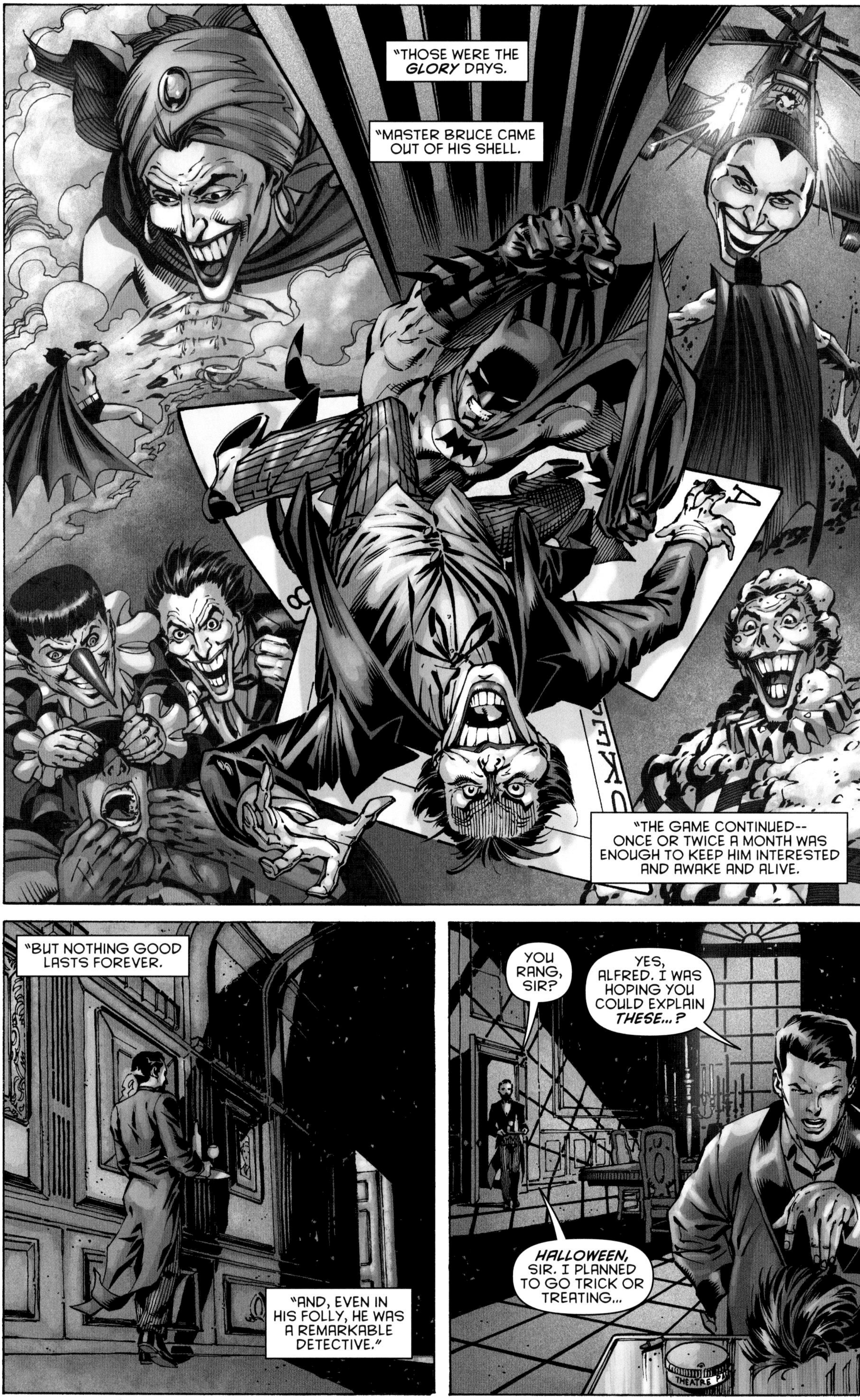
"THOSE WERE THE *GLORY* DAYS.
"MASTER BRUCE CAME OUT OF HIS SHELL.
"THE GAME CONTINUED-- ONCE OR TWICE A MONTH WAS ENOUGH TO KEEP HIM INTERESTED AND AWAKE AND ALIVE.
"BUT NOTHING GOOD LASTS FOREVER.
"AND, EVEN IN HIS FOLLY, HE WAS A REMARKABLE DETECTIVE."
YOU RANG, SIR?
YES, ALFRED. I WAS HOPING YOU COULD EXPLAIN *THESE...?*
HALLOWEEN, SIR. I PLANNED TO GO TRICK OR TREATING...

YOU DON'T HAVE TO LIE ANYMORE. OZZIE CHESTERFIELD, YOUR "PENGUIN". HE TOLD ME ABOUT THE *GAME.*

I KNOW ABOUT THE THEATRICAL TROUPE. I KNOW...I KNOW TOO MUCH...

AND *YOU* WERE THE JOKER.

YOU WERE *ALWAYS* THE JOKER.

WHY, ALFRED?

BECAUSE YOU *NEEDED* IT, SIR.

YOU'RE SAYING IT'S *ALL* BEEN A *LIE?* EVERYTHING I'VE *DONE?* ALL A *LIE?*

NOT AT *ALL,* SIR. IF YOU *BELIEVED* THAT YOU WERE FIGHTING EVIL, THEN YOU WERE *INDEED* FIGHTING EVIL.

I DON'T... BATMAN... *ALL* OF IT...IT'S JUST BEEN A HUGE *JOKE,* HASN'T IT?

I WOULD NOT HAVE PUT IT LIKE THAT, SIR. BUT PERHAPS IT MIGHT BE BEST TO LET IT *END,* NOW.

ALFRED... IT DOESN'T END.

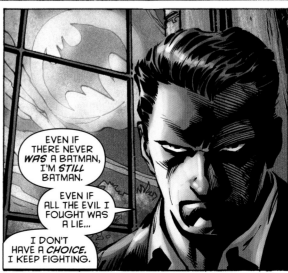

EVEN IF THERE NEVER *WAS* A BATMAN, I'M *STILL* BATMAN.

EVEN IF ALL THE EVIL I FOUGHT WAS A LIE...

I DON'T HAVE A *CHOICE.* I KEEP FIGHTING.

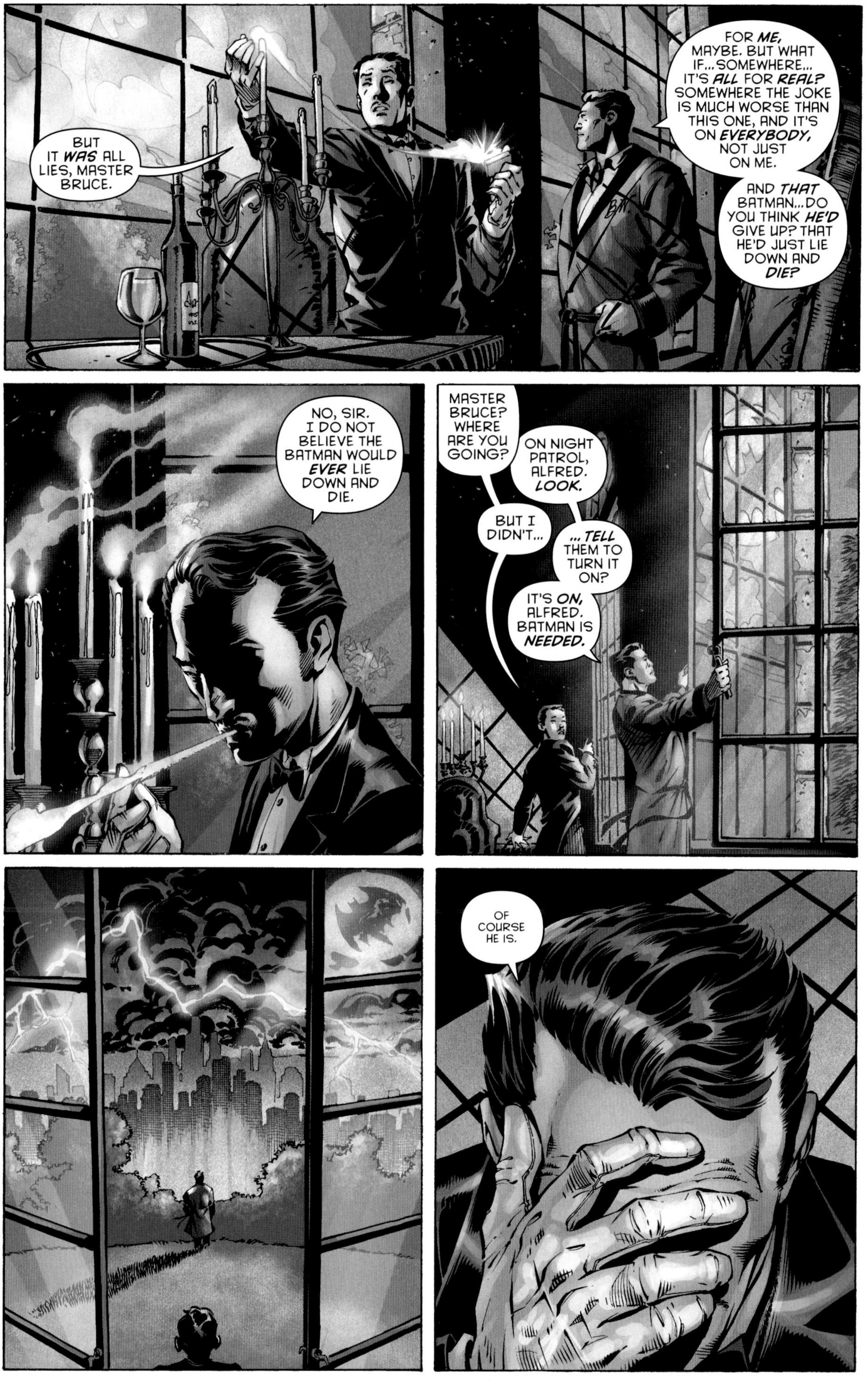
BUT IT WAS ALL LIES, MASTER BRUCE.
FOR ME, MAYBE. BUT WHAT IF... SOMEWHERE... IT'S ALL FOR REAL? SOMEWHERE THE JOKE IS MUCH WORSE THAN THIS ONE, AND IT'S ON EVERYBODY, NOT JUST ON ME.
AND THAT BATMAN... DO YOU THINK HE'D GIVE UP? THAT HE'D JUST LIE DOWN AND DIE?
NO, SIR. I DO NOT BELIEVE THE BATMAN WOULD EVER LIE DOWN AND DIE.
MASTER BRUCE? WHERE ARE YOU GOING?
ON NIGHT PATROL, ALFRED. LOOK.
BUT I DIDN'T...
...TELL THEM TO TURN IT ON?
IT'S ON, ALFRED. BATMAN IS NEEDED.
OF COURSE HE IS.

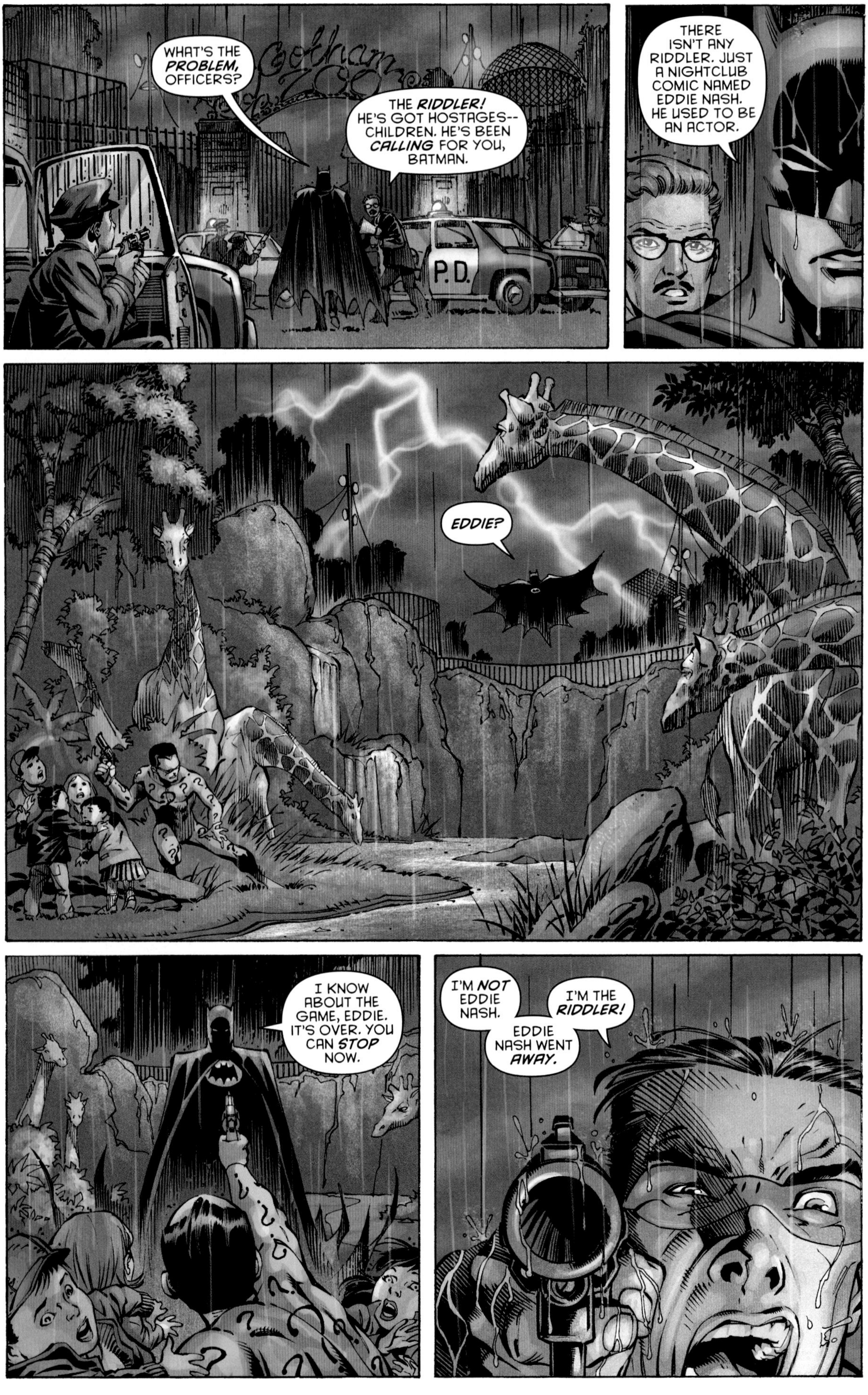
WHAT'S THE PROBLEM, OFFICERS?
THE RIDDLER! HE'S GOT HOSTAGES--CHILDREN. HE'S BEEN CALLING FOR YOU, BATMAN.
P.D.
THERE ISN'T ANY RIDDLER. JUST A NIGHTCLUB COMIC NAMED EDDIE NASH. HE USED TO BE AN ACTOR.
EDDIE?
I KNOW ABOUT THE GAME, EDDIE. IT'S OVER. YOU CAN STOP NOW.
I'M NOT EDDIE NASH.
I'M THE RIDDLER!
EDDIE NASH WENT AWAY.

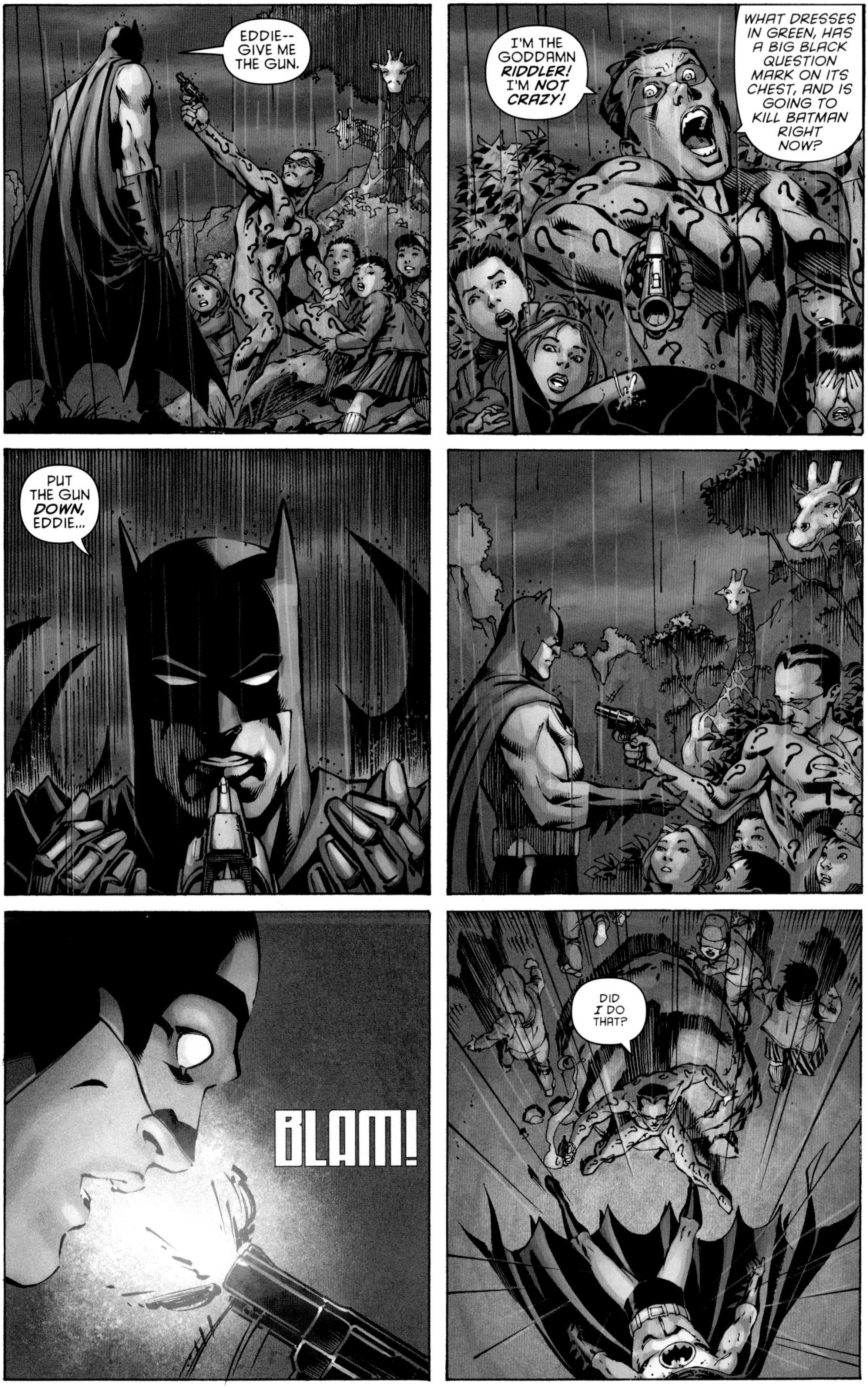
EDDIE-- GIVE ME THE GUN.
I'M THE GODDAMN RIDDLER! I'M NOT CRAZY!
WHAT DRESSES IN GREEN, HAS A BIG BLACK QUESTION MARK ON ITS CHEST, AND IS GOING TO KILL BATMAN RIGHT NOW?
PUT THE GUN DOWN, EDDIE...
BLAM!
DID I DO THAT?

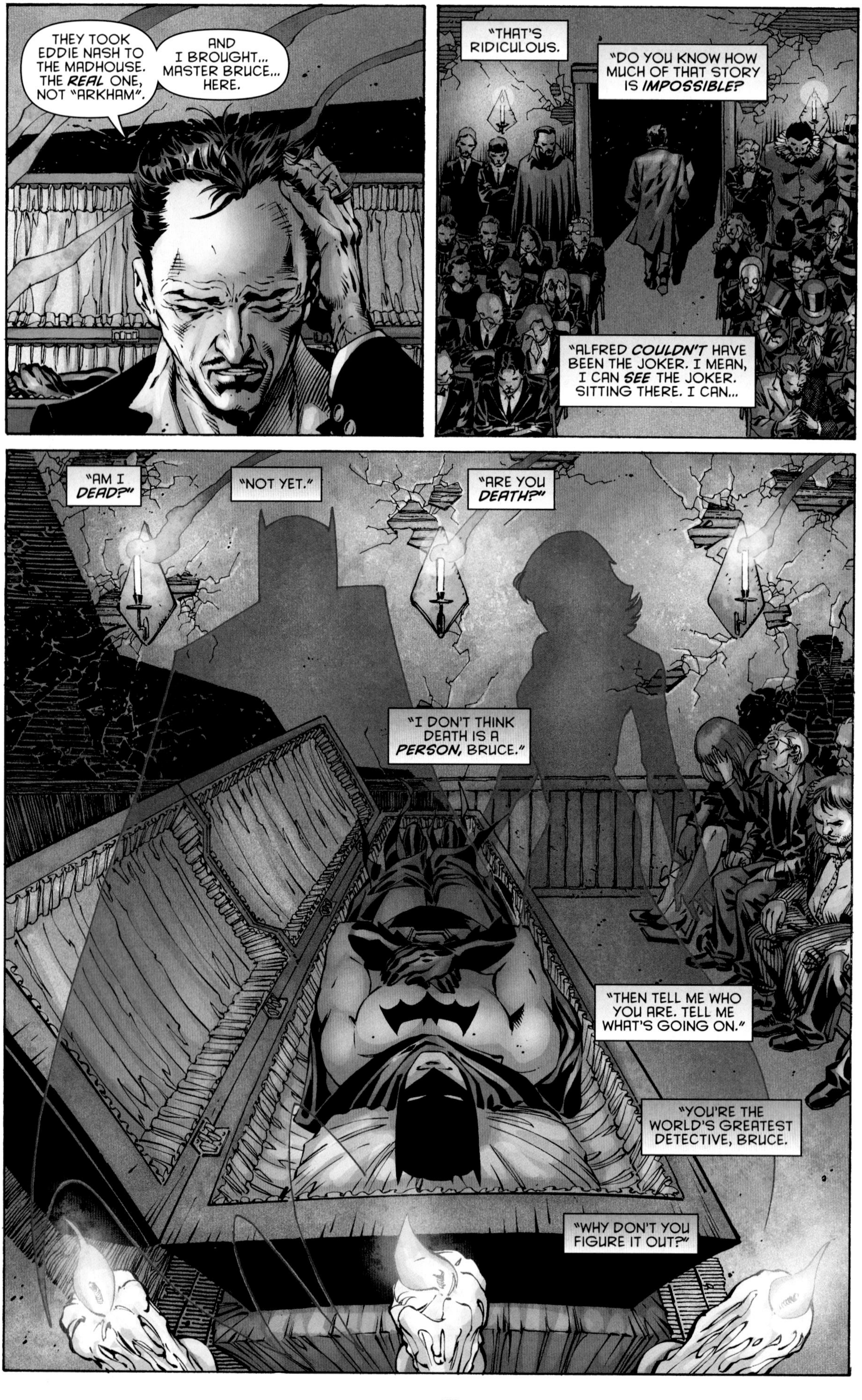
THEY TOOK EDDIE NASH TO THE MADHOUSE. THE *REAL* ONE, NOT "ARKHAM".
AND I BROUGHT... MASTER BRUCE... HERE.
"THAT'S RIDICULOUS.
"DO YOU KNOW HOW MUCH OF THAT STORY IS *IMPOSSIBLE?*
"ALFRED *COULDN'T* HAVE BEEN THE JOKER. I MEAN, I CAN *SEE* THE JOKER. SITTING THERE. I CAN...
"AM I *DEAD?*"
"NOT YET."
"ARE YOU *DEATH?*"
"I DON'T THINK DEATH IS A *PERSON,* BRUCE."
"THEN TELL ME WHO YOU ARE. TELL ME WHAT'S GOING ON."
"YOU'RE THE WORLD'S GREATEST DETECTIVE, BRUCE.
"WHY DON'T YOU FIGURE IT OUT?"

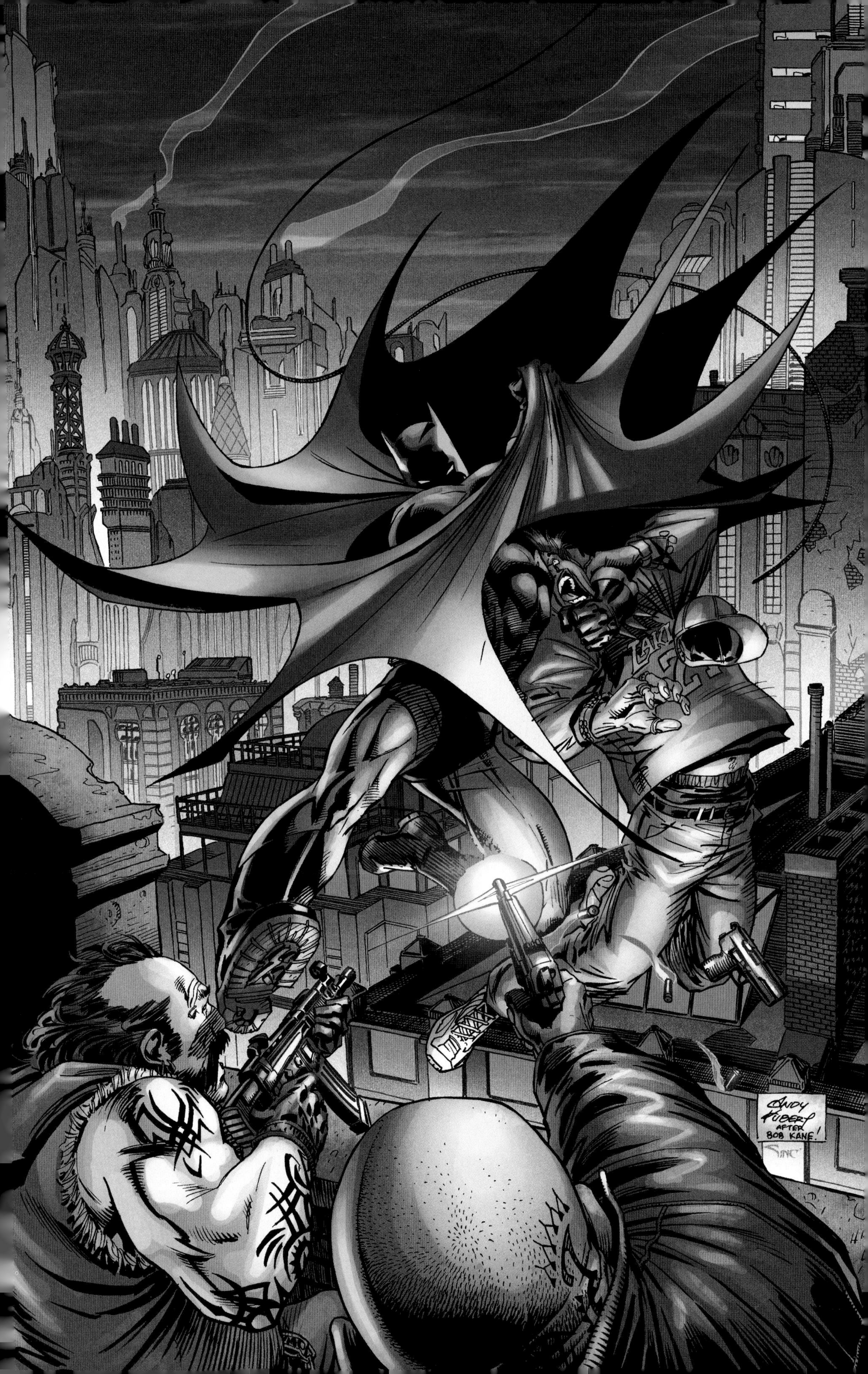
ANDY KUBERT
AFTER
BOB KANE!

DETECTIVE COMICS #853 variant cover art by Andy Kubert and Alex Sinclair

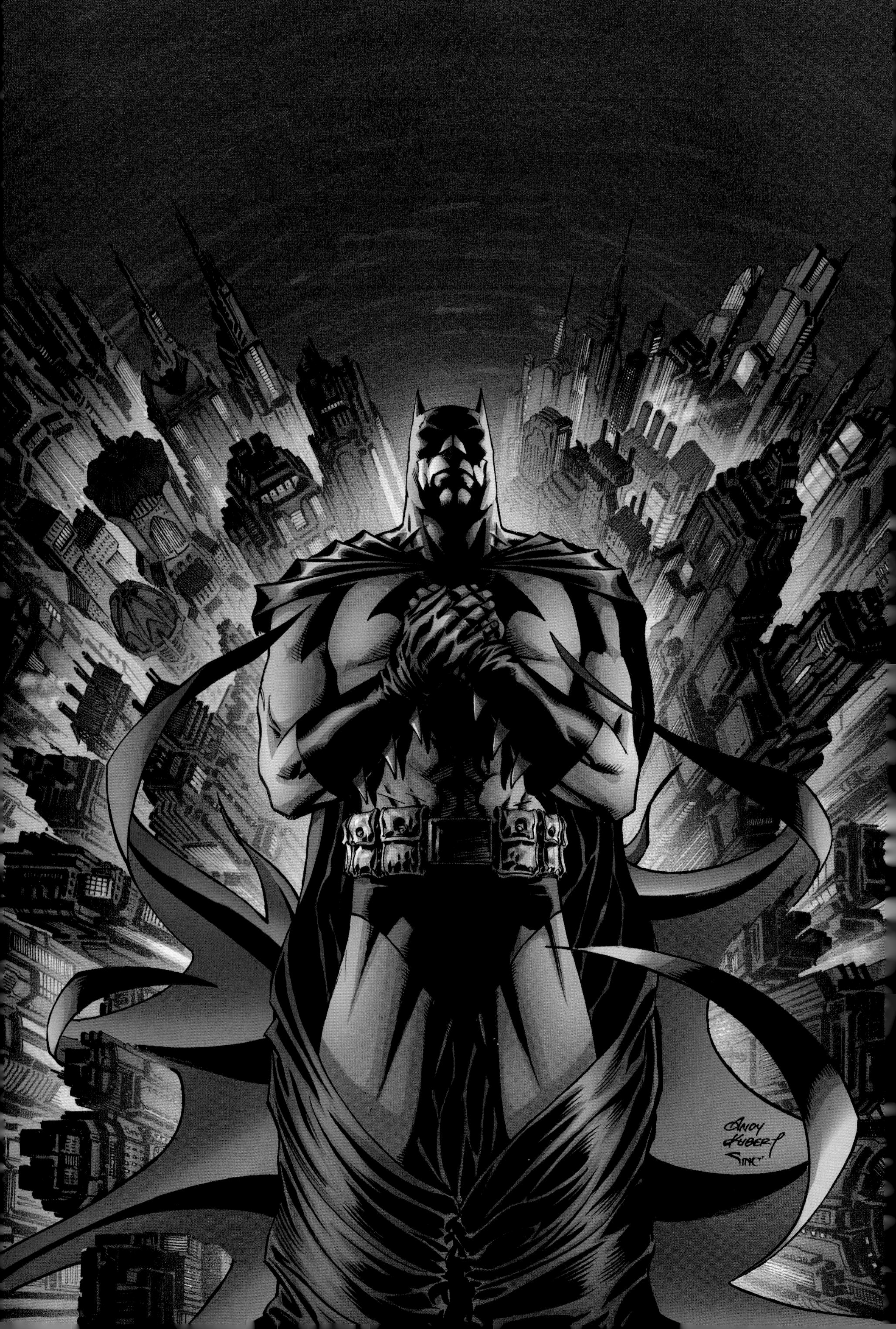

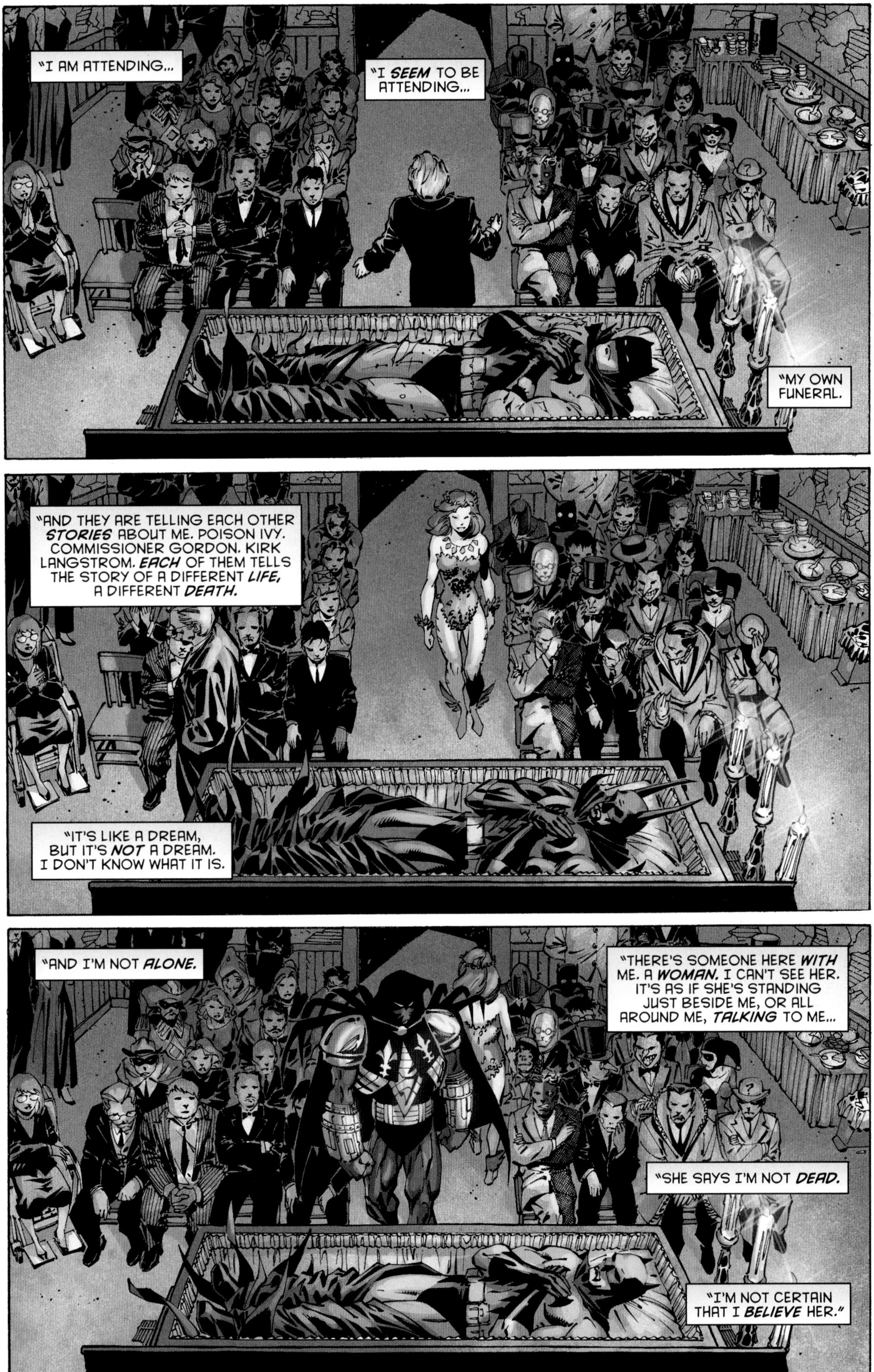
"I AM ATTENDING...
"I SEEM TO BE ATTENDING...
"MY OWN FUNERAL.
"AND THEY ARE TELLING EACH OTHER STORIES ABOUT ME. POISON IVY. COMMISSIONER GORDON. KIRK LANGSTROM. EACH OF THEM TELLS THE STORY OF A DIFFERENT LIFE, A DIFFERENT DEATH.
"IT'S LIKE A DREAM, BUT IT'S NOT A DREAM. I DON'T KNOW WHAT IT IS.
"AND I'M NOT ALONE.
"THERE'S SOMEONE HERE WITH ME. A WOMAN. I CAN'T SEE HER. IT'S AS IF SHE'S STANDING JUST BESIDE ME, OR ALL AROUND ME, TALKING TO ME...
"SHE SAYS I'M NOT DEAD.
"I'M NOT CERTAIN THAT I BELIEVE HER."

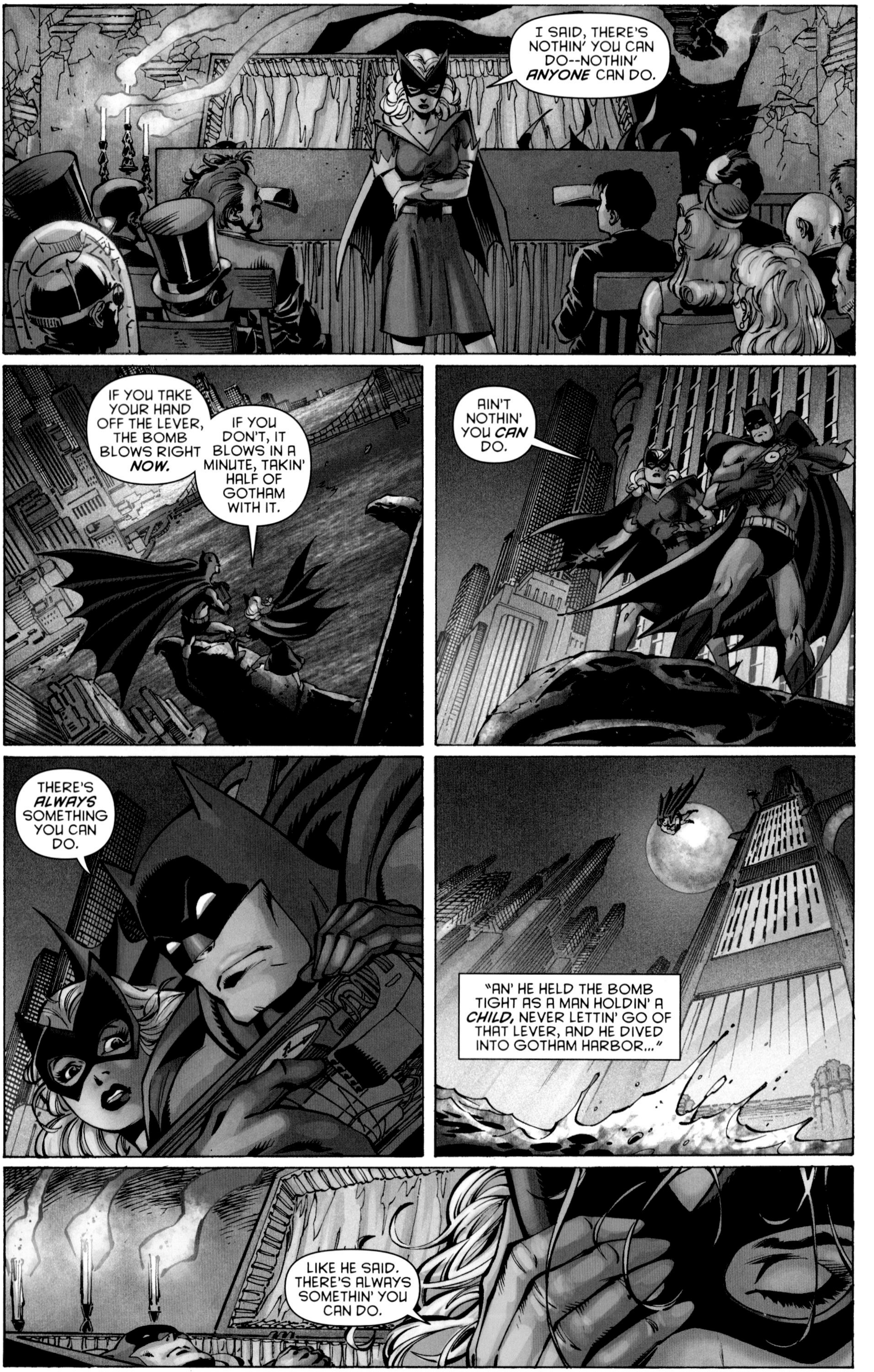
I SAID, THERE'S NOTHIN' YOU CAN DO--NOTHIN' ANYONE CAN DO.
IF YOU TAKE YOUR HAND OFF THE LEVER, THE BOMB BLOWS RIGHT NOW.
IF YOU DON'T, IT BLOWS IN A MINUTE, TAKIN' HALF OF GOTHAM WITH IT.
AIN'T NOTHIN' YOU CAN DO.
THERE'S ALWAYS SOMETHING YOU CAN DO.
"AN' HE HELD THE BOMB TIGHT AS A MAN HOLDIN' A CHILD, NEVER LETTIN' GO OF THAT LEVER, AND HE DIVED INTO GOTHAM HARBOR..."
LIKE HE SAID. THERE'S ALWAYS SOMETHIN' YOU CAN DO.

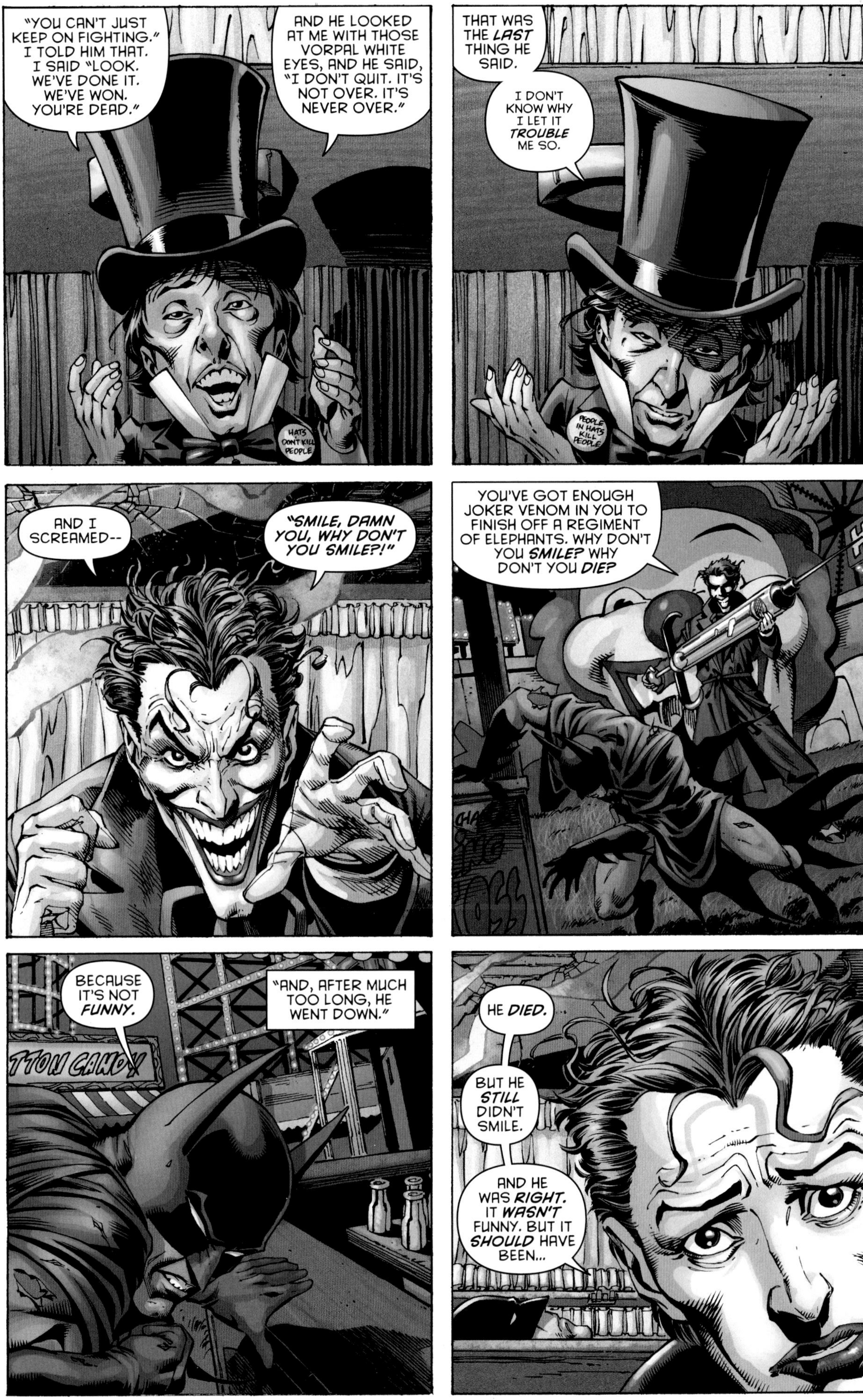
"YOU CAN'T JUST KEEP ON FIGHTING." I TOLD HIM THAT. I SAID "LOOK. WE'VE DONE IT. WE'VE WON. YOU'RE DEAD."
AND HE LOOKED AT ME WITH THOSE VORPAL WHITE EYES, AND HE SAID, "I DON'T QUIT. IT'S NOT OVER. IT'S NEVER OVER."
HATS DON'T KILL PEOPLE
THAT WAS THE LAST THING HE SAID.
I DON'T KNOW WHY I LET IT TROUBLE ME SO.
PEOPLE IN HATS KILL PEOPLE
AND I SCREAMED--
"SMILE, DAMN YOU, WHY DON'T YOU SMILE?!"
YOU'VE GOT ENOUGH JOKER VENOM IN YOU TO FINISH OFF A REGIMENT OF ELEPHANTS. WHY DON'T YOU SMILE? WHY DON'T YOU DIE?
BECAUSE IT'S NOT FUNNY.
"AND, AFTER MUCH TOO LONG, HE WENT DOWN."
TTON CANDY
HE DIED...
BUT HE STILL DIDN'T SMILE.
AND HE WAS RIGHT. IT WASN'T FUNNY. BUT IT SHOULD HAVE BEEN...

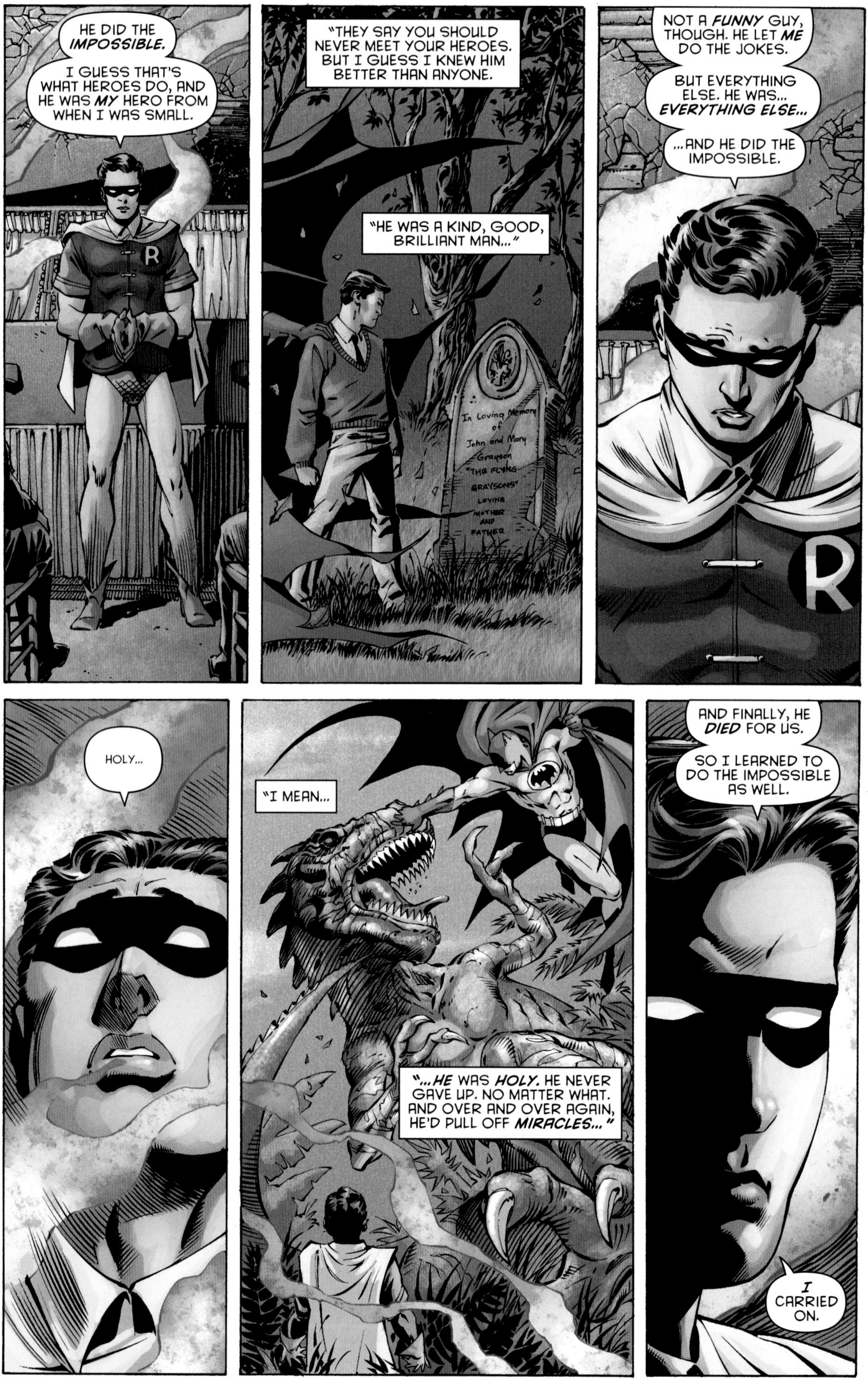

HE DID THE IMPOSSIBLE.
I GUESS THAT'S WHAT HEROES DO, AND HE WAS MY HERO FROM WHEN I WAS SMALL.
"THEY SAY YOU SHOULD NEVER MEET YOUR HEROES. BUT I GUESS I KNEW HIM BETTER THAN ANYONE.
"HE WAS A KIND, GOOD, BRILLIANT MAN..."
In Loving Memory of John and Mary Grayson "THE FLYING GRAYSONS" LOVING MOTHER AND FATHER
NOT A FUNNY GUY, THOUGH. HE LET ME DO THE JOKES.
BUT EVERYTHING ELSE. HE WAS... EVERYTHING ELSE...
...AND HE DID THE IMPOSSIBLE.
R
HOLY...
"I MEAN...
"...HE WAS HOLY. HE NEVER GAVE UP. NO MATTER WHAT. AND OVER AND OVER AGAIN, HE'D PULL OFF MIRACLES..."
AND FINALLY, HE DIED FOR US.
SO I LEARNED TO DO THE IMPOSSIBLE AS WELL.
I CARRIED ON.

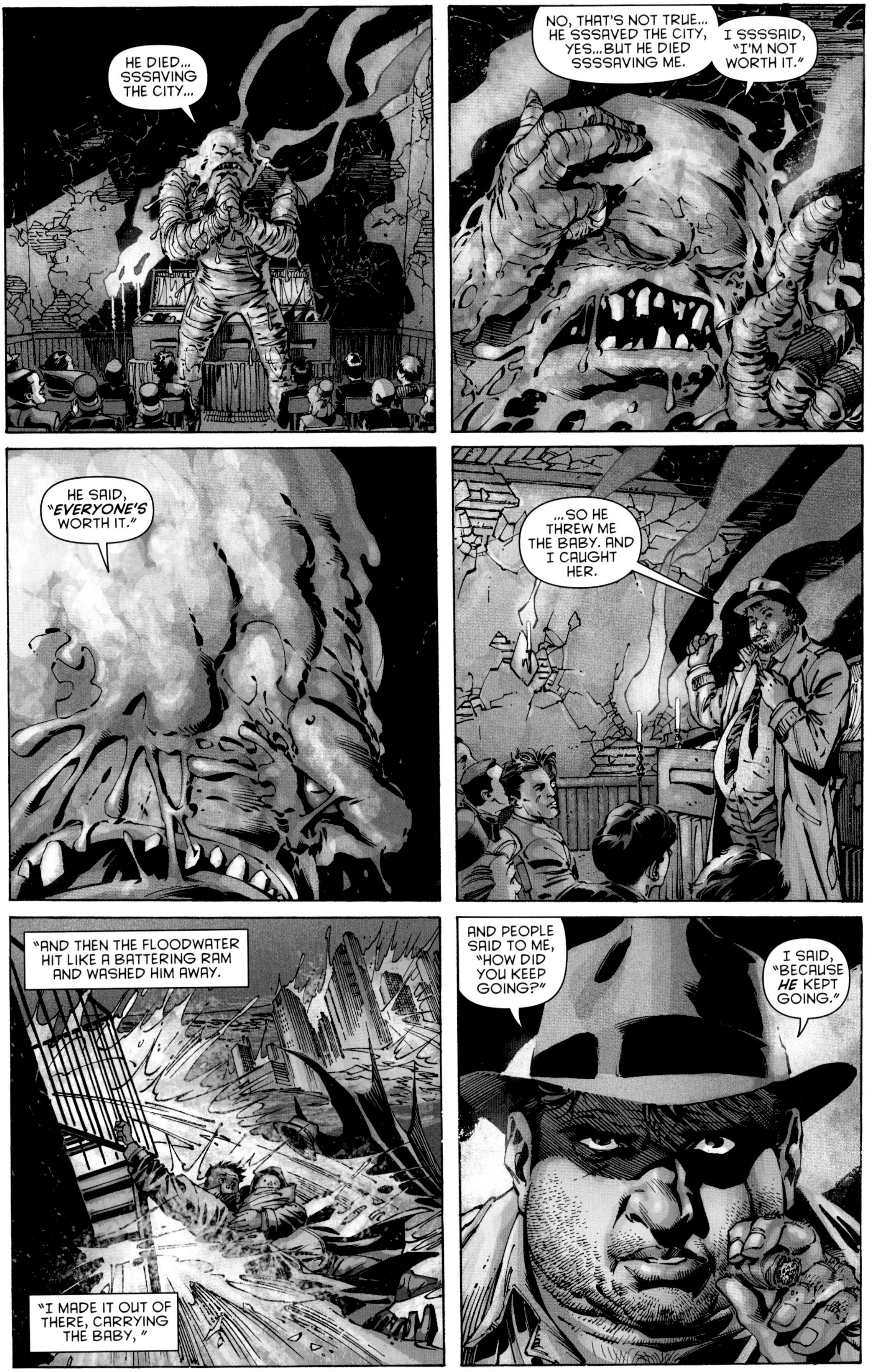
HE DIED... SSSAVING THE CITY...
NO, THAT'S NOT TRUE... HE SSSAVED THE CITY, YES...BUT HE DIED SSSSAVING ME.
I SSSSAID, "I'M NOT WORTH IT."
HE SAID, "EVERYONE'S WORTH IT."
...SO HE THREW ME THE BABY. AND I CAUGHT HER.
"AND THEN THE FLOODWATER HIT LIKE A BATTERING RAM AND WASHED HIM AWAY.
"I MADE IT OUT OF THERE, CARRYING THE BABY,"
AND PEOPLE SAID TO ME, "HOW DID YOU KEEP GOING?"
I SAID, "BECAUSE HE KEPT GOING."

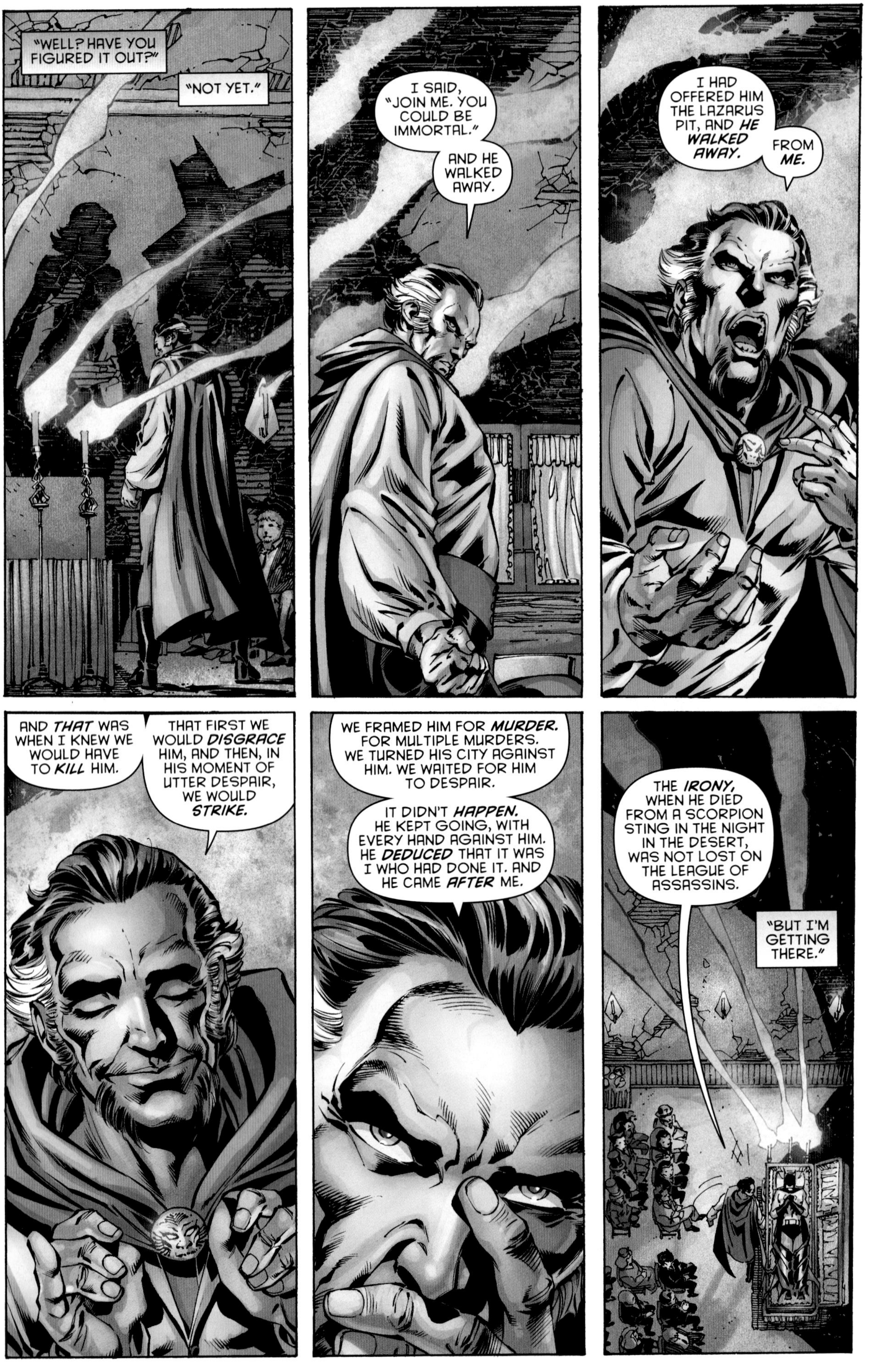
"WELL? HAVE YOU FIGURED IT OUT?"
"NOT YET."
I SAID, "JOIN ME. YOU COULD BE IMMORTAL."
AND HE WALKED AWAY.
I HAD OFFERED HIM THE LAZARUS PIT, AND HE WALKED AWAY.
FROM ME.
AND THAT WAS WHEN I KNEW WE WOULD HAVE TO KILL HIM.
THAT FIRST WE WOULD DISGRACE HIM, AND THEN, IN HIS MOMENT OF UTTER DESPAIR, WE WOULD STRIKE.
WE FRAMED HIM FOR MURDER. FOR MULTIPLE MURDERS. WE TURNED HIS CITY AGAINST HIM. WE WAITED FOR HIM TO DESPAIR.
IT DIDN'T HAPPEN. HE KEPT GOING, WITH EVERY HAND AGAINST HIM. HE DEDUCED THAT IT WAS I WHO HAD DONE IT. AND HE CAME AFTER ME.
THE IRONY, WHEN HE DIED FROM A SCORPION STING IN THE NIGHT IN THE DESERT, WAS NOT LOST ON THE LEAGUE OF ASSASSINS.
"BUT I'M GETTING THERE."

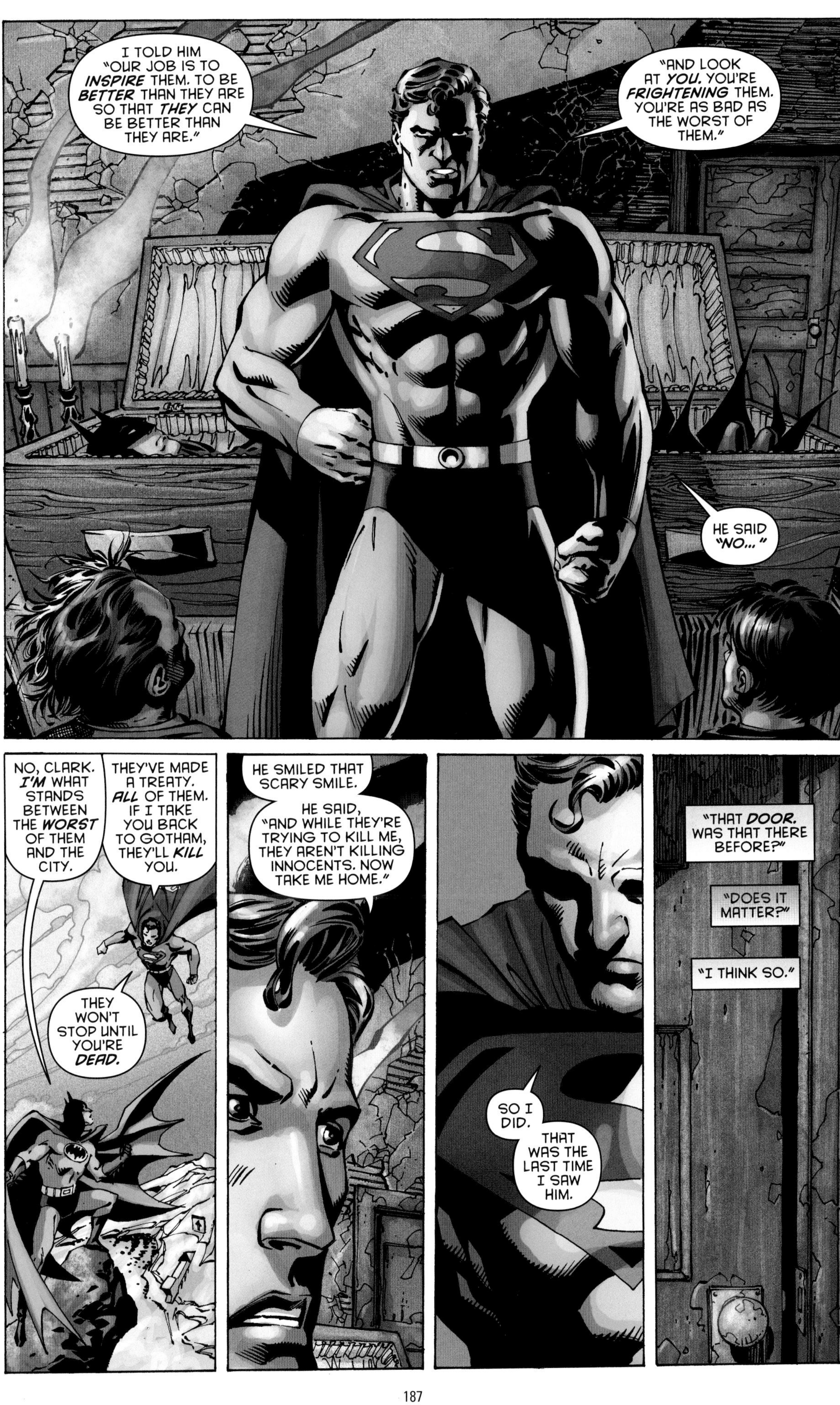
I TOLD HIM "OUR JOB IS TO INSPIRE THEM. TO BE BETTER THAN THEY ARE SO THAT THEY CAN BE BETTER THAN THEY ARE."
"AND LOOK AT YOU. YOU'RE FRIGHTENING THEM. YOU'RE AS BAD AS THE WORST OF THEM."
HE SAID "NO..."
NO, CLARK. I'M WHAT STANDS BETWEEN THE WORST OF THEM AND THE CITY.
THEY'VE MADE A TREATY. ALL OF THEM. IF I TAKE YOU BACK TO GOTHAM, THEY'LL KILL YOU.
THEY WON'T STOP UNTIL YOU'RE DEAD.
HE SMILED THAT SCARY SMILE.
HE SAID, "AND WHILE THEY'RE TRYING TO KILL ME, THEY AREN'T KILLING INNOCENTS. NOW TAKE ME HOME."
SO I DID.
THAT WAS THE LAST TIME I SAW HIM.
"THAT DOOR. WAS THAT THERE BEFORE?"
"DOES IT MATTER?"
"I THINK SO."

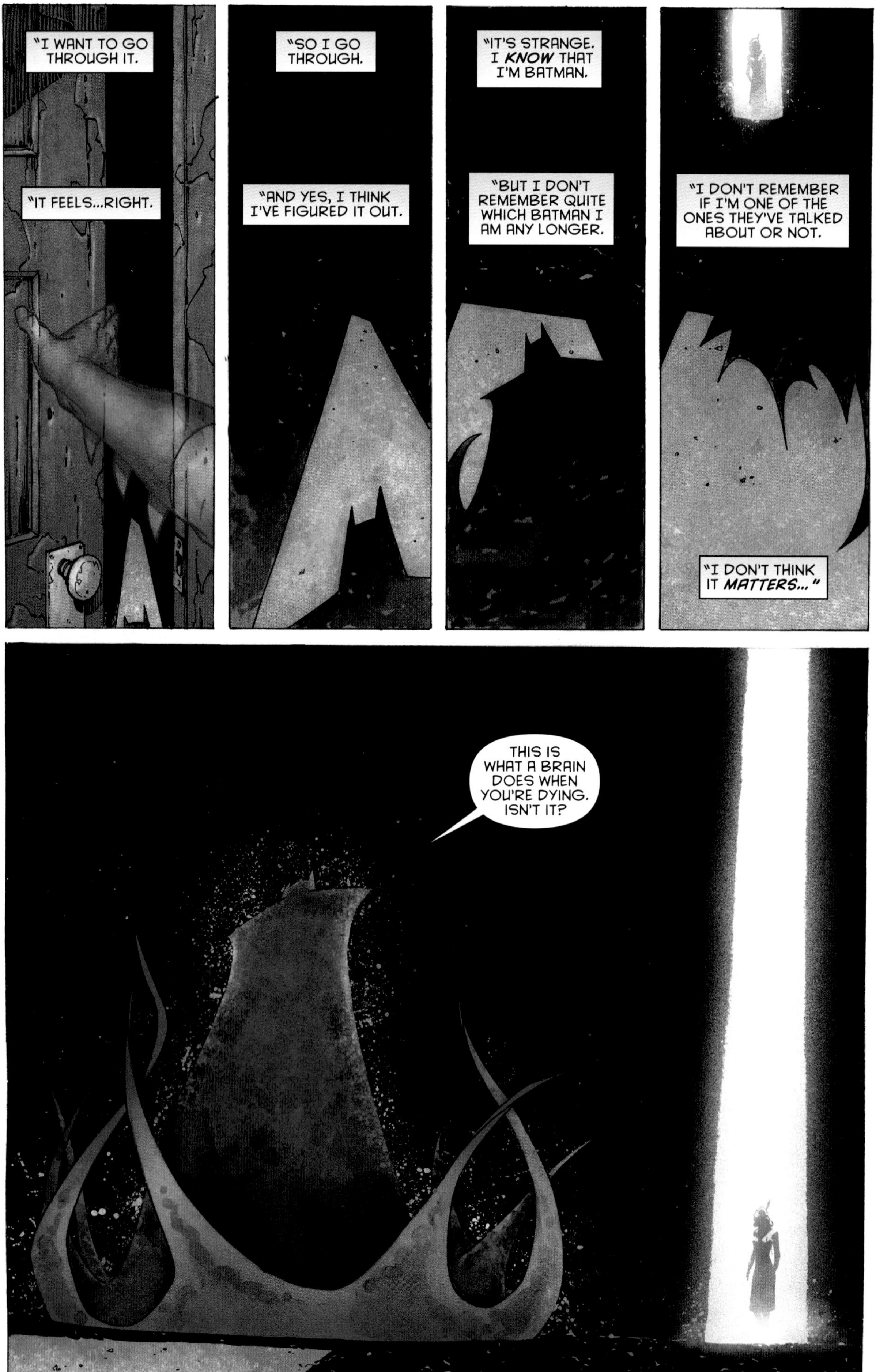
"I WANT TO GO THROUGH IT.
"IT FEELS...RIGHT.
"SO I GO THROUGH.
"AND YES, I THINK I'VE FIGURED IT OUT.
"IT'S STRANGE. I KNOW THAT I'M BATMAN.
"BUT I DON'T REMEMBER QUITE WHICH BATMAN I AM ANY LONGER.
"I DON'T REMEMBER IF I'M ONE OF THE ONES THEY'VE TALKED ABOUT OR NOT.
"I DON'T THINK IT MATTERS..."
THIS IS WHAT A BRAIN DOES WHEN YOU'RE DYING. ISN'T IT?

IT'S WHAT THEY CALL AN N.D.E.

A NEAR DEATH EXPERIENCE.

IT'S CLASSIC. MEETS ALL THE CRITERIA.

I FEEL SERENE AND CALM.

MY LIFE IS IN REPLAY OVER AND OVER. EVEN THOUGH IT'S NEVER QUITE MY LIFE... IS IT?

SO I'M NOT DEAD.

NOT YET.

BUT I'M CLOSE TO IT, AREN'T I?

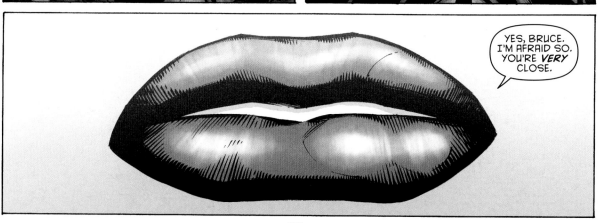

YES, BRUCE. I'M AFRAID SO. YOU'RE VERY CLOSE.

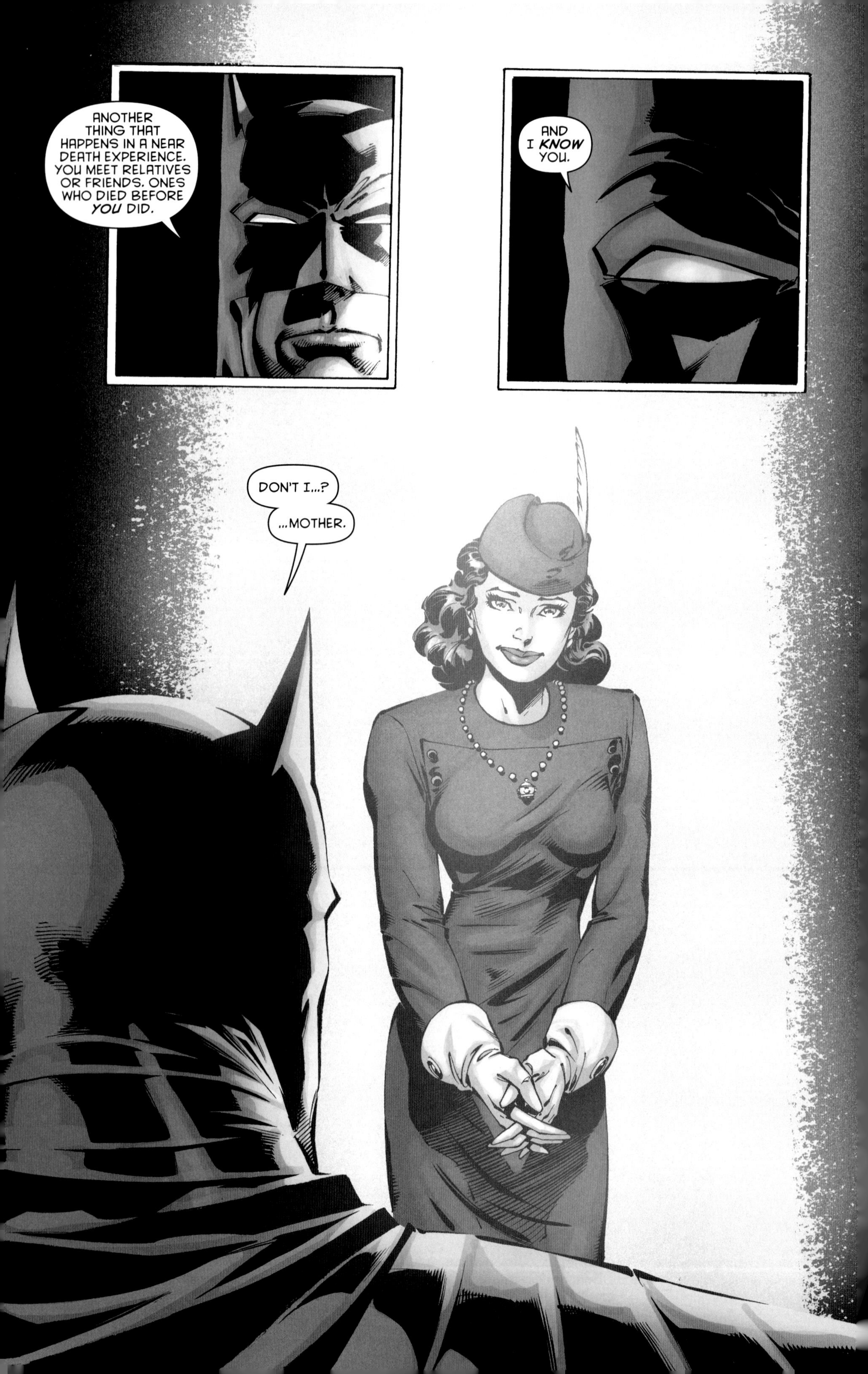
ANOTHER THING THAT HAPPENS IN A NEAR DEATH EXPERIENCE. YOU MEET RELATIVES OR FRIENDS. ONES WHO DIED BEFORE *YOU* DID.
AND I *KNOW* YOU.
DON'T I...?
...MOTHER.

YES, YOU DO, BRUCE.

SO ARE YOU *REAL?* OR JUST SOMETHING *ELSE* THAT'S HAPPENING IN MY HEAD, BEFORE THE END?

IS THERE ANY *DIFFERENCE,* AT THIS POINT?

I GUESS *NOT.* IT'S TOO SUBJECTIVE.

EXACTLY. SO WHAT HAVE YOU LEARNED FROM YOUR FUNERAL, BRUCE?

LEARNED?

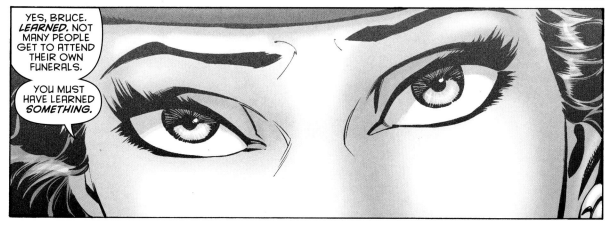

YES, BRUCE. *LEARNED.* NOT MANY PEOPLE GET TO ATTEND THEIR OWN FUNERALS.

YOU MUST HAVE LEARNED *SOMETHING.*

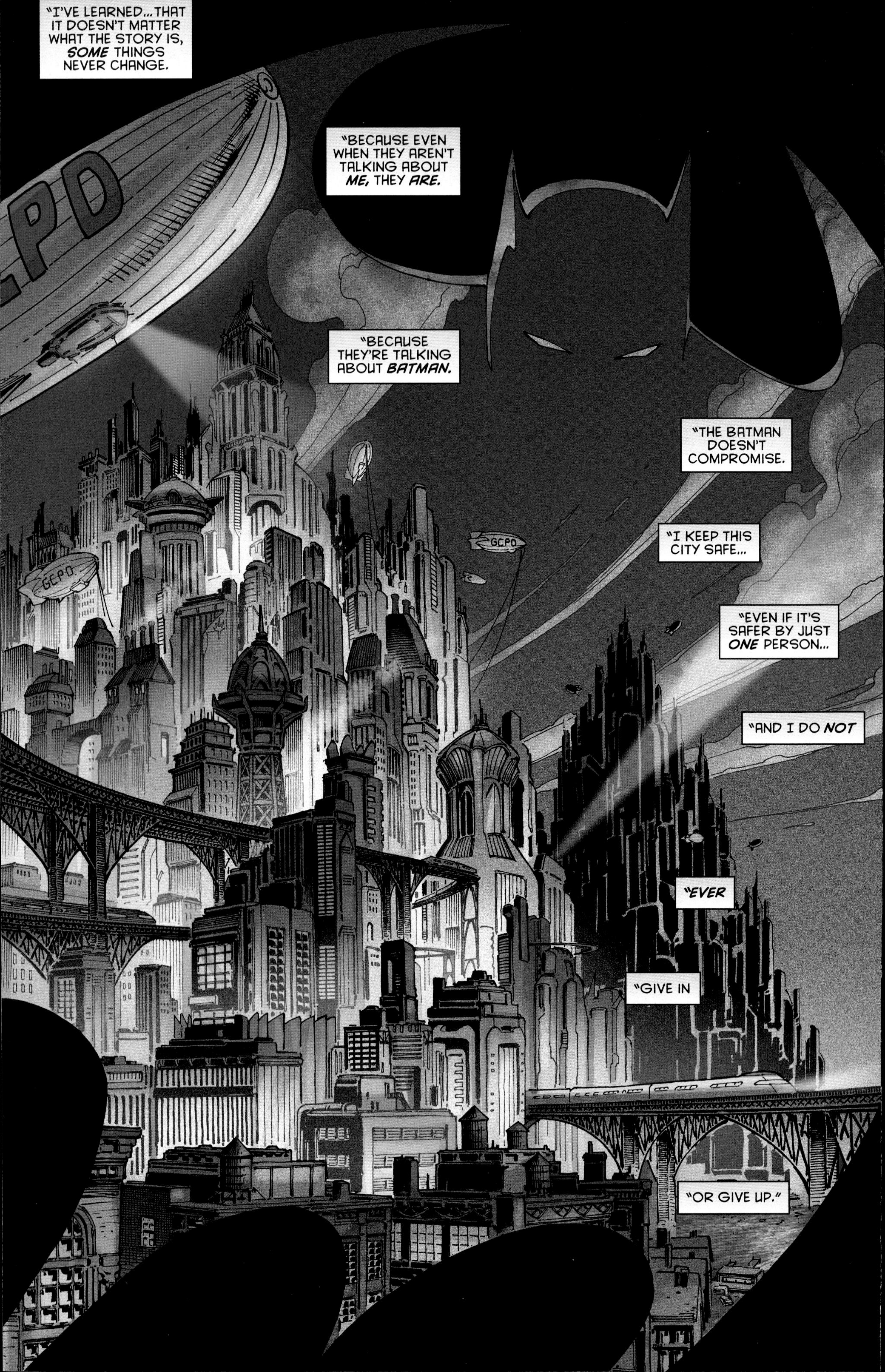
"I'VE LEARNED... THAT IT DOESN'T MATTER WHAT THE STORY IS, SOME THINGS NEVER CHANGE.
GCPD
"BECAUSE EVEN WHEN THEY AREN'T TALKING ABOUT ME, THEY ARE.
"BECAUSE THEY'RE TALKING ABOUT BATMAN.
"THE BATMAN DOESN'T COMPROMISE.
GCPD
GCPD
"I KEEP THIS CITY SAFE...
"EVEN IF IT'S SAFER BY JUST ONE PERSON...
"AND I DO NOT
"EVER
"GIVE IN
"OR GIVE UP."

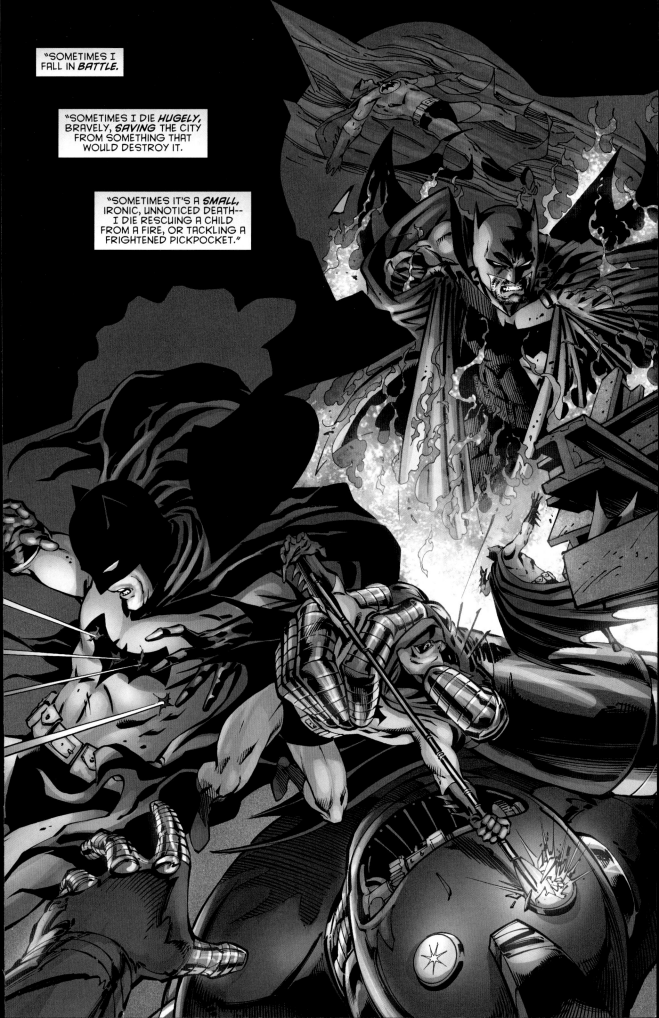

"SOMETIMES I FALL IN *BATTLE*.

"SOMETIMES I DIE *HUGELY*, BRAVELY, *SAVING* THE CITY FROM SOMETHING THAT WOULD DESTROY IT.

"SOMETIMES IT'S A *SMALL*, IRONIC, UNNOTICED DEATH-- I DIE RESCUING A CHILD FROM A FIRE, OR TACKLING A FRIGHTENED PICKPOCKET."

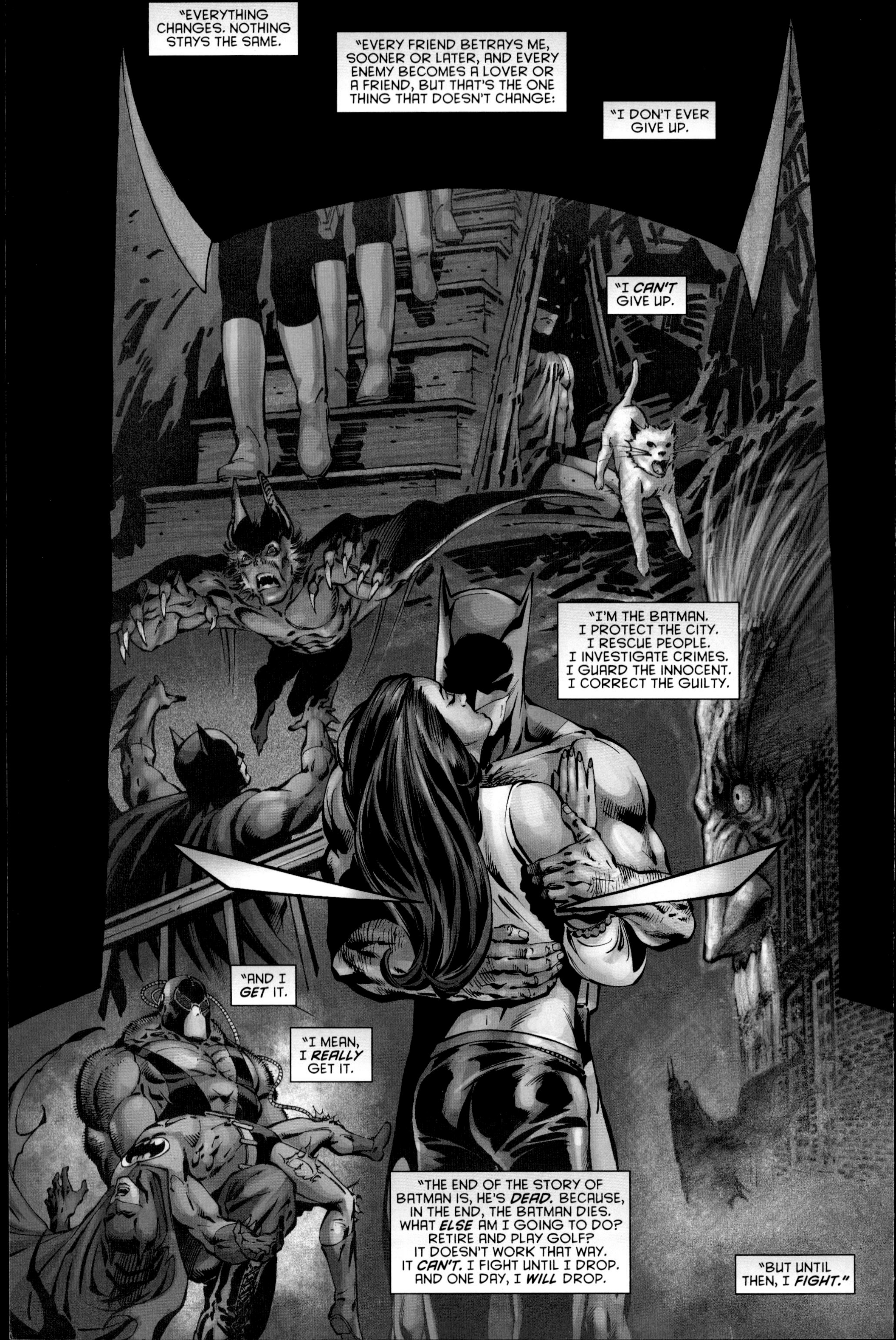
"EVERYTHING CHANGES. NOTHING STAYS THE SAME.
"EVERY FRIEND BETRAYS ME, SOONER OR LATER, AND EVERY ENEMY BECOMES A LOVER OR A FRIEND, BUT THAT'S THE ONE THING THAT DOESN'T CHANGE:
"I DON'T EVER GIVE UP.
"I *CAN'T* GIVE UP.
"I'M THE BATMAN. I PROTECT THE CITY. I RESCUE PEOPLE. I INVESTIGATE CRIMES. I GUARD THE INNOCENT. I CORRECT THE GUILTY.
"AND I *GET* IT.
"I MEAN, I *REALLY* GET IT.
"THE END OF THE STORY OF BATMAN IS, HE'S *DEAD.* BECAUSE, IN THE END, THE BATMAN DIES. WHAT *ELSE* AM I GOING TO DO? RETIRE AND PLAY GOLF? IT DOESN'T WORK THAT WAY. IT *CAN'T.* I FIGHT UNTIL I DROP. AND ONE DAY, I *WILL* DROP.
"BUT UNTIL THEN, I *FIGHT.*"

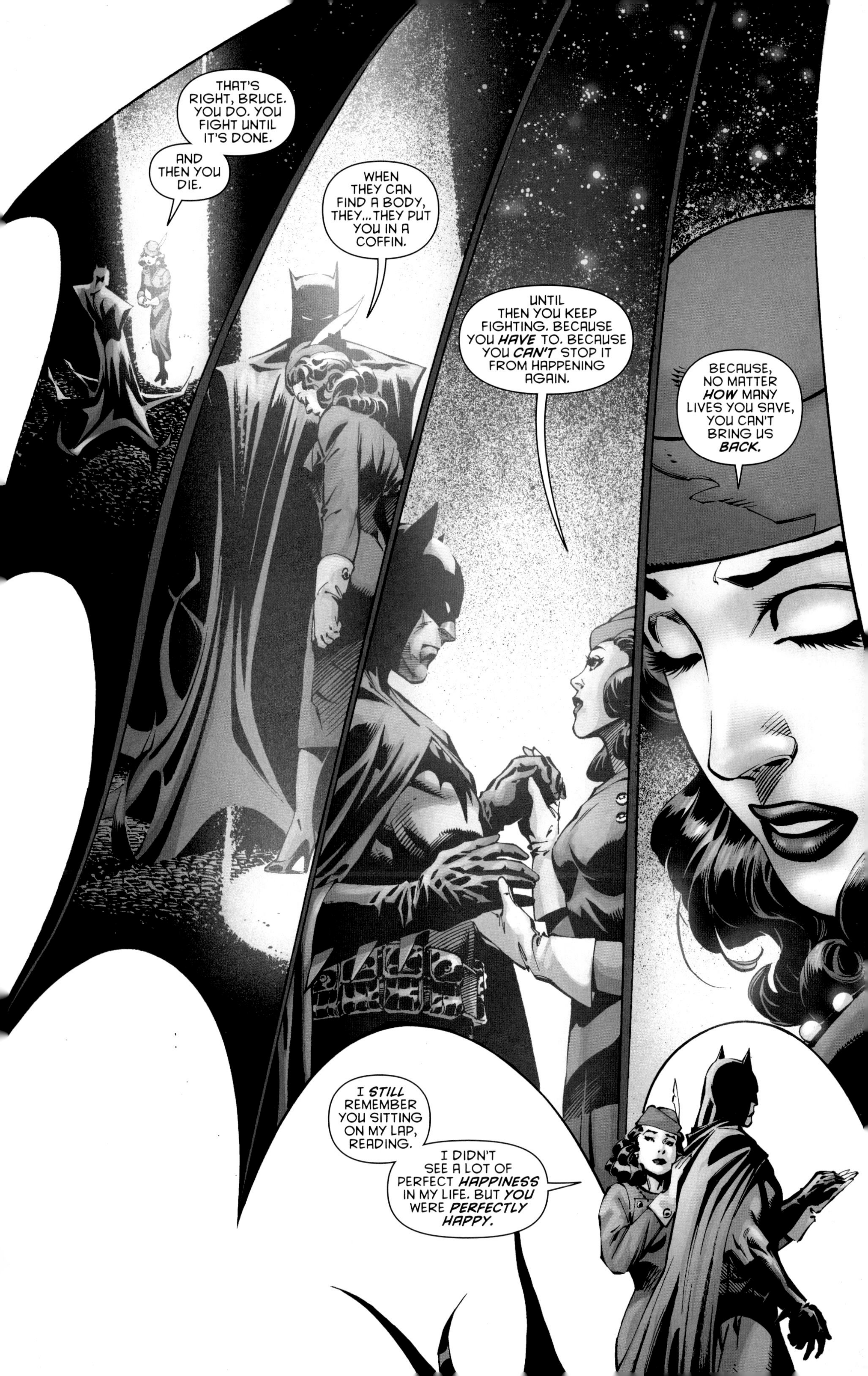

THAT'S RIGHT, BRUCE. YOU DO. YOU FIGHT UNTIL IT'S DONE.
AND THEN YOU DIE.
WHEN THEY CAN FIND A BODY, THEY... THEY PUT YOU IN A COFFIN.
UNTIL THEN YOU KEEP FIGHTING. BECAUSE YOU *HAVE* TO. BECAUSE YOU *CAN'T* STOP IT FROM HAPPENING AGAIN.
BECAUSE, NO MATTER *HOW* MANY LIVES YOU SAVE, YOU CAN'T BRING US *BACK.*
I *STILL* REMEMBER YOU SITTING ON MY LAP, READING.
I DIDN'T SEE A LOT OF PERFECT *HAPPINESS* IN MY LIFE. BUT *YOU* WERE *PERFECTLY HAPPY.*

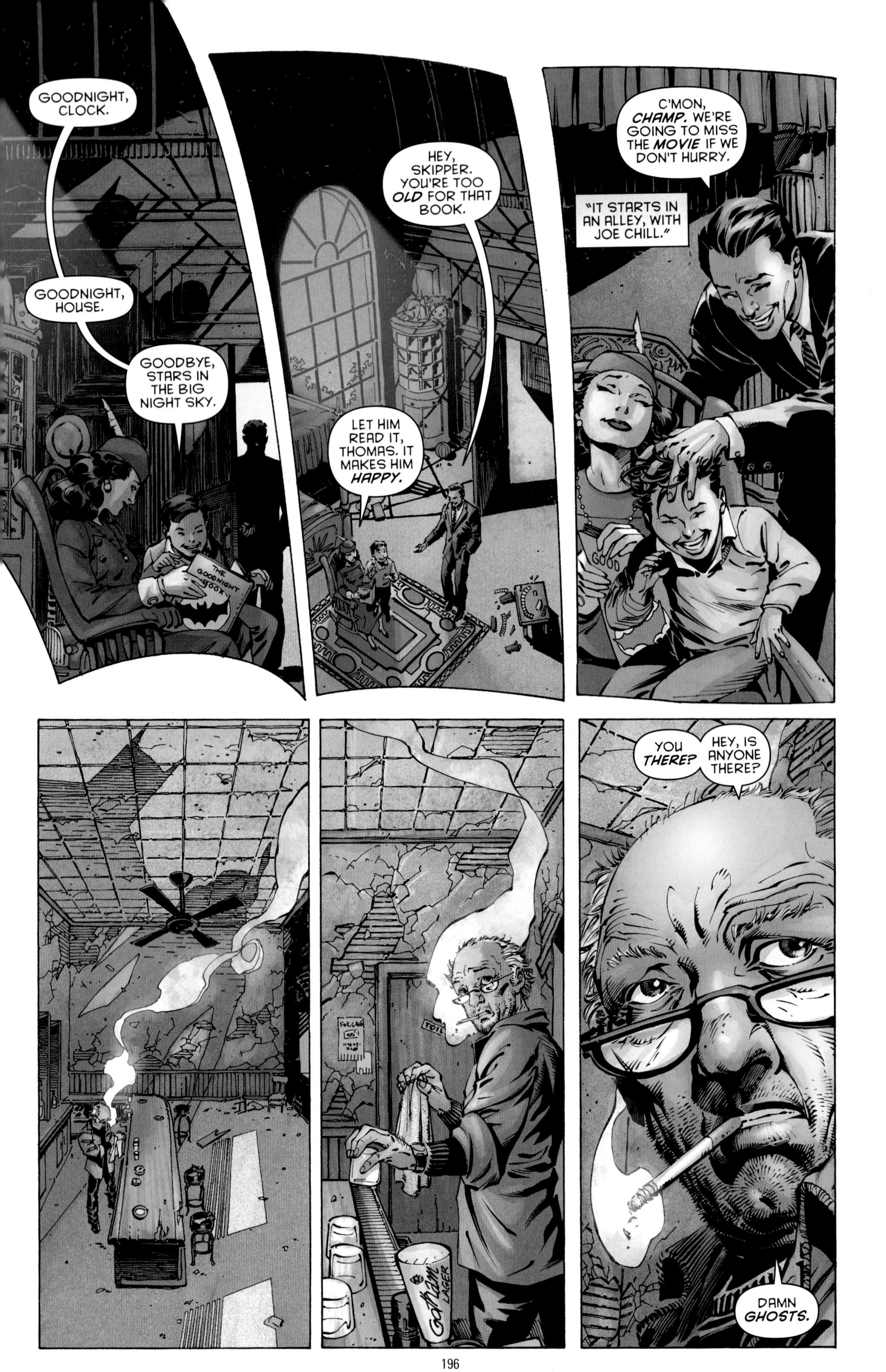
GOODNIGHT, CLOCK.
GOODNIGHT, HOUSE.
GOODBYE, STARS IN THE BIG NIGHT SKY.
THE GOODNIGHT BOOK
HEY, SKIPPER. YOU'RE TOO OLD FOR THAT BOOK.
LET HIM READ IT, THOMAS. IT MAKES HIM HAPPY.
C'MON, CHAMP. WE'RE GOING TO MISS THE MOVIE IF WE DON'T HURRY.
"IT STARTS IN AN ALLEY, WITH JOE CHILL."
YOU THERE?
HEY, IS ANYONE THERE?
DAMN GHOSTS.

HE WAS SO *BRAVE*, MOMMY.

IT WAS MORE VIOLENT THAN I WAS EXPECTING...

WELL, I *LOVED* IT. GOOD OLD-FASHIONED HEROICS NEVER GO OUT OF STYLE--

I'LL TAKE THAT PEARL NECKLACE YOU'RE WEARIN', LADY!

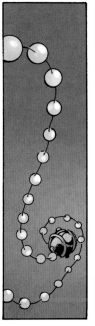

GET *AWAY* FROM HER...

"*PLEASE.* GET *AWAY* FROM HER.

"JUST THIS *ONCE.* TURN AROUND, LET IT GO."

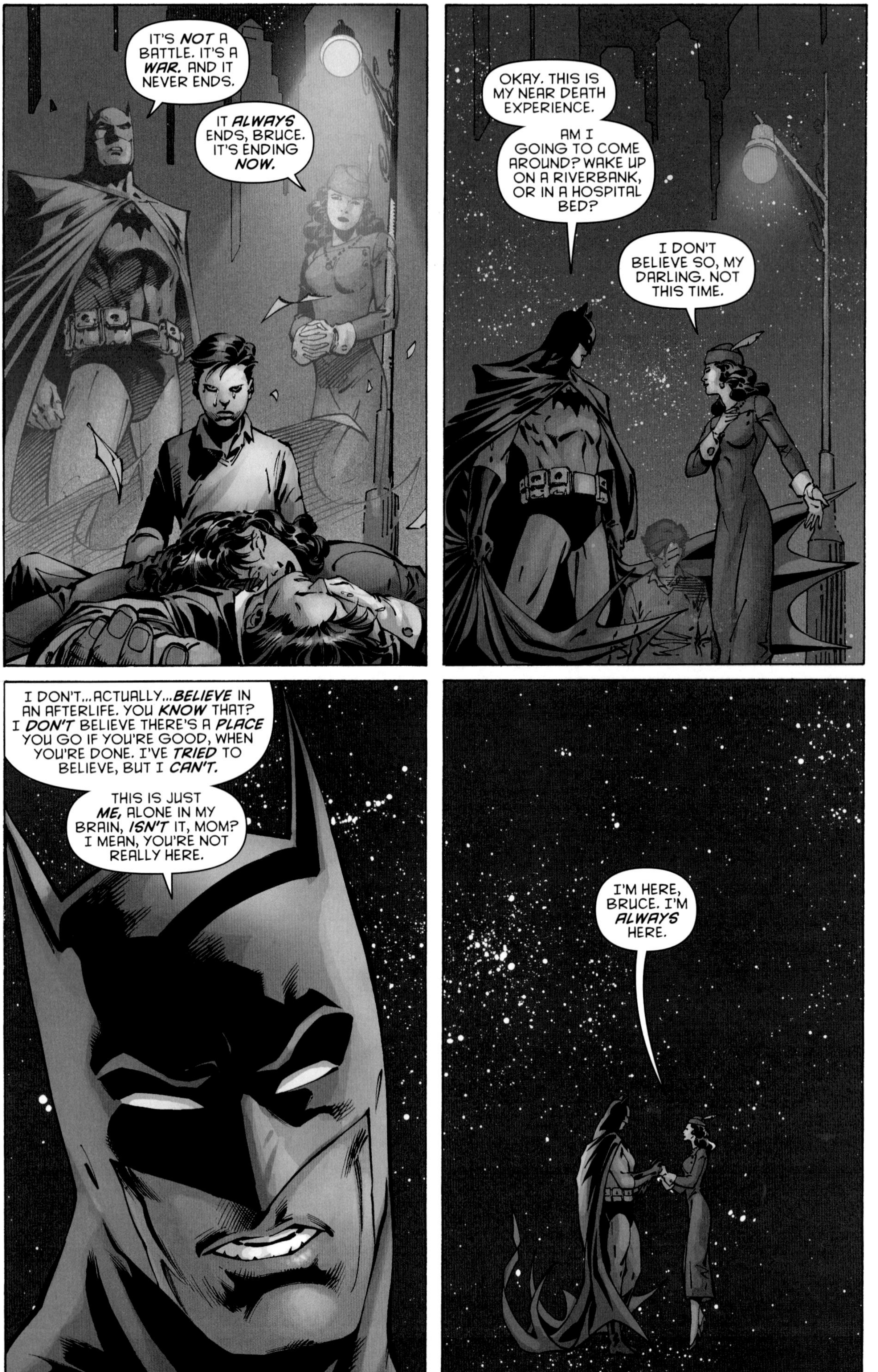
IT'S NOT A BATTLE. IT'S A WAR. AND IT NEVER ENDS.
IT ALWAYS ENDS, BRUCE. IT'S ENDING NOW.
OKAY. THIS IS MY NEAR DEATH EXPERIENCE.
AM I GOING TO COME AROUND? WAKE UP ON A RIVERBANK, OR IN A HOSPITAL BED?
I DON'T BELIEVE SO, MY DARLING. NOT THIS TIME.
I DON'T...ACTUALLY...BELIEVE IN AN AFTERLIFE. YOU KNOW THAT? I DON'T BELIEVE THERE'S A PLACE YOU GO IF YOU'RE GOOD, WHEN YOU'RE DONE. I'VE TRIED TO BELIEVE, BUT I CAN'T.
THIS IS JUST ME, ALONE IN MY BRAIN, ISN'T IT, MOM? I MEAN, YOU'RE NOT REALLY HERE.
I'M HERE, BRUCE. I'M ALWAYS HERE.

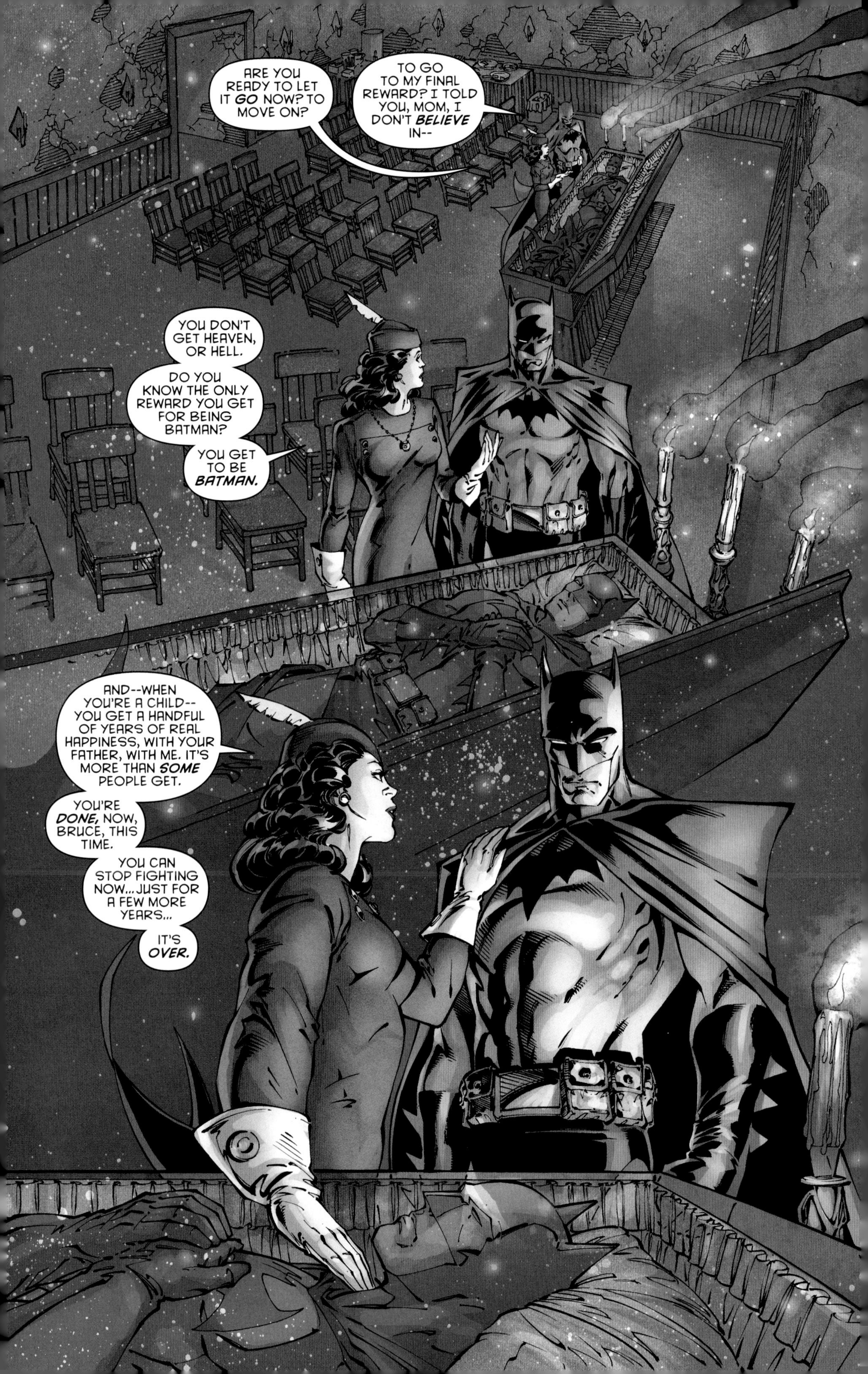
ARE YOU READY TO LET IT **GO** NOW? TO MOVE ON?
TO GO TO MY FINAL REWARD? I TOLD YOU, MOM, I DON'T **BELIEVE** IN--
YOU DON'T GET HEAVEN, OR HELL.
DO YOU KNOW THE ONLY REWARD YOU GET FOR BEING BATMAN?
YOU GET TO BE ***BATMAN.***
AND--WHEN YOU'RE A CHILD--YOU GET A HANDFUL OF YEARS OF REAL HAPPINESS, WITH YOUR FATHER, WITH ME. IT'S MORE THAN ***SOME*** PEOPLE GET.
YOU'RE ***DONE,*** NOW, BRUCE, THIS TIME.
YOU CAN STOP FIGHTING NOW... JUST FOR A FEW MORE YEARS...
IT'S ***OVER.***

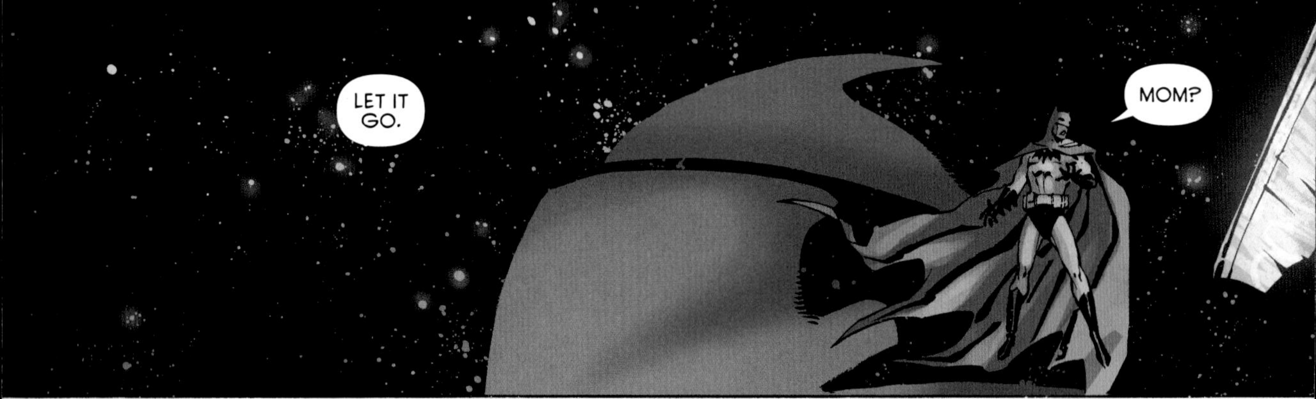
LET IT GO.
MOM?
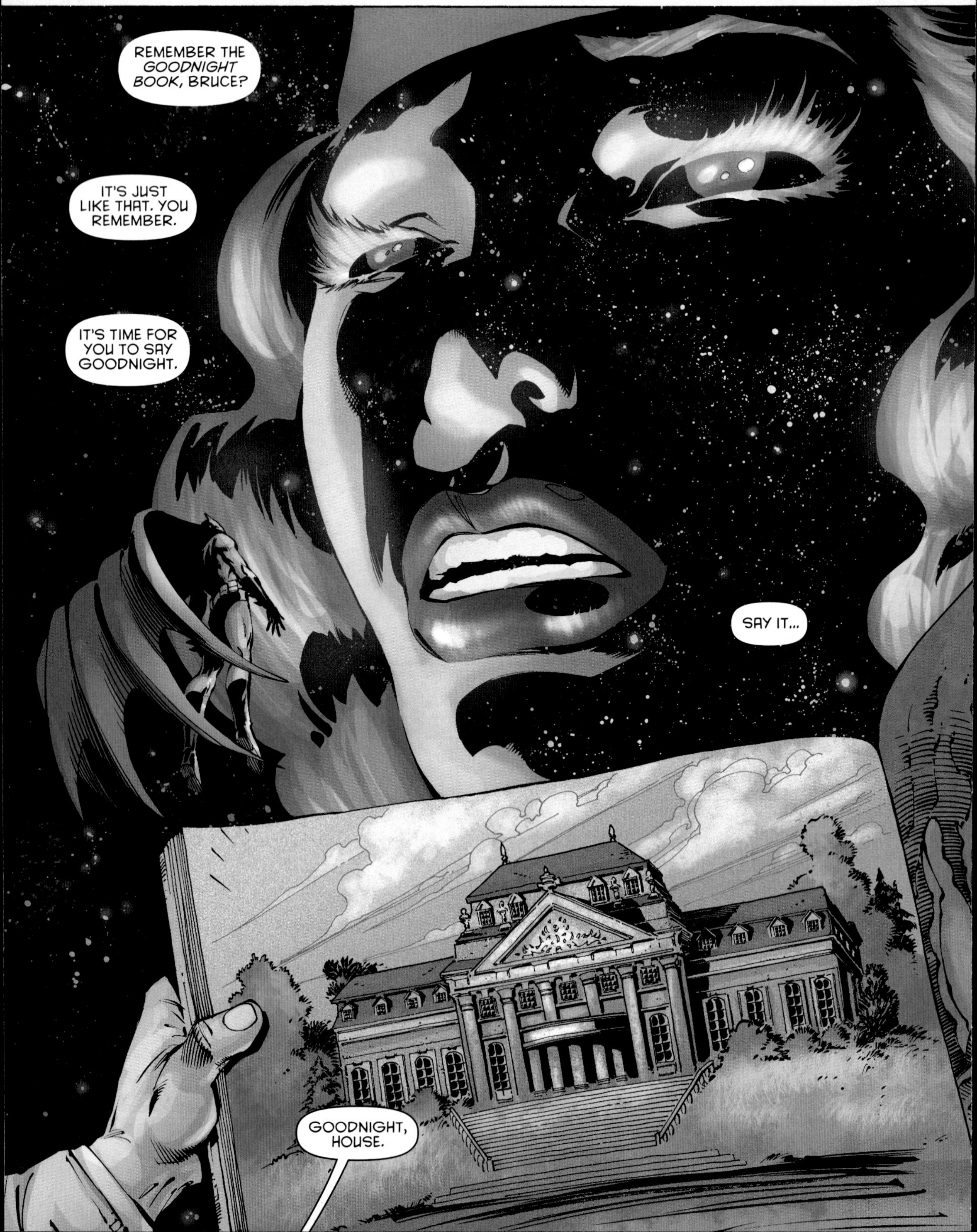
REMEMBER THE *GOODNIGHT BOOK*, BRUCE?
IT'S JUST LIKE THAT. YOU REMEMBER.
IT'S TIME FOR YOU TO SAY GOODNIGHT.
SAY IT...
GOODNIGHT, HOUSE.

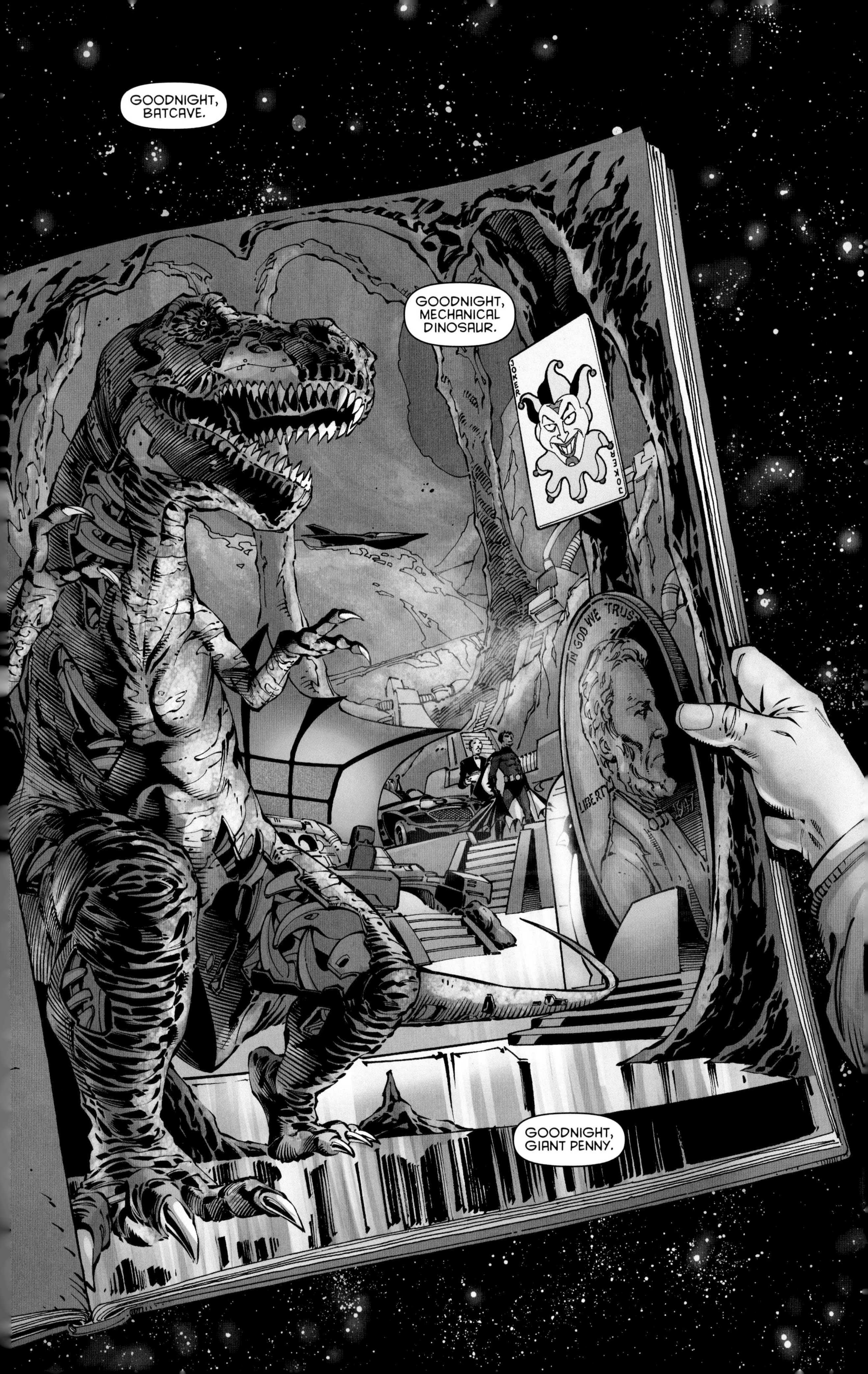
GOODNIGHT, BATCAVE.
GOODNIGHT, MECHANICAL DINOSAUR.
JOKER
LIBERTY
GOODNIGHT, GIANT PENNY.

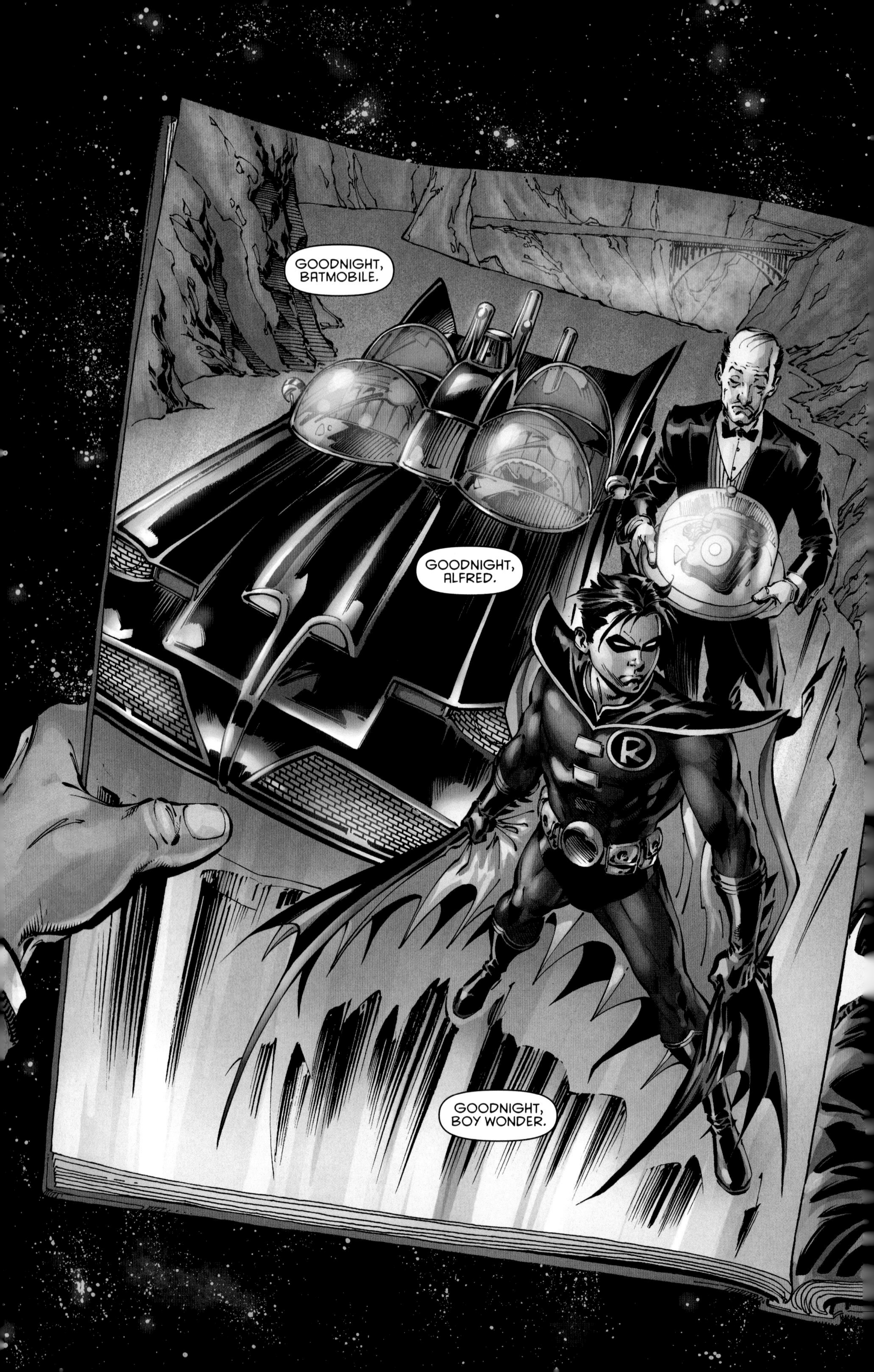
GOODNIGHT, BATMOBILE.
GOODNIGHT, ALFRED.
GOODNIGHT, BOY WONDER.

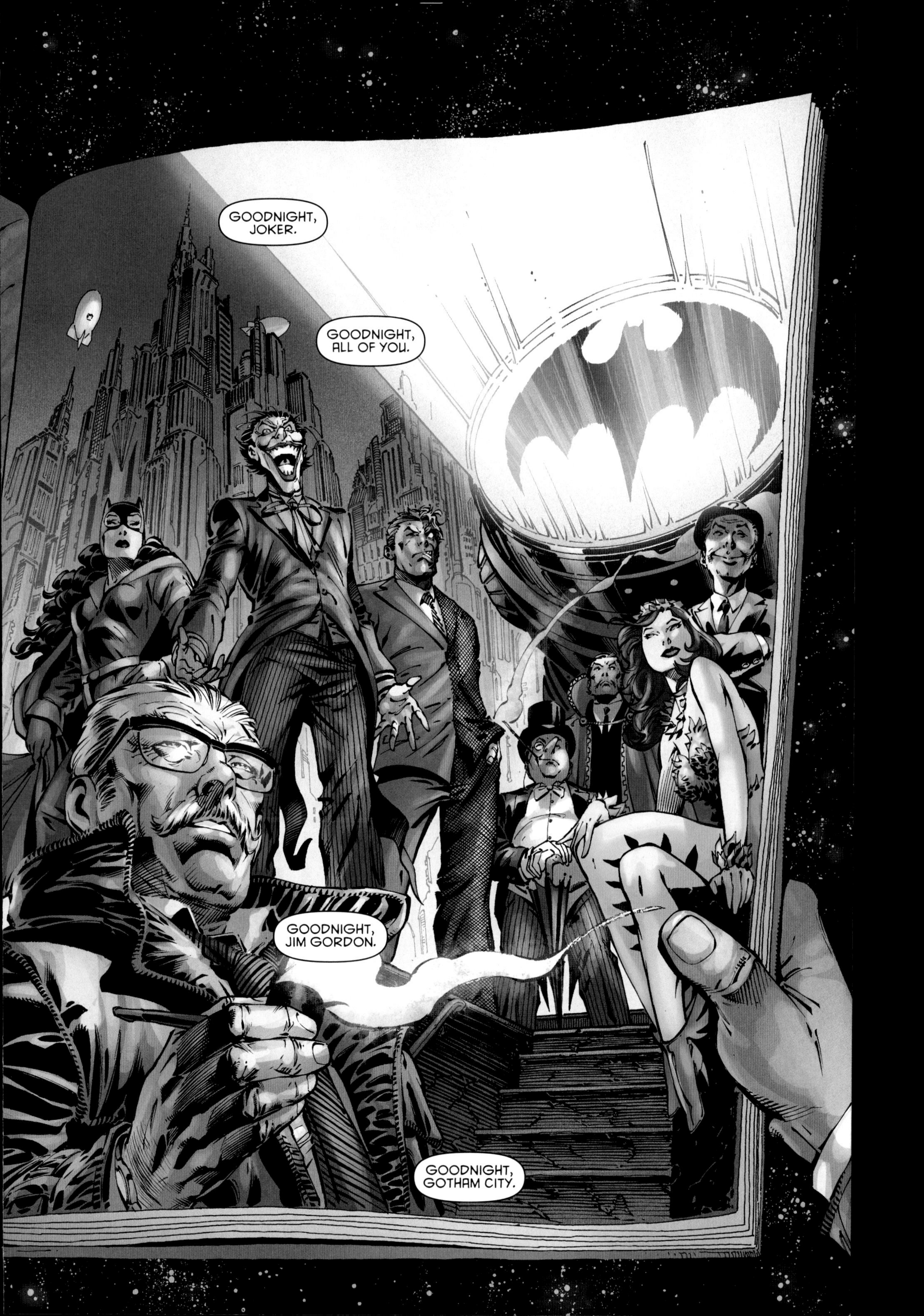
GOODNIGHT, JOKER.
GOODNIGHT, ALL OF YOU.
GOODNIGHT, JIM GORDON.
GOODNIGHT, GOTHAM CITY.

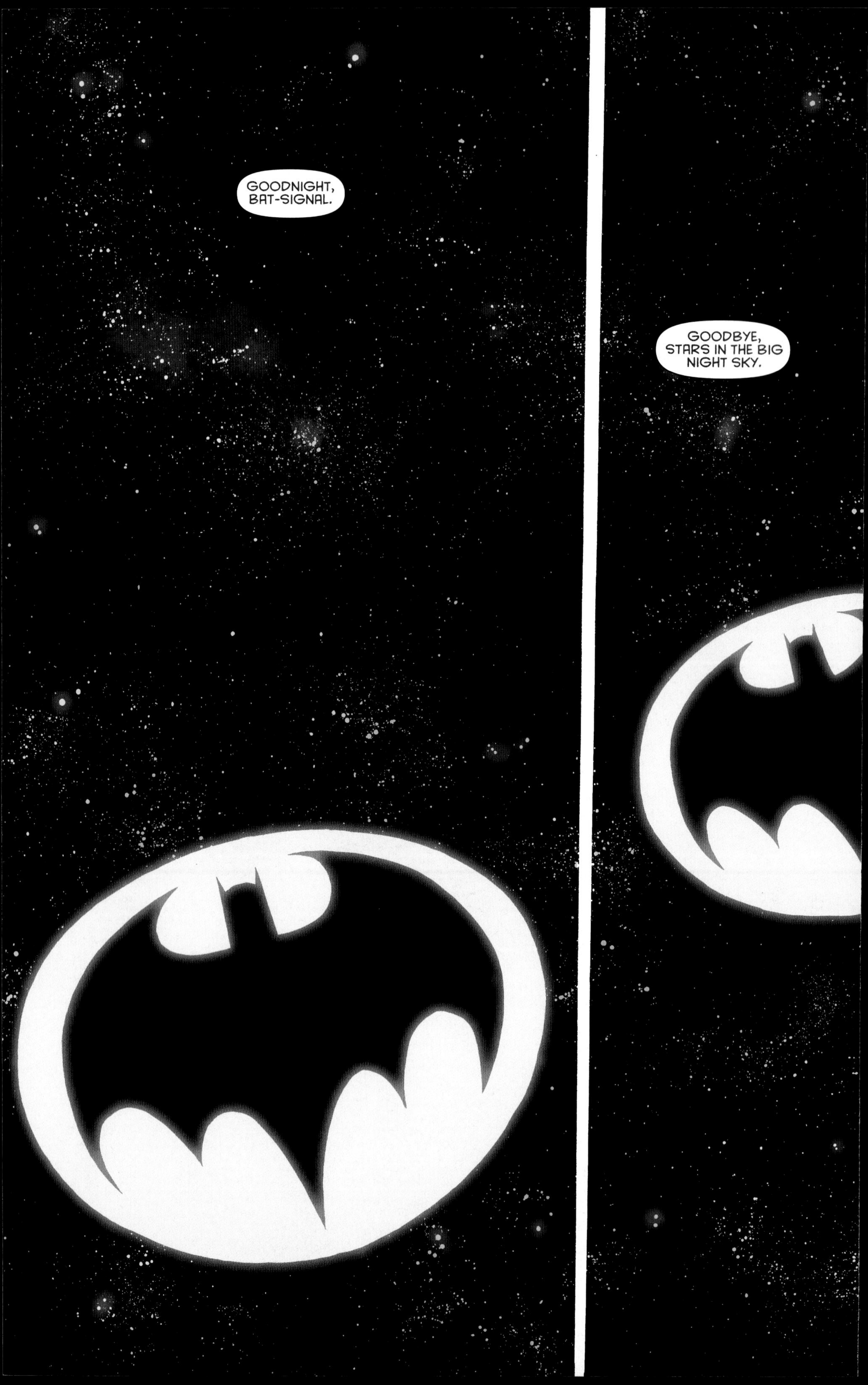
GOODNIGHT, BAT-SIGNAL.
GOODBYE, STARS IN THE BIG NIGHT SKY.

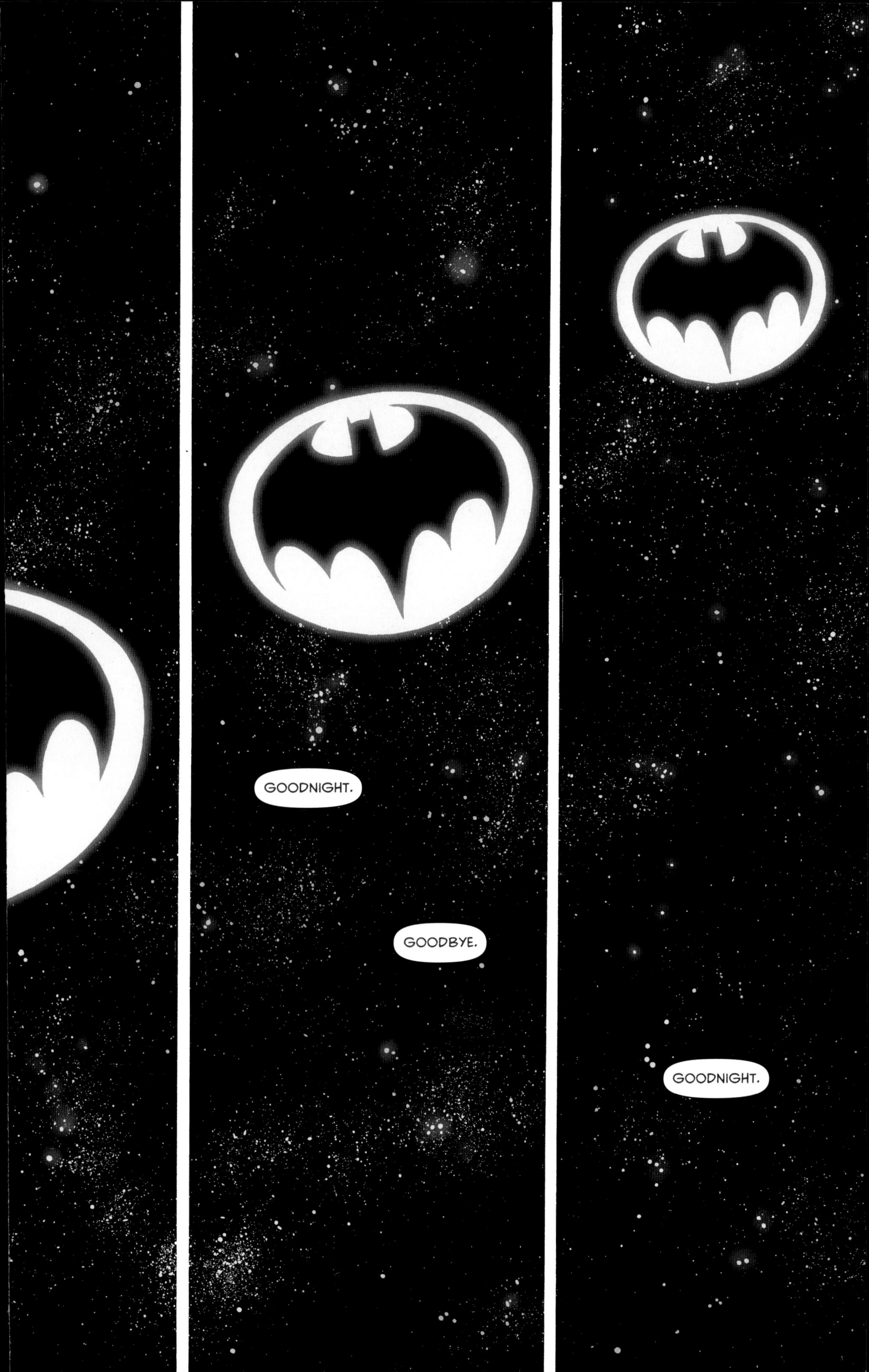
GOODNIGHT.
GOODBYE.
GOODNIGHT.

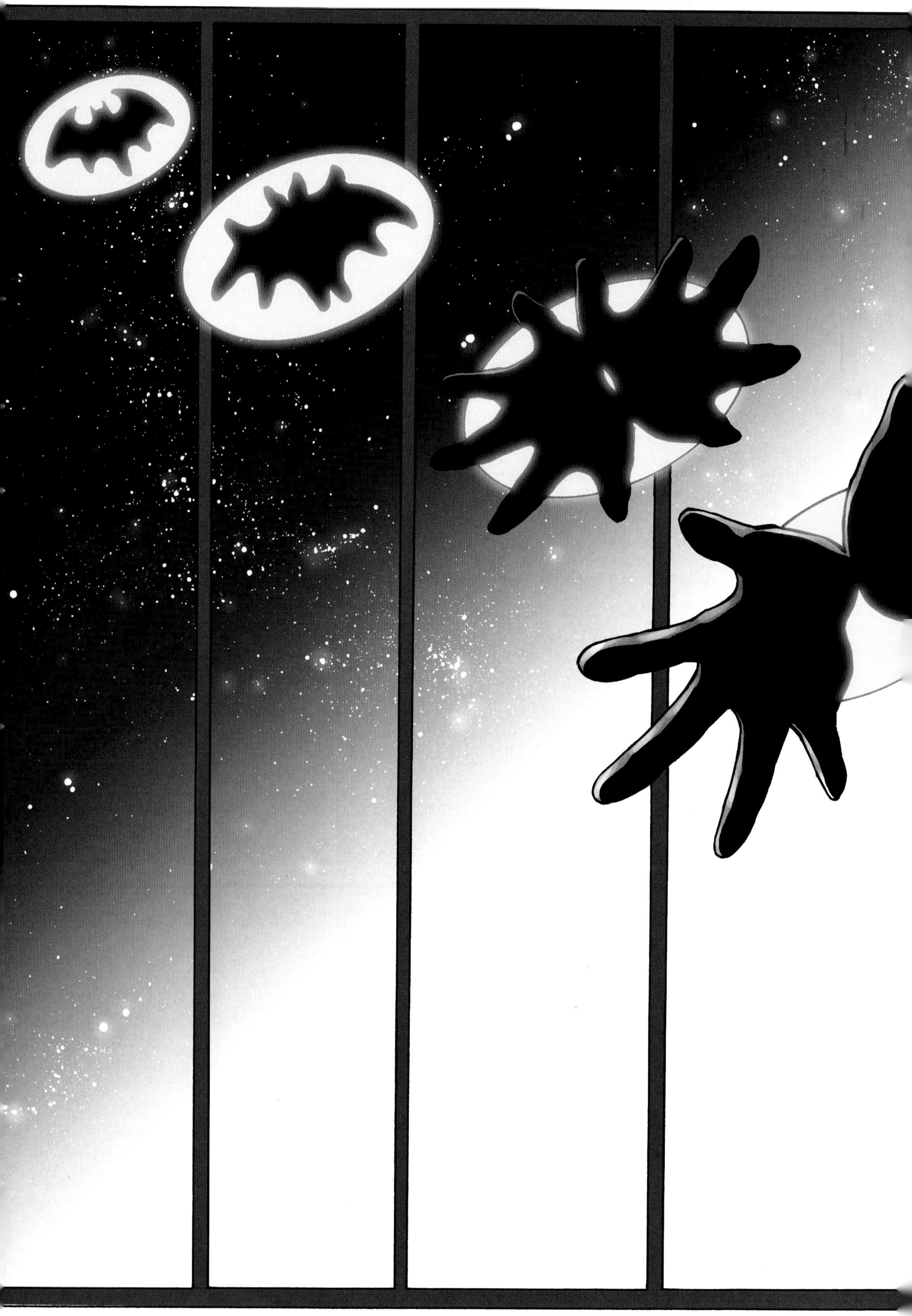

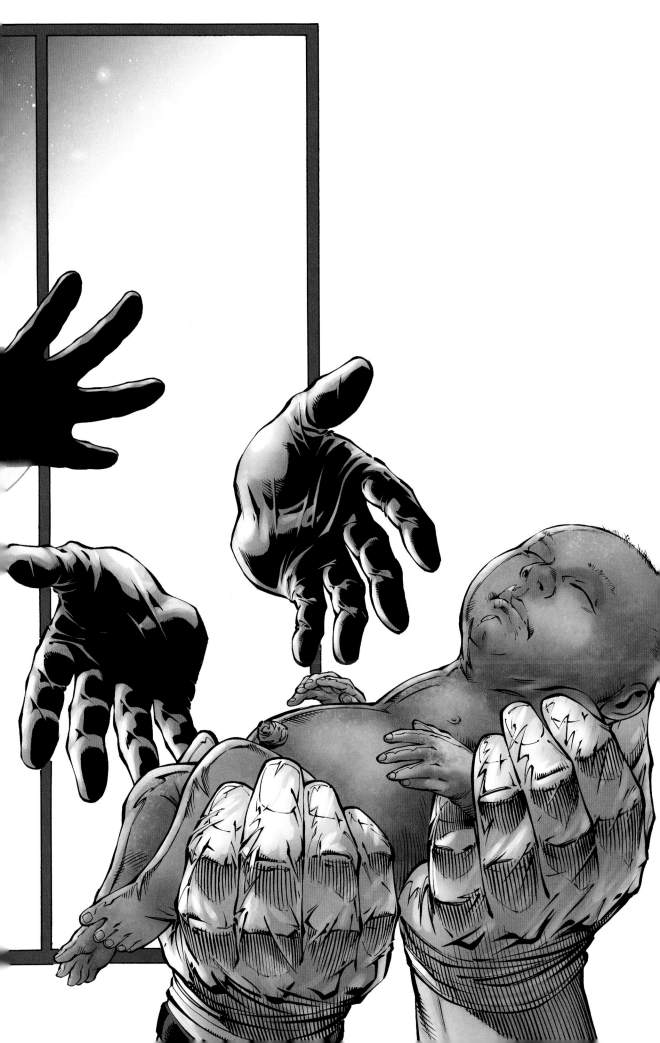

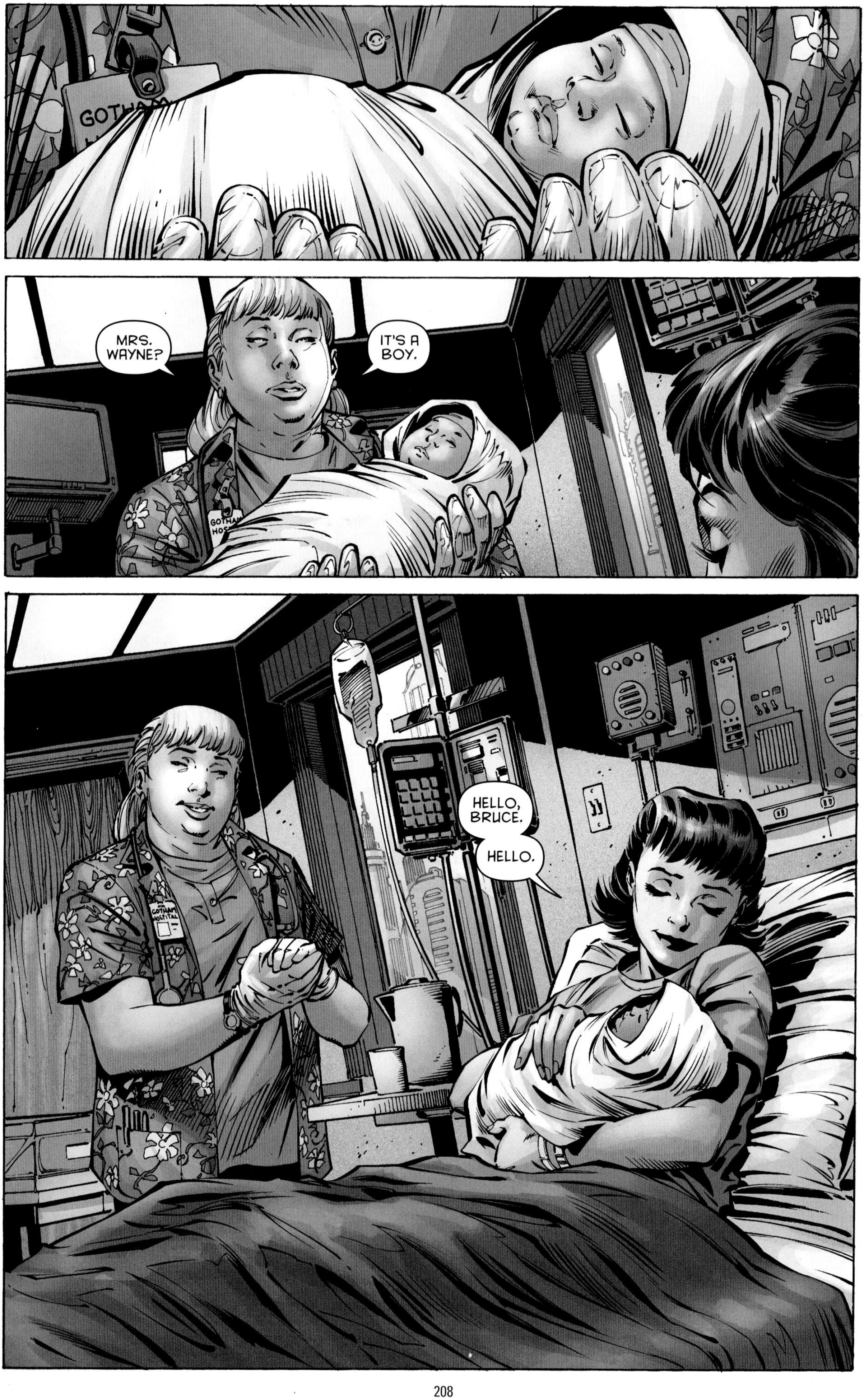
GOTHAM
MRS. WAYNE?
IT'S A BOY.
HELLO, BRUCE.
HELLO.

FOR DAVID GAIMAN (1933-2009)
Who bought me my first Batman comics, and who, some years later, figured he'd probably need to pick me up if the whole writing thing didn't work out. Thank you, Dad.
—Neil

FOR MURIEL KUBERT (1931-2008)
With unrelenting encouragement, she loved the fact that I followed in my father's footsteps and somehow got footprints of my own. This is for my mom, Muriel Kubert. We miss you so much.
—Andy

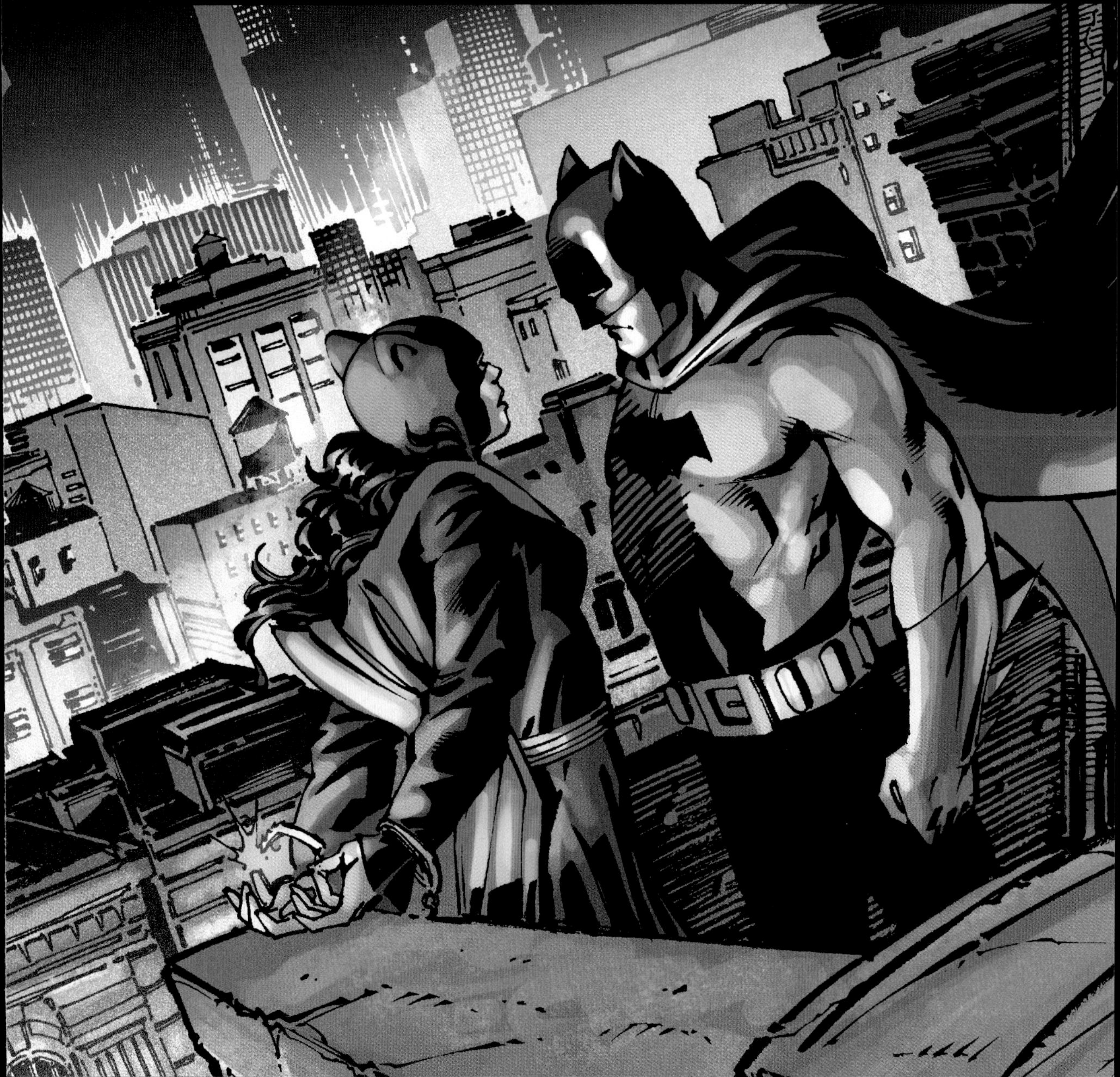

WHATEVER HAPPENED TO THE CAPED CRUSADER? AN AFTERWORD, OR A LOVE LETTER.

I love Batman. There are other characters I like. There may be other characters I like better. And there are characters I invented, and I love all of them like children. But I loved, and still love, Batman, unshakably, unquestioningly, as one loves a parent. He was the first. He's always been there.

Listen, I've loved him since the first time I heard his name. My father told me there was a television show in America about a man who dressed as a bat and fought crime. I was five years old, the only bats I had ever encountered were used to hit cricket balls, and I was still ridiculously interested. The TV show came to the UK next, and, honest, I used to worry about him. End of every first Bat-episode, he would be in the death trap and I would worry for a week. If I missed the second part I would have to get friends who saw it to fill me in on how he escaped ("He had a Bat bird-whistle in his utility belt, and got the birds to peck holes in the balloon, and got down safely...").

Batman hooked me on comics. I made my father buy me *Smash!* comics, which reprinted the U.S. newspaper strips and were the gateway drug to the American comics I found soon enough—first in a box of old issues, later in local newsagents. They were the real things: four-color dreams made real.

I loved the comics more than the TV show. I read other comics, too, and I liked other comics' characters, but Batman was best. He just was. He was Batman.

And the glorious thing about Batman was the way he kept pace with me as I grew up. There were the Neal Adams comics when I was twelve, which transmuted the reassuring Batman I'd grown up with into a lonelier, more shadowy creature, who kept pace with me through my early teens. There was Frank Miller's DARK KNIGHT RETURNS when I was twenty-five, the subject of my first big academic essay. All of it was Batman—all of it was glorious.

So, over Dave McKean's sighs, I put Batman into the first DC comic I ever wrote, BLACK ORCHID, as a shadowy figure, speaking in white-on-black lettering (something I liked so much I stole it for SANDMAN, causing untold heartache in the years to come for Todd Klein and DC Comics' production department). I wrote a SECRET ORIGINS of Poison Ivy. I wrote a SECRET ORIGINS SPECIAL—a framing story about Gotham, and a Riddler story inside, which said everything I thought about the loss of one kind of story. I even wrote a BATMAN BLACK AND WHITE story, with Batman and the Joker sitting around like off-duty Warner's cartoon characters, behind the scenes at a comic, waiting to go on and perform. I put a tiny Batman cameo in THE WAKE, the last Sandman story, just to remind people that, yes, this was still part of that.

Those were stories about Batman, though: he was there, but only seen from the outside, his effects on the world more important than his story.

There was one other Batman story, one that didn't happen: I proposed a story in about 1989 called (if memory serves) "Nights at the Circus." I was even paid a $900 advance for it. But for one reason or another

(mostly because the artist who was meant to draw it at the time signed an exclusive contract with another publisher), it never happened. It would have been a good Batman story, I think, about three nocturnal visits, over the course of Bruce Wayne's life, to a very strange circus indeed. But it never got written.

And then life happened, and one day I mostly wasn't writing comics anymore. I didn't have time, and, mostly, didn't have the smallest inclination. It would, I told people who asked, take something very special to get me to make the time to write something for comics. Or even, truthfully, to write something that I didn't own...

Then the phone rang and Dan DiDio asked if I would like to write a Batman story.

I asked Dan if this meant they were calling in their $900 and wanted me to write my "Nights at the Circus" story. He said, no, what he wanted was a two-part story—whatever I wanted to write, he said—that would be the final episode of BATMAN and the last episode of DETECTIVE. I could really write the last one of all.

told the story of how Alan Moore physically grabbed him, and would not let him go until Julie had agreed that Alan could write "Whatever Happened to the Man of Tomorrow?" And Alan said that it didn't matter that it wasn't actually true, and he had simply said yes when Julie asked—it was Julie's story and it was a good one.

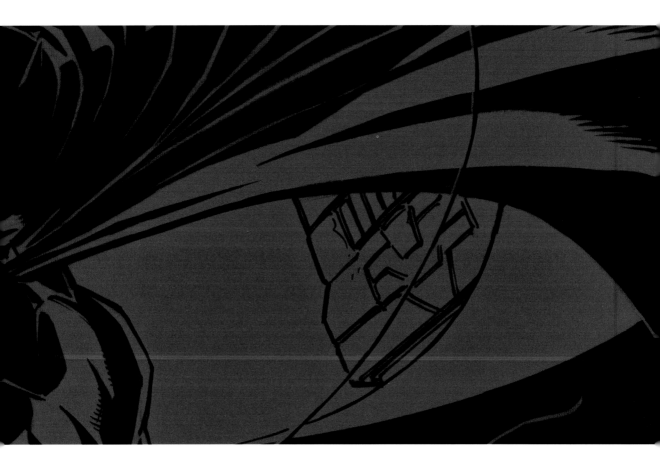

"It would be," he said, "kind of like 'Whatever Happened to the Man of Tomorrow?'" That was Alan Moore's two-part story that was the last issue of the original numbering of SUPERMAN and of ACTION COMICS, the story to mark the end of Superman's Silver Age, the Mort Weisinger–Julie Schwartz years. The end of an era. It was the best last Superman comic there could ever have been, a wonderful paean to a Superman who would soon be reimagined and reinvented, and whose comics would soon be renumbered, each starting at #1.

I don't remember thinking about it: I just said yes.

Honestly, what would you have said? I think I told Dan that I didn't have time, and didn't think I could pull it off, but sure. Until the day he died, Julie Schwartz

Probably in Dan's version of the story, he and editor Michael Marts were kidnapped, and blindfolded, and were tied to chairs in a basement, and then I walked in with henchmen and said, "Now listen up, youse guys. The Last Batman Story. Anyone else so much as tries to write it, and I'll have Lefty and Knuckles teach everyone a lesson, see?" which is actually really nice of me to suggest because it means that Dan DiDio doesn't have to attempt an English accent. It could have happened like that. You never know.

I got off the phone.

I thought about Alan Moore's "Whatever Happened to the Man of Tomorrow?" This was not that, and it would not even try to be what Alan did: a celebration of the end of an era, the swan song of the greatest of Superman artists, something that ended with a smile and a wink.

Batman stories don't end with smiles and winks. And Batman had survived many eras, and would, undoubtedly, survive many more. If I were going to tell the last Batman story, it would have to be something that would survive Batman's current death or disappearance, something that would still be the last Batman story in twenty years, or a hundred.

Because if there's one thing that Batman is, it's a survivor. He'll be around long after all of us are gone. So what could be more appropriate than the story of his death?

I was delighted and thrilled when editor Michael Marts told me that I would have Andy Kubert as my artist. I don't think there's anything Andy cannot do if you ask him to, and I asked him to do some very strange things in this issue. Where other artists might have traced or swiped or copied, Andy did something much odder and more interesting—as he explained to me, "I didn't try to draw like them. I tried to draw as if the artists you were talking about were trying to draw like me." And so we see Bob Kane and Dick Sprang and Carmine Infantino and Neal Adams and Dick Giordano and Brian Bolland and all the rest of them—so many amazing artists who had left their mark on Batman, so many wonderful artistic styles—through an Andy Kubert-shaped filter. (I even tried to write like other people, to sound like Bill Finger and Gardner Fox and Denny O'Neil and Steve Englehart and Bob Haney and Frank Miller and Alan Grant and many of the other fine writers who have stared at a blank sheet of paper and tried to think of something for the Dark Knight Detective to do, but I'm afraid mostly it just sounded like me.)

I was lucky to have Andy, and Andy was lucky to have Scott Williams, an excellent artist in his own right, and an inker's inker, taking what Andy had created in shaded pencils and turning it into beautiful inked comic book art. I wrote things just to see how they drew them, asked the impossible because I knew they could give it to me.

Alex Sinclair colored it with rapidity and aplomb, Jared K. Fletcher lettered the hell out of it, and I got my first-ever Alex Ross cover.

In my head, the story was simply called "Batman: The End," but the first time DC Comics people talked about it, they described it as "Whatever Happened to the Caped Crusader?" and the title sort of stuck.

Due to the strangeness of printing schedules, I'm writing this before the last issue has reached the stands. I have no idea if people will like it or hate it. And truly—and oddly—I don't mind.

It's my last Batman story, after all: if Batman had to end, I guess that, for me anyway, it would end like this.

And it's a small thank-you: to Batman, and to all the writers and artists and inkers and colorists and letterers and editors who gave him to us over the years.

—**Neil Gaiman**
2009

WHATEVER HAPPENED TO THE CAPED CRUSADER?

Sketchbook By Andy Kubert

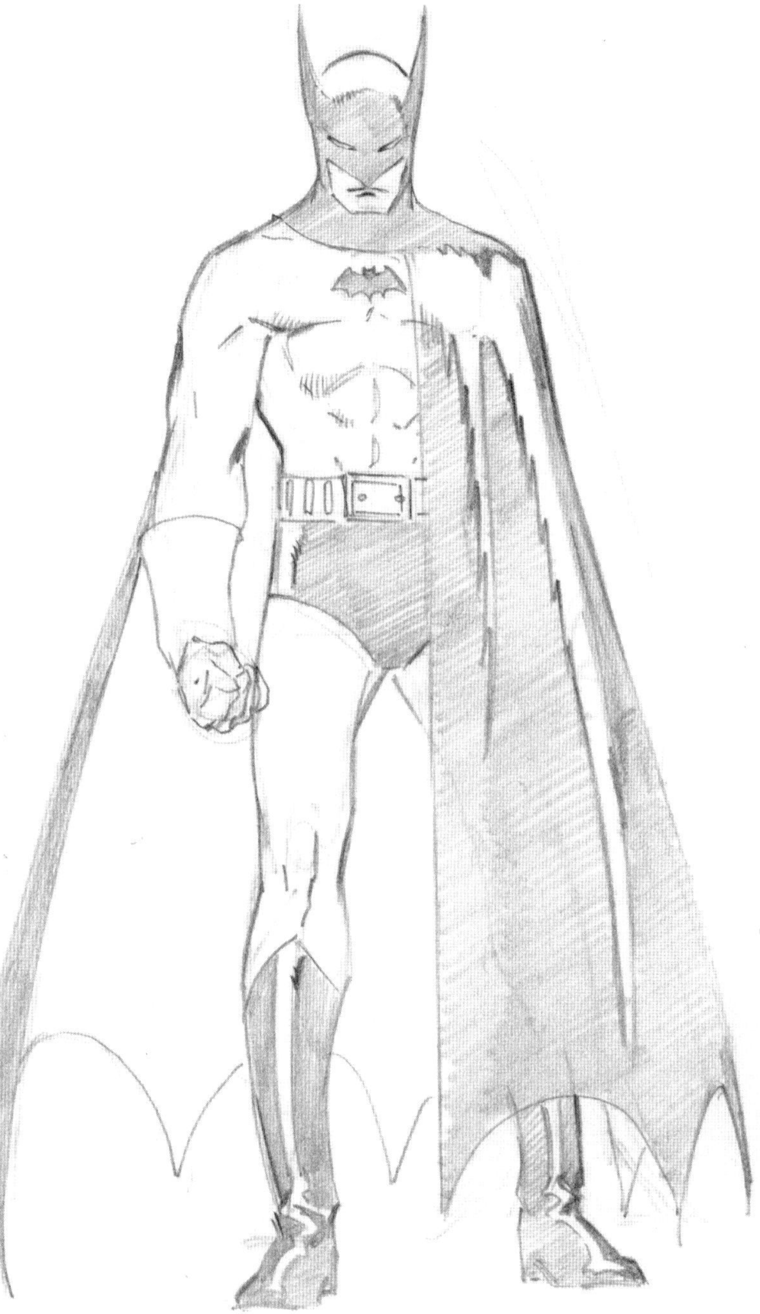

'BOB KANE' BATMAN 1939

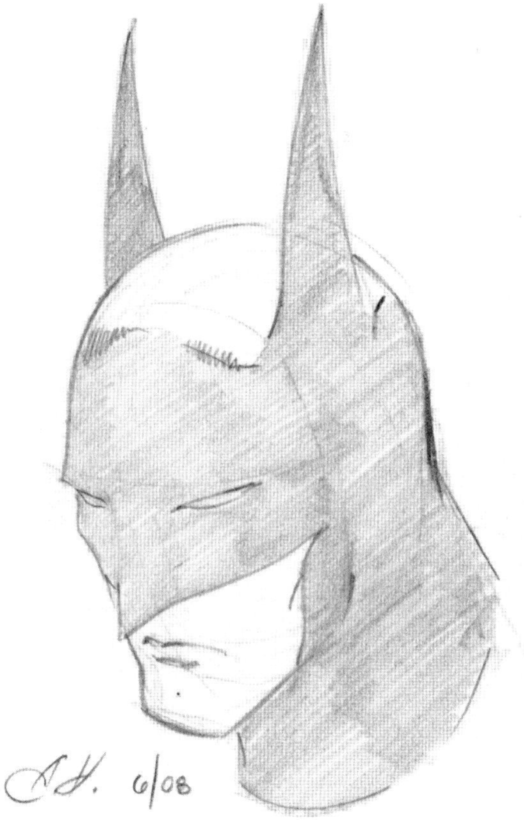
6/08

While developing "Whatever Happened to the Caped Crusader?" writer NEIL GAIMAN and artist ANDY KUBERT discussed showcasing different versions of Batman that would act as tributes to the artists who helped shape the Dark Knight, such as Bob Kane, Dick Sprang, Jim Aparo, Neal Adams and others.

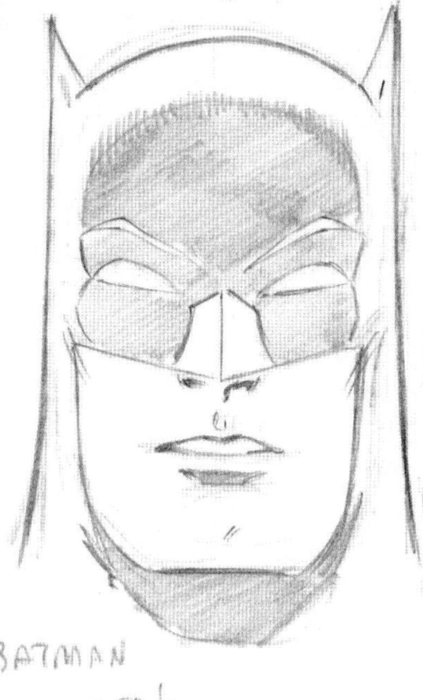

'DICK SPRANG' BATMAN 1950'S

shadow from blonde pg. 20

Shown here is Andy Kubert's initial rough layout for an interior page...

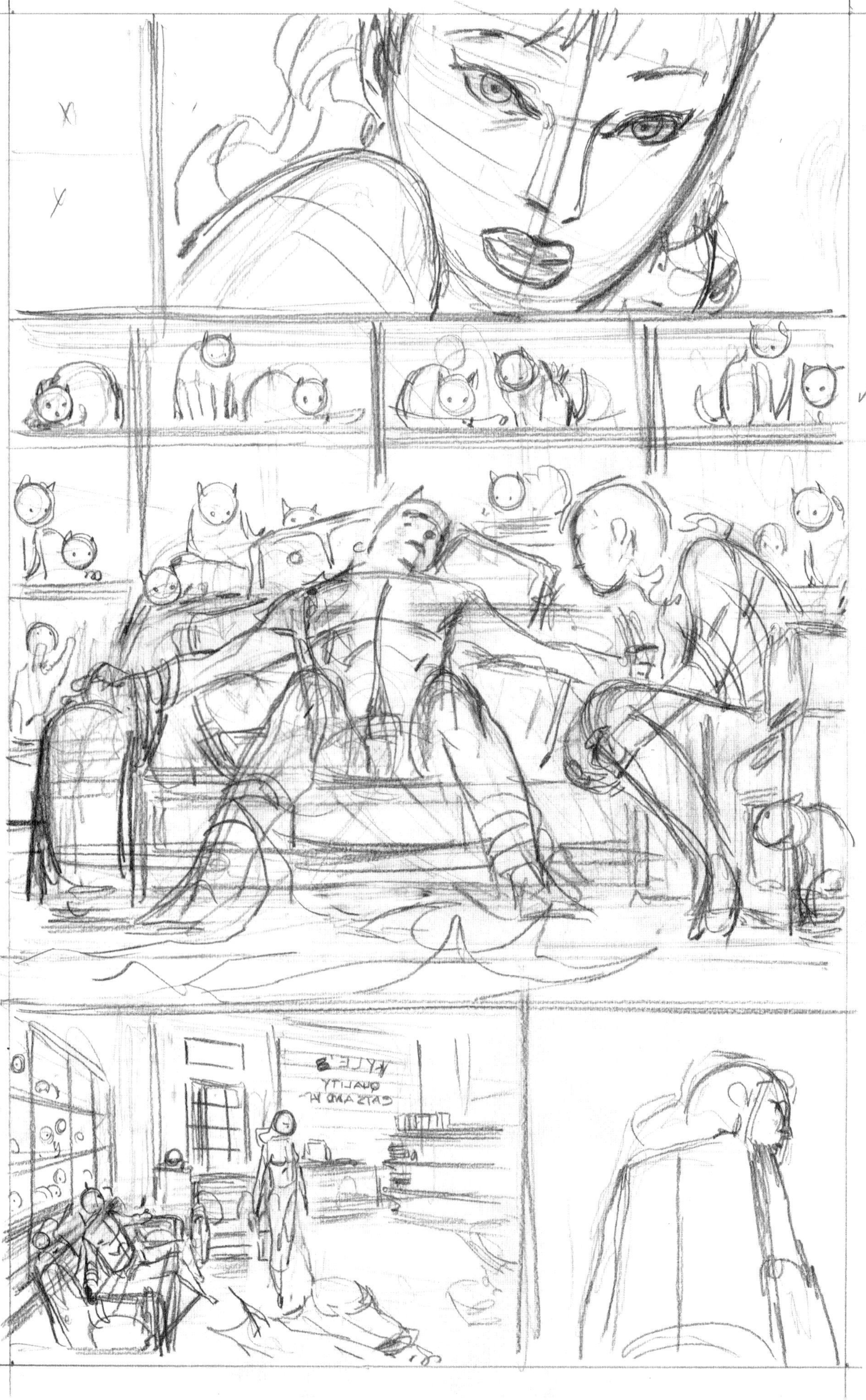

...and the completed, fully rendered pencilled version.

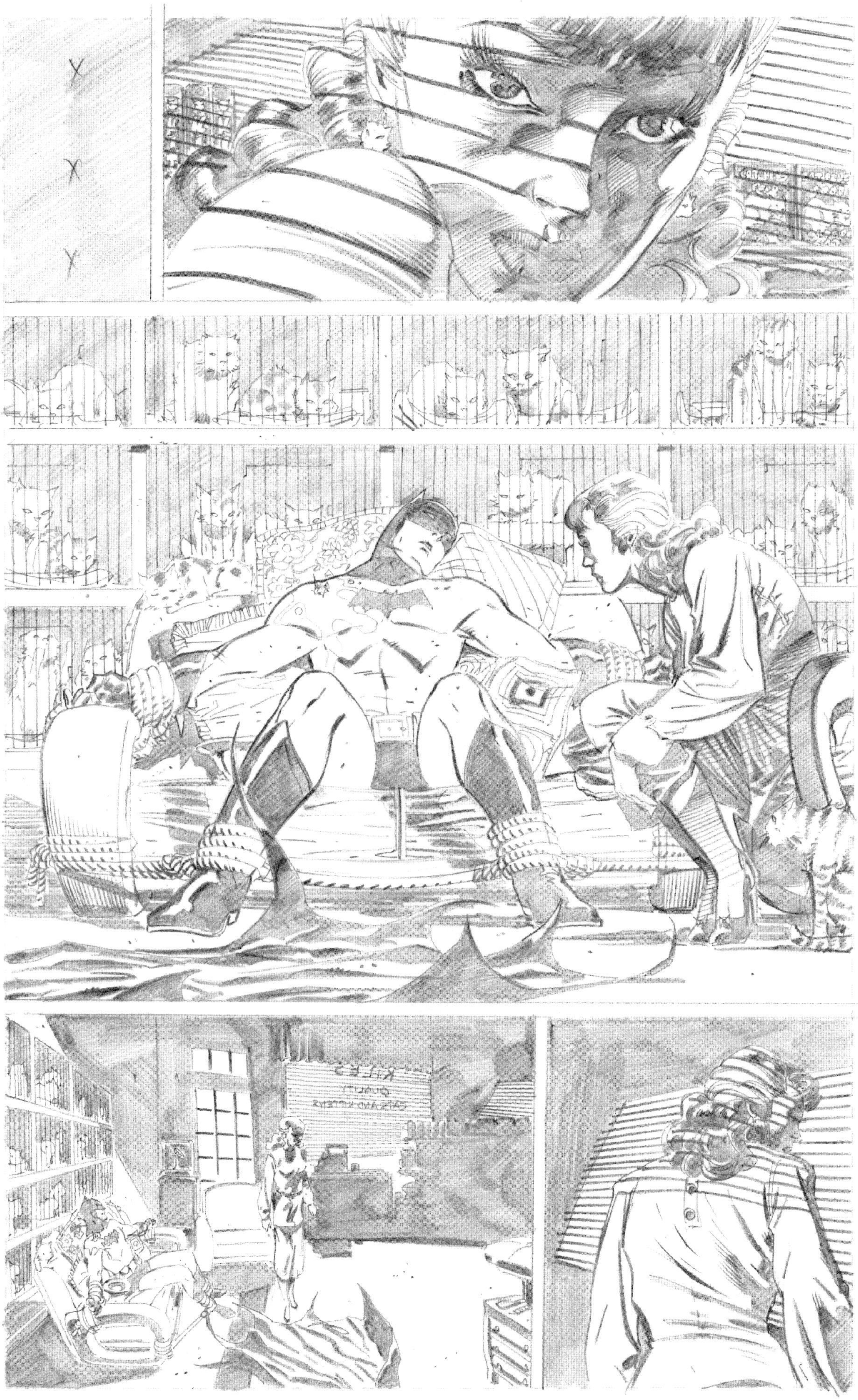

Here's an early concept sketch
for Selina Kyle, a.k.a. CATWOMAN.

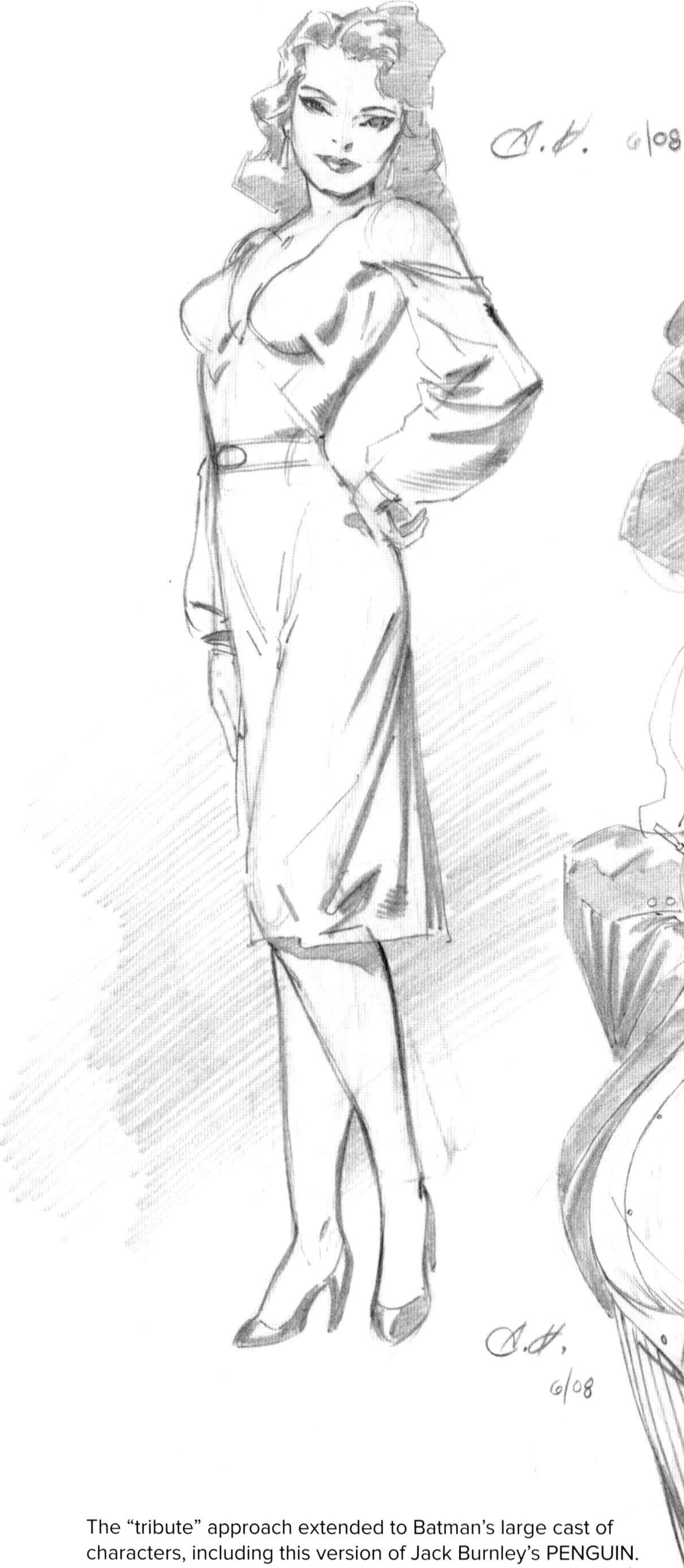
6/08

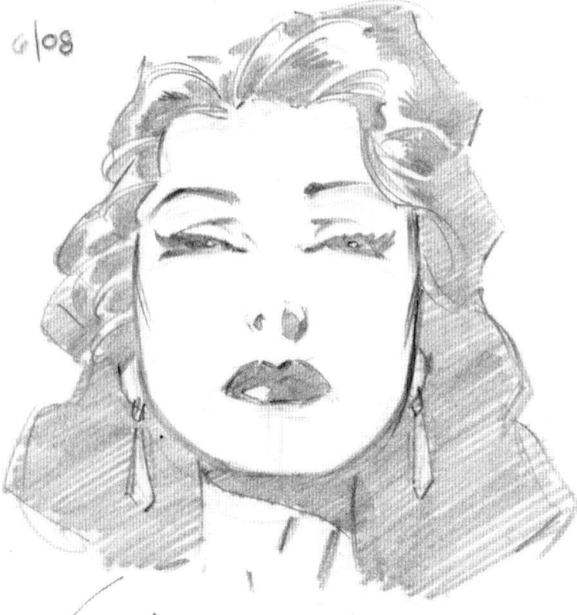
'CATWOMAN'

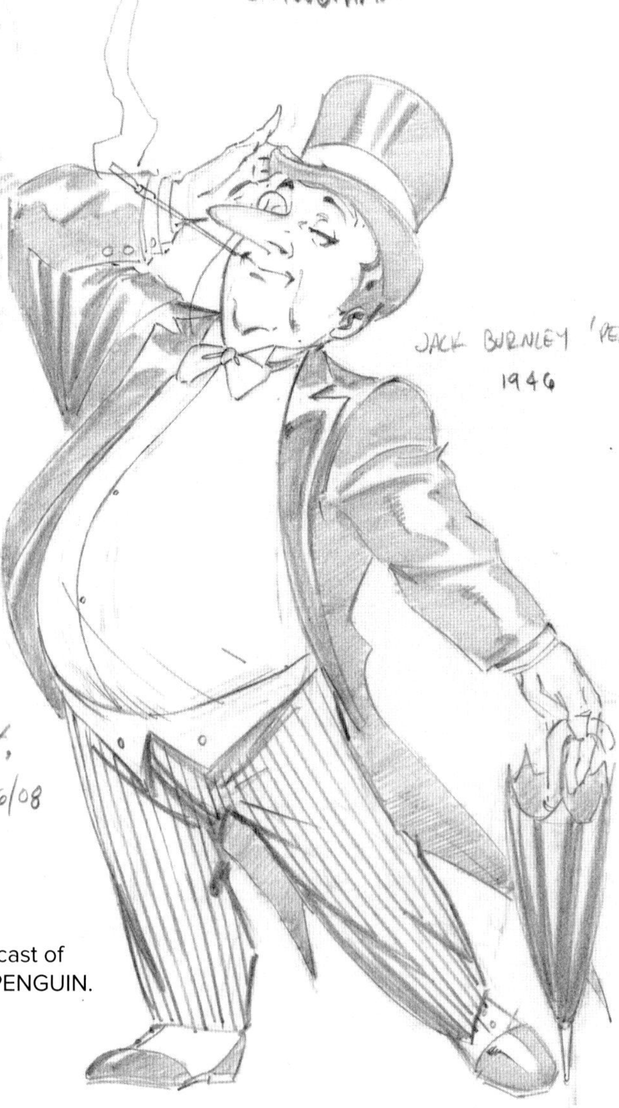
JACK BURNLEY 'PENGUIN
1946
6/08

The "tribute" approach extended to Batman's large cast of
characters, including this version of Jack Burnley's PENGUIN.

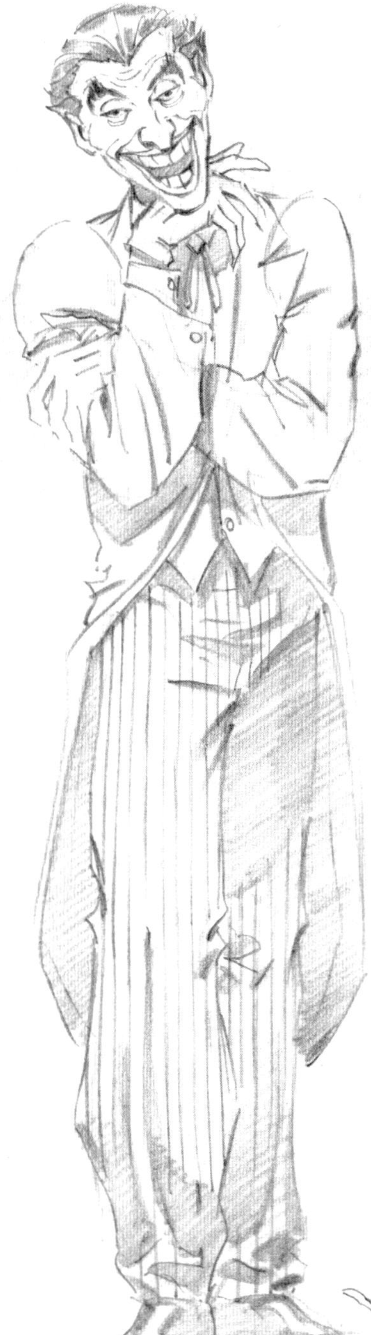

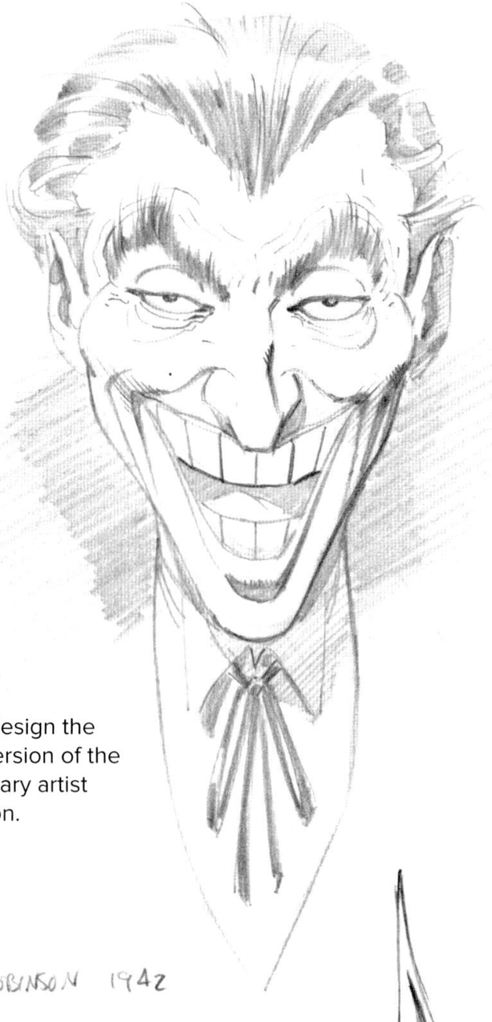

Neil asked Andy to design the JOKER based on the version of the character by legendary artist Jerry Robinson.

'JOKER' JERRY ROBINSON 1942

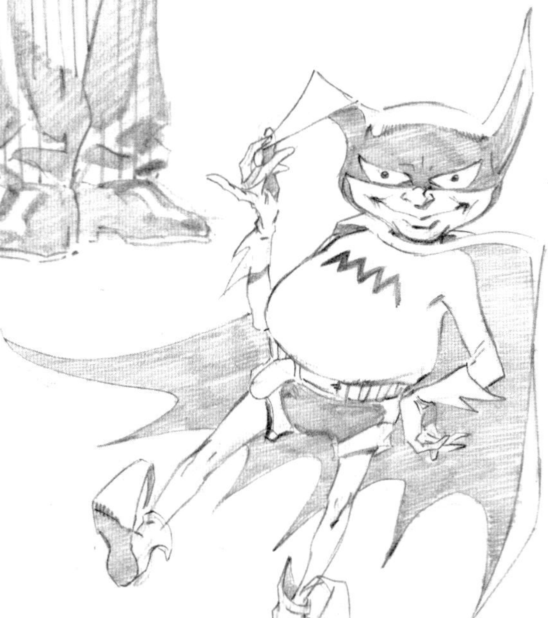

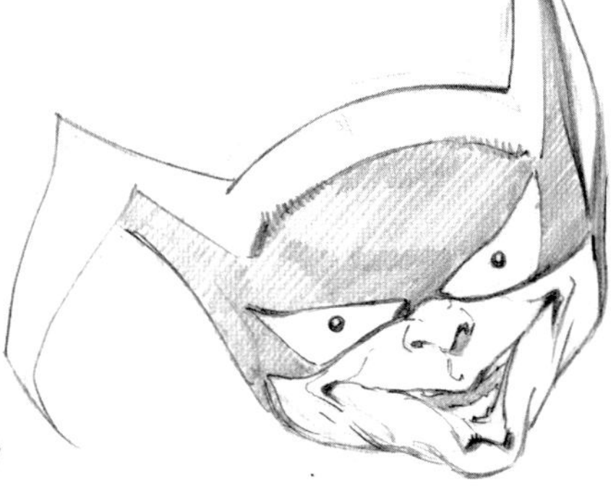

'BATMITE'

Here's a sketch that Andy did of BAT-MITE, who never made it into the actual story!

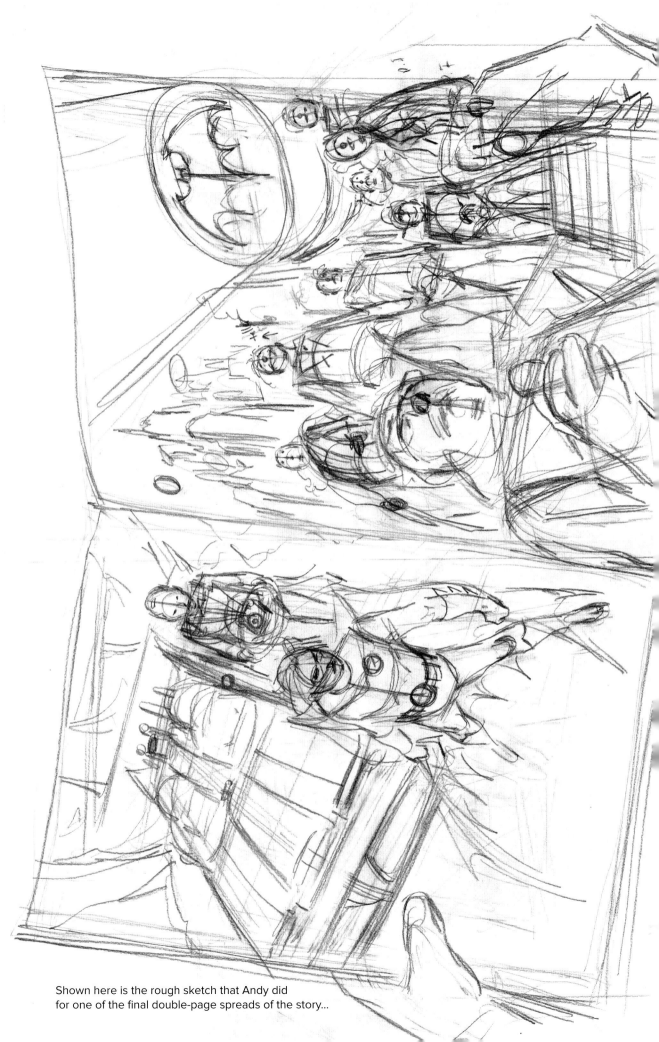

Shown here is the rough sketch that Andy did
for one of the final double-page spreads of the story...

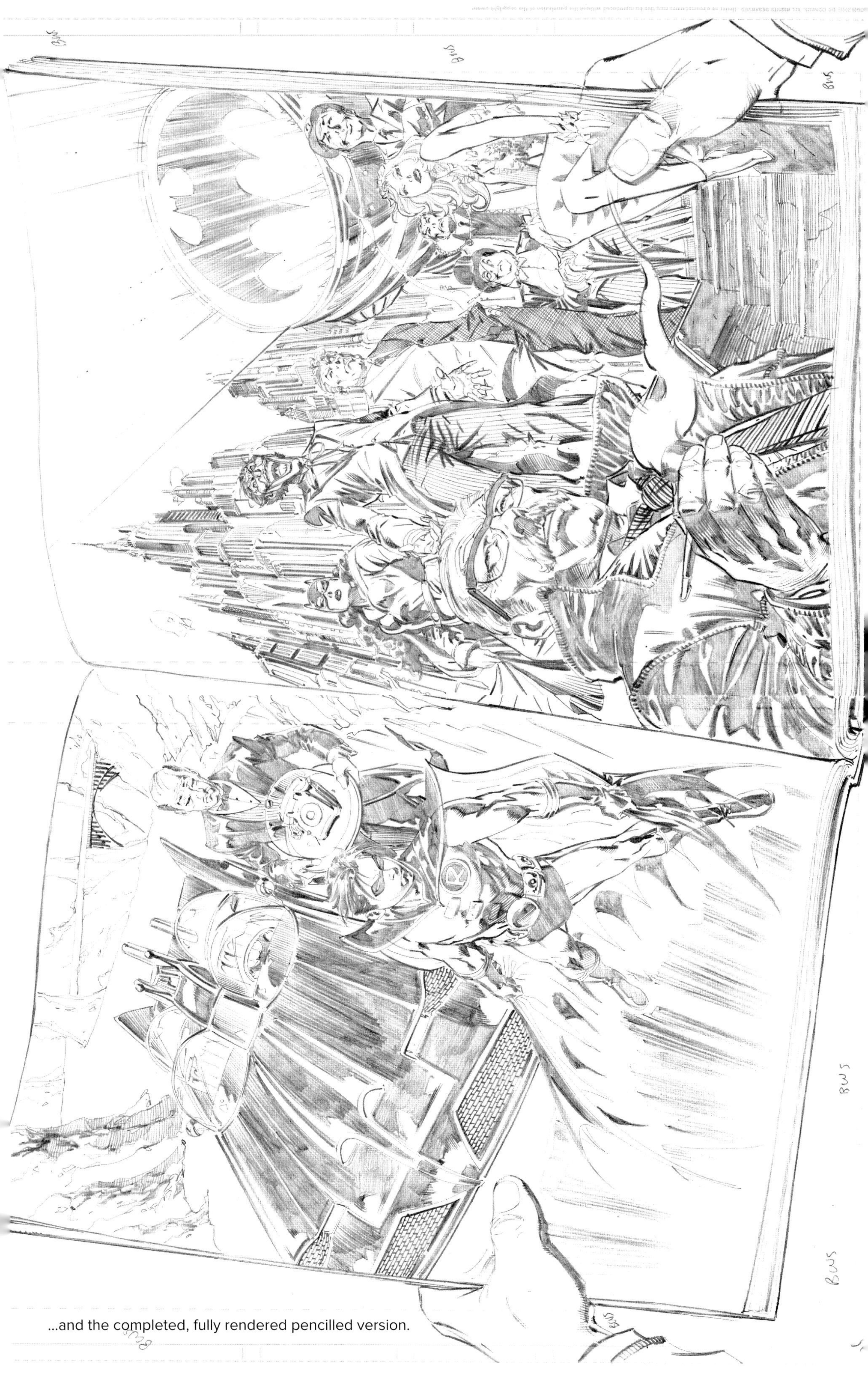

...and the completed, fully rendered pencilled version.

Andy uses a three-step approach to his pages:

First, he works out “rough pencils”...

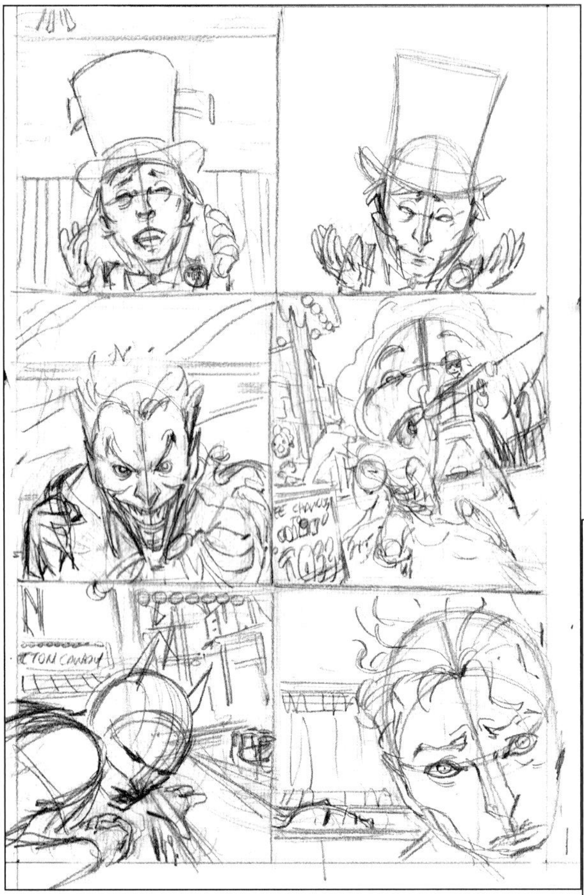

...then he refines the page to what he calls a “linear breakdown”...

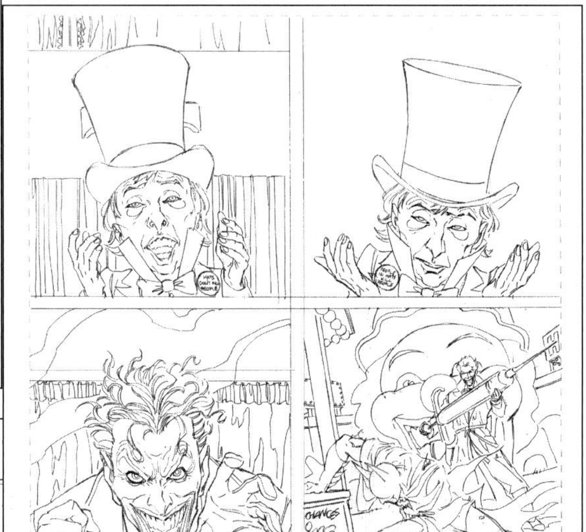

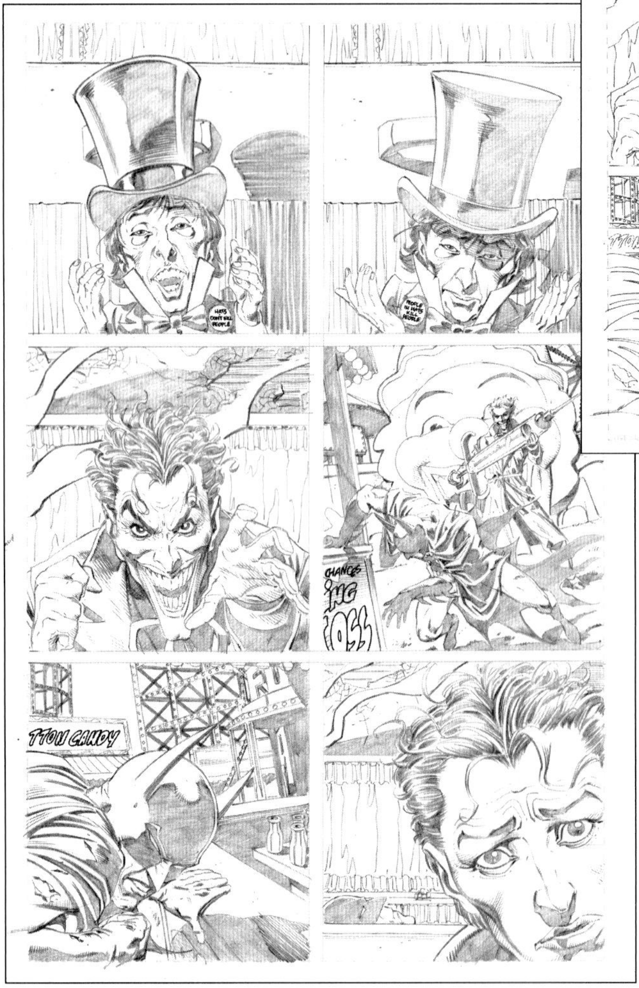
TTON CANDY

...and then finally he completes the page with “finished pencils.”

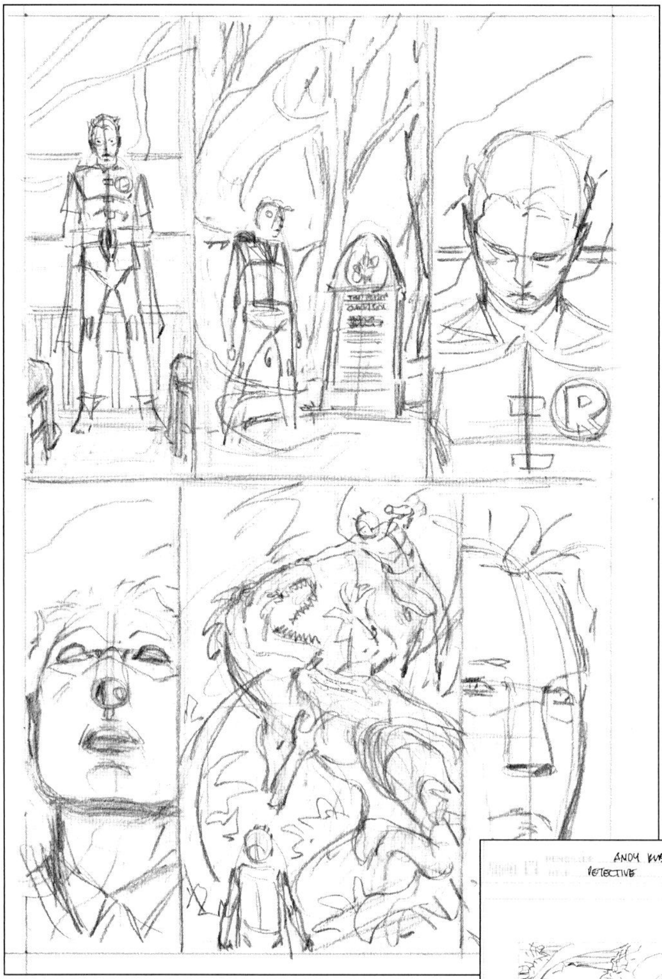

Here are Andy's roughs and finished pencils for page four of Part Two.

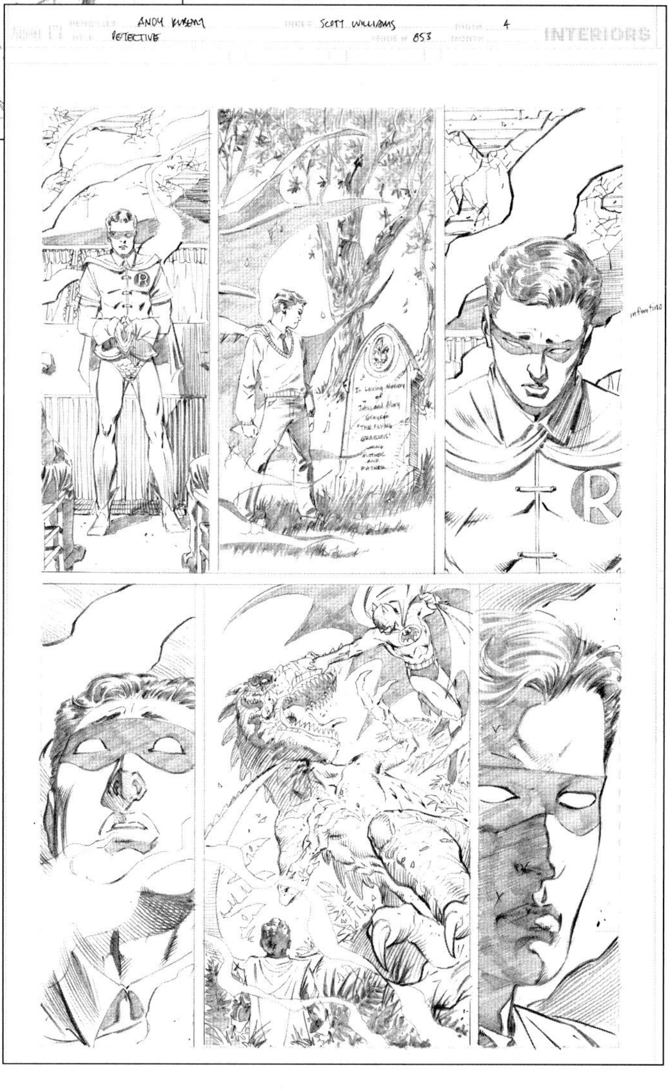
ANDY
SCOTT WILLIAMS
4
INTERIORS
DETECTIVE
853

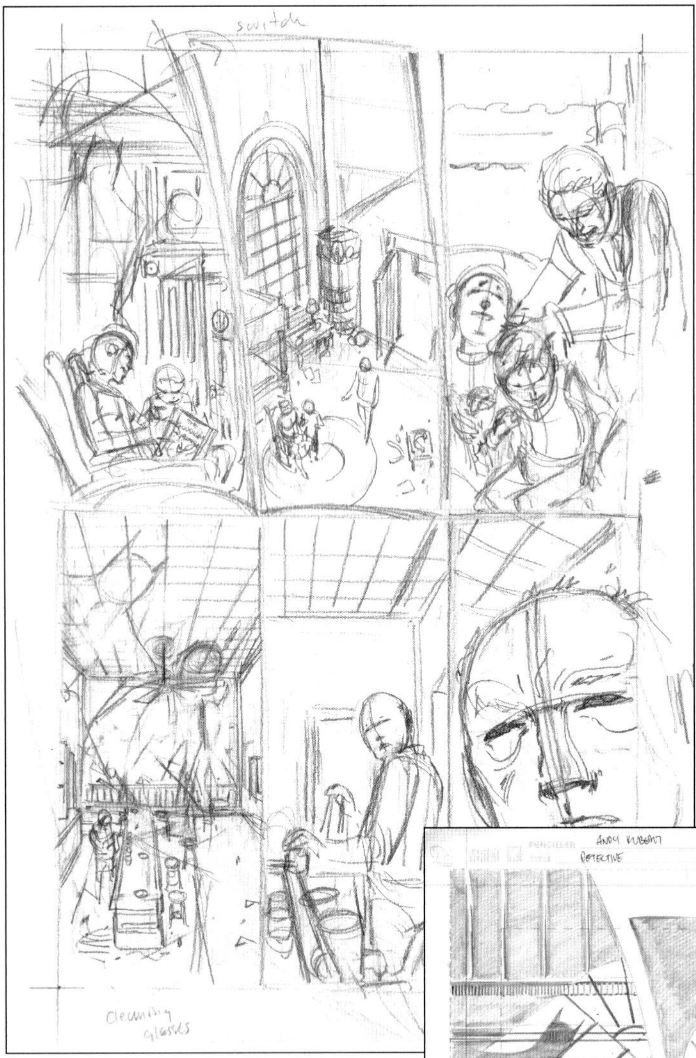
switch
cleaning glasses

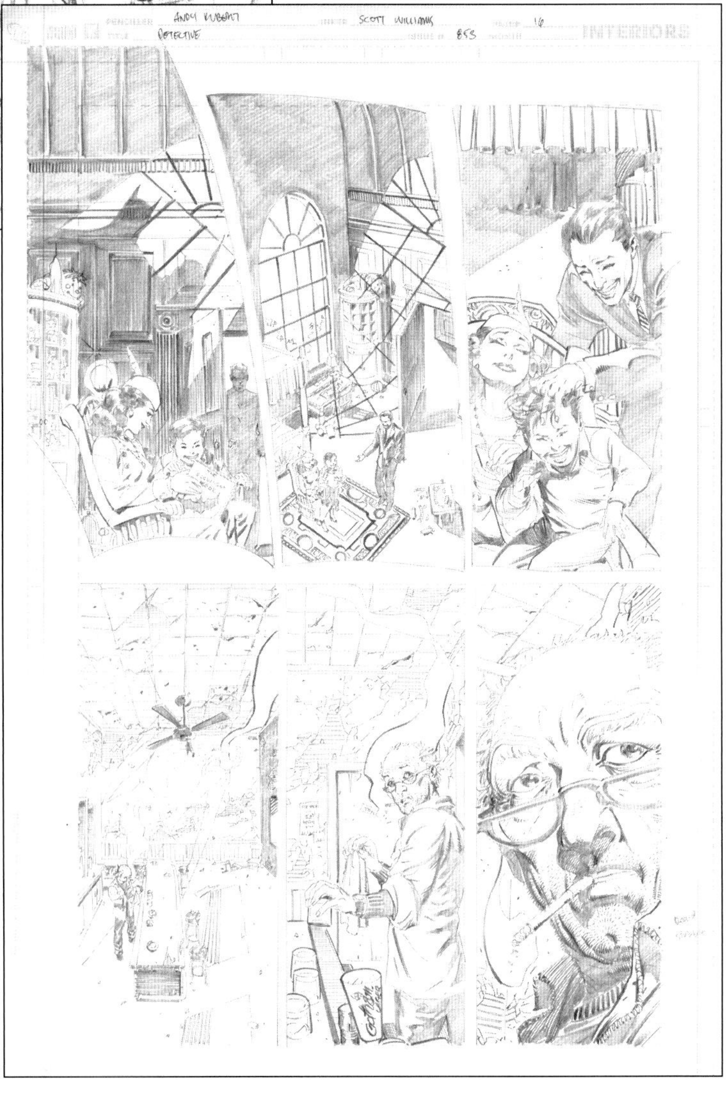
INTERIORS

And finally, the before and after versions, featuring young Bruce Wayne with his parents and an aging Joe Chill.

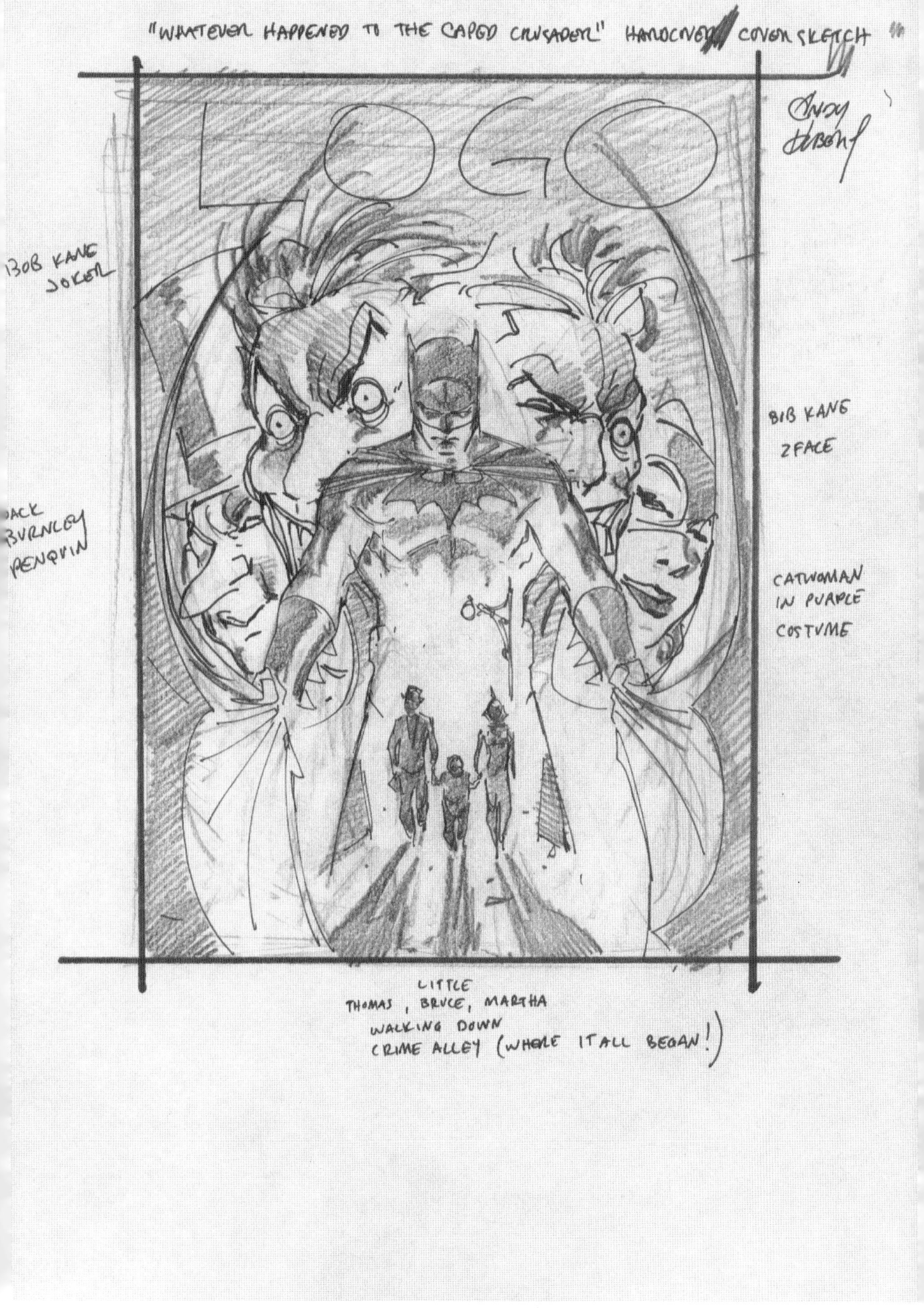
"WHATEVER HAPPENED TO THE CAPED CRUSADER" HARDCOVER COVER SKETCH
LOGO
BOB KANE JOKER
JACK BURNLEY PENGUIN
BOB KANE 2FACE
CATWOMAN IN PURPLE COSTUME
LITTLE THOMAS, BRUCE, MARTHA WALKING DOWN CRIME ALLEY (WHERE IT ALL BEGAN!)

Andy's cover sketch for the original BATMAN: WHATEVER HAPPENED TO THE CAPED CRUSADER? collection.

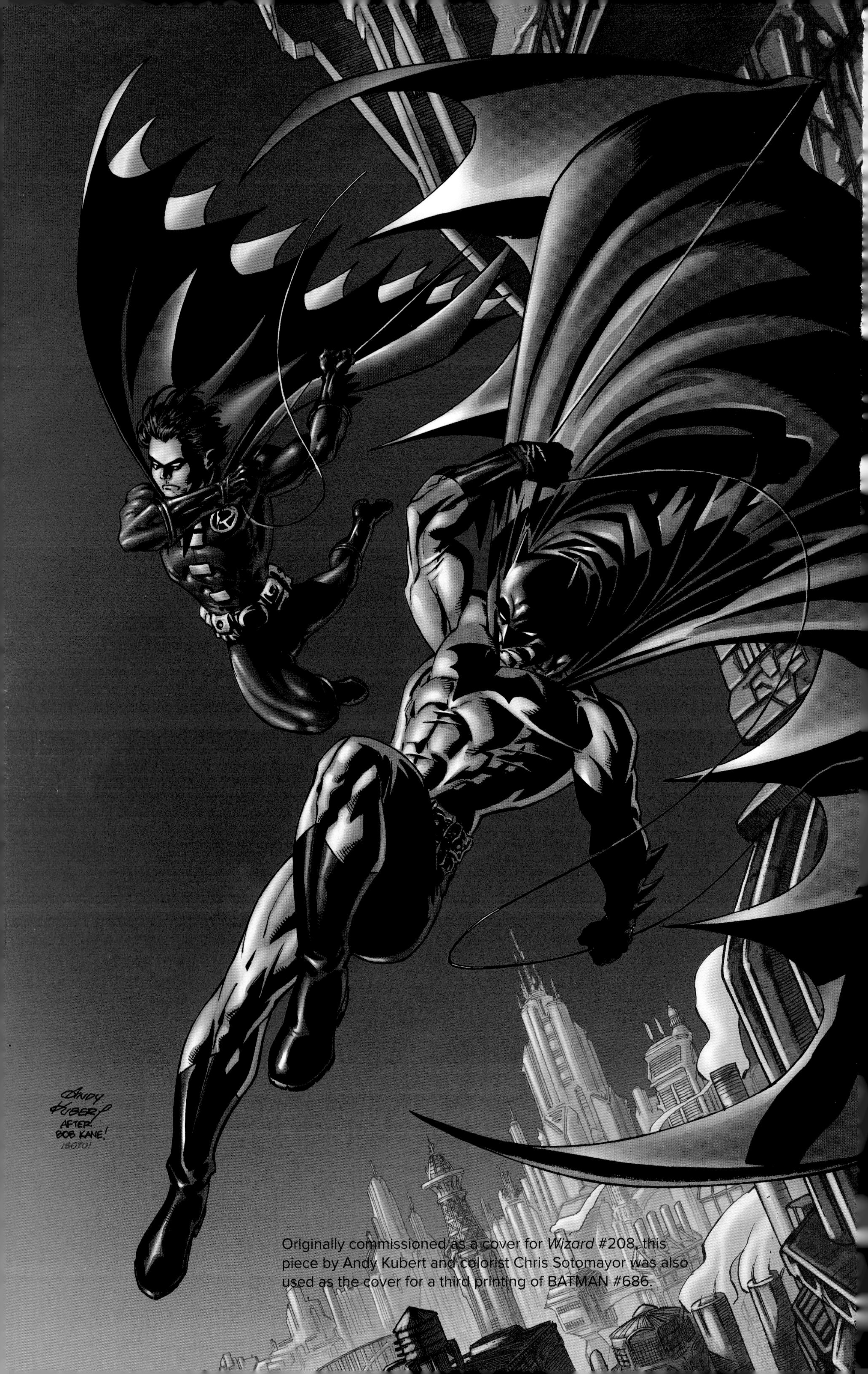
ANDY KUBERT AFTER BOB KANE!
¡SOTO!

Originally commissioned as a cover for *Wizard* #208, this piece by Andy Kubert and colorist Chris Sotomayor was also used as the cover for a third printing of BATMAN #686.